Lecture Notes in Computer Science 2672

Edited by G. Goos, J. Hartmanis, and J. van Leeuwen

D1717747

Springer
Berlin
Heidelberg
New York
Hong Kong
London
Milan
Paris
Tokyo

Markus Endler   Douglas Schmidt (Eds.)

Middleware 2003

ACM/IFIP/USENIX International Middleware Conference
Rio de Janeiro, Brazil, June 16-20, 2003
Proceedings

 Springer

Series Editors

Gerhard Goos, Karlsruhe University, Germany
Juris Hartmanis, Cornell University, NY, USA
Jan van Leeuwen, Utrecht University, The Netherlands

Volume Editors

Markus Endler
PUC-Rio
Departamento de Informática
Rua Marquês de São Vicente 225, 22453-900 Rio de Janeiro, Brazil
E-mail: endler@inf.puc-rio.br

Douglas Schmidt
Vanderbilt University
Department of Electrical Engineering and Computer Science
Box 1679,Station B Nashville 37235, TN, USA
E-mail: schmidt@uci.edu

Cataloging-in-Publication Data applied for

A catalog record for this book is available from the Library of Congress.

Bibliographic information published by Die Deutsche Bibliothek
Die Deutsche Bibliothek lists this publication in the Deutsche Nationalbibliografie;
detailed bibliographic data is available in the Internet at <http://dnb.ddb.de>.

CR Subject Classification (1998): C.2.4, D.4, C.2, D.1.3, D.3.2, D.2

ISSN 0302-9743
ISBN 3-540-40317-5 Springer-Verlag Berlin Heidelberg New York

Springer-Verlag Berlin Heidelberg New York
a member of BertelsmannSpringer Science+Business Media GmbH

http://www.springer.de

©IFIP International Federation for Information Processing, Hofstraße 3, A-2361 Laxenburg, Austria 2003
Printed in Germany

Typesetting: Camera-ready by author, data conversion by Olgun Computergrafik
Printed on acid-free paper   SPIN: 10927472   06/3142   5 4 3 2 1 0

Preface

Next-generation distributed applications and systems are increasingly developed using middleware. This dependency poses hard R&D challenges, including latency hiding, masking partial failure, information assurance and security, legacy integration, dynamic service partitioning and load balancing, and end-to-end quality of service specification and enforcement. To address these challenges, researchers and practitioners must discover and validate techniques, patterns, and optimizations for middleware frameworks, multi-level distributed resource management, and adaptive and reflective middleware architectures.

Following the success of the past IFIP/ACM Middleware conferences (Lake District/UK, Palisades/USA, and Heidelberg/Germany) and building upon the success of past USENIX COOTS conferences, the Middleware 2003 conference is the premier international event for middleware research and technology. The scope of the conference is the design, implementation, deployment, and evaluation of distributed system platforms, architectures, and applications for future computing and communication environments.

This year, we had a record of 158 submissions, among which the top 25 papers were selected for inclusion in the technical program of the conference. All papers were evaluated by at least three reviewers with respect to their originality, technical merit, presentation quality, and relevance to the conference themes. The selected papers present the latest results and breakthroughs on middleware research in areas including peer-to-peer computing, publish-subscriber architectures, component- and Web-based middleware, mobile systems, and adaptive computing.

We would like to express our thanks to the authors of the submitted papers and to all the reviewers and program committee members for their efforts in reviewing a large number of papers in a relatively short time. We would also like to thank ACM, IFIP, USENIX, and the corporate sponsors for their technical sponsorship and financial support, respectively. Finally, special thanks go to Alexandre Sztajnberg, Renato Cerqueira, Fabio Kon, and Fabio M. Costa and all the other organizing committee members for their hard work and efforts to bring Middleware 2003 to Brazil and make it a successful conference.

June 2003   Markus Endler and Douglas Schmidt

Organization

Middleware 2003 was organized under the auspices of IFIP TC6 WG6.1 (International Federation for Information Processing, Technical Committee 6 [Communication Systems], Working Group 6.1 [Architecture and Protocols for Computer Networks]).

Steering Committee

Gordon Blair (Lancaster University, UK)
Jan de Meer (condat AG, Germany)
Peter Honeyman (CITI, University of Michigan, USA)
Guy LeDuc (University of Liège, Belgium)
Kerry Raymond (DSTC, Australia)
Alexander Schill (TU Dresden, Germany)
Jacob Slonim (Dalhousie University, Canada)

Sponsoring Institutions

ACM (Association for Computing Machinery)
www.acm.org

IFIP (International Federation for Information Processing)
www.ifip.or.at

The Advanced Computing System Association
www.usenix.org

Supporting Companies

 IBM
www.ibm.com

 EA Industry

 Sony
www.sony.com

 BBN Technologies

 Sun Microsystems
www.sun.com

 Hewlett-Packart

 Boeing
www.boeing.com

 Petrobrás

Organizing Committee

General Chair: Carlos José Pereira de Lucena (PUC-Rio, Brazil)
Program Co-chairs: Markus Endler (PUC-Rio, Brazil)
                             Douglas Schmidt (Vanderbilt University, USA)

Work-in-Progress and
Posters Chair: Guruduth S. Banavar (IBM T.J. Watson, USA)
Advanced Workshops Chair: Gordon Blair (Lancaster University, UK)
Tutorials Chair: Frank Buschmann (Siemens AG, Germany)
Local Arrangements
Co-chairs: Alexandre Sztajnberg (UERJ, Brazil)
                             Renato Cerqueira (PUC-Rio, Brazil)
Student Travel Grant Chair: Hans-Arno Jacobsen (U. of Toronto, Canada)
Student Volunteer
Program Chair: Bruno Schulze (LNCC, Brazil)
Publicity Co-chairs: Fabio M. Costa (UF Goiás, Brazil)
                             Fabio Kon (University of São Paulo, Brazil)

Technical Program Committee

Gul Agha (University of Illinois, Urbana Champaign, USA)
Jean Bacon (Cambridge University, UK)
Gordon Blair (University of Lancaster, UK)
Don Box (Microsoft, USA)
Roy Campbell (University of Illinois, Urbana Champaign, USA)
Andrew Campbell (Columbia University, USA)
Geoff Coulson (Lancaster University, UK)
Naranker Dulay (Imperial College, UK)
Svend Frolund (HP Labs, USA)
Chris Gill (Washington University, St. Louis, USA)
Andy Gokhale (Vanderbilt University, USA)
Rashid Guerraoui (EPF Lausanne, Switzerland)
Arno Jacobsen (University of Toronto, Canada)
Peter Honeyman (CITI, University of Michigan, USA)
Fabio Kon (University of São Paulo, Brazil)
Doug Lea (SUNY Oswego, USA)
Guy LeDuc (University of Liège, Belgium)
Orlando Loques (UFF, Brazil)
Joe Loyall (BBN Technologies, USA)
Raimundo J. de Araujo Macedo (Federal University of Bahia, Brazil)
Edmundo R. Mauro Madeira (University of Campinas, Brazil)
Jan de Meer (condat AG, Germany)
Klara Nahrstedt (University of Illinois, Urbana Champaign, USA)
Priya Narasimhan (Carnegie Mellon University, USA)
Carlos Pereira (UFRGS, Brazil)
Vijay Raghavan (DARPA, USA)
Kerry Raymond (DSTC, Australia)
Luis Rodrigues (University of Lisboa, Portugal)
Isabelle Rouvellou (IBM, USA)
Bill Sanders (University of Illinois, Urbana Champaign, USA)
Rick Schantz (BBN Technologies, USA)
Alexander Schill (Technical University of Dresden, Germany)
David Sharp (The Boeing Company, USA)
Jacob Slonim (Dalhousie University, Canada)
Jean-Bernard Stefani (INRIA, Grenoble, France)
Joe Sventek (Agilent Labs, UK)
Janos Sztipanovits (Vanderbilt University, USA)
Nalini Venkatasubramanian (University of California, Irvine, USA)
Steve Vinoski (IONA Technologies, USA)
Werner Vogels (Cornell University, USA)
Martina Zitterbart (University of Karlsruhe, Germany)

Additional Reviewers

Filipe Araujo
Michael Atighetchi
Luciano Porto Barreto
Roberto Speicys Cardoso
Isidro Castineyra
Dan Cerys
Po-Hao Chang
Liping Chen
Joshua Chia
Renato Cerqueira
Nuno Correia
Fabio M. Costa
Lou Degenaro
Christo Devaraj
Gary Duzan
Paulo Ferreira
Marcelo Finger
Islene Calciolari Garcia
Jeff Gray
Andrei Goldchleger
Chris Jones
Richard King
Nirman Kumar
Youngmin Kwon
Soham Mazumdar
Kirill Mechitov

Thomas Mikalsen
Hugo Miranda
Gail Mitchell
Balachandran Natarajan
Dennis Noll
Partha Pal
Jeff Parsons
Irfan Pyarali
Smitha Reddy
Craig Rodrigues
Wendy Roll
Paul Rubel
Bruno R. Schulze
Koushik Sen
Rich Shapiro
Praveen Sharma
Flavio Assis Silva
Francisco J. Silva e Silva
Irineu Sotoma
Sameer Sundresh
Alexandre Sztajnberg
Stefan Tai
Maria Beatriz Felgar de Toledo
Nanbor Wang
Franklin Webber
John Zinky

Table of Contents

Peer-to-Peer Computing

Approximate Object Location and Spam Filtering
on Peer-to-Peer Systems 1
    *Feng Zhou, Li Zhuang, Ben Y. Zhao, Ling Huang, Anthony D. Joseph,
    and John Kubiatowicz*

Efficient Peer-to-Peer Keyword Searching 21
    Patrick Reynolds and Amin Vahdat

NaradaBrokering: A Distributed Middleware Framework and Architecture
for Enabling Durable Peer-to-Peer Grids 41
    Shrideep Pallickara and Geoffrey Fox

Publish-Subscribe Middleware I

A Framework for Event Composition in Distributed Systems 62
    Peter R. Pietzuch, Brian Shand, and Jean Bacon

Content Distribution for Publish/Subscribe Services 83
    Mao Chen, Andrea LaPaugh, and Jaswinder Pal Singh

Supporting Mobility in Content-Based Publish/Subscribe Middleware 103
    Ludger Fiege, Felix C. Gärtner, Oliver Kasten, and Andreas Zeidler

Adaptability and Context-Awareness

Fine-Grained Dynamic Adaptation of Distributed Components 123
    Frédéric Peschanski, Jean-Pierre Briot, and Akinori Yonezawa

A Middleware for Context-Aware Agents
in Ubiquitous Computing Environments 143
    Anand Ranganathan and Roy H. Campbell

Adaptable Architectural Middleware
for Programming-in-the-Small-and-Many 162
    Marija Mikic-Rakic and Nenad Medvidovic

Publish-Subscribe Middleware II

Opportunistic Channels: Mobility-Aware Event Delivery 182
    Yuan Chen, Karsten Schwan, and Dong Zhou

Congestion Control in a Reliable Scalable Message-Oriented Middleware . . 202
   Peter R. Pietzuch and Sumeer Bhola

On Shouting "Fire!": Regulating Decoupled Communication
in Distributed Systems 222
   Takahiro Murata and Naftaly H. Minsky

Web-Based Middleware

Performance Comparison of Middleware Architectures
for Generating Dynamic Web Content 242
   *Emmanuel Cecchet, Anupam Chanda, Sameh Elnikety,
   Julie Marguerite, and Willy Zwaenepoel*

Prefetching Based on Web Usage Mining 262
   *Daby M. Sow, David P. Olshefski, Mandis Beigi,
   and Guruduth Banavar*

Distributed Versioning: Consistent Replication
for Scaling Back-End Databases of Dynamic Content Web Sites 282
   Cristiana Amza, Alan L. Cox, and Willy Zwaenepoel

Component-Based Middleware

Abstraction of Transaction Demarcation
in Component-Oriented Platforms 305
   Romain Rouvoy and Philippe Merle

Optimising Java RMI Programs by Communication Restructuring 324
   Kwok Cheung Yeung and Paul H. J. Kelly

The JBoss Extensible Server 344
   Marc Fleury and Francisco Reverbel

Next Generation Middleware

Flexible and Adaptive QoS Control for Distributed Real-Time
and Embedded Middleware 374
   *Richard E. Schantz, Joseph P. Loyall, Craig Rodrigues,
   Douglas C. Schmidt, Yamuna Krishnamurthy, and Irfan Pyarali*

Large-Scale Service Overlay Networking with Distance-Based Clustering . . 394
   Jingwen Jin and Klara Nahrstedt

A Step Towards a New Generation of Group Communication Systems 414
   Sergio Mena, André Schiper, and Paweł Wojciechowski

Mobile and Ubiquitous Computing

A Middleware-Based Application Framework
for Active Space Applications 433
  Manuel Román and Roy H. Campbell

A Proactive Middleware Platform for Mobile Computing 455
  Andrei Popovici, Andreas Frei, and Gustavo Alonso

A Flexible Middleware System for Wireless Sensor Networks 474
  *Flávia Coimbra Delicato, Paulo F. Pires, Luci Pirmez,
  and Luiz Fernando Rust da Costa Carmo*

A Middleware Service for Mobile Ad Hoc Data Sharing,
Enhancing Data Availability 493
  Malika Boulkenafed and Valérie Issarny

Author Index 513

Approximate Object Location and Spam Filtering on Peer-to-Peer Systems

Feng Zhou, Li Zhuang, Ben Y. Zhao, Ling Huang,
Anthony D. Joseph, and John Kubiatowicz

Computer Science Division, U. C. Berkeley
{zf,zl,ravenben,hling,adj,kubitron}@cs.berkeley.edu

Abstract. Recent work in P2P overlay networks allow for decentralized object location and routing (DOLR) across networks based on unique IDs. In this paper, we propose an extension to DOLR systems to publish objects using generic *feature vectors* instead of content-hashed GUIDs, which enables the systems to locate similar objects. We discuss the design of a distributed text similarity engine, named *Approximate Text Addressing (ATA)*, built on top of this extension that locates objects by their text descriptions. We then outline the design and implementation of a motivating application on ATA, a decentralized spam-filtering service. We evaluate this system with 30,000 real spam email messages and 10,000 non-spam messages, and find a spam identification ratio of over 97% with zero false positives.

Keywords: Peer-to-peer, DOLR, Tapestry, spam filtering, approximate text matching

1   Introduction

Recent work on structured P2P overlay networks ([5, 18], [15], [11], [10]) utilize scalable routing tables to map unique identifiers to network locations, providing interfaces such as Decentralized Object Location and Routing (DOLR) and Distributed Hashtables (DHT). They allow network applications such as distributed file systems and distributed web caches to efficiently locate and manage object replicas across a wide-area network.

While these systems excel at locating objects and object replicas, they rely on known Globally Unique IDentifiers (GUID) for each object, commonly generated by applying a secure hash function to the object content. This provides a highly specific naming scheme, however, and does not lend itself to object location and management based on semantic features.

To address this problem, we propose an approximate location extension to DOLR systems to publish and locate objects using generic *feature vectors* composed of a number of values generated from its description or content. Any object can be addressed by a feature vector matching a minimal threshold number of entries with its original feature vector. Based on this extension, we propose an Approximate Text Addressing (ATA) facility, which instantiates the approximate location extension by using block text fingerprints as features to find matches between highly similar text documents. To validate the ATA design as well as the approximate object location extension, we design a decentralized spam-filtering application that leverages ATA to accurately identify junk

M. Endler and D. Schmidt (Eds.): Middleware 2003, LNCS 2672, pp. 1–20, 2003.

email messages despite formatting differences and evasion efforts by spammers. We evaluate the accuracy of our fingerprint vector scheme via simulation and analysis on real email data, and explore the trade-offs between resource consumption and search accuracy.

The rest of this paper is as follows: Section 2 briefly describes existing work in P2P overlays. Section 3 presents our approximation extension to DOLR systems and a prototype implementation. Section 4 describes the design of ATA and Section 5 discusses the design of the decentralized spam filter. Section 6 presents simulation and experimental results, followed by a discussion of related work in Section 7 and status and future work in Section 8. Finally, we provide a mathematical analysis of the robustness of text-based fingerprinting in Appendix A.

2   Background: Structured P2P Overlays

In this section, we first present background material on structured P2P overlays. Different protocols differ in semantics details and performance objectives. While we present our work in the context of Tapestry for performance reasons, our design is general, and our results can be generalized to most structured P2P protocols.

2.1   Routing

Tapestry is an overlay location and routing layer first presented in [18], with a rigorous treatment of dynamic algorithms presented in [5]. Like other structured P2P protocols, object and node IDs are pseudo-randomly chosen from the namespace of fixed-length bit sequences with a common base (e.g. Hex). Tapestry uses local routing tables at each node to route messages incrementally to the destination ID digit by digit (e.g., $4*** \implies 45** \implies 459* \implies 4598$ where $*$'s represent wildcards). A node N has a neighbor map with multiple levels, where each level represents a matching prefix up to a digit position in the ID. Each level of the neighbor map contains a number of entries equal to the base of the ID, where the ith entry in the jth level is the location of the node *closest in network latency* that begins with $prefix_{j-1}(N) + i$.

To forward on a message from its nth hop router, Tapestry examines its $n + 1^{th}$ level routing table and forwards the message to the link corresponding to the $n + 1^{th}$ digit in the destination ID. This routing substrate provides efficient location-independent routing within a logarithmic number of hops and using compact routing tables. Figure 1 shows a Tapestry routing mesh.

2.2   Data Location

In Tapestry, a server S makes a local object O available to others by routing a "publish" message to the object's "root node," the live node O's identifier maps to. At each hop along the path, a location mapping from O to S is stored. Mappings for multiple replicas are stored sorted according to distance from the local node. See Figure 2 for an example of object publication. Here two replicas of the same object are published. A client routes a query message towards the root node. The message queries each hop router along the

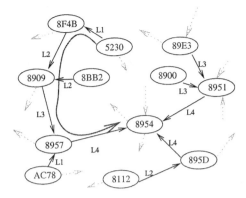

Fig. 1. *Tapestry routing example.* Path taken by a message from node 5230 for node 8954 in Tapestry using hexadecimal digits of length 4 (65536 nodes in namespace).

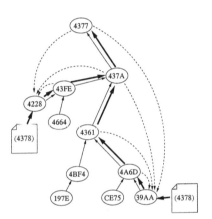

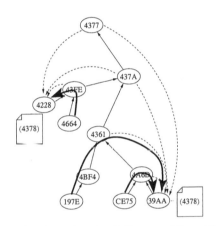

Fig. 2. *Publication in Tapestry.* To publish object 4378, server 39AA sends publication request towards root, leaving a pointer at each hop. Server 4228 publishes its replica similarly. Since no 4378 node exists, object 4378 is rooted at node 4377.

Fig. 3. *Object Location in Tapestry:* Three different location requests. For instance, to locate GUID 4378, query source 197E routes towards the root, checking for a pointer at each step. At node 4361, it encounters a pointer to server 39AA.

way, and routes towards S when it finds the O to S location mapping. Note that for nearby objects, query messages quickly intersect the path taken by publish messages, resulting in quick search results that exploit locality [18]. See Figure 3 for an example of object location. Notice how locality is exploited by directing location requests to nearby replicas.

3   Approximate DOLR

DOLR systems like Tapestry provide deterministic, scalable, and efficient location and routing services, making them attractive platforms for deploying wide-area network applications. Files, in particular, can be located efficiently if their canonical name is known. Previous approaches, however, generate Globally Unique IDentifiers (GUID) by a secure hash (e.g. SHA-1) of the content. This approach significantly limits the usability of the system in scenarios where users do not known exact names of objects, but rather perform searches based on general characteristics of the system. In particular, these scenarios might include searches for data that closely approximates, or is similar to known data with certain properties. Examples might include searching for audio or video that matches existing works in content features, or searching or lightly modified replicas of existing data.

3.1 Approximate DOLR Design

Here we propose an extension to DOLR, *Approximate DOLR*, as a generic framework to address some of the needs of these applications. In an ADOLR system, we apply application-specific analysis to given objects to generate *feature vectors* that describe its distinctive features, and provide a translation mechanism between these application-driven features and a traditional GUID obtained from a secure content hash of the object contents.

This query ability on features applies to a variety of contexts. In the world of multimedia search and retrieval, we can extract application-specific characteristics, and hash those values to generate feature vectors. Any combination of field to value mappings can be mapped to a feature vector, given a canonical ordering of those fields. For example, this can be applied to searching for printer drivers given printer features such as location, manufacturer, and speed. If features are canonically ordered as [location, manufacturer, speed], then an example feature vector might be [hash(443 Soda), hash(HP), hash(12ppm)].

Each member of the vector, a *feature*, is an application-specific feature encoded as a hashed identifier. For each feature f, an object (*feature object*) is stored within the network. The feature object is a simple object that stores the list of GUIDs of all objects whose feature vectors include f. Clients searching for objects with a given feature set finds a set of feature objects in the network, each associated with a single feature, and selects the GUIDs which appear in at least T feature objects, where T is a tunable threshold parameter used to avoid false positives while maintaining the desired generality of matches.

The "publication" of an object O in an ADOLR system proceeds as follows. First, its content-hash derived GUID is first published using the underlying P2P DOLR layer. This assures that any client can route messages to the object given its GUID. Next, we generate a feature vector for O. For each feature in the vector, we try to locate its associated feature object. If such an object is already available in the system, we append the current GUID to that object. Otherwise, we create a new feature object identified by the feature, and announce its availability into the overlay.

To locate an object in an ADOLR system, we first retrieve the feature object associated with each entry of the feature vector. We count the number of distinct feature objects each unique GUID appears in, and select the GUID(s) that appear in a number greater than some preset threshold. The GUID(s) are then used to route messages to the desired object.

The ADOLR API is as follows:

- **PublishApproxObject (FV, GUID).** This publishes the mapping between the **feature vector** and the GUID in the system. A feature vector is a set of feature values of the object, whose definition is application specific. Later, one can use the feature vector instead of the GUID to search for the object. Notice that **PublishApproxObject** only publishes the mapping from FV to GUID. It does not publish the object itself, which should be done already using publish primitive of Tapestry when **PublishApproxObject** is called.
- **UnpublishApproxObject (FV, GUID).** This removes the mapping from the FV to the GUID if this mapping exists in the network, which is the reverse of **PublishApproxObject**.
- **RouteToApproxObject (FV, THRES, MSG).** This primitive routes a message to the location of all objects which overlap with our queried feature vector FV on more than THRES entries. The basic operations involve for each feature, retrieving a list of GUIDs that share that feature, doing a frequency count to filter out GUIDs that match at least THRES of those features, and finally routing the payload message MSG to them. For each object in the system with feature vector FV^*, the selection criterion is:

$$|FV^* \bigcap FV| \geq THRES \ \ AND \ \ 0 < THRES \leq |FV|$$

The location operation is deterministic, which means all existing object IDs matching the criterion will be located and be sent the payload message. However, it is important to notice that this does not mean every matching object in the system will receive the message, because each object ID may correspond to multiple replicas, depending on the underlying DOLR system. The message will be sent to one replica of each matching object ID, hopefully a nearby replica if the DOLR utilizes locality.

With this interface, we reduce the problem of locating approximate objects on P2P systems to finding a mapping from objects and search criteria to feature vectors. The mapping should maintain similarity relationships, such that similar objects are mapped to feature vectors sharing some common entries. We show one example of such a mapping for text documents in Section 4.

3.2   A Basic ADOLR Prototype on Tapestry

Here we describe an Approximate DOLR prototype that we have implemented on top of the Tapestry API. The prototype serves as a proof of concept, and is optimized for simplicity. The prototype also allows us to gain experience into possible optimizations for performance, robustness and functionality.

The prototype leverages the DOLR interface for publishing and locating objects, given an associated identifier. When **PublishApproxObject** is called on an object O, it begins by publishing O's content-hashed object GUID using Tapestry. Then the client node uses Tapestry to send messages to all feature objects involved. Tapestry routes these messages to the nodes where these feature objects are stored. These nodes then add the new object GUID to the list of GUIDs inside the feature object. If any feature object

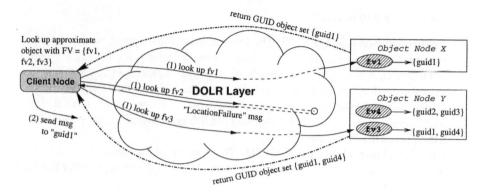

Fig. 4. *Location of an approximate object.* Client node wants to send a message to all objects with at least 2 feature in {fv1, fv2, fv3}. It first sends lookup message to feature fv1, fv2 and fv3. fv2 does not exists. A Location Failure message is sent back. fv1 is managed by object node X. It sends back a list of IDs of all objects having feature fv1, which is {guid1}. Similar operation is done for feature fv3, whose IDs list {guid1, guid4}. Client node counts the occurrence of all IDs in all lists and finds out guid1 to be the ID it is looking for. It then sends the payload message to object guid1 using Tapestry location message.

is not found in the network, the client node receives a LocationFailure message, creates a new feature object containing the new object, and publishes it.

For the **RouteToApproxObject** call, the client node first uses Tapestry location to send messages to all feature objects, asking for a list of IDs associated with each feature value. Nodes where these feature objects reside receive these messages, do the lookup in their maps and send back the result. **LocationFailure** messages are sent back for nonexistent feature objects, and are counted as an empty ID list. The client node counts the occurrence of each GUID in the resulting lists. GUIDs with less than the threshold number of counts are removed. Finally, the message in this call is sent to the remaining object GUIDs An example of executing a **RouteToApproxObject** call is shown in Figure 4.

Note that an analogous system can be implemented on top of a distributed hash table (DHT) abstraction on P2P systems. Instead of routing messages to previously published feature objects, one would retrieve each feature object by doing a **get** operation, appending the new GUID, and putting the object back using **put**.

3.3   Optimizing ADOLR Location

Our initial description of the **RouteToApproxObject** operation involves several round-trips from the client node to nodes where the feature objects are stored. We propose two optimizations here that eliminates a network round-trip, reducing overall latency to that of a normal **RouteToObject** in a DOLR system at the cost of keeping a small amount of state on overlay nodes. The first optimization involves a client node caching the result of translating a feature vector to a GUID. now all future messages to the same feature vector are routing to the cached GUID.

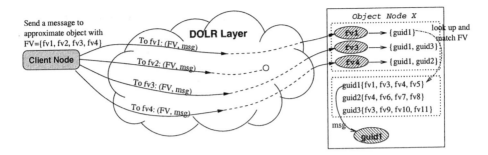

Fig. 5. *Optimized ADOLR location.* Client node wants to route a message to a feature vector {fv1, fv2, fv3, fv4}. It sends message to each identifier fv1, fv2, fv3, fv4. fv2 doesn't exist, so no object node receives this message. When object node X receives the messages to fv1, fv3 and fv4, it scans its local storage for all IDs matching fv1, fv3 and fv4, which is guid1. Then, object node X sends msg to guid1.

The second optimization is more complex, and illustrated in Figure 5. Normally, the client node retrieves a set of feature objects, counts GUID occurrences locally, then routes a message to the resulting GUID(s). The intuition here is that if features are identified as hashed keys with reasonably low collision rates, each feature will likely only identify a small number (one or two) of objects with that feature. Furthermore, multiple feature objects are likely to be colocated together along with the object they identify, because new feature objects are created by the same node where the object is stored. Another way to look at this is that the feature object is in most cases published at the same time with the object itself by the same node. This implies we can route the application-level message to each feature in the feature vector, and expect it to arrive at the node where the desired object is stored.

The key change here is that any node that is storing a feature object, (a file providing a mapping from a feature to all GUIDs that share that feature), also stores the feature vectors of each of those GUIDs. Routing a message to a feature vector $\{X, Y, Z\}$ means sending the message to each identifier $X, Y,$ and Z. Each message also includes the entire feature vector we're querying for. When a node receives such a message, it immediately scans its local storage for all feature objects matching X, Y, or Z. For each GUID in these feature objects, the node determines the amount of overlap between its feature vector and the queried feature vector. If the overlap satifies the query threshold, the message is delivered to that GUID's location.

This implies that any of the query messages contains enough information for a node to completely evaluate the ADOLR search on local information. If any locally stored feature objects contain references to matching objects, they can be evaluated immediately to determine if it satisfies the query. Because each message contains all necessary information to deliver the payload to the desired GUID, the set of messages sent to $X, Y,$ and Z provide a level of fault-resilience against message loss. Finally, the determination of the desired GUID can occur when the first message is received, instead of waiting for all messages to arrive.

The translation from the feature vector to one or more GUIDs occurs in the network, not the client node. This provides significant communication savings.

Nodes need to keep more state to support this optimization, however. In addition to storing feature objects (that keep the mapping between feature values and GUIDs), they also need to keep track of previously resolved feature vectors in order to drop additional requests for the same feature vector. This state can be stored on a temporary basis, and removed after a reasonable period of time (during which any other requests for the same feature vector should have arrived).

3.4   Concurrent Publication

There is one problem with the **PublishApproxObject** implementation described above. The lookup of feature objects and publication of new feature objects are not atomic. This can result in multiple feature objects for the same feature value being published if more than one node tries to publish an object with this feature value concurrently.

We propose two solutions. First, we can exploit the fact that every object is mapped to a unique root node and serialize the publication on the root node. Every node is required to send a message to the root node of the feature value to obtain a leased lock before publishing the feature object. After the lock is acquired by the first node, other nodes trying to obtain it will fail, restart the whole process, and find the newly published feature object. This incurs another round-trip communication to the root node.

In a more efficient "optimistic" way to solve this problem, the client node always assumes the feature object does not exist in the network. It tries to publish the object without doing a lookup beforehand. When the publication message travels through the network, each node checks whether it knows about an already published feature object with the same feature value. If such an object does exist, some node or at least the root will know about this. The node who detects this then cancels this publication and sends an message to the existing feature object to "merge" the new information. This process is potentially more efficient since conflicts should be rare. In general, the operation is accomplished with a single one-way publication message.

This optimistic approach can easily be implemented on top of DOLRs such as Tapestry using the recently proposed common upcall interface for peer to peer (P2P) overlays [2]. This proposed upcall interface allows P2P applications to override local routing decisions. Specifically, a node can "intercept" the publication message and handle conflicts as specified above.

4   Approximate Text Addressing

In this section, we present the design for the Approximate Text Addressing facility built on the Approximate DOLR extension, and discuss design decisions for exploring trade-offs between computational and bandwidth overhead and accuracy.

4.1   Finding Text Similarity

Our goal is to efficiently match documents distributed throughout the network that share strong similarities in their content. We focus here on highly similar files, such as modified email messages, edited documents, or news article published on different web sites.

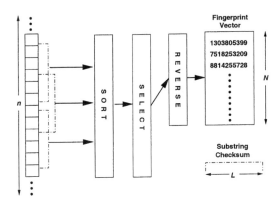

Fig. 6. *Fingerprint Vector.* A fingerprint vector is generated from the set of checksums of all substrings of length L, post-processed with sort, selection and reverse operations.

The algorithm is as follows. Given a text document, we use a variant of block text fingerprinting first introduced in [7] to generate a set of fingerprints. The fingerprint vector of a document is used as its feature vector in publication and location, using the Approximate DOLR layer.

To calculate a block text fingerprint vector of size N for a text document, we divide the document into all possible consecutive substrings of length L. A document of length n characters will have $(n - L + 1)$ such strings. Calculating checksums of all such substrings is a fast operation which scales with n. We sort the set of all checksums by value, select a size N subset with the highest values, and reverse each checksum by digit (i.e. $123 \Rightarrow 321$). This deterministically selects a random set without biasing the ID for prefix or numerical routing.

L is a parameterized constant chosen for each application to tune the granularity of similarity matches. For example, a size L of 50 might work well for email, where complete sentences might account for one substring; but less well for source code, where code fragments are often much longer in length. Figure 6 illustrates the fingerprint process. The calculation is not expensive. Our Java prototype has a processing throughput of $> 13MB/s$ for $L = 50$ on a 1Ghz PIII laptop.

4.2   Trade-offs

There are obvious trade-offs between network bandwidth used and the accuracy of the search. First, the greater the number of entries N in a vector, the more accurate the match (less false-positives), and also the greater number of parallel lookup requests for each document. Next, the distance each lookup requests travels directly impacts bandwidth consumption on the overall network. ATA-enabled applications[1] can benefit from exploiting network-locality by matching against similar documents nearby in the network via a DOLR/DHT with object location locality such as Tapestry. Finally, a trade-off exists

---

[1] Some example applications include spam filters, plagiarism detection and news article clustering.

between the number of publishers (those who indicate they have a particular document), and the resources required for a client to find a match in their query. Bandwidth and accuracy can be tuned by placing a Time-to-Live (TTL) field on the lookup query, constraining the scope of query messages. Clients who fail to find a match may publish their own documents, improving lookup performance for other clients. These are explored in detail in Section 6.

5 Decentralized Spam Filtering

Spam, or unsolicited email, wastes time and valuable network resources, causing headaches for network administrators and home users alike. Currently the most widely-deployed spam filtering systems scale to a university- or company- wide network, and use keyword matching or source address matching [13]. Although easy to deploy and manage, these systems often walk a fine line between letting spam through and blocking legitimate emails. Our observation is that human recognition is the only fool-proof spam identification tool. Therefore, we propose a decentralized spam filter that pools the collective spam recognition results of all readers across a network.

There already exist centralized collaborative spam filtering systems, such as Spam-Net [14], which claims to be peer-to-peer but actually uses a Napster-like architecture. To our knowledge ours is the first attempt to build a truly decentralized collaborative spam filtering system. Compared to alternative university-wide centralized collaborated designs, the most important benefit of our wide-area decentralized design lies in the fact that the effectiveness of the system grows with the number of its users. In such a system with huge number of users world-wide, it is highly probable that every spam email you receive has been received and identified by somebody else before because of the large number of users. The deterministic behavior of DOLR systems will prove useful, because when any single peer publishes information about a specific email, that piece of information can be deterministically found by all clients. Therefore we can expect this system to be more responsive to new spam than systems in which different nodes publish/exchange spam information at certain intervals, such as [3]. Additionally, decentralized systems provide higher availability and resilience to failures and attacks than similar centralized solutions such as SpamNet.

5.1 Basic Operation

The decentralized spam filtering system consists of two kinds of nodes, user agents and peers. User agents are extended email client programs that users use. They query peers when new emails are received and also send user's feedback regarding whether a certain email is or is not spam to peers. A peer is a piece of long-running software that is installed typically on a university, department or company server that speaks to other peers worldwide and forms a global P2P network.

When an email client receives a message from the server, the user agent extracts the body of the mail, drops format artifacts like extra spaces and HTML tags, generates a fingerprint vector, and sends it to a peer in the DOLR system. The peer in turn queries the network using the Approximate DOLR API to see if information on the email has been published. If a match is found, and it indicates the email is spam, the email will be filed separately or discarded depending on user preference. Otherwise, the message is delivered normally. If the user marks a new message as spam, the user agent *marks* the document, and tells the peer to publish this information into the network.

5.2   Enhancements and Optimizations

The basic design above allows human identification of spam to quickly propagate across the network, which allows all users of the system to benefit from the feedback of a few. There are several design choices and optimizations which will augment functionality and reduce resource consumption.

Our fingerprint vectors make reverse engineering and blocking of unknown emails very difficult. With the basic system, however, attackers can block well known messages (such as those from group mailing lists). We propose to add a voting scheme on top of the publish/search model. A count of positive and negative votes is kept by the system, and each user can set a threshold value for discarding or filing spam using the count as a confidence measure. A central authority controls the assignment and authentication of user identities. A user agent is required to authenticate itself before being able to vote for or against an email. Thus we can restrict the number of votes a certain user agent can perform on a certain email.

Another type of attack is for spammers to find arbitrary text segments with checksum values more likely to be selected by the fingerprint selection algorithm. By appending such "preferred" segments to their spam emails, spammers can fix the resulting email fingerprint vectors to attempt to avoid detection. Note that this attack can only succeed if a continuous stream of unique text segments are generated and an unique segment is appended to each spam message. This places a significant computational overhead on the spammer that scales with the number of spam messages sent. Additionally, mail clients can choose randomly from a small set of fingerprint calculation algorithms. Different fingerprinting methods can include transforming the text before calculating the checksums, changing the checksum method, or changing the fingerprint selection method. To circumvent this, the spammer would need to first determine the set of fingerprint algorithms, and then append a set of preferred segments, each segment overcoming a known selection algorithm. While different fingerprint algorithms generate distinct spam signatures for the same spam, partitioning the user population and reducing the likelihood of a match, it also requires significantly more computational overhead to overcome.

Optimizations can be made for centralized mail servers to compute fingerprint vectors for all incoming messages. These vectors can be compared locally to identify "popular" messages, and lookups performed to determine if they are spam. Additionally, the server can attach precomputed fingerprint vectors and/or spam filtering results as custom headers to messages, reducing local computation, especially for thin mail clients such as PDAs.

6   Evaluation

In this section, we use a combination of analysis, experimentation on random documents and real emails to validate the effectiveness of our design. We look at two aspects of fingerprinting, robustness to changes in content and false positive rates. We also evaluate fingerprint routing constrained with time-to-live (TTL) fields, tuning the trade-off between accuracy and network bandwidth consumption.

6.1   Fingerprint on Random Text

We begin our evaluation by examining the properties of text fingerprinting on randomly generated text. In particular, we examine the effectiveness of fingerprinting at matching text after small modifications to their originals, and the likelihood of matching unrelated documents (false positive rate).

Robustness to Changes in Content. We begin by examining the robustness of the fingerprint vector scheme against small changes in a document, by measuring the probability a fingerprint vector stays constant when we modify small portions of the document. We fix the fingerprint vector size, and want to measure the robustness against small changes under different threshold constants (THRES).

In experiments, we take 2 sets of random text documents of size 1KB and 5KB, which match small- and large-sized spam messages respectively, and calculate their fingerprint vectors before and after modifying 10 consecutive bytes. This is similar to text replacement or mail merge schemes often used to generate differentiated spam. We measure the probability of at least $THRES$ out of $|FV|$ fingerprints matching after modification as a function of threshold ($THRES$) and the size of the document (1KB or 5KB). Here, fingerprint vector size is 10, $|FV| = 10$. We repeat that experiment with a modification of 50 consecutive bytes, simulating the replacement of phrases or sentences and finally modifying 5 randomly placed words each 5 characters long.

In addition to the simulated experiments, we also developed a simple analytical model for these changes based on basic combinatorics. We present this model in detail in Appendix A. For each experiment, we plot analytical results predicted by our model in addition to the experimental results.

In Figure 7, we show for each scenario experimental results gathered on randomized text files, by comparing fingerprint vectors before and after modifications. From Figure 7, we can see the model in Appendix A predicts our simulation data almost exactly under all three patterns of modification. More specifically, modifying 10 characters in the text only impacts 1 or 2 fingerprints out of 10 with a small probability. This means setting any matching threshold below 8 will guarantee near 100% matching rate. When we increase the length of the change to 50 characters, the results do not change significantly, and still guarantee near perfect matching with thresholds below 7. Finally, we note that multiple small changes (in the third experiment) have the most impact on changing fingerprint vectors. Even in this case, setting a threshold value around 5 or less provides a near perfect matching rate.

Avoiding False Positives. In addition to being robust under modifications, we also want fingerprint vectors to provide a low rate of false positives (where unrelated documents generate matching entries in their vectors). In this section, we evaluate fingerprint vectors against this metric with simulation on random text documents. In Section 6.2, we present similar tests on real email messages.

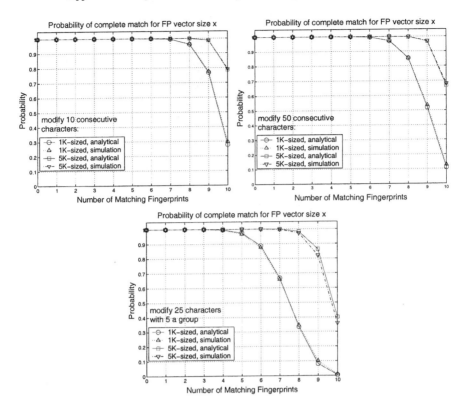

Fig. 7. *Robustness Test (Experimental and Analytical).* The probability of correctly recognizing a document after modification, as a function of threshold. $|FV| = 10$.

First, we generate 100,000 random text files and find document pairs that match 1 out of 10 fingerprint entries. This experiment is done for different file sizes ranging from 1KB to 64KB. Figure 8 shows the resulting false positive rate versus the file size. While the results for one fingerprint match are already low, they can be made statistically insignificant by increasing the fingerprint matches threshold ($THRESH$) for a "document match." Out of all our tests (5×10^9 pairs for each file size), less than 25 pairs of files (file size $> 32K$) matched 2 fingerprints, no pairs of files matched more than 2 fingerprints. This result, combined with the robustness result, tells us that on randomized documents, a threshold from 2 to 5 fingerprints gives us a matching mechanism that is both near-perfect in terms of robustness against small changes and absence of false positives.

6.2   Fingerprint on Real Email

We also repeat the experiments in Section 6.1 on real emails. We collected 29996 total spam email messages from http://www.spamarchive.org. Histogram and CDF representations of their size distribution are shown in Figure 9.

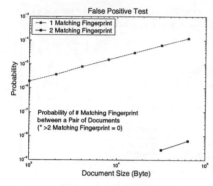

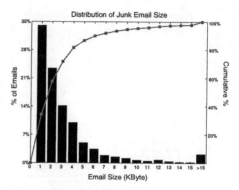

Fig. 8. *False Positives.* The probability of two random text files matching i ($i = 1, 2$) out of 10 fingerprint vectors, as a function of file size.

Fig. 9. *Spam Mail Sizes.* Size distribution of the 29996 spam email messages used in our experiments, using both histogram and CDF representations.

Table 1. *Robustness Test on Real Spam Emails.* Tested on 3440 modified copies of 39 emails, 5629 copies each. $|FV| = 10$.

THRES	Detected	Failed	Total	Succ. %
3	3356	84	3440	97.56
4	3172	268	3440	92.21
5	2967	473	3440	86.25

Table 2. *False Positive Test on Real Spam Emails.* Tested on $9589(normal) \times 14925(spam)$ pairs. $|FV| = 10$.

Match FP	# of Pairs	Probability
1	270	1.89e-6
2	4	2.79e-8
>2	0	0

In order to get an idea of whether small modifications on spam email is a common practice of spammers, we used a variant of our fingerprint techniques to fully categorize the email set for uniqueness. We personally confirmed the results. We found that, out of all these 29996 junk emails, there are:

- 14925 unique junk emails.
- 9076 modified copies of 4585 unique ones.
- 5630 exact copies of the unique ones.

From statistics above, we can see that about 1/3 junk emails have modified version(s), despite that we believe the collectors of the archive have already strive to eliminate duplicates. This means changing each email they sent is really a common technique used by spammers, either to prevent detection or to misdirect the end user.

We did the robustness test on 3440 modified copies of 39 most "popular" junk emails in the archive, which have $5 - 629$ copies each. The standard result is human processed and made accurate. The fingerprint vector size is set to 10, $|FV| = 10$. We vary threshold of matching fingerprint from 3 to 5, and collect the detected and failed number. Table 1 shows the successful detection rate with $THRES = 3, 4, 5$ are satisfying.

For the false positive test, we collect 9589 normal emails, which is compose of about half from newsgroup posts and half from personal emails of project members. Before doing the experiment, we expect collisions to be more common, due to the use of common words and phrases in objects such as emails. We do a full pair-wise fingerprint match (vector size 10) between these 14925 unique spam emails and 9589 legitimate email messages. Table 2 shows that only 270 non-spam email messages matched some spam message with 1 out of 10 fingerprints. If we raise the match threshold T to 2 out of 10 fingerprints, only 4 matches are found. For match threshold more than 2, no matches are found. We conclude that false positives for threshold value $T > 1$ are very rare ($\sim 10^{-8}$) even for real text samples.

6.3 Efficient Fingerprint Routing w/ TTLs

We want to explore our fingerprint routing algorithms in a more realistic context. Specifically, we now consider the additional factor *mark rate*, which is the portion of all users in the network that actively report a particular spam. A user who "marks" a spam message actives publishes this fact, thereby registering that opinion with the network. For example, a 10% mark rate means that 10% of the user population actively marked the same message as spam.

To simulate the trade-off between bandwidth usage, "mark" rate, and search success rate, we simulate the searching of randomly generated fingerprints on transit-stub networks, and vary the required number of overlay hops to find a match, as well as the mark rate. We assume users marking the spam are randomly distributed. With an efficient DOLR layer, the more users who mark a document as spam, the fewer number of hops we expect a query to travel before finding a match. We can set a TTL value on queries to conserve bandwidth while maintaining a reasonably high search success rate.

We performed experiments on 8 transit stub topologies of 5000 nodes, latency calibrated such that the network diameter is 400ms. Each Tapestry network has 4096 nodes, and each experiment was repeated with 3 randomized overlay node placements. By aggregating the data from all placements and all topologies, we reduced the standard deviation below 0.02 (0.01 for most data points).

The results in Figure 10 show the expected latency and success probability for queries as a function of the number of hops allowed per query (TTL). Since there is a high correlation between the TTL value and the network distance traveled in ms, we plot both the TTL used and the associated network distance. For example, we see that queries with TTL of 2 on these topologies travel a distance of approx. 60ms. Further, at 10% publication rate, we expect those queries to be successful 75% of the time. We note that a Time-to-Live value of 3 overlay hops results in a high probability of finding an existing document even if it has only been reported by a small portion of the participating nodes (2-5%).

7 Related Work

There has been a large amount of recent work on structured peer to peer overlays [18, 5, 11, 15, 10, 8, 4]. Recent work [2] has tried to clarify the interfaces these protocols export to applications, including distributed hash tables (DHTs) and decentralized object location and routing (DOLRs) layers. While our proposal is designed for DOLR systems, it can also be implemented on top of DHTs with minor modifications. Furthermore, protocols like Tapestry that use network proximity metrics to constrain network traffic will benefit the most from our performance optimizations.

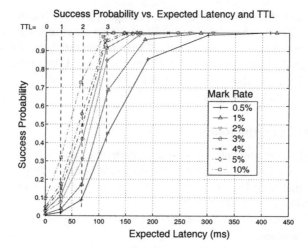

Fig. 10. *Finding an Ideal TTL.* A graph that shows, for a "marked" document, the correlation between TTL values on queries, probability of a successful search, and percentage of nodes in the network who "marked" it.

Recent work [6] discusses the feasibility of doing keyword-based web search in structured P2P networks, which can be thought of as an instantiation of our ADOLR proposal applied to text documents with keywords used as features. Both their scheme and our work use inverted indices of keywords/features assigned to different nodes and maintained using structured overlay location and routing primitives. Finally, this work tries to gauge feasibility, rather than to propose any specific implementation.

In the context of approximate text addressing, centralized text similarity search is a well-studied problem. Comprehensive discussion can be found in [17]. It includes discussion about using "n-grams" to do similarity search using exact search facility. One specific technique within this category [7] forms the basis of our approach of using checksum based fingerprints.

In [1], Broder examined the probability of two different strings colliding to an identical single fingerprint. In contrast, we focus on the collision probability of entire fingerprint vectors. In Appendix A, we also consider the probability of changes in a fingerprint vector under different document modification patterns.

Many spam filtering schemes have been proposed and some deployed. Schemes based on hashing and fuzzy hashes [16, 14, 3], including our proposal, are collaborative and utilize community consensus to filter messages. These systems include two main components: one or more hash functions to generate digests of email messages, and a repository of all known digests and whether the corresponding emails are spam. Our system differs from others in this group in that the digest repository is fully decentralized, and queries are deterministic by default (i.e. all existing results will be found no matter where it is). This ensures both scalability and accuracy.

Another big family of spam filtering schemes are machine learning-based [12, 9]. These schemes filter incoming messages based on symptoms or trails of spam emails identified explicitly or implicitly by the training process. They can be personalized according to user preferences and email content and therefore perform well on client machines. However, because the filters these systems use are only based on per-user local information and do not allow cross-user collaboration, they have difficulty in identifying new spam emails that are very different from those seen before by the local user.

8 Ongoing and Future Work

We have implemented the basic Approximate DOLR and Approximate Text Addressing prototype on a Java implementation of Tapestry, and are exploring additional optimizations and extensions. A prototype of the proposed P2P spam filtering system, SpamWatch, is implemented and available, including a per-node component implemented as a Tapestry application and the user interface implemented as a Microsoft Outlook plug-in[2]. One direction for future work is to deploy SpamWatch as a long-running service, both to provide a valuable service and also to collect valuable trace data. We are also considering extending the system to handle predicate queries.

In conclusion, we proposed the design of an approximate location extension to DOLR systems and described an Approximate Text Addressing facility for text-based objects. We discuss issues of data consistency and performance optimizations in the system design, and present a decentralized spam filtering system as a key application. We validate our designs via simulation and real data, and show how to tune the fingerprint vector size and query TTL to improve accuracy, reduce bandwidth usage and query latency, all while keeping a low false positive rate.

References

1. BRODER, A. Z. Some applications of rabin's fingerprint method. In *Sequences II: Methods in Communications, Security, and Computer Science*, R. Capocelli, A. D. Santis, and U. Vaccaro, Eds. Springer Verlag, 1993, pp. 143–152.
2. DABEK, F., ZHAO, B. Y., DRUSCHEL, P., KUBIATOWICZ, J., AND STOICA, I. Towards a common API for structured P2P overlays. In *Proceedings of IPTPS* (Berkeley, CA, February 2003).
3. Distributed checksum clearinghouse. http://www.rhyolite.com/anti-spam/dcc/.
4. HARVEY, N. J. A., JONES, M. B., SAROIU, S., THEIMER, M., AND WOLMAN, A. Skipnet: A scalable overlay network with practical locality properties. In *Proceedings of USITS* (Seattle, WA, March 2003), USENIX.
5. HILDRUM, K., KUBIATOWICZ, J. D., RAO, S., AND ZHAO, B. Y. Distributed object location in a dynamic network. In *Proceedings of ACM SPAA* (Winnipeg, Canada, August 2002).
6. LI, J., LOO, B. T., HELLERSTEIN, J., KAASHOEK, F., KARGER, D. R., AND MORRIS, R. On the feasibility of peer-to-peer web indexing and search. In *2nd International Workshop on Peer-to-Peer Systems* (Berkeley, California, 2003).
7. MANBER, U. Finding similar files in a large file system. In *Proceedings of Winter USENIX Conference* (1994).
8. MAYMOUNKOV, P., AND MAZIERES, D. Kademlia: A peer-to-peer information system based on the XOR metric. In *Proceedings of 1st International Workshop on Peer-to-Peer Systems (IPTPS)* (Cambridge, MA, March 2002).

---

[2] Fully functional prototypes of the ATA layer and spam filter are available for download at http://www.cs.berkeley.edu/~zf/spamwatch

9. Mozilla spam filtering. http://www.mozilla.org/mailnews/spam.html.

10. RATNASAMY, S., FRANCIS, P., HANDLEY, M., KARP, R., AND SCHENKER, S. A scalable content-addressable network. In *Proceedings of SIGCOMM* (August 2001).

11. ROWSTRON, A., AND DRUSCHEL, P. Pastry: Scalable, distributed object location and routing for large-scale peer-to-peer systems. In *Proceedings of IFIP/ACM Middleware 2001* (November 2001).

12. SAHAMI, M., DUMAIS, S., HECKERMAN, D., AND HORVITZ, E. A bayesian approach to filtering junk email. In *AAAI Workshop on Learning for Text Categorization* (Madison, Wisconsin, July 1998).

13. Spamassassin. http://spamassassin.org.

14. Spamnet. http://www.cloudmark.com.

15. STOICA, I., MORRIS, R., KARGER, D., KAASHOEK, M. F., AND BALAKRISHNAN, H. Chord: A scalable peer-to-peer lookup service for internet applications. In *Proceedings of SIGCOMM* (August 2001).

16. Vipul's razor. http://razor.sourceforge.net/.

17. WITTEN, I. H., MOFFAT, A., AND BELL, T. C. *Managing Gigabytes: Compressing and Indexing Documents and Images*, second ed. Morgan Kaufmann Publishing, 1999.

18. ZHAO, B. Y., KUBIATOWICZ, J. D., AND JOSEPH, A. D. Tapestry: An infrastructure for fault-tolerant wide-area location and routing. Tech. Rep. UCB/CSD-01-1141, U.C. Berkeley, April 2001.

A   Analysis of Robustness of Text Fingerprinting

Here we give mathematical analysis of how to compute the probability distribution of number of unchanged fingerprints of a text document after small modifications.

We define:

D : the original document
D' : the original document after modifications
L : the document is divided in consecutive substrings of length L characters
A : the set of checksums calculated from all substrings in D
B : the set of checksums calculated from all substrings in D'
X : $A - B$, checksums from D which are not present in checksums of D'
Y : $B - A$, checksums from D' not present in original checksums of D
$FP(A)$: the fingerprint vector generated from checksums of D, such that $FP(A) \subseteq A$, $|FP(A)| = N$
$FP(B)$: the fingerprint vector generated from checksums of D', such that $FP(B) \subseteq B$, $|FP(B)| = N$
$|S|$: if S is a set or vector, $|S|$ represents the size of S
z : $|FP(B) - FP(A)|$, number of checksums in new fingerprint vector which are not in the old fingerprint vector

Refer to Figure 11 for an illustration of X, Y, A and B.

Let's define $P_r(x)$ as the probability that x out of N checksums in $FP(A)$ are obsolete, that is, not in B; define $P_r(y)$ as the probability that y out of N checksums in $FP(B)$ are newly generated, that is, not in A. We have:

$$P_r(x) = P_r(|FP(A) \cap X| = x) = \frac{\binom{|X|}{x} \times \binom{|A| - |X|}{N - x}}{\binom{|A|}{N}} \tag{1}$$

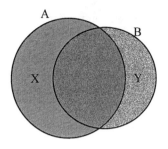

Fig. 11. *Relationship between X, Y, A and B.*

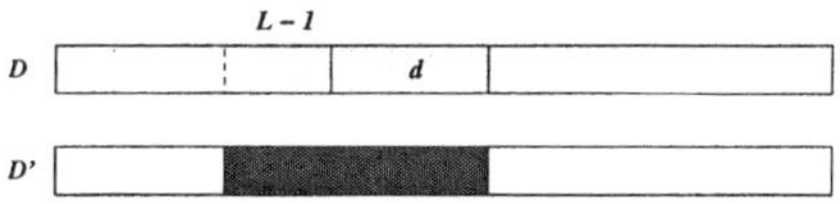

Fig. 12. *Update d chars.*

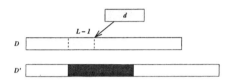

Fig. 13. *Insert d chars.*

Fig. 14. *Delete d chars.*

$$P_r(y) = P_r(|FP(B) \cap Y| = y) = \frac{\binom{|Y|}{y} \times \binom{|B| - |Y|}{N - y}}{\binom{|B|}{N}} \tag{2}$$

If:

1. $(N - x) + y < N$ (that is, $x > y$): $FP(B)$ is composed of $(N - x)$ checksums from $FP(A)$, y checksums from newly generated set Y, and others from $A \cap B$. That is, the y checksums from Y and others from $A \cap B$ are the new checksums in $FP(B)$ since $FP(A)$. Then, $z = N - (N - x) = x$.
2. $(N - x) + y \geq N$ (that is, $y \geq x$): $FP(B)$ is composed of y checksums from Y, other checksums from $FP(A) - X$. That is, the y checksums from Y are new checksums in $FP(B)$ since $FP(A)$. Then, $z = y$.

So, when $x > y$, $z = x$; when $y \geq x$, $z = y$. That is, $z = max(x, y)$. Then,

$$P_r(z) = P_r(y = z) \sum_{i=0}^{z} P_r(x = i) + P_r(x = z) \sum_{i=0}^{z} P_r(y = i) - P_r(x = z)P_r(y = z) \tag{3}$$

Let's define $P(|FP(A) \cap FP(B)| \geq k)$ to be the probability that at least k checksums are in common between fingerprint vector of new document and of old document. We have:

$$P_r(|FP(A) \cap FP(B)| \geq k) = P_r(|FP(B) - FP(A)| \leq N - k) = \sum_{i=0}^{N-k} P_r(z = i) \tag{4}$$

Knowing of $|X|$ and $|Y|$, we can apply results in equation (1)-(3) to equation (4), and then get the probability of the number of unchanged fingerprints after modification of the document.

While $|X|$ and $|Y|$ are related to modification pattern, we can further consider how to get $|X|$ and $|Y|$. $X = \bigcup X_i$ and $Y = \bigcup Y_i$, where X_i and Y_i are changes made to checksums because of one modification operation i.

We have three types of operations:

Update d characters : $|X_i| = L - 1 + d$, $|Y_i| = L - 1 + d$. This is illustrated in Figure 12.

Insert d characters : $|X_i| = L - 1$, $|Y_i| = L - 1 + d$. This is illustrated in Figure 13.

Delete d characters : $|X_i| = L - 1 + d$, $|Y_i| = L - 1$. This is illustrated in Figure 14.

X equals the union of each X_i and Y equals the union of each Y_i. So, if there is only one modification, we can exactly compute $|X|$ and $|Y|$. If there are more than one modification, $|X|$ ranges from $max_i|X_i|$ to $\sum_i |X_i|$, $|Y|$ ranges from $max_i|Y_i|$ to $\sum_i |Y_i|$. We can compute approximate average $|X|$ and $|Y|$ for a specific pattern of modification operations according to equations above.

Thus, we can use equation (4) to compute the probability distribution of number of unchanged fingerprints in fingerprint vector.

Efficient Peer-to-Peer Keyword Searching*

Patrick Reynolds and Amin Vahdat

Department of Computer Science, Duke University
{reynolds,vahdat}@cs.duke.edu

Abstract. The recent file storage applications built on top of peer-to-peer distributed hash tables lack search capabilities. We believe that search is an important part of any document publication system. To that end, we have designed and analyzed a distributed search engine based on a distributed hash table. Our simulation results predict that our search engine can answer an average query in under one second, using under one kilobyte of bandwidth.

Keywords: search, distributed hash table, peer-to-peer, Bloom filter, caching

1 Introduction

Recent work on distributed hash tables (DHTs) such as Chord [19], CAN [16], and Pastry [17] has addressed some of the scalability and reliability problems that plagued earlier peer-to-peer overlay networks such as Napster [14] and Gnutella [8]. However, the useful keyword searching present in Napster and Gnutella is absent in the DHTs that endeavor to replace them. In this paper, we present a symmetrically distributed peer-to-peer search engine based on a DHT and intended to serve DHT-based file storage systems.

Applications built using the current generation of DHTs request documents using an opaque key. The means for choosing the key is left for the application built on top of the DHT to determine. For example, the Chord File System, CFS [6], uses hashes of content blocks as keys. Freenet [5, 9], which shares some characteristics of DHTs, uses hashes of filenames as keys. In each case, users must have a single, unique name to retrieve content. No functionality is provided for keyword searches.

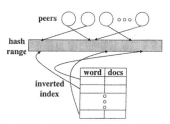

Fig. 1. Distributing an inverted index across a peer-to-peer network.

The system described in this paper provides keyword search functionality for a DHT-based file system or archival storage system, to map keyword queries to the unique routing keys described above. It does so by mapping each keyword to a node in the DHT that will store a list of documents containing that keyword. Figure 1 shows how keywords in the index map into the hash range and, in turn, to nodes in the DHT.

* This research is supported in part by the National Science Foundation (EIA-99772879, ITR-0082912), Hewlett Packard, IBM, Intel, and Microsoft. Vahdat is also supported by an NSF CAREER award (CCR-9984328), and Reynolds is also supported by an NSF fellowship.

M. Endler and D. Schmidt (Eds.): Middleware 2003, LNCS 2672, pp. 21–40, 2003.

We believe that end-user latency is the most important performance metric for a search engine. Most end-user latency in a distributed search engine comes from network transfer times. Thus, minimizing the number of bytes sent and the number of times they are sent is crucial. Both bytes and hops are easy to minimize for queries that can be answered by a single host. Most queries, however, contain several keywords and must be answered by several cooperating hosts. Using a trace of 99,405 queries sent through the IRCache proxy system to Web search engines during a

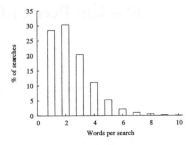

Fig. 2. Number of keywords per search operation in the IRCache for a ten-day period in January 2002.

ten-day period in January 2002, we determined that 71.5% of queries contain two or more keywords. The entire distribution of keywords per query is shown in Figure 2. Because multiple-keyword queries dominate the search workload, optimizing them is important for end-user performance. This paper focuses on minimizing network traffic for multiple-keyword queries.

1.1   Non-goals

One extremely useful feature of distributed hash tables is that they provide a simple service model that hides request routing, churn costs, load balancing, and unavailability. Most DHTs route requests to nodes that can serve them in expected $O(\lg n)$ steps, for networks of n hosts. They keep churn costs [11] – the costs associated with managing node joins and departures – logarithmic with the size of the network. Using consistent hashing [10] they divide load roughly evenly among available hosts. Finally, they perform replication to ensure availability even when individual nodes fail. Our design uses a DHT as its base; thus, it does not directly address these issues.

1.2   Overview

This paper describes our search model, design, and simulation experiments as follows. In Section 2 we describe several aspects of the peer-to-peer search problem space, along with the parts of the problem space we chose to explore. Section 3 describes our approach to performing peer-to-peer searches efficiently. Section 4 details our simulation environment, and Section 5 describes the simulation results. We present related work in Section 6 and conclude in Section 7.

2   System Model

Fundamentally, search is the task of associating keywords with document identifiers and later retrieving document identifiers that match combinations of keywords. Most text searching systems use inverted indices, which map each word found in any document to a list of the documents in which the word appears. Beyond this simple description, many design trade-offs exist. How will the index be partitioned, if at all? Should

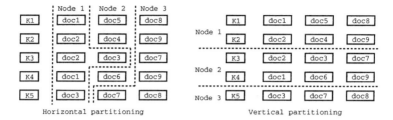

Fig. 3. A horizontally partitioned index stores part of every keyword match-list on each node, often divided by document identifiers. Here we divide the index into document identifiers 1-3, 4-6, and 7-9. A vertically partitioned index assigns each keyword to a single node.

it be distributed, or would a centralized index suffice? In what order will matching documents be listed? How are document changes reflected in the index? We address these questions below.

2.1 Partitioning

Although a sufficiently small index need not be partitioned at all, our target application is a data set large enough to overwhelm the storage and processing capacities of any single node. Thus, some partitioning scheme is required. There are two straightforward partitioning schemes: horizontal and vertical.

For each keyword an index stores, it must store a match-list of identifiers for all of the documents containing the keyword. A horizontally partitioned index divides this list among several nodes, either sequentially or by partitioning the document identifier space. Google [3] operates in this manner. A vertically partitioned index assigns each keyword, undivided, to a single node. Figure 3 shows a small sample index partitioned horizontally and vertically, with $K1$ through $K5$ representing keywords and $doc1$ through $doc9$ representing documents that contain those keywords.

A vertically partitioned index minimizes the cost of searches by ensuring that no more than k servers must participate in answering a query containing k keywords. A horizontally partitioned index requires that all nodes be contacted, regardless of the number of keywords in the query. However, horizontal indices partitioned by document identifier can insert or update a document at a single node, while vertically partitioned indices require that up to k servers participate to insert or update a document with k keywords. As long as more servers participate in the overlay than there are keywords associated with an average document, these costs favor vertical partitioning. Furthermore, in file systems, most files change rarely, and those that change often change in bursts and may be removed shortly after creation, allowing us to optimize updates by propagating changes lazily. In archival storage systems, files change rarely if at all. Thus, we believe that queries will outnumber updates for our proposed uses, further increasing the cost advantage for vertically partitioned systems.

Vertically partitioned indices send queries to a constant number of hosts, while horizontally partitioned indices must broadcast queries to all nodes. Thus, the throughput of a vertically partitioned index theoretically grows linearly as more nodes are added.

Query throughput in a horizontally partitioned index does not benefit at all from additional nodes. Thus, we chose vertical partitioning for our search engine.

2.2 Centralized or Distributed Organization

Google has had great success providing centralized search services for the Web. However, we believe that for peer-to-peer file systems and archival storage networks, a distributed search service is better than a centralized one. First, centralized systems provide a single point of failure. Failures may be network outages; denial-of-service attacks, as plagued several Web sites in February of 2000; or censorship by domestic or foreign authorities. In all such cases, a replicated distributed system may be more robust. Second, many uses of peer-to-peer distributed systems depend on users voluntarily contributing computing resources. A centralized search engine would concentrate both load and trust on a small number of hosts, which is impractical if those hosts are voluntarily contributed by end users.

Both centralized and distributed search systems benefit from replication. Replication improves availability and throughput in exchange for additional hardware and update costs. A distributed search engine benefits more from replication, however, because replicas are less susceptible to correlated failures such as attacks or network outages. Distributed replicas may also allow nodes closer to each other or to the client to respond to queries, reducing latency and network traffic.

2.3 Ranking of Results

One important feature of search engines is the order in which results are presented to the user. Many documents may match a given set of keywords, but some may be more useful to the end user than others. Google's PageRank algorithm [15] has successfully exploited the hyperlinked nature of the Web to give high scores to pages linked to by other pages with high scores. Several search engines have successfully used words' proximity to each other or to the beginning of the page to rank results. Peer-to-peer systems lack the linking structure necessary for PageRank but may be able to take advantage of word position or proximity heuristics. We will discuss specific interactions between ranking techniques and our design in Section 3.5 after we have presented the design.

2.4 Update Discovery

A search engine must discover new, removed, or modified documents. Web search engines have traditionally relied on enumerating the entire Web using crawlers, which results in either lag or inefficiency if the frequency of crawling differs from the frequency of updates for a given page. Popular file-sharing systems use a "push" model for updates instead: clients that have new or modified content notify servers directly. Even with pushed updates, the process of determining keywords and reporting them to server should occur automatically to ensure uniformity.

The Web could support either crawled or pushed updates. Crawled updates are currently the norm. Peer-to-peer services may lack hyperlinks or any other mechanism for enumeration, leaving them dependent on pushed updates. We believe that pushed updates are superior because they promote both efficiency and currency of index information.

2.5   Placement

All storage systems need techniques for placing and finding content. Distributed search systems additionally need techniques for placing index partitions. We use a DHT to map keywords to nodes for the index, and we claim that the placement of content is an orthogonal problem. There is little or no benefit to placing documents and their keywords in the same place. First, very few documents indicated as results for a search are later retrieved; thus, most locality would be wasted. Second, there is no overlap between an index entry and the document it indicates; both still must be retrieved and sent over the network. A search engine is a layer of indirection. It is expected that documents and their keywords may appear in unrelated locations.

3   Efficient Support for Peer-to-Peer Search

In the previous section, we discussed the architecture and potential benefits of a fully distributed peer-to-peer search infrastructure. The primary contribution of this work is to demonstrate the feasibility of this approach with respect to individual end user requests. Conducting a search for a single keyword consists of looking up the keyword's mapping in the index to reveal all of the documents containing that keyword. This involves contacting a single remote server, an operation with network costs comparable to accessing a traditional search service. A boolean "AND" search consists of looking up the sets for each keyword and returning the intersection. As with traditional search engines, we return a small subset of the matching documents. This operation requires contacting multiple peers across the wide area, and the requisite intersection operation across the sets returned by each peer can become prohibitively expensive, both in terms of consumed network bandwidth and the latency incurred from transmitting this data across the wide area.

Consider the example in Figure 4(a), which shows a simple network with servers s_A and s_B. Server s_A contains the set of documents A for a given keyword k_A, and server s_B contains the set of documents B for another keyword k_B. $|A|$ and $|B|$ are the number of documents containing k_A and k_B, respectively. $A \cap B$ is the set of all documents containing both k_A and k_B.

The primary challenge in performing efficient keyword searches in a distributed inverted index is limiting the amount of bandwidth used for multiple-keyword searches. The naive approach, shown in Figure 4(a), consists of the first server, s_A, sending its entire set of matching document IDs, A, to the second server, s_B, so that s_B can calculate $A \cap B$ and send the results to the client. This is wasteful because the intersection, $A \cap B$, is likely to be far smaller than A, resulting in most of the information in A getting discarded at s_B. Furthermore, the size of A (i.e., the number of occurrences of the keyword k_A) scales roughly with the number of documents in the system. Thus, the cost of naive search operations grows linearly with the number of documents in the system. We

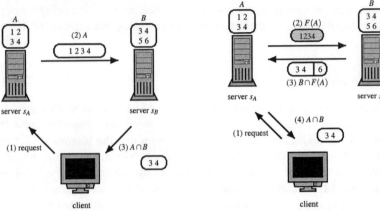

(a) A simple approach to "AND" queries. Each server stores a list of document IDs corresponding to one keyword.

(b) Bloom filters help reduce the bandwidth requirement of "AND" queries. The gray box represents the Bloom filter $F(A)$ of the set A. Note the false positive in the set $B \cap F(A)$ that server s_B sends back to server s_A.

Fig. 4. Network architecture and protocol overview.

propose three techniques to limit wasted bandwidth, to ensure scalability, and to reduce end-client latency: Bloom filters, caches, and incremental results. We discuss each of these approaches in turn and present analytical results showing the potential benefits of each technique under a variety of conditions before exploring these tradeoffs in more detail through simulation in Section 5.

3.1   Bloom Filters

A Bloom filter [2, 7, 13] is a hash-based data structure that summarizes membership in a set. By sending a Bloom filter based on A instead of sending A itself, we reduce the amount of communication required for s_B to determine $A \cap B$. The membership test returns false positives with a tunable, predictable probability and never returns false negatives. Thus, the intersection calculated by s_B will contain all of the true intersection, as well as a few hits that contain only k_B and not k_A. The number of false positives falls exponentially as the size of the Bloom filter increases.

Given optimal choice of hash functions, the probability of a false positive is

$$p_{fp} = .6185^{m/n}, \tag{1}$$

where m is the number of bits in the Bloom filter and n is the number of elements in the set [7]. Thus, to maintain a fixed probability of false positives, the size of the Bloom filter must be proportional to the number of elements represented.

Our method for using Bloom filters to determine remote set intersections is shown in Figure 4(b) and proceeds as follows. A and B are the document sets to intersect, each containing a large number of document IDs for the keywords k_A and k_B, respectively.

The client wishes to retrieve the intersection $A \cap B$. Server s_A sends a Bloom filter $F(A)$ of set A to server s_B. Server s_B tests each member of set B for membership in $F(A)$. Server s_B sends the matching elements, $B \cap F(A)$, back to server s_A, along with some textual context for each match. Server s_A removes the false positives from s_B's results by calculating $A \cap (B \cap F(A))$, which is equivalent to $A \cap B$.

False positives in $B \cap F(A)$ do not affect the correctness of the final intersection but do waste bandwidth. They are eliminated in the final step, when s_A intersects $B \cap F(A)$ against A.

It is also possible to send $B \cap F(A)$ directly from s_B to the client rather than first sending it to s_A and removing the false positives. Doing so eliminates the smaller transfer and its associated latency at the expense of correctness. Given reasonable values for $|A|$, $|B|$, the size of each document record, and the cache hit rate (see Section 3.2), the false-positive rate may be as high as 0.05 or as low as 0.00003. This means that $B \cap F(A)$ will have from $0.00003|B|$ to $0.05|B|$ extra elements that do not contain k_A. For example, if 5% of the elements of B actually contain k_A, then returning the rough intersection $B \cap F(A)$ to the client results in between $\frac{0.00003|B|}{(0.05+0.00003)|B|} = 0.06\%$ and $\frac{0.05|B|}{(0.05+0.05)|B|} = 50\%$ of the results being incorrect and not actually containing k_A, where each expression represents the ratio of the number of false positives to the total number of elements in $B \cap F(A)$. The decision to use this optimization is made at run time, when the parameters are known and p_{fp} can be predicted. Server s_A may choose an m value slightly larger than optimal to reduce p_{fp} and improve the likelihood that s_B can return $B \cap F(A)$ directly to the client.

The total number of bits sent during the exchange shown in Figure 4(b) is $m + p_{fp}|B|j + |A \cap B|j$, where j is the number of bits in each document identifier. For this paper, we assume that document identifiers are 128-bit hashes of document contents; thus, j is 128. The final term, $|A \cap B|j$, is the size of the intersection itself. It can be ignored in our optimization, because it represents the resulting intersection, which must be sent regardless of our choice of algorithm.

The resulting total number of excess bits sent (i.e., excluding the intersection itself) is

$$m + p_{fp}|B|j.$$

Substituting for p_{fp} from Equation 1 yields the total number of excess bits as

$$m + .6185^{m/|A|}|B|j. \tag{2}$$

Taking the first derivative with respect to m and solving for zero yields an optimal Bloom filter size of

$$m = |A| \log_{.6185}\left(2.081\frac{|A|}{|B|j}\right). \tag{3}$$

Figure 5(a) shows the minimum number of excess bits sent for three sets of values for $|A|$, $|B|$, and j. The optimal m for any given $|A|$, $|B|$, and j is unique and directly determines the minimum number of excess bits sent. For example, when $|A|$ and $|B|$ are $10,000$ and j is 128, m is $85,734$, and the minimum number of excess bits sent is

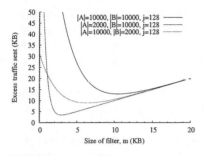
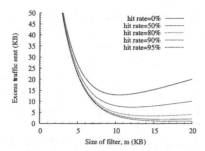

(a) Expected excess bits sent as a function of m

(b) Improving cache hit rates reduces the amount of data sent and increases the size of the optimal Bloom filter.

Fig. 5. Effects of Bloom filter size and cache hit rate.

$106,544$, representing $12.01 : 1$ compression when compared to the cost of sending all $1,280,000$ bits ($10,000$ documents, each with a 128-bit ID) of either A or B.

As also shown in Figure 5(a), performance is not symmetric when A and B differ in size. With j constant at 128, the minimum number of excess bits for $|A| = 2,000$ and $|B| = 10,000$ is $28,008$, lower than the minimum number for $|A| = 10,000$ and $|B| = 2,000$, which is $73,046$. $28,008$ bits represents $9.14 : 1$ compression when compared with the $256,000$ bits needed to send all of A. The server with the smaller set should always initiate the transfer.

Our Bloom filter intersection technique can be expanded to arbitrary numbers of keywords. Server s_A sends $F(A)$ to server s_B, which sends $F(B \cap F(A))$ to s_C, and so on. The final server, s_Z, sends its intersection back to s_A. Each server that encoded its transmission using a Bloom filter must process the intersection once more to remove any false positives introduced by its filter. Thus, the intersection is sent to each server except s_Z a second time. As above, the expected number of excess bits is minimized when $|A| \le |B| \le |C| \le \ldots \le |Z|$.

3.2 Caches

Caching can eliminate the need for s_A to send A or $F(A)$ if server s_B already has A or $F(A)$ stored locally. We derive more benefit from caching Bloom filters than from caching entire document match lists because the smaller size of the Bloom representation means that a cache of fixed size can store data for more keywords. The benefit of caching depends on the presence of locality in the list of words searched for by a user population at any given time. To quantify this intuition, we use the same ten-day IRCache trace described in Section 1 to determine word search popularity. There were a total of $251,768$ words searched for across the $99,405$ searches, $45,344$ of them unique. Keyword popularity roughly followed a Zipf distribution, with the most common keyword searched for $4,365$ times. The dominance of popular keywords suggests that even a small cache of either the Bloom filter or the actual document list on A is likely to produce high hit rates.

When server s_B already has the Bloom filter $F(A)$ in its cache, a search operation for the keywords k_A and k_B may skip the first step, in which server s_A sends its Bloom filter to s_B. On average, a Bloom filter will be in another server's cache with probability r equal to the cache hit rate.

The excess bits formula in Equation (2) can be adapted to consider cache hit rate, r, as follows:

$$(1-r)m + .6185^{m/|A|}|B|j \qquad (4)$$

Setting the derivative of this with respect to m to zero yields the optimal m as

$$m = |A|\log_{.6185}\left[(1-r)2.081\frac{|A|}{|B|j}\right]. \qquad (5)$$

Figure 5(b) shows the effect of cache hit rates on the excess bits curves, assuming $|A|$ and $|B|$ are both $10,000$ and j is 128. Each curve still has a unique minimum. For example, when the hit rate, r, is 0.5, the minimum excess number of bits sent is $60,486$, representing $21.16 : 1$ compression when compared with sending A or B. Improvements in the cache hit rate always reduce the minimum expected number of excess bits and increase the optimal m. The reduction in the expected number of excess bits sent is nearly linear with improvements in the hit rate. The optimal m increases because as we become less likely to send the Bloom filter, we can increase its size slightly to reduce the false-positive rate. Even with these increases in m, we can store hundreds of cache entries per megabyte of available local storage. We expect such caching to yield high hit rates given even moderate locality in the request stream.

Cache consistency is handled with a simple time-to-live field. Updates only occur at a keyword's primary location, and slightly stale match list information is acceptable, especially given the current state of Internet search services, where some degree of staleness is unavoidable. Thus, more complex consistency protocols should not be necessary.

3.3   Incremental Results

Clients rarely need all of the results of a keyword search. By using streaming transfers and returning only the desired number of results, we can greatly reduce the amount of information that needs to be sent. This is, in fact, critical for scalability: the number of results for any given query is roughly proportional to the number of documents in the network. Thus, the bandwidth cost of returning all results to the client will grow linearly with the size of the network. Bloom filters and caches can yield a substantial constant-factor improvement, but neither technique eliminates the linear growth in cost. Truncating the results is the only way to achieve constant cost independent of the number of documents in the network.

When a client searches for a fixed number of results, servers s_A and s_B communicate incrementally until that number is reached. Server s_A sends its Bloom filter in chunks and server s_B sends a block of results (true intersections and false positives) for each chunk until server s_A has enough results to return to the client. Because a single Bloom filter cannot be divided and still retain any meaning, we divide the set A into chunks and send a full Bloom filter of each chunk. The chunk size can be set adaptively based on how many elements of A are likely to be needed to produce the desired number of results. This protocol is shown in Figure 6. Note that s_A and s_B overlap their communication: s_A sends $F(A_2)$ as s_B sends $B \cap F(A_1)$. This protocol can be extended logically to more than two participants. Chunks are streamed in parallel from server s_A to s_B, from s_B to s_C, and so on. The protocol is an incremental version of the multi-server protocol described at the end of Section 3.1.

When the system streams data in chunks, caches can store several fractional Bloom filters for each keyword rather than storing the entire Bloom filter for each keyword. This allows servers to retain or discard partial entries in the cache. A server may get a partial cache hit for a given keyword if it needs several chunks but already has some of them stored locally. Storing only a fraction of each keyword's Bloom filter also reduces the amount of space in the cache that each keyword consumes, which increases the expected hit rate.

Sending Bloom filters incrementally substantially increases the CPU costs involved in processing a search. The cost for server s_B to calculate each intersection $B \cap F(A_i)$ is the same as the cost to calculate the entire intersection $B \cap F(A)$ at once because each element of B must be tested against each chunk. This added cost can be avoided by sending

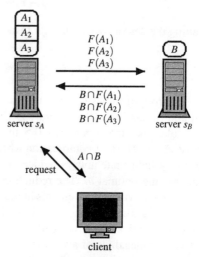

Fig. 6. Servers s_A and s_B send their data one chunk at a time until the desired intersection size is reached.

contiguous portions of the hash space in each chunk and indicating to s_B which fraction of B (described as a portion of the hash space) it needs to test against $F(A)$.

3.4   Virtual Hosts

One key concern in a peer-to-peer system is the inherent heterogeneity of such systems. Randomly distributing functionality (e.g., keywords) across the system runs the risk of assigning a popular keyword to a relatively under-provisioned machine in terms of memory, CPU, or network capacity. Further, no hash function will uniformly distribute functionality across a hash range. Thus, individual machines may be assigned disproportionate numbers of keywords (recall that keywords are assigned to the host whose ID is closest to it in the hash range). Virtual hosts [6] are one technique to address this potential limitation. Using this approach, a node participates in a peer-to-peer system as several logical hosts, proportional to its request processing capacity. A node that participates as several virtual hosts is assigned proportionally more load, addressing heterogeneous node capabilities. Thus, a node with ten times the capacity of some baseline measure would be assigned ten virtual IDs (which means that it is mapped to ten different IDs in the hash range). An optional system-wide scaling factor for each node's number of virtual hosts further reduces the probability that any single node is assigned a disproportionately large portion of the hash range. This effect is quantified in Section 5, but consider the following example: with 100 hosts of equal power, it is likely that one or more hosts will be assigned significantly more than 1% of the hash range. However, with a scaling factor of 100, it is much less likely that any host will be assigned much more than 1% of the range because an "unlucky" hash (large portion of the hash region) for one virtual host is likely to be canceled out by a "lucky" hash (small portion of the hash region) for another virtual host on the same physical node.

3.5   Discussion

Two of the techniques described here, Bloom filters and caching, yield constant-factor improvements in terms of the number of bytes sent and the end-to-end query latency. Bloom filters compress document ID sets by about one order of magnitude, in exchange for either added latency or a configurable probability of false positives. Caching exploits re-referencing and sharing in the query workload to reduce the probability that document ID sets need to be sent. However, even together, these techniques leave both bytes sent and end-to-end query time roughly proportional to the number of documents in the system.

The third technique, incremental results, reduces the number of bytes sent and the end-to-end query latency to a constant in most cases. As long as the user wants only a constant number of results, only a constant amount of work will be done, regardless of how many possible results exist in the system. Incremental results yield no improvement in some unusual cases, however. If the user searches for several keywords that are individually popular but mostly uncorrelated in the document space, there may be a small but nonzero number of valid results[1]. If the number of results is nonzero but smaller than the number that the client requests, the system must consider the entire search space, rendering incremental results useless. In cases such as this, the entire search space must be considered, and incremental results will increase, rather than decrease, the number of bytes sent and the end-to-end query latency. However, caching may alleviate the problem if the words used are popular in search queries, and Bloom filters still yield approximately a ten-to-one compression factor.

We expect that searches containing popular but uncorrelated keywords will be rare. In our IRCache search trace, most of the queries with small numbers of results had uncommon (often misspelled) keywords. Uncommon keywords—i.e., those with few matching documents—are easy to handle, as discussed in Section 3.1. The system considers the least common keyword first, bounding the maximum size of any intersection set sent for the remainder of the query.

3.6   Ranking of Results

Two of our optimization techniques, Bloom filters and incremental results, complicate problem of ranking results. Bloom filters roughly convey membership in a set, but they

---

[1] One example of a difficult search is "OpenBSD birthday pony," suggested by David Mazières at New York University. In recent Google searches, these three keywords match two million, eight million, and two million documents, respectively. Only fifteen documents contain all three.

do not provide the ability to order set members or to convey additional data with each member, such as a word's position in a document. The uncompressed response message containing $B \cap F(A)$ can contain document-ranking or word-position information, which would give server s_A enough information to generate rankings based on both keywords, k_A and k_B. However, in Section 3.1, we suggested eliminating this uncompressed response message. Doing so eliminates the ability to consider k_A in any ranking techniques.

Incremental results can alleviate the problems with Bloom filters. If each chunk sent contains document IDs with strictly lower rankings than in previous chunks, then the first results returned to the client will be the best, though order within a chunk will not be preserved. However, in Section 3.3 we suggested sending contiguous portions of the hash space in each chunk to save processing time on server s_B. These two techniques are mutually exclusive.

We believe that ranking documents is more important than eliminating one additional message or saving processing time. However, this trade-off can be determined at run time according to user preference.

3.7   Load Balancing

A vertically partitioned index distributes keywords randomly, resulting in a binomial (roughly normal) distribution of the number of keywords on each node. However, keyword appearance popularity (i.e., the size of the keyword's match-list) and search popularity are both roughly Zipf-distributed. Keyword appearance popularity determines the storage required, and keyword search popularity determines processing loads. Both contribute to network loads. The resulting storage, processing, and network loads are less evenly distributed than with a horizontally partitioned index. Virtual hosts alleviate the problem by assigning larger loads to more capable nodes, but they do not make load any more balanced. Increasing the size of the network and the number of documents results in somewhat more balanced load. As long as the network is over-provisioned, which many peer-to-peer networks are, we believe that load balancing will not be a problem.

4   Simulation Infrastructure

The simple analysis described above in Section 3 provides some insight into the potential benefits of our three approaches toward efficiently supporting peer-to-peer search. However, the actual benefits and tradeoffs depend heavily upon target system characteristics and access patterns. To test the validity of our approach under a range of realistic circumstances, we developed a simulation infrastructure implementing our three techniques. In this section, we discuss the details of this simulation infrastructure before presenting the results of our evaluation in Section 5.

4.1   Goals

Our goal in writing the simulator was to test the system with a realistic workload and to test the effects of parameters and features that did not lend themselves to tractable analysis. In particular, we tested the effects of the number of hosts in the network, the use of virtual hosts, the Bloom filter threshold, Bloom filter sizes, caching techniques, and the use of incremental results. We also tested the system's sensitivity to varying network characteristics.

The Bloom filter threshold refers to the document set size below which a host transmits a full list rather than a Bloom-compressed set. For small documents, the total bandwidth consumed for transmission to a remote host (for set intersection) may be so small that it may not be worth the CPU time required to compress the set. Eliminating the Bloom step further eliminates the need to return to the transmitting host to eliminate false positives from the intersection. Typically, we find that the extra CPU overhead and network overhead of returning the result is worth the substantial saving in network bandwidth realized by using Bloom filters. In Section 5, we quantify this effect for a variety of Bloom thresholds.

Bloom filter sizes affect the number of false positives transmitted during the search process. If the client is willing to accept some probability of false positives (a returned document containing only a subset of the requested keywords), sufficiently large Bloom filters can meet the client's accepted false-positive rate and eliminate the need to revisit nodes to remove false positives, as described in Section 3.1. That is, small Bloom filters result in significant compression of a keyword-set size at the cost of either generating more false positives in the result returned to the client or requiring the transmission of the intersection back to the originating host for false positive elimination.

4.2   Design

The simulator runs as a single-threaded Java application. We implement the inverted index, word-to-host mapping, and host measurement (in this case, random generation) in separate classes so that much of the simulator could be reused in a full implementation of our protocol. Our simulations use a real document set and search trace. The document set totals 1.85 GB of HTML data, comprising 1.17 million unique words in 105,593 documents, retrieved by crawling to a recursion depth of five from 100 seed URLs [4]. The searches performed are read from a list of 95,409 searches containing 45,344 unique keywords. The search trace is the IRCache log file described in Section 1. Note that the results presented in this paper are restricted to these particular traces. However, we do not expect the benefits of our techniques to differ significantly for other workloads.

Hosts in the network are generated at random based on configurable distributions for upload speed, download speed, CPU speed, and local storage capacity. We use three distributions for network speeds: one with all modems, one with all backbone links, and one based on the measurements of the Gnutella network performed by Saroiu et al [18]. This last heterogeneous set contains a mixture of modems, broadband connections (cable/DSL) and high-speed LAN connections. Our CPU speed distribution is roughly a bell curve, with a mean of 750 MIPS, and our local storage distribution is a heavy-tailed piece-wise function ranging from 1 MB to 100 MB. We experimented with a broad range of host characteristics and present the results for this representative subset in this paper. To generate random latencies, we place hosts at random in a 2,500-mile square grid and assume that network packets travel an average of 100,000 miles per second.

The time required to send a network message is the propagation time, as determined by the distance between the hosts involved, plus the transmission time, as determined by the minimum of the sender's upload speed and the recipient's download speed, and the size of the packet. The total network time for a search is the sum of the latency and transmission time for all packets sent among server nodes processing the query. We ignore the time spent by the client sending the initial query and receiving the results because these times are constant and independent of any search architecture, whether centralized or distributed.

Document IDs are assumed to be 128 bits. The time required to look up words in a local index or perform intersections or Bloom filter operations is based on the CPU speed and the following assumptions for operation costs: 1,500 simple operations per hit to look up words in an index, 500 simple operations per element to intersect two result sets, and 10,000 simple operations per document ID inserted into a Bloom filter or checked against a Bloom filter received from another host. We believe that in general, these assumptions place an upper bound on the CPU cost of these operations. Even with these assumptions, we find that network time typically dominates CPU time for our target scenarios.

We determine the number of virtual hosts to assign each simulated node based on its network and CPU speeds when compared to a baseline host. The baseline host has a 57.5 MIPS CPU and 30 Kbit/s network links. These speeds were chosen as those required to compute and transmit 5,000 Bloom operations per second. Each node is compared to the baseline host in three categories: upload speed, download speed, and CPU speed. The nodes's minimum margin over the baseline host in these three categories is rounded down and taken to be its number of virtual hosts.

To perform each query, the simulator looks up each keyword in the inverted index, obtaining up to M results for each, where M is the incremental result size. Each host intersects its set with the data from the previous host and forwards it to the subsequent host, as described in Section 3.1. Each node forwards its current intersected set as either a Bloom filter or a full set, depending on whether or not the set is larger than the Bloom threshold. After each peer performs its part of the intersection, any node that sent a Bloom filter in the first pass is potentially revisited to remove false positives. If the number of resulting documents is at least as large as the the desired number, the search is over. Otherwise, M is increased adaptively to twice what appears to be needed to produce the desired number of results, and the search is rerun.

At each step, a host checks its cache to see if it has data for the subsequent host's document list in its local cache. If so, it performs the subsequent host's portion of the intersection locally and skips that host in the sending sequence.

4.3 Validation

We validated our simulator in two ways. First, we calculated the behavior and performance of short, artificial traces by hand and confirmed that the simulator returns the same results. Second, we varied the Bloom filter size, m, in the simulator and compared the results to the analytical results presented in Section 3.1. The analytical results shown in Figure 5(b) closely resemble the simulated results shown in Figure 9(a).

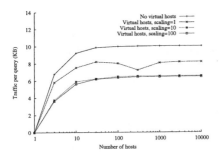 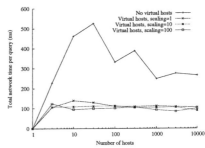

(a) The number of bytes sent increases very little beyond networks of 100 hosts. Enabling virtual hosts reduces the number of bytes sent by about 18%. Scaling the number of virtual hosts reduces the number of bytes sent by an additional 18%.

(b) Virtual hosts cut the amount of time spent transmitting by up to 60%. Scaling the number of virtual hosts yields a small additional improvement.

Fig. 7. Network scaling and virtual hosts.

5   Experimental Results

The goal of this section is to understand the performance effects of our proposed techniques on a peer-to-peer search infrastructure. Ideally, we wish to demonstrate that our proposed peer-to-peer search system scales with system size (total resource consumption per search grows sub-linearly with the number of participating hosts) and that techniques such as Bloom filters and caching improve the performance of individual requests. Primarily, we focus on the metric of bytes sent per request. Techniques such as caching and the use of Bloom filters largely serve to reduce this metric. Reducing bytes per request has the added benefit of reducing total time spent in the network and hence end-to-end client perceived latency. We also study the effects of the distribution of network and CPU characteristics on overall system performance. One challenge with peer-to-peer systems is addressing the subset of hosts that have significantly less computation power and network bandwidth than is required to support a high-performance search infrastructure.

Finally, although we implemented incremental results, we do not present results for this technique here because our target document set is not large enough to return large numbers of hits for most queries. For our workload, this optimization reduces network utilization by at most 30% in the best case. However, we believe this technique will be increasingly valuable as the document space increases in size.

5.1   Scalability and Virtual Hosts

A key goal of our work is to demonstrate that a peer-to-peer search infrastructure scales with the number of participating hosts. Unless otherwise specified, the results presented in this section all assume the heterogeneous distribution [18] of per-peer network connectivity and the default distribution of CPU power described in Section 4. Caching and Bloom filters are both initially turned off. As shown in Figure 7(a), increasing the number of hosts in the simulation has little effect on the total number of bytes sent. With very small networks, several keywords from a query may be located on a single host, resulting in entirely local handling of parts of the query. However, beyond 100 hosts, this probability becomes insignificant, and each n-keyword query must contact n hosts, independent of the size of the system.

In addition to demonstrating the scalability of the system, Figures 7(a) and 7(b) also quantify the benefits of the use of virtual hosts in the system. Recall that when virtual hosts are turned on, each node is assigned a number of hosts based on its capacity relative to the predefined baseline described in Section 4. The virtual host scaling factor further multiplies this number of hosts by some constant value to ensure that each physical host is assigned a uniform portion of the overall hash range as discussed in Section 4. Overall, virtual hosts have a small effect on the number of total bytes sent per query. This is because enabling virtual hosts concentrates data mostly on powerful hosts, increasing the probability that parts of a query can be handled entirely locally. Virtual host scaling results in better expected load balancing, which very slightly decreases the amount of data that must be sent on average.

Although virtual hosts have little effect on how much data must be sent, they can significantly decrease the amount of time spent sending the data, as shown in Figure 7(b). By assigning more load to more capable hosts, the virtual hosts technique can cut network times by nearly 60%. Using virtual host scaling further decreases expected network times by reducing the probability that a bottleneck host will be assigned a disproportionate amount of load by mistake. Thus, while total bytes sent decreases only slightly as a result of better load balancing, total network time decreases significantly because more capable hosts (with faster network connections) become responsible for a larger fraction of requests.

5.2   Bloom Filters and Caching

Having established the scalability of our general approach, we now turn our attention to the additional benefits available from the use of Bloom filters to reduce network utilization. In particular, we focus on how large the Bloom filter should be and for what minimum data set size it should be invoked. Using Bloom filters for every transfer results in substantial unnecessary data transmissions. Any time a Bloom filter is used, the host using it must later revisit the same query to eliminate any false positives. Thus, Bloom filters should only be used when the time saved will outweigh the time spent sending the

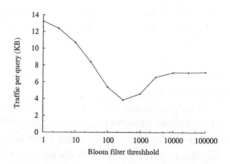

Fig. 8. Using Bloom filters less often significantly reduces the amount of data sent by eliminating the need to revisit nodes to eliminate false positives.

clean-up message. Figure 8 shows the total bytes transmitted per query as a function of the Bloom filter threshold, assuming the default value of 6 bits per Bloom entry. We find that the optimal Bloom filter threshold for our trace was approximately 300. Any set below this size should be sent in its entirety as the savings from using Bloom filters

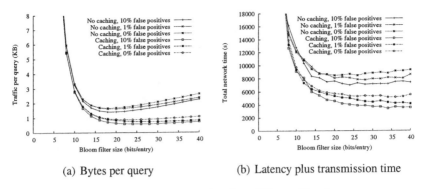

(a) Bytes per query   (b) Latency plus transmission time

Fig. 9. Network costs as a function of Bloom filter size.

do not outweigh the network (not to mention latency) overhead of revisiting the host to eliminate false positives.

Next, we consider the effects of varying the number of bits per entry in the Bloom filter and of caching on total network traffic. Figure 9(a) plots the total number of bytes transmitted as a function of the Bloom filter size. The two sets of curves represent the case when we enable and disable caching. Within each set, we set a maximum rate of allowable false positives in the set of documents returned to the user for a particular query, at 0%, 1%, and 10%. When the client allows 1% or 10% false positives, false-positive removal steps may sometimes be eliminated; increasing the Bloom filter size enhances this effect. Figure 9(b) shows that allowing false positives has significantly more effect on varying total network time than it does on bytes transferred as it eliminates a number of required message transmissions.

The effects of caching shown in Figure 9(a) are similar to those derived analytically in Figure 5(b). Caching decreases the total amount of data sent and increases the optimal Bloom filter size: in this case, from 18 bits per entry to 24 bits per entry. For optimal Bloom filter sizes of 18 and 24 bits per entry in the no-caching and caching cases respectively, our caching technique introduces more than a 50% reduction in the total number of bytes transmitted per query.

5.3 Putting It All Together

We now present the end-to-end average query times considering all of our optimizations under a variety of assumed network conditions. We break down this end-to-end time into the three principal components that contribute to end-to-end latency: CPU processing time, network transmission time (bytes transferred divided by the speed of the slower network connection speed of the two communicating peers), and latency (determined by the distance between communicating peers). Recall from Section 4 that we do not measure the time associated with either the client request or the final response as the size of these messages is independent of our optimization techniques.

Figure 10 shows three bar charts that break down total end-to-end search time under the three network conditions described in Section 4: WAN, Heterogeneous, and Modem. For each network setting there are four individual bars, representing the effects of virtual hosts on or off and of caching on or off. Each bar is further broken down into network transmission time, CPU processing time, and network latency. In the case of an all-modem network, end-to-end query time is dominated by network transmission time. The use of virtual hosts has no effect on query times because the network set is homogeneous. Caching does reduce the network transmission portion by roughly 30%. All queries still manage to complete in 1 second or less because, as shown in Figure 9(a) the use of all our optimizations reduces the total bytes transferred per query to less than 1,000 bytes for our target workload; a 56K modem can transfer 6 KB/sec in the best case. However, our results are limited by the fact that our simulator does not model network contention. In general, we expect the per-query average to be worse than our reported results if any individual node's network connection becomes saturated. This limitation is significantly mitigated under different network conditions as individual nodes are more likely to have additional bandwidth available and the use of virtual hosts will spread the load to avoid underprovisioned hosts.

In the homogeneous WAN case, network time is negligible in all cases given the very high transmission speeds. The use of caching reduces latency and CPU time by 48% and 30%, respectively, by avoiding the need to calculate and transmit Bloom filters in the case of a cache hit. Enabling virtual hosts reduces the CPU time by concentrating requests on the subset of WAN nodes with more CPU processing power. Recall that although the network is homogeneous in this case we still have heterogeneity in CPU processing power as described in Section 4.

Finally, the use of virtual hosts and caching together has the most pronounced effect on the heterogeneous network, together reducing average per-query response times by 59%. In particular, the use of virtual hosts reduces the network transmission portion of average query response times by 48% by concentrating keywords on the subset of nodes with more network bandwidth. Caching uniformly reduces all aspects of the average query time, in particular reducing the latency components by 47% in each case by eliminating the need for a significant portion of network communication.

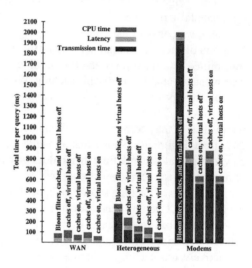

Fig. 10. Isolating the effects of caching, virtual hosts, and different network characteristics for optimal Bloom threshold (300) and Bloom filter sizes (18/24 for caching on or off).

6   Related Work

Work related to ours can be divided into four categories: the first generation of peer-to-peer systems; the second-generation, based on distributed hash tables; Web search engines; and database semijoin reductions. We dealt with DHT-based systems in Section 1. The others, we describe here.

The first generation of peer-to-peer systems consists of Napster [14], Gnutella [8], and Freenet [5,9]. Napster and Gnutella both use searches as their core location determination technique. Napster performs searches centrally on well-known servers that store the metadata, location, and keywords for each document. Gnutella broadcasts search queries to all nodes and allows each node to perform the search in an implementation-specific manner. Yang and Garcia-Molina suggest techniques to reduce the number of nodes contacted in a Gnutella search while preserving the implementation-specific search semantics and a satisfactory number of responses [20]. Freenet provides no search mechanism and depends instead on well-known names and well-known directories of names.

Web search engines such as Google [3] operate in a centralized manner. A farm of servers retrieves all reachable content on the Web and builds an inverted index. Another farm of servers performs lookups in this inverted index. When the inverted index is all in one location, multiple-keyword searches can be performed with entirely local-area communication, and the optimizations presented here are not needed. Distributing the index over a wide area provides greater availability than the centralized approach. Because our system can take advantage of the explicit insert operations in peer-to-peer systems, we also provide more up-to-date results than any crawler-based approach can.

The general problem of remotely intersecting two sets of document IDs is equivalent to the database problem of performing a remote natural join. We are using two ideas from the database literature. Sending only the data necessary for the intersection (i.e., join) comes from work on semijoin reductions [1]. Using a Bloom filter to summarize the set of document IDs comes from work on Bloom joins [12, 13].

7   Conclusions

This paper presents the design and evaluation of a peer-to-peer search infrastructure. In this context we make the following contributions. First, we show that our architecture is scalable; global network state and message traffic grows sub-linearly with increasing network size. Next, relative to a centralized search infrastructure, our approach can maintain high performance and availability in the face of individual failures and performance fluctuations through replication. Finally, through explicit document publishing, our distributed keyword index delivers improved completeness and accuracy relative to traditional spidering techniques.

One important consideration in our architecture is reducing the overhead of multi-keyword conjunctive searches. We describe and evaluate a number of cooperating techniques—Bloom filters, virtual hosts, caching, and incremental results—that, taken together, reduce both consumed network resources and end-to-end perceived client search latency by an order of magnitude for our target workload.

Acknowledgments

We are grateful to Duane Wessels of the IRCache project (supported by NSF grants NCR-9616602 and NCR-9521745) for access to their trace data files. We would also like to thank Lipyeow Lim for access to the 1.85 GB HTML data set we used for our document trace. Finally, Rebecca Braynard, Jun Yang, and Terence Kelly provided helpful comments on drafts of this paper.

References

1. Philip Bernstein and Dah-Ming Chiu. Using semi-joins to solve relational queries. *Journal of the Association for Computing Machinery*, 28(1):25–40, January 1981.
2. Burton H. Bloom. Space/time trade-offs in hash coding with allowable errors. *Communications of the ACM*, 13(7):422–426, 1970.
3. Sergey Brin and Lawrence Page. The anatomy of a large-scale hypertextual web search engine. In *7th International World Wide Web Conference*, 1998.
4. Junghoo Cho and Hector Garcia-Molina. The evolution of the web and implications for an incremental crawler. In *The VLDB Journal*, September 2000.
5. I. Clarke. A distributed decentralised information storage and retrieval system, 1999.
6. Frank Dabek, M. Frans Kaashoek, David Karger, Robert Morris, and Ion Stoica. Wide-area cooperative storage with CFS. In *Proceedings of the 18th ACM Symposium on Operating Systems Principles (SOSP'01)*, October 2001.
7. Li Fan, Pei Cao, Jussara Almeida, and Andrei Broder. Summary cache: A scalable wide-area web cache sharing protocol. In *Proceedings of ACM SIGCOMM'98*, pages 254–265, 1998.
8. Gnutella. http://gnutella.wego.com/.
9. T. Hong. Freenet: A distributed anonymous information storage and retrieval system. In *ICSI Workshop on Design Issues in Anonymity and Unobservability*, 2000.
10. David R. Karger, Eric Lehman, Frank Thomson Leighton, Rina Panigrahy, Matthew S. Levine, and Daniel Lewin. Consistent hashing and random trees: Distributed caching protocols for relieving hot spots on the World Wide Web. In *ACM Symposium on Theory of Computing*, pages 654–663, 1997.
11. David Liben-Nowell, Hari Balakrishnan, and David Karger. Analysis of the evolution of peer-to-peer systems. In *Proceedings of ACM Conference on Principles of Distributed Computing (PODC)*, 2002.
12. Lothar Mackert and Guy Lohman. R^* optimizer validation and performance evaluation for local queries. In *ACM-SIGMOD Conference on Management of Data*, 1986.
13. James Mullin. Optimal semijoins for distributed database systems. *IEEE Transactions on Software Engineering*, 16(5):558–560, May 1990.
14. Napster. http://www.napster.com/.
15. Lawrence Page, Sergey Brin, Rajeev Motwani, and Terry Winograd. The PageRank citation ranking: Bringing order to the web. Technical report, Stanford University, 1998.
16. Sylvia Ratnasamy, Paul Francis, Mark Handley, Richard Karp, and Scott Shenker. A scalable content-addressable network. In *Proceedings of ACM SIGCOMM'01*, 2001.
17. Antony Rowstron and Peter Druschel. Storage management and caching in PAST, a large-scale, persistent peer-to-peer storage utility. In *Proceedings of the 18th ACM Symposium on Operating Systems Principles (SOSP'01)*, 2001.
18. Stefan Saroiu, P. Krishna Gummadi, and Steven D. Gribble. A measurement study of peer-to-peer file sharing systems. In *Proceedings of Multimedia Computing and Networking 2002 (MMCN'02)*, January 2002.
19. Ion Stoica, Robert Morris, David Karger, M. Frans Kaashoek, and Hari Balakrishnan. Chord: A scalable peer-to-peer lookup service for Internet applications. In *Proceedings of ACM SIGCOMM'01*, 2001.
20. Beverly Yang and Hector Garcia-Molina. Efficient search in peer-to-peer networks. Technical Report 2001-47, Stanford University, October 2001.

NaradaBrokering:
A Distributed Middleware Framework and Architecture
for Enabling Durable Peer-to-Peer Grids

Shrideep Pallickara and Geoffrey Fox

Community Grid Labs, Indiana University, 501 N. Morton St, Suite 224
Bloomington, IN-47404. USA
{spallick,gcf}@indiana.edu

Abstract. A Peer-to-Peer (P2P) Grid would comprise services that include those of Grids and P2P networks and naturally support environments that have features of both limiting cases. Such a P2P grid integrates the evolving ideas of computational grids, distributed objects, web services, P2P networks and message oriented middleware. In this paper we investigate the architecture, comprising a distributed brokering system that will support such a hybrid environment. Access to services can then be mediated either by the middleware or alternatively by direct P2P interactions between machines.

1   Introduction

The Grid [1-4] has made dramatic progress recently with impressive technology and several large important applications initiated in high-energy physics [5,6], earth science [7,8] and other areas [9,10]. At the same time, there have been equally impressive advances in broadly deployed Internet technology. We can cite the dramatic growth in the use of XML, the "disruptive" impact of peer-to-peer (P2P) approaches [11] that have resulted in a slew of powerful applications, and the more orderly, but still widespread adoption, of a universal Web Service approach to Web based applications [12,13]. There are no crisp definitions of Grids and P2P Networks that allow us to unambiguously discuss their differences and similarities and what it means to integrate them. However these two concepts conjure up stereotype images that can be compared. Taking "extreme" cases, Grids are exemplified by the infrastructure used to allow seamless access to supercomputers and their datasets. P2P technology facilitates sophisticated resource sharing environments between "consenting" peers over the "edges" of the Internet, enabling ad hoc communities of low-end clients to advertise and access resources on communal computers. Each of these examples offers services but they differ in their functionality and style of implementation. The P2P example could involve services to set-up and join peer groups, browse and access files on a peer, or possibly to advertise one's interest in a particular file. The "classic" grid could support job submittal and status services and access to sophisticated data management systems.

Grids typically have structured robust security services while P2P networks can exhibit more intuitive trust mechanisms reminiscent of the "real world". Grids typically offer robust services that scale well in pre-existing hierarchically arranged organizations. P2P networks are often used when a best effort service is needed in a

M. Endler and D. Schmidt (Eds.): Middleware 2003, LNCS 2672, pp. 41–61, 2003.

dynamic poorly structured community. If one needs a particular "hot digital re-cording", it is not necessary to locate all sources of this, a P2P network needs to search enough plausible resources to ensure that success is statistically guaranteed. On the other hand, a 3D simulation of the universe might need to be carefully sched-uled and submitted in a guaranteed fashion to one of the handful of available super-computers that can support it. There are several attractive features in the P2P model, which motivate the development of hybrid systems. Deployment of P2P systems is entirely user driven, obviating the need for any dedicated management of these sys-tems. Resource discovery and management is an integral part of P2P computing with peers exposing the resources that they are willing to share and the system (sometimes) replicating these resources based on demand. Grids might host different persistent services and they must be able to discover these services and the interfaces they sup-port. Peers can form groups with the fluid group memberships and are thus very rele-vant for collaboration [14, 15]. This is an area that has been addressed for the Grid in Ref [16] and also in a seminal paper by Foster and collaborators [17] addressing broad support for communities.

A P2P Grid would comprise services that include those of Grids and P2P networks while naturally supporting environments that have features of both limiting cases. We can discuss two examples where such a model is naturally applied. In the High En-ergy Physics data analysis (e-Science [18]) problem discussed in [19], the initial steps are dominated by the systematic analysis of the accelerator data to produce summary events roughly at the level of sets of particles. This Grid-like step is followed by "physics analysis", which can involve many different studies and much debate be-tween involved physicists regarding the appropriate methods to study the data. Here we see some Grid and some P2P features. As a second example, consider the way one uses the Internet to access information – either news items or multimedia entertain-ment. Perhaps the large sites like Yahoo, CNN and future digital movie distribution centers have Grid like organization. There are well-defined central repositories and high performance delivery mechanisms involving caching to support access. Security is likely to be strict for premium channels. This structured information is augmented by the P2P mechanisms popularized by Napster with communities sharing MP3 and other treasures in a less organized and controlled fashion. These simple examples suggest that whether for science or commodity communities, information systems should support both Grid and P2P capabilities [20,21].

The proposed P2P grid, which integrates the evolving ideas of computational grids, distributed objects, web services, P2P networks and message oriented middleware, comprises resources such as relatively static clients, high-end resources and a dy-namic collection of multiple P2P subsystems. We investigate the architecture, com-prising a distributed brokering system that will support such a hybrid environment. Services can be hosted on such a P2P grid with peer groups managed locally and arranged into a global system supported by core servers. Access to services can then be mediated either by the "broker middleware" or alternatively by direct P2P interac-tions between machines "on the edge". The relative performance of each approach (which could reflect computer/network cycles as well as the existence of firewalls) would be used in deciding on the implementation to use. Such P2P Grids should seamlessly integrate users to themselves and to resources, which are also linked to each other. We can abstract such environments as a distributed system of "clients" which consist either of "users" or "resources" or proxies thereto. These clients must be linked together in a flexible fault tolerant efficient high performance fashion. The messaging infrastructure linking clients (both users and resources of course) would provide the backbone for the P2P grid.

The smallest unit of this messaging infrastructure should be able to intelligently process and route messages while working with multiple underlying communication protocols. We refer to this unit as a *broker*, where we avoid the use of the term *servers* to distinguish it clearly from the application servers that would be among the sources/sinks to messages generated within the integrated system. For our purposes (registering, transporting and discovering information), we use the term events/messages interchangeably where events are just messages – typically with time stamps. We may enumerate the following requirements for the messaging infrastructure –

1. *Scaling*: This is of paramount importance considering the number of devices, clients and services that would be aggregated in the P2P grid. The distributed broker network should scale to support the increase in these aggregated entities. However the addition of brokers to aid the scaling should not degrade performance by increasing communication *pathlengths* or ineffective bandwidth utilizations between broker nodes within the system. This calls for efficient organization of the broker network to ensure that the aforementioned degradations along with concomitant problems such as increased communication latencies do not take place.

2. *Efficient disseminations*: The disseminations pertain to routing content, queries, invocations etc. to the relevant destinations in an efficient manner. The routing engine at each broker needs to ensure that the paths traversed within the broker network to reach destinations are along efficient paths that eschew failed broker nodes.

3. *Guaranteed delivery mechanisms*: This is to ensure persistent delivery and reliable transactions within P2P grid realms.

4. *Location independence*: To eliminate bandwidth degradations and bottlenecks stemming from entities accessing a certain known broker over and over again to gain access to services, it must be ensured that any broker within the broker network is just as good as the other. Services and functionality would then be accessible from any point within the broker network.

5. *Support for P2P interactions*: P2P systems tend to be autonomic, obviating the need for dedicated management. P2P systems incorporate sophisticated search and subsequent discovery mechanisms. Support for P2P interactions facilitates access to information resources and services hosted by peers at the "edge" of the network.

6. *Interoperate with other messaging clients*: Enterprises have several systems that are built around messaging. These clients could be based on enterprise vendors such as IBM's MQSeries or Microsoft's MSMQ. Sometimes these would be clients conforming to mature messaging specifications such as the Java Message Service (JMS) [22]. JMS clients, existing in disparate enterprise realms, can utilize the distributed broker network as a JMS provider to communicate with each other.

7. *Communication through proxies and firewalls*: It is inevitable that the realms we try to federate would be protected by firewalls stopping our elegant application channels dead in their tracks. The messaging infrastructure should thus be able to communicate across firewall, DHCP and NAT boundaries. Sometimes communications would also be through authenticating proxies.

8. *Extensible transport framework*: Here we consider the communication subsystem, which provides the messaging between the resources and services. Examining the

growing power of optical networks we see the increasing universal bandwidth that in fact motivates the thin client and server based application model. However the real world also shows slow networks and links(such as dial-ups), leading to a high fraction of dropped packets. We also see some chaos today in the telecom industry which is stunting, somewhat, the rapid deployment of modern "wired' (optical) and wireless networks. We suggest that key to future federating infrastructures will be messaging subsystems that manage the communication between external re-sources, services and clients to achieve the highest possible system performance and reliability. We suggest this problem is sufficiently hard that we only need solve this problem "once" i.e. that all communication – whether TCP/IP, UDP, RTP (A Transport Protocol for Real-Time Applications) [23], RMI, XML/SOAP [24] or you-name-it be handled by a single messaging or event subsystem.

9. *Ability to monitor the performance of P2P grid realms*: State of the broker network fabric provides a very good indicator of the state of the P2P grid realm. Monitoring the network performance of the connections originating from individual brokers enables us to identify bottlenecks and performance problems, if any, which exist within a P2P grid realm.

10. *Security Infrastructure*: Since it is entirely conceivable that messages (including queries, invocations and responses) would have to traverse over hops where the underlying communication mechanisms are not necessarily secure, a security infra-structure that relies on message level security needs to be in place. Furthermore, the infrastructure should incorporate an authentication and authorization scheme to ensure restricted access to certain services. The infrastructure must also ensure a secure and efficient distribution of keys to ensure access by authorized clients to content encapsulated in encrypted messages.

In this paper we base our investigations on our messaging infrastructure, NaradaBro-kering [25-31], which addresses or provides the foundations for the issues discussed above. The remainder of this paper is organized as follows. In section 2.0 we discuss broker network organization, routing of events and support for durable interactions in the NaradaBrokering system. Section 3.0 presents the rationale, and our strategy, to support P2P interactions. Section 4.0 presents an extensible transport framework that addresses the transport issues alluded to earlier. A performance aggregation frame-work for monitoring and responding to changing network conditions is discussed in Section 5.0. Section 6.0 presents an overview of the message based security frame-work in the system. Finally, in section 7.0 we present our conclusions and outline future work.

2   NaradaBrokering

To address the issues [31] of scaling, load balancing and failure resiliency, NaradaB-rokering is implemented on a network of cooperating brokers. Brokers can run either on separate machines or on clients, whether these clients are associated with users or resources. This network of brokers will need to be dynamic for we need to service the needs of dynamic clients. Communication within NaradaBrokering is asynchronous and the system can be used to support different interactions by encapsulating them in specialized events. Clients reconnecting after prolonged disconnects, connect to the local broker instead of the remote broker that it was last attached to. This eliminates bandwidth degradations caused by heavy concentration of clients from disparate geographic locations accessing a certain known remote broker over and over again.

NaradaBrokering goes beyond other operational publish/subscribe systems [32-37] in many (support for JMS, P2P interactions, audio-video conferencing, integrated performance monitoring, communication through firewalls among others) ways. The messaging system must scale over a wide variety of devices – from hand held computers at one end to high performance computers and sensors at the other extreme. We have analyzed the requirements of several Grid services that could be built with this model, including computing and education. Grid Services (including NaradaBrokering) being deployed in the context of Earthquake Science can be found in [29]. NaradaBrokering supports both JMS and JXTA [44] (from juxtaposition), which are publish/subscribe environments with very different interaction models. NaradaBrokering also provides support for legacy RTP clients.

2.1   Broker Organization

Uncontrolled broker and connection additions result in a broker network susceptible to network-partitions and devoid of any logical structure thus making the creation of efficient broker network maps (BNM) an arduous if not impossible task. The lack of this knowledge hampers the development of efficient routing strategies, which exploit the broker topology. Such systems then resort to "flooding" the entire broker network, forcing clients to discard events they are not interested in. To circumvent this, NaradaBrokering incorporates a broker organization protocol, which manages the addition of new brokers and also oversees the initiation of connections between these brokers.

In NaradaBrokering we impose a hierarchical structure on the broker network, where a broker is part of a cluster that is part of a super-cluster, which in turn is part of a super-super-cluster and so on. Clusters comprise strongly connected brokers with multiple links to brokers in other clusters, ensuring alternate communication routes during failures. This organization scheme results in "small world networks" [38,39] where the average communication "pathlengths" between brokers increase logarithmically with geometric increases in network size, as opposed to exponential increases in uncontrolled settings. This cluster architecture allows NaradaBrokering to support large heterogeneous client configurations that scale to arbitrary size.

Creation of BNMs and the detection of network partitions are easily achieved in this topology. We augment the BNM hosted at individual brokers to reflect the cost associated with traversal over connections, for e.g. intra-cluster communications are faster than inter-cluster communications. The BNM can now be used not only to compute valid paths but also for computing shortest paths. Changes to the network fabric are propagated only to those brokers that have their broker network view altered. Not all changes alter the BNM at a broker and those that do result in updates to the routing caches, containing shortest paths, maintained at individual brokers.

2.2   Dissemination of Events

Every event has an implicit or explicit destination list, comprising clients, associated with it. The brokering system as a whole is responsible for computing broker destinations (targets) and ensuring efficient delivery to these targeted brokers en route to the intended client(s). Events as they pass through the broker network are updated to snapshot its dissemination within the network. The event dissemination traces eliminate continuous echoing and in tandem with the BNM –computes shortest paths – at each broker, is used to deploy a near optimal routing solution. The routing is near optimal since for every event the associated targeted brokers are usually the only ones involved in disseminations. Furthermore, every broker, either targeted or en route to one, computes the shortest path to reach target destinations while eschewing links and brokers that have failed or have been failure-suspected.

In NaradaBrokering topics could be based on tag-value pairs, Integer and String values. Clients can also specify SQL queries on properties contained in a JMS message. Finally, NaradaBrokering currently incorporates a distributed XML matching engine, which allows clients to specify subscriptions in XPath queries and store advertisements in XML encapsulated events. Real-time XML events are evaluated against the stored XPath subscriptions, while stored XML advertisements are evaluated against a real-time XPath query for discovery purposes.

Figures 2 and 3 illustrate some results [14] from our initial research where we studied the message delivery time as a function of load. The results are from a system comprising 22 broker processes and 102 clients in the topology outlined in Figure 1. Each broker node process is hosted on 1 physical Sun SPARC Ultra-5 machine (128 MB RAM, 333 MHz), with no SPARC Ultra-5 machine hosting more than one broker node process. The publisher and the *measuring* subscriber reside on the same SPARC Ultra-5 machine. In addition to this there are 100 subscribing client processes, with 5 client processes attached to every other broker node (broker nodes **22** and **21** do not have any other clients

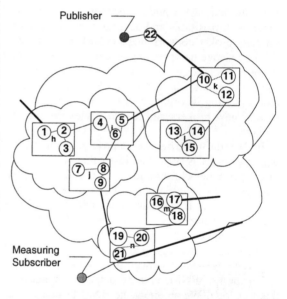

Fig. 1. The NaradaBrokering Test Topology

besides the publisher and measuring subscriber respectively) within the system. The 100 client node processes all reside on a SPARC Ultra-60 (512 MB RAM, 360 MHz) machine. The run-time environment for all the broker node and client processes is Solaris JVM (JDK 1.2.1, native threads, JIT). The machines involved in the experiment reside on a 100 Mbps network.

We measure the latencies at the client under varying conditions of publish rates, event sizes and matching rates. In most systems where events are continually generated a "typical" client is generally interested in only a small subset of these events. This behavior is captured in the matching rate for a given client. Varying the matching rates allows us to perform measurements under conditions of varying selectivity. The 100% case corresponds to systems that would flood the broker network. In systems that resort to flooding (routing a message to every router node) the system performance does not vary with changes in the match rate. Furthermore, in most cases a given message would only be routed to a small set of targeted client nodes.

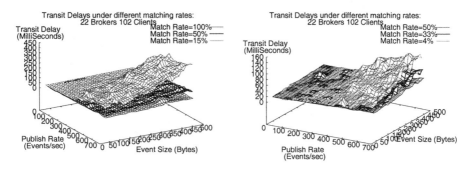

Fig. 2. NaradaBrokering Performance at match rates of 100%, 50% and 15%

Fig. 3. NaradaBrokering Performance at match rates of 50%, 33% and 4%

As the results demonstrate, the system performance improves significantly with increasing selectivity from subscribers. The distributed broker network scaled well, with adequate latency, unless the system became saturated at very high publish rates.

2.3   Failures and Recovery

In NaradaBrokering, stable storages existing in parts of the system are responsible for introducing state into the events. The arrival of events at clients advances the state associated with the corresponding clients. Brokers do not keep track of this state and are responsible for ensuring the most efficient routing. Since the brokers are stateless, they can fail and remain failed forever. The guaranteed delivery scheme within NaradaBrokering does not require every broker to have access to a stable store or DBMS. The replication scheme is flexible and easily extensible. Stable storages can be added/removed and the replication scheme can be updated. Stable stores can fail but they do need to recover within a finite amount of time. During these failures the clients that are affected are those that were being serviced by the failed storage.

2.4   JMS Compliance

NaradaBrokering is JMS compliant and provides support not only for JMS clients, but also for replacing single/limited server JMS systems transparently [28] with a distributed NaradaBrokering broker network. Since JMS clients are vendor agnostic, this JMS integration has provided NaradaBrokering with access to a plethora of applications built around JMS, while the integrated JMS solution provides these applications with scaling, availability and dynamic real time load balancing. Among the applications ported to this solution are the Anabas distance education conferencing system [40] and the Online Knowledge Center (OKC) portal [41].

2.4.1   JMS Performance Data

To gather performance data, we run an instance of the SonicMQ (version 3.0) [42] broker and NaradaBrokering broker on the same dual CPU (Pentium-3, 1 GHz, 256MB) machine. We then setup 100 subscribers over 10 different JMS TopicConnections on another dual CPU (Pentium-3, 866MHz, 256MB) machine. There is also a *measuring* subscriber and a publisher that are set up on a third dual CPU (Pentium 3, 866MHz, 256MB RAM) machine. The three machines (residing on a 100 Mbps network) have Linux (version 2.2.16) as their operating system. The runtime environment for all the processes is Java 2 JRE (Blackdown-FCS).

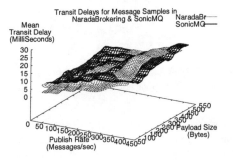

Fig. 4. Transit Delays for messages   **Fig. 5.** Standard Deviation for messages

The topic, which the subscribers subscribe to and the publisher publishes to, is the same. We vary the rates at which the publisher publishes messages while varying the payload sizes associated with these messages. We compute the transit delays associated with individual messages and also the standard deviation in the delays (used to compute the mean transit delay) associated with messages in a given test case. Figure 4 depicts the mean transit delays for the measuring subscriber under NaradaBrokering and SonicMQ for high publish rates and smaller payload sizes. Figure 5 depicts the standard deviation associated with message samples under the same conditions.

As can be seen NaradaBrokering compares very well with SonicMQ. Also, the standard deviation associated with message samples in NaradaBrokering were for the most part lower than in SonicMQ. Additional results can be found in [28].

3   Support for P2P Interactions in NaradaBrokering

Issues in P2P systems pertaining to the discovery of services and intelligent routing can be addressed very well in the NaradaBrokering system. The broker network would be used primarily as a delivery engine, and a pretty efficient one at that, while locating peers and propagating interactions to relevant peers. The most important aspect in P2P systems is the satisfaction of peer requests and discovery of peers and associated resources that could handle these requests. The broker network forwards these requests only to those peers that it believes can handle the requests. Peer interactions in most P2P systems are achieved through XML-based data interchange. XML's data description and encapsulation properties provide easy access to specific elements of data. Individual brokers routing interactions could access relevant elements, cache this information and use it subsequently to achieve the best possible routing characteristics. The brokering system, since it is aware of advertisements, can also act as a hub for search and discovery operations. These advertisements when organized into "queryspaces" allow the integrated system to respond to search operations more efficiently.

Resources in NaradaBrokering are generally within the purview of the broker network. P2P systems replicate resources in an ad hoc fashion, the availability of which is dependent on the peer's active digital presence. Some resources, however, are best managed by the brokering system rather than being left to the discretion of peers who may or may not be present at any given time. An understanding of the network topology and an ability to pin point the existence of peers interested in that resource are paramount for managing the efficient replications of a resource. The distributed broker network, possessing this knowledge, best handles this management of resources while ensuring that these replicated resources are "closer" and "available" at locations with a high interest in that resource. Furthermore, the broker network is also better suited, than a collection of peers, to eliminate race conditions and deadlocks that could exist due to a resource being accessed simultaneously by multiple peers. The broker network can also be responsive to changes in peer concentrations, volumes of peer requests, and resource availability.

There are also some issues that need to be addressed while incorporating support for P2P interactions. P2P interactions are self-attenuating with interactions dying out after a certain number of hops. These attenuations in tandem with traces of the peers, which the interactions have passed through, eliminate the continuous echoing problem that result from loops in peer connectivity. However, attenuation of interactions sometimes prevents peers from discovering certain services that are being offered. This results in P2P interactions being very "localized". These attenuations thus mean that the P2P world is inevitably fragmented into many small subnets that are not connected. Furthermore, sophisticated routing schemes are seldom in place and interactions are primarily through simple forwarding of requests with the propagation range determined by the attenuation indicated in the message. NaradaBrokering could also be used to connect islands of peers together. Peers that are not directly connected through the peer network could be indirectly connected through the broker network. Peer interactions and resources in the P2P model are traditionally unreliable, with interactions being lost or discarded due to peer failures or absences, overloading of peers and queuing thresholds being reached.

Guaranteed delivery properties existing in NaradaBrokering can augment peer behavior to provide a notion of reliable peers, interactions and resources. Such an integrated brokering solution would also allow for hybrid interaction schemes to exist alongside each other. Applications could be built around hybrid-clients that would exhibit part peer behavior and part traditional client behavior (e.g. JMS). P2P communications could be then used for traffic where loss of information can be sustained. Similarly, hybrid-clients needing to communicate with each other in a "reliable" fashion could utilize the brokering system's capabilities to achieve that. Sometimes, hybrid-clients satisfy each other's requests, obviating the need for funneling interactions through the broker network. Systems tuned towards large-scale P2P systems include

Pastry [43] from Microsoft, which provides an efficient location and routing substrate for wide-area P2P applications. Pastry provides a self-stabilizing infrastructure that adapts to the arrival, departure and failure of nodes. The JXTA [44] project at Sun Microsystems is another effort to provide such large-scale P2P infrastructures.

3.1   JXTA

JXTA is a set of open, generalized protocols [45] to support P2P interactions and core P2P capabilities such as indexing, file sharing, searching, peer grouping and security. The JXTA peers, and rendezvous peers (specialized routers), rely on a simple forwarding of interactions for dissemination. Time-to-live (TTL) indicators and peer traces attenuate interaction propagations. JXTA interactions are unreliable and tend to be localized. It is expected that existing P2P systems would either support JXTA or have bridges initiated to it from JXTA. Support for JXTA would thus enable us to leverage other P2P systems along with applications built around those systems.

3.2   JXTA & NaradaBrokering

In our strategy for providing support for P2P interactions within NaradaBrokering, we impose two constraints. First, we make no changes to the JXTA core and the associated protocols. We make additions to the rendezvous layer for integration purposes. Second, this integration should entail neither any changes to the peers nor a straitjacketing of the interactions that these peers could have had prior to the integration.

The integration is based on the proxy model, which essentially acts as the bridge between the NaradaBrokering system and JXTA. The Narada-JXTA proxy, operating inside the JXTA rendezvous layer, serves in a dual role as both a rendezvous peer and as a NaradaBrokering client providing a bridge between NaradaBrokering and JXTA. NaradaBrokering could be viewed as a service by JXTA. The discovery of this service is automatic and instantaneous due to the Narada-JXTA proxy's integration inside the rendezvous layer. Any peer can utilize NaradaBrokering as a service so long as it is connected to a Narada-JXTA proxy. Nevertheless, peers do not know that the broker network is routing some of their interactions. Furthermore, these Narada-JXTA proxies, since they are configured as clients within the NaradaBrokering system, inherit all the guarantees that are provided to NaradaBrokering clients.

3.2.1 The Interaction Model
Different JXTA interactions are queued at the queues associated with the relevant layers comprising the JXTA protocol suite. Each layer performs some operations including the addition of additional information. The rendezvous layer processes information arriving at its input queues from the peer-resolving layer and the pipe-binding layer. Since the payload structure associated with different interactions is different we can easily identify the interaction types associated with the payloads. Interactions pertaining to discovery/search or communications within a peer group would be serviced both by JXTA rendezvous peers and also by Narada-JXTA proxies.

Interactions that peers have with the Narada-JXTA proxies are what are routed through the NaradaBrokering system. JXTA peers can continue to interact with each other and of course some of these peers can be connected to pure JXTA rendezvous peers. Peers have multiple routes to reach each other and some of these could include the NaradaBrokering system and some of them need not. Such peers can interact directly with each other during the request/response interactions.

3.2.2   Interaction Disseminations

Peers can create a peer group; request to be part of a peer group; perform search/request/discovery all with respect to a specific targeted peer group. Peers always issue requests/responses to a specific peer group and sometimes to a specific peer. Peers and peer groups are identified by UUID [46] (IETF specification guarantees uniqueness until 3040 A.D.) based identifiers. Every peer generates its own peer id while the peer that created the peer group generates the associated peer group id. Each rendezvous peer keeps track of multiple peer groups through peer group advertisements that it receives and is responsible for forwarding interactions.

Narada-JXTA proxies are initialized both as rendezvous peers and also as NaradaBrokering clients. During its initialization as a NaradaBrokering client every proxy is assigned a unique connection ID by the NaradaBrokering system, after which the proxy subscribes to a topic identifying itself as a Narada-JXTA proxy. This enables NaradaBrokering to be aware of all the Narada-JXTA proxies that are present in the system. The Narada-JXTA proxy in its role as a rendezvous peer to peers receives –

1) Peer group advertisements
2) Requests from peers to be part of a certain peer group and responses to these requests
3) Messages sent to a certain peer group or a targeted peer
4) Queries and responses to these queries

To ensure the efficient dissemination of interactions, it is important to ensure that JXTA interactions that are routed by NaradaBrokering are delivered only to those Narada-JXTA proxies that should receive them. This entails that the Narada-JXTA proxy perform a sequence of operations, based on the interactions that it receives, to ensure selective delivery. The set of operations that the Narada-JXTA proxy performs comprise gleaning relevant information from JXTA's XML encapsulated interactions, constructing an event based on the information gleaned and finally in its role as a NaradaBrokering client subscribing (if it chooses to do so) to a topic to facilitate selective delivery. By subscribing to relevant topics, and creating events targeted to specific topics each proxy ensures that the broker network is not flooded with interactions routed by them. The events constructed by the Narada-JXTA proxies include the entire interaction as the event's payload. Upon receipt at a proxy, this payload is deserialized and the interaction is propagated as outlined in the proxy's dual role as a rendezvous peer. Additional details pertaining to this integration can be found in [27].

3.3   Performance Measurements

For comparing JXTA performance in NaradaBrokering we setup the topologies depicted in Figure 6. We then compare the performance of the pure JXTA environment, the integrated Narada-JXTA system and the native NaradaBrokering system. The rendezvous peers connected to brokers in topology 6.(b) are Narada-JXTA proxies.

To compute communication delays while obviating the need for clock synchronizations and the need to account for clock drifts, the receiver/sender pair is setup on the same machine (Pentium-3, 1 GHz, 256 MB RAM). In all the test cases, a message published by the sender is received at the receiver and the delay is computed. For a given message payload this is done for a sample of messages and we compute the mean delay and the standard deviation associated with the samples. This is repeated for different payload sizes. For every topology every node (broker or rendezvous peer) involved in the experimental setup is hosted on a different machine (Pentium-3, 1 GHz, 256MB RAM). The run-time environment for all the processes is

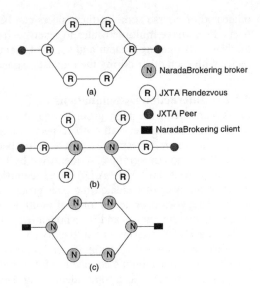

Fig. 6. The JXTA Test Topologies

(JDK-1.3 build Blackdown-1.3.1, Red Hat Linux 7.3). The machines involved in the experimental setup reside on a 100 Mbps LAN. Figures 7 and 8 depict the mean transit delay and standard deviation for the message samples under the different test topologies. These results indicate the superior performance of the integrated Narada-JXTA system compared to that of the pure JXTA system. The results [27] follow the same general pattern for measurements under other test topologies.

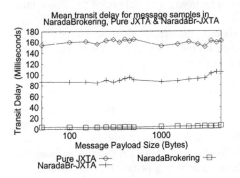

Fig. 7. Mean Transit Delay for samples

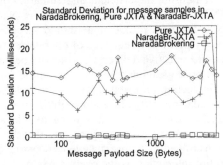

Fig. 8. Standard Deviation for samples

4   NaradaBrokering's Transport Framework

In the distributed NaradaBrokering setting it is expected that when an event traverses an end-to-end *channel* across multiple broker *hops* or *links* the underlying transport protocols deployed for communications would vary. The NaradaBrokering Transport framework aims to abstract the operations that need to be supported for enabling efficient communications between nodes. These include support for –

1) Easy addition of transport protocols within the framework.
2) Deployments of specialized links to deal with specific data types.
3) Negotiation of the best available communication protocol between two nodes
4) Adaptability in communications by responding to changing network conditions.
5) Accumulating performance data measured by different underlying protocol implementations.

TCP, UDP, Multicast, SSL, HTTP and RTP based implementations of the transport framework are currently available in NaradaBrokering. It is also entirely conceivable that there could be a JXTA link, which will defer communications to the underlying JXTA pipe mechanism. NaradaBrokering can also tunnel through firewalls such as Microsoft's ISA [47] and Checkpoint [48] and proxies such as iPlanet [49]. The user authentication modes supported include Basic, Digest and NTLM. Operations that need to be supported between two communication endpoints are encapsulated within the "link" primitive in the transport framework. The adaptability in communications is achieved by specifying network constraints and conditions under which to migrate to another underlying protocol. For e.g. a UDP link may specify that when the loss rates increase substantially communication should revert to TCP. Though there is support for this adaptability in the transport framework, this feature is not yet implemented in the current release. Figure 9 provides an overview of the NaradaBrokering transport framework.

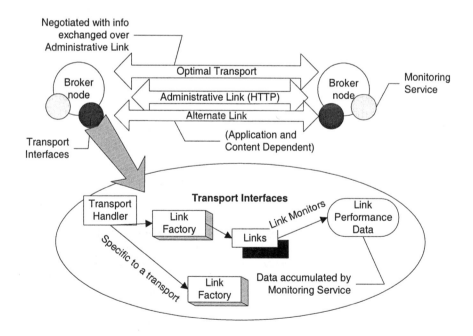

Fig. 9. Transport Framework Overview

A **Link** is an abstraction that hides details pertaining to communications. A Link has features, which allow it to specify a change in the underlying communications and the conditions under which to do so. An implementation of the Link interface can incorporate its own handshaking protocols for setting up communications. The Link also contains methods, which allow for checking the status of the underlying communication mechanism at specified intervals while reporting communication losses to the relevant error handlers within the transport framework. Each implementation of the Link interface can expose and measure a set of performance factors. Measurement of performance factors over a link requires cooperation from the other end-point of the communication link; this particular detail should be handled within the Link implementation itself. How the Link implementation computes round trip delays, jitter factors, bandwidth, loss rates etc. should be within the domain of the implementer. The Link also has methods which enable/disable the measurement of these performance factors. Links expose the performance related information in the **LinkPerformanceData** construct using which it is possible to retrieve information (*type, value, description*) pertaining to the performance factors being measured.

In the distributed NaradaBrokering setting it is expected that when an event traverses across multiple broker hops it could be sent over multiple communication links. In places where links optimized to deal with the specialized communication needs of the event exist (or can exist) they will be used for communications. While routing events between two NaradaBrokering brokers (that already have a link established between them) it should be possible for the event routing protocol to specify the creation of alternate communication links for disseminations. Support for this feature arises when routing handlers request the deployment of specific transport protocols for routing content, for e.g. a NaradaRTP event router could request that RTP links be used for communication. Sometimes such links will be needed for short durations of time. In such cases one should be able to specify the time for which the link should be kept alive. Expiry of this timer should cause the garbage collection of all resources associated with the link. The *keepalive* time corresponds to the period of inactivity after which the associated link resources must be garbage collected.

All broker locations need not have support for all types of communication links. Information regarding the availability of a specific link type could be encapsulated in an URI. This information could be exchanged along with the information regarding supported link types (at a given node) exchanged over the **AdministrativeLink**, which is different from that of a link in the methods that can be invoked on it. This URI could then possibly be used to dynamically load services. The AdministrativeLink exchanges information regarding the various communication protocols (along with information pertaining to them such as server, port, multicast group etc) that are available at a broker/client node. This is then used to determine the best link to use to communicate with the broker. Communication over the AdministrativeLink will be HTTP based to ensure the best possibility for communications between two nodes. All link implementations need to have an implementation of the **LinkNegotiator** interface. Based on the information returned on the AdministrativeLink, the LinkNegotiators are initialized for the common subset of communications and then deployed to negotiate the transport protocol for communications. The LinkNegotiator determines whether communication is possible over a specified link and also returns metrics that would enable the AdministrativeLink in arriving at a decision regarding the deployment of the best possible link.

All links of a specific communications *type* are managed by a **LinkFactory** instance. The LinkFactory for a particular communications protocol enables communications to and from other nodes over a specific link type. The LinkFactory also controls the intervals at which all its *managed* links check their communication status. Links also allow the specification of constraints (usually on the set of performance factors that it measures) and the link type that the communication must migrate to when those conditions are satisfied. This feature allows a link to revert to an alternate underlying transport protocol when communication degrades or is impossible to achieve. For example, it is conceivable that while communicating using TCP, bandwidth and latency constraints force a switch to UDP communications. The LinkFactory is also used to manage the migration of communication protocols from links of different types. Based on the set of supported communication protocol migrations, which a LinkFactory exposes, adaptive communications between nodes is enabled.

Protocol layers use the **TransportHandler** interface to invoke methods for communications with other NaradaBrokering nodes. LinkFactories are loaded at run-time by the TransportHandler implementation and it is then that TransportHandler interface is passed to the LinkFactory implementation. The reference to the transport handler is passed to every link created by the link factory. This is the reference that is used by individual links to report the availability of data on a link. Individual links use this interface to report data streams that are received over the link, loss of communications and requests to migrate transport protocols if the migration constraint is satisfied. Based on the LinkFactories that are loaded at run-time the transport handler can expose the set of link types (generally corresponding to transport types) that it supports. Transport Handler manages all Link factories and Links. LinkFactories are responsible for the creation of links. Links have methods for sending data (while also indicating the data type). Data received on a communication link is reported to the TransportHandler by invoking the appropriate methods within the interface.

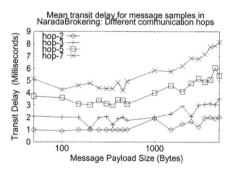
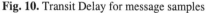
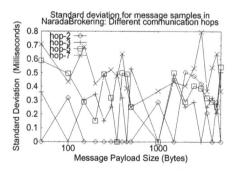

Fig. 10. Transit Delay for message samples   **Fig. 11.** Standard deviation for samples

4.1   Some Performance Measurements

Figures 10 and 11 depict results for the TCP implementation of the framework. The graphs depict the mean transit delays, and the accompanying standard deviations, for native NaradaBrokering messages traversing through multiple (2, 3, 5 and 7) hops with multiple brokers (1, 2, 4 and 6 respectively) in the path from the sender of the message to the receiver. For each test case the message payload was varied. The transit delay plotted is the average of the 50 messages that were published for each payload. The sender/receiver pair along with every broker involved in the test cases were hosted on different physical machines (Pentium-3, 1 GHz, 256 MB RAM). The machines reside on a 100 Mbps LAN. The run-time environment for all the processes is JRE-1.3 build Blackdown-1.3.1, Red Hat Linux 7.3

The average delay per inter-node (broker-broker, broker-client) hop was around 500-700 microseconds. The standard deviation varies from 0 microseconds for 50 byte messages traversing a hop to 800 microseconds over 7 hops.

5   Performance Monitoring and Aggregation

The performance monitoring scheme within the distributed broker network needs to have two important characteristics. First, it should be able to work with different transport protocols with no straitjacketing of the performance factors being measured. The Link and LinkPerformanceData primitives that abstract transport details and performance data respectively, as outlined in the preceding section, ensure the ability to work with unlimited performance factors over different transport protocols. Different nodes, with different

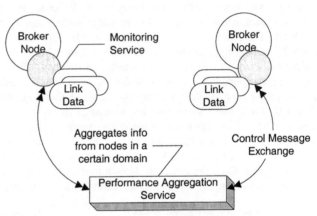

Fig. 12. Performance Aggregation Overview

types of links originating from them, can end up measuring a different set of performance factors. Second, the scheme should be to federate with other network measurement services such as the network weather service (NWS) [50]. An added feature would be to allow administrators to monitor specific realms or domains.

Every broker in NaradaBrokering incorporates a monitoring service (as shown in Figure 12) that monitors the state of the links originating from the broker node. Metrics computed and reported over individual links, originating from a broker node, include *bandwidth, jitter, transit delays, loss rates* and *system throughputs*. Factors are measured in a non-intrusive way so as to ensure that the measurements do not further degrade the metrics being measured in the first place. Factors such as bandwidth measurements, which can pollute other metrics being measured, are measured at lesser frequencies. Furthermore, once a link is deemed to be at the extreme ends of the performance spectrum (either very good or very bad) the measurement of certain factors are turned off while others are measured at a far lower frequency. Each link can measure different set of parameters. So the set of parameters being measured would be extensible and flexible. The monitoring service that runs at every node encapsulates performance data gathered from each link in an XML structure. The monitoring service then reports this data to a performance aggregator node, which aggregates information from monitoring services running at other nodes.

Performance aggregators monitor the state of the network fabric at certain realms; the aggregators themselves may exchange information with each other to provide a state of the integrated network realm. The performance aggregators exchange information with the monitoring services pertaining to the measurement and reporting of performance factors. For example, the aggregator can instruct the monitoring service running at a broker node to stop (or modify the intervals between) the measurement of certain factors. Similarly, an aggregator may instruct the monitoring service to report only certain performance factors and that too, only if the factors have varied by the amount (absolute value or a percentage) specified in it's request.

Information accumulated within the aggregators is accessible to administrators via a portlet residing in a portal such as Apache Jetspeed [51]. Note that, since the information returned to the aggregators in encapsulated in an XML structure, it is very easy to incorporate results gathered from another network monitoring service such as NWS. All that needs to be done is to have a proxy, residing at a NWS node that encapsulates the monitored data into an XML structure. The aggregated XML performance data (from the monitoring service at each node and other third-party services) would be mined to generate information, which would then be used to achieve to certain objectives.

(a) *The ability to identify, circumvent, project and prevent system bottlenecks:* Different transports would reveal this in different ways. As system performance degrades UDP loss rates may increase, TCP latencies increase. Similarly as available bandwidths decrease the overheads associated with TCP error correction and in order delivery may become unacceptable for certain applications.

(b) *To aid routing algorithms:* Costs associated with link traversals in BNM's would be updated to reflect the state of the fabric and the traversal times associated with links in certain realms. Routes computed based on this information would then reveal "true" faster routes.

(c) *To be used for Dynamic topologies to address both (a) and (b):* The aggregated performance information would be used to identify locations to upgrade the network fabric of the messaging infrastructure. This upgrade would involve brokers/connections be instantiated/purged dynamically to assuage system bottlenecks and to facilitate better routing characteristics. Although multicasting and bandwidth reservation protocols such as RSVP [52] and ST-II [53] can help in better utilizing the network they require support at the router level, more conceited effort is need at higher levels, and dynamic topologies coupled with efficient routing protocols can help in the efficient utilization of network resources.

(d) *To determine the best available broker to connect to:* Based on the aggregated information it should be possible to determine the best broker that a client can connect to within a certain realm. Scaling algorithms, such as the one derived from item (c), would benefit greatly from this strategy by incorporating newly added broker nodes (which would be the best available ones) into the routing solution.

(e) *Threshold notifications:* Administrators can specify thresholds, which when reached by specific monitored factors, results in notifications being sent to them.

6   Security Framework

Since it is entirely conceivable that messages (including queries, invocations and responses) would have to traverse over hops where the underlying communication mechanisms are not necessarily secure, a security infrastructure that relies on message level security needs to be in place. The security framework in NaradaBrokering tries to address the following issues

1. *Authentication:* Confirm whether a user is really who he says he is.
2. *Authorization:* Identify if the user is authorized to receive certain events
3. *Key distribution:* Based on the authentication and authorization, distribute keys, which ensure that only the valid clients are able to decrypt encrypted data.
4. *Digital Signing:* Have the ability to verify the source of the event and whether the source is authorized to publish events conforming to the specified template.
5. *Communication Protocol Independence:* Have the ability to work over normal communication channels. Communications need not to be over unencrypted links.
6. *End-to-End integrity:* Ensure that the only place where the unencrypted event is seen at the authorized publisher of the event and the authenticated (and authorized) subscribers to the event.
7. *Detection of security compromise:* Check whether the publisher's signature is a valid one. This approach would be similar to the Certificate Revocation Lists (CRL) scheme.
8. *Qualities of Service detecting compromise:* Clients may be asked to answer questions to verify its authenticity at regular intervals to facilitate detection of compromise.
9. *Response to security compromise:* This would involve invalidating certain signatures and discarding the use of certain keys for encrypted communications.

In our approach we secure messages independently of any transport level security. This provides a fine-grained security structure suitable for distributed systems and multiple security roles. For example, parts of the message may be encrypted differently, allowing users with different access privileges to access different parts of the message. Basic security operations such as authentication should be performed in a mechanism-independent way, with specific mechanisms (Kerberos [54], PKI) plugged into specific applications. The message level security framework allows us to deploy communication links where data is not encrypted. Furthermore, this scheme also ensures that no node/unauthorized-entity ever sees the unencrypted message. In our strategy we incorporate schemes to detect and respond to security compromises while also dealing with various attack scenarios.

Security specifications for Web Services [55, 56] are just starting to emerge, but generally follow the same approach: the message creator adds a signed XML message containing security statements to the SOAP envelope. The message consumer must be able to check these statements and the associated signature before deciding if it can execute the request. Legion (http://www.cs.virginia.edu/ ~legion/) is a long-standing research project for building a "virtual computer" out of distributed objects running on various computing resources. Legion objects communicate within a secure messaging framework [57] with an abstract authentication/identity system that may use either PKI or Kerberos. Legion also defines an access control policy on objects. Additional details pertaining to the NaradaBrokering security infrastructure can be found in [58].

7   Conclusions and Future Work

This paper outlined an extensible messaging framework that, we propose, would be appropriate to host P2P grids. Our results demonstrate that the framework can indeed be deployed for both synchronous and asynchronous applications while incorporating performance-functionality trade-offs for different scenarios (centralized, distributed and peer-to-peer mode). We believe we are now well positioned to incorporate support, within the messaging infrastructure, for Web/Grid Services.

We have recently incorporated an XML matching engine within the distributed brokering framework. This allows us to facilitate richer discovery mechanisms. Trade-offs in performance versus functionality inherent in such matching engines is a critical area that needs to be researched further. Another area that we intend to investigate is the model of dynamic resource management. A good example of a dynamic peer group is the set of Grid/Web Services [59, 60] generated dynamically when a complex task runs – here existing registration/discovery mechanisms are unsuitable. A P2P like discovery strategy within such a dynamic group combined with NaradaBrokering's JMS mode between groups seems attractive. We have also begun investigations into the management of distributed lightweight XML databases using P2P search and discovery mechanisms. Another area amenable to immediate investigation and research is the federation of services in multiple grid realms.

Bibliography

1. The Grid Forum http://www.gridforum.org
2. GridForum Grid Computing Environment working group(http://www.computingportals.org) and survey of existing grid portal projects. http://www.computingportals.org/
3. "The Grid: Blueprint for a New Computing Infrastructure", Ian Foster and Carl Kesselman (Eds.), Morgan-Kaufman, 1998. See especially D. Gannon, and A. Grimshaw, "Object-Based Approaches", pp. 205-236, of this book.
4. Globus Grid Project http://www.globus.org
5. GriPhyN Particle Physics Grid Project Site, http://www.griphyn.org/
6. International Virtual Data Grid Laboratory at http://www.ivdgl.org/
7. NEES Earthquake Engineering Grid, http://www.neesgrid.org/
8. SCEC Earthquake Science Grid, http://www.scec.org
9. W. Johnston, D. Gannon, B. Nitzberg, A. Woo, B. Thigpen, L. Tanner, "Computing and Data Grids for Science and Engineering," Proceedings of Super Computing 2000.
10. DoE Fusion Grid at http://www.fusiongrid.org
11. Oram, A. (eds) 2001. Peer-To-Peer: Harnessing the Power of Disruptive Technologies. O'Reilly, CA 95472.
12. Web Services Description Language (WSDL) 1.1 http://www.w3c.org/TR/wsdl
13. Definition of Web Services and Components http://www.stencilgroup.com/ideas_scope_200106wsdefined.html#whatare
14. Geoffrey Fox and Shrideep Pallickara, An Event Service to Support Grid Computational Environments. Concurrency and Computation: Practice and Experience. Volume 14(13-15) pp 1097-1129.
15. Fox, G. Report on Architecture and Implementation of a Collaborative Computing and Education Portal. http://aspen.csit.fsu.edu/collabtools/updatejuly01/erdcgarnet.pdf. 2001.
16. V. Mann and M. Parashar, Middleware Support for Global Access to Integrated Computational Collaboratories, Proc. of the 10th IEEE symposium on High Performance Distributed Computing (HPDC-10), CA, August 2001.

17. Ian Foster, Carl Kesselman, Steven Tuecke, The Anatomy of the Grid: Enabling Scalable Virtual Organizations http://www.globus.org/research/papers/anatomy.pdf
18. Kingdom e-Science Activity http://www.escience-grid.org.uk/_
19. Julian Bunn and Harvey Newman. Chapter on *Data Intensive Grids for High Energy Physics* in Grid Computing: Making the Global Infrastructure a Reality. Editors Berman, Fox and Hey. John Wiley. April 2003.
20. Hasan Bulut et al. An Architecture for e-Science and its Implications. Proceedings of the *International Symposium on Performance Evaluation of Computer and Telecommunication Systems (SPECTS 2002)* July 17 2002.
21. Geoffrey Fox, Ozgur Balsoy, Shrideep Pallickara, Ahmet Uyar, Dennis Gannon, and Aleksander Slominski, "Community Grids" invited talk at *International Conference on Computational Science*, April, 2002, Netherlands.
22. Java Message Service Specification". Mark Happner, Rich Burridge and Rahul Sharma. Sun Microsystems. 2000. http://java.sun.com/products/jms.
23. RTP: A Transport Protocol for Real-Time Applications (IETF RFC 1889) http://www.ietf.org/rfc/rfc1889.txt.
24. XML based messaging and protocol specifications SOAP. http://www.w3.org/2000/xp/.
25. The NaradaBrokering System http://www.naradabrokering.org
26. Geoffrey Fox and Shrideep Pallickara. "The Narada Event Brokering System: Overview and Extensions". Proceedings of the *International Conference on Parallel and Distributed Processing Techniques and Applications*, June 2002. pp 353-359.
27. Geoffrey Fox, Shrideep Pallickara and Xi Rao. "A Scaleable Event Infrastructure for Peer to Peer Grids". *Proceedings of ACM Java Grande ISCOPE Conference 2002*. Seattle, Washington. November 2002.
28. Geoffrey Fox and Shrideep Pallickara. "JMS Compliance in the Narada Event Brokering System". Proceedings of the *International Conference on Internet Computing*. June 2002. pp 391-402.
29. "Grid Services For Earthquake Science". Geoffrey Fox et al. *Concurrency & Computation: Practice and Experience*. 14(6-7): 371-393 (2002).
30. Hasan Bulut, Geoffrey Fox, Shrideep Pallickara, Ahmet Uyar and Wenjun Wu. "*Integration of NaradaBrokering and Audio/Video Conferencing as a Web Service*". Proceedings of the IASTED International Conference on Communications, Internet, and Information Technology, November, 2002, in St.Thomas, US Virgin Islands.
31. Geoffrey Fox and Shrideep Pallickara "An Approach to High Performance Distributed Web Brokering", *ACM Ubiquity* Volume2 Issue 38. November 2001.
32. Gurudutt Banavar, et al. An Efficient Multicast Protocol for Content-Based Publish-Subscribe Systems.In *Proceedings of the IEEE International Conference on Distributed Computing Systems*, Austin, Texas, May 1999.
33. Bill Segall and David Arnold. Elvin has left the building: A publish/subscribe notification service with quenching. In *Proceedings AUUG97*, pages 243–255, Australia, 1997.
34. Fiorano Corporation. A Guide to Understanding the Pluggable, Scalable Connection Management (SCM) Architecture - White Paper. Technical report, http://www.fiorano.com/products/fmq5 scm wp.htm, 2000.
35. Talarian Corporation. Smartsockets: Everything you need to know about middleware: Mission critical interprocess communication. Technical report, URL: http://www.talarian.com/products/smartsockets, 2000.
36. TIBCO Corporation. TIB/Rendezvous White Paper. Technical report, URL: http://www.rv.tibco.com/whitepaper.html, 1999.
37. The Object Management Group (OMG). OMG's CORBA Event Service. URL: http://www.omg.org/.
38. D.J. Watts and S.H. Strogatz. "Collective Dynamics of Small-World Networks". *Nature*. 393:440. 1998.

39. R. Albert, H. Jeong and A. Barabasi. "Diameter of the World Wide Web". *Nature* 401:130. 1999.
40. The Anabas Conferencing System. http://www.anabas.com
41. The Online Knowledge Center (OKC) Web Portal http://ptlportal.ucs.indiana.edu
42. SonicMQ JMS Server http://www.sonicsoftware.com/
43. Antony Rowstron and Peter Druschel. Pastry: Scalable, decentralized object location and routing for large-scale peer-to-peer systems. Proceedings of Middleware 2001.
44. Sun Microsystems. The JXTA Project and Peer-to-Peer Technology http://www.jxta.org
45. The JXTA Protocol Specifications. http://spec.jxta.org/v1.0/docbook/JXTAProtocols.html
46. Paul J. Leach and Rich Salz. Network Working Group. UUIDs and GUIDs. February, 1998.
47. Microsoft Internet Security and Acceleration (ISA) Server. http://www.microsoft.com/isaserver/
48. Checkpoint Technologies. http://www.checkpoint.com/
49. iPlanet. http://www.iplanet.com/
50. The Network Weather Service: A Distributed Resource Performance Forecasting Service for Metacomputing Rich Wolski, Neil Spring, and Jim Hayes, Journal of Future Generation Computing Systems,Volume 15, Numbers 5-6, pp. 757-768, October, 1999
51. Apache Jetspeed. http://jakarta.apache.org/jetspeed/site/index.html
52. Zhang, L. et al. "ReSource ReserVation Protocol (RSVP) – Functional Specification", Internet Draft, March 1994.
53. Topolcic, C., "Experimental Internet Stream Protocol: Version 2 (ST-II)", Internet RFC 1190, October 1990.
54. J. Steiner, C. Neuman, and J. Schiller. "Kerberos: An Authentication Service For Open Networked Systems". In *Proceedings of the Winter 1988 USENIX Conference.*
55. B.Atkinson, et al. "Web Services Security (WS-Security) Version 1.0 05 April 2002," Available from http://www-106.ibm.com/developerworks/webservices/library/ws-secure/.
56. "Assertions and Protocol for the OASIS Security Assertion Markup Language," P. Hallam-Baker and E. Maler, eds. Available from http://www.oasis-open.org/committees/security/docs/ cs-sstc-core-01.pdf.
57. Adam Ferrari et al. "A Flexible Security System for Metacomputing Environments". (HPCN Europe 99), pp 370-380. April 1999
58. Pallickara et. al. A Security Framework for Distributed Brokering Systems available at http://www.naradabrokering.org
59. Semantic Web from W3C to describe self organizing Intelligence from enhanced web resources. http://www. w3c.org/2001/sw/
60. Berners-Lee, T., Hendler, J., and Lassila, O., "The Semantic Web," Scientific American, May2001.

A Framework for Event Composition in Distributed Systems

Peter R. Pietzuch*, Brian Shand**, and Jean Bacon

University of Cambridge Computer Laboratory
Cambridge CB3 0FD, UK
{Peter.Pietzuch,Brian.Shand,Jean.Bacon}@cl.cam.ac.uk

Abstract. For large-scale distributed applications such as internet-wide or ubiquitous systems, event-based communication is an effective messaging mechanism between components. In order to handle the large volume of events in such systems, composite event detection enables application components to express interest in the occurrence of complex patterns of events. In this paper, we introduce a general composite event detection framework that can be added on top of existing middleware architectures – as demonstrated in our implementation over JMS. We argue that the framework is flexible, expressive, and easy to implement. Based on finite state automata extended with a rich time model and support for parameterisation, it provides a decomposable core language for composite event specification, so that composite event detection can be distributed throughout the system. We discuss the issues associated with automatic distribution of composite event expressions. Finally, tests of our composite event system over JMS show reduced bandwidth consumption and a low notification delay for composite events.

1 Introduction

Event-based communication has become a new paradigm for building large-scale distributed systems. It has the advantages of loosely coupling communication partners, being extremely scalable, and providing a simple application programming model. In event-based systems, events are the basic communication mechanism. An event can be seen as a notification that something of interest has occurred within the system. Components either act as *event sources* and *publish* new events, or *event sinks* and *subscribe* to events by providing a specification of events that are of interest to them. A *publish/subscribe* (pub/sub) communication layer [1] is then responsible for disseminating events; for efficiency, it can often also filter events by topic or content, according to client specifications.

Many existing pub/sub systems [2–4] restrict subscriptions to single events only and thus lack the ability to express interest in the occurrence of *patterns of events*. However, especially in large-scale applications, event sinks may be

---

* Research supported by UK EPSRC and QinetiQ, Malvern.
** Research supported by ICL, now part of Fujitsu, and the SECURE EU consortium.

M. Endler and D. Schmidt (Eds.): Middleware 2003, LNCS 2672, pp. 62–82, 2003.

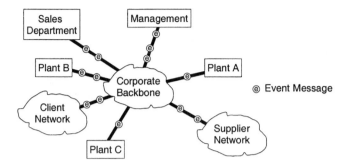

Fig. 1. A publish/subscribe system in a corporate network

overwhelmed by the vast number of primitive, low-level events, and would benefit from a higher-level view. Such a higher-level view is given by *composite events* (CE) that are published when an event pattern occurs. To date, it is usually left to the event sink to implement a detector for composite events making it unnecessarily complex and error-prone.

In this paper, we address the problem by proposing a general framework for composite event detection that works on top of a range of pub/sub systems. This framework includes a generic language for specifying composite events and CE detectors that can detect composite events in a distributed way.

The paper is organised as follows: Section 2 motivates the necessity of composite event detection in large-scale distributed systems. After related work (Sect. 3), we discuss prerequisites of the detection framework (Sect. 4) such as the pub/sub infrastructure requirements, the time model and the event model. The CE detectors and the associated core language are presented in Sect. 5, and Sect. 6 discusses distributed detection. In Sect. 7, we present our implementation over JMS, and evaluate its performance. The paper finishes with an introduction to higher-level specification languages (Sect. 8) and conclusions (Sect. 9).

2   Motivation

Large-scale event systems need to support CE detection, in order to quickly and efficiently notify their clients of new, relevant information in the network. This is particularly important for widely distributed systems where bandwidth is limited and components are loosely coupled. In such systems, distributed CE detection can improve efficiency and robustness.

For example, consider a large corporate network which connects disparate information systems, illustrated in Fig. 1. The computer system at one site might use the network to notify a supplier that more raw materials were required. At the same time, the sales department might notify all plants of projected regional demand for each product, in order to guide production. Finally, management might want to be informed of all orders over £10 000 from new clients, or of plants increasing production when demand was falling.

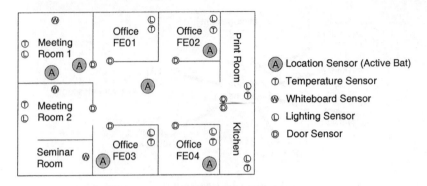

Fig. 2. An Active Office environment

In a small company, simple point-to-point messaging between departments would be sufficient. However, this would require considerable administration in a larger organisation, as each information producer would need a list of all intended recipients. A pub/sub system would reduce this overhead, allowing more flexible communication and easier bootstrapping of the system.

Nevertheless, without CE detection, many messages would still be sent unnecessarily, because specific event combinations or patterns could not be expressed by recipients. Instead, in the example above, management would have to be notified independently of all large orders and of all new clients. Furthermore, reuse of common subexpressions would be impossible, if for example both management and accounting were interested in orders over £10 000.

For reliability and efficiency, each CE detector should be distributed near to its event sources. Otherwise, if one site's connection to the rest of the network failed, local notification of composite events might fail unnecessarily. Besides, sending these events off-site for detection would have been a waste of bandwidth, if all relevant events were known to be locally produced.

Just as a general purpose pub/sub system supports flexible messaging, so too can a generic CE framework extend this support. Therefore, this paper proposes a general purpose middleware system for CE detection, independent of the specific underlying pub/sub infrastructure. By making CE detection closely interoperate with the underlying communication infrastructure, we obtain a system that is more efficient than an *ad hoc* implementation of CE detectors at the application level.

2.1   Application Scenario: The Active Office

The Active Office is a computerised building which is aware of its inhabitants' behaviour (cf. Fig. 2). Workers wear Active Bats [5] to inform the building of their movements at least once a minute. Other sensors monitor doors, office temperatures, electronic whiteboard usage, and lighting. A content-based pub/sub system is used so that applications can be notified of specific events, such as 'location events where Peter is seen in room FE04'. We used the following two application scenarios to test our CE detection framework:

Scenario 1. The building services manager wants to know about temperature events under 15 °C in an occupied room.

Scenario 2. Jean wants the list of participants and the electronic whiteboard contents of any meeting she attended to be sent to her wireless PDA, but only if she does not login to the workstation in her office within 5 min of the meeting.

There are many advantages of using a CE middleware for services in an Active Office, instead of (or perhaps as well as) offering predefined composite subscriptions on dedicated servers. The most important are the flexibility with which recipients can compose personal subscriptions, and the ease with which composite patterns can be reused and distributed close to event sources. The cost of establishing this network of CE detection broker nodes is then offset by the simplicity of configuring it for new CE subscriptions.

3   Related Work

Historically, composite event detection first arose in the context of triggers in active databases. Early languages for specifying composite events follow the Event-Condition-Action (ECA) model and resemble database query algebras with an expressive, yet complex syntax. In general, the detection process is not distributed.

In the Ode object database [6], composite events are specified with a regular-expression-like language and detected using finite state automata (FSA). Equivalence between the CE language and regular expressions is shown. Since a composite event has a single timestamp of the last event that led to its detection, a total event order is created that makes it difficult to deal with clock synchronisation issues. The pure FSAs do not support parameterised events.

CE detectors based on Petri Nets are used in the SAMOS database [7]. Coloured Petri Nets can represent concurrent behaviour and manage complex data such as event parameters during detection. However, even for simple expressions, they quickly become complicated. SAMOS does not support distribution and has a simple time model that is not suitable for distributed systems.

The motivation for Snoop [8] was to design an expressive CE specification language with powerful temporal support. A CE detector is a tree that reflects the structure of the event expression. Its nodes implement language operators and conform to a particular *consumption policy*. A consumption policy influences the semantics of an operator by resolving which events are consumed from the event history in case of ambiguity. For example, under a *recent* policy only the most recently occurring event is considered; others are ignored. Detection propagates up the tree with the leaves of the tree being primitive event detectors. A disadvantage is that the nodes are essentially Turing-complete making it difficult to formalise their semantics and to reason about their behaviour. The use of consumption policies can be non-intuitive and operator-dependent.

In [9], Schwiderski presents a distributed CE architecture based on the 2g-precedence model for monitoring distributed systems. This model makes strong assumptions about the clock granularity in the system and thus does not scale to large, loosely-coupled distributed systems. The language and the detection algorithm used are similar to Snoop and suffer from the same shortcomings. It addresses the issue of events being delayed during transport by *evaluation policies*: *asynchronous evaluation* enables a detector to consume an event as soon as it arrives sometimes leading to incorrect detection, whereas *synchronous evaluation* forces a detector to delay evaluation until all earlier events have arrived, and assumes a heartbeat infrastructure. Although detection is distributed, no decision on the efficient placement of detectors in the network is made.

The GEM system [10] has a rule-based event monitoring language. It follows a tree-based detection approach and assumes a total time order. Communication latency is handled by annotating rules with tolerable delays. Such an approach is not feasible in an environment with unpredictable delays.

Research efforts in ubiquitous computing have led to CE languages that are intuitive to use in environments such as the Active Office. The work by Hayton [11] on composite events in the Cambridge Event Architecture (CEA) [12] is similar to ours in the sense that it defines a language that non-programmers can use to specify occurrences of interest. Hayton uses push-down FSAs to handle parameterised events. However, the language itself can become non-intuitive as the semantics of some operators is not obvious. Even though detectors can use composite events as their input, distributed detection is not dealt with explicitly. As in previous work, scalar timestamps are used.

Distributed pub/sub architectures such as Hermes [4], Gryphon [3,13], and Siena [2] only provide parameterised primitive events and leave the task of CE detection to the application programmer. Siena supports restricted *event patterns*, but it does not define a complete pattern language.

In our CE detection framework, we adopt the interval timestamp model introduced in [14]. The partial order of timestamps in a distributed system is made explicit by having timestamps associated with an uncertainty interval. A CORBA-based detection architecture is presented in [14] that implements this time model. The notion of *event stability* is defined in order to handle communication delays. We extend this to cope with delays in wide-area systems.

4   Design and Architecture

The CE detectors in our framework recognise concurrent patterns of simpler events, generating a composite event whenever a match is found. The component layers of our detection architecture are illustrated in Fig. 3: Distributed CE detectors are compiled from expressions in our *core CE language*. Patterns can be specified using higher-level languages, which are first translated into the core CE language before compilation and execution.

The CE framework relies on and interacts with the underlying event system, in order to detect complex patterns of events. This section outlines the prereq-

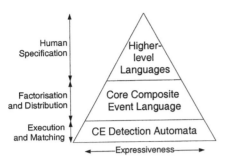

Fig. 3. Components of the composite event detection framework

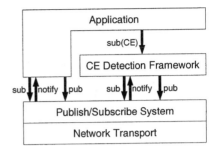

Fig. 4. Interface between the CE detection framework and the pub/sub system

uisites for this interaction: an interface to a pub/sub infrastructure, and formal models of events and time. Given these prerequisites, the full expressive power of our CE languages can be used.

4.1 Publish/Subscribe Infrastructure Support

One of our design goals was to keep the CE detection framework strictly separated from the pub/sub infrastructure used. The interface to the event system (Fig. 4) makes only minimal assumptions about the functionality supported allowing our framework to be deployed on a large variety of pub/sub systems. Our current test-bed uses the Java Message Service (JMS) [15], but other pub/sub systems could equally be used: earlier work was based on Hermes [4], a distributed event-based middleware architecture, and CORBA Events would also be suitable.

In addition to the time and event model described below, the underlying pub/sub system needs to support (1) publication of primitive events by event sources, (2) subscription to these events by event sinks, and (3) relaying of events from sources to sinks. Many systems also filter events en route for efficiency; our CE framework uses this if available, but no particular publication or subscription model is assumed. Our event model uses the abstraction of a *describable event set* as an atom for CE detection. If the pub/sub system supports content-based filtering, a describable event set will be defined by a parameterised filtering expression. In a topic-based system, it will conform to a certain event type only.

In particular, the pub/sub system does not need to be aware of CE types. As illustrated in Fig. 4, application event sources submit CE subscriptions to the CE detection layer. Any composite events that are then detected by a CE detector are published to the pub/sub system disguised as primitive events. It is then the responsibility of the pub/sub system to disseminate these encapsulated CE occurrences to all interested event sources. The same mechanism is used for the communication between distributed event detectors (cf. Sect. 6).

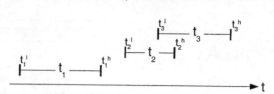

Fig. 5. Illustration of interval timestamps for events

4.2   Composite Event Detection Framework

The Java interface to the CE detection service, presented to applications, is shown below in part. Applications may use this for all event services, or contact the underlying pub/sub infrastructure directly for primitive event subscriptions.

```
public interface DistCEDServiceInf {
   public void registerCEType(CEType type, CEPublisherInf publisher);
   public void unregisterCEType(CEType type, CEPublisherInf publisher);
   public CEInf createCE(CEType ceType);
   public CEType createCEType(String typeName);
   public void publish(CEInf ce, CEPublisherInf publisher);
   public void subscribe(CEType type, CESubscriberInf subscriber,
                         CEQoSInf qos, CESubscriberCallbackInf callback);
   public void unsubscribe(CEType type, CESubscriberInf subscriber);
}
```

Before an event type can be published it must be `registered` with the CE detection service so that e.g. an appropriate type/topic is created in the underlying pub/sub system. After that, a new event instance can be created using the `createCE` method. The `publish` method will pass the publication down to the pub/sub system. A call to `subscribe` subscribes to primitive or composite events. A CE subscription may trigger the instantiation of new CE detectors.

Time Model. Each event in our framework has an associated timestamp, denoting when it occurred. In a large-scale system, it may often be impossible to decide which of two events occurred first. Therefore we assume that there is a *partial* order relation on timestamps '$<$', showing which events definitively occurred before others. This is extended to a total order '$\prec$', using a tie-breaker convention (see App. A) allowing events to be treated as a well ordered sequence of symbols for detection.

This may be illustrated using a two-part interval timestamp for events, rather than a single conventional timestamp. These interval timestamps are used implicitly throughout the rest of the paper. They can represent the clock uncertainty of a distributed time service such as NTP, and also the time interval associated with a composite event. The intervals can factor in the estimated receiver-specific delay on receiving UTC, including radio transmission lag or network delays.

Figure 5 illustrates three interval timestamps t_1, t_2 and t_3. Here, $t_1 < t_2$, $t_1 < t_3$ but $t_2 \not< t_3$ and $t_3 \not< t_2$. On the other hand, using the total order, $t_1 \prec t_2 \prec t_3$; these operators are formally defined in App. A.

Event Model. Events provide notification of observations in a distributed system. *Primitive events* represent observations from outside the event system, while *composite events* represent patterns of events. The constituents of a composite event may be primitive events, or other, simpler composite events. Despite this distinction, all events are treated homogeneously; we assume only that events have timestamps, and can be consistently ordered for each subscriber (e.g. by interval timestamp, source IP address and local event generation count).

In an Active Office [5], primitive events might be 'The door opens' and 'Peter is seen in the room'. Similarly, 'The door opens, then Peter is seen in the room' could be a composite event. Thus event sequences, of interleaved primitive and composite events, can be used to formalise the detection of composite events (cf. App. A). Furthermore, our event ordering still supports distributed detection, since each CE detector's subscription is used to sequence only the events needed for its composite event pattern.

5 Composite Event Detection

The CE detectors in our framework are simple automata, with a regular structure. Unlike conventional FSAs, these automata provide support for a rich time model and parameterisation, as well as the ability to detect concurrent event patterns. A novel language is used to express these patterns; this *core CE language* can then be compiled into automata for matching.

Distribution support is important for communication efficiency; Section 6 discusses how each pattern may be factorised into subexpressions. These subexpressions can then be matched independently on distributed nodes – these mobile detectors were discussed in an earlier paper [16]. Patterns may also be more intuitively defined using higher-level specification languages, described in Sect. 8. However, this is only a matter of convenience, not expressiveness; any patterns described in a higher-level language are first translated into the core CE language, before being compiled into automata. Figure 3 illustrates the relationship between these different aspects of the CE framework.

For example, in Scenario 1, the building services manager subscribes to temperature events under 15 °C in an occupied room. (For simplicity, we consider the movement, door and temperature events of only a single room, although multiple rooms could be represented in a single CE expression using parameterisation. We also prefilter the `PersonEvents`, limiting repeat notifications to one per minute.) We consider a room to be occupied if it has exhibited movement or door events within the last 5 min. In our core CE language, we might represent the primitive events (as exposed by JMS) using:

- `[PersonEvent(location='Office FE02')]`
- `[DoorEvent(location='Office FE02')]`
- `[TempEvent(location='Office FE02' AND temp<15)]`

Scenario 1 could be written (using $[\text{Pers}(f_1)]$, $[\text{Door}(f_1)]$, $[\text{Temp}(f_2)]$ for the expressions above, for brevity) as: $([\text{Pers}(f_1)] \mid [\text{Door}(f_1)], [\text{Temp}(f_2)])_{t=5\,\text{min}}$. This would be compiled into the following automaton, for use as a detector:

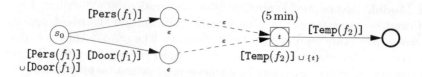

We based our core language and automata on regular expressions and FSAs for a number of reasons. Firstly, their expressive power is well understood, but they require only limited, predictable resource usage, and are thus a safer tool for distributed detection than a more general language. Still, they are powerful, and are frequently used for pattern detection and matching. Furthermore, regular expressions may also easily be factorised into subexpressions, for distributed detection of independent expressions. Finally, we felt that it would be more sensible to extend the commonly accepted regular expression operators with necessary additions, rather than arbitrarily define new operators, with the concomitant risks of redundancy or incompleteness. Our core CE language and automata therefore only minimally extend regular expressions and FSAs, to allow temporal relationships, input filtering, and parallel detection to be expressed.

5.1   Composite Event Detectors

The automata which detect composite events contain a finite number of states and state transitions, but each state also maintains the timing information of the previous symbol detected. In a given state, the automaton decides when to make the transition to another state by considering new input symbols only from a per state describable subset of the global event input sequence I (cf. App. A.2).

Structure of Automata. Our automata have two types of state: *ordinary* and *generative*. A generative state causes a new event to be created, either a composite of the events matched so far (with a specified type), or an instantaneous time event in the future (with a freshly allocated local identity). The timestamp of the composite event will start at the earliest start time of the constituent events, and end at the latest end time. A time event may be used later in the automaton, to progress or fail after a given timeout (cf. App. A.2). Each state has an *input domain of describable events*, the family of events it can match. When in a given state, the automaton processes only those new events that lie within the state's domain. The diagram below shows four states: an initial (ordinary) state, an ordinary state, a generative state for a composite event of type '$A;B$', and a generative state for a time event. The input domains are $\Sigma_0 \dots \Sigma_3$.

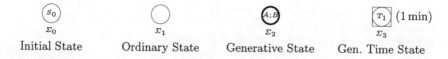

Each state can have any number of outward transitions. There are two types of transition: *strong* and *weak*, which can match events which strongly or weakly follow the previously detected event. These correspond to the partial and total event orderings '$<$' and '$\prec$' respectively. Each transition has a describable family of events attached, any of which will cause it to be taken.

New events in the input domain of a state but not in any transitions will cause the match to fail. These new events must strongly follow the previous event if all outgoing transitions are strong, or weakly follow otherwise. If there are two or more matching transitions, they will be followed nondeterministically. When a state with no outgoing transitions is reached, an event is generated if it is generative, then the machine (or the current nondeterministic branch) immediately terminates. The diagram below illustrates both strong and weak state transitions. If a, b, c are the events which matched A, B and C, then $a < b$ and $b \prec c$. Furthermore, $b \in B$ is the first event in the input stream I_{Σ_1} for which $a < b$. Similar constraints apply to c.

Limitations of Automata. The extended automata address many of the disadvantages of standard FSAs. Firstly, temporal support is provided by explicit event timestamps and special timer events. Concurrent events are also supported; the following automaton generates a new event when composite events $C_1, C_2 \in \mathcal{D}$ occur in parallel within 1 min of each other. C_1 might represent 'Peter is seen in the building but not in his office' and C_2 'Peter's phone rings'. The resulting event could be used to divert the call to wherever Peter was last seen.

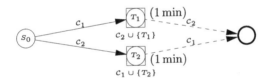

Conventional FSAs have other limitations too. Most importantly, they cannot handle event interrelationships such as event parameterisation. For example, to detect how long each door in a building is left open, a mechanism is needed for expressing free parameters which apply the same expression to all rooms: detect opening (x) followed by closing(x). Our framework can resolve this issue by filtering on the CE attributes of all opening and closing event pairs as soon as they are detected, reporting only matching pairs. This is still efficient, since the unnecessary composites are discarded as soon as they are detected, and every possible pairing would have been considered.

Finally, when nondeterministic FSAs are made deterministic, the number of states can grow exponentially. Although our automata potentially exhibit this behaviour, it does not happen in practice: since distribution takes place at the level of CE expressions (see Sect. 5.2), not automata, resolution to deterministic automata is not required; instead, a list of active states is held. Furthermore, in typical composite expressions this list is usually short, since distributed detection makes parallel detection of independent subexpressions the norm.

Formal Definition of Automata. Each automaton consists of a set of states S, state domains $a_S : S \to \mathcal{D}$, and strong and weak transition domains $a_{TS}, a_{TW} : S \times S \to \mathcal{D}$. There is also a start state $S_0 \in S$. Finally, $G \subseteq S \times (\mathbb{T} \uplus \mathcal{D})$ defines the generative states (an extension of accepting states) and their actions.

The current state of an automaton is $C \subseteq S \times T \times \mathbb{P}(\mathbb{E})$ where T is the set of possible timestamps. In other words, the current state consists of a number of triples, each representing a state, a timestamp, and a list of detected events. From the perspective of the automaton, the list of events is opaque, except that extra detected events may be added to it, when a transition is made.

5.2   Core Composite Event Language

A CE language allows expression of CE patterns. In this section, we introduce our core CE language, which can easily be compiled into automata, but is still human readable, and outline its grammar. This language also defines the level at which subexpressions are chosen for distributed detection. App. B contains the transformation from expressions into automata, and gives precise operator semantics. The operators of the core CE language extend those found in regular languages, namely concatenation, alternation, and iteration, with operators for timing control, parallelisation, and weak/strong event sequencing. In contrast with other CE languages, we avoided redundant operators to simplify analysis.

Atoms. $[A, B, C, \cdots \subseteq \Sigma_0]$. Atoms detect individual events in the input stream. Here, only events in $A \cup B \cup C \cup \ldots$ will be successfully matched. Other events in Σ_0 will cause a failed detection, and events outside Σ_0 will be ignored. We abbreviate negation using $[\neg E \subseteq \Sigma]$ for $[\Sigma \setminus E \subseteq \Sigma]$, and also write $[E]$ instead of $[E \subseteq E]$. (Negation ensures any other events in Σ will stop the detection, such as timeouts or stopper events.)

Concatenation. $C_1 C_2$. Detects expression C_1 *weakly* followed by C_2.

Sequence. $C_1 ; C_2$. This detects expression C_1 *strongly* followed by C_2. Thus C_1 and C_2 must not overlap in a sequence, but they may in a concatenation.

Iteration. C_1^*. Detects any number of occurrences of expression C_1. If C_1 detects a symbol which causes it to fail, then C_1^* will fail too. (So $[A][A \subseteq \{A,B\}]^*[C]$ would match input AAC but not $AABC$.)

Alternation. $C_1 \mid C_2$. This expression will match if either C_1 or C_2 is matched.

Timing. $(C_1, C_2)_{T_1 = \text{timespec}}$. The timing operator detects event combinations within, or not within, a given interval. The second expression C_2 can then use T_1 in its event specification.

Parallelisation. $C_1 \parallel C_2$. Parallelisation detects two composite events in parallel, and succeeds only if both are detected. Unlike alternation, any order is allowed, and the events may overlap in time.

The following examples illustrate the use of the core CE language to describe composite events. Let B be the events corresponding to 'Brian enters the room', let P be 'Peter enters the room', and let A be 'anyone enters the room'.

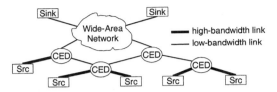

Fig. 6. Illustration of distributed composite event detection

1. Brian enters the room followed by Peter: $[B]; [P]$
2. Brian enters the room before Peter: $[B \subseteq \{B, P\}]$
3. Brian enters and Peter follows within an hour: $([B], [P \subseteq \{P, T_1\}])_{T_1 = 1\,\mathrm{h}}$
4. Someone else enters the room when Brian is away: $[B] [\neg B \subseteq A] [B]$

6 Distributed Detection

In a large-scale distributed application, events are published at geographically dispersed sites. A centralised CE detector would have to subscribe to all primitive events that are part of a CE expression in order to detect occurrences of composite events. This could become a bottleneck and a single point of failure.

Instead, our framework provides a mechanism for distributing CE detectors. Detectors can be installed at various locations in the network and cooperate with each other. This cooperation is achieved by decomposing CE expressions stated in the core language into subexpressions that are then detected by detectors running at different nodes. Figure 6 shows an example of a network of cooperating CE detectors. The detectors are located close to event sources that publish events at a high rate, thus requiring high-bandwidth links. After CE detection, bandwidth consumption is reduced since composite events occur less frequently. Composite events are then sent to remote event sinks over a low-bandwidth, wide-area network. No CE detector is overwhelmed by the rate of primitive events, as it subscribes to at most two event sources.

The main difficulty when distributing detectors is to decide on their optimal placement within the system. This is complicated by the fact that the reasons for distributing detectors are potentially conflicting. For example, to minimise bandwidth usage, existing detectors should be reused for subexpressions as much as possible – even between applications, if this is appropriate. However, if minimum latency is required, detectors should be replicated at various regions in the network which leads to higher bandwidth consumption. As a result, an optimal solution must be a trade-off that takes the static and dynamic characteristics of the system and the requirements of the application into account.

In our framework, mobile CE detectors (Sect. 6.1) detect composite events in a distributed fashion. A distribution policy (Sect. 6.2) ensures that detectors are installed at sensible locations and specifies a policy for their movement and behaviour during their lifetime. Network delays that can lead to incorrect detection are addressed by a detection policy (Sect. 6.3).

6.1   Mobile Composite Event Detectors

We introduce the concept of a *mobile composite event detector* to add distributed detection to our framework. A mobile CE detector is an agent-like entity encapsulating an automaton that detects an expression from our core language. It subscribes to event sources to receive event input streams and publishes the composite events detected by the automaton. The detector is capable of moving from one location to another in the network. This assumes the existence of a logical overlay network of nodes that supports the migration of components. Consequently, our work is built on top of a network of *event brokers*, for example corresponding to Hermes brokers or JMS nodes, where each event broker is capable of running one or more mobile detectors.

Whenever a CE subscription is added and no detector for this expression can be found in the system, a new mobile CE detector is created at an existing broker. It can carry out a number of actions: the detector can *factorise* the CE expression along its abstract syntax tree and *delegate detection* of subexpressions to other (already existing) detectors. For this, it can *instantiate new detectors* if it needs to reduce its own load. It can *migrate to another node* in the network that is for example closer to the event sources that it has subscribed to. Finally, the detector can *destroy* itself once it is no longer required.

Consider the Active Office application scenario introduced in Sect. 2.1. Let B be the event type corresponding to 'Brian enters the room', let P be 'Peter enters the room', and let M be 'a meeting takes place in the room'. A user is interested in occurrences of 'Brian enters the room followed by Peter'. The corresponding mobile CE detector C_1 for the expression $[B];[P]$ is shown below.

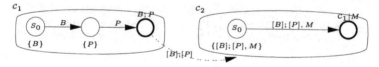

When another user subscribes to occurrences of the composite event 'Brian enters the room followed by Peter or a meeting takes place', this new expression $([B];[P])|M$ can be rewritten as $C_1|M$. Therefore, the new detector C_2 can reuse the existing detector C_1 by subscribing to $[B];[P]$. The communication between the two detectors happens exclusively through the underlying pub/sub system.

6.2   Distribution Policy

The behaviour of a mobile CE detector with respect to its actions is governed by a *distribution policy* – a set of heuristics to be followed by the detector. Several dimensions are addressed by a distribution policy:

(1) The location of mobile CE detectors must be determined. On the one hand, bandwidth usage can be reduced by moving detectors close to event sources. Primitive events that constitute a composite event may be of interest only to the CE detector and should therefore not be widely disseminated throughout the entire system unnecessarily. On the other hand, CE detectors

should be close to application components that subscribe to them to improve reliability and detection delay. (2) The degree of decomposition and distribution must be stated in the policy (with optional hints from the application). Whenever a new CE subscription is created, existing detectors for this subexpression should be reused to save bandwidth and computational effort. (3) Detectors must be replicated since, in a typical system, certain composite events will be more common than others. Detection for very common composite events should therefore be shared among several detectors for scalability.

6.3   Detection Policy

In a distributed system, events from different event sources travel along separate network routes to a mobile CE detector. Even if we assume that the network itself does not reorder events, out-of-order arrival of events at the detector can occur because of the different associated network delays. Whenever a new event arrives, it has to be inserted at the correct position in the totally-ordered event input stream before the stream is fed into the automaton.

The problem is to decide when the next event in the event input stream can be safely consumed by the automaton without risking that an event with an older timestamp is still being delayed by the network. Premature consumption could lead to an incorrect detection or non-detection of a composite event. Thus, each CE subscription is annotated with a *detection policy* that specifies when a detector can consume an event from an event input stream.

Best-Effort Detection. A best-effort detection policy states that events are consumed from event input streams without delay. Whenever an event is available, it will cause a state transition (or failure) in the automaton. Although this policy may lead to incorrect detection, it can be applied by applications that are sensitive to detection delay and are willing to ignore false positives.

Guaranteed Detection. Under a guaranteed detection policy, an event is consumed from an event input stream only once it has become *stable*[1] [14]. The consumption of only stable events ensures that no spurious composite events are detected. A detector knows that an event is stable after another event with a later timestamp from the same event source has been inserted in the event input stream. An event source that does not publish events at a high enough frequency can publish dummy *heartbeat events* that are used to 'flush the network'.

In an asynchronous distributed system, a guaranteed detection policy potentially introduces an unbounded delay at the detector. For instance, an event source might fail or decide not to cooperate by not sending heartbeat events. To avoid this problem, we are currently investigating a *probabilistic stability* metric. As opposed to a simple binary stability measure, a detector attempts to model the probability that a particular event in an event input stream is stable and the event is only consumed if its stability metric is above a certain threshold.

---

[1] An event is stable if there is no other event with an earlier timestamp in the system that should be part of this event input stream and should thus be consumed instead.

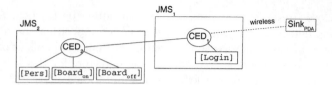

Fig. 7. Implementation of Scenario 2 using the CE framework

7 Implementation Using JMS

This section describes the implementation and performance results of our CE framework over JMS using JORAM [17], an open-source implementation of the JMS API. Application programs can then publish and subscribe to composite events using the `DistCEDServiceInf` interface, presented in Sect. 4.1, that is provided by the event brokers in the system. In the pub/sub messaging model supported by JMS, a publisher registers a topic with a particular JMS provider, such as a JORAM or J2EE server. Whenever a message is published on the topic, topic subscribers are notified by the JMS provider via a callback mechanism. Content-based filtering on the fields in the message header is supported.

Although a JMS provider can be a distributed service, most current implementations are centralised, though they may provide redundancy through replication and clustering. Thus, clients may need to connect to several providers, such as a local and a remote message server. Therefore, the binding of our CE framework to JMS does not assume that all events (primitive or composite) have a single JMS provider. Instead, our implementation uses a JNDI directory to look up the JMS server for a particular topic. For composite events, we use this to ensure that we establish only a single CE detector for a given CE type, since all such detectors will produce the same events. Since the directory may itself be distributed, this does not imply unnecessary centralisation.

To support automatic distribution of CE detection, all event brokers subscribe to a common *administration topic* (`DistCEDAdminTopic`) that is hosted by an *admin JMS server*. When a new CE expression needs to be detected, the event brokers collectively decide how and where to instantiate the mobile CE detector (i.e. the expression's automata), and register the locations of newly created detectors with the JNDI directory. In the following experiments, the distribution policy is a simple choice function derived from the hash of the CE type name, although we are investigating the more complex policies outlined in Sect. 6.2.

7.1 Evaluation and Results

To test the CE framework implementation on JMS, we simulated the Active Office Scenario 2 described in Sect. 2.1. The movement of people was treated as a Markov process, with a probability matrix describing the likely movements in each time interval. We used the office layout shown in Fig. 2 with 9 rooms and 15 occupants. Eight of the occupants were classed as residents, predisposed to use the offices, while the remainder were visitors preferring the meeting rooms.

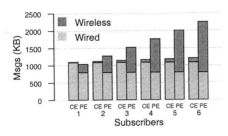

Fig. 8. Amount of data sent

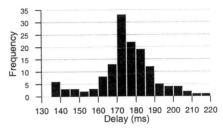

Fig. 9. Delay distribution of C

The event sinks in the scenario were PDAs connected by an (expensive) wireless link with limited bandwidth. The goals of the experiment were to minimise the usage of that link and to achieve a low notification delay for composite events.

The CE subscription C that was presented to our CE framework as the subscription submitted by the event sinks was as follows:

$$C \equiv ([C_1(f_1)]\,,\ [T_1] \subseteq \{T_1, \text{Login}(f_2)\})_{T_1 = 5\,\text{min}} \tag{1}$$

$$C_1 \equiv [\text{Board}_{\text{on}}]\ [[\text{Pers}(f_3)]\ [\text{Pers}(f_3)]^* [\text{Board}_{\text{off}}] \subseteq \{\text{Pers}(f_3), \text{Board}_{\text{off}}\}] \tag{2}$$

where f_{1-3} are JMS filter expressions that are omitted for brevity. Figure 7 shows how the detection of C was distributed over two event brokers by the CE framework. The detector CED_2 was responsible for the subexpression C_1. All the primitive events that it subscribed to and the resulting composite events were located on the server JMS_2. CED_2 then detected the complete expression C and output its composite events to a different server JMS_1.

We compared our CE framework (CE) against a JMS-only solution (PE), in which the wireless PDAs subscribed to all the primitive events and performed the CE detection themselves in an *ad hoc* manner. Figure 8 shows the total data transferred over the wireless and wired networks with a changing number of subscribers. As expected, there is a small overhead when using our CE framework for a single subscriber. However, as the number of subscribers increases, less data needs to be sent over the wireless network because CE detectors can be reused. For 6 subscribers, our CE framework generates 53% of the total traffic generated by the primitive *ad hoc* solution, and only 8% of the wireless traffic. Note that the traffic over the wired network stays roughly constant as it is mainly caused by primitive event sources sending messages to the JMS servers.

The additional notification delay introduced by our CE framework is small. The plot in Fig. 9 shows the distribution of delay that it takes for a subscriber to be notified of an occurrence of C after the composite event logically happened in the system, i.e. its last primitive event was published. The notification delay stays below 220 ms and is fairly constant during the course of the experiment.

8   Further Work: Higher-Level Specification Languages

When designing a language for the specification of composite events for ubiquitous applications, two conflicting requirements arise: Primarily, the language should facilitate the implementation of efficient detectors and be decomposable for distributed detection, i.e. the language should be optimised to be *machine-processable*. On the other hand, the syntax and semantics of the CE language should be clean and intuitive so that it is *human-processable*. Therefore, we introduce the idea of *higher-level specification languages* for humans to express composite events in a natural and domain-dependent way. These languages are then compiled down into our automata. Whereas our core CE language is optimised for machine detection, the higher-level languages focus on CE specification by end users or programmers. The following are three examples for such languages:

The Pretty Language. The 'pretty' language has a verbose syntax similar to many current rule-based specification languages. It does not have a minimal set of operators. CE specifications in the pretty language, such as `'Event A' followed_by 'Event B' within '1h'` resemble English language statements making it easier for non-programmers to express composite events.

Programming Language Binding. A binding of composite events to a programming language such as C++ or Java attempts to hide CE specification by integrating it into the programming language making its usage easier for programmers. This can be achieved with a sequence of method calls on event objects that build a CE expression: `eventA.after(eventB.repeated(3))` At runtime, these method calls are translated into a core CE language expression.

Graphical Composition. In the Active Office, users may interact with the system at runtime by specifying its behaviour with rules based on composite events such as 'Turn off the office light after 7pm'. A graphical composition tool could be used that is based on a simple model that is familiar to users. For instance, CE streams could be visualised as water flows in pipes allowing different types of piping to be composed to build composite events.

9   Conclusions

In a world with many mobile entities and complex, internet-based applications, events will become the dominant communication paradigm. CE detection in these large-scale systems provides a means of managing the complexity of a vast number of events. We consider our work as a first step to face this challenge, by providing novel scalable middleware services such as generic CE detection.

In this paper, we have presented a general CE detection framework as an extension of an existing pub/sub middleware. The framework assumes a realistic, interval-based time model and its event model makes few assumptions about the pub/sub communication infrastructure employed. Our CE detectors are an easily-implementable extension of conventional FSAs. They can handle timestamps, concurrent events, and come with a core CE language that is expressive and decomposable. Higher-level specification languages can provide more domain-specific ways to specify composite events. The abstraction of mobile CE detectors allows distributed CE detection, making the framework more scalable and robust. We introduced the concept of distribution and detection policies that control the distributed behaviour of detectors. Finally, the implementation of our CE framework over JMS demonstrates that it can improve performance in a real pub/sub application, compared to client-side JMS subscriptions.

In further work, we plan to extend our simulation environment to experiment with various distribution policies and determine how these depend on the application, the distribution of event flows, the location of event sources and event sinks, and the topology of the network.

References

1. Eugster, P.T., Felber, P., Guerraoui, R., Kermarrec, A.M.: The Many Faces of Publish/Subscribe. Technical report, EPFL, Lausanne, Switzerland (2001)
2. Carzaniga, A., Rosenblum, D.S., Wolf, A.L.: Design and Evaluation of a Wide-Area Event Notification Service. ACM Trans. on Comp. Sys. **19** (2001) 332–383
3. IBM T J Watson Research Center: Gryphon: Publish/Subscribe Over Public Networks. Whitepaper (2002)
4. Pietzuch, P.R., Bacon, J.M.: Hermes: A Distributed Event-Based Middleware Architecture. In: Proc. of the 1st Int. Workshop on Distributed Event-Based Systems (DEBS'02), Vienna, Austria (2002) 611–618
5. Addlesee, M., Curwen, R., Hodges, S., Newman, J., et al.: Implementing a Sentient Computing System. IEEE Computer Mag. **34** (2001) 50–56
6. Gehani, N.H., Jagadish, H.V., Shmueli, O.: Event Specification in an Active Object-Oriented Database. In: Proc. of the ACM SIGMOD International Conference on Management of Data. (1992) 81–90
7. Gatziu, S., Dittrich, K.R.: Detecting Composite Events in Active Database Systems Using Petri Nets. In: Proc. of the 4th RIDE-AIDS. (1994) 2–9
8. Chakravarthy, S., Mishra, D.: Snoop — An Expressive Event Specification Language For Active Databases. Technical Report UF-CIS-TR-93-007, Dept. of Computer and Information Sciences, Univ. of Florida (1993)
9. Schwiderski, S.: Monitoring the Behaviour of Distributed Systems. PhD thesis, Computer Laboratory, University of Cambridge (1996)
10. Mansouri-Samani, M., Sloman, M.: GEM: A Generalised Event Monitoring Language for Distributed Systems. IEE/IOP/BCS Distributed Systems Engineering Journal **4** (1997) 96–108
11. Hayton, R.: OASIS — An Open Architecture for Secure Interworking Services. PhD thesis, Computer Laboratory, Univ. of Cambridge (1996)
12. Bacon, J., Moody, K., Bates, J., Hayton, R., Ma, C., McNeil, A., Seidel, O., Spiteri, M.: Generic Support for Distributed Applications. IEEE Computer (2000) 68–77
13. Banavar, G., et al.: Information Flow Based Event Distribution Middleware. In: Middleware Workshop at ICDCS'99. (1999) 114–121
14. Liebig, C., Cilia, M., Buchmann, A.: Event Composition in Time-dependent Distributed Systems. In: Proc. of the 4th Int. Conf. on Coop. Inf. Sys. (1999) 70–78
15. Sun: Java™ Message Service. http://java.sun.com/products/jms/ (2001)
16. Pietzuch, P.R., Shand, B.: A Framework for Object-Based Event Composition in Dist. Sys. In: Pres. at PhDOOS Workshop (ECOOP'02). http://www.cl.cam.ac.uk/Research/SRG/opera/pub/phdoos02-ced.pdf, Malaga, Spain (2002)
17. ObjectWeb Open Source Middleware: JORAM Java Open Reliable Asynchronous Messaging 3.2.0 Release. http://www.objectweb.org/joram (2002)

A   Appendix: Formalising the Time and Event Models

A.1   Definition of Interval Timestamps

This appendix formalises our notion of an interval timestamp, while App. A.2 presents our model of the event subscriptions available to the CE service, in terms of describable events and event input sequences.

Conventional timestamps are often inappropriate for distributed event systems. In a distributed system, node clocks may have unknown jitter within a known synchronisation distance. As a result, if two nodes detect events A and B respectively, it may be impossible to decide which occurred first. An interval timestamp, consisting of a start time and an end time, can make this ambiguity explicit, yet remains consistent with the physical time order of the events [14].

Let $t = [t^l; t^h]$ be an interval time stamp with start and end times t^l and t^h $(t^l \leq t^h)$. We define the order relations $<$ and $\prec$ and union operator $\cup$ as:

$$t_1 < t_2 \triangleq t_1^h < t_2^l \tag{3}$$

$$t_1 \prec t_2 \triangleq (t_1^h < t_2^h) \vee (t_1^h = t_2^h \wedge t_1^l < t_2^l) \tag{4}$$

$$t_1 \cup t_2 \triangleq [\min(t_1^l, t_2^l); \max(t_1^h, t_2^h)] \tag{5}$$

A.2   Formalising Describable Events and Input Sequences

Users of event systems subscribe for notification of relevant events. Our CE detectors use the same subscription mechanism to describe which events they need to receive. In a sense, therefore, subscriptions (and the associated filter expressions) represent the atomic input streams available to CE detectors.

Let $\mathbb{E} = \{e_1, e_2, \dots\}$ be the space of possible events in the system. Each event e has timestamp $T(e)$, and a unique identifier $u(e)$ ordered by '$<$'. We write $e_1^{t_1}$ to show $T(e_1) = t_1$. Events are then ordered, consistently with their timestamps:

$$\forall e_1, e_2 \in \mathbb{E}, \; e_1 < e_2 \triangleq T(e_1) < T(e_2) \tag{6}$$

$$e_1 \prec e_2 \triangleq (T(e_1) \prec T(e_2)) \vee (T(e_1) = T(e_2) \wedge u(e_1) < u(e_2)) \tag{7}$$

The space of events may be further categorised. The special *empty event* $\varepsilon \in \mathbb{E}$ is always detected. *Time events* $\mathbb{E}_T \subseteq \mathbb{E}$ are made to occur at a given future instant or after a certain interval, when timers expire. With instantaneous timestamps $(t^l = t^h)$, they help detect composite events with time restrictions. If not supported by the pub/sub infrastructure, CE detectors can generate them as needed.

Event systems often allow us to differentiate types of event, by subscribing to subspaces of the event space $\mathbb{E}$, e.g. 'events where a door opens', or 'events where FE04's door opens'. These sets of events are denoted by an upper case letters: E, A, B. (In pub/sub systems, these are often called event types.) Individual event instances, on the other hand, take lower case letters: e_1, e_2, a, b.

Subscriptions also need certain properties, to be useful for CE detection. For example, if subscriptions A and B are valid, then it should be possible to detect events matching both or either of the subscriptions, $A \cap B$ or $A \cup B$. (If this is not supported by the underlying event framework, it can be simulated by detectors, if the event input streams are well ordered together under the total order $\prec$.)

There should be a maximal subscription $\mathbb{E}_D$, of all events that can be matched. There is also a subscription to detect any predefined, matchable event alone (and the special empty event ε is always matched); see (8) below. Finally, CE detectors should also be able to detect events matching one subscription but not another.

Each subscription can be associated with the set of events that would match it. The theoretical collection of all of these subscription sets is the family of *describable event sets* $\mathcal{D} \subseteq \mathbb{P}(\mathbb{E})$. This is a special collection of subsets of $\mathbb{E}$: those which can be detected within the CE framework. $\mathcal{D}$ is closed under finite union, finite intersection and element complementing relative to $\mathbb{E}_D$:

$$\text{Let } \mathbb{E}_D = \bigcup_{E \in \mathcal{D}} E. \text{ Then } \mathbb{E}_D \in \mathcal{D},\ \varepsilon \in \mathbb{E}_D, \text{ and } \forall e \in \mathbb{E}_D, \{e, \varepsilon\} \in \mathcal{D} \qquad (8)$$

The automata which detect composite events need to be able to treat incoming events as a well ordered stream, in order to match sequential patterns of events. By totally ordering events with '$\prec$' this can be achieved, resulting in the *global event input sequence* $I = (e_1, e_2, e_3, \dots)$, where $e_n \prec e_{n+1}\ \forall n \in \mathbb{N}$.

However, not all events are relevant to all patterns, or at all stages of a particular pattern. Describable event sets provide partial views of the input events, selecting subsequences of I. Thus CE detectors can restrict their view of the input sequence to only the relevant symbols. For example, if $E \in \mathcal{D}$ then $I_E = (e_{E_1}, e_{E_2}, e_{E_3}, \dots)$ denotes the subsequence consisting of elements of E.

B   Appendix: Generating Composite Event Detectors

This appendix details how expressions in our core CE language are transformed into CE detection automata, as outlined in Sect. 5.2. The grammatical components of our core language are listed below, with corresponding automata.

Atoms. $[A, B, \dots \subseteq \Sigma_0]$. Atoms detect individual events in the input stream. The resulting automaton considers an input stream of all events that are elements of Σ_0. Any input event in $A \cup B \dots$ will be successfully detected; an event in Σ_0 but not in $A \cup B \dots$ is a failure which stops expression matching (cf. Fig. 10(a)).

Negation. $[\neg E \subseteq \Sigma] \triangleq [\Sigma \backslash E \subseteq \Sigma]$.   **Trivial Input.** $[E] \triangleq [E \subseteq E]$.

Concatenation. $\mathcal{C}_1 \mathcal{C}_2$. Detects expression $\mathcal{C}_1$ *weakly* followed by $\mathcal{C}_2$. In the diagram, the shaded boxes are automata matching $\mathcal{C}_1$ and $\mathcal{C}_2$. An empty transition is then added for each generative state of $\mathcal{C}_1$ or $\mathcal{C}_2$, and those states become ordinary (cf. Fig. 10(b)). If $\mathcal{C}_1$ or $\mathcal{C}_2$'s detection were distributed, each submachine could be replaced by a single transition. Removing empty transitions[2] gives:

---

[2] Outgoing transitions from the second submachine's start state inherit the strength or weakness of the empty transition, but keep their original labellings.

Sequence. $C_1; C_2$. This detects C_1 *strongly* followed by C_2. Thus C_1 and C_2 must not overlap in a sequence, but they may in a concatenation (cf. Fig. 10(c)).

Iteration. C_1^*. Detects any number of occurrences of expression C_1. If C_1 detects a symbol which causes it to fail, then the composite machine C_1^* stops detecting iterations – even when C_1 is distributed to another node (cf. Fig. 10(d)).

Alternation. $C_1 | C_2$. This expression will match if either C_1 or C_2 is matched by the input stream. This may result in nondeterminism for the number of input symbols which are matched by both C_1 and C_2 (cf. Fig. 10(e)).

Timing. $(C_1, C_2)_{T_1 = \text{timespec}}$. The timing operator can be used to detect event combinations within, or not within, a given interval. In the above expression, event T_1 will be generated at a certain time after C_1 is detected – either a relative time, such as a minute later, or an absolute time. The second expression C_2 may then use T_1 as an event specification, in detecting composite events. Furthermore, C_2 is extended so that all states include T_1 in their input domain. For distribution or reuse, the modified C_2 detector is treated as distinct from the original, and it should be on the same node as the $(C_1, C_2)_{T_1}$ detector (cf. Fig. 10(f)).

Parallelisation. $C_1 \parallel C_2$. This can be used to detect composite expressions C_1 and C_2 in parallel. The diagram assumes that separate detectors for C_1 and C_2 already exist. They must be separate, to maintain the two independent timestamps needed for proper order restrictions on the two input sequences (cf. Fig. 10(g)).

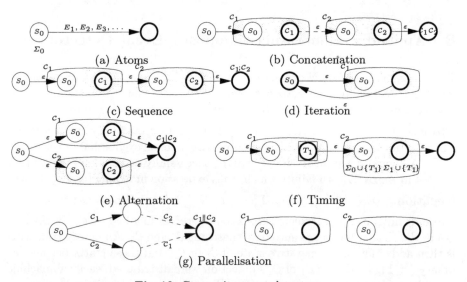

Fig. 10. Composite event detectors

Content Distribution for Publish/Subscribe Services

Mao Chen, Andrea LaPaugh, and Jaswinder Pal Singh

Department of Computer Science, Princeton University
35 Olden Street, Princeton, NJ 08544, USA
{maoch,aslp,jps}@cs.princeton.edu

Abstract. Caching and content delivery are important for content-intensive publish/subscribe applications. This paper proposes several content distribution approaches that combine match-based pushing and access-based caching, based on users' subscription information and access patterns. To study the performance of the proposed approaches, we built a simulator and developed a workload to mimic the content and access dynamics of a busy news site. Using a purely access-based caching approach as the baseline, our best approaches yield over 50% and 130% relative gains for two request traces in terms of the hit ratio in local caches, while keeping the traffic overhead comparable. Even when the subscription information is assumed not to reflect users' accesses perfectly, our best approaches still have about 40% and 90% relative improvement for the two traces. To our knowledge, this work is the first effort to investigate content distribution under the publish/subscribe paradigm.

1 Introduction

The information needs of content consumers form a key to driving content delivery over the Internet. Typically, these information needs are determined based on access patterns and pre-determinations of popular resources.

Many web-based notification services are based on users' subscriptions, which are statements of interest. The stated interest can therefore also be used as a basis for caching and content distribution. Little exploration of this use has been done.

An example is the notification services at news sites. A user indicates the categories or keywords of the news of interest; the news site notifies the user with a list of titles when it publishes news that matches the user's subscription. If the user wants to read an article in the list, the user requests the actual content from the origin site. These types of services are usually known as publish/subscribe applications.

In the literature, most work on publish/subscribe systems examines event routing and efficient matching. However, content distribution in publish/subscribe services is an important module that has not been adequately studied. Content delivery is usually ignored because the existing publish/subscribe applications assume subscribers are only interested in short messages rather than large-size contents. However, this assumption does not hold for many applications, such as news delivery, in which the object of interest (to which the notification might only carry a link) may embed long

M. Endler and D. Schmidt (Eds.): Middleware 2003, LNCS 2672, pp. 83–102, 2003.

texts, images and video/audio streams. In addition to this need, the time decoupling in publish/subscribe services, which means information producing and consuming occur asynchronously, creates an opportunity for early content distribution. Of course, because of the constraints on the storage at subscriber-side machines and on the Internet bandwidth, it is neither realistic to store all the matched contents at the subscriber side until users read them nor efficient to leave all the contents at the publisher side until users request them, so dynamic content distribution strategies must be developed.

This paper presents a set of content distribution strategies for publish/subscribe systems. The different approaches can be classified along two axes, which also expose the key design issues: (i) *when* is the opportunity for placing a page into a cache; (ii) *how* (on what basis) the placement and replacement decisions are made at evaluation time. The two major possibilities for *when* are (a) at match time, i.e. when a page is determined to match certain subscriptions and (b) at access time, as in traditional caching systems. The two major possibilities for *how* are (a) based on access patterns only, as in traditional caching systems, and (b) based on subscription information and matching.

A major challenge in such a study is that of developing workloads. No real-world publish/subscribe workloads are available for such studies. We therefore have developed workloads based on studies of observed access patterns at busy sites, extrapolating from there to publish/subscribe workloads. In particular, to study the performance of our approaches, we simulate the news delivery to subscribers who are geographically distributed. The publishing pattern and the access dynamics are simulated according to a study on one of the busiest media sites, MSNBC [24].

In our experiments, the performance metrics are: (i) the hit ratio in the local proxy servers, since the major goal of this work is to reduce the response time perceived by end-users, and (ii) the traffic overhead, which is measured using the network traffic for transferring contents from the publisher site to the proxies of subscribers. Using a purely access-based caching approach as the baseline, our approaches improve the hit ratio dramatically while keeping the traffic overhead comparable.

The major contributions of this paper are as follows:

1. Presenting the first study of content delivery and caching that uses publish-subscribe information;
2. Proposing and comparing a set of solutions for content delivery in publish-subscribe services, based on subscription information as well as access patterns;
3. Experimentally demonstrating the benefit of our approaches in reducing the response time to end users without extra overhead in network traffic;
4. Developing realistic workloads for evaluation, a major challenge given that publish/subscribe workloads are not generally available;
5. Building a simulator to study content delivery in globally distributed servers.

The rest of this paper is organized as follows. Section 2 outlines the architecture of a content delivery system that this paper addresses. Section 3 presents several information delivery mechanisms in the system. Section 4 discusses a news delivery workload and a simulator that are used to evaluate the approaches. The simulation results are demonstrated and analyzed in section 5. Section 6 discusses related work. Section 7 draws conclusions and indicates future directions for this research.

2   A Publish/Subscribe System
with Content Distribution Engine

Publish/subscribe is an asynchronous communication paradigm for information producers and information consumers. The producers and consumers are globally distributed and do not have to know each other. Information consumers declare their information needs to a publish/subscribe system that notifies the subscribers when published information matches the users' subscriptions.

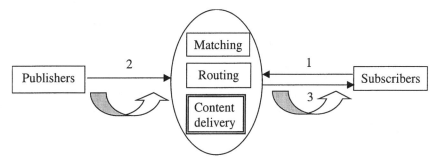

Publish/subscribe brokering system

Fig. 1. Architecture of a publish/subscribe system

Figure 1 outlines a conceptual architecture of a publish/subscribe system. Publishers and subscribers (end-users) are connected via the publish/subscribe system. Notification services are usually implemented through three basic communication streams as labeled in the figure:

1. Users subscribe, announcing their interests to the system;
2. Producers publish contents to the system;
3. The system notifies the users whose subscriptions match the contents.

A typical system consists of a matching engine and a routing engine. After a piece of content is published into the system (flow 2), the matching engine finds the users who are interested in the events according to their interest profiles, and the routing engine delivers events to those users. These engines may be centralized or distributed.

This paper adds a content distribution and caching (or content delivery) engine, which is not discussed in the literature. After step 3, the notified users may choose to read the actual content of the event; the content distribution module in figure 1 is in charge of deciding when to deliver which content to the subscribers.

In this study, the caching/content-delivery servers are deployed as proxy servers close to the end-users. Each proxy server connects to a group of clients/subscribers. A proxy server aggregates its users' subscriptions and processes notifications for its users. It also serves as the cache that is consulted when one of its users accesses content. In this paper, the terms proxy, proxy server and server are used synonymously for content distribution server.

3   Content Delivery Strategies

As discussed earlier, content delivery strategies can be classified along two axes, namely *when* and *how* pages are evaluated for placement in caches.

Regarding *when*, the content distribution engine has two obvious opportunities to deliver content from a publisher to a proxy server. In the first case, the publisher proactively forwards a page to a proxy for potential placement when the matching engine determines that the content of the page matches the subscriptions of some users at the proxy. This approach, which we call the *push-time* strategy, assumes that the subscribers are likely to request the page later after receiving the notifications. The second scenario, which we call the *access-time* strategy, is like traditional caching and is based on the fact of rather than the prediction of users' accesses to a page.

Since a server is limited in physical storage capacity, when a page is delivered to a server in either the push-time or the access-time approaches, the server may need to replace some content at the server if the server's cache is already full. Replacement is based on values given to pages. Regarding *how* the value is determined, it can be done based on subscription and matching information or on actual access information.

This paper focuses on the following interesting combinations of when and how evaluations are made for page placement in caches:

1. Access-time strategy based on usage pattern only
2. Push-time strategy based on subscription and matching information only
3. Push-time and access-time strategy based on subscription and access pattern

The first combination is the traditional caching approach and is the baseline used in this study. The second case is a simple pushing mechanism driven by matching. This paper puts the emphasis on the third class of schemes that exploit both placement opportunities and both types of information about the value of pages.

3.1   Access-Time Strategy Based on Access Pattern

This paper uses a new caching replacement algorithm called Greedy-Dual* (GD*) [17] as the baseline algorithm, since it yields higher hit ratio than LRU, Greedy-Dual-Size (GDS) [7] and LFU-DA in an experimental study [17]. GD* determines the value of a page $V(p)$ based on the access frequency, the access recency, the cost to fetch a page, and the size of the page, as represented in equation 1:

$$V(p) = L + \left(\frac{f(p) \cdot c(p)}{s(p)} \right)^{1/\beta}. \tag{1}$$

Where
L: inflation value to capture the access recency
$f(p)$: number of accesses on the page
$c(p)$: cost to fetch a page from the publisher
$s(p)$: page size
β: balance factor of popularity and temporal correlation

In our implementation, the reference count of a page is discarded when the page is evicted, as in the In-Cache LFU algorithm [17]. As suggested by [7], our implementation uses the network distance to the origin publisher to measure the cost to fetch a page for a given proxy, where the network topology of proxy servers and the publishers is a random graph built using BRITE [6]. The constant parameter β is set manually as discussed in the experiment section (section 5).

On an access hit of page p, the replacement algorithm GD* increases the reference count $f(p)$ and re-evaluates the page based on the current inflation value L. On a cache miss, all the pages in the cache are sorted by values and are evicted from the least valuable one, until there is room for the requested page; the inflation value L is set to be the value of the page that is evicted last. The following is the pseudo-code of GD*:

```
Replacement algorithm in GD*
    L←0.0
    For each request in turn:
        The current request is for page p:
            If p is already in memory
                Increase f(p);
            Else
                While there is not enough room
                    L ← min {V(k) ∈ pages in the cache}
                    Evict q s.t. V(q) = L
                Bring p into cache;
```
$$V(p) \leftarrow L + \left(\frac{f(p) \bullet c(p)}{s(p)} \right)^{1/\beta} ;$$
```
end.
```

3.2   Push-Time Strategy Based on Subscription Information and Matching

For a page that matches some subscriptions aggregated on a proxy, the number of the subscriptions indicates the number of requests of the page in future. The value of a page in a push-time replacement is based on the number of end-users' subscriptions that match the page, the cost and the size of the page as described in equation 2.

$$V(p) = \frac{f_S(p) \cdot c(p)}{s(p)}. \tag{2}$$

Where
$f_S(p)$: the number of subscriptions matching the content of page p
$c(p)$ and $s(p)$ have the same meaning as in equation 1

If the cache of a destination proxy is full in a push-time placement, the new page is evaluated and compared to the existing pages in the proxy. The pages whose values are less than that of the new page are candidates for replacement. The candidate pages are sorted by value and are evicted one by one until the available storage on the proxy is large enough for the new page. This placement algorithm using the subscription-based push-time strategy is denoted as SUB in this paper.

When an event is generated and routed to a destination proxy, SUB may decide not to store the new page if the total size of all the candidate pages (the pages whose values are smaller than that of the new page) is less than that of the new page. As a push-time only strategy, on a cache miss, SUB fetches the requested page from the publisher and forwards the page to the user without caching it in the local server.

3.3   Push-Time and Access-Time Schemes Based on Subscription Information and Access Pattern

We developed several approaches within the category that performs both push-time and access-time placement. The approaches run two independent placement modules at push-time and access-time, and are distinct in whether the same replacement algorithm is used in the two modules and in how a server's cache is configured.

Single Cache and Single Replacement Method. Using this type of approach, the push-time and the access-time placement modules share a server's cache and use the same replacement algorithm. Like SUB, whether to store a page on a server is purely based on the value of the page. As a consequence, the push-time placement does not store a new page in the local server if the page's size is larger than the total size of the candidate pages for eviction; on a cache miss, the replacement module discards the requested page immediately after forwarding it to the user if the page's value is not high enough to reside in the server's cache.

Within this framework, the evaluation function used in the replacement algorithm can analyze and combine the subscription and the usage information in several ways.

GD*-based Approaches. Since GD* provides a general framework to combine several factors related to a page's value, it is used as the basis to incorporate the subscription information. Two evaluation functions are developed based on GD*.

For a given page, the number of end-user subscriptions that match the page indicates the amount of references of the page in the future, while the number of accesses in the past exhibits the usage pattern of users. A direct way to combine the prediction and the history information is adding the two numbers together. The evaluation function based on this idea is as in equation 1 after replacing the frequency factor $f(p)$ by the sum of the number of subscriptions and of the accesses as in equation 3. This approach is referred to as Subscription-GD*-1 or *SG1* in this paper.

$$f(p) = s + a. \tag{3}$$

Where
s : the number of subscriptions matching page p
a : the number of accesses of page p

SG1 ignores the relationship between the references and the subscriptions of a page. Ideally, if every subscriber reads any page that matches his/her subscription exactly once, the difference between the number of subscriptions and that of past requests is equal to the number of future references of a page. Based on this idea, an alternative uses the following equation to calculate $f(p)$, while keeping the other factors the same as in equation 1. The alternative is called Subscription-GD*-2 or *SG2*.

$$f(p) = s - a. \qquad (4)$$
Where
  s : the number of subscriptions matching page p
  a : the number of accesses of page p

Frequency-based Approach. Using GD* as the framework, SG2 integrates the estimation of a page's reference frequency in the future with the access recency in the past. However, there is lack of proof about the correlation between the two factors. Therefore a new evaluation function that relies only on the frequency prediction is developed. This evaluation function is defined in equation 5. The approach using this evaluation method is referred to as *subscription-request* or *SR* in this paper.

$$V(p) = \frac{f(p) \cdot c(p)}{s(p)}. \qquad (5)$$
Where
  $f = s - a$

Single Cache and Dual Replacement Methods. The approaches that combine the subscription and the usage pattern into a single evaluation function are based on some assumptions on the relationship between the two patterns. For example, SG2 and SR assume every user requests all the pages that match his/her subscription exactly once.

An alternative is to use independent replacement algorithms as well as evaluation functions at push-time and access-time. Namely, GD* is applied in an access-time replacement, while SUB is used in a push-time placement. Since the two replacement algorithms use either access analysis or subscription information, the two types of information are used separately in different placement modules. This approach is referred to as Dual-Methods or *DM* in this paper.

Dual Caches and Dual Replacement Methods. A potential problem within *DM* is that a page that is in hot use will be replaced in a push-time placement if the number of subscriptions matching the page is not large enough. Or, on the other hand, a new page with a high future use indicated by subscription matching will be replaced on a cache miss just because of the few references up to the replacing time. This problem is due to the overlapping operations of the push-time and access-time placement modules in the same cache space.

To deal with the problem associated with *DM*, the cache on a proxy can be divided into two portions that are used by the push-time and the access-time modules independently. Under this scheme, the cache portion used by the push-time module is called *Push-Cache* or *PC* in this paper, while the portion used by the access-time module is called *Access-Cache* or *AC*. The new mechanism is denoted as *Dual-*

Caches or *DC* in the following discussions. Like *DM*, *Dual-Caches* runs GD* in the access-time module and SUB in the push-time module. But different from *DM*, each replacement algorithm runs only on the corresponding portion of a proxy cache.

Dual Caches with Fixed Partition (DC-FP). A simple way to handle a dual-cache is keeping a fixed partition on the storage. This approach is denoted as *Dual-Caches with Fixed Partition* or *DC-FP* in this paper.

When a page is pushed into a server, the push-time module tries to store the page into *PC* using SUB. When serving a request, *DC-FP* first checks *PC*. If the requested page is in *PC*, the page is moved from *PC* to *AC*; meaning that the page should be henceforth evaluated based on the access pattern and be compared with other referenced pages in *AC* in the cache replacement algorithm. Otherwise, GD* is called to handle the replacement on *AC* as a standard caching algorithm.

Dual Caches with Adaptive Partition (DC-AP). A fixed partition in a dual-cache lacks flexibility in adjusting the effectiveness of pushing and caching according to the content publishing dynamics and the access dynamics. For example, when a page in the push cache *PC* is requested, the page is moved to the access cache *AC*, which may trigger a replacement in *AC* if *AC* is full. However, the storage in *PC* that was cleared by moving out the requested page is unused at least until the next new page is published. In such a case, a better strategy is to reassign the storage of the requested page to the access cache. On the other hand, some storage in the access cache can be "devoted" to the push cache if there is no room to store a new page in *PC* **and** several old pages in *AC* have not been referenced for a while.

The approach that labels the storage of each page according to the publishing and request patterns is called *Dual-Caches with Adaptive Partition* or *DC-AP* in our discussion. Using *DC-AP*, when a page cannot be stored into *PC* based on *SUB* at push time, the push-time placement module checks the pages in *AC*. If some pages in *AC* have not been referenced since the last replacement in *AC*, these pages are assumed to be less important than the new page and thus become candidates for eviction. The storage of those pages is labeled as belonging to *PC* and is used to store the new page. The placing algorithm of *DC-AP* is as follows:

```
Placing in DC-AP
  Page P is pushed to the server:
    Run SUB on the push cache PC;
    If SUB fails to store P
      S ← pages in AC that have not been accessed since
the last replacement in AC;
      If Size(S) ≥ Size(P)
        While the available storage in PC < Size(P)
          Pm s.t. VPm = Min{Vi : i ∈ S};
          Label the storage of Pm as PC Label;
        Store P in PC;
  end.
```

Recall that *DC-FP* moves a page from *PC* to *AC* when the page in *PC* is accessed for the first time. This "Moving" operation may trigger the replacement in *AC*. To avoid the unnecessary replacements in *AC*, in the same scenario, the locating algorithm in *DC-AP* labels the storage of the page as *AC*, assuming that the pushing frequency in *PC* is relatively low as compared to the replacement frequency in *AC*.

Recall that the Dual-Methods (*DM*) strategy labels each page with two values and considers each value only in the corresponding module. In contrast, *DC-AP* labels each page with a 2-tuple (o, v) at any time, where o indicates the module that should process the page and v refers to the page's value under the corresponding operation. Both elements o and v are updated with time.

In *DC-AP*, the fraction of the storage assigned to each portion can be any value between 0 and 1. If either *PC* or *AC* dominates the storage on a server, pushing or caching consequently dominates the content distribution at that server. To avoid the possible imbalance in the effects of the two modules, a boundary should be set on the fraction of storage that can be assigned to each portion. A variant of *DC-AP* sets the upper boundary and the lower boundary on the fraction that can be *PC* at any given time. We call this variant *Dual-Caches with Limited Adaptive Partition (DC-LAP)*. In *DC-LAP*, the re-partition in the placing and locating algorithms is performed only when the new partition does not violate the boundary setting.

3.4 Summary of Strategies

The above caching and content delivery approaches can be classified based on when and how content is delivered from the publisher to a proxy server. Table 1 categorizes all the approaches discussed in this paper.

Table 1. Categorization of content distribution schemes

When \ How	Access	Subscription	Access + Subscription
Access-time	GD*		
Push-time		SUB	
Access-time + Push-time			SG1, SG2, SR, DM, DC-FP, DC-AP, DC-LAP

As discussed in the literature [27], the performance of the cache replacement algorithms depends highly on the traffic characteristics of accesses. It is worth pointing out that although we use *GD** as the framework in forming our push-time and access-time combined schemes based on subscription as well as usage patterns, our approaches can be also incorporated with other cache replacement algorithms.

4   Workload and Simulator

Because of the difficulty of obtaining meaningful commercial data, the approaches discussed in this paper are validated using a simulator. The simulator is built based on analysis and observations about the real-world data in the literature.

We chose news delivery to be the application scenario for our simulation because of its challenges. News publishing and reading have high temporal dynamics. In addition, news pages are of significant size, especially for multimedia news (e.g., video, audio, and images). Gadde et al. indicate that content distribution is more beneficial when a large number of popular objects have large sizes and high update frequencies [15]. Therefore, news delivery can demonstrate the power of the content distribution strategies that this paper focuses on.

The simulator in figure 2 assumes a single publisher as a news site and a group of proxy servers, each of which connects to a set of users who are close to the server. The input of the simulator includes a publishing stream, a request sequence at each proxy-server, and the subscriptions collected from the end-users at each proxy-server. The publishing and request streams are temporal sequences, while the subscription information is assumed to be static. Our workload is for a 7-day simulation.

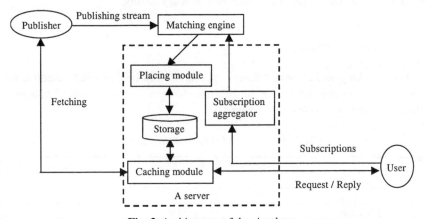

Fig. 2. Architecture of the simulator

As in the models presented in [5, 29], our workload parameterizes the request rate, the document rate of change, the total number of the information objects, and the popularity distribution for objects. As an extension, we model the sizes of pages and simulate a more realistic scenario in which every server has a limited storage capacity. Furthermore, we incorporate subscription distribution that has not been addressed in the literature. Finally, the formulae and the parameters used to build our workload are based mainly on a set of observations and analyses of the content generation and access patterns at the publishing server MSNBC ([23]), rather than on observations at a proxy as in most trace analyses.

4.1   Publishing Stream Generation

As observed in [24], the total number of pages published in 7 days is about 30,000, and about 24,000 pages are modified versions of 2,400 out of 6,000 distinct pages. Our publishing sequence consists of 30,147 pages in total.

In [24], 5% of the modification intervals are less than 1 hour and 5% are greater than 1 day, while others are between 1 hour and 1 day. Based on that, we generate the modification intervals of the 2400 pages using a step-wise random number distribution, assuming a fixed modification interval for any updated page. The first publishing time of the 6000 original pages are randomly chosen from the period (0, 7 days). The generation times of the 24,000 modified versions are then decided based on the modification intervals and the generation times of the first versions.

The sizes of the pages are generated using a log-normal distribution [3][1]. All the pages are assumed to be cacheable in our simulation.

4.2   Request Stream Generation

Scaling Down the Number of Requests. The MSNBC site receives about 25 million requests every day [24], so a 7-day trace should contain about 175 million requests. To scale down the simulation, we consider only 100 proxy-servers as representatives of all the servers sending requests to the publisher from all over the world. In [24], a 5-day trace includes the requests from several hundreds of thousands of institutional domains, hence we assume the 100 servers issue about 1/1000 of all the requests to the site. In this way, the request rate in our trace is scaled down to around 195,000.

The request generator uses Zipf's Law[2] with a homogeneity parameter α of 1.5 to model the popularity distribution of the pages, as observed in [24]. The popularity ranks are randomly assigned to the pages with the assumption that popularity is independent of the publishing time and the size of the page.

Deciding Request Times. The reference times are generated based on the correlation between a page's age and the probability that the page is requested. According to the observations in [24], most news pages are requested when they are fresh, but popular pages are still referenced even if they have been generated for a long time.

The request generator groups the pages into four classes according to their popularity so that the request rate drops about one order of magnitude from one class to the next. For a page in any given class, the probability for the page to be requested at a given time is inversely correlated to the page's age. The more popular a page is, the stronger the negative correlation between the access probability and the page's age is.

---

[1] $p(x) = \dfrac{1}{x\sigma\sqrt{2\pi}} e^{-(\ln x - \mu)^2 / 2\sigma^2}$, $\mu = 9.357; \sigma = 1.318$.

[2] $R_i = \dfrac{1}{i^\alpha}$, the request rate on the page with rank i .

Splitting Requests by Server. As observed in the literature [24, 28], the frequently referenced pages are usually accessed by more organizations. As the first step, the server assignment procedure decides the maximum number of servers requesting a given page in a day as a function of the page's popularity using equation 6.

$$S_i = 100 \cdot \left(P_i \middle/ P_{max} \right)^{0.5}.$$

(6)

Where

P_i :   the popularity of page i

P_{max} :   the maximum popularity of all the pages

For the first day that a page is requested, S_i servers are randomly chosen from the 100 servers to make up a pool of potential servers. After that, every request to that page in that day is randomly assigned to one of the S_i servers.

As observed in [24], the server group requesting a page in one day and that in the next day overlap. Assuming the overlapping ratio is 60%, 40% of the candidate servers for a page in one day are replaced by the servers that are not in the current pool when generating the candidate servers for the page in the second day.

Generating Request Traces with α = 1.0. While news delivery is the focus of our validation study, the performances of our content delivery strategies for more general scenarios are also of interest. As a comparison, another request trace is built using a more popular α value of 1.0 in the Zipf's Law popularity distribution. The trace built using 1.5 as α is called NEWS, and that using 1.0 is called ALTERNATIVE.

4.3   Subscription Generation

Since the subscriptions are static, the only subscription information of interest is the number of subscriptions matching every page at every server.

This paper assumes that the users only request pages based on notification. For a page i, the ratio of the requests to the number of subscriptions matching i at a server j is called *subscription quality*, denoted as $SQ_{i,j}$. When any user reads a page at most once, $SQ_{i,j}$ is the probability for a subscriber of a page to actually request the page.

The number of subscriptions matching a page at a server can be inferred using equation 7, given an *estimate subscription quality (SQ)*. SQ being 1 is the special case that every user will in fact access any page matching the user's interest. More generally, users may only access a subset of pages that match their stated interest (SQ < 1).

$$SF_{i,j} = P_{i,j} \middle/ SQ_{i,j}.$$

(7)

Where

$P_{i,j}$:   number of requests of page i from server j

$SQ_{i,j}$: a random number in $[2 \cdot SQ - 1, 1]$ if $SQ > 0.5$ or in $[0, 2 \cdot SQ]$ if $SQ \leq 0.5$

5   Experiments

5.1   Metrics and Experiment Setup

The motivation of this study is to reduce the response time perceived by the end users. A high hit ratio in a local server generally means a smaller response time hence the *global hit ratio* (*H*) on the 100 servers is the major performance metric as follows:

$$H = \frac{\sum_{i=1}^{100} H_i}{\sum_{i=1}^{100} R_i}. \tag{8}$$

Where
H_i : the number of hits on server i
R_i : the number of request on server i

An elegant content delivery strategy should improve H without introducing a big overhead into the network traffic between the publishing site and proxy servers. The networking cost is measured using the amount of contents transferred between the publishers and the servers in terms of the number of pages or the number of bytes.

Our simulation experiments model a quite realistic scenario in which the storage capacity of each cache is limited. The storage capacity of a server's cache is set based on the unique bytes requested at the server in the whole simulation. In the experiments, the performances of the methods are tested under three settings for cache capacity: 1% of the total number of unique bytes requested by a server, 5%, and 10%.

According to experimental results [17], the parameter β (see equation 1) that balances the long-term popularity and the short-term temporal correlation in GD* may be different from trace to trace. On the other hand, when β is learned on-line from the past accesses seen at different times, β is quite stable for a given trace. To decide the suitable value of β, GD* and the two GD*-based approaches SG1 and SG2 are evaluated by varying β from 0.0625 to 4, under three capacity settings for both traces.

In the following experiments, the value of β is set in such a way that the hit ratio of the given algorithm achieves the highest hit ratio. Namely, β is 2 in the three methods for the trace NEWS; for ALTERNATIVE, β is 2 in GD* and SG1 when the capacity setting is 5% or 10% and 1 for 1%, while the value of β is always 0.5 in SG2.

5.2   Comparing Dual-Methods and Dual-Caches

Figure 3 compares Dual-Methods (DM), Dual-Caches with Fixed Partition (DC-FP), Dual-Caches with Adaptive Partition (DC-AP), and Dual-Caches with Limited Adaptive Partition (DC-LAP) for trace NEWS. DC-FP uses a 50%-50% partition. DC-AP starts from a 50%-50% partition but adjusts the partition dynamically. DC-LAP is like DC-AP but bounds the fraction of the pushing cache between 25% and 75%.

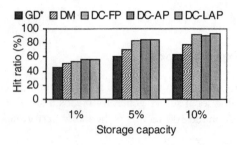

Fig. 3. Hit ratios of Dual-Methods and Dual-Caches algorithms (NEWS)

All the Dual* approaches have better hit ratio than GD*, but DC-LAP outperforms DM and other Dual-Caches approaches in all the cases. The observations hold for the trace ALTERNATIVE and for SQ < 1. Therefore, DC-LAP is chosen as the representative of the Dual* family in the following comparison experiments.

More adaptive approaches DC-AP and DC-LAP only yield marginal improvement over DC-FP. Recall that DC-AP assumes a difference between the publishing rate in the push-cache and the reference rate in the access-cache. Therefore, we conjecture that the little improvement using DC-AP and DC-LAP is due to the high publishing frequency and high re-access frequency in our traces.

5.3   Overall Hit Ratio with Perfect Subscriptions

Figure 4 compares the hit ratios of the major algorithms in this paper in the ideal case that the subscription information perfectly reflects users' request patterns ($SQ = 1$).

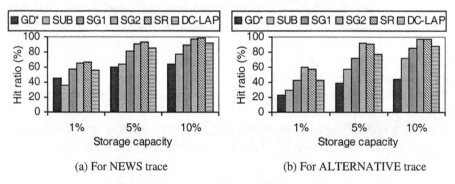

(a) For NEWS trace   (b) For ALTERNATIVE trace

Fig. 4. Hit ratios of all the methods ($SQ = 1$)

The only case in which any of our new approaches that incorporate subscription-based pushing are worse than the access-based caching-only scheme GD* is when the cache capacity is low (1%). Then GD* outperforms the simple subscription-based pushing-only scheme SUB for the trace NEWS. NEWS has a set of very popular pages and thus exaggerates the performance of the caching-only algorithm.

While the hit ratio increases with the capacity setting for any method, the relative performance ranks of the approaches are quite stable under different capacity settings. All the other new approaches shown in the figure outperform SUB under any setting.

SG2 and SR, which use the estimation of the number of requests of a page in the future, provide the highest hit ratios. The temporal analysis in SG2 does **not** provide extra benefit to SR, which exhibits the difficulty of combining the analyses of history information and of future usage. SG1 has a lower hit ratio than SG2 and SR, which implies the importance to take into account the relation between the subscriptions and the accesses of a page. DC-LAP has a hit ratio similar to SG1, and yields around 4% higher hit ratio than SG1 only when the storage capacity is high (5% or 10%).

When α becomes smaller (ALTERNATIVE trace), the hit ratio of the caching approach GD* is much lower than that when α is high (NEWS trace). The degradation in hit ratio results from a more uniform popularity distribution implying fewer repeated references to the same page. However, the relative improvements using subscription-based pushing-enhanced methods are much higher when α is 1.0 than when α is 1.5, as summarized in table 2. The much higher gains for ALTERNATIVE mean that the push-time placement module benefits the non-homogeneous request streams (characterized by low α) more.

Table 2. Relative improvement over GD* (%) (capacity = 5%)

α	SUB	SG1	SG2	SR	DM	DC-FP	DC-LAP
1.5	6	34	50	54	17	37	40
1.0	47	84	133	133	34	93	96

5.4   Influence of Subscription Quality

At the 5% capacity level, figure 5 reveals the effect of subscription quality (SQ) that is defined in equation 7 in section 4.3. All the approaches are affected by SQ, except for GD* which does not use the subscription information at all.

SR, which is one of the best approaches in the ideal case, is most affected by SQ and its superiority disappears quickly as SQ decreases. Both SG1 and DC-LAP are not sensitive to SQ, and they are similarly good approaches as SQ decreases. DC-LAP has about 3% higher hit ratio than SG1 when SQ is as low as 0.25.

One major distinction between the results for the two traces is the behavior of SG2. By incorporating the analysis of access patterns, SG2 outperforms SR by remaining highly effective when SQ varies. For NEWS trace, when SQ $\leq$ 0.5, whether one is using the sum (SG1) or the difference (SG2) of the number of subscriptions and that of accesses becomes less important because the number of subscriptions dominates the frequency factor in equation 1. For ALTERNATIVE trace, however, the hit ratio of SG2 drops more quickly and it is even worse than SG1 when SQ is 0.25 or 0.5.

One possible reason for the above distinction is that since the request frequencies of pages are getting more similar with smaller α, the subscription frequency dominates the frequency factor in the evaluation method in SG2. Therefore, the accuracy of subscription information becomes more important for SG2.

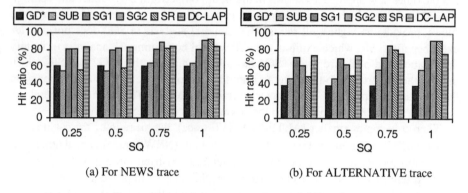

(a) For NEWS trace   (b) For ALTERNATIVE trace

Fig. 5. Hit ratios of the algorithms with different subscription qualities (capacity = 5%)

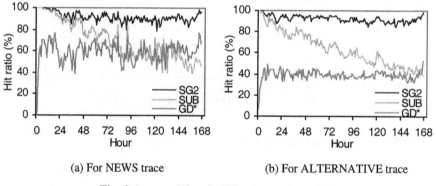

(a) For NEWS trace   (b) For ALTERNATIVE trace

Fig. 6. Average H hourly (SQ = 1, capacity = 5%)

5.5   Hit Ratio versus Time

Figure 6 demonstrates the average H of three algorithms in every hour, given that the subscription quality is 1 and the cache capacity setting is 5%. SG2, the best push-time and access-time placement approach in general, is compared against the subscription-based pushing-only method SUB and the access-based caching-only method GD*.

After the first couple of hours, GD* behaves stably. At the beginning, SUB has a high hit ratio by proactively pushing contents before users request them. However, the hit ratio of SUB drops with time because SUB only uses static subscription in-formation but does not adjust the pushing policy according to the usage pattern. SG2 keeps a high hit ratio by combining the subscription and access pattern in placement.

5.6   Traffic Overhead

The push-time module can use either of the following two schemes to push contents:

1. *Always Pushing*: the push-time module always transfers a page to a server when the page is generated and matched to the subscriptions from the server; the server then decides whether to store the page in its local cache based on the replacement algorithm. The bandwidth is wasted if the server decides not to store the page.

2. *Pushing When Necessary*: the push-time module notifies the server of the meta-information such as page size when a page matches the subscriptions from the server; then the server performs its evaluation to decide whether to store the page and sends the result to the push-time module; if the reply is "will store it in cache", the push-time module notifies the publisher to forward the page to the server. This scheme is designed to reduce unnecessary pushing from the publisher to the server.

Figures 7 shows the traffic for pushing pages and fetching pages on cache misses versus time, considering each of the above two pushing schemes. The amount of traffic in terms of the number of pages is measured when using GD*, SUB and SG2.

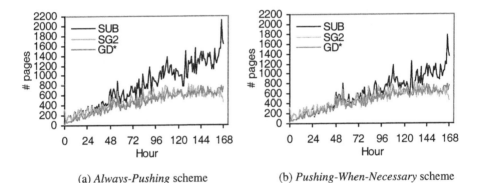

(a) *Always-Pushing* scheme   (b) *Pushing-When-Necessary* scheme

Fig. 7. Traffic in number of pages for two traces (SQ = 1, capacity = 5%, NEWS trace)

The traffic overhead of GD* does not change with pushing scheme hence it can be used as the baseline to compare the two pushing schemes. Interestingly, SG2 is not sensitive to pushing scheme, which implies that SG2 is biased toward new pages. In any case, the traffic overhead of SG2 is comparable to GD*. SUB always introduces the highest traffic overhead, because it suffers from fetching-on-miss due to its low hit ratio. The difference between the curves of SUB and GD* is smaller when using Pushing-When-Necessary than when using Always-Pushing, which means the former benefits SUB a lot in reducing the traffic overhead. The above observations hold for both traces when considering number of pages or number of bytes.

6   Related Work

Siena [8] is a distributed publish/subscribe system that makes use of the coverage relation of messages and subscriptions to achieve scalability. Efficient matching is important to publish/subscribe systems, either in a centralized or a distributed matching scheme [2, 13]. As a complement to topic-based and content-based systems, type-based publish/subscribe enables the integration of middleware and language [11]. The publish/subscribe paradigm can support event notification [14], communication in sensor networks [21], etc. To our knowledge, the storage management problem in content-intensive publish-subscribe services has not been investigated sufficiently.

Web caching passively keeps the most useful information in a capacity-limited proxy server. Many caching replacement algorithms have been presented in the literature. The GreedyDual-Size algorithm combines factors such as temporal locality and popularity as well as fetching cost and page size in caching replacement [7]. Greedy-Dual* is a generalization of GDS and balances the effects of long-term popularity and short-term reference correlation in a reference stream [17].

Prefetching is used to proactively pull information from an original site to a proxy server [10], or from a proxy to a browser cache [17]. Fan et. al. [17] propose a pre-fetching mechanism by mining the reference dependency between pages. Browsing agents can pull the pages that link to the current page and/or are similar in contents [9, 22]. Combining access pattern and link structure together, Duchamp proposes a mechanism to prefetch the popular embedded components [10].

Besravros [4] proposes a server-initiated pushing algorithm that places the most popular pages at the layer closer to the end users in a hierarchical caching system. Based on geographical information, Gwertzman and Seltzer [16] present a system that pushes the popular pages to the proxy servers that request the pages frequently.

Caching, prefetching and pushing are mainly based on inferred user interest. In a publish/subscribe application, user preference is stated in their subscriptions and pre-known by the publish/subscribe system. Our work addresses how to exploit the stated user interest as well as the inferred interest in content distribution.

The push-time placement algorithms in this paper belong to replication technique according to the definition in [26]. More importantly, our content delivery is on behalf of the content producers as for content delivery networks (CDN).

Most commercial products and research in CDN focus on hashing-based request redirection to achieve load balance among servers and thus reduce the response time [1, 19]. Gadde et al. [15] indicate a natural limit to the benefits of redirection-based hierarchical CDNs, since the hit ratio in proxy caches increases dramatically as ISPs serve larger user communities. This paper addresses server-based populating that helps to improve the hit ratio even when passive caching achieves its upper limit.

Regarding the placement problem in CDN, the previous work has mainly concentrated on optimum solutions for space-constrained problems. The optimum solution in an overlay network with a graph topology has been proved to be NP-hard, while there exist polynomial solutions for other topologies like trees [20]. The optimum solutions usually assume precise global and stable information known in advance, and thus are infeasible for many web-applications.

Kangasharju et al. [18] propose four heuristics, but the best one needs global knowledge about the network topology, the reference distribution and the content distribution at different times. Qiu et al. [25] propose several heuristics to choose M replica sites from N candidates for a given site, assuming a relatively stable reference pattern at the candidate sites. For bandwidth-constraint placement, Venkataramani et al. [30] present a solution whose expected response time is within a constant factor of the optimal placement if the information objects have uniform size. However, the algorithm is not designed for a highly dynamic environment in which the object update rate is high and demand-readings proceed in parallel with publishing.

This paper focuses on the coordination between a publisher and a proxy server; hence the placement decision at each proxy server is based on local knowledge only. Therefore, our solutions are suitable for a highly dynamic scenario, which is distinctive from the placement algorithms based on global and static information.

7   Conclusion

We have proposed several content distribution mechanisms for content-intensive publish/subscribe systems. Our approaches combine push-time and access-time content delivery based on subscriptions as well as access patterns. The simulation study demonstrates great improvement in hit ratio by applying our best approaches as compared to the access-based caching method, even if the subscription information does not match requests perfectly. The improvement in hit ratio translates into a reduction in user perceived response time. The traffic introduced by adding the pushing module is not significantly more than that needed to fetch pages on cache misses when using caching only. Our approaches benefit request streams with both regular-popularity and news-based distributions, even benefiting the former more.

Future work is on extending the content delivery schemes to more general scenarios in which not all requests to pages are driven through notification services.

References

1. Akamai. http://www.akamai.com.
2. Altinel, M. and Franklin, M. J. Efficient Filtering of XML Documents for Selective Dissemination of Information. In Proceedings of VLDB 2000, 2000.
3. Barford, P. and Crovella, M. Generating Representative Workloads for Network and Server Performance Evaluation. In Proceedings of ACM Sigmetrics'98, 1998.
4. Besravros, A. Demand-based Document Dissemination to Reduce Traffic and Balance Load. In Proceedings of SPDP'95, 1995.
5. Breslau, L., Cao, P., Li, F., Phillips, G., and Shenker, S. Web Caching and Zipf-like Distributions: Evidence and Implications. In Proceedings of IEEE Infocom '99, 1999.
6. BRITE. http://www.cs.bu.edu/brite/
7. Cao, P. and Irani, S. Cost-Aware WWW Proxy Caching Algorithms. In Proceedings of USENIX Symposium on Internet Technology and Systems, 1997.

8. Carzaniga, A., Rosenblum, D. S., and Wolf, A. L. Design of a Scalable Event Notification Service: Interface and Architecture. Tech. Rep. CU-CS-863-98, Department of Computer Science, Univ. of Colorado at Boulder, Sept. 1998.

9. Chi, E. H., Pirolli, P., Chen, K., and Pitkow, J. Using Information Scent to Model User Information Needs and Actions on the Web. CHI 2001, Vol. 3(1), 490-497.

10. Duchamp, D. Prefetching Hyperlinks. In Proc. of USENIX Symp. on Internet Technologies and Systems, 1999.

11. Eugster, P.T., Guerraoui, R., and Sventek, J. Type-based publish/subscribe. Technical Report, Swiss Federal Institute of Technology, June 2000.

12. Fan, L., Cao, P., Lin, W., and Jacobson, Q. Web Prefetching Between Low-Bandwidth Clients and Proxies: Potential and Performance. SIGMETRICS, 1999.

13. Fabret, F., Jacobsen, H. A., Llirbat, F., Pereira, J., Ross, K. A., and Shasha, D. Filtering Algorithms and Implementation for Very Fast Publish/Subscribe Systems. In proceedings of SIGMOD, 2001.

14. Fitzpatrick, G., Kaplan, S, Mansfield, T., Arnold, D., and Segall, B. Supporting public availability and accessibility with Elvin: Experiences and Reflections. ACM TOC 11(3): 447 – 474, 2002.

15. Gadde, S., Chase, J., and Rabinovich, M. Web Caching and Content Distribution: A View From the Interior. In Proceedings of WCW '00, 2000.

16. Gwertzman, J. and Seltzer, M. An Analysis of Geographical Push-Caching. 1997.

17. Jin, Shudong and Bestavrous, A. GreedyDual* Web Caching Algorithm: Exploiting the Two Sources of Temporal Locality in Web Request Streams. Computer Comm., vol. 24(2), pp. 174-183, Feb. 2001.

18. Kangasharju, J., Roberts, J., and Ross, K. W. Object Replication Strategies in Content Distribution Networks. In Proceedings of WCW'01, 2001.

19. Karger, D., Lehman, E., Leighton, F. T., Levine, M., Lewin, D., and Panigrahy, R. Consistent Hashing and Random Trees: Distributed Caching Protocols for Relieving Hot Spots on the World Wide Web. In Proceedings of the ACM STOC, 1997.

20. Krishnan, P., Raz, D., and Shavitt, Y. The cache location problem. IEEE/ACM Transactions on Networking, 8(5): pages 568-582, October 2000.

21. Huang, Y.-Q. and Garcia-Molina, H. Publish/Subscribe in a Mobile Environment. MobiDE 01.

22. Lieberman, H. Letizia: An Agent That Assists Web Browsing. Proceedings of the 1995 International Joint Conference on Artificial Intelligent, 1995.

23. MSNBC. http://www.msnbc.com/news

24. Padmanabhan, V. N. and Qiu, L.-L. The Content and Access Dynamics of a Busy Web Site: Findings and Implications. In Proceedings of ACM SIGCOMM 2000.

25. Qiu, L., Padmanabham, V. N., and Voelker, G. M. On the placement of web server replicas. In Proceedings of 20th IEEE INFOCOM, 2001.

26. Rabinovich, M. Issues in Web Content Replication.

27. Wang, J. A Survey of Web Caching Schemes for the Internet. ACM Computer Communication Review, 29(5):36-46, October 1999.

28. Wolman, A., Voelker, G., Sharma, N., Cardwell, N., Brown, M., Landray, T., Pinnel, D., Karlin, A., and Levy, H. Organization-Based Analysis of Web-Object Sharing and Caching. In Proceedings of USITS'99, 1999.

29. Wolman, A., Voelker, G., Sharma, N., Cardwell, N., Karlin, A., and Levy, H. On the Scale and Performance of Cooperative Web Proxy Caching. In Proc. of SOSP, 1999.

30. Venkataramani, A., Weidmann, P., and Dahlin, M. Bandwidth Constrained Placement in a WAN. In Proceedings of ACM PODC 2001.

Supporting Mobility in Content-Based Publish/Subscribe Middleware

Ludger Fiege[1], Felix C. Gärtner[2], Oliver Kasten[3], and Andreas Zeidler[1]

[1] Darmstadt University of Technology (TUD), Department of Computer Science
Databases and Distributed System Group, D-64283 Darmstadt, Germany
{fiege,az}@dvs1.informatik.tu-darmstadt.de
[2] Swiss Federal Institute of Technology (EPFL)
School of Computer and Communication Sciences
Distributed Programming Laboratory, CH-1015 Lausanne, Switzerland
fcg@acm.org
[3] Swiss Federal Institute of Technology (ETH Zurich)
Department of Computer Science, Distributed Systems Group
CH-8092 Zurich, Switzerland
oliver.kasten@inf.ethz.ch

Abstract. Publish/subscribe (pub/sub) is considered a valuable middleware architecture that proliferates loose coupling and leverages reconfigurability and evolution. Up to now, existing pub/sub middleware was optimized for static systems where users as well as the underlying system structure were rather fixed. We study the question whether existing pub/sub middleware can be extended to support *mobile* and *location-dependent applications*. We first analyze the requirements of such applications and distinguish two orthogonal forms of mobility: the system-centric physical mobility and an application-centric logical mobility (where users are aware that they are changing location). We introduce *location-dependent subscriptions* as a suitable means to exploit the power of the event-based paradigm in mobile applications. Briefly spoken, location-dependency refines a subscription to accept only events related to a mobile user's current location. Implementations for both forms of mobility are presented within the content-based pub/sub middleware REBECA, drawing from its refined routing capabilities (namely, covering and merging).

1 Introduction

Location-Based Services. The emergence of mobile computing has opened up a whole new field of services provided for the benefit of the mobile user. Many such services can exploit the fact that the mobile device is aware of its current location. For example, car navigation systems use knowledge about current and past locations to aid drivers find their way through unknown cities. Location information can even be combined with other sources of data, e.g., the weather report, information on traffic jams or free parking spaces. In such cases, the system can propose routes that avoid places where traffic is high or weather

M. Endler and D. Schmidt (Eds.): Middleware 2003, LNCS 2672, pp. 103–122, 2003.
© IFIP International Federation for Information Processing 2003

conditions are unpleasant, or can direct the driver to the nearest free parking space. All these are examples for *location-based services*.

Publish/Subscribe Systems. A convenient way to construct location-based services is to build them using event infrastructures, such as those provided by *publish/subscribe systems*. Here, producers and consumers are enabled to exchange information based on message type or content rather than particular destination identifiers or addresses. This *loose coupling* of producers and consumers is the premier advantage of pub/sub systems, which facilitates mobile communication. Producers are relieved from managing interested consumers, and vice versa. In this paper we study how to exploit these advantages and what extensions are eligible in the context of mobile services.

Supporting Mobility in pub/sub Middleware. We argue that support for mobility should be an issue of the pub/sub middleware itself and not be delegated to the application layer. Three kinds of application scenarios have to be supported: i) existing applications in a static environment, ii) existing applications in a mobile environment, iii) mobility-aware applications. Since pub/sub systems and applications have been deployed very successfully, extending existing systems and models is preferred to creating new "mobile" middleware from scratch in order to facilitate the integration of the first two scenarios. As a consequence, the middleware must transparently handle some of the new mobility issues. This allows existing event-based applications to directly interact with and even to be deployed as mobile applications. On the other hand, the third scenario requires the middleware to support a (semi-)automated handling of location changes. If no such support is available, mobility is actually controlled by the application and not by the movement of the client.

We provide support for two different and orthogonal types of mobility. The first type of mobility is called *physical* mobility, where clients may temporarily disconnect from the pub/sub system (due to power-saving requirements or the network characteristics). This means that applications are not necessarily aware of the fact that the client is moving, allowing existing applications to be transferred to mobile environments. The second type of mobility is called *logical mobility*, where clients remains attached to the their broker and have an application-level notion of location, which is described by *location-dependent subscriptions* introduced in this paper. As an example, consider a car looking for a free parking space in the street it is currently driving along. In this situation it may subscribe to "New free parking space on Rebeca Drive". However, if Rebeca Drive is a very long street, the same driver will also receive notifications about free parking spaces very far down the road (or behind him), which are impossible to reach in good time. What the user would like to do is to specify a subscription such that he receives all notifications about "vacancies in the vicinity of his current location". We call these subscriptions *location-dependent*.

Related Work. Work on middleware for mobile computing usually concentrated on classical synchronous middleware like CORBA, see [4] for a survey. Only recently, position papers have stated that pub/sub systems have an enormous potential to better accommodate the needs of large mobile communities [16, 6]. Research in pub/sub systems has mainly focused on *static* systems, where clients do not move and the pub/sub infrastructure remains relatively stable throughout the system's lifetime, e.g., Elvin [23], Gryphon [15], REBECA [12], and Siena [5]. If present at all, mobility support is a concern of the application layer. Applications detect the need to change a subscription and have to react explicitly and manually to this detection.

Huang and Garcia-Molina [13, 14] provide a good overview of possible options for supporting mobility in pub/sub systems. They describe algorithms for a "new" middleware system tailored and optimized to mobile and ad hoc networks, not so much an extension of an existing system. CEA [1] and JEDI [7], too, address problems of mobility. JEDI uses explicit moveIn and moveOut operations to relocate clients. Hence, mobility is controlled by the application, which is not transparent and even unrealistic since clients usually only can react *after* having been moved. The mobility extensions of SIENA [3] are very similar. Explicit sign-offs are required and interim notifications stored during disconnectedness are directly forwarded to a new location upon request. Cugola et al. [6] proposes a leader election and group management protocol for dynamic dispatching trees to dynamically adapt the internals of the JEDI event system, their implementation model is based on multicast and it groups identical subscribers. An extension for Elvin allows for disconnectedness using a central caching proxy [24], which is a potential performance bottleneck. Jacobsen [16] presents some very interesting ideas on location-based services and the possible expressiveness of subscription languages. STEAM [18] is an event service designed for wireless ad hoc networks. Subscribers consume only events produced by geographically close-by publishers. It relies on proximity-based group communication.

Outline. This paper is structured as follows: We provide some basic background and terminology on content-based pub/sub and the REBECA system in Section 2. We then discuss in more detail the issues involved when supporting mobility using existing content-based pub/sub middleware in Section 3. We present a solution for physical mobility in Section 4 and a solution for logical mobility in Section 5. Section 6 concludes the paper.

2   Content-Based Publish/Subscribe

The following gives an introduction to publish/subscribe systems and the system model we used as basis for the proposed mobility support. It is based on the REBECA notification service [11, 20].

2.1   Publish/Subscribe Systems

Processes in pub/sub systems (also known as *event-based systems* [12]) are clients of an underlying notification service and can act both as producers and consumers of messages, called event notifications or notifications for short. The communication interface to the system consists of four primitives only: *pub,*

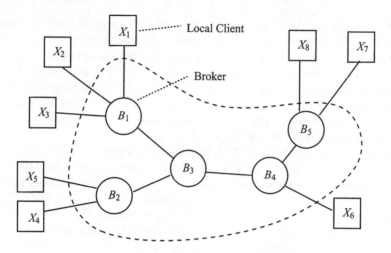

Fig. 1. The router network of REBECA.

sub, *unsub*, and *notify*. The latter is a function provided by consumers that the event system calls to deliver notifications. A *notification* is a message that reifies and describes an occurred event. Notifications are injected into the event system rather than being published towards a specific receiver. They are conveyed by the underlying notification service to those consumers that have registered a matching subscription (*sub*). Subscriptions describe the kind of notifications consumers are interested in. In some systems producers are required to issue advertisements to describe the notifications they are about to publish.

The expressiveness of the notification service is determined by its language used for specifying subscriptions and the data model of the transmitted notifications. Subject- and type-based addressing exists [22, 2, 8], but the most flexible scheme is offered by content-based filtering [19]. Filters are boolean functions on the entire content of a notification and a common way to implement subscriptions. Together with the typically used name/value-pairs data model, subscriptions look like: (*service* = "parking"), (*location* = "100 Rebeca Drive"), (*cost* < "3 EURO"), (*car-type* ≥ "compact"). The Java Message Service (JMS), for example, uses a combination of subjects and content-based addressing.

The notification service for our scenario is distributed, of course, to meet the mobility scenario and scalability considerations. The communication topology of the pub/sub system is given by a graph, which is assumed to be acyclic and connected (Fig. 1). The graph consists of brokers and clients. The edges are point-to-point, FIFO order communication links, e.g., TCP connections, that are error-free, a common assumption that can be relieved later. This model simplifies the presentation and opens up implementation-dependent options, like using Multicast, to improve communication performance. Brokers are processes that route the notifications along multiple hops to the appropriate clients. Three types of brokers are distinguished: *Local brokers* constitute the clients' access point to the middleware and are part of the communication library loaded into the clients; they are not represented in the graph, but only used for implementation issues. A local broker is connected to at most one border broker. *Border brokers* form the boundary of the distributed communication middleware and maintain connections to local brokers, i.e., the clients. *Inner brokers* are connected to other inner or border brokers and do not maintain any connections to clients.

The individual processes are assumed to have local real-time clocks that are synchronized using a standard protocol like NTP. While we postulate that there is no upper bound on the message delivery delay, we assume that the delays satisfy some probability distribution so that an expected delivery time can be computed statistically.

2.2   Content-Based Routing

Each broker maintains a routing table that determines the decision in which directions a notification is forwarded. Each table entry is a pair (F, L) containing a filter and the link from which it was received, denoting that a matching subscription is to be forwarded along L. The routing decision is assumed to be an atomic operation so that the end-to-end sender FIFO characteristic holds. The routing tables are maintained to correspond to the available information about active consumers and their subscriptions. Each broker forwards these information according to the routing algorithm used.

The simplest form of routing is *simple routing*: active filters are simply added to the routing tables with the link they originated from. Obviously, this is not optimal with respect to routing table sizes, which grow with the number of subscriptions. A first improvement is to check and combine filters that are equal. More generally, the *covering* routing strategy [5] tests whether a filter F_1 accepts a superset of notifications of a second filter F_2, and in this case replaces all occurrences of F_2 assigned to the same link in the routing table, significantly decreasing the table size. In a second step, if no cover can be found in a given set of filters, *merging* can be used to create new filters that are covers of existing ones [19]. Only the resulting merged filter is forwarded to neighbor brokers, where it covers and replaces the base filters.

3   Publish/Subscribe Systems and Mobility

In this section we analyze and discuss the basic issues involved when adding mobility support to a pub/sub infrastructure. We identify and define two orthogonal forms of mobility (physical and logical mobility) and discuss the requirements of a system supporting both types of mobility.

3.1   Mobility Issues in Publish/Subscribe Middleware

Mobile clients have many characteristics, among them the need to disconnect from the network for different reasons. Be it for geographical, administrative, or power saving reasons, being connected to the same broker all the time is no longer possible. Hence, we have to take into account that clients will disconnect from their border broker once in a while. The middleware has to deal with moving clients and the possibility that a disconnected client reconnects at the same or a different broker later.

A first step towards mobility is to enhance existing pub/sub middleware to allow for roaming clients so that existing applications can be used in mobile environments. This means that the interfaces for accessing the middleware and the applications on top are not required to change. More importantly, the quality of service offered by the middleware must not degrade substantially. The resulting location transparency is necessary to make existing applications mobile, e.g., stock quote monitoring seamlessly transferred from PCs to PDAs.

On the other hand, future applications do not want complete transparency, but rely on awareness of mobility. More specifically, mobility support should blend out unwanted phenomena, like disconnectedness, and enforce wanted behavior, like the location awareness in location-based services. Consequently, extending the interface of the pub/sub middleware to facilitate location awareness is a promising open issue, since most existing work concentrated on the transparency only.

When roaming, clients change (at least some portion of) the context they are operating in, and they might want to react to these changes, e.g., to adapt their subscriptions. However, an appropriate infrastructure support has to relieve the application from having to react "manually" to all changes. The middleware should rather offer an automated adaptation to context changes, i.e., facilitating location dependency. This leads to a different notion of mobility and we distinguish:

- *Physical mobility*: A client that is physically mobile disconnects for certain periods of time and has different border brokers along its itinerary through the infrastructure. The main concern of physical mobility is *location transparency*.
- *Logical mobility*: A client that is logically mobile is aware of its location changes. In order to relieve the client from adapting *manually* to new locations, the main concern of logical mobility is *automated* location awareness within the pub/sub middleware.

Physical and logical mobility are two orthogonal aspects of mobility. Since the physical layout of a pub/sub system is usually fixed and its layout does usually not correspond to geographical realities, it seems reasonable to separate the two notions of mobility. In this paper, we assume logical mobility to be a refinement of physical mobility in that a client remains connected to the same broker when roaming logically. The two notions have different quality of service requirements and therefore different solutions are developed to match both.

3.2   Physical Mobility

Physical mobility is similar to what in the area of mobile computing is called *terminal mobility* or *roaming*. A client accesses the system through a certain number of *access points* (GSM base stations, WLAN access points, or border brokers). When moving physically, the client may get out of reach of one access point and move into the reach of a second access point which are not necessarily overlapping. In general we cannot expect to have seamless access to the broker network but more a sequence of phases of connectedness, e.g., on the daily route between home and office. In this setting we analyze the quality of service requirements from the viewpoint of roaming clients:

- Interface. Obviously, the interface to the pub/sub system must not change as legacy applications are not aware of mobility.
- Completeness. Despite intermittent disconnects, the pub/sub middleware delivers all notifications for a client eventually. This is the core requirement for transparency.
- Ordering. Sender FIFO ordering was guaranteed in Section 2 and it is an eligible feature in the mobile case, too.
- Responsiveness. The delay of relocating a roaming client should be minimal to maximize the responsiveness of the system. This has to be taken into account when designing a relocation protocol.

Possible Solutions. One solution would be to rely on Mobile IP [17] for connecting clients to border brokers, hiding physically mobility in the network layer. The drawback, however, is that the communication is also hidden from the pub/sub middleware, which is then not able to draw from any notification delivery localities or routing optimizations, thereby possibly violating the requirement of responsiveness. Such an approach might only be feasible if the physical and logical layout of a given system is completely orthogonal.

A different, naïve solution to implement physical mobility would be to use sequences of *sub-unsub-sub* calls to register a client at a new broker. When a client moves from border broker B_1 to B_2, it simply unsubscribes at B_1 and (re-) subscribes at B_2, without any support in the middleware. But a client may not detect leaving the range of a broker and is in this case not able to unsubscribe at its old location. Even more severely, during its time of disconnectedness, the client might miss several notifications or get duplicates, even if notifications are flooded in the network and the location change is instantaneous. This problem is depicted in Figure 2. Hence, this solution is not complete and we outline an algorithm in Section 4 that takes into account all requirements stated above. The complete algorithm is detailed in [25].

3.3   Logical Mobility

While physical mobility is a rather technical issue invisible to the application, logical mobility involves location awareness. An example for logical mobility is when clients move around a house or building that is served by only one border broker. In this case, the user might be interested to receive just those notifications that refer to the room he is currently located in. Note that a client can be both logically and physically mobile at the same time.

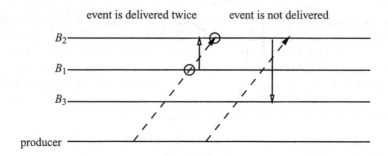

Fig. 2. Missing notifications in a flooding scenario.

A logically mobile client moving from one location to another, e.g., from one room to the other in a company building, will expect a frictionless change of location explicitly without a notable setup time after having changed from its own office to the conference room next door. The adaptation of some location-dependent subscription should take place "instantaneously". Intuitively, we would like to experience the notion of being subscribed to "everything, every-where, all the time" and increase the reactivity of the system to moving clients.

Location-Dependent Filters. A pub/sub system that offers location-dependent filters has the same interface as a regular pub/sub system (i.e., it offers the *pub*, *sub*, *unsub*, *notify* primitives). However, in specifying subscription filters for name/value pairs referring to *"location"* it supports a new primitive to spec-ify things like "all notifications where the attribute *location* equals my current location". More precisely, we postulate a specific marker *myloc* that can be used in a subscription. The marker stands for a specific set of locations that depend on the current location of the client. For example, a client could issue a subscrip-tion for all free parking spaces in the vicinity of his current location as follows: (*service* = "parking"), (*location* ∈ *myloc*), (*car-type* ≥ "compact").

The set of locations associated with the marker is taken from a particular range L of locations. This set is application dependent and can, for instance, contain all the different rooms of a building, all the streets of a town, or all the geographical coordinates given by a GPS system up to a certain granularity. Given a notification with the attribute *location*, the subscription (*location* ∈ *myloc*) will evaluate to true for a particular client at location y if and only if $x \in myloc(y)$ where $myloc(y)$ is the specific set of locations associated with y. In this case we say that the notification matches the location-dependent filter.

The simplest form of $myloc(y)$ is simply the set $\{y\}$. In this case a notification matches the subscription if $x = y$. But in the car example, the car driver looking for a parking space might want to specify:

(*location* = "at most two blocks away from *myloc*")

In this case, *myloc* corresponds to all elements of L that satisfy this requirement.

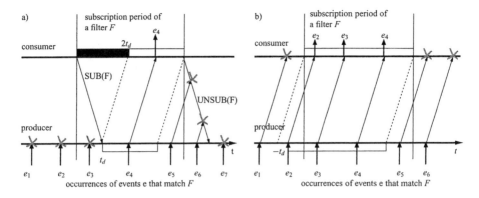

Fig. 3. Blackout period after subscribing with simple routing a) and flooding with client-side filtering b).

A Tentative but Incomplete Solution for Logical Mobility. While location-dependent filters are not directly supported by current pub/sub middleware, one might argue that it is not very difficult to emulate them on top of currently available systems in this case. The idea would be to build a wrapper around an existing system that follows the location changes of the users and transparently unsubscribes to the old location and subscribes to the new one when the user moves. However, depending on the internal routing strategy of the event system, it may lead to unexpected results. The routing strategies deployed in many existing content-based event systems such as Siena [5], Elvin [23], and REBECA [10] lead to blackout periods where no notifications are delivered. The problem is that it usually takes an unnegligible time delay to process a new subscription. After subscribing to a filter, it takes some time t_d until the subscription is propagated to a potential source. Then it takes at least another t_d time until a notification reaches the subscriber. This phenomenon is depicted in Figure 3a. (Note that the delay t_d may be different for different notification sources and may change over time.) If the client remains at any new location less than $2t_d$ time, then the subscriber will "starve", i.e., it will receive little or no notifications.

An Intuitive but Inefficient Solution. Another basic solution that can be immediately built using existing technology is again based on flooding. The local broker can then decide to deliver a notification to a client depending on the client's current location (see Figure 3b). Obviously, flooding prevents the blackout periods, which were present in the previous solution, but it should be equally clear that flooding is a very expensive routing strategy especially for large pub/sub systems [21].

Quality of Service of Logical Mobility. Interestingly, while flooding is very expensive and therefore not desirable, it comes very close to the quality of service that we would like to achieve for logical mobility, namely to the notion of being subscribed to "everything, everywhere, all the time". The problem is that

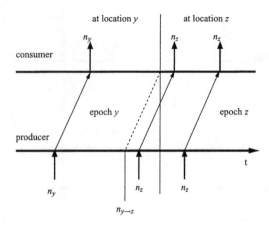

Fig. 4. Defining the quality of service for logical mobility using virtual notifications $n_{y \to z}$ that arrives at the consumer just at the time of the location change from y to z.

it is hard to precisely define the behavior of flooding without reverting to some unpleasantly theoretical constructions of operational semantics.

With logical mobility there is, however, no danger of receiving a notification twice because the consumer remains attached to the same "delivery path". The quality of service we require for logical mobility therefore is simply stated as follows: On change of location from x to y, all notifications should be delivered to the consumer "as if" flooding were used as underlying routing strategy. This statement is made a little more concrete in Figure 4 where the sequence of notifications generated by any consumer is divided into epochs that correspond to when the notification actually arrives at the consumer (the epoch borders between location y and z are drawn as a virtual notification $n_{y \to z}$). We require that all notifications matching the current location-dependent subscription from every such epoch must be delivered. Intuitively, the epochs define the semantics of flooding.

4   Notification Delivery with Roaming Clients

In this section we sketch an algorithm for extending standard REBECA brokers to cope with roaming mobile clients, maintaining their subscriptions as well as guaranteeing the required quality of service described in the previous section.

Apart from guaranteeing uninterrupted notification delivery together with transparency of mobility, our algorithm also guarantees that the "old" border broker (i.e., the broker to which the roaming client was formaly attached) will eventually receive an equivalent to an explicit *sign-off* from the client, so that it can garbage collect all resources allocated to this specific client. In this process the algorithm also guarantees that any routing path to the old location related to the client will be deleted.

4.1   Main Idea

The basic idea is to maintain a "virtual counterpart" of a roaming client at the last known location until some broker at a new location is claiming responsibility and then merge "actual" and "virtual" client in such a way that no notification is lost or delivered twice.

In the light of the quality of service requirements from the previous section, a realistic choice to devise such an algorithm has to employ the following features:

- Reactive model. The relocation algorithm has to be *reactive*, i.e., no explicit MoveOut or un-subscribe at the old location should be needed.
- Distribution. To enhance responsiveness, the algorithm adheres to strict locality; the approach is completely distributed, buffers notifications wherever necessary, and restricts reconfiguration of the broker network to the smallest possible subgraph.
- Completeness. By introducing distributed buffers within the border brokers the algorithm guarantees completeness within the boundaries of time and/or space limitations of buffering approaches.
- Pub/sub adherence. All communication related to the relocation protocol is done within and based on the broker network. Other approaches using some sort of direct, out-of-band communication between old and new broker might introduce problems of ordering, duplicate detection, or even message loss. This can be avoided by only using communication mechanisms offered by the pub/sub middleware.

Example. We illustrate the relocation process using the simple example scenario on the left of Fig. 5 for a single producer and consumer; the generalization for multiple producers is indicated on the right of Fig. 5 and a more detailed description can be found in [25].

Assume client C is moving from the location at broker B_6 to another location at broker B_1. This refers to step 1 in the figure. After the client has detected the change of location and broker it automatically re-issues a subscription together with the last received sequence number for this subscription (e.g., $(C, F, 123)$, with 123 being the last known sequence number annotated by the former border broker; step 3). Broker B_1 will detect that this client has moved and must be relocated. Note that neither client nor broker need to have any knowledge about the old location B_6. Broker B_1 then starts the relocation process by sending a special message to its neigboring brokers.

The goal of the relocation process is to divert the delivery paths from producer P to C to the new location. During this process, the brokers propagate the subscription through B_2 and B_3 to broker B_4. Here the old and new path from producer P to client C meet (dotted and dashed line, respectively). Broker B_4 is aware of this by inspecting its routing table and its list of received advertisements, and comparing it to the subscription received. As B_4 has an old entry for this subscription, B_4 sends a fetch request $(C, F, 123, B_4)$ along the old path to B_6 and already starts routing all newly received notifications from P along the *new* path.

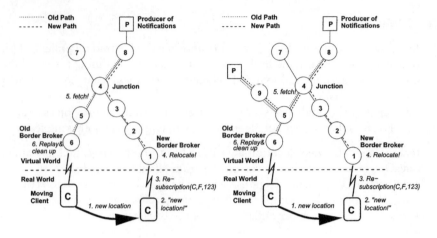

Fig. 5. A moving client scenario with one producer (left) and more than one producer (right).

When receiving the fetch request along the path to the old broker B_6, all brokers along this path update their routing tables such that they are pointing into the direction of B_4. B_6 as last recipient replays all events buffered in the virtual counterpart of (C, F) beginning with the sequence number initially given by C to B_1 (here 124). The counterpart sends a message with a replay of all notifications received in the meantime along the path into the direction of B_4. As all intermediate brokers have already updated their routing tables, the replay eventually reaches B_1 via B_4 and is delivered to C. In the meantime, B_1 has buffered all notifications that have arrived for C and delivers the old messages from B_6 first before delivering the "new" messages from its own buffer to guarantee the correct delivery order.

Broker B_6 at the old location can garbage collect all resources formerly associated with C, and so can B_5, resulting in the new routing path between P and C as shown in Fig. 5.

4.2 Discussion

This example should give a feeling of how relocation and adaptation of the delivery paths is performed in a fully distributed fashion. Through the use of administrative control messages, and buffering and replay mechanisms the algoritm makes good use of the already builtin features of REBECA. Covering and merging can be exploited, too, if the fetch request sent by B_4 is directed towards both matching advertisments and covering filters.

5   Location-Dependent Filters for Logical Mobility

We now describe the algorithmic solution to the scenario where clients are only logically mobile, i.e., they remain attached to a single border broker.

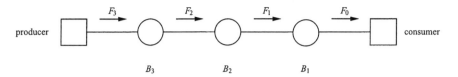

Fig. 6. Network setting for the example.

5.1 Main Idea

Consider an arbitrary routing path between a producer (publisher) and a consumer (subscriber). This path consists of a sequence of brokers $B_1, B_2, \ldots, B_{k-1}$, B_k where B_1 is the local broker of the consumer and B_k is the local broker of the producer (Figure 6 shows the setup for $k = 3$). Assume the consumer has issued a location-dependent subscription F. Using the "usual" content-based routing algorithms, the current value $\tilde{F}$ of F, which instantiates the marker variable with the current location, would permeate the network in such a way that the filters along the routing path allow a matching subscription published by the producer to reach the consumer. Formally, the filters $F_1, F_2, \ldots, F_k$ along the links between the brokers should maintain a set-inclusion property

$$F_k \supseteq F_{k-1} \supseteq \ldots \supseteq F_2 \supseteq F_1 \supseteq F_0 = \tilde{F}.$$

If F is the only active subscription in the network and if the subscription has permeated the network, the above formula can be simplified to

$$F_k = F_{k-1} = \ldots = F_2 = F_1 = F_0 = \tilde{F}.$$

Obviously, if for any new value $\tilde{F}$ of F a new subscription must flow through the network towards the producers, notifications published in the meantime might go unnoticed. The idea of the proposed scheme is to always have the local broker of the consumer do perfect client-side filtering (i.e., set $F_0 = \tilde{F}$), but to let possible future notifications reach brokers that are nearer to the consumer so that their delay to reach the consumer is lower once the consumer switches to a new location.

Let T denote the set of time values, which for simplicity we will assume to be the set of natural numbers $\mathbb{N}$. Let L denote the set of all consumer locations. Then we define a function $loc : T \rightarrow L$ that describes the movement of the consumer over time. For example, for a location set $L = \{a, b, c, d\}$ a possible value of loc is $\{(1, a), (2, b), (3, d), \ldots\}$ meaning that at time 1, the consumer's location is a, at time 2 it is b and so on.

We assume that loc is subject to some movement restrictions, which in effect define a maximum speed of movement for the consumer. We assume that such a restriction is given by a *movement graph* such as the one depicted in Figure 7. The graph formalizes which locations can be reached from which locations in one movement step of the consumer. One movement step has some application-defined correspondence to one time step.

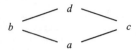

Fig. 7. Movement graph defining movement restrictions of a consumer.

Given the function *loc* and a movement graph, it is possible to define a function $ploc : L \times \mathbb{N} \rightarrow 2^L$ of possible (future) locations (the notation 2^L denotes the powerset of L, i.e., the set of all subsets of L). The function takes a current location x and a number of consumer steps $q \geq 0$ and returns the set of possible locations, which the consumer could be in starting from x after q steps in the movement graph.

Since a possible move of the consumer always is to remain at the same location, for all locations $x \in L$ and all $q \in \mathbb{N}$ we should require that

$$ploc(x, q) \subseteq ploc(x, q + 1). \tag{1}$$

Taking the example values from above, possible values for *ploc* are as follows:

$$ploc(a, 0) = \{a\} \qquad ploc(a, 1) = \{a, b, c\} \qquad ploc(a, 2) = \{a, b, c, d\}$$

Now, if the consumer is at location a, for example, every broker B_i along the path towards a producer should subscribe for $ploc(a, q)$ for some q, which is an increasing sequence of natural numbers depending on i and the network characteristics. If the time it takes for a broker to process a new subscription is in the order of the time a client remains at one particular location, then the individual filters F_i along the sample network setting in Figure 6 should be set as $F_i = ploc(a, i)$, e.g., $F_0 = ploc(a, 0) = \{a\}$, $F_1 = ploc(a, 1) = \{a, b, c\}$ and so on. This requirement should be maintained throughout location changes by the consumer. For example, whenever a consumer moves from an old location x to a new location y, the corresponding client node must declare the new location by sending a message to its broker B_1. This will cause B_1 to change the location-dependent part of filter F_0 for client-side filtering from the old to the new location. Broker B_1 updates its routing table appropriately.

In general, broker B_i sends a message with the new location to B_{i+1} instructing it to change F_i from $ploc(x, i)$ to $ploc(y, i)$ and consequently to update the routing table by removing certain locations and adding new locations. Removing and adding new locations corresponds to unsubscribing and subscribing to the corresponding filters. The normal REBECA administration messages can be used to do this. Note that Equation 1 guarantees the subset relationship, which should always hold on every path between producer and consumer.

5.2 Example

As an example, consider the value of *loc* where at time 1 the client is in location a, at time 2 at b and at time 3 at d in the movement graph depicted in Figure 7.

Table 1. Values of $ploc(x, t)$ for the example setting.

t	$x = a$	$x = b$	$x = c$	$x = d$
0	$\{a\}$	$\{b\}$	$\{c\}$	$\{d\}$
1	$\{a, b, c\}$	$\{a, b, d\}$	$\{a, c, d\}$	$\{b, c, d\}$
2	$\{a, b, c, d\}$	$\{a, b, c, d\}$	$\{a, b, c, d\}$	$\{a, b, c, d\}$
3	$\{a, b, c, d\}$	$\{a, b, c, d\}$	$\{a, b, c, d\}$	$\{a, b, c, d\}$

Table 2. Values of filters in example setting.

time t	F_3	F_2	F_1	F_0
0	$\{a, b, c, d\}$	$\{a, b, c, d\}$	$\{a, b, c\}$	$\{a\}$
1	$\{a, b, c, d\}$	$\{a, b, c, d\}$	$\{a, b, d\}$	$\{b\}$
2	$\{a, b, c, d\}$	$\{a, b, c, d\}$	$\{b, c, d\}$	$\{d\}$

Table 1 gives the values of *ploc* for all locations and the first four time instances. For $t = 0$ the value of *ploc* is equal to the current location. For $t = 1$ it returns all locations reachable in one time step in the movement graph, etc.

Now assume again the setting depicted in Figure 6. The values of Table 1 directly determine the filter settings for $F_0, \ldots, F_3$ as shown in Table 2. At time $t = 1$ the client moves to location b. This means that F_0 changes from $\{a\}$ to $\{b\}$ and that F_1 must unsubscribe to c and subscribe to d, yielding $F_1 = \{a, b, d\}$. At time $t = 2$ the client moves to d, causing F_0 to change to $\{d\}$ and F_1 to unsubscribe to a and subscribe to c. All other filters remain unchanged.

The example nicely shows that the method does some sort of "restricted flooding", i.e, all notifications reach broker B_2 but from there the uncertainty is restricted and so is the flow of notifications forwarded by B_2. In fact, the method described above using the *ploc* function can be regarded as an abstraction of both "trivial" implementations discussed in Section 3 (i.e., both implementations are instantiations of our scheme), as we explain in the following section.

5.3   Adaptivity

The example setting above assumes that processing a new subscription by a broker takes about as long as a consumer stays at one particular location. Obviously, it will usually take much less time to process a subscription even if slow or wireless network connections are used (user movement will be in the order of seconds while network delay will be in the order of milliseconds). We now present a scheme that adapts the level of "buffering" in the network to the average movement time of the client. Our algorithm, which for lack of space is detailed in [9], satisfies this form of adaptivity.

In the following, we denote the average time a client remains at one location by Δ and the time it takes to process a sufficiently large batch of *sub/unsub* messages between brokers B_i and B_{i+1} by δ_i. If the client moves very slowly, meaning that the sum of all δ_i is still less than Δ, we would like the scheme to behave like the trivial *sub/unsub* solution. For the example setting from the

Table 3. Values of $ploc(x, t)$ for trivial *sub/unsub* implementation (top) and flooding with client-side filtering (bottom).

$ploc(x, t)$ for global *sub/unsub*			
t \ $x = a$	$x = b$	$x = c$	$x = d$
0 \ $\{a\}$	$\{b\}$	$\{c\}$	$\{d\}$
1 \ $\{a, b, c\}$	$\{a, b, d\}$	$\{a, c, d\}$	$\{b, c, d\}$
2 \ $\{a, b, c\}$	$\{a, b, d\}$	$\{a, c, d\}$	$\{b, c, d\}$
3 \ $\{a, b, c\}$	$\{a, b, d\}$	$\{a, c, d\}$	$\{b, c, d\}$

$ploc(x, t)$ for flooding			
t \ $x = a$	$x = b$	$x = c$	$x = d$
0 \ $\{a\}$	$\{b\}$	$\{c\}$	$\{d\}$
1 \ $\{a, b, c, d\}$	$\{a, b, c, d\}$	$\{a, b, c, d\}$	$\{a, b, c, d\}$
2 \ $\{a, b, c, d\}$	$\{a, b, c, d\}$	$\{a, b, c, d\}$	$\{a, b, c, d\}$
3 \ $\{a, b, c, d\}$	$\{a, b, c, d\}$	$\{a, b, c, d\}$	$\{a, b, c, d\}$

Table 4. Values of $ploc(x, t)$ for the example setting with concrete timing values.

t \ $x = a$	$x = b$	$x = c$	$x = d$
0 \ $\{a\}$	$\{b\}$	$\{c\}$	$\{d\}$
1 \ $\{a, b, c\}$	$\{a, b, d\}$	$\{a, c, d\}$	$\{b, c, d\}$
2 \ $\{a, b, c\}$	$\{a, b, d\}$	$\{a, c, d\}$	$\{b, c, d\}$
3 \ $\{a, b, c, d\}$	$\{a, b, c, d\}$	$\{a, b, c, d\}$	$\{a, b, c, d\}$

previous section this would mean that *ploc* has values like in the top part of Table 3 (note that the algorithm always has to provide information for "the next" user location to maintain the semantics of flooding). On the other hand, if the client moves very fast and Δ is much smaller than δ_1, the method should revert to flooding (i.e., *ploc* values like in the bottom part of Table 3).

If Δ is neither very large nor very small, what values should *ploc* acquire? The idea is to relate multiples of Δ to the increasing sum of the δ_i as follows: Whenever the sum of δ_i results in a value larger than the next multiple of Δ then the value of *ploc* must "take a step". As an example, assume the following values (all in milliseconds): $\Delta = 100$, $\delta_1 = 120$, $\delta_2 = 50$, $\delta_3 = 50$, $\delta_4 = 20$. Now consider Figure 8 where the sums of these values have been put on a single scale. The *ploc* value for client-side filtering (F_0) is fixed to the current location of the client. Since it takes longer for the brokers B_1 and B_2 to process a location change than the client moves, the system must insert a level of buffering at this point, i.e., *ploc* must cater for one additional step of uncertainty at this stage.

Considering that $\delta_1 + \delta_2 < 2 \cdot \Delta$, a location change can be processed fast enough between B_2 and B_3 so that no additional buffering is necessary at this point. However, the sum $\delta_1 + \delta_2 + \delta_3 > 2 \cdot \Delta$, and so *ploc* must have one additional step between B_3 and B_4. The resulting values in the example setting for *ploc* are shown in Table 4.

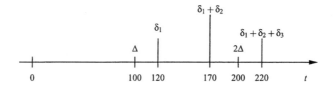

Fig. 8. Estimating *ploc* steps with respect to concrete timing bounds.

5.4 Discussion

The operations "subscribe" and "unsubscribe" in the algorithm refer to operations performed on the original routing table of the corresponding broker. In REBECA, these operations exploit the optimizations of the underlying routing strategy. For example, in covering-based routing, subscribing to a filter $\tilde{F}$ may have no effect on the routing table if there already exists a filter F' that covers $\tilde{F}$. The messages about location changes replace the administrative messages that are sent to spread the information about new subscriptions.

We have informally analyzed the total number of messages (notifications and administrative messages) generated by our new algorithm for an arguably realistic network setting, exactly one consumer and two different speeds of consumer movement: fast movement ($\Delta = 1s$) and slow ($\Delta = 10s$). We compare the results of these calculations with the total number of messages generated by flooding in Figure 9 (see [9] for a detailed description of the system assumptions and the derivation of these numbers). It is interesting to see that although our algorithm generates administrative messages on all network links for every location change of the consumer, the fraction of messages saved is still considerable. We also note that many of the assumptions made in calculating these figures have been very conservative. For example, we assume that there is only one consumer in the network and that notifications are generated by the producers according to a uniform distribution over set of locations. Both assumptions prevent the routing strategy optimizations of REBECA to play to their strengths.

6 Conclusions

This paper has presented an approach to support mobility in existing publish/subscribe middleware. We have analyzed the problem of mobility from the viewpoint of the event-based paradigm and have identified two separate flavors of mobility. While physical mobility is tied to the notion of rebinding a client to different brokers and can be implemented transparently, logical mobility refers to a certain form of location awareness offering a client a fine-grained control over notification delivery in the form of location-dependent filters. We have sketched how both notions can be implemented within the existing REBECA event system to exploit its refined routing strategies.

It is quite obvious that even both of our solutions together cannot claim to solve *all* problems related to mobility or together with REBECA constitute

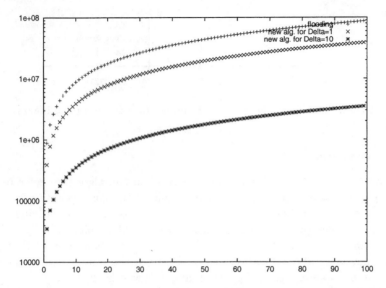

Fig. 9. Total number of messages generated for flooding and two scenarios of the new algorithm ($\Delta = 1s$ and $\Delta = 10s$). Note that the y axis has a logarithmic scale. The x axis denotes time in seconds.

a *complete* mobile computing middleware. In some worst case scenarios both algorithms may lead to undesirable behavior like missing notifications or even starvation of a client, i.e., where a client does not receive notifications due to the latency of the event middleware. For example, this is the case if a client is just too fast for the infrastructure to adapt or if some network links within the broker network are too slow. We have attempted to alleviate these problems by designing adaptive solutions that should work in and can be tuned to most real world scenarios. A detailed analysis of the behavior of the solutions in more extreme and dynamic network settings is a point for future research.

Many other interesting problems concerning the combination of mobility and pub/sub infrastructures remain. For example, location-dependent filters may be generalized to "dynamic filters" that depend on a function of the local state of the client (not only its current location), like a client interested in receiving notifications for sales that he still can afford. Currently, we are investigating how logical and physical mobility can be integrated to allow for logically mobile clients roaming beyond the boundaries of a single broker. First results using the *idea* of logical mobility to deal with the uncertainty of roaming with mobile clients and "pre-subscribe" to information at brokers at *possible* next locations seem promising but need further investigation.

Acknowledgments

We thank Gero Mühl for his cooperation in the REBECA project, and Alejandro Buchmann and Sidath Bandara Handurukande for helpful comments on an earlier version of this paper. Also we would like to thank the anonymous referees for their suggestions.

References

1. J. Bacon, K. Moody, J. Bates, R. Hayton, C. Ma, A. McNeil, O. Seidel, and M. Spiteri. Generic support for distributed applications. *Computer*, 33(3):68–76, 2000.
2. J. Bates, J. Bacon, K. Moody, and M. Spiteri. Using events for the scalable federation of heterogeneous components. In P. Guedes and J. Bacon, editors, *Proceedings of the 8th ACM SIGOPS European Workshop: Support for Composing Distributed Applications*, Sintra, Portugal, Sept. 1998.
3. M. Caporuscio, P. Inverardi, and P. Pelliccione. Formal analysis of clients mobility in the Siena publish/subscribe middleware. Technical report, Department of Computer Science, University of L'Aquila, Oct. 2002.
4. L. Capra, W. Emmerich, and C. Mascolo. Middleware for mobile computing (a survey). Research Note RN/30/01, University College London, July 2001.
5. A. Carzaniga, D. S. Rosenblum, and A. L. Wolf. Design and evaluation of a wide-area event notification service. *ACM Transactions on Computer Systems*, 19(3):332–383, 2001.
6. G. Cugola and E. Di Nitto. Using a publish/subscribe middleware to support mobile computing. In *Proceedings of the Workshop on Middleware for Mobile Computing*, Heidelberg, Germany, Nov. 2001.
7. G. Cugola, E. Di Nitto, and A. Fuggetta. The JEDI event-based infrastructure and its application to the development of the OPSS WFMS. *IEEE Transactions on Software Engineering*, 27(9), 2001.
8. P. T. Eugster, R. Guerraoui, and C. H. Damm. On objects and events. In L. Northrop and J. Vlissides, editors, *Proceedings of the OOPSLA '01 Conference on Object Oriented Programming Systems Languages and Applications*, pages 254–269, Tampa Bay, FL, USA, 2001. ACM Press.
9. L. Fiege, F. C. Gärtner, O. Kasten, and A. Zeidler. Supporting mobility in content-based publish/subscribe middleware. Technical Report IC/2003/11, Swiss Federal Institute of Technology (EPFL), School of Computer and Communication Sciences, Lausanne, Switzerland, Mar. 2002.
10. L. Fiege and G. Mühl. Rebeca Event-Based Electronic Commerce Architecture, 2000. http://www.gkec.informatik.tu-darmstadt.de/rebeca.
11. L. Fiege, G. Mühl, and F. C. Gärtner. A modular approach to build structured event-based systems. In *Proceedings of the 2002 ACM Symposium on Applied Computing (SAC'02)*, pages 385–392, Madrid, Spain, 2002. ACM Press.
12. L. Fiege, G. Mühl, and F. C. Gärtner. Modular event-based systems. *The Knowledge Engineering Review*, 17(4), 2003. to appear.
13. Y. Huang and H. Garcia-Molina. Publish/subscribe in a mobile environment. In *Proceedings of the 2nd ACM International Workshop on Data Engineering for Wireless and Mobile Access (MobiDE01)*, Santa Barbara, CA, May 2001.
14. Y. Huang and H. Garcia-Molina. Publish/subscribe tree construction in wireless ad-hoc networks. In M.-S. Chen, P. Chrysanthis, M. Sloman, and A. Zaslavsky, editors, *4th International Conference on Mobile Data Management (MDM 2003)*, volume 2574 of *LNCS*, pages 122–140, Melbourne, Australia, 2003. Springer-Verlag.
15. IBM. Gryphon: Publish/subscribe over public networks. Technical report, IBM T. J. Watson Research Center, 2001.

16. H.-A. Jacobsen. Middleware services for selective and location-based information dissemination in mobile wireless networks. In *Proceedings of the Workshop on Middleware for Mobile Computing*, Heidelberg, Germany, Nov. 2001.
17. D. Johnson. Scalable support for transparent mobile host internetworking. *Wireless Networks*, 1:311–321, Oct. 1995.
18. R. Meier and V. Cahill. STEAM: Event-based middleware for wireless ad hoc networks. In *Proceedings of the International Workshop on Distributed Event-Based Systems (ICDCS/DEBS'02)*, pages 639–644, 2002.
19. G. Mühl. Generic constraints for content-based publish/subscribe systems. In C. Batini, F. Giunchiglia, P. Giorgini, and M. Mecella, editors, *Proceedings of the 6th International Conference on Cooperative Information Systems (CoopIS '01)*, volume 2172 of *LNCS*, pages 211–225, Trento, Italy, 2001. Springer-Verlag.
20. G. Mühl. *Large-Scale Content-Based Publish/Subscribe Systems*. PhD thesis, Darmstadt University of Technology, 2002.
21. G. Mühl, L. Fiege, F. C. Gärtner, and A. P. Buchmann. Evaluating advanced routing algorithms for content-based publish/subscribe systems. In A. Boukerche and S. Majumdar, editors, *The Tenth IEEE/ACM International Symposium on Modeling, Analysis and Simulation of Computer and Telecommunication Systems (MASCOTS 2002)*, Fort Worth, TX, USA, October 2002. IEEE Press.
22. B. Oki, M. Pfluegl, A. Siegel, and D. Skeen. The information bus—an architecture for extensible distributed systems. In B. Liskov, editor, *Proceedings of the 14th Symposium on Operating Systems Principles*, pages 58–68, Asheville, NC, USA, Dec. 1993. ACM Press.
23. W. Segall and D. Arnold. Elvin has left the building: A publish/subscribe notification service with quenching. In *Proceedings of the 1997 Australian UNIX Users Group*, Brisbane, Australia, Sept. 1997.
24. P. Sutton, R. Arkins, and B. Segall. Supporting disconnectedness – transparent information delivery for mobile and invisible computing. In *First International Symposium on Cluster Computing and the Grid*, pages 277–287, Brisbane, Australia, May 2001. IEEE/ACM.
25. A. Zeidler and L. Fiege. Mobility support with REBECA. In *Proceedings of the 23rd International Conference on Distributed Computing Systems Workshop on Mobile Computing Middleware*, 2003.

Fine-Grained Dynamic Adaptation
of Distributed Components*

Frédéric Peschanski[1], Jean-Pierre Briot[2], and Akinori Yonezawa[1]

[1] University of Tokyo
{pesch,yonezawa}@yl.is.s.u-tokyo.ac.jp
[2] Laboratoire d'Informatique de Paris 6
Jean-Pierre.Briot@lip6.fr

Abstract. Dynamic adaptability of distributed components, nowadays scarcely supported, should become a basic principle of future middleware platforms. While most related work envisage somewhat large software reconfigurations, we explore in this paper fine-grained adaptations which intervene within component boundaries. Our experiments are conducted in the framework of the Comet middleware. Dynamic adaptability is supported in Comet through distributed protocols that can be applied at runtime. These protocols may locally denote intrusive modifications which are abstracted through the notion of role. Functional roles are used to describe all-purpose adaptations. We use hook roles as wrappers around existing functionalities. Finally, filter roles interfere with the communication layer. The expressiveness of these complementary abstractions are illustrated in various examples involving non-trivial system adaptations for distributed debugging and communication flow synchronization. A preliminary but promising quantitative evaluation of our adaptation engine under real-world conditions is proposed. We also discuss the difficult but crucial issue of verifying such dynamic adaptations in terms of type, access and security contracts.

Keywords: Dynamic Adaptability, Component-based Middleware, Fine-grain adaptations, Event-based Asynchronous Communications, Strong typing

1 Introduction

The *dynamic adaptability* of computer systems – their ability to be modified at runtime – represents nowadays a prominent research topic [5].

In mainstream middleware platforms such as CORBA or RMI, introducing a new distributed service (i.e. *common service*) in a running application represents a fairly complex process. Some components of the system must be updated so that they can participate to the new envisaged interactions. To do so, these components must be stopped as well as all their interacting counterparts. Then,

---

* This work is supported by the Japan Society for the Promotion of Science (JSPS) under Research Grant #14-02748.

M. Endler and D. Schmidt (Eds.): Middleware 2003, LNCS 2672, pp. 123–142, 2003.

developers may add the code needed to support the new service. Finally, the application must be deployed again. But in many recent systems and most especially Internet-based applications, a *continuous* mode of service delivery is expected from both providers and clients. Put in other words, the components of such systems cannot be stopped so easily. There are also cases where components may not be stopped for safety reasons.

In order to adress these issues, it is our belief that next-generation middleware environments should provide extensive support for dynamic adaptatability. However, the participation for already deployed components to new distributed services in a dynamic manner may involve intrusive functional and control-level changes. This challenges in a fundamental way the well-established middleware environments. Obviously, these mainstream infrastructures lack abstractions and mechanisms to support dynamic changes [4].

Researchers mostly investigated dynamic adaptability by means of software reconfigurations such as component replacements. We adopt in this paper a complementary point of view by focusing on finer-grained dynamic adaptations. To explore this direction, we conceived an experimental middleware platform called Comet [11]. Adaptation requirements are abstracted in Comet through the notion of *protocol*. At the operational level, such protocols can be dynamically applied on already-deployed and running components. The problem in this setting is that the components possess no knowledge about the protocols they are supposed to participate in. In consequence, we have to (1) allow the simple and *independent* description of the implied local adaptations as well as (2) ensure their consistent and efficient operationalization. We address these requirements by abstractions called *roles* which fall in three complementary categories. *Functional roles* support general-purpose adaptations. *Hook roles* are wrappers around existing functionalities that can be plugged-in dynamically. Finally, *filter role* interfere with the communication layer and support behavioral changes. Fine-grain dynamic adaptation is obtained through the runtime assignment of such roles within component boundaries. Kernel-level mechanisms must be proposed in order to verify this profound impact on the system. It is also decisive to evaluate this impact in terms of performance.

The organization of this paper is as follows. Sect. 2 presents an overview of the Comet middleware using a distributed multimedia system as an example. Through this case study, we introduce the important concepts of *component* and *event*, which are ubiquitous in our approach. The fundamental abstractions for dynamic adaptation, namely the *protocols* and *roles*, are then presented in Sect. 3. The foundations of an adaptive service for distributed debugging is presented as an illustration. We propose in Sect. 4 to evaluate our adaptation engine using a somewhat more sophisticated protocol for adaptive event flow synchronization. We then address the difficult but crucial issue of verifying these fine-grained adaptations in Sect. 5. Finally, we present an overview of related work and then conclude the discussion.

2   The Comet Middleware

2.1   Principles

As for other distributed event-based systems [8], the Comet middleware is based
on the *component/event* dichotomy. While components perform local computations, the data they exchange with each other are described by *typed events*.
The main originality of the approach is to enforce the extraction of the coupling
relation among components using two fundamental principles : structural and
control-level decoupling. By *structural decoupling*, we mean that components are
transparently localized and may not reference directly other components. The
coupling relation is expressed using typed connections that are established at
runtime. The type information attached to connections completely capture the
routing semantics. While we do not discuss this feature in the present paper, we
show in [12] that this added to the introduction of a proper subtyping relation
results in a powerful *type-based multicast* communication model. *Control-level
decoupling* between components relies on *asynchronous* communications. When
a component emits an event, there is no impact on its local control-flow. As a
consequence of fulfilling these two decoupling principles, it is possible to dynamically change the structure of the applications by adding/removing components
and connections. This represents the proper definition of dynamic adaptability
in Comet.

The original semantics of the Comet middleware are captured by constructs
of the language substrate of the platform, namely Scope. The Scope language
is to Comet what is, for example, Java to RMI : the language layer of the
middleware environment. Scope programs are compiled to standard java source
code[1]. The basic Scope features are discussed more thoroughly in [12].

2.2   Example: Distributed Multimedia

The example described in this section is a simple distributed multimedia application. It consists in client components requesting multimedia streams to dedicated servers. Despite its simplicity, this example captures interestingly the
client/server semantics expressed in Comet terms.

Components. The following definition shows the structure of the multimedia
clients we will deploy:

```
component MMClient {
receive MMEvent; send MMRequest;
when(MMEvent event) {
 // show the multimedia contents
 show(event); }
void askServer(MMRequest request) {
 // send a server request
 send(request); } }
```

---

[1] Source-to-source Scope compilers are also available for Scheme and Common Lisp.

The `receive` declaration and the corresponding `when` construct together define a *reactive block* for type `MMEvent`[2]. Clients *react* by showing the contents of received multimedia events (`show` method). The `askServer` method is used to send a request event to a server. Note that the `send` primitive does not here references any explicit destination and as such follows our structural decoupling principle. In a similar way, we can give definition for servers:

```
component MMServer {                    component VideoServer extends MMServer {
  receive MMRequest; send MMEvent;        receive MMRequest; send VideoEvent;
  when(MMRequest request) {               double _frame_rate; // Frame rate field
    // subclasses refine this method      void doRequest(MMRequest req) {
    doRequest(request);                     ... In a loop for the whole video
  }                                         send(req.sender, new VideoEvent(...)
}                                           ... } }
```

The general structure of a multimedia server is described by the left definition. Events of type `MMRequest`, when received, denote client requests for multimedia streams. Operational servers must refine the `doRequest` method to generate the corresponding contents. A refinement for video servers is described partially on the right. Such a server will emit a serie of unicast video frames to the requesting client[3]. Of course, there are many details we do not explain here. Note however the declaration of the `_frame_rate` field, which represents as expected the current "speed" of the server; we will refer to this field later on.

Events. As explained previously, events represent the data exchanged by components at runtime. These are abstracted through the definition of an *event type*. For example, we can describe video frames using the following event type definition:

```
event VideoEvent is MMEvent {
  slot _contents type DeltaImage;
  slot _serial type int;
  slot _gentime type long;
  VideoEvent(DeltaImage ic, int is, long ig) {
    _contents = ic; _serial = is; _gentime = ig;
  }
  DeltaImage getContents() { return _contents;}
  int getSerial() { return _serial; }
  long getGenTime() { return _gentime; } }
```

The type `VideoEvent` describes differential frames within video streams. In order to support different categories of multimedia contents, we take advantage of the *subtyping relation* among event types. We may for example define subtypes

---

[2] `Receive`/`when` declarations seems redundant but in fact address different problems: respectively type negotiations among component and reaction semantics. For example, one `receive` declaration might refer to multiple `when` constructs.

[3] Events are of course not multicast from servers to clients. We use the `sender` slot of events to identify the request's origin. Since it is a relative reference, we do not break the structural decoupling rule.

for sound and voice streams, as well as synchronization events [13]. There also exists a most-generic event-type called Event which is a supertype of all the event types.

Instantiation and Connection. In order to start a distributed application from the previous definitions, we first have to deploy some client and server components. This is done using a simple instantiate primitive whose syntax is:

comp = **instantiate**(*ComponentType, location*)

Suppose for example that we have deployed two clients (mmclient and mmclient2 of type MMclient) as well as a video server (vserver of type VideoServer). We then have to connect *dynamically* our components altogether. Analyzing the *component type* is an important preliminary for connection. This type is decomposed into an *input type* (received events) and an *output type* (emitted events). To connect the server to the client, we may use the MMRequest since it is emitted by the client and received by the server. This connection establishment is performed using the connect primitive as follows[4]:

connect(mmclient, vserver, MMRequest)

Similarly, we can connect back the server to the client for the video frame communications:

connect(vserver, mmclient, VideoEvent)

Here, the connection is granted since we used a subtype for connection: clients can interpret events of type MMEvent denoting more general events than just video frames. If we connect our two clients this way, we obtain the architecture depicted on Fig. 1.

2.3   Component Internals

The client and server components described in the previous section are in fact higher-order components. If we look inside each of these components, we reveal an internal architecture of sub-components. These inner architectures expose very similar properties if compared to the higher-order ones: explicit coupling relation and event-based communication. They differ only in the fact that sub-components are not distributed and can communicate synchronously as well as asynchronously.

By default, the internal architecture of a component denotes an actor-like behavior with asynchronous semantics [1]. These semantics are captured by the sub-components depicted on Fig. 2. For the sake of simplicity, we do not show the input and output types of the sub-components which is always the most generic Event type. First, events are received and queued by the Receive and

---

[4] As we explain in [12], we also propose an inference algorithm to determine possible connection types automatically. Also note that connections are unidirectional, source and destination components are distinguished.

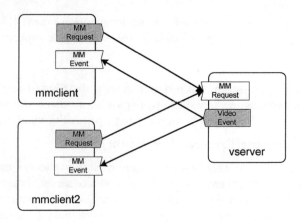

Fig. 1. Distributed multimedia architecture

InQueue sub-components. Concurrently[5], the InFetch component passes the queued events to Exec. The latter will deterministically associates the events to a (most) compatible reactive block (i.e. when construct) for execution. The Send component then handles the potential event emission requests using the implicit type-based multicast algorithm introduced previously. At that level, when an event of type t is sent, a copy of this event is emitted to all destinations compatible with type t: itself or some super-type. Of course, other sub-components can be introduced like the State sub-components which captures the interaction with the component internal state.

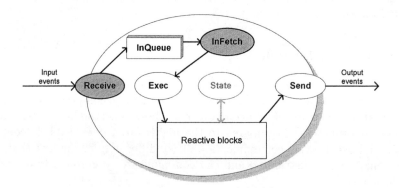

Fig. 2. Behavioral sub-components

As we explained in the previous section, the Comet middleware supports dynamic adaptability by ensuring that distributed components can be added, removed or interconnected at runtime. By designing the internal architectures

---

[5] The concurrent or *active* components which own a thread of control are emphasized on Fig. 2. The other sub-components use synchronous communications.

of components as if they were regular architectures, we also support the modification of the component internals at runtime by means of adding or removing sub-components. As such, a structural modification at this level will be perceived, from the outside, as a change in the way the associated distributed component is behaving. This represents the operational foundation for the fine-grained adaptations we will discuss in the remainder of the paper.

3   Dynamic Adaptation in Comet

Comet components open their internal architecture to support fine-grained adaptations. However, this does not explain how such adaptations are described. In order to capture these conceptual requirements, we propose abstractions called *protocols* and *roles*.

3.1   Protocols and Roles

We write protocol definitions to describe dynamic adaptations of running Comet applications. Such a definition is composed of *roles* and *functionalities*, as well as of an optional *internal state*. Functionalities describe the protocol properties that are shared among the components which will participate in it. These can be seen as methods or scripts explaining how to use the protocol. In contrast, roles describe local conventions that each participating component should follow so that the protocol can be used in practice. As a matter of fact, roles capture the essence of the protocols. They describe what will effectively change in the running system when the protocol will be applied. As hinted previously, these roles correspond to sub-components which will be plugged in dynamically within distributed component internals.

Example. To illustrate these notions, we propose to design a protocol for on-the-fly inspection of component fields. The definition of this protocol is written as follows:

```
protocol ComponentInspection {
ComponentRef _inspector; // Internally managed component
ComponentInspection() { // Creation of the internal component
  _inspector = instantiate_local(InspectorClient);
}
Object inspect(ComponentRef component, String fieldname) {
  assign(component, InspectorRole);
  connect(component, _inspector, Ask);
  connect(_inspector, component, Answer);
  return _inspector.getLocalRef().inspect(fieldname); // Perform the inspection
} }
```

The inspect functionality is used to remotely read the value of a component field. The component we would like to inspect is referenced through the

component parameter and the name of the field to read is `fieldname`. This protocol manages an internal state in the form of a component that will act as a client for the inspection process. We need this component because protocols themselves are not able to receive events.

The client for inspection is defined as follows:

```
component InspectorClient {
  receive Answer; send Ask;
  Object inspect(String varname) {
    Answer ans = sendreceive(new Ask(varname));
    return ans.getValue(); } }
```

We use the event type `Ask` to inspect fields remotely and `Answer` to denote the replied value. The protocol can invoke the `inspect` method of this component to perform a remote inspection. The use of the `sendreceive` primitive allows to send an event and receive a reply in an atomic way[6]. This simplifies greatly the description of client-side computations.

The problem here is that Comet components, such as our multimedia clients and servers, do not support the inspection event types by default. We thus propose to add the necessary code at runtime; and only on the components we would like to remotely inspect. This is done by assigning them dynamically a role for inspection using the `assign` primitive. But for this we first have to define the inspector role as follows:

```
role InspectorRole {
  receive Ask; send Answer;
  when(Ask ask) {
    send(new Answer(outer.getFieldValue(ask.getFieldName()))); } }
```

As a sub-component, it is not surprising a role looks similar to the definition of a regular component. However, the operational identity of such role (`this`, as usual) cannot be considered independently from the component it is supposed to be assigned to (referenced as `outer`). On this example, we define a reactive block for events of type `Ask` which carry the name of the component's field(s) to inspect. In reply to such requests, the role sends a reply with the value resulting from the inspection. The standard method `getFieldValue` of the `outer` component is used to locally perform the inspection. Of course, this intrusive invocation must be precisely controlled. We will discuss this in Sect. 5.

In our terminology, we classify the `InspectorRole` as a *functional role*. The purpose of such a role is to dynamically add new functionalities – or reactive blocks – to already running components. This represents of course the most versatile form of dynamic adaptation. We will see other forms of adaptation in the following section but let us first describe the use of protocols.

To begin with, we have to create an instance of the protocol as follows:

```
ComponentInspection inspector = new ComponentInspection()
```

---

[6] Because we rely on multicast semantics, the `sendreceive` primitive supports atomic distributed *rendez-vous*. This interesting aspect is discussed in [12].

It is then possible to ask for the inspection of some component's internal state such as our previously deployed **vserver** component:

```
println(inspector.inspect(vserver, "_frameRate");
==¿ [float] 29.9673
```

Here, the value of the internal field **_frameRate** is inspected whereas the inspected component itself has not been tailored at the origin for such fine-grain access. Fig. 3 shows the resulting architecture after inspection.

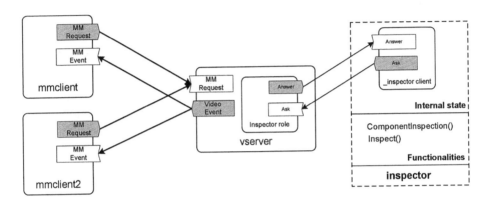

Fig. 3. Dynamic application of the inspection protocol

We can see that an instance of the inspection role has been plugged dynamically within the boundary of the inspected – or dynamically adapted – component. On Fig. 4, we describe the generic modification involved at the level of the inner architecture.

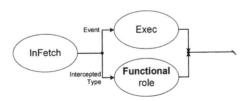

Fig. 4. Functional roles assignments

After the instantiation of the functional role as a sub-component, it is connected from the **InFetch** sub-component for the type **Ask** and also to **Send** so that events of type **Answer** can be sent. This is done as follows:

```
role = instantiate(InspectorRole);
connect(InFetch, role, Ask);
connect(role, Send, Answer);
```

We can see that only structural changes, triggered by standard primitives, are used to realize the dynamic adaptation.

3.2   Other Role Categories

In complement to functional roles, we also provide *prehook* and *posthook* roles to allow the wrapping of *existing* functionalities. And we introduce *filter* roles to be able to interfere with the communication layer of Comet. We argue that these three complementary role categories cover a very large spectrum of dynamic adaptations.

Hook Roles. Hooks are fine-grained wrappers that can dynamically decorate functionalities. They can be used for example to implement resource management schemes. The way these resources are managed can be modified without touching their functional usage. Another interesting use of a hook is to reflect at the global level things that are happening locally within some running component. To illustrate this, we will develop in this section a protocol for *event interception*. The idea is to inform external components (or roles) when events are received by a given component. This can be used to create replication protocols or, in our case, to complement our debugging techniques with a transparent trace protocol.

In the example of Sect. 2, the events received by the generic multimedia servers are of type `MMRequest`. Suppose that we want to trace such events and also all types that derive from a more generic `Request` type used by all server components. We thus use the latter type for the interception mechanism, defined as a role:

```
role InterceptorRole {
  prehook Request; send Request;
  before (Request request) {
    send(request); // Send a copy
} }
```

Here, we define a prehook (`prehook/before` reactive block) for events of type `Request`. The only operation performed here is simply to send a copy of the received request to all compatible destinations (i.e. multicast send).

The corresponding fine-grained process for such assignment is depicted on Fig. 5. The hook roles, as sub-components, are plugged as wrappers around reactive blocks. This means that unlike with functional roles, the `Exec` sub-component will here also get the event and process it as usual. If compared to Corba interceptors [9], note that changes are here performed within component boundaries. Hooks may interfere with internal properties such as the component's state.

Filter Roles. Similarly to prehooks, filters denote computations that are done at event reception time. However, the latter may adjust the delivery semantics

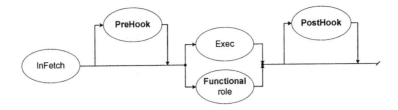

Fig. 5. Hook roles assignments

for the so-called filtered events. There exist various delivery semantics such as instantaneous delivery (no filter), cancellation and so on. The main use of filter roles, as shown in [12], is to apply content-based filtering protocols to complement the default type-based routing algorithm of the Comet middleware. However, one can find many other interesting uses for filter roles. In this section, we will implement a postponing scheme to support a demand-driven execution mode for components. A generic filter role for such purpose is presented below:

```
role StepFilter {
  filter Event, Step; // Filter all events and Step
  LinkedList _stepList = new LinkedList(10); int _maxStep = 10;

  Event filter (Event event) {
    _stepList.addFirst(event); // Queue the event
    if(_stepList.size()¿=_maxStep-1) // Fairness condition
      return _stepList.removeLast(); // Return the oldest event
    else // Step-mode event-flow
      return null; // Cancel the current delivery
  }

  Event filter (Step s) {
    return _stepList.removeLast(); // Replaces by the oldest event
} } }
```

In this example (and once the role has been assigned to some host component), every reception of an event (except Step) will be postponed for later delivery. This is performed using a bounded buffer in which we record the received events. To cancel the current delivery, the filter reactive block simply has to return a null reference. When events of type Step are received, then the oldest recorded event is processed instead of the step event. While simple, this algorithm completely changes the behavior of the host component which is not reactive anymore. The use of a bounded buffer (of size _maxStep) guarantees that the modification preserves the *liveness* property of event delivery.

Internally, the role is plugged between the InQueue and InFetch sub-components, as depicted on Fig. 6.

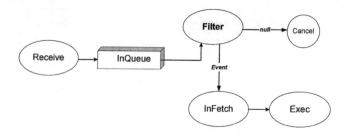

Fig. 6. Filter role assignment

3.3   Put It All Together: Dynamic Distributed Debugging

We may now summarize our mechanisms for distributed debugging. This results in a versatile protocol defined as follows:

```
protocol DebugProtocol extends ComponentInspection {
  void stepMode(ComponentRef comp) { // Step-mode
    assign(comp, StepFilter); }
  void step(ComponentRef comp) { // Atomic delivery
    send(comp, new Step()); }
  void reactiveMode(ComponentRef comp) { // Standard reactive mode
    unassign(comp, StepFilter); } // Unplug the role
  void trace(ComponentRef comp, EventType type) { // Trace mode
    assign(comp, InterceptorRole);
    connect(comp, _inspector, type); } // Connection to the inherited
                                       // internal component
  void unTrace(ComponentRef comp, EventType type) { // End of trace
    disconnect(_inspector, comp, type); // Disconnection
    unassign(comp, InterceptorRole); } }
```

Using this protocol, we can trace the execution of a given component (using the `trace` functionality). It is also possible to put this execution in a demand-driven mode. To do so, we first have to invoke the `stepMode` functionality. Then, every time we want to "move" one step further in the execution process, we just have to invoke `step`. The protocol above also inherits from the previous `ComponentInspection` definition. Thus, on-the-fly component inspection is also available. Of course, all the modifications needed to support the debugging facilities, which may slow down the system, can be undone using the disconnection (`disconnect`) and role removal (`unassign`) primitives.

4   Quantitative Evaluation

In the previous sections, we mainly explored the expressiveness of protocol and role constructs. We will now argue in a more quantitative way and measure the impact of their operationalization. To conduct this evaluation, we will use

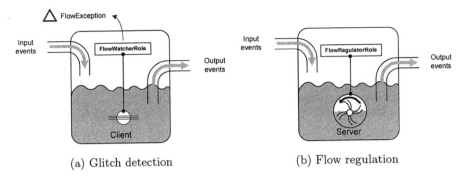

(a) Glitch detection   (b) Flow regulation

Fig. 7. Protocol for event flow synchronization

a protocol whose purpose is to synchronize the flow of events among components. Usually, such fine-grained flow synchronization is not needed since most transport protocols ensure some level of fairness. However, if we want to guarantee client-specific quality of service (such as minimal frame-rate for video), then user-level synchronization techniques may be required.

Protocol Definition. The synchronization scheme we propose is based on flow analysis and regulation mechanisms. For the analysis part, we first define a role for the detection of event flow glitches (see Fig. 7(a)).

Our criterion for flow analysis is the interval between event reception times. We say that a glitch occurs when the average interval time crosses a given threshold. The Scope definition of this role is given below:

```
role FlowWatcher {
  prehook Event; send FlowException;
  long _event_count=0; long _avg_limit=100; long _avg_time=0;
  before(Event event) {
    _event_count++;
    long current = System.currentTimeMillis();
    _total_time = _total_time + current;
    _avg_time = _total_time / _event_count;
    if(_avg_time ¿ _avg_limit)
      send(new FlowException(_avg_time));
} }
```

This definition implements a prehook for all the events (generic `Event` type) that are received by the host component. When the hook is performed, the total number of received events (`_event_count` variable) is incremented. Then, the local time is fetched from the operating system and added to the total execution time recored in `_total_time`. We can then compute our criterion (average execution time `_avg_time`) and test if it crosses the threshold `_avg_limit`. If so, an exception (event of type `FlowException`) is raised by the role. This exception encapsulates a proposed rate for regulation.

In order to complete the synchronization algorithm, we also need a role for flow regulation that will take decisions when flow exceptions will be raised (see Fig. 7(b)). A possible solution is to delay the event emissions from the regulated host component through the following definition:

```
role FlowRegulator {
  prehook Event; posthook Event;
  receive FlowException;
  long _start_time; long _end_time; long _rate=1000;
  before(Event event) {
    _start_time = System.currentTimeMillis();
  } after(Event event) {
    _end_time = System.currentTimeMillis();
    if(_end_time - _start_time ¡ _rate)
      Thread.sleep(min_rate - (_end_time - _start_time));
  }
  when(FlowException except) {
    _rate = except.getRate(); // Detected anomaly
  } }
```

Here, we use another prehook to record the time when a given event has been received by the host component. Then, a corresponding posthook computes the execution time for this particular event and sees if a delay is necessary (comparison to the _rate variable) so that the next event won't be processed too early; that is, we perform regulation. When a flow exception is received, the event rate is updated to meet the client proposition.

A minimal definition for the whole synchronization protocol can be written as follows:

```
protocol FlowSyncProtocol {
  void sync(ComponentRef server, ComponentRef client) { // Synchronizing
    assign(client, FlowWatcher); // Client watching
    assign(server, FlowRegulator); // Server regulation
    connect(client, server, FlowException); // Protocol connection
  } }
```

The sync functionality applies the synchronization algorithm through the assignment of the detection and regulation roles to a couple of host components.

Evaluation. The graph depicted on Fig. 8 illustrates the impact of such dynamic adaptation on our multimedia client/server application.

The vertical axis of the graph shows the immediate event handling time on the client (or detection) side. The darkened curve corresponds to the client that will be source of glitches. Another "normal" client is measured by the lighter curve. The (1) mark shows a manually triggered glitch before system adaptation[7]. We can see that the client becomes suddenly less efficient since it cannot handle

---

[7] We instrumented the role and component code to support the manual generation of such "deficiency". In fact, we simply conceived a generic protocol that can be used to slow down any component.

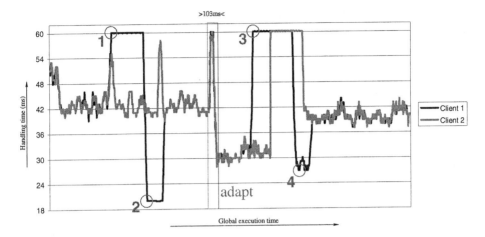

Fig. 8. Dynamic adaptation for event flow synchronization

any received video event in less than 60 ms. We can also note that the second (unmodified) client is taking advantage of the situation (its performance slowly increases). At mark (2), we perform the converse operation: accelerating the instrumented client. We can see now that the second client becomes drastically less efficient. This shows that the event flow between the server and the clients is not synchronized by default.

The central part of the graph (*adapt* label) shows the impact of dynamically applying the synchronization protocol on the instrumented client and on the server. Both the clients are notably affected by this dynamic adaptation. However, we can see on table 1 that the adaptation duration itself, if observed from the client-side, is of about 100 ms and so hardly noticeable from the global point of view. As a matter of fact, this adaptation time is in the same order of magnitude as the average handling time for atomic events. Table 1 shows also that the global adaptation time has a rather limited cost (about 18 times less) if compared to the application deployment time. Mark (3) reproduces the glitch period triggered on the instrumented client. About 150 ms later (adaptation latency), we notice that the second client, albeit not itself adapted, is slowed down to obtain an approximatively equivalent shared quality of service. At mark (4), we try to accelerate our instrumented client but the system now avoids such anomaly and both clients eventually converge at the best throughput from the system's point of view: synchronization is now active.

5   Verification Contracts

As we can conclude from the preceding discussion, the fine-grained runtime modifications we support in Comet are highly intrusive and thus potentially harmful for the system's integrity. The verification of the dynamic role assignment process is in consequence a critical issue. Role/component contracts are established

Table 1. Impact of dynamic adaptation

Operation	Duration
Application deployment	9934 ms
Adaptation time (global)	541 ms
Adaptation time (client)	103 ms
Average time for event handling	42 ms

for verification from three different perspectives: *typing, internal access* and *security*.

5.1   Typing Contracts

The first level of verification is built upon the versatile type system of the scope language. From a formal point of view, we saw previously that component types where composed of input/output type pairs. A *role type* is composed of such input and output types as well as pre/posthook and filtering types. A typing contract will then establish the conditions so that a role R of type $\langle R_{in}, R_{out}, R_{pre}, R_{post}, R_{filter} \rangle$ may be assigned to a host component C of type $\langle C_{in}, C_{out} \rangle$. What we have to verify is that all the types that are intercepted by the role are compatible[8] with the input types of the host component. In formal terms, we write:

$$\forall t \in R_{pre} \cup R_{post} \cup R_{filter}, \exists t' \in C_{in}, t' \sim t$$

The establishment of such typing contracts is performed through *static analysis* of the role and component source code. It is then generated and transmitted at assignment time as an XML document. For example, the interceptor role described in Sect. 3.2 is associated to the following contract:

```
<role type="InterceptorRole">
 <type>
  <prehook>Request</prehook>
  <out>Request</out>
 </type></role>
```

This document, when transmitted as a preamble to the role assignment, is compared to a corresponding host component type contract. In the case of our multimedia server, this contract is:

```
<component type="MMServer">
 <type><in>MMRequest</in><out>MMEvent</out></type>
</component>
```

Intuitively, we see that both definitions match since the intercepted type is Request which is compatible (as a supertype) with the host input type MMRequest.

---

[8] We define type compatibility between types t and t' through the relation $t \sim t'$, t being a subtype of t' ($t \preceq t'$) or the converse ($t \succeq t'$).

5.2   Access Contracts

The contracts we describe in this section firstly establish the modality for sub-components – most notably the roles – to access the internals of their outer component. In order to allow or disallow a role from accessing parts of the host component internal state and methods, we define two complementary contracts. The first one is associated to the role we try to assign. This role contract must indicate which fields or methods should be accessible. For example, the InspectorRole described in Sect. 3.1 proposes the following access contract:

```
<role type="InspectorRole">
 <type> <in>InspectReq</in>
        <out>InspectRep</out></type>
 <access><all-fields mode="read"></access>
 </role>
```

Here, we request the access to all fields for reading only. In order to satisfy this request from the host component point of view, we must allow at least access to some fields. In our example, we will only grant access for _frameRate which is the one we use for inspection. This is written as follows:

```
<component type="VideoServer">
 <access><field type="float" name="_frameRate" mode="read"></access>
 </component>
```

As we can see, the `<field>` discriminates fields using either their type, their name or a combination of both. The access mode can be either read, write or readwrite. It is also possible to access/restrict method invocations and instance creations. For example, the synchronization protocol of Sect. 4 may only be plugged in if the sleep method of the standard class Thread is accessible. This is requested from the flow regulator side as follows:

```
<role type="FlowRegulator">
 <access> <method class="java.lang.Thread" name="sleep" </access>
 </role>
```

By default, methods are requested/granted either as invoked from the outer (host component reference) or static contexts. On the host component side, access rights are established in the same way. The instance creations are controlled using the same scheme by considering their constructors as methods.

5.3   Security Contracts

We employ low-level security rules when both type and access contracts are not enough to prevent unexpected runtime modifications. For example, it seems important to restrict the adaptability features to well-authenticated sources when potentially unsafe mechanisms are employed. In Sect. 4, the use of the sleep method is for example a way to slow down a system so that only an authorized person should be able to plug and control the synchronization protocol. This can be done through authentication or domain restriction. The latter would for example be expressed like this:

```
<component type="Dummy">
  <access><method class="java.lang.Thread" name="sleep" />
  <domain ip="127.0.0.*" /></access></component>
```

Here, we only grant the access rule from domains within a range of IP addresses. In order to implement these low-level security contracts, we integrally rely on the Java security API [14].

6   Related Work

Several other researchers have addressed the problem of modifying computer systems at runtime [5]. In the case of middleware environments, studies such as X-RMI [2] focus on large-grain reconfigurations. This allows existing RMI applications to be preserved while introducing dynamic reconfiguration features. Corba interceptors [9] have also been used to support runtime changes in a portable way. Reflective approaches such as [6] show that more intrusive modifications can be obtained at the price of deriving from standards (like with Comet). However, most of these propositions seem to focus on *mechanisms* for dynamic adaptation. In contrast, we think that finding *abstractions* to capture adaptation requirements should be the priority. The Drastic approach [3] seems to fit more closely this vision of dynamic adaptability. It proposes a proper frontier between the abstractions for adaptation and the operational mechanisms that support them. In this work, runtime modifications are abstracted by type contracts among distributed objects. At the operational level, these contracts are matched against physical zones that need to be temporarily frozen (using persitency) for update. Meanwhile, every components of the system outside such zones carry on their computations unaware of the runtime modification in progress. The main difference in our approach is the much finer granularity level of the changes we support. We also focus more on minimizing the impact on the system performances.

The CodA framework [7] once demonstrated that metal-level architectures could be introduced to circumvent the rigidity of most (distributed) object models. We took our inspiration from CodA to design the inner architecture of Comet components. But we (finally) found no need to convey the hardly tractable reflective concepts since both inner and outer architectures use the same fundamental concepts. This makes our work diverge from approaches such as [10] where reflection plays an essential role. Of course, the implementation of the middleware itself relies heavily on reflective mechanisms.

Actor-based languages [1] were also an important source of inspiration. The DIL approach [13], most notably, introduced similar concepts of protocol and role that we use. However, Comet is an event-based middleware relying on typed and multicast communications. This diverges in an important way from actor-based message-passing semantics. We can also note that Comet components may denote multiple internal activities (depending on the number of active subcomponents) whereas actor-based languages identify the activity and actor concepts.

7   Conclusion

The Comet middleware we designed and implemented supports a development model which we argue is innovating because it is tailor-made for dynamic adaptability. From a structural point of view, runtime system reconfigurations are made (1) *possible* thanks to the extraction of the coupling relations among components and (2) *controllable* through strong typing. Relying on the same principles but within component boundaries, we were able to support dynamic adaptability at a finer granularity level. This is in our opinion the most objective contribution described in this paper.

Fine-grained adaptations are manipulated at the language level as role and protocol abstractions. We think that such domain-specific abstractions foreshadow tomorrow's *adaptive* middleware environments. The three categories of role we introduce form in our opinion a quite *expressive* model. Functional roles, for example, are particularly versatile since they support incremental and dynamic functionality enhancements. We saw how prehooks or posthooks could even change the way a particular functionality is handled. Filter roles go even further and allow incremental changes in the way events are communicated, using content-based analysis. Our expressiveness argument represents of course a more subjective contribution. But we think our example protocols are particularly illustrative in this respect. They denote less than trivial changes in a quite concise manner.

Moreover, we began to evaluate the cost of such dynamic adaptations which deeply modify the system semantics. Despite the prototype status of our implementation, these evaluations reveal promising results. Of course, this evaluation is relative to the performances of the Comet middleware itself. We are currently conducting an extensive benchmark to optimize its prototype implementation so that we may compare to industrial-strength approaches (most notably Java RMI).

In the mean time, it is very important to keep in mind that the *arbitrary* modification of a distributed system at runtime remains a mostly open research topic. Of course, type-related negotiations, if useful, are not enough to verify such intrusive changes. We discussed the complementary access and security contracts as "compensations" here. The security layer seems to be yet the only operational mechanism at our disposal to envisage the support of dynamic adaptation in today's real-world applications. But we find this quite unsatisfactory: more solid foundations are in our opinion needed to address the problem of safety in the presence of dynamic adaptations. In this perspective, we currently address the problem of describing properly the semantics of the language substrate of our middleware. We hope this would then ease the definition of properties regarding dynamic adaptations as well as their verification using, for example, theorem-proving or model checking techniques.

Acknowledgements

We would like to thank the anonymous reviewers for their useful comments. A special thanks also to Reynald Affeldt who carefully read and commented the paper.

References

1. G. Agha. *Actors : A Model of Concurrent Computation in Distributed Systems.* Series in Artificial Intelligence. MIT Press, 1986.
2. X. Chen. Extending rmi to support dynamic reconfiguration of distributed systems. In *Proceedings of ICDCS'02.* IEEE, July 2002.
3. H. Evans and P. Dickman. Zones, Contracts and Absorbing Changes: An Approach to Software Evolution. In *Proceedings of OOPSLA'99.* ACM Press, November 1999.
4. K. Geihs. Middleware challenges ahead. *IEEE Computer*, 34(6):24–31, June 2001.
5. X. Liu and H. Yang, editors. *International Symposium on Principles of Software Evolution (ISPSE 2000), Kanazawa, Japan.* IEEE computer society, November 2000.
6. J. Malenfant, M.-T. Segarra, and F. André. Dynamic adaptability: The molène experiment. In *Proceedings of Reflection 2001*, volume LNCS 2192. Springer Verlag, September 2001.
7. J. McAffer. *Metalevel Programming with Coda.* In *Proceedings of the European Conference on Object-Oriented Computing (ECOOP)*, LNCS 952, pages 190–214. Springer Verlag, August 1995.
8. R. Meyer. State of the art of distributed event models. Technical report, University of Dublin, Trinity College, 2000.
9. Object Management Group. *Common Object Request Broker Architecture (CORBA) 2.6 Specifications.* http://www.corba.org, 2001.
10. N. Parlavantzas, G. Coulson, M. Clarke, and G. Blair. Towards a reflective component-based middleware architecture. In *Proceedings of Workshop on Reflection and Metalevel Architectures*, June 2000.
11. F. Peschanski. A reflective middleware architecture for adaptive, component-based distributed systems. *IEEE DS Online*, 1(7), 2001.
12. F. Peschanski. A versatile event-based communication model for generic distributed interactions. In *Proceedings of DEBS'01 (ICDCS International Workshop on Distributed Event-based Systems)*. IEEE, July 2002.
13. D. C. Sturman. *Modular Specification of Interaction Policies in Distributed Computing.* PhD thesis, University of Illinois at Urbana-Champaign, May 1996.
14. Sun Microsystems. *Java Security Model.* http://java.sun.com/security, 2001.

A Middleware for Context-Aware Agents in Ubiquitous Computing Environments[*]

Anand Ranganathan and Roy H. Campbell

Department of Computer Science
University of Illinois at Urbana-Champaign, USA
{ranganat,rhc}@uiuc.edu

Abstract. Ubiquitous Computing advocates the construction of massively distributed systems that help transform physical spaces into computationally active and intelligent environments. The design of systems and applications in these environments needs to take account of heterogeneous devices, mobile users and rapidly changing contexts. Most importantly, agents in ubiquitous and mobile environments need to be context-aware so that they can adapt themselves to different situations. In this paper, we argue that ubiquitous computing environments must provide middleware support for context-awareness. We also propose a middleware that facilitates the development of context-aware agents. The middleware allows agents to acquire contextual information easily, reason about it using different logics and then adapt themselves to changing contexts. Another key issue in these environments is allowing autonomous, heterogeneous agents to have a common semantic understanding of contextual information. Our middleware tackles this problem by using ontologies to define different types of contextual information. This middleware is part of Gaia, our infrastructure for enabling Smart Spaces.

1   Introduction

Ubiquitous Computing Environments consist of a large number of autonomous agents that work together to transform physical spaces into smart and interactive environments. In order for an agent to function effectively in these environments, they need to perform two kinds of tasks – they need to sense and reason about the current context of the environment; and they need to interact smoothly with other agents. In this paper, we propose a middleware for Ubiquitous Computing Environments that meets these two needs of agents in the environment.

The role of context has recently gained great importance in the field of ubiquitous computing. "Context" is any information about the circumstances, objects, or conditions by which a user is surrounded that is considered relevant to the interaction between the user and the ubiquitous computing environment [1]. A lot of work has been done in trying to make applications in ubiquitous computing environments context aware so that they can adapt to different situations and be more receptive to users' needs[1][2][3][8][13].

Humans behave differently in different contexts. They are able to sense what their context is and they adapt their behavior to their current context. The way humans

---

[*] This research is supported by a grant from the National Science Foundation, NSF CCR 0086094 ITR and NSF 99-72884 EQ

M. Endler and D. Schmidt (Eds.): Middleware 2003, LNCS 2672, pp. 143–161, 2003.

adapt themselves is based on rules that they learn over the course of their experiences. Humans are, thus, able to follow socially and politically correct behavior that is conditioned by their past experiences and their current context.

Automated agents (which may be applications, services and devices) too, can follow contextually-appropriate behavior, if they are able to sense and reason about the context in which they are operating. Ubiquitous computing environments are characterized by many sensors that can sense a variety of different contexts. The types of contexts include physical contexts (like location, time), environmental contexts (weather, light and sound levels), informational contexts (stock quotes, sports scores), personal contexts (health, mood, schedule, activity), social contexts (group activity, social relationships, other people in a room), application contexts (email received, websites visited) and system contexts (network traffic, status of printers)[9]. Agents in these environments should be able to acquire and reason about these contexts to adapt the way they behave.

In this paper, we argue that ubiquitous computing environments must provide middleware support for context awareness. A middleware for context awareness would provide support for most of the tasks involved in dealing with context. Context-aware agents can be developed very easily with such a middleware. A middleware for context-awareness would also place different mechanisms at the disposal of agents for dealing with context. These mechanisms include reasoning mechanisms like rules written in different types of logic (first order logic, temporal logic, fuzzy logic, etc.) as well as learning mechanisms (like Bayesian networks, neural networks or reinforcement learning). Developers of context-aware agents would not have to worry about the intricate details of getting contextual information from different sensors or developing reasoning or learning mechanisms to reason about context.

Another important requirement of middleware in ubiquitous computing environments is that they allow autonomous, heterogeneous agents to seamlessly interact with one another. While a number of protocols and middlewares (like TCP/IP, CORBA, Jini, SOAP, etc.) have been developed to enable distributed agents to talk to one another, they do not address the issues of syntactic and semantic interoperability among agents. They do not provide a common terminology and shared set of concepts that agents can use when they interact with each other. This problem is especially acute in the realm of contextual information since different agents could have different understandings of the current context. They might use different terms to describe context, and even if they use the same terms, they might attach different semantics to these terms. A middleware for context-awareness must address this problem by ensuring that there is no semantic gap between different agents when they exchange contextual information.

We have identified several requirements for a middleware for context-awareness in ubiquitous computing environments. These are:

1. Support for gathering of context information from different sensors and delivery of appropriate context information to different agents.
2. Support for inferring higher level contexts from low level sensed contexts
3. Enable agents use different kinds of reasoning and learning mechanisms
4. Facilities for allowing agents to specify different behaviors in different contexts easily.
5. Enable syntactic and semantic interoperability between different agents (through the use of ontologies)

In this paper, we propose a middleware for promoting context-awareness among agents in ubiquitous computing environments. This middleware is based on a predicate model of context. The model of context and the middleware also supports the use of different reasoning mechanisms like first order logic and temporal logic by agents to reason about context and decide how to behave in different contexts. Agents can alternatively employ learning mechanisms like Bayesian learning and reinforcement learning to learn different behaviors in different contexts. Different logics have different power, expressiveness and decidability properties. Agents can choose the appropriate logic that best meets their reasoning requirements.

The middleware uses ontologies to define the semantics of various contexts. The ontologies define the structure and the properties of different types of contextual information. They allow different agents in the environment to have a common semantic understanding of different contexts.

Ontologies have been used extensively in the Semantic Web[14] to allow semantic interoperability among different web-based agents. DAML+OIL[20] has emerged as one of the premier languages for describing ontologies in the Semantic Web. Our ontologies are also written in DAML+OIL. The use of standard technologies for semantics allows semantic interoperability between agents in our environment and other external agents (in other environments or on the web). The use of ontologies, thus, dramatically increases the scalability of the environment.

Our middleware allows rapid prototyping of context-aware agents in ubiquitous computing environments. It also allows agents the use of powerful reasoning mechanisms to handle contextual information and ensures syntactic as well as semantic interoperability between different agents through the use of ontologies. The middleware has made it very easy for us to develop a variety of context-aware applications and services.

In the rest of the paper, we describe how our middleware achieves context awareness in and semantic interoperability between agents in ubiquitous computing environments. In Section 2, we provide motivation for middleware support for context-awareness. In Section 3, we describe our predicate model for context, which forms the basis of the various reasoning and learning mechanisms that we use. Section 4 introduces Gaia, our infrastructure for Smart Spaces, into which our middleware for context awareness and semantic interoperability has been integrated. Section 5 describes how context awareness has been achieved among agents. Section 6 describes the use of ontologies in the middleware. Section 7 describes our current implementation status; Section 8 has related work; Section 9 has future work and Section 10 concludes the paper.

2   Why a Middleware for Context-Awareness?

Different approaches have been suggested for promoting context-awareness among agents. Anind Dey et al[1] have proposed the Toolkit approach, which provides a framework for the development and execution of sensor-based context-aware applications and provides a number of reusable components. The toolkit supports rapid prototyping of certain types of context-aware applications.

The other approach is developing an infrastructure or a middleware for context-awareness. A middleware would greatly simplify the tasks of creating and maintaining context-aware systems[2]. A middleware would provide uniform abstractions and reliable services for common operations. It would, thus, simplify the development of context-aware applications. It would also make it easy to incrementally deploy new sensors and context-aware agents in the environment. A middleware would be independent of hardware, operating system and programming language. Finally, a middleware would also allow us to compose complex systems based on the interactions between a number of distributed context-aware agents.

While traditional middleware like CORBA and Jini do provide the basic mechanisms for different objects (or agents) to communicate with each other, they fall short in providing ways for agents to be context aware. Context-awareness involves acquisition of contextual information, reasoning about context and modifying one's behavior based on the current context. A middleware for context-awareness would provide support for each of these tasks. It would also define a common model of context, which all agents can use in dealing with context. It would also ensure that different agents in the environment have a common semantic understanding of contextual information.

Our middleware for context-awareness does use CORBA to enable distributed agents to find and communicate with one another. It, however, provides extra functionality to enable context-awareness. It is based on a predicate model of context and uses ontologies to describe different types of contexts. It also provides various services and libraries to enable agents acquire and reason about contextual information easily.

3   Context Model

In order to allow applications to be context-aware, we first need a model for context. We have developed a context model that is based on predicates. We use ontologies to describe the properties and structure of different context predicates. This context model provides the basis for reasoning about contexts using various mechanisms.

3.1   The Context Predicate

We represent a context as a predicate. We follow a convention where the name of the predicate is the type of context that is being described (like location, temperature or time). This convention allows us to have a simple, uniform representation for different kinds of contexts. Besides, it also allows us to easily describe the different contexts in an ontology, as we shall see later. It is also possible to have relational operators like "=" and "<" as arguments of a predicate.

Example context predicates are:

- Location (chris , entering , room 3231)
- Temperature (room 3231 , "=" , 98 F)
- Sister(venus , serena)
- StockQuote(msft , ">" , $60)
- PrinterStatus(srgalw1 printer queue , is , empty)
- Time(New York , "<" , 12:00 01/01/01)

The values that the arguments of a predicate can take are actually constrained by the type of context. For example, if the type of context is "location", the first argument has to be a person or object, the second argument has to be a preposition or a verb like "entering," "leaving," or "in" and the third argument must be a location. We perform type-checking of context predicates to make sure that the predicate does make sense.

3.2   Ontologies to Describe Context Predicates

The structures of different context predicates are specified in an ontology[15]. Each context type corresponds to a class in the ontology. This ontology defines various context types as well as the arguments that the predicates must have. The ontology is written in DAML+OIL[20], which is fast becoming the de-facto language of the semantic web[14].

For example, many context predicates are defined to have arguments in an SVO (Subject Verb Object) format. Thus, the structure of these predicates is ContextType(<Subject>,<Verb>,<Object>). For instance, the ontology declares that the Location predicate must have a subject which belongs to the set of persons or things, a verb or preposition like "inside" or "entering" and a location, which may be a room or a building.

The ontology is used to check the validity of context predicates. It also makes it easier to write different context predicates since we know what the structure of the predicate is and what kinds of values different arguments can take. It also allows different ubiquitous computing environments to inter-operate since it is possible to define translations between the terms used in the ontologies of these environments. Section 6 has more details about the use of ontologies.

This logical model for context is quite powerful. It allows us to describe the context of a system in a generic way, which is independent of programming language, operating system or middleware. Since the structure and the semantics of context predicates are specified in an ontology, it allows different components in the system to have a common understanding of the semantics of different contexts.

The predicate model of context is also generic enough to allow different reasoning mechanisms. For example, it is possible to write rules using these context predicates that describe application behavior using different logics like first order logic or temporal logic. It is also possible to perform other kinds of inferencing based on these predicates using Bayesian networks, neural networks or other approaches.

4   Gaia

Our middleware for context awareness and semantic interoperability has been integrated into Gaia[16][17]. Gaia is our infrastructure for Smart Spaces, which are ubiquitous computing environments that encompass physical spaces. The main aim of Gaia is to make physical spaces like rooms, homes, buildings and airports intelligent, and aid humans in these spaces. Gaia converts physical spaces and the ubiquitous computing devices they contain into a programmable computing system. It offers services to manage and program a space and its associated state. Gaia is similar to traditional operating systems in that it manages the tasks common to all applications built for physical spaces. Each space is self contained, but may interact with other spaces. Gaia provides core services, including events, entity presence (devices, users and services), discovery and naming. By specifying well defined interfaces to services, applications may be built in a generic way so that they are able to run in arbitrary active spaces. The core services are started through a bootstrap protocol that starts the Gaia infrastructure. Gaia uses CORBA to enable distributed computing.

Gaia consists of a number of different types of agents performing different tasks. There are agents that perform various core services required for the functioning of the environment like discovery, context-sensing, event distribution, etc. There are agents associated with devices that enable them be a part of the environment. Each user also has an agent that keeps personal information and acts as his proxy in a variety of settings. Finally there are application agents that help users perform various kinds of tasks in the environment. Examples of application agents include PowerPoint applications, music playing applications and drawing applications.

5   Enabling Context-Awareness

The Gaia middleware provides different ways for agents to acquire various types of contextual information and then reason about it. A diagram of our infrastructure for context-awareness is shown in Fig 1.

5.1   Overview of Context Infrastructure

There are different kinds of agents that are involved in the Context Infrastructure within Gaia (Fig. 1). These are:

- *Context Providers*. Context Providers are sensors or other data sources of context information. They allow other agents (or Context Consumers) to query them for context information. Some Context Providers also have an event channel where they keep sending context events. Thus, other agents can either query a Provider or listen on the event channel to get context information.
- *Context Synthesizers*. Context Synthesizers get sensed contexts from various Context Providers, deduce higher-level or abstract contexts from these simple sensed contexts and then provide these deduced contexts to other agents. For example, we have a Context Synthesizer which infers the activity going in a room based on the number of people in the room and the applications that are running.
- *Context Consumers*. Context Consumers (or Context-Aware Applications) are agents that get different types of contexts from Context Providers or Context Synthesizers. They then reason about the current context and adapt the way they behave according to the current context.
- *Context Provider Lookup Service*. Context Providers advertise the context they provide with the Context Provider Lookup Service. This service allows agents to find appropriate Context Providers. There is one such service in a single ubiquitous computing environment.

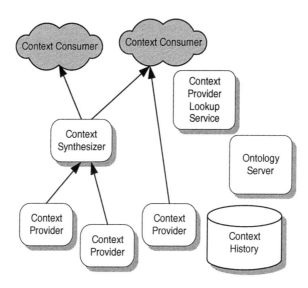

Fig. 1. Gaia Context Infrastructure

- *Context History Service.* Past contexts are logged in a database. The Context History Service allows other agents to query for past contexts. There is one such service in a single ubiquitous computing environment.
- *Ontology Server.* The Ontology Server maintains ontologies that describe different types of contextual information. There is one Ontology Server per ubiquitous computing environment.

These different kinds of agents are described in further detail in the following sections.

5.2   Use of Different Reasoning Mechanisms by Different Agents

A key feature of our middleware is that it endows agents with a variety of reasoning and/or learning mechanisms to help them reason about context appropriately. Using these reasoning or learning mechanisms, agents can infer various properties about the current context, answer logic queries about context or adapt the way they behave in different contexts.

Agents can reason about context using rules written in different types of logic like first order logic, temporal logic, description logic, higher order logic, fuzzy logic, etc. Different agents have different logic requirements. Agents that are concerned with the temporal sequence in which various events occur would need to use some form of temporal logic to express the rules. Agents that need to express generic conditions using existential or universal quantifiers would need to use some form of first order logic. Agents that need more expressive power (like characterizing the transitive closure of relations) would need higher order logics. Agents that deal with specifying terminological hierarchies may need description logic. Agents that need to handle uncertainties may require some form of fuzzy logic.

Instead of using rules written in some form of logic to reason about context, agents can also use various machine learning techniques to deal with context. Learning techniques that can be used include Bayesian learning, neural networks, reinforcement learning, etc. Depending on the kind of concept to be learned, different learning mechanisms can be used. If an agent wants to learn the appropriate action to perform in different states in an online, interactive manner, it could use reinforcement learning or neural networks. If an agent wants to learn the conditional probabilities of different events, Bayesian learning is appropriate. The decision on what kind of logic or learning mechanism to use depends not only on the power and expressivity of the logic, but also on other issues like performance, tractability and decidability.

Our middleware provides agents a choice of reasoning and learning mechanisms that they can use to understand and react to context. Our current implementation allows reasoning based on many-sorted first order logic, propositional linear-time temporal logic or probabilistic propositional logic. It also allows agents to learn using Bayesian methods or through reinforcement learning. These mechanisms are provided in the form of libraries that the agent can use. We discuss the power, expressivity and decidability of these logics in the implementation section. In the following sections, we describe how Context Providers, Context Synthesizers and Context Consumers use various reasoning mechanisms to perform their tasks.

5.3   Context Providers

Context Providers sense various types of contexts and allow these contexts to be accessed by other agents. We have a number of Context Providers in our infrastructure providing various types of contexts like location, weather, stock price, calendar and schedule information, etc.

Different Context Providers use different reasoning or learning mechanisms for reasoning about the contexts they sense and for answering queries. For example, Context Providers that deal with uncertain contexts could use fuzzy logic, while those that require the ability to quantify over variables could use first order logic. Our Location Context Provider, for instance, uses first order logic so that it can quantify over people or over locations. It can thus answer queries concerning all the people in a room, or all the locations in a building. Our Weather Forecast Context Provider uses a form of fuzzy logic to attach probabilities with different contexts. For instance, it says that precipitation could occur with a certain probability the next day.

Context Providers provide a query interface for other agents to get the current context. Depending on the type of logic or learning mechanism used, Context Providers have different ways of evaluating queries. However, all reasoning and learning mechanisms are based on the predicate model of context, which is defined in the ontology. So, in spite of different Providers using different logics, their common grounding on the predicate model makes it easy for Context Consumers to query them in a uniform way.

The query interface is similar to that of Prolog. If the query is a predicate with no variables, then the result is expected to be the truth value of that predicate. The result is, thus, either a "yes" or a "no" (or a probability of the context predicate being true). If the query is a predicate with variables, then the result must include any unifications of the variable with constants that make the predicate true (if there are any). The resulting unified context predicates that are returned may have additional attributes like time or probability depending on the type of logic used.

Some Context Providers (like those that provide dynamic contexts and are associated with sensors) also send events about their context on an event channel. Consumers can listen on this channel. For example, our room-based location service sends an event like *"Location(Bob, Entering, Room 3231)"* when Bob enters Room 3231. Exactly when a Context Provider generates an event is set by a policy for the Context Provider. In some cases, the provider keeps sending events periodically. For example, our weather service keeps sending temperature updates every 5 minutes. In other cases, the provider sends an event whenever a change in context is detected.

All Context Providers support a similar interface for getting contexts and listening to context events. So, consumers don't have to worry about the actual type of Context Provider they are querying. This greatly aids development of context-aware applications.

5.4   Context Synthesizers

Context Synthesizers are agents that provide higher-level contexts based on simpler sensed contexts. A Context Synthesizer gets source contexts from various Context Providers, applies some sort of logic to them and generates a new type of context. A Context Synthesizer is both a Context Provider and a Context Consumer. Just like Context Providers, Context Synthesizers also support a Prolog-like query interface which other agents can use to get the current context. They may also send events in an event channel.

We follow two basic approaches for inferring new contexts from existing contexts. The first uses static rules to deduce higher-level contexts and the other uses machine learning techniques.

Rule Based Synthesizers. Rule-based synthesizers use pre-defined rules written in some form of logic to infer different contexts. For example, we have a Room Activity Context Provider that based on the number of people in the room and the applications running in the room deduces what kind of activity is going on in the room. It uses rules written in first order logic to perform the deduction. Some of the rules that this Room Activity Context Provider employs are:

1. #People(Room 2401, ">=" , 3)   AND Application(PowerPoint, Running) => RoomActivity(2401, Presentation)
2. #People(Room 2401, ">=" , 1) AND Application(MPEG Player, Running) => RoomActivity(2401, Movie Screening)
3. #People(Room 2401, ">=" , 3) AND NOT $\exists_{Entertainment\text{-}Application}$ x Application(x, Running) => RoomActivity(2401, Meeting)
4. #People(Room 2401, "=" , 1) AND Application(Visual Studio, Running) => RoomActivity(2401, Individual Development)
5. #People(Room 2401, "=" , 2) AND Application(Visual Studio, Running) => RoomActivity(2401, Extreme Programming)
6. #People(Room 2401, "=" , 0) => RoomActivity(2401, Idle)

Each of the rules also has a priority associated with it – so if more than one rule is true at the same time, exactly what the activity in the room is determined using the priorities of the rules. If two rules are true at the same time and they have the same priority, then one of them is picked at random.

Even the context concerning the number of people in the room is an inferred context. So, the Room Activity Context Provider has to keep track of these entered and exited context events and infer the number of people in the room based on these events. Whenever the Room Activity Context Provider deduces a change in the activity in the room, it sends an event with the new activity.

We found that a fairly small set of rules are sufficient for deducing the activity in a room in most circumstances. The Room Activity Context Provider did accurately deduce the activity in the room most of the times. This proves, at least empirically, that rule-based synthesizers are fairly useful in deducing some types of contexts.

The middleware provides mechanisms for developers to specify the rules of inference for these Synthesizers very easily. The developer can browse the ontology to get the terminology used in the environments. He can then make use of this terminology to frame the rules. The middleware also abstracts away many tasks like getting references to appropriate Context Providers, querying them or listening to their event channels and sending context events at appropriate times. The developer is thus free to concentrate on the task of writing the rules.

Synthesizers that Learn. Rule based synthesizers have the disadvantage that they require explicit definition of rules by humans. They are also not flexible and can't adapt to changing circumstances. Making use of machine learning techniques to deduce the higher-level context enables us to get around this problem.

One type of context that is extremely difficult to sense is the mood of a user. It is difficult to write rules for predicting user mood since each user is different. There are such a large number of factors that can influence a user's mood. We attempted to use a learning mechanism that took some possible factors into account like his location, the time of day, which other people are in the room with him, the weather outside and how his stock portfolio is faring.. Our User Mood Context Provider uses the Naïve Bayes algorithm for predicting user mood. We make use of past contexts to train the learner. During the training phase, we ask the user for his mood periodically. We construct a training example by finding the values of the features (ie. location, weather, etc.) for each time the user entered his mood. We train the learner for a week. Once the training phase is over, the learner can predict the mood of the user given the values of the feature contexts (which are represented as predicates). The result of a Naïve Bayes algorithm is probabilistic. It would be possible to retain the probabilities associated with different user moods and thus some form of fuzzy logic or probabilistic reasoning in handling these contexts. However, we just consider the mood with the highest probability and assume that to be true.

We found that this user mood predictor did predict the moods of user fairly well in different situations after some training. Humans are fairly repetitive creatures –their moods in different contexts follow certain predictable patterns. Of course, the predictions are not always perfect – we can only make good guesses based on the information we have available. It is quite difficult to take into account all possible factors that can influence the mood of a user.

The middleware aids the training and the actual operation of the agent. It provides support for many tasks like getting references to appropriate Context Providers, querying them or listening to their event channels and sending context events at appropriate times. The developer is thus free to concentrate on the task of learning.

5.5   Context Consumers (or Context-Aware Applications)

Context Consumers are agents that consume various types of contexts and adapt their behavior depending on the current context. As mentioned earlier, consumers can obtain contexts by either querying a Context Provider or by listening for events that are sent by Context Providers. Our middleware makes it very easy to develop and deploy context aware applications. It is easy for applications to get the contexts they require to make decisions. In our infrastructure, Context Consumers get references to Context Providers using the Context Provider Lookup Service.

Specifying Context-Sensitive Behavior. One common way in which applications can be made context sensitive is to specify actions to be performed whenever the context of the environment changes. Thus, whenever the context of the environment changes, the application reconfigures itself to meet the requirements of the new context. For example, a jukebox application in a smart room may reconfigure itself whenever a person enters or leaves the room by changing the song it is playing, the volume of the song or the speakers it uses to play the music. This application model is based on the ECA (event-condition-action) execution model[24].

Our context framework provides a number of ways for developers to specify different behaviors in different contexts. Just as in the case of Context Synthesizers, there are two broad ways in which these behaviors can be described. The first is to allow application developers to write rules that indicate what actions are to be performed in different contexts. The second is to use machine learning approaches that learn what actions to perform in different contexts.

Rule-Based Approaches. Using rules to specify application behavior is a very simple way to make applications context-sensitive. These rules consist of conditions and actions. Whenever the context of the environment changes, the conditions in all the rules are evaluated. If any of the conditions become true, then the actions corresponding to these rules are evaluated. Each rule is also associated with a certain priority, which is used in case there is a conflict in the actions.

The conditions in the rules are expressions in some form of logic like first order logic, temporal logic, description logic, higher order logic, fuzzy logic, etc. Our framework for context awareness is flexible enough to allow the use of any form of logic for writing rules. Depending on the kind of logic used to express the condition, different evaluation engines are used to decide whether a condition is true or false.

The middleware makes it very easy to develop rule-based Context Consumers. These agents have a configuration file that lists all the rules. Actions are specified as methods in the agent that are invoked when the context becomes true. The middleware provides support for getting references to appropriate Context Providers, getting context information from them, evaluating the rules and invoking appropriate methods in different contexts. It also makes available different evaluation engines in the form of libraries, which aid in the reasoning process. The job of the agent developer is, thus, very simple. He can concentrate on writing the rules that govern agent behavior without worrying about other things.

A sample configuration file for a jukebox application agent is shown in Table 1. This agent plays appropriate music in a room depending on who is in the room, what the weather is outside and how the stock portfolio of the user is faring. The rules of this agent are written in first order logic.

In our current implementation, developers of context-aware applications need to write such a configuration file (using the appropriate kind of logic) for describing behavior in different contexts. However, we are also working on a graphical interface, which simplifies the developer's task. This graphical interface would show the various types of contexts available (as defined in the ontology), allow the developer to construct complex rules involving these contexts in different types of logics and also present him with a list of possible behaviors of the application for these different contexts.

Another example, which uses temporal logic, is a slideshow agent. One of its rules is that it starts playing a particular ppt file on a large plasma screen when Chris enters the room and continues playing until the Activity in the room is Meeting. This rule is written as:

```
Condition: Location(Chris, Entered, 2401) AND (TRUE UNTIL Ac-
tivity(2401, Meeting))

Action: PlayOnPlasmaScreen("scenery.ppt")

Priority: 2
```

Machine Learning Approaches. The disadvantage of using rule-based approaches for developing context sensitive applications is that they are not flexible and cannot adapt themselves to changing circumstances. Use of machine learning techniques helps us get around this problem. Developers need not specify the behavior of applications in different scenarios; the application can learn the most appropriate behavior in different contexts.

A variety of machine learning techniques can be employed for learning appropriate behavior. These include Bayesian approaches, neural networks, Support Vector Machines, various clustering algorithms, reinforcement learning, etc.

Learning can take place either in a batch-processing or in an online fashion. Batch-processsing approaches (like Naïve Bayes, etc.) require a number of training examples. Gaia stores all events that are sent in the environment in a database. These include events with context information, events that describe user and application actions, etc. The stored past events act as training examples for our learner. This approach is especially useful for learning user behavior by studying his actions over a period of time. If user behavior is learned well, applications can take proactive actions on behalf of the user depending on the context and thus save the user's valuable time.

Online learning mechanisms (like reinforcement learning) can learn their concepts while operating in the environment. These mechanisms involve trying out different actions, observing the user's reaction to these actions and learning which actions are better in different situations. For example, we have developed an intelligent Notification Service that tries to learn the most appropriate times to send different types of notifications. It can send different types of notifications like stock prices, weather

Table 1. First Order Rules for deducing activity in a room

```
ThereExists(Person) x Location(x, Entered, 2401).
PlayWelcomeMessage().
Priority:1.

Location(Manuel, Entered, 2401) OR Location(Chris, Entered,
2401).
ShowInterface().
Priority:1.

Location(Manuel,In, 2401).
PlayRockMusic().
Priority:1.

Location(Manuel,In,2401)AND Temperature(Champaign,>,50)
PlaySoftMusic()
Priority:2

Location(Bhaskar,In, 2401) AND Location(Chris,In, 2401)
PlayPopMusic()
Priority:2

Location(Bhaskar,In, 2401) AND Location(Chris,In, 2401) AND
Temperature(Champaign,>,50)
PlayHiphopMusic()
Priority:4

Location(Bhaskar,In, 2401) AND
StockPrice(MSFT,>,50)
PlayHappyMusic()
Priority:2
```

information, news headlines and error messages on different kinds of media like on tickertape, by speech or by email. The Notification Service learns by sending a notification in some situation and observing the user's reaction to the notification. The user can give feedback about the notification by rating its usefulness (or even by stopping the notification midway). Depending on the feedback of the user, the Notification Service either increases or decreases the probability that it would send the same type of notification in a similar situation again.

As in the case of rules, the middleware provides support for getting references to appropriate Context Providers, getting context information from them, evaluating the concept learned and invoking appropriate actions in different contexts. It also provides libraries and utilities that aid the learning process.

5.6 Context Provider Lookup Service

The Context Provider Lookup Service allows searches for different context providers. Providers advertise the set of contexts they provide with the Context Provider Lookup Service. This advertisement is in the form of a first order expression. Agents can query the Lookup Service for a context provider that provides contextual information it needs. The Lookup Service checks if any of the context providers can provide what the agent needs and returns the results to the application.

For example, a location context provider that tracks Bob's location around the building advertises itself as $\forall_{Location} y\ Location(\ Bob,\ In,\ y)$. An application that wants to know when Bob enters room 3231, would send the query *Location(Bob, In, Room 3231)*to the Lookup Service. The Lookup Service sees that the context provider does provide the context that the application is interested in (the advertisement is a superset of the query) and returns a reference to the context provider to the application.

5.7   Context History

Applications can make use of not just the current context, but also past contexts to adapt their behavior for better interacting with users. We thus store contexts continuously, as they occur, in a database. The Gaia event service allows event channels to be "persistent", ie. all events sent on these channels are stored in a database along with a timestamp indicating when the event was sent.

It is thus possible to store all context events (or a certain subset of them) in a database. Since all context events have a well-determined structure (as given by the ontology), it is relatively simple to automatically develop schemas for storing them into a database. Storing past contexts enables the use of data mining to learn and discover patterns in user behavior, room activities and other contexts. This sort of data mining can, for example, be used in security applications like intrusion detection, where any observed behavior way outside the ordinary can be construed as an intrusion.

6   Ontologies for Semantic Interoperability

Ubiquitous Computing Environments feature a large number of autonomous agents. Various types of middleware (based on CORBA, Java RMI, SOAP, etc.) have been developed that enable communication between different entities. However, existing middleware have no facilities to ensure semantic interoperability between the different entities. Since agents are autonomous, it is infeasible to expect all of them to attach the same semantics to different concepts on their own. This is especially true for context information, since different agents could have a different understanding of the current context and can use different terms and concepts to describe context.

In order to enable semantic interoperability between different agents, we take recourse to methods used in the Semantic Web[14]. Ontologies establish a joint terminology between members of a community of interest. These members can be humans or automated agents. Each agent in our environment uses the vocabulary and concepts defined in one or more ontologies. When two different agents talk to each other, they know which ontology the other agent uses and can thus understand the semantics of what the other agent is saying.

Another advantage of using standard technologies employed in the Semantic Web for describing semantics is scalability. Since agents in our environment use ontologies described in the same language (DAML+OIL) as those on the web, we enable semantic interoperability between our agents and other external agents (in other environments or on the web).External agents can refer to ontologies used in our environment while interacting with our agents. They can, thus, find out what terms and concepts are used by our agents and communicate meaningfully with them. Similarly, agents in our environment can refer to the ontologies used by external agents while communicating with them. The use of ontologies, thus, enables agents in different ubiquitous computing environments to have a common vocabulary and a common set of concepts while interacting with one another.

6.1   Ontologies in Gaia

We have developed ontologies for describing various concepts in a Ubiquitous Computing Environment. We have ontologies that describe the different kinds of agents and their properties. These ontologies define different kinds of applications, services, devices, users, data sources and other agents. They also define all terms used in the environment and the relationships between different terms. They establish axioms on the properties of these agents and terms (written in Description Logic) that must always be satisfied.

We also have ontologies that define the structure of contextual information. These are useful for checking the validity of context information. They also makes it easier to specify the behavior of context-aware applications since we know the types of contexts that are available and their structure. They ensure that all agents in the system have the same semantic understanding of different pieces of contextual information.

6.2   The Ontology Server

All the ontologies in Gaia are maintained by an Ontology Server. Other agents in Gaia contact the Ontology Server to get descriptions of agents in the environment, meta-information about context or definitions of various terms used in Gaia. It is also possible to support semantic queries (for instance, classification of individuals or subsumption of concepts). Such semantic queries require the use of a reasoning engine that uses description logics like the FaCT reasoning engine[21]. We plan on providing support for such queries in the near future.

The Ontology Server also provides an interface for adding new concepts to existing ontologies. This allows new types of contexts to be introduced and used in the environment at any time. The Ontology Server ensures that any new definitions are logically consistent with existing definitions.

The use of ontologies also makes it possible for agents in different environments to inter-operate. To support such an inter-operation, mappings need to be developed between concepts defined in the ontologies of the two environments. We plan on developing a framework for supporting such inter-operation very soon.

6.3   Ontologies for Smoother Interaction between Agents

Since the ontologies clearly define the structure of contextual information, different agents can exchange different types of context information easily. Context Consumer agents can get the structure of contexts they are interested in from the Ontology Server. They can then frame appropriate queries to Context Providers to get the contexts they need.

Context Providers and Context Synthesizers can also get the structure of contexts that they provide from the Ontology Server. So, they know the kinds of queries they can expect. They also know the structure of events that they need to send on event channels.

Finally, ontologies also help the developer when he is writing rules or developing learning mechanisms for context aware agents. The developer has access to the set of terms and concepts that describe contextual information. He can thus use the most appropriate terms and concepts while developing context aware agents.

7   Implementation

All agents in the Context Infrastructure are implemented on top of CORBA and are a part of Gaia. This means they can be instantiated in any machine in the system, can access event channels, can be moved from one machine to another and can be discovered using standard mechanisms like the CORBA Naming Service and the CORBA Trading Service. The Context History Service uses the MySQL database for storing past contexts.

We currently support a number of reasoning mechanisms including many sorted first order logic and linear time propositional temporal logic. For reasoning in first order logic, we use XSB[19] as the reasoning engine. XSB is a more powerful form of Prolog which uses tabling and indexing to improve performance and also allows limited higher order logic reasoning. We use the many-sorted logic model where quantification is performed only over a specific domain of values. The ontology defines various sets of values (like Person, Location, Stock Symbol, etc). Thus, the Person set consists of the names of all people in our system. The Location set consists of all valid locations in our system (like room numbers and hallways). Stock Symbol consists of all stock symbols that the system is interested in (e.g. IBM, MSFT, SUNW, etc.). Each of these sets is finite. Quantification of variables is done over the values of one of these sets. Since quantification is performed only over finite sets, evaluations of expressions with quantifications will always terminate. More discussion on the issues of decidability and expressiveness can be found in [10][11][12].

For temporal logic, we have developed our own reasoning engine that is based on Templog[23]. Templog is a logic programming language, similar to Prolog, which allows the use of temporal operators. We restrict the power of this logic to propositional logic, which makes it decidable and also simpler to evaluate.

We also currently support some machine learning mechanisms, viz. Naïve Bayes learning and reinforcement learning. The Naïve Bayes approach involves learning conditional probabilities between different events from a large number of training examples. Thus given a certain context, it gives the conditional probability that some action should be performed or some other context should be true. The reinforcement learning approach involves trying to learn appropriate actions based on user feedback.

An ontology of all terms used in the context infrastructure has been developed in DAML+OIL. The Ontology Server uses the FaCT reasoning engine[21] for checking the validity of context expressions.

We have implemented a number of Context Providers in our system such as providers of location, weather, stock price, calendar contexts and authentication contexts. We also have some context synthesizers as described earlier. Some examples are a Synthesizer which deduces the mood of a user using Naïve Bayes learning; and another which deduces the activity in the room using rules. The middleware has allowed us to develop a number of context aware applications very easily. Some context-aware applications we have developed are a context-sensitive jukebox, a context-sensitive chat application[18] and a context-sensitive notification service.

One of the main features of our middleware is that it greatly helps in the development of context-aware applications. The benefits of using the middleware include reduced development times of context-aware applications and great ease in specifying complex behaviors of these applications. Developers do not have to worry about the details of getting contextual information from different sources or the mechanics of triggering different actions in different situations. This helps in rapid development and prototyping of applications.

The middleware also makes it pretty simple to insert new sensors and new Context Synthesizers, which infer different contexts, into the system. Since all the terms used in the environment are defined in the ontology, it is easy to frame rules for inferring contexts based on these terms. The developer does not have to worry about not using inappropriate terms or concepts, since he can refer to the definitions in the ontology when in doubt.

8   Related Work

A lot of work has been done in the area of context-aware computing in the past few years. Seminal work has been done by Anind Dey, et al. in defining context-aware computing, identifying what kind of support was required for building context aware applications and developing a toolkit that enabled rapid prototyping of context-aware applications[1]. While the Context Toolkit does provide a starting point for applications to make use of contextual information, it does not provide much help on how to reason about contexts. It does not provide any generic mechanism for writing rules about contexts, inferring higher-level contexts or organizing the wide range of possible contexts in a structured format.

In [2], Jason Hong, et. al., make the distinction between a toolkit and an infrastructure. An infrastructure, according to Hong, is a well-established, pervasive, reliable set of technologies providing a foundation for other systems. Our middleware for context-awareness builds on Hong's notion of an infrastructure and provides a foundation for developing context-aware applications easily.

Bouquet, et al. [4] address the problem of contexts in autonomous, heterogeneous distributed applications, where ach entity has its own notion of context depending on its viewpoint. To interact with other entities, an entity should know the relationship between its viewpoint and other entities' viewpoint. Our middleware uses ontologies to achieve this inter-operability in a more generic fashion. Paul Castro and his colleagues [5] have worked on developing "fusion services" which extract and infer useful context information from sensor data using Bayesian networks. Our middleware provides a more generic framework where such learning approaches can be used.

Terry Winograd compares different architectures for context[6] and proposes one that uses a centralized Event Heap[7]. Our system, however, provides a framework where distributed reasoning can take place. In [3], Brumitt, et al describe their experiences with multi-modal interactions in context-aware environments and how such an environment can respond automatically to different contexts. Our middleware provides an easy way for developers to specify how an environment should automatically respond to different contexts.

Reconfigurable Context-Sensitive Middleware [22] provides context-sensitive applications with adaptive object containers (ADCs) for runtime context data acquisition, monitoring and detection. Applications can specify behavior using a context-aware IDL. Our middleware provides a more generic way of specifying the behavior of context-aware applications using different reasoning and learning mechanisms.

9   Future Work

There are a number of possible enhancements to our middleware. A new approach to developing context-sensitive applications is by modeling them as state machines. This allows their behavior to be determined by specific sequences of context changes. State machine approaches to modeling applications are useful especially when a sequence of changes in context needs to trigger a sequence of actions by the application.

We have not yet tackled the issues of privacy and security. Some context information may be private and hence, all agents may not have access to them. The ontology can potentially encode such privacy and security constraints. It can thus be used to ensure that the rules developed for applications do not violate security restrictions.

We are also working on better user interfaces for developing context-aware applications, so that any ordinary user can program his or her own context-aware agent. These interfaces can make use of the ontologies to get the structures of different types of contexts and thus allow the user to develop rules with context information.

One aspect which we haven't studied as yet is the usability of context-aware applications. How will ordinary users deal with applications that try to learn their behaviors and their preferences? Will users take the time to write rules for specifying context-sensitive behavior of applications? Will users respond positively to the fact that the behavior of applications can change according to the context, and is hence not as predictable as current applications?

10   Conclusion

In this paper, we have described our middleware for developing context-aware applications. The middleware is based on a predicate model of context. This model enables agents to be developed that either use rules or machine learning approaches to decide their behavior in different contexts. The middleware uses ontologies to ensure that different agents in the environment have the same semantic understanding of different context information. This allows better semantic interoperability between different agents, as well as between different ubiquitous computing environments. Our middleware allows rapid prototyping of context-sensitive applications. We have developed a number of context-sensitive agents on our middleware very easily.

References

1. Dey, A.K., et al. "A Conceptual Framework and a Toolkit for Supporting the Rapid Proto-typing of Context-Aware Applications", anchor article of a special issue on Context-Aware Computing, Human-Computer Interaction (HCI) Journal, Vol. 16, 2001.
2. Hong, J. I., et al. "An Infrastructure Approach to Context-Aware Computing". HCI Journal, '01, Vol. 16

3. Shafer, S.A.N., et al. "Interaction Issues in Context-Aware Interactive Environments." Special issue on Context-Aware Computing, Human-Computer Interaction (HCI) Journal, Vol. 16, 2001.
4. Bouquet, P., et al. "Context-Aware Distributed Applications" IRST Technical Report 0101-04, Instituto Trentino di Cultura, January 2001
5. Castro, P., et al. "Managing Context for Internet Video Conferences: The Multimedia Internet Recorder and Archive". Multimedia and Computer Networks 2000, San Jose, CA, January 2000
6. Winograd T. "Architectures for Context" In Human-Computer Interaction (HCI) Journal, '01, Vol. 16.
7. Johanson, B., et al. "The Event Heap: An Enabling Infrastructure for Interactive Workspaces" https://graphics.stanford.edu/papers/eheap/
8. Pascoe, J., et al. "Issues in Developing Context-Aware Computing" Proceedings of the International Symposium on Handheld and Ubiquitous Computing, Sept. 1999, Springer-Verlag, pp. 208-221.
9. Korkea-aho, M. "Context-Aware Applications Survey", http://www.hut.fi/~mkorkeaa/doc/context-aware.html
10. Shmueli O., "Decidability and expressiveness aspects of logic queries", Proceedings of the sixth ACM SIGACT-SIGMOD-SIGART Symposium on Principles of database systems, March 23 - 25, 1987, San Diego, CA USA , pp 237 - 24
11. Chandra, A.K., et al. "Horn Clauses Queries and Generalization", J Logic Programming 1985
12. Jarke, M., et al. "An Optimizing PROLOG Front-End to a Relational Query System", in Proceedings of ACM SIGMOD '84 Conference, pp296-306, Boston, MA, June 1984
13. Schilit, W. N., "A Context-Aware System Architecture for Mobile Distributed Computing", PhD Thesis, Columbia University, May 1995.
14. Berners-Lee T., et al. "A new form of Web content that is meaningful to computers will unleash a revolution of new possibilities" http://www.scientificamerican.com/2001/0501issue/0501berners-lee.html
15. Guarino N. "Formal Ontology in Information Systems" Proc. of FOIS'98, Trento, Italy
16. Román, M., et al, "Gaia: A Middleware Infrastructure to Enable Active Spaces". In *IEEE Pervasive Computing*, pp. 74-83, Oct-Dec 2002..
17. Hess, C.K.,et al, "Building Applications for Ubiquitous Computing Environments" In *International Conference on Pervasive Computing (Pervasive 2002)*, pp. 16-29, Zurich, Switzerland, August 26-28, 2002.
18. Ranganathan, A., et al, "ConChat: A Context-Aware Chat Program" . In *IEEE Pervasive Computing*, pp. 52-58, July-Sept 2002.
19. XSB – http://xsb.sourceforge.net
20. Harmelon, F., et al " Reference Description of the DAML+OIL ontology markup language", http://www.daml.org/2001/03/reference.html
21. Horrocks, I., "The FaCT System", Automated Reasoning with Analytic Tableaux and Related Methods, 1998
22. Yau, S., et al, "Reconfigurable Context-Sensitive Middleware for Pervasive Computing". In *IEEE Pervasive Computing*, pp. 33-40, July-Sept 2002.
23. Abadi, M. et al. "Temporal Logic Programming" Journal of Symbolic Computation, 8:277-295, 1989
24. Dayal, U., et al. "The Architecture of an Active Database Management System". ACM SIGMOD Conference 1989, pp 215-224

Adaptable Architectural Middleware
for Programming-in-the-Small-and-Many

Marija Mikic-Rakic and Nenad Medvidovic

Computer Science Department, University of Southern California
Los Angeles, CA 90089-0781 USA
{marija,neno}@usc.edu

Abstract. A recent emergence of small, resource-constrained, and highly-mobile computing platforms presents numerous new challenges for software developers. We refer to development in this new setting as programming-in-the-small-and-many (Prism). This paper provides a description and evaluation of a middleware intended to support software architecture-based development in the Prism setting. The middleware, called Prism-MW, provides highly efficient and scalable implementation-level support for the key aspects of Prism application architectures. Additionally, Prism-MW is easily extensible to support different application requirements suitable for the Prism setting. Prism-MW is accompanied with design, analysis, deployment, and run-time monitoring tool support. It has been applied in a number of applications and used as an educational tool in a graduate-level embedded systems course. Recently, Prism-MW has been successfully evaluated by a major industrial organization for use in one of their key distributed embedded systems. Our experience with the middleware indicates that the principles of architecture-based software development can be successfully, and flexibly, applied in the Prism setting.

1 Introduction

The software systems of today are rapidly growing in size, complexity, amount of distribution, and numbers of users. We have recently witnessed a rapid increase in the speed and capacity of hardware, a decrease in its cost, the emergence of the Internet as a critical resource, and a proliferation of hand-held consumer electronics devices. In turn, this has resulted in an increased demand for software applications, outpacing our ability to produce them, both in terms of their sheer numbers and the sophistication demanded of them. One can now envision a number of complex software development scenarios involving fleets of mobile devices used in environment monitoring, freeway-traffic management, damage surveys in times of natural disaster, and so on. Such scenarios present daunting technical challenges: effective understanding of existing or prospective software configurations; rapid composability and dynamic reconfigurability of software; mobility of hardware, data, and code; scalability to large amounts of data, numbers of data types, and numbers of devices; and heterogeneity of the software executing on each device and across devices. Furthermore, software often must execute on "small" devices, characterized by highly constrained resources such as limited power, low network bandwidth, slow CPU speed, limited memory, and small display size. We refer to the development of software systems in the described setting as _pro-_

M. Endler and D. Schmidt (Eds.): Middleware 2003, LNCS 2672, pp. 162–181, 2003.

gramming-in-the-small-and-many (Prism), in order to distinguish it from the commonly adopted software engineering paradigm of programming-in-the-large (PitL) [6].

Recent studies [11,16,33] have shown that a promising approach to developing software systems in the Prism setting is to employ the principles of software architectures. *Software architectures* provide abstractions for representing the structure, behavior, and key properties of a software system [29]. They are described in terms of software *components* (computational elements) [36], software *connectors* (interaction elements) [19], and their *configurations* (also referred to as *topologies*) [18].

Software architectures provide design-level models and guidelines for composing software systems. For these models and guidelines to be truly useful in a development setting, they must be accompanied by support for their implementation [15,28]. This is particularly important in the Prism setting: Prism systems may be highly distributed, decentralized, mobile, and long-lived, increasing the risk of architectural drift [25] unless there is a clear relationship between the architecture and its implementation.

This paper describes the design and evaluation of *Prism-MW*, a middleware developed to support the implementation of software architectures in the Prism setting. We say that the middleware is *architectural* because it provides programming language-level constructs for implementing software architecture-level concepts such as component, connector, configuration, and event. This allows software developers to directly transfer architectural decisions into implementations, thus distinguishing Prism-MW from existing middleware solutions.

Another key contribution of Prism-MW is its highly modular design that employs an extensive separation of concerns. This results in a middleware that is flexible, efficient, scalable, and extensible. The middleware is *flexible* in its support for independent selection, variation, and composition of implementation-level concerns. The middleware is *efficient* in its size, speed, and overhead added to an application. The middleware is *scalable* in the numbers of components, connectors, events, execution threads, and hardware devices. Finally, the middleware is easily *extensible* to support new development concerns and situations in the Prism setting.

These properties of Prism-MW have been successfully evaluated using a series of example applications, benchmark tests performed both within our group and by external users, and a large-scale feasibility study conducted in collaboration with an industrial organization. At the same time, our evaluations of Prism-MW have suggested several areas of improvement, including an entirely novel approach to designing architectural middleware. We intend to explore these issues in our future work.

The rest of the paper is organized as follows. Section 2 presents our objectives for Prism-MW. Section 3 presents the design and implementation of Prism-MW's core capabilities, and evaluates them with respect to the objectives. Section 4 discusses the extensibility of Prism-MW and presents several specific extensions completed to date. Section 5 describes our tool support. Section 6 presents additional evaluation of the middleware conducted in collaboration with external users. The paper concludes with overviews of related and future work.

2 Middleware Objectives

As discussed above, there are a number of significant challenges faced by software developers in the Prism setting. We believe those challenges to fall within four general categories, comprising our objectives for Prism-MW. Three of the four objectives directly derive from the "Prism" acronym: support for _pr_ogramming (i.e., development) of Prism applications on _m_any _s_mall computing platforms. We consider these three to be the core objectives. The fourth objective reflects the variation and constant evolution of development situations in the Prism setting. Each objective is further discussed below.

- _Architectural abstractions_ – A key observation guiding this research is that an effective way of supporting the development of Prism applications is to explicitly focus on software architectures [11,16,33]. _Pr_ism-MW should thus provide direct implementation-level support for architectural abstractions (components, connectors, communication events, and so on).
- _Efficiency_ – Pri_sm_-MW should impose minimal overhead on an application's execution. Our current goal is to enable efficient execution of applications on platforms with varying characteristics (e.g., speed, capacity, network bandwidth). The ultimate goal is to extend this support to include efficient access to and sharing of hardware resources (e.g., battery, peripheral devices).
- _Scalability_ – Pris_m_-MW should be scalable in order to effectively manage the large numbers of devices, execution threads, components, connectors, and communication events present in Prism systems.
- _Extensibility_ – There are several additional capabilities that may be required for different (classes of) Prism applications. These include awareness, mobility, dynamic reconfigurability, security, real-time support, and delivery guarantees [2,3,7,11,12,24]. Prism-MW should be easily extensible to provide support for (arbitrary combinations of) these capabilities.

3 Middleware Core

In this section we discuss the design, implementation, and evaluation of Prism-MW's core capabilities. The discussion is organized around the three core objectives.

3.1 Architectural Abstractions

Prism-MW's core supports architectural abstractions by providing classes for representing each architectural element, with methods for creating, manipulating, and destroying the element. These abstractions enable direct mapping between an architecture and its implementation. Figure 1 shows the class design view of Prism-MW. The shaded classes constitute the middleware core, with dark gray classes being relevant to the application developer. Our goal was to keep the core compact, reflected in the fact that it contains only eight classes and six interfaces. Furthermore, the design of the core (and the entire middleware) is highly modular: the only dependencies among classes are via interfaces and inheritance; the only exception is the _Architecture_ class, which contains multiple _Bricks_ for reasons that are explained below.

3.1.1 Middleware Core's Design

Brick is an abstract class that encapsulates common features of its subclasses (_Architecture, Component,_ and _Connector_). The _Architecture_ class records the configuration of its constituent components and connectors, and provides facilities for their addition, removal, and reconnection, possibly at system runtime. A distributed applica-

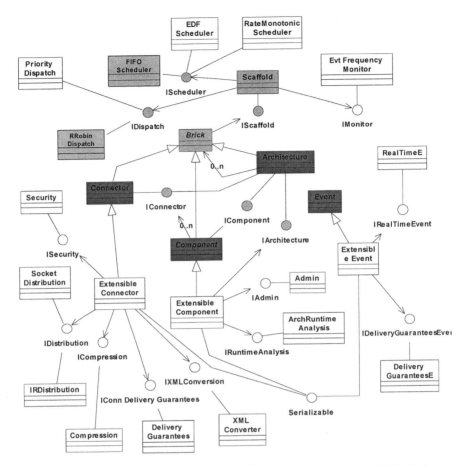

Fig. 1. UML class design view of Prism-MW. Middleware core classes are highlighted.

tion is implemented as a set of interacting *Architecture* objects. *Component*s in an architecture communicate by exchanging *Event*s, which are routed by *Connector*s. In order to support different topologies, each component may be attached to an arbitrary number of connectors. In order to support the needs of dynamically changing applications, each Prism-MW connector is capable of servicing varying numbers of components [21]. This property of connectors, coupled with event-based interaction, has proven to be a highly-effective mechanism for addressing system reconfigurability.

Each subclass of the *Brick* class has an associated interface. The *IArchitecture* interface exposes a *weld* method for attaching components and connectors to one another. The *IComponent* interface exposes *send* and *handle* methods used for exchanging events. We have implemented several versions of this interface to support asynchronous, synchronous unicast, and synchronous multicast of events. The *IConnector* interface provides a *handle* method for routing of events. To address the needs of different applications in the Prism setting, we have implemented two versions of this interface, supporting both symmetric (i.e., peer-to-peer) and asymmetric (i.e., request-response) interaction. Each *Architecture* object implements both *IConnector* and *IComponent* interfaces, thus allowing construction of complex components and connectors with internal architectures.

Finally, Prism-MW's core associates the *IScaffold* interface with every *Brick*. Scaffolds are used to schedule events for delivery (via the *IScheduler* interface) and pool threads (via the *IDispatch* interface) in a decoupled manner. Prism-MW's core provides default implementations of *IScheduler* and *IDispatch*: FIFO and round-robin, respectively. The novel aspect of our design is that this separation of concerns allows us to select the most suitable event scheduling policy independently of the dispatching policy for a given application. Additionally, dispatching and scheduling are decoupled from the *Architecture*, allowing one to easily compose many sub-architectures (each with its own scheduling and dispatching policies) in a single application. *IScaffold* also directly aids architectural awareness [2] by allowing probing of the runtime behavior of a *Brick*.

To date, Prism-MW's core has been implemented in Java JVM and KVM [35], C++ and Embedded Visual C++ (EVC++). Each implementation of the middleware core is quite small, averaging 1,750 SLOC, which aids Prism-MW's understandability and ease of use.[1]

3.1.2 Using Prism-MW

Prism-MW's core provides the necessary support for developing arbitrarily complex applications, so long as they rely on the provided default facilities (e.g., event scheduling, dispatching, and routing) and stay within a single address space. The first step a developer takes is to subclass from the *Component* class for all components in the architecture and to implement their application-specific methods. The next step is to instantiate the *Architecture* class and define the needed instances of thus created components, and of connectors selected from the reusable connector library.[2] Finally, attaching component and connector instances into a configuration is achieved by using the *weld* method of the *Architecture* class. This process can be partially automated using our tool support described in Section 5.

For illustration, Figure 2 shows a simple usage scenario of the Java version of Prism-MW. The application consists of two components communicating through a single connector. The *DemoArch* class's *main* method instantiates components and connectors and composes (*weld*s) them into a configuration. Figure 2 also demonstrates event-based communication between the two components. *Component A* creates and sends an event, in response to which *Component B* sends a response event. An event need not identify its recipient components; they are uniquely defined by the topology of the architecture and routing policies of the employed connectors [16].

3.2 Efficiency

Since Prism applications frequently run on resource-constrained devices, with low amounts of memory (e.g., 256 KB on the Palm Pilot) and slow processing speed, we have performed several optimizations on Prism-MW's core. While there are common techniques for ensuring efficient implementations of distributed systems, Prism-MW

---

[1] The interfaces used in Prism-MW's core are directly supported in Java. In C++ and EVC++ they have been implemented using abstract classes with pure virtual functions.

[2] Recall that Prism-MW's core provides several connectors through the implementations of the *IConnector* interface.

presented unique challenges in this regard because of its objective of *directly* supporting architectural abstractions in highly resource-constrained settings. Some of the optimization techniques we applied are novel, while others have been adapted from existing work. A contribution of our work on optimizing Prism-MW lies in their combination: it results in a highly efficient architectural middleware that introduces minimal overhead in terms of dynamic memory usage and shows good performance. In the remainder of this section we describe these optimizations and provide a series of benchmark results that evaluate them.

3.2.1 Initial Implementation

In our initial implementation of Prism-MW's core, each component maintained dynamically allocated queues of its incoming and outgoing events. Each component also owned an internal thread of control that was used to process incoming events and place outgoing events on the queue (as implemented in *IComponent*'s *send* and *handle* methods, respectively). The encompassing *Architecture*'s dispatcher then ensured that the outgoing events are routed to their destinations. Furthermore, the *Architecture*'s implementation of the *IScheduler* interface was trivial since all the scheduling was handled at the individual component level. How-

Architecture initialization

```
class DemoArch {
  static public void main(String argv[]) {
  Architecture arch = new Architecture ("DEMO ");
    // create components here
    ComponentA a = new ComponentA ("A");
    ComponentB b = new ComponentB ("B");

    // create connectors here
    Connector conn = new Connector("Conn");

    // add components and connectors to the architectu
    arch.addComponent(a);
    arch.addComponent(b);
    arch.addConnector(conn);

    // establish the interconnections
    arch.weld(a, conn);
    arch.weld(b, conn);
    arch.start();
  }
}
```

Component A sends an event

```
e - new Event ("Event_a");
e.addParameter("param_1", p1);
send (e);
```

Component B handles the event and sends a response

```
public void handle(event e)
{
  if (e.equals("Event_a")) {
    ...
    event e1= new Event("Response_to_a");
    e1.addParameter("response", resp);
    send(e1);
  }...
}
```

Fig. 2. Illustration of application implementation fragments.

ever, this implementation had several problems, including unacceptable application size and speed. Prism-MW's highly modular design allowed us to significantly improve efficiency by radically altering the manner in which events are exchanged and processed. At the same time, we were able to confine our modifications to the implementations of *IComponent* (specifically, its *send* method), *IScheduler*, and *IDispatch*. These modifications are discussed below.

3.2.2 Optimizing for Size and Speed

We observed that a large amount of dynamic system memory usage was a result of the exchange of events among components and connectors. We minimized the required memory for event passing by exchanging read-only events in the same address space by reference, rather than by copy. We further optimized memory usage by adopting a fixed-sized, circular array for storing all events in a single address space. This reduced overall memory usage by a factor of 20 or more over the initial solution described above [15].

Another modification addressed event processing. A pool of shepherd threads (implemented in Prism-MW core's *RoundRobinDispatcher* class) was introduced to handle events sent by any component in a given address space. The size of the thread pool is parameterized and, hence, adjustable. It should be noted that the concurrency management of the circular array used to implement the event queue slightly impacts the speed of processing by applying a producer-consumer algorithm to keep event production under control, and supply shepherd threads with a constant stream of events to process.

To process an event, a shepherd thread removes the event from the head of the queue. For local communication, the shepherd thread is run through the connector attached to the sending component; the connector dispatches the event to relevant components using the same thread (see Figure 3). If a recipient component generates further events, they are added to the tail of the event queue; different threads are

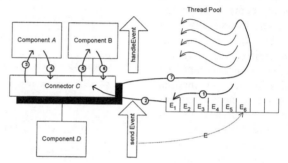

Fig. 3. Event dispatching in Prism-MW for a single address space. Steps (1)-(7) are performed by a single shepherd thread.

used for dispatching those events to their intended recipients. An alternative design, which required modification of only the *IDispatch* interface's implementation, allows separate threads to be used for dispatching an event from the connector to each intended recipient component (steps 3-6 in Figure 3). This increases parallelism, but also resource consumption, in the architecture. We are currently implementing and evaluating this design.

Prism-MW uses the same basic mechanism for communication that spans address spaces as it does for local communication: a shepherd thread transports the event from the queue to its recipients via a connector. However, in this case the connector is a specialized *DistributionConnector* (further discussed in Section 4.1), which manages a set of network (e.g., socket or infrared) connections. Thus, instead of routing the event through the components attached to the connector (steps 3-6 in Figure 3), the shepherd thread simply deposits the event on all communication ports managed by the *DistributionConnector*. As the event is propagated across the network, the *DistributionConnector* on each recepient device uses its internal thread to retrieve the incoming event from the communication port and place it on its local event queue.

This solution represents an adaptation of an existing worker thread pool technique [31] that results in several unique benefits:

1. By leveraging explicit architectural topology an event can be routed to multiple destinations using a single shepherd thread. This minimizes resource consumption, since events need not be tagged with their recipients;

2. We further optimize resource consumption by using a single event queue for storing both locally and remotely generated events; and
3. Since Prism-MW does not process local and remote events differently, and all routing is accomplished via the multiple and explicit software connectors, Prism-MW also allows for easy redeployment and redistribution of existing applications onto different hardware topologies.

3.2.3 Evaluation

The above optimizations have resulted in very light-weight Prism-MW implementations that have shown several orders of magnitude in performance improvement over the original implementation described above. More importantly, the performance of Prism-MW is now comparable to solutions using a plain programming language (PL): each Prism-MW event exchange causes five PL-level method invocations and, a comparatively much more expensive, context switch if the architecture is instantiated with more than one shepherd thread (roughly corresponding to steps 1-4 and 7 in Figure 3); analogous functionality would be accomplished in a PL with two invocations and, assuming concurrent processing is desired, a context switch. It should also be noted that it is unlikely that a plain PL could support a number of development situations for which Prism-MW is well suited (e.g., asynchronous event multicast) and due to which it introduces its performance overhead in the first place.

For illustration, we describe the results from one series of evaluations used to measure the size and performance of the Java Prism-MW implementation.[3] The benchmarking applications consisted of n (n = 1, 10, and 50) identical components communicating via a connector with a single component, but not with each other (Figure 3 shows such a scenario for n = 2). The applications used a pool of 10 shepherd threads and a queue of 1000 events (*q_size*). Between 1 and 100,000 simple (parameter-less)

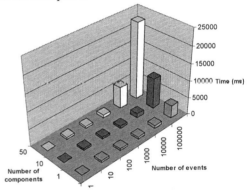

Fig. 4. The results of the performance benchmark.

events were sent asynchronously by the single component to the n components, resulting in between 1 and 5,000,000 handled events for the three applications. The results of this benchmark are shown in Figure 4.

Memory usage of Prism-MW core (*mw_mem*), recorded at the time of architecture initialization, is 4.6 KB. The overhead of a "base" Prism component (*comp_mem*), without any application-specific methods or state, is 0.8 KB. Memory overhead of creating and sending a single event (*evt_mem*) can be estimated using the following formula, obtained empirically:

evt_mem (in KB) = 0.16 + 0.24 * num_of_parameters

---

[3] The benchmarks presented throughout the paper were performed on an Intel Pentium III 700 MHz processor with 256 MB of RAM running JDK 1.1.8 on Microsoft Windows 2000.

The formula assumes that the parameters do not contain complex objects, but may contain simple objects (e.g., Java Integer or String).[4] Therefore, for example, the maximum memory overhead (assuming the event queue is full) induced by using Prism-MW in the largest benchmark application described above is approximately

mw_mem + num_comps * comp_mem + q_size * evt_mem =

4.6 + (51 * 0.8) + (1000 * (0.16 +(0.02 * 0))) ≈ 205 KB

3.3 Scalability

Prism-MW's modularity and separation of concerns directly aid its scalability in the numbers of supported devices, components, connectors, threads, and events. Prism-MW's support for large numbers of devices is a consequence of its support for large numbers of connectors. Similarly, its scalability in the number of events is fostered by scalability in the number of threads. The below discussion reflects these relationships.

3.3.1 Connectors and Devices

Unlike the existing middleware platforms (e.g., CORBA [40], LIME [12], .NET [20]), which support a single, implicit connector in a system, Prism-MW supports an arbitrary *number of connectors*. Prism-MW's explicit, flexible connectors allow an architecture to be deployed onto an arbitrary number of hosts, by repeated splitting of the connectors using the technique described in [5]. In a highly degenerate case, this would result in some devices serving only as routers, without containing any components. For this reason, the *number of devices* supported by Prism-MW is unlimited in principle. It should be noted, however, that the deployment choice directly affects efficiency: the performance gain of using the centralized event queue is achieved only if the components are residing in the same address space.

3.3.2 Components

Realistically, the *number of components* on a given device is limited and can be estimated using the following simple formula: n = (M - MS) / ACS, where *M* is the available memory on the device, *MS* is the memory occupied by Prism-MW, and *ACS* is the average component size. Recall from Section 3.2 that the impact of MS and the middleware-induced portion of ACS on the device's memory consumption is very low. We have performed a series of benchmarks in order to assess the behavior of Prism-MW in cases where large numbers of components is used.[5] Figure 5 shows the

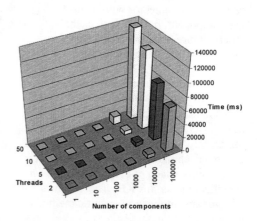

Fig. 5. The results of the scalability benchmark.

---

[4] In this sense, the measure represents minimum event overhead. Use of complex objects as event parameters is independent of the middleware, but is an application-level decision.

[5] We have run benchmark tests with up to 1,000,000 components.

results of a test in which a varying number of identical components (n) communicated with a single component through a connector. 100 parameter-less events were sent asynchronously by the single component to all other components, resulting in $n*100$ events being handled. We have also performed a benchmark test with two end-point components that communicated using a "chain" consisting of 100,000 components that simply forward incoming events through 100,001 connectors. The total round-trip time for a single event was 2.7 seconds.

3.3.3 Threads and Events

Prism-MW supports as many *threads* as the underlying platform supports. Finally, the *number of events* supported by Prism-MW is not limited by the middleware itself, but by the properties of the underlying hardware platform. This limit can be characterized by the following two parameters: (1) the maximum number of events that can simultaneously be present in a system and (2) the rate of event delivery. The maximum number of events is limited by the available memory on a given host (or set of hosts) and event size (recall Section 3.2), while the rate of event delivery depends on the CPU speed, the number of threads servicing the event queue, the ratio of event production to consumption by the components, and the network bandwidth for events that traverse machine boundaries.

4 Middleware Extensions

The design of Prism-MW's core provides extensive separation of concerns both via its explicit architectural constructs and its pervasive use of interfaces. The design is highly extensible. The unshaded classes and interfaces in Figure 1 show various extensions to the Prism-MW core we have built to date. These include support for architectural awareness, real-time, distributability, security, heterogeneity, data compression, delivery guarantees, and mobility [2,3,7,11,12,24]. In this section we describe our approach to supporting these extensions. Our experience indicates that other extensions can be easily added to the middleware in the same manner.

Our support for extensibility is built around the objective that Prism-MW's core remains unchanged. Instead, the core constructs (*Component, Connector,* and *Event*) are subclassed via specialized classes (*ExtensibleComponent, ExtensibleConnector,* and *ExtensibleEvent*), each of which composes a number of interfaces. Each interface can have multiple implementations, thus enabling selection of the desired functionality inside each instance of a given *Extensible* class. If an interface is installed in a given class instance, that instance will exhibit the behavior realized inside the interface's implementation. Multiple interfaces may be installed in a single *Extensible* class instance. In that case, the instance will exhibit the combined behavior of the installed interfaces.

Below we describe four classes of extensions supported by Prism-MW, with an explicit focus on the extensions we have completed to date. Further details on these extensions may be found in [21]. With the exception of Prism-MW's support for distribution (see below as well as Sections 5.2 and 6.3), we do not discuss the efficiency aspects of these extensions for two reasons. First, our primary goal to date has been to assess the extensibility of Prism-MW, and we have not optimized our implementations of many of its extensions. Secondly, in most cases our implementations employed known algorithms and techniques, such that any performance measures would be a function of those algorithms and techniques rather than the inherent properties of Prism-MW.

4.1 Connector Extensions

In order to address different aspects of interaction the *ExtensibleConnector* class composes a number of interfaces that support various interaction services. In turn, each interface can have multiple implementations.

Figure 1 shows five different interfaces we have implemented thus far. The *IDistribution* interface has been implemented in two classes, one supporting socket-based and the other infrared port-based inter-process communication (IPC). We refer to an *ExtensibleConnector* with instantiated *IDistribution* interface as *DistributionConnector*. A single *DistributionConnector* can be attached to an arbitrary numbers of remote hosts, as well as local components and connectors. Similarly to the "base" Prism-MW connector discussed in Section 3.1.1, a *DistributionConnector* is capable of supporting runtime addition and removal of local components and connectors, as well as remote devices. The base size of the (more frequently used) socket-based *DistributionConnector* is 1.27 KB. In addition to this, each socket connection adds 2.7 KB on average. Finally, the PL's support for IPC introduces additional overhead. In Java this overhead is 9.5 KB for loading the `java.net` package.

The *ISecurity* interface has several implementations that perform combinations of authentication, authorization, encryption, and event integrity. These services are implemented using three major cryptographic algorithms: symmetric key, asymmetric key, and event digest function. The *IConnDeliveryGuarantees* interface supports event delivery guarantees. We have implemented this interface to support at most once, at least once, exactly once, and best effort delivery semantics. In order to support communication across PLs, we have added the *IXMLConversion* interface and implemented XML encoding/decoding of events inside the *XMLConverter* class. Finally, we have added the *ICompression* interface with the goal of minimizing the required network bandwidth for event dispatching. To this end, we have implemented the Huffman coding technique [27] inside the *Compression* class.

Addition of a new interface to the *ExtensibleConnector* requires adding a pointer to the interface and performing method calls on it inside *ExtensibleConnector*'s *handle* method. The change to the *ExtensibleConnector* class is minimal, averaging three new lines of code for each new interface. However, it is important to know the right ordering of method calls to achieve the desired behavior. For example, when combining *ISecurity* and *IXMLConversion* interfaces, *IXMLConversion*'s *convert* method is invoked before *ISecurity*'s *encrypt* method when sending the event; on the receiving end, the *ISecurity*'s *decrypt* method is invoked before *IXMLConversion*'s *reconstitute* method.

The overhead introduced by this solution is that an *ExtensibleConnector* instance may have many *null* pointers, corresponding to interfaces that have not been installed. The values of these pointers will be checked each time the *handle* method is invoked. An alternative solution, which would trade-off the extensibility for efficiency, is to subclass the *Connector* class directly and to have the references only to the desired interfaces. We are planning to implement a tool that would perform this task automatically, given a specification of features that a connector should support.

4.2 Component Extensions

To support various aspects of architectural awareness and middleware-level reflection, we have provided the *ExtensibleComponent* class that composes several interfaces. Additionally, *ExtensibleComponent* contains a reference to *IArchitecture*, allowing its instances to act as meta-level components and to effect runtime changes on the system's architecture. To date, we have augmented the *ExtensibleComponent* class with two interfaces. The *IAdmin* interface is used for performing component deployment and mobility (see Section 5.2). The *IRuntimeAnalysis* interface is used for analyzing the architectural descriptions and assessing proposed architectural changes during the application's execution. We have recently implemented several versions of this interface that encapsulate different subsets of our DRADEL [17] environment (see Section 5.1).

4.3 Event Extensions

To support various facets of event delivery we have provided the *ExtensibleEvent* class that can compose multiple interfaces. To date, we have created three interfaces inside the *ExtensibleEvent* class. The *IDeliveryGuaranteesEvent* interface is used to assign a delivery guarantee policy to an event (i.e., at most once, at least once, exactly once, best effort). This interface is used in tandem with the *IConnDeliveryGuarantees* interface of the *ExtensibleConnector* class. The *IRealTimeEvent* interface is used to assign a real-time deadline to an event. We have implemented this interface to support both aperiodic and periodic real-time events. In support of real-time event delivery we have additionally provided three classes that implement the *IScheduler* and *IDispatch* interfaces, discussed below. Finally, to support communication across PL boundaries the *IXMLRepresentation* interface provides XML-based representation of an event.

4.4 Other Extensions

In addition to the *IDistribution* interface inside the *ExtensibleConnector* class, to support distribution and mobility we have implemented the *Serializable* interface inside each one of the *Extensible* classes. This allows us to send data as well as code across machine boundaries.

In support of real-time event delivery we have provided two additional implementations of the *IScheduler* interface. *EDFScheduler* implements scheduling of aperiodic events based on the earliest-deadline-first algorithm, while *RateMonotonicScheduler* implements scheduling of periodic events.

5 Tool Support

We augment Prism-MW with tools for architectural modeling, analysis, deployment, and run-time monitoring and evolution. These tools themselves have been implemented using Prism-MW. As such, the tools provide additional evaluation of Prism-MW.

5.1 Modeling and Analysis

In adding support for architecture modeling and analysis to Prism-MW, we have integrated xADL 2.0 [4], a highly extensible XML-based architecture description language (ADL) [18], into our existing analysis environment, DRADEL [17]. Our support for architectural description is reasonably general: we model interacting components simply as collections of provided and required services whose semantics are represented in first-order logic. DRADEL's *TopologicalConstraintChecker* and *TypeChecker* components use this information to ensure architectural consistency. While the details of DRADEL have been reported elsewhere [17], DRADEL is relevant in this context because it has been reengineered using Prism-MW: it consists of nine components and four connectors, comprising 13,000 Java SLOC, not counting Prism-MW itself. Furthermore, DRADEL's *CodeGenerator* component generates Prism-MW compatible application skeletons from xADL descriptions, directly aiding the transfer of architectural decisions into application code.

5.2 Deployment and Run-Time Monitoring

Our support for deployment and run-time monitoring directly leverages Prism-MW's services. We have integrated and extended the COTS MS Visio tool to develop Prism-DE, the deployment environment for Prism applications, shown in Figure 6. Prism-DE contains several toolboxes (left side of Figure 6). The top toolbox enables an architect to specify a configuration of hardware devices by dragging their icons onto the canvas and connecting them. The next toolbox enables the specification of processes that will be executing on each device. The remaining toolboxes supply the software components and connectors that may be placed inside the processes. The *Connectors* toolbox is populated with connector types that represent various combinations of *Extensible-Connector* interface implementations we have built to date. The *Components* toolboxes have to be populated with application components for each new application. This task only requires specifying the location of each component's implementation (either a collection of Java classes or a C++ DLL). Prism-DE actively analyzes the specified configurations, ensuring that each architectural element has a container process and a valid instance name, and that C++ modules are not be in the same process as Java modules. Additionally, Prism-DE contains a pluggable DRADEL *Topological-ConstraintChecker* to ensure conformance of a desired set of topological rules. Our future goal is to integrate DRADEL's entire modeling and analysis capabilities inside Prism-DE.

Once a desired software configuration is created in Prism-DE, it can be deployed onto the depicted hardware configuration with a simple button click. In order to deploy the desired architecture on a set of target hosts, we assume that a skeleton configuration is preloaded on each host. The skeleton configuration consists of Prism-MW's *Architecture* object that contains a *DistributionConnector* (recall Section 4.1) and an *ExtensibleComponent* with instantiated *IAdmin* interface (referred to as *AdminComponent* below), that is attached to the connector. The skeleton configuration is extremely lightweight. For example, in our Java implementation, the skeleton uses under 11 KB of dynamic memory.[6] Since Prism-MW itself, the *Architecture* object, and *Distribu-*

---

[6] This figure does not include the additional overhead discussed in Section 4.1: 9.5 KB needed to load the java.net package and 2.7 KB per socket connection.

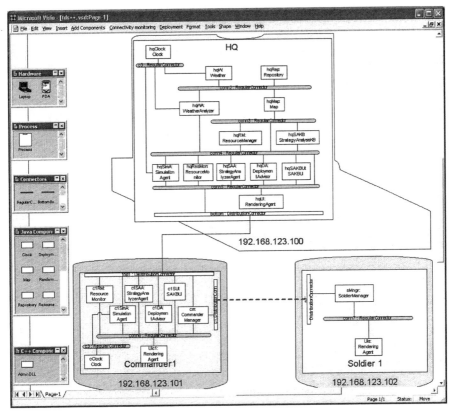

Fig. 6. *The Prism-DE* deployment and run-time monitoring environment.

tionConnector are also used at the application level, the actual memory overhead of our basic deployment support (i.e., the *Admin Component*) is only around 5 KB.

As shown in Figure 1, the *ExtensibleComponent* on each device contains a pointer to its *Architecture* object and is thus able to effect run-time changes to its local subsystem's architecture: instantiation, addition, removal, connection, and disconnection of components and connectors with the help of *DistributionConnectors*. *Admin Components* are able to send and receive from any device to which they are connected the events that contain application-level components (sent between address spaces using the *Serializable* interface).

Prism-DE supports run-time monitoring of connectivity between application processes. If communication between two *DistributionConnectors* is disabled for any reason (e.g., failed connection or failed container process), that information is propagated via an event to Prism-DE, which, in turn, highlights the disconnection (dotted line in Figure 6). A future enhancement to the run-time monitoring aspects of Prism-DE will include discovery of alternate paths between the disconnected nodes and automatic reconfigurations to enable their continued communication.

6 Further Evaluation and Experience

Over twenty applications have been implemented using Prism-MW to date, involving traditional desktop platforms, PalmOS- and WindowsCE-compatible devices, digital cameras, and motion sensors. Several of these applications were developed in the context of three graduate-level courses at USC. They include distributed digital image capture and processing, map visualization and navigation, location tracking, and instant messaging for hand-held devices. We do not provide additional details of these applications here due to space constraints; several of them are described in [23]. Instead, in this section we focus on experiences resulting from a project involving multiple teams of graduate students and our collaborations with two industrial organizations. The student-led project assessed Prism-MW's ease of use and resulted in different implementations of a dynamic service discovery capability. The first external collaboration resulted in a large-scale military application in support of one organization's specific needs in the ground vehicle domain. The second collaboration resulted in an extensive further evaluation of Prism-MW in the context of the other organization's distributed airborne system.

6.1 Dynamic Service Discovery

Eight teams, each consisting of three graduate students, were tasked with developing a distributed application, called dynamic service discovery (DSD), using the Java implementation of Prism-MW. The application was to be deployed on a set of Compaq iPAQ PDAs running WindowsCE and connected into a wireless LAN. In DSD, each host provides and requires a set of services. The goal of the application is to satisfy the greatest number of service requests in the shortest amount of time given the below requirements. In order to allow the students to focus on the important aspect of the project, the services were simple arithmetic and trigonometric operations provided by Java (e.g., $+$, $-$, sin, cos, and so on).

DSD assumes that the sets of provided and required services will vary across hosts. Furthermore, the sets of provided and required services on each host may change at any time. Each host is connected to and has access to only a subset of other hosts. However, a host may use one of its neighbors as a "relay" to indirectly access the desired host. The connectivity among the hosts may be altered at any time during the application's execution. New hosts may enter the network at any time, while existing hosts may leave and reenter the network at any time.

The eight student teams implemented DSD's requirements by extending the Prism-MW with implementations of IDistribution interface that allows monitoring of the network for new devices and for changes in connectivity among existing devices. Each team also implemented meta-level components in support of the varying set of services requested.

DSD was a reasonably simple application, but one that had some interesting properties representative of the Prism setting. The functionality described above was developed over a ten-week period. While just under one half of the students had exposure to Java prior to starting the project, only one student was somewhat familiar with a previous version of Prism-MW, four students had some experience with component-based software development, three had experience with developing for WindowsCE, and none had any experience with the Compaq iPAQ. The students were asked to estimate the amounts of time spent on the various aspects of the project, including "*Under-standing/Learning Prism-MW*". The teams reported that this aspect of the project required between 8% and 21% of the total project time, with 15% being the average. While many additional case studies are required to draw definitive conclusions, we view these results as indicative of Prism-MW's understandability, particularly in light of the fact that the students were not only asked to use Prism-MW, but also to *modify* it, as described above.

6.2 Military Deployment

Figure 7 depicts the application for distributed military troops deployment and battle simulations (TDS). A computer at *Headquarters* gathers information from the field and displays the current battlefield status: the locations of friendly and enemy troops, vehicles, and obstacles such as mine fields. The headquarters computer is networked via secure links to a set of PDAs used by *Commanders* in the field. The

Fig. 7. TDS application.

commander PDAs are connected directly to each other and to a large number of *Soldier* PDAs. Each commander is capable of controlling his own part of the battlefield: deploying troops, analyzing the deployment strategy, transferring troops between commanders, and so on. In case the *Headquarters* device fails, a designated *Commander* assumes the role of *Headquarters*. Soldiers can only view the segment of the battlefield in which they are located, receive direct orders from the commanders, and report their status. Figure 6 shows the partial architecture of TDS consisting of single *Headquarters*, *Commander*, and *Soldier* subsystems, while Figure 7 shows one possible deployment with single *Headquarters*, four *Commanders*, and 36 *Soldiers*.

TDS has provided an effective platform for demonstrating a number of Prism-MW services and assessing its scalability in a real application setting. TDS has been designed, analyzed, implemented, deployed, monitored, and dynamically evolved using the techniques described in this paper. It has been implemented in four dialects of two programming languages: Java JVM and KVM, C++ and EVC++, with on-going plans to integrate it with legacy software implemented in Ada. TDS has been deployed to 105 mobile devices and mobile device emulators running on PCs, with plans for further scaling it up to 1,000 devices. The dynamic size of the application is approximately 1 MB for the *Headquarters* subsystem, 600 KB for each *Commander*, and 90 KB for each *Soldier* subsystem. The devices on which TDS has been deployed are of several different types (Palm Pilot Vx and VIIx, Compaq iPAQ, HP Jornada, NEC

MobilePro, Sun Ultra, PC), running four OSs (PalmOS, WindowsCE, Windows 2000, and Unix). The performance of TDS has been acceptable, easily surpassing user reaction time after the initial delay caused by application deployment. We are currently in the process of designing tests to quantify that performance.

6.3 Airborne System

In order to assess the maturity and suitability of Prism-MW for use in one of their key distributed airborne systems, our second industrial collaborator conducted a series of benchmark tests. The tests were designed to be representative of usage scenarios in the reference system's existing implementation. Once it was established that application speed using Prism-MW was satisfactory,[7] our collaborator became particularly interested in the overhead induced on application size by Prism-MW. One example test involved exchanging 100,000 records of proprietary structure (totalling over 13 MB) between Prism-MW components distributed over a LAN (i.e., using Prism-MW's *DistributionConnector*s discussed in Section 5.2). The base, unoptimized implementation of Prism-MW resulted in a 20% increase of the amount of exchanged data in comparison to the reference implementation. A relatively simple specialization of the *DistributionConnector* class (modifying the implementation of two methods of the *IDistribution* interface), without any other modifications to the middleware, reduced that overhead down to 5%. As a result, our collaborator has deemed Prism-MW "very efficient and flexible" and is planning on adopting it.

7 Related Work

Our work on Prism-MW has been primarily influenced by two research areas: architectural styles and middleware. Architectural styles were discussed in the Introduction. Below we discuss two most closely related approaches in the middleware arena. Additionally, we briefly discuss a preliminary comparison of Prism-MW with several representative middleware solutions.

ArchJava [1] is an extension to Java that unifies software architecture with implementation, ensuring that the implementation conforms to architectural constraints. ArchJava currently has several limitations that would likely limit its applicability in the Prism setting: communication between ArchJava components is achieved solely via method calls; ArchJava is only applicable to applications running in a single address space; it is currently limited to Java; and its efficiency has not yet been assessed.

Aura [33] is an architectural style and supporting middleware for ubiquitous computing applications with special focus on user mobility, context awareness, and context switching. Aura is only applicable to certain classes of applications in the Prism setting. Similarly to Prism-MW, Aura has explicit, first-class connectors. Aura also provides a set of components that perform management of tasks, environment monitoring, context observing, and service supplying. This suggests that the Aura style could be successfully supported using Prism-MW augmented with a set of Aura-specific extensions. This would eliminate the need for performing optimizations of Aura's current

---

[7] We were not appraised of the details of the tests assessing the application speed, only of their outcome.

implementation support, which has to date only been tested on traditional, desktop platforms.

We have performed a preliminary comparison of Prism-MW with several representative middleware solutions with respect to the objectives identified in Section 2. The results of these comparisons are shown in Table 1.[8] TAO and Orbix/E do well in supporting scalability,[9] security, and delivery guarantees, but do so at the expense of the middleware size. Jini, .NET, XMIDDLE, RCSM, and LIME do well in supporting awareness and mobility, while all of them lack support for delivery guarantees. Finally, none of the representative middleware solutions support explicit architectural abstractions, thus clearly distinguishing them from Prism-MW .

8 Conclusions and Future Work

This paper presented the design, implementation, and evaluation of Prism-MW, a middleware targeted at applications in highly distributed, resource constrained, heterogeneous, and mobile settings. The key properties of the middleware are its native, and flexible, support for architectural abstractions, efficiency, scalability, and extensibility. These properties were enabled by Prism-MW's extensive separation of concerns that spans several dimensions:

Table 1: Comparison of existing middleware solutions. ? denotes unavailable data; ✓✓✓ denotes extensive support; ✓✓ denotes solid support; ✓ denotes some support; empty cells denote no support.

Property		Orbix/E [10]	TAO [32]	JXTA [26]	.NET [20]	JINI [34]	XMIDDLE [14]	RCSM [39]	LIME [12]	Prism-MW
Architectural abstractions										✓✓✓
Efficiency [a]		16,6K	8K	?	?	?	?	?	?	20K
		95KB	0.5MB	?	?	?	156KB	?	?	4.6KB
Scalability		✓✓	✓✓	✓✓	✓✓	✓✓	?	?	?	✓✓✓
Extensibility	Awareness		✓	✓	✓✓	✓✓	✓	✓✓	✓✓	✓✓
	Delivery guarantees	✓	✓✓✓							✓✓
	Mobility					✓✓	✓✓✓	✓✓	✓✓✓	✓✓
	Reconfig.		✓✓			✓✓		✓✓	✓✓	✓✓
	Security	✓✓	✓✓	✓✓	✓✓	✓		✓✓		✓✓

a. Number of events per second (top) and memory usage (bottom).

- By adopting an explicit architectural perspective, Prism-MW has inherited the separation of computation (handled by components) from interaction (handled by connectors) intrinsic to software architectures.
- Furthermore, Prism-MW's extensive use of interfaces and complete lack of direct dependencies among its classes also allows tailoring implementation-level concerns (e.g., the ability to select different schedulers independently of dispatchers or to compose distribution, XML encoding, and compression facilities for network-based interactions).

---

[8] The results of performance benchmarks are taken from the available online documentation. The hardware platforms on which these benchmarks were ran are comparable, but the OSs and PLs used are different. However, since both OrbixE and TAO are implemented in C++ running on Linux, we expect that their performance results would not significantly improve when run on Windows2000 using Java (the test platform for Prism-MW).

[9] Recall from Section 3.3 that an aspect of the existing middleware platforms which hampers their scalability is their support for only one software connector.

- The middleware also separates an application's conceptual architecture from its implementation: each component may be implemented in multiple PLs; those implementations are fully interchangeable if *ExtensibleConnectors* with the appropriate implementations of the *IXMLConversion* interface are used.
- Finally, the Prism-DE environment enables the complete separation of an application's architecture from its deployment.

In turn, this separation of concerns across multiple dimensions enables easy selection and tailoring of the exact middleware features needed for each development situation in the Prism setting.

While our experience thus far has been very positive, a number of pertinent issues remain unexplored. One such issue is the role Prism-MW may play in supporting different architectural styles (e.g., client-server, push-based, peer-to-peer) [25,29], perhaps even in the same application. We are also in the process of further evaluating Prism-MW by applying it in the mobile robotics domain in collaboration with USC's Center for Robotics and Embedded Systems. Our future work will span issues such as adding configuration management support to Prism-MW and automatically generating an optimized version of Prism-MW given a desired set of features (i.e., eliminating the need to store and check interface pointers even when they are not used in a given Prism-MW class implementation). Another alternative we are considering to address the latter problem is to parameterize Prism-MW's variation points instead of using interfaces. We are not aware of any comparable attempts at parameterizing middleware to this extent, and consider this to be an interesting research challenge.

References

1. J.Aldrich, C. Chambers, D. Notkin. ArchJava: Connecting Software Architecture to Implementation. International Conference on Software Engineering 2002, Orlando, Florida, May 2002.
2. L. Capra, W. Emmerich and C. Mascolo. Middleware for Mobile Computing. UCL Research Note RN/30/01.
3. A. Carzaniga, D. S. Rosenblum, and A. L. Wolf. Design and Evaluation of a Wide-Area Event Notification Service. ACM Transactions on Computer Systems, 19(3), August 2001.
4. E. Dashofy, A. Hoek, and R. N. Taylor. An Infrastructure for the Rapid Development of XML-based Architecture Description Languages. International Conference on Software Engineering 2002, Orlando, Florida, May 2002.
5. E. Dashofy, N. Medvidovic, and R. N. Taylor. Using Off-the-Shelf Middleware to Implement Connectors in Distributed Software Architectures. International Conference on Software Engineering'99, Los Angeles, May 1999.
6. F. DeRemer and H. Kron. Programming-in-the-Large Versus Programming-in-the-Small. IEEE Transactions on Software Engineering, June 1976.
7. W. Emmerich. Software Engineering and Middleware: A Roadmap. In The Future of Software Engineering, ACM Press 2000.
8. R. Fielding. Architectural Styles and the Design of Network-Based Software Architectures. Ph.D Thesis, UCI, June 2000.
9. M. Hauswirth and M. Jazayeri. A Component and Communication Model for Push Systems. Joint European Software Engineering Conference (ESEC) and Foundations of Software Engineering (FSE) '99, September 1999.
10. IONA Orbix/E Datasheet. http://www.iona.com/whitepapers/orbix-e-DS.pdf
11. E. A. Lee. Embedded Software. Revised from UCB/ERL Memorandum M01/26, UC Berkeley, CA, November 1, 2001.
12. LIME http://lime.sourceforge.net/

13. T. Lindholm and F. Yellin. The Java Virtual Machine Specification. 2nd Edition Java Series. Addison Wesley 1999.
14. C. Mascolo et. al. XMIDDLE: A Data-Sharing Middleware for Mobile Computing. To appear in Personal and Wireless Communications, Kluwer.
15. N. Medvidovic, N. R. Mehta, M. Mikic-Rakic: A Family of Software Architecture Implementation Frameworks. The Working IEEE/IFIP Conference on Software Architecture 2002, Montreal, Canada, August 2002.
16. N. Medvidovic and M. Mikic-Rakic. Architectural Support for Programming-in-the-Many. TR USC-CSE-2001-506.
17. N. Medvidovic, et al. A Language and Environment for Architecture-Based Software Development and Evolution. International Conference on Software Engineering '99, Los Angeles, CA, May 1999.
18. N. Medvidovic and R. N. Taylor. A Classification and Comparison Framework for Software Architecture Description Languages. IEEE Transactions on Software Engineering, vol. 26, no. 1, pages 70-93 (January 2000). Reprinted in Rational Developer Network: Seminal Papers on Software Architecture. Rational Software Corporation, (July 2001).
19. N. R. Mehta, N. Medvidovic, and S. Phadke. Towards a Taxonomy of Software Connectors. International Conference on Software Engineering (ICSE 2000), pages 178-187, Limerick, Ireland, June 4-11, 2000.
20. Microsoft.NET. http://www.microsoft.com/net/
21. M. Mikic-Rakic and N. Medvidovic. A Connector-Aware Middleware for Distributed Deployment and Mobility. ICDCS Workshop on Mobile Computing Middleware, Rhode Island, May, 2003.
22. M. Mikic-Rakic and N. Medvidovic. Middleware for Software Architecture-Based Development in Distributed, Mobile, and Resource-Constrained Environments. TR USC-CSE-2002-501.
23. M. Mikic-Rakic and N. Medvidovic. Software Architecture-Based Development Support for Ubiquitous Systems. TR USC-CSE-2002-508.
24. P. Oreizy, et al. An Architecture-Based Approach to Self-Adaptive Software. IEEE Intelligent Systems and Their Applications, 14(3), May/June 1999.
25. D. Perry and A.L. Wolf. Foundations for the Study of Software Architecture. ACM SIGSOFT Software Engineering Notes, October 1992.
26. Project JXTA. http://www.jxta.org/
27. D. Salomon. Data Compression: The Complete Reference. Springer Verlag, December 1997.
28. M. Shaw et al. Abstractions for Software Architecture and Tools to Support Them. IEEE Transactions on Software Engineering, 21(4), April 1995.
29. M. Shaw and D. Garlan. Software Architecture: Perspectives on an Emerging Discipline. Prentice Hall, 1996.
30. D. Schmidt. ACE. http://www.cs.wustl.edu/~schmidt/ACE-documentation.html
31. D. Schmidt et. al. Software Architectures for Reducing Priority Inversion and Non-determinism in Real-time Object Request Brokers. Kluwer Journal of Realtime Systems, Volume 21, Number 2, 2001.
32. D. Schmidt. TAO. http://www.cs.wustl.edu/~schmidt/TAO.html
33. J. P. Sousa, and D. Garlan: Aura: an Architectural Framework for User Mobility in Ubiquitous Computing Environments. The Working IEEE/IFIP Conference on Software Architecture 2002 2002, Montreal, Canada, August 2002.
34. Sun Microsystems. JINI(TM) Network technology. http://wwws.sun.com/software/jini/
35. Sun Microsystems. K Virtual Machine (KVM). http://java.sun.com/products/kvm.
36. C. Szyperski. Component Software – Beyond Object-Oriented Programming. Addison-Wesley / ACM Press, 1998
37. R.N. Taylor, et al. A Component- and Message-Based Architectural Style for GUI Software. IEEE Transactions on Software Engineering, June 1996.
38. The x-kernel Protocol Framework. http://www.cs.arizona.edu/xkernel/
39. S. S. Yau and F. Karim, Context-Sensitive Middleware for Real-time Software in Ubiquitous Computing Environments. Proceedings of the International Symposium on Object-oriented Real-time distributed Computing 2001, Magdeburg, Germany.
40. A Discussion of the Object Management Architecture (OMA) Guide, OMG, 1997.

Opportunistic Channels: Mobility-Aware Event Delivery

Yuan Chen[1], Karsten Schwan[1], and Dong Zhou[2]

[1] College of Computing, Georgia Institute of Technology, Atlanta, GA 30332, USA
{yuanchen,schwan}@cc.gatech.edu
[2] DoCoMo USA Labs, San Jose, CA 95110, USA
zhou@docomolabs-usa.com

Abstract. The delivery of data in pervasive systems has to deal with end host mobility. One problem is how to create appropriate, application-level data provisioning topologies, termed data brokers, to best match underlying network connectivity, end user locations, and the locales of their network access. Another problem is how to balance workloads in such overlay networks, in response to mobility and to changes in available processing and communication resources. This paper improves the performance of data provisioning by dynamically changing broker topologies and end users' assignments to brokers. Specifically, using publish/subscribe as a communication paradigm, a new abstraction, termed an *opportunistic* event channel, enables dynamic broker creation, deletion, and movement. Experimental and simulation results demonstrate the ability of opportunistic channels to optimize event delivery and processing when end users move across different network access points. The technique is to 'opportunistically' follow network-level handoffs across network access points with application-level handoffs of a user's broker functionality to a new, 'closer' broker. The potential load imbalances across brokers caused by such handoffs are also addressed. Opportunistic channels are realized with the JECho event infrastructure. Performance advantages attained from their use can be substantial, with the cost of sending a message from a publisher to a mobile subscriber improved by up to 50%. Load balancing improves event delivery even for moderate numbers of event subscribers.

1   Introduction

Publish/subscribe is a widely used paradigm for interconnecting applications in distributed environments. It provides anonymous, inherently asynchronous group communication, where event providers and consumers interact via event brokers, as illustrated in Figure 1. Subscription means that an event consumer declares its interest in receiving certain events, using some predicate or more generally, in content-based subscription, a filter/conversion function defined on event contents (e.g., see the ECho and JECho infrastructures developed in our research [9, 38]). An event provider generates and publishes events, where message brokers are responsible for collecting event subscriptions and routing events from

M. Endler and D. Schmidt (Eds.): Middleware 2003, LNCS 2672, pp. 182–201, 2003.
© IFIP International Federation for Information Processing 2003

publishers to interested consumers. Each provider/consumer connects to one of the brokers, where broker networks can be organized in multiple ways, ranging from single central broker (Elvin [31]), to hierarchical topologies (JEDI [7], Gryphon [24]), to general graphs (SIENA [3], READY [11]). Once a topology of brokers has been defined, appropriate routing paths must be established to ensure the correct and efficient delivery of events to all interested consumers.

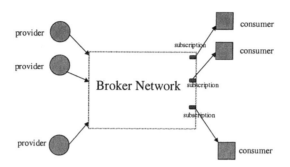

Fig. 1. Publish/Subscribe Communication Model

The issue addressed in this paper is that publish/subscribe systems' broker infrastructures or more generally, overlay networks [20] used in distributed applications do not take into account the unique needs of mobile systems. Problems include (1) which interconnection topology may currently best suit the underlying mobile system's communication paths [26] and how to dynamically construct such a topology, (2) selecting the numbers and capabilities of brokers to match the mobile platform's configuration, and (3) dynamic changes in (1) and (2) to match changes in mobile node locations [35], configurations, and resources. For publish/subscribe systems, this implies the need to use dynamically varying topologies with a changing number of brokers, and it requires runtime changes to providers' and consumers' assignments to brokers. A specific example is one in which a location change by an event provider or consumer results in a consequent change of the network access point used by the underlying Mobile IP protocol [25,17]. This can lead to inefficiencies in broker communications, as depicted in Figure 2, where a mobile client's crossing of a network boundary results in a circuitous path from publisher to home broker to event subscriber.

Opportunistic channels is an event channel concept that addresses the mobility of event producers, consumers, and of the dynamic changes in the pervasive systems where they operate. The following attributes of opportunistic channels differentiate them from previous work:

- *Network and location awareness.* The event broker associated with an opportunistic channel is aware of the underlying network topology used for transporting events from providers to consumers. It is also aware of the respective locations of both.
- *Dynamic broker adaptation.* Brokers can be created, deleted, and moved at runtime, resulting in the ability of opportunistic channels to react to changes

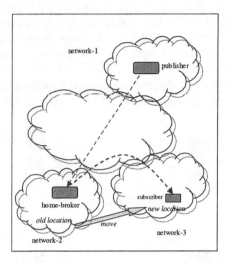

Fig. 2. Inefficient Event Delivery after Subscriber Migration

in end user locations and also to secondary effects of such changes, such as broker overloads due to changes in client/broker assignments.

The algorithm used for dynamic broker deployment and movement is one that evaluates the performance opportunities presented by current network connectivities and broker loads/node capabilities. Specifically, it attempts to optimize the event delivery path when a mobile user moves out of range of its old network access point by 'opportunistically' following the network level handoff [25, 35] with an application-level handoff of the user's brokering functionality to a broker that is 'closer' to the new client location, hence the term 'opportunistic' event channel. The potential load imbalances across brokers caused by such middleware-level handoffs are addressed by dynamic broker creation. In effect, we aim to dynamically construct portions of the event dispatch trees used in static broker architectures [24].

Opportunistic channels are realized with the JECho peer-to-peer pub/sub infrastructure [38]. A unique extension of JECho is that its current peer-based broker infrastructure (i.e., each peer runs its own broker) is enhanced with dynamically created 'third party' brokers, which can run on machines and/or in address spaces not used by event publishers or subscribers [38]. Moreover, generalizing the capabilities of other event systems, brokers perform tasks in addition to the event routing permitted by other systems [24], using subscriber-provided functions, termed *event modulators* [37]. The intent is to address the severe resource limitations existing in many mobile and embedded systems, by permitting event consumers to deploy application-specific functions that manipulate event content into event sources and/or brokers, so as to precisely meet their current needs, and to avoid needless data transfers [38]. Finally, since JECho is constructed with Java, the realization of opportunistic channels presented in this paper has some limitations, including the need for a reasonably sized Java footprints on the target mobile nodes [38]. Opportunistic channels, however, also benefit from certain JECho functionality, such as the relative ease with which third party brokers may be created, deployed, and migrated.

The performance advantages attained from the use of opportunistic channels can be substantial. For instance, simulation results indicate that the cost of sending a message from a fixed publisher to a mobile subscriber can be improved by up to 50%. Experimental results show that the end-to-end latency can be improved by 20% with microbenchmarks, when a mobile devices uses a 802.11a-based wireless network, where access points are connected via a high performance network backbone. Furthermore, broker load balancing can deliver events at two times the speed of a non-load balancing solution when the number of subscribers reaches 16, as demonstrated with microbenchmarks. Finally, even for a moderate number of video players (i.e., 8 players), load balancing and dynamic broker creation permits video playout to be improved by a factor of 3.

In the remainder of this paper, Section 2 briefly reviews the JECho event system, clarifying the basic software architecture of opportunistic channels. In Section 3, opportunistic channels are used in a mobile environment, including experimental measurements with campus wireless network. Section 4 describes load balancing in opportunistic channels. Related work is discussed in Section 5, and conclusions and future work appear in Section 6.

2   System Architecture

2.1   Overview of JECho

JECho implements a publish/subscribe communication paradigm, providing interactive services to distributed, concurrently executing components via event channels. JECho's efficient implementation enables it to move events at rates higher than other Java-based event system implementations [38, 37]. In addition, using JECho's modulator concept [38, 37], individual event subscribers can dynamically tailor event flows to their own needs, and adapt to runtime changes in component behaviors and needs and/or changes in platform resources. JE-Cho's implementation is in pure Java, its group-cast communication layer is based on Java Sockets, and it runs with both standard and embedded JVMs. A *modulator* is a Java object that executes in a source's or broker's address space, on behalf of some client. The basic communication model in JECho is shown in Figure 3.

Fig. 3. JECho Communication Model

Client-defined customization in modulators, including event conversion or transformation, is performed prior to delivering the event to the consumer. Event conversion may reduce their sizes and hence reduce network traffic. Modulators can also be used for offloading computation from constrained mobile devices. An example is a modulator that pre-converts events to the forms needed by specific client's graphical displays, thereby eliminating the costs of data conversion in the client. In fact, it is sometimes impossible to display data appropriately without performing such conversions, as with rendering OpenGL-based graphical data on a PalmTop or when applying server-resident business rules to data prior to its display on cellphones [6]. Other reasons for such conversion include the delivery of data with certain Quality of Service or to conserve power on battery-limited handheld devices [28].

2.2   Broker Adaptation Architecture

The notion of *opportunistic channel* (OC) generalizes upon JECho's modulators in three ways. First, OC modulators can run in consumers, intermediate brokers, or in providers. Second, brokers may be created dynamically. Third, for load balancing and migration, each broker is associated with a Java object called an *adaptor*. The idea is for a modulator and adaptor to adapt event dispatching to the dynamic needs of the clients, as shown in Figure 4.

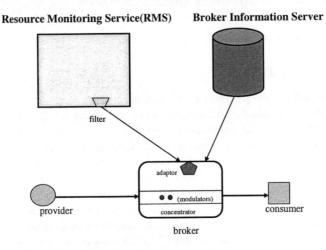

Fig. 4. Opportunistic Channel Architecture

The adaptation framework constructed with brokers and adaptors utilizes a resource monitoring service (RMS), which collects, aggregates, processes, and delivers data about the current execution environment. The RMS is able to monitor any nodes in the mobile system, using daemon processes connected via their own communication links. Monitoring data is captured from objects (including devices) at these nodes, and it is distributed to RMS clients via a customizable push-based interface. As with other monitoring systems [12], such data is contained in events, with current events containing information about CPU loads, memory availability, handoff actions occurring at the network level (to capture client mobility), and application-level communication latency and bandwidth experienced between RMS clients. RMS clients can selectively register their interests in the data being captured, by providing a filter function installed at the source of a monitoring data stream. For example, a broker may provide a function that evaluates captured data and then provides it with a notification event only when the network topology changes and when the broker's own current CPU load exceeds 80%. Our current prototype implementation uses a central RMS server.

Another component of the architecture is a broker information server, which maintains information about current brokers, including their names, certain attributes (e.g., CPU and memory loads, IP addresses, network-related parameters,etc.) and their interconnections. A broker can get these information by sending a query to the broker information server.

A sample adaptor used by a broker is shown below. Its method 'subscribe()' registers the broker with the RMS and specifies its interest in certain monitoring data, using the object 'filter'. Adaptation code is implemented in the event handler method 'push()', which is invoked whenever an interesting event is received. Using adaptors, RMS, and filters, system developers can create potentially complex adaptation policies [34].

```
public class MyAdaptor implements BrokerAdaptor {
        //join the resource channel
        public void subscribe( ) {
          registerToRMS("CPU_Load", filter);
        }

        public void push(Object e) {
              //adaptation code
        }
```

In summary, the adaptation model used for realization of opportunistic channels is seamlessly integrated with the JECho publish/subscribe system. Adaptation involves broker registration with a resource monitoring service and the use of potentially broker-specific adaptors. The adaptor can perform simple tasks like recording certain resource changes, to complex adaptations like changing the topology of broker interconnection.

3   Opportunistic Channels in Mobile Environments

While the concept of opportunistic channels may be applied to a wide variety of wireless networks, this paper assumes that there exists a reliable underlying network with guaranteed connectivity, where links are subject to dynamic variations in available communication bandwidth. In the presence of end user mobility, connectivity is guaranteed by Mobile IP, which performs network-level handoff actions [25, 17, 35]. The resulting transparent mobility exists in both deployed and experimental systems, including Berkeley's BARWAN and CMU's wireless Andrew systems [20, 15], which provide such support within a network (horizontal handoff) and across heterogeneous networks (vertical handoff) across substantial geographical areas. For simplicity, in the remainder of this paper, we ignore any transient disconnection, which may happen during mobile suppliers' or consumers' migration. Furthermore, brokers are pre-created onto all nodes of the underlying network, thereby ignoring the costs of dynamic broker creation.

3.1   Mobility Adaptation

The network topologies of mobile systems change in response to mobile users' movements. When using base stations, this implies that the router (network access point) to which a mobile host connects may change when the mobile host moves across network boundaries. In Figure 5, M is a mobile host whose home network is network-2. M receives events from a source residing in network-1. There are two brokers in the system: broker-2 in network-2 and broker-3 in network-3. When M first subscribed to the event channel, it specified broker-2 as its broker and placed its modulator into broker-2. The event was delivered from the source to broker-2 through the network and finally reached M. The resulting delivery path was network-1(source)→network-2(broker-2→M). At some point in time, M moved from network-2 to network-3. If M still used broker-2, the resulting delivery path would be network-1(source)→network-2(broker-2)→network-3(M). However, if M changed its broker from broker-2 to broker-3, then the event delivery path would become network-1(source)→network-3(broker-3→M), which is much shorter.

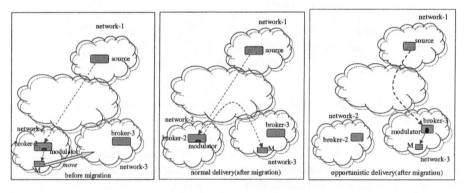

Fig. 5. Event Delivery in a Mobile Environment

In most cases, using the old, longer dispatching path (i.e., triangle delivery) results in higher event delivery latency and in the consumption of additional, often scarce network capacity. A solution is to change event delivery paths along with changes in underlying network message delivery. In particular, when a mobile consumer moves out of range of its previous network and into the range of a new one, the mobile host should connect to the broker that is 'closest' to the new network access point. This is the basic idea of opportunistic channels (OC): to 'opportunistically' move broker activities as end users move. Specifically, using the adaptation mechanism described in Section 2.2, a simple adaptor transparently relocates the mobile client's modulator to the new broker in response to a network-level handoff, the latter detected via online monitoring. The basic steps performed by this adaptor are:

1. search for an alternative broker via the broker information server;
2. send a handoff request to the remote broker; and
3. if the remote broker agrees to accept the request, then execute the broker-level handoff protocol.

The modulator handoff protocol, described in detail in Section 3.2 and implemented by the adaptor, ensures that the dynamic handoff of a modulator is performed without losing or duplicating events. The broker information server lists the available brokers, including their names and certain attributes (e.g., CPU and memory loads, IP addresses, network-related parameters,etc.). The current implementation uses a central broker information server. More detail on scalable directory services appears in [2].

Two different adaptors are implemented and evaluated in this research. The 'simple' adaptor always performs modulator handoff, with the intent of using the broker that is closest to the current location of the mobile client. A more realistic adaptor takes into account additional factors. First, it may also consider the new broker's load. Second, it evaluates the network path to the new broker. This is important because the latency from network-1 to network-3 may actually be larger than the latency of network-1 to network-2 plus network-2 to network-3 shown in Figure 5. Specifically, the 'complex' adaptor evaluated next compares the old path with the potential new path when network handoff is detected. It schedules the modulator handoff only when the new path is shorter than the old one. In the current implementation, latency is measured by sending a ping' message between two nodes and using one-half of the round-trip time as an approximation. The source of events can be achieved from broker information server.

3.2 Modulator Handoff

Modulator handoff is illustrated in Figures 6. Our algorithm guarantees correctness properties that include (1) in order event delivery, (2) no lost or duplicate events, and (3) consistent modulator state in the presence of migration:

1. The source broker initiates a handoff by sending a HANDOFF request to the destination broker.
2. Upon receiving the handoff request, the destination broker adds the mobile client to its consumer list and sends an ACK to the source broker.
3. After receiving the ACK from the destination broker, the source broker sends a DETOUR request, which includes the name of the destination broker, to all of the event providers.
4. Upon receiving the DETOUR request, each provider atomically replaces the source broker from its consumer list with the destination broker; it then sends an ACK to the source broker and the destination broker.
5. The source broker receives events from each provider, applies the client's modulator to these event, and forwards them to the client until it receives the ACK from the provider.

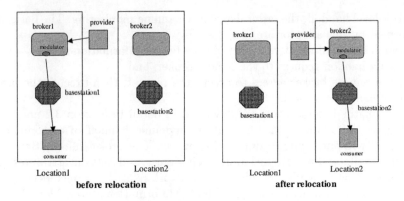

Fig. 6. Modulator Relocation

6. The destination broker buffers events from each provider after it receives the ACK.
7. After ACKs from all providers are received by the source broker, it removes the client from its consumer list and sends a HANDOFF along with the current modulator to the destination broker.
8. Upon receiving the HANDOFF, the destination broker applies the modulator received from the source broker to the buffered events and starts forwarding events to the client.

This protocol ensures that no events are lost or duplicated, since the old broker processes all events from a provider before receiving the provider's ACK mark, while the new broker processes only those events after the ACK message. The order of events from the same provider is maintained, since both the old broker and new broker process the events in the order delivered by the provider. Since modulators are stateful and since event processing may change their states, the protocol described above also ensures the consistency of modulator state. Finally, the algorithm is non-disruptive, in that the relocation procedure does not directly affect the other consumers of the providers handled by a certain broker. This is because it requires neither the providers nor the brokers to temporarily stop event delivery.

3.3   Experimental Evaluation

This section establishes the basic performance of opportunistic channels, and it demonstrates that opportunistic channels can improve the performance of event delivery in mobile environments.

Relocation Overhead. When measured on a cluster of 300Mhz Pentium II Linux PCs connected with dual 100Mbps fast Ethernet, the times required to complete a relocation for a varying number of suppliers (see Figure 7) demonstrate that relocation cost increases linearly with the number of event suppliers. This is explained by the underlying peer-to-peer communications occurring in

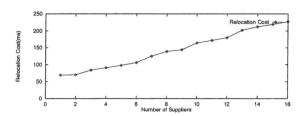

Fig. 7. Relocation Overhead

JECho, where brokers are integrated with event suppliers unless otherwise specified. The intent, of course, is to separate the broker infrastructure from the remainder of the JECho system, so that solutions like opportunistic channels can specialize their broker behavior for the target environments being addressed. Interestingly, even for the simple peer-to-peer interconnections, total relocation cost remains small even for a moderate number of suppliers (i.e., 16 suppliers). In these measurements, each supplier is located on a different machine, and the event consumer moves across two Linux machines in the same cluster.

Simulation Results. For the purpose of simulation, a 100 node network is generated using the BRITE (Internet topology generator developed at Boston University [21]). Nodes are assumed to be geographically distributed, and each link is assigned a cost corresponding to the distance between the nodes it connects. The cost of sending a message between any pair of nodes is the cost of the shortest path between the nodes, computed with Dijkstra's algorithm. There are multiple fixed sources and one mobile host in the network, all located on network nodes. Brokers also reside on these nodes. In the simulation, the mobile host stays on the same node for some varying time period, which is generated from an exponential distribution. When the period expires, the mobile host moves to the 'next' location, according to the mobility model used. In the simulation, four mobility models characterize different user behaviors. The random model chooses the next location randomly. The traveling salesman model moves to one of its neighbors, which is randomly chosen. The pop-up model is similar to the traveling salesman one, except that it sometimes roams to a randomly chosen remote node. The fixed model has two fixed locations which the mobile host visits more frequently than others. The mobile host moves between these two locations most of the time. Occasionally, the mobile host roams to a different node. More detail about the client behavior models used in our experimentation appears in [30].

The simulation uses a mobility-to-communication ratio to measure the mobile host's movement speed. This ratio captures the rate at which a mobile host changes its location to the rate at which it receives messages. The higher the mobility-to-communication ratio, the faster the mobile host's movement. For each relocation, adaptation cost is measured by multiplying the number of messages used by the relocation protocol by the distance between suppliers, consumer, source brokers or destination broker.

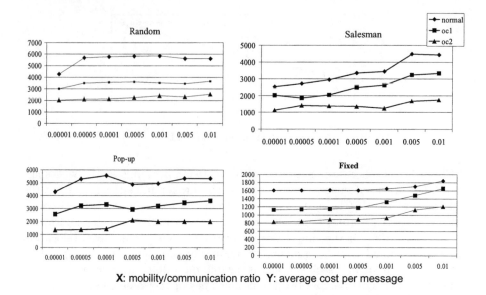

Fig. 8. Simulation Results for Single Supplier

The first simulation uses one fixed source and a single mobile client. We compare the performance of using a 'normal' channel, a 'simple' opportunistic channel (oc1) and a 'complex' opportunistic channel (oc2). oc1 uses a simple adaptor, which always performs a modulator handoff when the mobile client moves to a new location. oc2's adaptor compares the distances of old path and new path when the mobile client moves to a new location. If the new path is shorter, the adaptor relocates the modulator to the new broker. Otherwise, the old broker is used. Figure 8 shows the average cost per message of three channels, respectively, using the random model, traveling salesman and fixed model. In the figure, the X-axis indicates the mobility/communication ratio, and the Y-axis indicates the average cost of receiving a message. The results show that opportunistic channels achieve better performance than normal ones, even for random walks with very high mobility. In all cases, complex opportunistic channels (oc2) perform better than simple ones (oc1). In general, when the mobility/communication ratio increases, relocation cost and hence, average cost, increases accordingly.

The second simulation involves five fixed sources and one mobile client. The results are shown in Figure 9. They demonstrate that the opportunistic channel with the complex adaptor has the best performance, and that even the simple adaptor still outperforms non-opportunistic channels.

End-to-End Delay. To substantiate our claims, experiments are performed with a microbenchmark used in three different locations on the Georgia Tech campus, as shown in Figure 10. The achieved end-to-end delays using opportunistic vs. normal channels are compared, with an event publisher running on a SUN Ultra 30 machine (H1) at subnet1. An IPAQ is the event consumer, and it

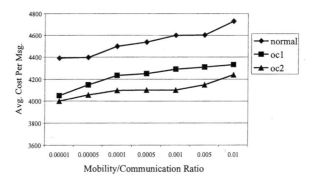

Fig. 9. Simulation Results for Multiple Suppliers

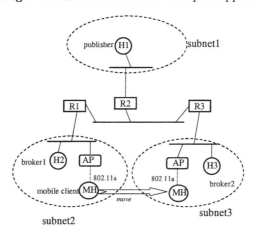

Fig. 10. Experiment Configuration for End-to-End Delay

accesses the network via 802.11a access points (802.11a devices offer a maximum of 56Mb bandwidth). Initially, the mobile client runs in subnet2 and connects to the event broker running on H2, with network connectivity provided via a wireless network access point attached to subnet2. When the mobile client moves to another location (subnet3), with non-adaptive channels, the mobile client continues to connect to the old broker (H2), whereas the opportunistic channel uses a local broker (H3). With opportunistic channels, the mobile client and its broker have access to the same local network (subnet2), hence resulting in a shorter path between them. The experiment is performed at midnight in order to avoid high levels of variation in network usage. The results presented here are the average performance achieved over 50,000 events. The standard deviation for the measurements is less than 10% of the average latency.

The experiment measures the end-to-end delay with data of size 25KB in two different locations, as shown in Figure 11. Since the opportunistic channel can always connect the mobile client to a local broker, the latency is nearly identical after moving to new location. In comparison, with the non-opportunistic channel, latency increases by more than 20% after migration. This is due to

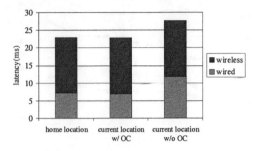

Fig. 11. Microbenchmark End-to-End Delay

the fact that event delivery for a non-opportunistic channel follows the path subnet1→subnet2→subnet3, whereas an opportunistic channel directly delivers the event from subnet1 to subnet3. The figure also shows a breakdown of the costs involved in event latency. The portions labeled 'wired' represent the latencies from the event publisher to the wireless access points. The 'wireless' times are the delays in transmitting data from access point to mobile client. This breakdown is useful for understanding the performance differences between non-adaptive and opportunistic channels. Namely, in all of these scenarios, the wireless times are nearly identical, since all network accesses use the same 802.11a devices. The difference is the time from the publisher to the access point, that is, the 'wired' times. In this scenario, therefore, the opportunistic channel optimizes 'wired' times.

Clearly, even in realistic scenarios within a campus like Georgia Tech, performance advantages can be derived from using opportunistic channels. The numeric benefits attained here are somewhat small, however, because the dominant factor in the scenario studied is the communication between broker (access point) and the mobile client. Even with 802.11a, this wireless communication is more than 2 times slower than the wired communications. This will not be the case for wide area mobility or in adhoc wireless networks, with potentially large delays between the publisher and the broker. Actually, in ad-hoc wireless networks, the delay between a publisher and a broker should be comparable to the delay between a broker to a mobile client, since both communications use wireless links. Finally, even the relatively modest 20% improvement in latency shown here can be important to applications that require real-time response. Examples include web portals [27] and the interactive virtual workbench for remote machine monitoring and control [6] evaluated in our previous research.

4   Load Balancing in Opportunistic Channels

Mobile hosts are known to be limited in computing power, storage, display, network bandwidth, etc. One approach to dealing with such limitations is per client service differentiation, that is, to customize service delivery to the needs of individual clients. JECho enables such customization by deploying modulators into event sources and/or brokers, where modulators range from simple event filters to complex time-consuming event transcoding engines. With consumers and sup-

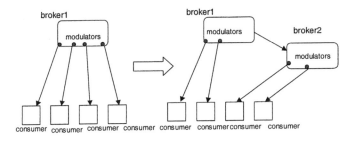

Fig. 12. Modulator Relocation for Load Balancing

pliers joining and leaving dynamically, broker loads are also subject to runtime variation, including overloads caused by modulator migration in opportunistic channels. One reason is the arrival of a large numbers of local users, as when many mobile units converge, such as during meetings. Another reason is the use of complex modulators by 'thin' clients, such as modulators that implement the flexible data transcoding required by such clients [38].

4.1 Adaptations for Load Balancing

Opportunistic channels use a load balancing adaptor that permits a broker to distribute its load (i.e., modulator execution) to a less heavily loaded broker. This adaptor works as follows. The broker monitors the total execution time of all modulators in its address space, using broker-resident timers maintained by the resource monitoring service (RMS) described in Section 2. When the broker's modulator execution time exceeds some limit, which can be specified when the broker is started, it will try to find a less loaded broker and relocate some of its load (i.e., modulators) to that broker. In the current implementation, adaptors simply contact a directory service to identify a lightly loaded broker. The directory service finds a lightly loaded broker as follows. First, it has information about each broker's location, current load, status indicating whether it can receive the load balancing request and network distances between all pairs of brokers. Second, using the RMS, it collects information that includes remote brokers' CPU loads, modulator execution times, and total execution times. The frequency with which such monitoring information is exchanged is also set when the broker is started. Third, given this information, the directory executes the following, simple algorithm to identify a suitable broker:

- check all available brokers in the order of the distance from the requesting broker;
- if a less loaded broker is found, stop the search and return the broker's id;
- if no such broker exists, terminate with failure.

The broker initiating the request contacts the target broker and executes the relocation protocol described in Section 3.2. To reduce the frequency with which relocations are performed, our current implementation simply relocates half of the modulators from the overloaded broker to the target broker. The result of these actions is depicted in Figure 12.

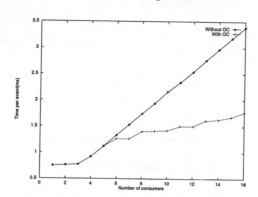

Fig. 13. Load Balancing Microbenchmark Results

4.2   Experimental Evaluation

Benchmarks. Figure 13 compares the performance of event distribution for opportunistic vs. normal channels. The events being passed are arrays of 100 floats. A for() loop is used to emulate the behavior of complex modulator runtimes. When brokers and consumers reside on different machines, with opportunistic channels, one intermediate broker is added after 6 consumers have joined the channel, and a second broker is added after 14 consumers have joined. In comparison, with the non-opportunistic channel, all consumers use the same broker for the entire duration of the experiment. The results clearly establish the importance of dynamic load distribution across brokers.

Performance of a Video Player. A more realistic experiment is one that measures the frame rate of a video player, varying the number of players and comparing the results with a single broker vs. dynamically 'split', multiple brokers. In the experiment, a video server runs on a Linux machine and multiple players each running on a different Linux machine receive video stream from the server. The results are shown in Figure 14. For 8 players, opportunistic channel permits the frame rate to be improved by a factor of 3.

5   Related Work

5.1   Publish/Subscribe Systems

Most current publish/subscribe systems permit subscribers to specify their interests, storing these interests at providers or intermediate brokers. Typical interest expressions result in predicate-based event filtering, sometimes also enabling limited forms of event transformation. However, most such subscription are stateless and therefore, do not support the general event processing needed for the complex data conversions occurring in multimedia, business, or scientific applications. In addition, a client's subscriptions cannot be changed at runtime. JECho and opportunistic channels generalize upon these systems' capabilities

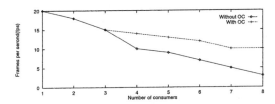

Fig. 14. Frame Rate Comparison

in our support for dynamic broker creation, load balancing across brokers and most importantly, in our ability to make broker behavior platform-aware, by dynamically monitoring and adapting to changes in platform capabilities and client behaviors.

There has been substantial research on interconnection topologies, event routing, and event matching (to eliminate redundant event transmission) in order to scale publish/subscribe systems to large numbers of publishers, subscribers, and events. Typically addressing wide area networks (e.g., Gryphon [24], SIENA [3], JEDI [7], READY [11]), The main goal in such work is to 'send' an event only towards brokers with consumers that are currently interested in that event, and to use shortest such path available. In comparison to our work, fixed topologies are used for broker interconnection, and there is no dynamic support for changing topologies or broker locations. More specifically, JEDI offers moveout and movein operations to change its dispatching system somehow, but the applications have to explicitly call those operations [8]. Elvin supports disconnection and reconnection in a mobile environment by using proxies, but the mobile client must connect to the same proxy even after it moves to a new location [33]. Neither system provides general adaptation support for dynamic reconfiguration and redeployment of the event system itself. [16] discusses general ideas about how to adapt a publish/subscribe system to mobile environments, but does not describe an implementation. Solar [5] provides a flexible and scalable data-fusion infrastructure for delivering context information in ubiquitous computing systems. Its concept of operator is similar to modulators in our systems, but modulator in JECho can perform more general operations. Furthermore, Solar focuses on how to delivery context information efficiently, whereas JECho is a general event system.

5.2 Mobile IP and Its Location Management

Optimization of location management for Mobile IP [19] is similar to the way in which opportunistic channels operate. Namely, both attempt to optimize event routing paths after a mobile host changes its location, by changing the 'triangle' delivery to direct delivery. Multiple handoff algorithms have been proposed for Mobile IP [19,13], all of which require location registration with clients' home agent or a regional agent. In comparison, opportunistic channels use directory services in place of home or regional agent, which implies that handoff performance depends on that of the directory service. Furthermore, modulator handoff is somewhat more complex than link handoff, especially for stateful modulators. Finally, since opportunistic channels are realized on top of Mobile IP, its performance benefits and overheads depend on the underlying Mobile IP implementation.

5.3   Adaptations in Mobile Environments

Several network-level efforts address mobility issues. As already mentioned, Mobile IP (e.g., Mobile IPv6 [25, 17]) enables a mobile user to stay connected when moving across network boundaries without changing its IP address. Berkeley's BARWAN project [20] provides seamless roaming across heterogeneous networks. Furthermore, BARWAN enables data forms to be changed to suit end system or wireless network limitations, by permitting application-level, type-specific data transformation and data compression [20]. JECho offers the same functionality, but in addition, provides dynamic support for handler partitioning [37]. Zhao, Castelluccia and Baker [36] describe a general-purpose mechanism at the network level, which supports multiple packet delivery methods and multiple network interfaces, where the system adaptively selects the most appropriate method and interface. Similarly, the CMU Monarch project aims to enable adaptive mobile host communications, to make the most efficient use of the network connectivity available to the mobile host at any time [18]. The adaptors used in opportunistic channels would interact with such network-level mechanisms. Resilient Overlay Networks [1] optimize application-specific routing metrics, by monitoring the functioning and quality of network paths. Opportunistic channels could implement the same mechanisms, if appropriate. Finally, there are several TCP enhancements for wireless networks [4].

Our work focuses on middleware-level and application-level adaptations, and it can benefit from the network level research mentioned above. Since such adaptations require information about network-level changes, we can also benefit from the substantial ongoing work on real-time network monitoring, including the work performed in the Monarch [18] and net100 [22] projects.

At application-level, the Odyssey projects extends the Unix System call interface to support flexible application-aware adaptations [23], as also done in our own work addressing interactive applications [29]. The system monitors resource levels, notifies applications of relevant changes, and enforces resource allocation decision. Each application independently decides how best to adapt when notified. This is similar to JECho's adaptations where an application can be notified of resource changes and responds to such changes according to its adaptation strategy defined in a modulator.

Some adaptations based on application semantics can be provided only at application level. For example, datatype-specific data transformation and data compression must depend on the application. Similarly, HRL's Intelligent information dissemination services use bandwidth-aware filtering to adapt information streams to resource bandwidth availability [32]. Our own previous work with JECho has addressed these problems by supporting general application-level adaptations via the dynamic deployment and partitioning of event modulators [38]. Opportunistic channels, as well as our related research on coordinating network- with application-level adaptations [14] complement these efforts, by providing models and mechanisms for linking network- or broker-level changes in resource availability with suitable application- and middleware-level adaptations.

6 Conclusions and Future Work

This paper describes how a content-based event dispatching system may be extended to cope with end user mobility and with the changing computational resources and network conditions of mobile systems. Our approach is to dynamically deploy and reconfigure the underlying event distribution infrastructure (i.e., the 'broker' overlays). The approach is realized with the novel abstraction of *opportunistic* event channels. Their implementation involves dynamically created event brokers, the runtime installation of event modulators in brokers, and the dynamic relocation of such modulators. Adaptation policies are realized by adaptors that interact with a runtime resource monitoring system. Essentially, opportunistic channels implement a middleware-level analogue of the channel handoff protocol used in wireless communications. More importantly, by coordinating network- with middleware-level handoffs, opportunistic channels can attain substantial performance improvements over non-adaptive event channels. Such improvements are due to their use of shorter network paths and the better balancing of loads across event brokers.

Future work should address some deficiencies of our current implementation, as well as generalize upon the basic concept of opportunistic channels. First, the current implementation assumes that there is only one intermediate broker between a provider and a consumer and therefore, cannot handle multi-level broker topologies. We are extending our implementation and algorithm to address this limitation. Second, our current experimentation uses wireless networks that employ base stations, with only the last hop being a wireless link. Future work will use opportunistic channels over ad-hoc wireless networks. In addition, the current implementation assumes a reliable network environment and therefore, does not consider dynamic disconnection and reconnection. Our intent is to add application-specific failure recovery to brokers, an example being the mirroring and failure recovery described for business transaction systems in [10].

References

1. D. G. Andersen, H. Balakrishnan, M. F. Kaashoek, and R. Morris. Resilient overlay networks. In *Proceedings of the 18th ACM Symposium on Operating Systems Principles(SOSP-18)*, October 2001.
2. F. E. Bustamante. *The Active Streams Approach to Adaptive Distributed Applications a nd Services*. PhD thesis, Georgia Institute of Technology, 2001.
3. A. Carzaniga, D. S. Rosenblum, and A. L. Wolf. Achieving scalability and expressiveness in an internet-scale event notification service. In *Proceedings of the Nineteenth Annual ACM Symposium on Principles of Distributed Computing(PODC 2000)*, pages 219–227, Portland, Oregon, July 2000.

4. M. C. Chan and R. Ramjee. Tcp/ip performance over 3g wireless links with rate and delay variation. In *Proceedings of The Eighth ACM International Conference on Mobile Computing and Networking(MobiCom 2002)*, Atlanta, GA, September 2002.

5. G. Chen and D. Kotz. An open platform for context-aware mobile applications. In *Proceedings of the First International Conference on Pervasive Computing (Pervasive 2002)*, August 2002.

6. Y. Chen, K. Schwan, and D. W. Rosen. Java mirrors: Building blocks for remote interaction. In *Proceedings of the 2002 International Parallel and Distributed Processing Symposium (IPDPS 2002)*, April 2002.

7. G. Cugola, E. D. Nitto, and A. Fuggetta. The "jedi" event-based infrastructure and its application to the development of the opss wfms. In *IEEE Transactions on Software Engineering in 2001*, 2001.

8. G. Cugola, E. D. Nitto, and G. P. Picco. Content-based dispatching in a mobile environment. In *In Workshop su Sistemi Distribuiti: Algorithms, Architecture e Linguaggi (WSDAAL)*, 2000.

9. G. Eisenhauer, F. Bustamente, and K. Schwan. Event services for high performance computing. In *Proceedings of High Performance Distributed Computing-9(HPDC-9)*, August 2000.

10. A. Gavrilovska, K. Schwan, and V. Oleson. A practical approach for 'zero' downtime in operational information systems. In *Proceedings of the 22nd International Conference on Distributed Computing Systems (ICDCS-22)*, July 2002.

11. R. Gruber, B. Krishnamurthy, and E. Panagos. The architecture of the READY event notification service. In *Proceedings of the 19th IEEE International Conference on Distributed Computing Systems Middleware Workshop*, Austin, Texas, USA, May 1999.

12. W. Gu, G. Eisenhauer, and K. Schwan. Falcon: On-line monitoring and steering of parallel programs. *Concurrency: Practice and Experience*, 10(9):699–736, August 1998.

13. E. Gustafsson and et al. *Mobile IPv4 Regional Registration*. draft-ietf-mobileip-reg-tunnel-05,IETF,September 2001.

14. Q. He, , and K. Schwan. Iq-rudp: Coordinating application adaptation with network transport. In *Proceedings of High Performance Distributed Computing-9(HPDC-9)*, July 2002.

15. A. Hills. Wireless andrew. *IEEE Spectrum*, 36(6), June 1999.

16. Y. Huang and H. Garcia-Molina. Publish/subscribe in a mobile environment. In *2nd ACM International Workshop on Data Engineering for Wireless and Mobile Access (MobiDE'01)*, Santa Barbara, California, USA, 2001.

17. D. Johnson and C. Perkins. *Mobility Support in IPv6*. Internet Draft, IETF, draft-ietf-mobileip-ipv6-12.txt(work in progress), September 2000.

18. D. B. Johnson and D. A. Maltz. Protocols for adaptive wireless and mobile networking. *IEEE Personal Communications*, 3(1):34–42, 1995.

19. D. B. Johnson and C. Perkins. *Route Optimization in Mobile IP*. In Internet Draft(work in progress), 1998.

20. R. Katz and E. Brewer. The case for wireless overlay networks. In *SPIE Multimedia and Networking Conference*, January 1996.

21. A. Medina, A. Lakhina, I. Matta, and J. Byers. Brite: An approach to universal topology generation. In *Proceedings of the International Workshop on Modeling, Analysis and Simulation of Computer and Telecommunications Systems- MASCOTS '01*, Cincinnati, Ohio, August 2001.

22. Net100. *The Net100 Project - Development of Network-Aware Operating Systems*. www.net100.org.

23. B. D. Noble, M. Satyanarayanan, D. Narayannan, J. Tilton, J. Flinn, and K. Walker. Agile application-aware adaptation for mobility. In *Proceedings of the 16th ACM Symposium on Operating Systems Principles(SOSP-16)*, October 1997.
24. L. Opyrchal, M. Astley, J. Auerbach, G. Banavar, R. Strom, , and D. Sturman. Exploiting ip multicast in content-based publish-subscribe systems. In *Proceedings of IFIP/ACM International Conference on Distributed Systems Platforms and Open Distributed Processing(Middleware 2000)*, April 2000.
25. C. Perkins. *IP Mobility Support*. IETF, Request for Comments 2002, Oct., 1996.
26. T. Phan, L. Huang, and C. Dulan. Integrating mobile wireless devices into the computational grid. In *Proceedings of The Eighth ACM International Conference on Mobile Computing and Networking(MobiCom 2002)*, Atlanta, GA, September 2002.
27. M. Pierce, C. Youn, and G. Fox. The gateway computational portal: Developing web services for high performance computing. In *Proceedings of 2002 International Conference on Computational Science(ICCS2002)*, April 2002.
28. C. Poellabauer and K. Schwan. Power-aware video decoding using real-time event handlers. In *Proceedings of the 5th International Workshop on Wireless Mobile Mult imedia (WoWMoM)*, September 2002.
29. C. Poellabauer, K. Schwan, and R. West. Coordinated cpu and event scheduling for distributed multimedia applications. In *Proceedings of the 9th ACM Multimedia Conference*, October 2001.
30. S. Rajagopalan and B. Badrinath. An adaptive location management strategy for mobile ip. In *Proceedings of the first annual international conference on Mobile computing and networking(MobiCom 1995)*, December 1995.
31. B. Segall and D. Arnold. Elvin has left the building: A publish/subscribe notification service with quenching. In *Proceedings of A UUG97*, September 1997.
32. E. C. Shek, S. K. Dao, Y. Zhang, and etc. Intelligent information dissemination services in hybrid satellite-wireless networks. *ACM Mobile Networks and Applications(MONET) Journal*, 5(4), December 2000.
33. P. Sutton, R. Arkins, and B. Segall. Supporting disconnectedness - transparent information delivery for mobile and invisible computing. In *CCGrid 2001 IEEE International Symposium on Cluster Computing and the Grid*, May 2001.
34. R. West, K. Schwan, and C. Poellabauer. Scalable scheduling support for loss and delay constrained media streams. In *Proceedings of 5th IEEE Real-Time and Embedded Technology and Applications Symposium (RTAS 1999)*, June 1999.
35. H. Yokota, A. Idoue, and T. Kat. Link layer assisted mobile ip fast handoff method over wireless lan networks. In *Proceedings of The Eighth ACM International Conference on Mobile Computing and Networking(MobiCom 2002)*, Atlanta, GA, September 2002.
36. X. Zhao, C. Castelluccia, and M. Baker. Flexible network support for mobility. In *Proceedings of The Fourth ACM International Conference on Mobile Computing and Networking(MobiCom 1998)*, October 1998.
37. D. Zhou, S. Pande, and K. Schwan. Method partitioning - runtime customization of pervasive programs without design-time application knowledge. In *Proceedings of the 23nd International Conference on Distributed Compu ting Systems (ICDCS-23)*, 2003.
38. D. Zhou, K. Schwan, G. Eisenhauer, and Y. Chen. Supporting distributed high performance application with java event channels. In *Proceedings of the 2001 International Parallel and Distributed Processing Symposium (IPDPS 2001)*, April 2001.

Congestion Control in a Reliable Scalable Message-Oriented Middleware

Peter R. Pietzuch[1,*] and Sumeer Bhola[2]

[1] University of Cambridge Computer Laboratory
Cambridge, UK
Peter.Pietzuch@cl.cam.ac.uk
[2] IBM T.J. Watson Research Center
Hawthorne, NY, USA
sbhola@us.ibm.com

Abstract. This paper presents congestion control mechanisms for reliable and scalable message-oriented middleware following the publish/subscribe communication model. We identify the key requirements of congestion control in this environment, how it differs from congestion control for the Internet, and propose a combination of two congestion control mechanisms, (1) driven by a publisher hosting broker (PDCC), (2) driven by a subscriber hosting broker (SDCC). SDCC decouples the notion of a receive window and a NACK window, and is used by subscriber hosting brokers in recovery mode. PDCC implements a scalable and low latency feedback loop between a publisher hosting broker and all subscriber hosting brokers, which is used to adjust the rate of publishing new messages, to allow brokers in recovery to eventually catch up, and other brokers to keep up. We present a detailed experimental evaluation of our implementation of these mechanisms in the Gryphon system by injecting network failures and link congestion.

1 Introduction

Message-oriented middleware is an important building block for enterprise applications. Its asynchronous model is preferable to tight synchronization, for application integration and information dissemination to many users. Reliability of message delivery, despite failures in the messaging middleware, and scalability of the middleware, are important requirements for many such applications.

This paper focuses on congestion control mechanisms for reliable and scalable messaging middleware. Our mechanisms are developed in the context of a publish/subscribe messaging model, since it is a challenging model due to its one-to-many nature and message filtering semantics. Subscribers express interest in messages by providing a predicate/filter, that can be executed on each message, and only messages that match the filter are delivered to the subscriber. Scalable messaging middleware is deployed as an overlay network of application-level routers, which we refer to as *brokers*. Typically, multiple routing paths are

---

* Work done while at IBM T.J. Watson Research Center.

M. Endler and D. Schmidt (Eds.): Middleware 2003, LNCS 2672, pp. 202–221, 2003.

possible between a pair of brokers, and the routing protocol used in the overlay both (1) balances the load amongst the available paths, and (2) routes around failed paths, for high availability. However, the overlay routing protocol cannot ensure that the system has enough capacity, say after some failure, to continue processing messages at the rate at which they are being published. In addition, messages lost due to failures need to be resent, which requires more capacity for retrieving them (potentially from stable storage), processing them at intermediate brokers, and network bandwidth for sending them on each network link.

Congestion control has been an active research area for Internet protocols, especially for point-to-point communication using TCP. There is also work that addresses end-to-end congestion control for IP multicast, such as using layered multicast [1], or single-rate schemes that adjust the sender's rate to the slowest receiver [2, 3]. However, these schemes are for best-effort delivery, and assume that all receivers get the same set of messages. In contrast, for reliable publish/-subscribe, (1) the congestion control mechanism needs to ensure that the overlay network allocates enough capacity for message retransmission to satisfy receivers who are lagging behind, (2) message filtering may occur at intermediate brokers, due to which each receiver may get a different subset of messages from the sender, and (3) message retransmissions, to overcome losses, can originate not only at the sender, but from caches located on the path from the sender to the receiver.

There are also important differences in the system environment compared with Internet protocols running on IP routers, such as:

1. Message processing is bursty due to (1) application-level scheduling, since brokers run on commercial off-the-shelf (COTS) hardware and software, and (2) variable processing cost of performing content filtering on a message.
2. The ratio of maximum queue size at a node, to the message processing throughput, is typically much higher for a broker compared to an Internet router. This is due to (1) lower routing throughput because of content filtering, and (2) larger queues to handle burstiness. Hence queue overflows occur only when significant congestion already exists. Since the congestion control mechanism should not allow significant congestion to build up, it cannot use message loss caused by queue overflows as a trigger for congestion control.
3. Broker software and inter-broker routing protocols are completely under the control of the messaging vendor. Hence, we are not constrained to a congestion control scheme which treats the entire overlay network as a black-box. At the same time, the congestion control scheme should not depend intimately on a particular broker architecture, since that would hinder congestion control being part of a future protocol standard for publish/subscribe routing.

1.1 System Model

We assume a model where brokers can perform 3 roles (1) *publisher hosting broker* (PHB) is an edge of the network broker to which publishing clients connect, (2) *subscriber hosting broker* (SHB) is an edge broker to which subscribing clients connect, and (3) *intermediate broker* (IB) is a broker which is inside the network and does not host clients. Brokers can perform multiple roles, but for simplicity of exposition we will assume that each broker has only one.

Each PHB hosts one or more publishing endpoints, referred to as *pubends*. Each pubend represents an ordered stream of messages, and maintains this stream in persistent storage. Messages published from different publishing clients may be assigned to the same pubend. This pubend decides on a position for the message in the persistent stream and logs the message to persistent store. After that, the pubend sends the message downstream towards SHBs. The IBs forward data and control messages to the SHBs, and may also perform filtering on data messages such that an SHB does not receive messages that do not match any of its subscribers' filters. One approach to performing such filtering, while preserving the guarantee of in-order exactly-once delivery to subscribers, is described in our previous work [4]. IBs also cache stream data and can respond to NACKs. NACKs not satisfied by an IB are forwarded towards the pubend.

The congestion control protocols presented here deal with congestion starting from the pubend upto and including the SHBs that receive messages from the pubend. The goal is to ensure that eventually all SHBs are being able to receive and deliver in-order *recent* messages from a pubend's stream. Hence, the protocols adjust the message rate to the slowest link or broker inside the system, but not to the slowest subscribing application. This design choice allows the system to protect itself against very slow or malicious subscribers by disconnecting them. The number of brokers is typically 3–4 orders of magnitude lower than the number of clients. We assume that the brokers are trusted.

We perform adaptation at both PHBs and SHBs to control congestion, such that broker queues do not overflow. Adaptation at an SHB is done by

- decoupling the notion of a NACK window and a receive window, where the receive window is used to bound the memory consumption at an SHB and the NACK window is used for congestion control.
- using a NACK throughput metric (similar to the send throughput metric in TCP Vegas [5]) to adjust the NACK window. Adjustment is additive increase and additive decrease. The NACK throughput adjusts to NACK responses received from the pubend or intermediate caches at IBs.

Adaptation at a PHBs is done using explicit feedback from the SHBs. Lack of feedback is not used as a trigger for congestion control since it can give false positives if some SHBs are down or partitioned from the rest of the network.

- The messages in a pubend stream are assigned timestamps based on real-time, and the message rate at SHBs is computed in terms of these timestamps. This normalizes the rate at different SHBs regardless of which subset of messages they receive, and the current pubend rate[1].

---

[1] The brokers do not need to have synchronized clocks, but the difference in clock rates should be small.

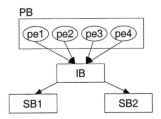

Fig. 1. A simple broker topology

- The protocol distinguishes between SHBs that are in recovery and those not in recovery, and scalably monitors the slowest SHB rate for both recovery and non-recovery using high-priority congestion-alert messages that get consolidated at intermediate brokers. The target rate for SHBs in recovery mode is such that they will eventually catch up to the current time.
- The PHB shapes the rate of new messages sent by a pubend when congestion occurs, using an additive increase and hybrid (multiplicative and additive) decrease that accounts for burstiness in the overlay network.

These protocols have been implemented in the context of the Gryphon system [6, 7, 4], which supports highly-scalable content-based publish/subscribe. The Gryphon system has been deployed for information dissemination in a wide-area environment, such as score updates for tennis Grand Slam events, and the Sydney Olympics, for tens of thousands of concurrently connected subscribers.

The paper is organized as follows: Section 2 illustrates the congestion problem using some examples of congestion collapse. Section 3 describes our congestion control protocols, and Sect. 4 discusses their implementation in the Gryphon broker. Section 5 describes experimental results that show the effectiveness of our protocols. Section 6 describes related work and we conclude in Sect. 7.

2 The Congestion Control Problem

In this section, we illustrate the congestion control (cc) problem in publish/-subscribe overlay networks by showing two instances of congestion collapse in Gryphon without any congestion control mechanism. This helps to characterize the points of congestion, and motivates the design presented in the next section.

Figure 1 shows a simple overlay network with 1 publisher hosting broker, PB, that hosts 4 pubends, connected to 2 SHBs, SB1 and SB2, through an intermediate broker IB. In this example there is only 1 path from PB to SB1, but in general there could be multiple paths. For instance, the Gryphon system organizes the overlay network into trees of cells [4], where each cell can have multiple equivalent brokers which balance the load and provide lightweight failover. The load balancing is accomplished by routing messages from different pubends on different paths through the same cell. We allow for the path from a pubend to a particular SHB to change, but assume that paths change infrequently.

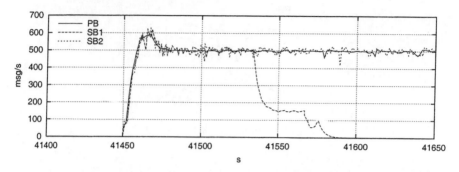

Fig. 2. Collapse with IB-SB1 link restricted to 60 KB/s

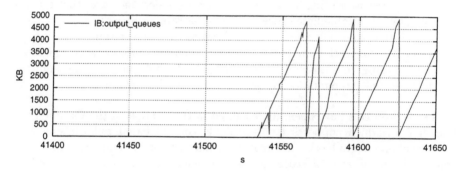

Fig. 3. Queue utilization at broker IB during collapse

In Gryphon, links between brokers are implemented using TCP connections, which means that there is a congestion control protocol running on each link. This is not sufficient to prevent congestion collapse in the system as a whole. We illustrate this for a simple overlay using two examples. In both examples, the PB is handling an aggregate publish rate of 500 msg/s, split over the 4 pubends, where each message has a message header and carries a 100 byte application payload. The trivial filter of 'true' is used on all inter-broker links, i.e., all data messages need to be eventually received at both SB1 and SB2. Each subscriber receives 2 msg/s and there are 250 subscribers each at SB1, SB2, which is an aggregate subscriber rate of 500 msg/s at each SHB. This is a modest rate, and the CPU at the SHBs is 95% idle in the steady-state.

In Fig. 2, after running the system without any congestion, we throttle the bandwidth on the IB-SB1 link to 60 KB/s [2]. The X-axis is elapsed time in seconds, and the Y-axis shows the aggregate smoothed rate for the pubends (PB) and the subscribing applications at SB1 and SB2 respectively. With no congestion control the pubends continue accepting published messages, and sending them, at the same rate. This causes queues to build up at IB (cf. Fig. 3) and eventually overflow which causes message loss. Lost messages need to be recov-

---

[2] KB/s stands for (binary) Kilo Bytes per second.

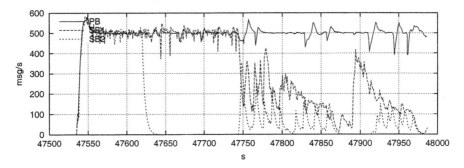

Fig. 4. Collapse with PB-IB link restricted to 250 KB/s

ered (using NACKs) before delivering later messages, but many of the messages retransmitted due to NACKs also get lost. The result is that the aggregate rate for subscribers connected to SB1 drops to zero.

In Fig. 4, the bandwidth on the PB-IB link is restricted to 250 KB/s. In the absence of failure, this does not cause congestion. We then fail the link IB-SB2 for 120 s. When the link comes back, the NACKs initiated by SB2 cause congestion on the PB-IB link and the rate for subscribers at both SB1 and SB2 drops much below the rate at which pubends are sending new messages, and never recovers.

These examples demonstrate how congestion on a network link can cause collapse. Congestion at an IB or SHB, due to not having enough CPU capacity, can also appear to be network congestion to an upstream broker since its outgoing queues will build up. However, CPU congestion at a PHB due to the overhead of processing NACKs may not readily appear as queue buildup, since NACKs are small and each NACK message can request retransmission of a large number of data messages. We want to control all three kinds of congestion (1) on a network link, (2) at an IB or SHB, (3) at the PHB, while ensuring that all SHBs that are trying to recover messages they missed due to failure are eventually successful.

3   Congestion Control Protocols

In this section, we present our congestion control mechanism in detail. The solution consists of two parts: (1) The *PHB-driven cc protocol (PDCC)* ensures that pubends do not cause congestion due to a too high publication rate. A feedback loop between pubends and SHBs with downstream and upstream messages is created to monitor congestion in the broker network. (2) The *SHB-driven cc protocol (SDCC)* handles the rate at which SHBs try to recover after a failure. This protocol only involves the SHBs by monitoring their recovery rate. These two congestion control mechanisms can be used independently from each other. Both protocols need to distinguish between recovering and non-recovering SHBs in order to ensure that SHBs will eventually manage to recover successfully[3].

---

[3] Informally, an SHB is recovering when it is re-requesting previous messages sent by the pubend. A non-recovering SHB is only receiving new messages.

3.1   PHB-Driven Congestion Control

The PDCC mechanism regulates the rate at which new messages are published by a pubend. The publication rate is adjusted depending on the observed throughput at the SHBs. It is the responsibility of the SHBs to calculate their own congestion metric based on throughput and notify the pubend whenever they think that they are suffering from congestion. The PDCC protocol uses two kinds of control messages between brokers to exchange congestion information:

Downstream Congestion Query Messages (DCQ). DCQ messages trigger the congestion control mechanism. They are generated by a pubend and sent down the message dissemination tree to all SHBs. DCQ messages carry a (1) pubend identifier (`pubendID`), (2) a monotonically increasing sequence number (`sequenceNo`), and (3) the current position in the pubend's message stream (`m_pubend`), e.g. the latest assigned message timestamp.

Upstream Congestion Alert Messages (UCA). UCA messages tell the pubend about congestion. They flow upwards the message dissemination tree from SHBs to the pubend and are generated by SHBs in response to DCQ messages. They are aggregated at IBs so that the pubend eventually receives a single UCA message. Apart from a pubend identifier and a sequence number, they contain the (3) minimum throughput rates observed at recovering (`minRecSHBRate`) and (4) non-recovering (`minNonRecSHBRate`) SHBs. The sequence number associates a UCA message with the DCQ message that triggered it.

For the PDCC scheme to be efficient, it is important that (1) DCQ and UCA messages have very low loss rates and (2) their queuing delays are much lower than the maximum delays that can occur in the system, even when the system in congested. Since DCQ and UCA messages are small in size and are sent at a larger time-scale compared to data messages, they consume little resources in the system. In our implementation, described in Sect. 4, DCQ and UCA messages are treated as high-priority messages in the event broker. Note that for fairness with other applications sharing the network, we rely on the fairness properties of TCP for inter-broker connections. We will describe the behavior of the three types of brokers (PHB, IB, and SHB) when processing these messages in turn[4].

Publisher Hosting Brokers (PHB). The PHB triggers the PDCC mechanism by periodically sending out DCQ messages. The sequence number in the DCQ message is used to match it to the corresponding response coming from the SHBs in form of a UCA message. The interval (e.g. 1 s) at which DCQ messages are dispatched determines the interval at which the pubend will receive UCA responses when there is congestion. The higher the rate of responses, the quicker the protocol will adapt to congestion.

When the PHB has not received any UCA messages for a certain period of time (t_{nouca}), it assumes that the system is currently not congested. It then increases the publication rate when the rate is throttled (i.e. the publishers could publish at a higher rate). For the increase of the publication rate, we use a hybrid

---

[4] To simplify the discussion, we will assume that each PHB only hosts a single pubend.

scheme with additive and multiplicative increase. The new rate r_{new} is calculated from the old rate r_{old} according to

$$r_{\text{new}} = \max \left[\, r_{\text{old}} + r_{\text{min}}, \; r_{\text{old}} + f_{\text{incr}} * (r_{\text{old}} - r_{\text{decr}}) \, \right]. \tag{1}$$

In (1), r_{decr} is the publication rate at the time of the last decrease in rate, f_{incr} is a multiplicative increment, and r_{min} is the minimum increase in rate. Initially, we used a purely additive scheme that resulted in a very slow increment, but experiments showed that a more optimistic approach gave a higher message throughput. The multiplicative use of f_{incr} allows the increase to be faster than a fixed additive increase. However, when the publication rate is already close to the optimal value, it is necessary to limit the increase. This done by keeping track of the publication rate at which the increase started (r_{decr}) and using it to restrict the multiplicative increase. As shown in the experiments in Sect. 5, this scheme leads to the publication rate probing whether the congestion condition has disappeared and, if not, oscillating around the optimal operating point.

When the PHB receives a UCA message, a decision is made whether to decrease the current publication rate. The rate is kept constant if the sequence number of the received UCA message is smaller than the sequence number of the DCQ message that was sent after the last decrease. This means that the system did not have enough time to adapt to the last decrease in rate and more time should pass before another congestion control decision can be made. Moreover, the rate is not reduced if the throughput value in the UCA message is larger than the value in the previous message. In this case, the congestion situation is improving, and further reduction in rate is deemed to be unnecessary. Otherwise, the publisher rate is decreased according to

$$r_{\text{new}} = \max \left[\, f_{\text{decr1}} * r_{\text{old}}, \; (r_{\text{decr}} + f_{\text{decr2}} * (r_{\text{old}} - r_{\text{decr}})) \, \right] \text{ iff } r_{\text{decr}} \neq r_{\text{old}} \tag{2}$$

$$r_{\text{new}} = f_{\text{decr1}} * r_{\text{old}} \text{ otherwise} \tag{3}$$

where f_{decr1} and f_{decr2} are two multiplicative decrement factors. The first term in (2) multiplicatively reduces the rate by a factor f_{decr1}, whereas the second term reduces the rate relative to the previous decrement r_{decr}. As in (1), the second term prevents an aggressive reduction in rate when congestion is encountered for the first time after an increase. Since the PDCC mechanism constantly tries to increase the publication rate in order to achieve a higher rate, it will eventually cause SHBs to send UCA messages. This should not result in a strong reduction of the rate. Taking the maximum of the two decrement values tries to keep the publication rate close to the optimal operating point that is supported by the system. However, if the congestion level does not improve after a reduction, the publication rate is reduced again. This time a multiplicative decrease is performed (3) since the condition $r_{\text{decr}} = r_{\text{old}}$ now holds.

Intermediate Brokers (IB). The aggregation logic of UCA messages at IBs must ensure that (1) multiple UCA messages from different SHBs are consolidated such that the minimum rate at any SHB is passed upstream in a UCA

```
1    processDCQ(dcqMsg):
2      sendDownstream(dcqMsg)
3
4    initialization:
5      minNonRecSHBRate ← ∞, minRecSHBRate ← ∞, seqNo ← 0
6
7    processUCA (ucaMsg):
8      minNonRecSHBRate ← MIN(minNonRecSHBRate, ucaMsg.minNonRecSHBRate)
9      minRecSHBRate ← MIN(minRecSHBRate, ucaMsg.minRecSHBRate)
10     IF ucaMsg.seqNo > seqNo THEN
11       sendUpstream(ucaMsg.seqNo, minNonRecSHBRate, minRecSHBRate)
12       minNonRecSHBRate ← ∞, minRecSHBRate ← ∞, seqNo ← ucaMsg.seqNo
```

Fig. 5. Processing logic for DCQ and UCA messages at IBs

message. This enables the pubend to adjust its publication rate to provide for the worst congested SHB in the system. Moreover, (2) when UCA messages occur for the first time, they should be immediately sent upstream so that the pubend responds to new congestion as quickly as possible.

The algorithm for processing DCQ/UCA messages is shown in Fig. 5: IBs relay DCQ messages down to their children (line 2) and aggregate UCA responses. An IB keeps track of the minimum observed throughput values for non-recovering and recovering SHBs, and the maximum sequence number of the UCA messages that it has received (line 5). When a new UCA message arrives, the throughput minima are potentially updated (lines 8–9). A new UCA message is only sent upstream if the sequence number of the received message is larger than the maximum sequence number stored at the IB (line 10). This ensures that UCA messages with the same sequence number coming from different SHBs are aggregated before being sent upstream. However, the first UCA message with a new sequence number immediately triggers a new UCA message so that the pubend is quickly informed about newly detected congestion. Future UCA messages from other SHBs having the same sequence number will be aggregated, and will contribute towards the throughput minima in the next UCA message. After a UCA message is sent, both minimum throughput values are reset (line 12).

Subscriber Hosting Brokers (SHB). A SHB uses the ratio of pubend and SHB message rate as a metric for detecting congestion.

$$t = \frac{r_{\text{pubend}}}{r_{\text{SHB}}} \tag{4}$$

To allow for burstiness in the throughput due to application-level scheduling and network anomalies, we smooth t using a standard first-order low pass filter with an (empirical) value of $\alpha = 0.1$ and obtain $\bar{t}$.

$$\bar{t} = (1 - \alpha)\,\bar{t} + \alpha t \tag{5}$$

In addition, we need to distinguish between recovering and non-recovering SHBs. We describe how a SHB detects that it is recovering in Sect. 4.

Non-recovering Brokers. A non-recovering SHB should receive messages at the *same rate* at which they are sent by the pubends. If the smoothed throughput ratio $\bar{t}$ drops below unity by a threshold, the SHB assumes that it has started falling behind because of congestion.

$$\bar{t} < 1 - \Delta t_{\text{nonrec}} \tag{6}$$

In rare cases, an SHB could be slowly falling behind because $\bar{t}$ stays below 1 (but above $1 - \Delta t_{\text{nonrec}}$) for a long time. Unless there is already significant congestion in the system, this will not cause overflow if queue sizes are large. Nevertheless, an SHB needs a mechanism to detect even very slow queue build-up. Therefore, an SHB periodically compares its current position in its message stream m_{SHB} to the pubend's message stream position (m_{pubend}), as given in the last DCQ message. If the difference is larger than Δt_s, the SHB will send a UCA message, even though its throughput ratio $\bar{t}$ is above the threshold:

$$m_{\text{SHB}} < m_{\text{pubend}} + \Delta t_s \tag{7}$$

Recovering Brokers. A recovering SHB must receive messages at a *higher rate* than the publication rate, otherwise it will never manage to successfully catch-up and recover all previous messages. Often, there is an additional requirement to maintain a minimum recovery rate $1 + \Delta t_{\text{rec}}$ that ensures a timely recovery. Thus, a recovering SHB will send a UCA message if

$$\bar{t} < 1 + \Delta t_{\text{rec}} \tag{8}$$

holds. The value of Δt_{rec} influences how much of the congested resource will be used for recovery messages instead of new data messages.

3.2   SHB-Driven Congestion Control

The SDCC mechanism manages the rate at which an SHB requests missed data by sending NACKs upstream. An SHB maintains a NACK window to decide which parts of the message stream should be requested. Then, the NACK window is opened and closed additively depending on the level of congestion in the broker network. The change in recovery rate throughput is used for detecting congestion.

An SHB starts with a small NACK window size $nwnd_0$. During recovery, the NACK window is adjusted depending on the change in recovery rate r_{SHB},

$$r_{\text{SHB}} = \frac{nwnd}{RTT}, \tag{9}$$

where $nwnd$ is the NACK window size and RTT is an estimate of the round trip time needed to satisfy a NACK.

The NACK window is managed in a similar fashion to TCP Vegas [5]: When r_{SHB} increases by at least a factor α_{NACK}, the NACK window is opened by one additional NACK per RTT. When r_{SHB} decreases by at least a factor β_{NACK}, the NACK window is reduced by one NACK:

$$nwnd_{\text{new}} = nwnd_{\text{old}} \pm size_{\text{NACK}} \tag{10}$$

Table 1. Configuration parameters for the PDCC and SDCC protocols

Param.	Description	Value
$size_{NACK}$	minimum size of NACK	100 tickms
$t_{silence}$	interval for sending explicit silence messages	1000 ms
t_{nouca}	interval without UCA messages before rate increase for PDCC	2000 ms
r_{min}	minimum rate increase for PDCC scheme	2 msgs
f_{incr}	multiplicative increment for PDCC scheme	0.05
f_{decr1}	multiplicative decrement for PDCC scheme	0.5
f_{decr2}	multiplicative decrement w.r.t. previous increment for PDCC	0.25
α	smoothing factor for low pass filter	0.1
Δt_{nonrec}	threshold value for UCA messages for non-recovering SHBs	50 tickms
Δt_{rec}	threshold value for UCA messages for recovering SHBs	1000 tickms
Δt_s	threshold value for lag in message stream for SHBs	4000 tickms
$nwnd_0$	initial size of NACK window	100 tickms
α_{NACK}	recovery rate increase before NACK window is increased	0.1
β_{NACK}	recovery rate decrease before NACK window is decreased	0.3

4 Implementation in the Gryphon Broker

We have implemented the PDCC and SDCC mechanisms as an extension on top of the guaranteed delivery service provided by the Gryphon Broker [4]. The implementation comes with a number of configuration parameters (cf. Table 1) that influence the congestion control protocols. They were either explained in Sect. 3 or are referred to below. We begin by giving an introduction to Gryphon's guaranteed delivery service and then discuss the SHB and PHB implementation.

Guaranteed Delivery Service. Under exactly-once delivery semantics, the message stream is subdivided into discrete intervals called *ticks*. Each tick potentially holds a data message and is in one of four states: (1) (d)ata, when it contains a published message, (2) (s)ilence, when no message was published or was filtered upstream, (3) (f)inal, when it is no longer needed, and (4) (q) unknown, when its state is unknown. Ticks are fine-grained such that no two data messages can be assigned to the same tick. This is achieved by using a millisecond granularity clock that is enhanced with a counter to assign unique timestamps to messages. Therefore, a tick can be converted into a real-time timestamp assigned by the pubend.

When no messages are published, ticks in the stream are assigned the silence state. A data message is prefixed with all silence ticks since the last message so that brokers can update their message streams. A pubend will send an explicit silence message containing silence ticks when no data messages were published for a certain interval. This is done every $t_{silence}$ ms (cf. Table 1). Explicit silence messages ensure that SHBs know that no messages were published.

The message stream at an SHB is initialized with all ticks in the unknown state. The SHB then attempts to resolve all unknown ticks to either data or silence states by sending NACK messages upstream. Once a tick has been successfully

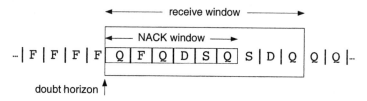

Fig. 6. Example of an `EdgeOutputStream` at an SHB

processed by the SHB, the receipt is acknowledged and its state changes to final. Each SHB maintains a *doubt horizon*, which is the position in the stream until which there are no unknown ticks. All ticks before the doubt horizon either already were or can be delivered to the client applications.

SHB Implementation. In our PDCC implementation, SHBs use the rate of progress of the doubt horizon in the message stream (dh_{rate}) to detect congestion. Since the message stream contains seconds worth of ticks, the rate is measured as "tick seconds" per second:

$$t = dh_{\mathrm{rate}} = \frac{\mathrm{ticks}}{\mathrm{time}} \tag{11}$$

An SHB maintains a consolidated message stream that is used to service all subscribers, and is represented using an `EdgeOutputStream` object. This stream maintains two windows, a *receive window* and a *NACK window*. The lower bound of both windows is the doubt horizon, and so they advance together with the doubt horizon. The receive window is a range of ticks such that only ticks that fall within this window are processed, and messages containing information about ticks outside the window are ignored. Thus, the receive window bounds the memory usage of the `EdgeOutputStream`. In the SDCC mechanism, the NACK window is a subset of the receive window that determines which unknown ticks in the `EdgeOutputStream` can be NACKed. The NACK window size (*nwnd*) is altered depending on the rate of progress of the window through the stream (cf. Sect. 3.2). Figure 6 shows an example of an `EdgeOutputStream` with a receive window and a NACK window. The doubt horizon points to the first unknown tick. The three unknown ticks that are within the NACK window will trigger NACK messages. Any messages referring to ticks outside the receive window will be ignored and, consequently, NACKed once the receive window has advanced.

As mentioned previously, an SHB must be able to determine whether it is currently recovering or not. A solution where the SHB considers whether it is sending NACK messages would be too sensitive because a single lost message would force the PDCC mechanism to go into recovery mode. Instead, we implemented a scheme in which an SHB claims to be recovering only if it has been ignoring messages with ticks outside its receive window. This means that its doubt horizon has been lagging behind by a significant amount and the SHB is recovering all previous ticks in its receive window.

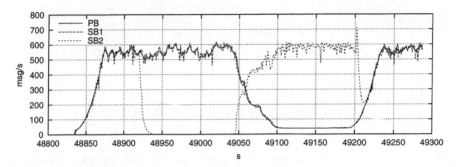

Fig. 7. E1: Congestion control after a IB-SB1 link failure

PHB Implementation. The PDCC protocol requires pubends to be able to shape the rate of messages coming from publishers. We implemented a simple scheme that is compatible with the Java Message Service (JMS) API [8] used between clients and a Gryphon broker. The pubend keeps track of the number of messages published by a publisher in a time interval and stops sending ACK messages once the target rate has been reached. Holding back acknowledgments to publishers prevents them from publishing new messages. In the future, we plan to implement window flow control between clients and brokers.

5   Experimental Results

In this section, we discuss our experiments that evaluate the PDCC and SDCC mechanisms under congestion in two different topologies. The experimental setup was a network of dedicated broker machines running AIX connected via Ethernet links. Various broker metrics were used to create the plots shown here. Physical link failure was simulated by flushing a broker's output queues and closing its TCP connection. Network congestion was created as bandwidth limits on links. In all experiments, the PHB had 4 pubends and the broker queue sizes were large to maximize throughput (input queues: $\sim 24\,\mathrm{MB}$; output queues: $5\,\mathrm{MB}$).

E1: CC after Link Failure (Simple Topology). The first experiment is a re-run of the failure experiment from Sect. 2. However, now the PDCC and SDCC schemes ensure that the system recovers successfully. Figure. 7 shows that the publication rate of PB is reduced by the PDCC mechanism after the IB-SB2 link comes back up ($t = 49045$) because most of its bandwidth is used by the broker SB2 for recovery. After SB2 has finished recovering ($t = 49205$), PB can increase its publication rate. The spike in SB2's rate close to the end of the recovery phase occurs because the IB caches recent ticks in its message stream and is therefore able to satisfy some of the final NACKs more quickly.

The plot in Fig. 8 [5] shows the behavior of the NACK window during recovery, as controlled by the SDCC mechanism. Initially, the NACK window has a small

---

[5] This plot is a re-run of E1 with a b/w limit on the PB-IB link of $500\,\mathrm{KB/s}$.

value (200 tickms) and is progressively increased until an optimal operation point ($\sim$ 900 tickms) is found. The NACK window further increases towards the end of the recovery process because of cached ticks at the IB.

E2: CC with B/W Limits (Simple Topology). We investigated how well the PDCC mechanism can adapt to an alternating bandwidth limit. At first, the IB-SB1 link is restricted to 60 KB/s for 120 s ($t = 63500..63620$). After that, the limit is increased to 150 KB/s for 120 s ($t = 63620..63740$), and then reduced to 60 KB/s again. As can be seen from the publication rate in Fig. 9, the PDCC scheme attempts to determine the optimal rate that can be supported by the link bottlenecks. It quickly adapts to new bottlenecks and keeps the queue utilization low (Fig. 10). Even when the available bandwidth is severely restricted ($t = 63500, 63740$), the output queues at the IB do not increase above 1 MB. The publication rate oscillates around the optimal point since the PHB is constantly probing the system to see whether the congestion situation has improved. The r_{decr} mechanism ensures that it stays close to the optimal value.

Figure 11 shows the doubt horizon rate from UCA messages received at the pubend. When there is no congestion during the first 120 s, no UCA messages are received except for transient messages at start-up. These messages occur when the doubt horizons at the SHBs start advancing causing the doubt horizon rate to stay below the threshold for a short time. At $t = 63540$, the doubt horizon rate decreases to half its previous value because of the link bottleneck. Once the publication rate at the pubend has been reduced sufficiently, the doubt horizon rate starts increasing again. When the link bottleneck is constant, UCA messages with doubt horizon rates slightly below the "real-time" rate of 1 ticksec/s are received periodically and prevent the publication rate from increasing further.

E3: CC with B/W Limits and Link Failures (Complex Topology). To evaluate how multiple sources of congestion in different parts of the network are handled, we set up a complex broker topology. This topology consists of 1 PHB, 3 IBs, and 5 SHBs (Fig. 12). It is asymmetric with different paths lengths from the SHBs to PHB. IBs have to perform a non-trivial amount of aggregation of UCA messages that are sent upstream by SHBs in different parts of the network. The following experiments had 100 subscribers per SHB so that under normal conditions the message rate at an SHB was 2/5 of the PHB's rate.

The first experiment consists of link bottlenecks and link failures (leading to subsequent recovery phases). Throughout the entire run, the IB1-SB1 link is restricted to 250 KB/s, which does not cause congestion in the absence of failures. The PB-IB1 link is limited to 150 KB/s at $t = 56590$, and, after 120 s, the IB3-SB5 link is failed ($t = 56710..56830$). The message rates observed at the SHBs and PHB are shown in Fig 13. At the beginning, the PB broker publishes messages at a rate of around 500 msgs/s. The subscribers connected to each SHB observe an aggregate message rate of 200 msg/s. When the first bandwidth limit comes into effect, all SHBs receive messages at a reduced rate because PB adjusts its publication rate. After the failure of the IB3-SB5 link, PB drops its rate even further to enable SB5 to recover all lost messages. Even though the link

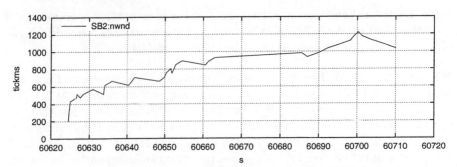

Fig. 8. E1: NACK window behavior after the IB-SB1 link failure

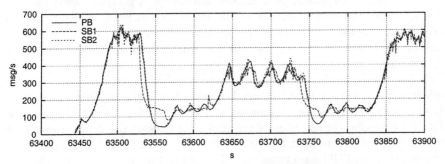

Fig. 9. E2: Congestion control with dynamic bandwidth restrictions

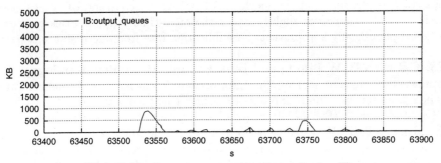

Fig. 10. E2: Output queue utilization at broker IB

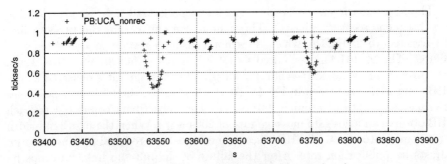

Fig. 11. E2: UCA messages received at pubend

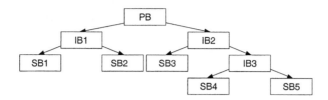

Fig. 12. A complex broker topology

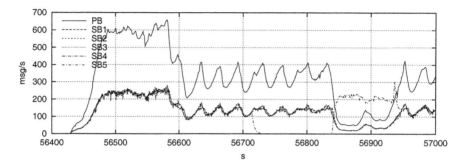

Fig. 13. E3: Congestion control with bandwidth restrictions and link failures

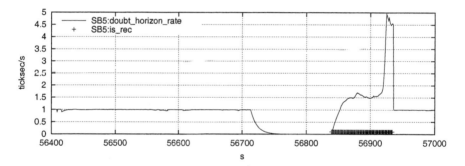

Fig. 14. E3: Doubt horizon rate with bandwidth restrictions and link failures

bottleneck and failure occur in different parts of the network at the same time, the PDCC scheme drives the publication rate by the worst congestion point in the system and successfully prevents queues from building up.

The doubt horizon rate, as observed at SB5, is shown in Fig. 14. Since the doubt horizon rate is independent from the publication rate, it stays close to 1 ticksec/s until the IB3-SB5 link is failed at $t = 56710$. The value of $\Delta t_{\rm rec}$ in this experiment is 0.5 ticksec/s. After the link failure, the SHB switches to recovery mode (is_rec in Fig. 14) and the doubt horizon rate is kept above $\Delta t_{\rm rec}$. Close to the end, the rate peaks to about 5 ticksec/s when SB5 reaches the point in the message stream at which the pubend reduced its rate. Now, more ticks in the stream are silence ticks without data, which enables the SHB to recover faster.

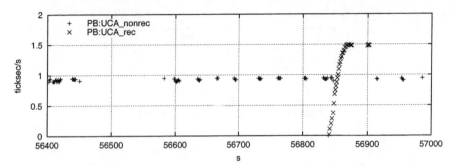

Fig. 15. E3: UCA messages received at pubend

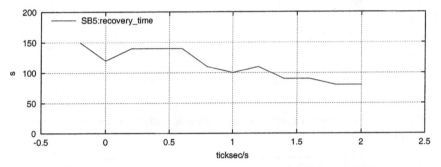

Fig. 16. E4: Variation of recovery time with Δt_{rec} threshold

Figure 15 shows the consolidated UCA messages received at PB from recovering and non-recovering SHBs. After a startup effect, messages from the non-recovering SHBs (UCA_nonrec) arrive at regular intervals due to the link bottleneck PB-IB1. When SB5 starts recovering ($t = 56830$), it sends UCA messages (UCA_rec) in recovery mode whenever its rate drops below Δt_{rec}.

E4: CC with Different Recovery Times (Simple Topology). The next experiments show how the duration of recovery is influenced by the threshold value Δt_{rec}. The higher this value, the earlier the SHB will send UCA messages so that more of the congested resource is used for recovery messages. Figure 16 plots how recovery time varies with the Δt_{rec} values ranging from $-0.2 .. 2.0$ ticksec/s at 0.2 ticksec/s steps. A value $\Delta t_{\mathrm{rec}} \leq 0$ is not used in practice, as it can result in an infinite recovery time. The PB-IB1 link was throttled to 500 KB/s.

The plot shows a clear correlation between Δt_{rec} and the recovery duration. However, it is not linear for two reasons: (1) With Δt_{rec} above 1.8 ticksec, the bandwidth-restricted link PB-IB is saturated with resent data messages. (2) When Δt_{rec} is less than or equal to 1 ticksec/s, there is an interaction between the 4 pubends: Even though the low threshold value does not require the pubends to reduce their publication rate by much, some pubends tend to consume a larger fraction of the bottleneck bandwidth, reducing the available bandwidth for the remaining pubends. These pubends observe a very low doubt horizon rate and thus reduce their publication rate more than necessary. The reason for this unfairness between pubends is that we employ first-come first-serve scheduling of messages in brokers and the PDCC protocol cannot synchronize rate reduction at different pubends inside a distributed system. We intend to investigate if the unfairness properties of the TCP Vegas equation are causing this [9].

6   Related Work

TCP. TCP comes with a point-to-point, end-to-end cc algorithm with a congestion window that uses additive increase, multiplicative decrease (AIMD) [10]. *Slow start* helps to open the congestion window more quickly. Packet loss is the only indicator for congestion in the system and *fast retransmit* enables the receiver to signal packet loss by ACK repetition. Modern TCP implementations such as TCP Vegas [5] attempt to detect congestion before packet loss occurs by using a throughput-based congestion metric. Since TCP Vegas is widely used, we decided to base our NACK throughput metric on this.

Reliable Multicast. Multicast protocols are comparable to pub/sub due to their one-to-many semantics, but typically have no filtering at intermediate nodes, and do not ensure that all leaves in the tree will eventually catch up to the sender. Congestion control is usually implemented at the transport level relying on router support. It must often adhere to existing standards to ensure fairness and compatibility with TCP [11, 12]. Since there are many receivers, scalable feedback processing is important, e.g. by feedback suppression [13]. Our approach does not discard information by consolidating feedback in a scalable way. Multicast cc schemes can be divided into (1) *sender-based*, in which all receivers support the same rate, and (2) *receiver-based* schemes, in which receivers have different rates by requesting transcoded versions of the data [14]. Since we can make few assumptions about our data, a receiver-based approach is hard.

The pgmcc [2] protocol forms a feedback loop between the sender and the "worst" congested receiver. The sender chooses this receiver depending on receiver reports in NACKs. The cc protocol for SRM [15] is similar except that here the feedback agent can give positive and negative feedback, and a receiver locally decides whether to send a congestion notification upstream to compete for becoming the new agent. An approach that does not rely on network support except minimal congestion feedback in NACKs is LE-SBCC [3]. A cascaded filter model transforms the NACKs from the multicast tree to appear like unicast NACKs before feeding them into an AIMD module. However, no consolidation of NACKs can be performed. All these schemes use a loss-based congestion metric that is not a good indicator for congestion in an application-level network.

Multicast ABR ATM. The ATM Forum Traffic Management Spec. [16] includes an available bit rate (ABR) category for traffic through an ATM network. At connection set-up, Forward and Backward Resource Management (FRM/-BRM) cells are exchanged between the sender and the receiver and modified at intermediate ATM switches depending on their resource availability. All involved parties agree on an acceptable cell rate depending on congestion in the system.

Multicast ABR requires flow control for one-to-many communication: A FRM cell is sent by the source and all receivers in the multicast tree respond with BRM cells that are consolidated at ATM switches [17]. Different ways of consolidating feedback cells have been proposed [18]. These algorithms have a trade-off between timely responsive and the creation of "consolidation noise" when new BRM cells do not include feedback from all downstream branches. Our consolidation logic at the IBs tries to balance this trade-off by aggregating UCA messages with the same sequence number and short-cutting new UCA messages. The scalable flow control protocol in [19] follows a "soft" synchronization approach where BRM cells triggered by different FRM cells can be consolidated at a branch point.

Overlay Networks. Congestion control for application-level overlay networks is sparse, mainly because application-level routing is a new research focus. A hybrid system for application-level reliable multicast in heterogeneous networks that addresses congestion control is RMX [20]. Here, a receiver-based scheme with the transcoding of application data is suggested. In general, global flow control in an overlay network can be viewed as a dynamic optimization problem [21] where a cost-benefit approach helps to find an optimal solution.

7   Conclusion

The problem of congestion control in messaging systems has received little attention so far. In this paper, we have presented a scalable congestion control scheme for a reliable message-oriented middleware. We have separated our scheme into a PHB-driven protocol that restricts the rate of new data messages, and a SHB-driven protocol that limits the rate of NACKs. Both protocols were implemented as part of the Gryphon Broker, an industrial-strength message-oriented middleware. The proposed solution addresses the special requirements of application-level overlay routing of messages, and filtering of messages at intermediate brokers in the network, and introduces little overhead into the system. A number of experiments with simple and complex topologies were used to show that the system quickly adapts to congestion and ensures that queue utilization is low.

Future work will investigate how to dynamically adapt the interval between DCQ messages and how to take advantage of the doubt horizon rate in UCA messages. Using the doubt horizon rate will help the system realize the severity of the congestion and allow it to adjust its rate faster to adapt to it.

References

1. McCanne, S., Jacobson, V., Vetterli, M.: Receiver-driven Layered Multicast. In: Proc. of ACM SIGCOMM. Volume 26,4. (1996) 117–130
2. Rizzo, L.: pgmcc: A TCP-Friendly Single-Rate Multicast Congestion Control Scheme. In: Proc. of ACM SIGCOMM, Stockholm, Sweden (2000)
3. Thapliyal, P., Li, S., Kalyanaraman, S.: LE-SBCC: Loss-Event Oriented Source-based Multicast Congestion Control. Technical report, RPI-ECSE (2001)

4. Bhola, S., Strom, R., Bagchi, S., Zhao, Y., Auerbach, J.: Exactly-once Delivery in a Content-based Publish-Subscribe System. In: Proc. of the Int. Conf. on Dependable Systems and Networks (DSN'2002). (2002) 7–16

5. Brakmo, L.S., O'Malley, S.W., Peterson, L.L.: TCP Vegas: New Techniques for Congestion Detection and Avoidance. In: Proc. of ACM SIGCOMM. (1994)

6. Banavar, G., Chandra, T., Mukherjee, B., Nagarajarao, J., Strom, R.E., Sturman, D.C.: An Efficient Multicast Protocol for Content-based Publish-Subscribe Systems. In: Proc. of the 19th IEEE Int. Conf. on Distributed Computing Systems, 1999. (1999) 262–272

7. Aguilera, M.K., Strom, R.E., Sturman, D.C., Astley, M., Chandra, T.D.: Matching Events in a Content-based Subscription System. In: Proc. of the Principles of Distributed Computing, 1999. (1999) 53–61

8. Sun: Java^{TM} Message Service. In: http://java.sun.com/products/jms/. (2001)

9. Hasegawa, G., Murata, M., Miyahara, H.: Fairness and Stability of Congestion Control Mechanisms of TCP. In: Proc. of INFOCOM'99. (1999)

10. Jacobson, V., Karels, M.J.: Congestion Avoidance and Control. In: Proc. of ACM SIGCOMM. (1988) 314–332

11. Floyd, S., Fall, K.: Promoting the Use of End-to-end Congestion Control in the Internet. IEEE/ACM Trans. on Networking 7 (1999) 458–472

12. Golestani, S.J., Sabnani, K.K.: Fundamental Observations on Multicast Congestion Control in the Internet. In: INFOCOM (2). (1999) 990–1000

13. DeLucia, D., Obraczka, K.: Multicast Feedback Suppression Using Representatives. In: INFOCOM (2). (1997) 463–470

14. Yang, Y.R., Lam, S.S.: Internet Multicast Congestion Control: A Survey. In: Proc. of ICT, Acapulco, Mexico (2000)

15. Shi, S., Waldvogel, M.: A Rate-based End-to-end Multicast Congestion Control Protocol. In: Proc. of 5th IEEE Symposium on Comp. and Comm. (ISCC). (2000)

16. Sathaye, S.: ATM Forum Traffic Management Specification 4.0. ATM Forum af-tm-0056.000 (1996)

17. Roberts, L.: Rate-based Algorithm for Point to Multipoint ABR Service. ATM Forum Contribution 94-0772R1 (1994)

18. Fahmy, S., Jain, R., Goyal, R., et al.: Feedback Consolidation Algorithms for ABR Point-to-Multipoint Connections in ATM Networks. In: Proc. of IEEE INFOCOM. Volume 3. (1998) 1004–1013

19. Zhang, X., Shin, K.G., Saha, D., Kandlur, D.D.: Scalable Flow Control for Multicast ABR Services in ATM Networks. IEEE/ACM Trans. on Netw. 10 (2002)

20. Chawathe, Y., McCanne, S., Brewer, E.A.: RMX: Reliable Multicast for Heterogeneous Networks. In: INFOCOM, Tel Aviv, Israel, IEEE (2000) 795–804

21. Amir, Y., Awerbuch, B., Danilov, C., et al.: Global Flow Control for Wide Area Overlay Networks: A Cost-Benefit Approach. In: OpenArch'02. (2002) 155–166

On Shouting "Fire!": Regulating Decoupled Communication in Distributed Systems*

Takahiro Murata and Naftaly H. Minsky

Dept. of Computer Science, Rutgers University
Piscataway, NJ, 08854 USA
{murata,minsky}@cs.rutgers.edu

Abstract. Decoupled communication, which requires no direct association between the producers of information and its consumers – as under the *publish/subscribe* (P/S) middleware – is often essential for the integration of distributed and heterogeneous applications. But the indefinite, and potentially global, reach of decoupled communication – the very reason for its power – has a dark side, which may complicate the system using it, making it less predictable, more brittle, and less safe. Just think about the effect of shouting "fire" in a packed theatre, particularly, but not only, if it is a false alarm.

It is our thesis that the inherent drawbacks of decoupled communication can be tamed by decentralized regulation of its use. We show how such regulation can be carried out scalably by means of a distributed control mechanism called Law-Governed Interaction (LGI), and a middleware called Moses that implements this mechanism. Along the way, we illustrate the importance of such regulation, and its effectiveness, by considering the treatment of alarms in a large hospital.

1 Introduction

The issue addressed in this paper is that of communication in large heterogeneous distributed systems, under which, the communicators may not know the location, identity, or even the presence, of those they communicate with. Among several techniques that have been developed to support such communication – which effectively *decouples* the producers of information from its consumers, both in time and in space [5] – the most prominent are: the *publish/subscribe* (P/S, for short) [6, 14], and the Linda-like *tuple-space* [4, 12] middlewares. The publish/subscribe paradigm, which we will take here as a representative of what enables decoupled communication, provides *mediators* between the producers of information (which we call here *informers*), and its consumers (the *clients*, or *subscribers*). Under this paradigm, when an informer has some information to

---

* Work supported in part by NSF grants Nos. CCR-97-10575 and CCR-98-03698, and by the NJ Commission on Science and Technology "excellence award."

M. Endler and D. Schmidt (Eds.): Middleware 2003, LNCS 2672, pp. 222–241, 2003.

impart, it sends it to the mediator[1] – an act called *publishing*. The mediator, in turn, would communicate the published information (often called an *event-notice*) to all its clients who previously expressed interest in it by *subscribing* to a certain kind of event-notices.

As an example of decoupled communication, consider a large hospital, where various kinds of emergency situation may arise, such as: fire, low level of blood supply, a blackout in some regions of the facility, etc. When such an emergency is discovered by some agent – which may be an employee, a patient, a visitor, or some system component – it needs to be communicated to the various agents that might be concerned with it, whose identity, or its very existence, is likely not to be known to the discoverer of the emergency. Such communication can be carried out effectively via a P/S service, which allows the discoverer of an emergency to raise an alarm by publishing it, and allows anybody concerned with a given type of alarms to subscribe to it.

But the indefinite, and potentially global, reach of decoupled communication – the very reason for its power – has a dark side, which may complicate the system using it, making it less predictable, more brittle, and less safe. For example, raising an alarm that warns of a low level of blood supply may disrupt various routine activities, anywhere in the hospital – and may, therefore, be very harmful, particularly if it is a false alarm. Or, just think about the effect of shouting "fire" in a packed theatre. Even a valid alarm of low blood supply may cause harm by creating unnecessary panic, if it is communicated to the wrong people, like to patients waiting for an operation, or to their relatives. Moreover, an individual agent is in no position to evaluate the effect of an alarm he (or it) is about to publish, since he does not know who, if anybody, may be listening to it; nor will he be able to rely on any feedback from his listeners. So, this mode of communication is conducted, in a sense, in the dark, making its consequences unpredictable, and potentially dangerous.

It is the thesis of this paper that these drawbacks of decoupled communication can be alleviated by a suitable regulation of its use. We will motivate this thesis by presenting, in Sect. 2, a policy for regulating alarms in a hospital, which specifies, in particular: (a) who is qualified, and under what condition, to raise which kind of alarms; (b) who should be able to, or ought to, subscribe to which alarm; and (c) how should certain agents respond when they receive an alarm. In general, a policy that regulates decoupled communication needs to govern a large, heterogeneous, and indefinite community of agents, which might be dispersed throughout a system. The specification, and the scalable enforcement, of such *communal* policies is the subject of this paper.

The need to regulate decoupled communication – long ignored by the research community – has been recently addressed by some researchers working on publish/subscribe middleware [10, 8], by providing P/S mediators with access-control capabilities. Some commercial P/S mediators, particularly those that

---

[1] We assume here, for simplicity, a single mediator, but, as explained later, the technique of regulation proposed in this paper can be straightforwardly applied to multiple mediators working in concert.

implement JMS [7], also provide rudimentary access-control, based on conventional access-control lists (ACLs). However, as we will demonstrate later, policies required to regulate decoupled communication go beyond access-control, and we will contend that it is not appropriate to implement such policies in the servers of such communication mode. Therefore, we take here an alternative approach, which, in the context of the publish/subscribe paradigm, can be characterized as follows: Instead of having the P/S mediator define and enforce an access-control policy over all publications and subscriptions made through it, we have a substantially richer policy defined and enforced directly over the agents attempting to communicate via the P/S mediator. This is done by means of a distributed coordination and control mechanism called Law-Governed Interaction (LGI) [13], and a middleware called Moses that implements this mechanism – an overview of which is provided in Sect. 3.

We will also show that the proposed regulatory mechanism, which is entirely decentralized, is more scalable than the centralized access-control built into the P/S mediator, and that it can better protect the mediator from abuse by careless or buggy users. Finally, we will demonstrate that our regulatory mechanism is more powerful than the mediator-based alternative, in particular, in that it is able to: (a) impose obligations on the informers, or on the recipients, of certain event-notices; and (b) ensure the qualification of the mediators themselves.

The rest of this paper is organized as follows. Sect. 2 is a study of the nature of regulation that may be required over decoupled communication, using the treatment of alarms within a hospital as a case in point. Sect. 3 is an overview of law-Governed Interaction (LGI) – the computation mechanism on which this paper is based. In Sect. 4 we show how our example alarm policy of Sect. 2 is formulated, and scalably enforced under LGI. In Sect. 5 we consider the performance of our control mechanism; and we conclude in Sect. 6.

2   An Institutional Alarm Policy – A Motivating Example

We start this section with an elaboration on the alarm example introduced above, by stipulating a detailed policy for the treatment of alarms within a large hospital. We will then argue that this policy cannot be implemented effectively by P/S mediators alone, requiring a degree of control over the community of users of the P/S services.

2.1   An Alarm Policy for a Hospital

Before we present the policy itself, some comments about our assumptions and terminology are in order. First, we will distinguish between various *kinds* of alarms, for emergencies such as: fire, low level of blood supply, etc. – assuming, for simplicity, that the sets of alarms of different kinds are disjoint. Alarms of kind K are called K-alarms. Second, we assume that for each kind K of emergency, there are some designated *experts*, called K-experts, who take the primary responsibility for recognizing the occurrence of this emergency, and for dealing with the associated alarms. Agents that are not thus designated as experts, on a given type of emergency, are called *laymen* with respect to it.

Third, we recognize certain roles that various agents may play in this context. These include: (a) P/S servers, also called *mediators*; (b) the above mentioned *experts* on various kinds of emergencies and alarms; (c) *K-inspectors*, who have special responsibility with respect to *K*-alarms, to be discussed below; (d) a *facility manager*, whose function is to regulate dynamically various aspects of the system, as we shall see; and (e) a *certification authority* (CA) called admin, whose certification would be required for the authentication of most of the above roles.

Fourth, we assume all alarms to have the following form:

```
alarm(kind(K), time(T), informer(I), status(S), text(X))
```

where, K is the kind of the alarm; T marks the time when this alarm was raised; I identifies the informer who has raised this alarm; S specifies the status of this informer – either expert or layman – with respect to the current alarm kind K; and, finally, X is the text describing the specific alarm. Finally, regarding subscriptions to alarms, we consider here, for simplicity, only exact matching with a specified list of attribute values; e.g., subscription to

```
alarm([kind(fire), status(expert)])
```

means to capture all fire alarms published by experts.

We now introduce a detailed example of an alarm policy for a hospital, to be called simply *AP*. The statement of this policy is followed by a discussion of its rationale.

1. *The status of the following roles must be certified by the CA* admin: *the facility manager, a mediator, and a K-expert.*
2. *The publishing of alarms, and subscription to them, must be done via agents duly certified as valid P/S mediators.*
3. *Alarms published by experts are receivable by everyone, while alarms published by laymen are receivable by experts, but not by laymen (Fig. 1).*
4. *A layman can publish the same alarm only once within any 5 minute period, and the facility manager can prevent laymen from publishing alarms altogether.*
5. *The facility manager can appoint an expert on alarms of type K as a K-inspector. The duty of such an inspector would be to examine all K-alarms raised by laymen, and decide what to do with them; their behavior is governed by the following rules:*
   *(a) Every K-inspector is **obliged to subscribe** to all K-alarms.*
   (b) Each K-inspector is supposed to acknowledge the receipt of every K-alarm issued by a layman, within 10 minutes after receiving this alarm, by sending the copy of this alarm to the facility manager.
   (c) If an inspector failed to acknowledge the receipt of an alarm in a timely manner, as specified above, an alarm of kind metaAlarm ***must be published**, identifying the unacknowledged alarm, and the inspector that failed to acknowledge it. Alarms of kind* metaAlarm *are receivable only by experts.*

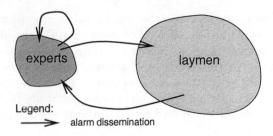

Fig. 1. Alarm dissemination between experts and laymen

Rationale: Point 1 of this policy requires the holders of a role – such as a facility manager, an expert on alarms of a specific kind, and, in particular, the P/S mediator – certify themselves via the specified CA. In other words, such certification process reflects the organizational decision as to which agents should play these roles. The certification of mediators, and the requirement of Point 2 that only mediators thus certified be used for the dissemination of alarms, provide some assurance of the quality and trustworthiness of the mediators. This is, in part, a way to deal with concerns such as confidentiality of information handled by the P/S mediators, raised by [18].

Point 3 is concerned with the distinction between experts and laymen. The reason for this distinction is that a widely disseminated alarm can be as dangerous as shouting "Fire!" in a crowded theatre. Therefore, this policy limits the ability to make such alarms to those who are certified as "experts," and presumably able to recognize a true emergency condition that requires the raising of an (real) alarm. Of course, an emergency condition may be first observed by a layman, which is why laymen are allowed to raise alarms. But because laymen's alarms are not very trustworthy, they are visible only by the appropriate experts, who can examine the situation and, if necessary, issue an alarm to the entire client base.

The role of inspector is introduced, by Point 5, in an attempt to ensure that there are some responsible agents that listen to all laymen's alarms, and in a timely fashion. This assurance, which is, of course, not absolute, is achieved as follows. First, once a K-inspector is appointed by a certified facility manager, he is *obliged*, by Point 5a, to subscribe to all K-alarms, so that no such alarms would be left unseen. Second he is expected, by Point 5b, to send a copy of each such alarm to the facility manager, serving here as an auditor, as a proof that he actually noticed it. Third, if such a copy is not sent within a specified deadline – perhaps because this inspector is not attentive, or is disconnected – then, by Point 5c, an appropriate `metaAlarm` is to be raised automatically, in the hope that it will be picked up by the `metaAlarm`-inspector, or by some other expert on such alarms. We believe such monitoring of responses to certain publications is often essential for the reliability of the system composed of potentially unreliable components.

Finally, Point 4 is an attempt to protect the P/S mediator from large numbers of unnecessary alarms – which might be issued by an overzealous, or faulty, layman. This is done by: (a) limiting the frequency of publishing repeated alarms by every layman; and (b) by allowing the facility-manager to prevent certain laymen from publishing alarms altogether.

2.2   On the Communal Nature of Policy AP

We explain here our contention that policy AP – and other such policies, by implication – is inherently communal, governing the entire community involved with alarms, and that it does not lend itself to effective implementation by P/S mediators alone. This contention has several reasons.

First, the mediators (or P/S servers) cannot ensure by themselves that publish and subscribe messages are sent only to servers duly certified as mediators, as required by Point 2. This, clearly, requires a degree of control over the operation of the agents that publish and subscribe, not allowing them to use uncertified servers.

Second, Point 4 of policy AP limits the frequency of alarms from any layman. As we already pointed out, the purpose of this provision is to reduce congestion on the mediators by protecting them from overzealous alarmists, which may be in a loop sending thousands of alarm notices. This purpose cannot be achieved if the mediator itself has to enforce policy AP, because it might still be congested, just by having to receive, and then reject, all such useless alarms.

Third, besides the client/server interactions between the users and the mediators, the regulation of policy AP ranges also over some interactions between users themselves. This is the case, in particular, for the assignment of K-inspectors for duty, which, under Point 5, is carried out by messages from facility managers to the agents in question. Such messages do not involve the mediators, which are, therefore, in no position to regulate them.

It is, of course, possible to require the assignment messages from managers be sent via the mediator, which would then be able to regulate them. But this is undesirable for two reasons: First, such message traffic might constitute a relatively large increase in the number of messages that the mediator has to process. Relatively large, because the assignment of agents to various duties is a routine matter of administration, which is likely to be much more frequent than alarms. Given such large background traffic, the mediator may not be able to react rapidly enough to an emergency situation. Secondly, and more importantly, organizational activities, such as the assignment of inspectors for duty, are orthogonal to the functionality of the P/S mediator – efficiently disseminating event-notices to matching subscribers. Attempting to couple these functionalities together would complicate the mediator, and make it less efficient, and less secure. Note further that, as seen immediately below, the scope of the regulation over such organizational activities is not just restricted to the maintenance of roles that are used to render access permissions, as is the case with traditional access-control.

Finally, requirements concerning the behavior of K-inspectors, imposed by Point 5, are *not*, by and large, suitable for implementation via the P/S mediator. First, Point 5a requires the obligation of every K-inspector to subscribe to all K-alarms be fulfilled. Second, Point 5b implies a requirement that each K-inspector be monitored for his acknowledgement of the receipt of every K-alarm issued by a layman. Finally, Point 5c requires a K-inspector's failure to fulfill such duty result in the publication of a suitable meta-alarm. In essence, these points require an enforcement mechanism (a) that maintains the status of communication between users (not necessarily involving the mediator), and (b) that, based on such status, exercises further regulation on the communication, including fulfilling the obligation to publish, or to subscribe to, a specified event-notice on behalf of certain users – which are, again, largely orthogonal to the core functionality of P/S service.

In conclusion, we argue that a policy like AP, which regulates alarms within a hospital, represents one of possibly many administrative aspects of the hospital that are inextricably intertwined with its general operation at large; thus, the implementation of such a policy does not belong in its entirety to the P/S mediator – a means of transporting event-notices. Moreover, as seen above, some provisions of policy AP just do not lend themselves to effective implementation by the P/S mediators. Indeed, none of the existing P/S services can handle the entire scope of policy AP. In Sect. 4 we will show how policy AP can be formulated and enforced in a decentralized, communal manner, with only marginal involvement of the P/S mediator.

3   Law-Governed Interaction (LGI) – An Overview

Broadly speaking, LGI [11] is a message-exchange mechanism that allows an *open* group of distributed agents to engage in a mode of interaction *governed* by an explicitly specified policy, called the *interaction-law* (or simply the "law") of the group. The messages thus exchanged under a given law $\mathcal{L}$ are called $\mathcal{L}$-messages, and the group of agents interacting via $\mathcal{L}$-messages is called an $\mathcal{L}$-community $\mathcal{C}_\mathcal{L}$ (or, simply, a *community* $\mathcal{C}$) .

We refer to entities that participate in an $\mathcal{L}$-community as *agents*[2], by which we mean autonomous actors that can interact with each other, and with their environment. An agent might be an encapsulated software entity, with its own state and thread of control, or a human that interacts with the system via some interface. A community under LGI is *open* in the following sense: (a) its membership can change dynamically, and can be very large; and (b) its members can be heterogeneous. For more details about LGI than provided by this overview, the reader is referred to [13, 1, 2].

3.1   On the Nature of LGI Laws
and Their Decentralized Enforcement

The function of an LGI law $\mathcal{L}$ is to regulate the exchange of $\mathcal{L}$-messages between members of a community $\mathcal{C}_\mathcal{L}$. Such regulation may involve (a) restriction

---

[2] Given the currently popular usage of the term "agent", it is important to point out that we do not imply either "intelligence" nor mobility by this term, although we do not rule out either of these.

of the kind of messages that can be exchanged between various members of C_L, which is the traditional function of access-control; (b) transformation of certain messages, possibly rerouting them to different destinations; and (c) causing certain messages to be emitted spontaneously, under specified circumstances, via a mechanism we call *obligations*.

A crucial feature of LGI is that its laws can be *stateful*. That is, a law L can be sensitive to some function of the history of the interaction among members of C_L, called the *control-state* (CS) of the community. The dependency of this control-state on the history of interaction is defined by the law L itself.

But the most salient and unconventional aspects of LGI laws are their strictly *local* formulation, and the *decentralized* nature of their enforcement. This architectural decision is based on the observation that a centralized mechanism to enforce interaction-laws in distributed systems is inherently unscalable, as it can become a bottleneck, and a dangerous single point of failure. The replication of such an enforcement mechanism, as seen in the Tivoli system [9], would not scale either, due to the required synchronous update of CS at all the replicas, when dealing with stateful policies.

The local nature of LGI laws: An LGI law is defined over a certain types of events occurring at members of a community C subject to it, mandating the effect that any such event should have. Such a mandate is called the *ruling* of the law for the given event. The events subject to laws, called *regulated events*, include (among others): the *sending* and the *arrival* of an L-message; the coming due of an *obligation*; and the occurrence of an *exception* in executing an operation in the ruling for another event. The agent at which a regulated event has occurred is called the *home agent* of the event. The ruling for a given regulated event is computed based on the local control state CS_x of the home agent x – where CS_x is some function, defined by law L, of the history of communication between x and the rest of the L-community. The operations that can be included in the ruling for a given regulated event, called *primitive operations*, are all local with respect to the home agent. They include: operations on the control-state of the home agent, such as insertion (+t), removal (-t), and replacement (t<-s) of terms; operations on messages, such as forward and deliver; and the imposition of an obligation on the home agent.

To summarize, an LGI law satisfies the following locality properties: (a) a law can regulate explicitly only *local events* at individual home agents; (b) the ruling for an event e can depend only on e itself, and on the *local control-state* CS_x of the home agent x; and (c) the ruling for an event can mandate only *local operations* to be carried out at the home agent x.

Decentralization of law-enforcement: The enforcement of a given law is carried out by a distributed set $\{T_x \mid x \in C\}$ of *controllers*, one for each member of community C. Structurally, all these controllers are generic, with the same law-enforcer $\mathcal{E}$, and all must be trusted to interpret correctly any law they might operate under. When serving members of community C_L, however, they all carry the *same law* L. And each controller T_x associated with an agent x of this

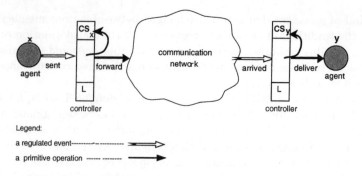

Legend:
a regulated event ·········· ········· ⟹
a primitive operation ····· ········ ⟶

Fig. 2. enforcement of the law

community carries only the *local control-state* CS_x of x, while every $\mathcal{L}$-message exchanged between a pair of agents x and y passes through a pair of controllers, $\mathcal{T}_x$ and $\mathcal{T}_y$ (see Fig. 2).

Due to the local nature of LGI laws, each controller $\mathcal{T}_x$ can handle events that occur at its client x strictly locally, with no explicit dependency on anything that might be happening with other members in the community. It should also be pointed out that controller $\mathcal{T}_x$ handles the events at x strictly sequentially, in the order of their occurrence, and atomically. These greatly simplify the structure of the controllers, making them easier to use as our *trusted computing base* (TCB).

Finally we point out that the law-enforcement mechanism ensures that a message received under law $\mathcal{L}$ has been sent under the same law; i.e., that it is not possible to forge $\mathcal{L}$-messages. As described in [2], this is assured by the following: (a) The exchange of $\mathcal{L}$-messages is mediated by correctly implemented controllers, certified by a CA specified by law $\mathcal{L}$; (b) these controllers are interpreting the *same law* $\mathcal{L}$, identified by a one-way hash [15] H of law $\mathcal{L}$; and (c) $\mathcal{L}$-messages are transmitted over cryptographically secured channels between such controllers. Consequently, how each member x gets the text of law $\mathcal{L}$ is irrelevant to the assurance that all members of $\mathcal{C}_\mathcal{L}$ operate under the same law.

3.2   The Deployment of LGI

The mechanism of LGI, and particularly that of controllers as the law-enforcer, has been implemented (in Java) as a messaging middleware called Moses[3]. Thus, all one needs for the deployment of LGI is the availability of a set of such trustworthy controllers, which run as distinct processes from each other, and from any clients, and a way for a prospective client to locate a running controller. For this purpose, we have also implemented a *controller-service* to maintain a set of controllers, as part of Moses.

For an agent x to engage in LGI communication, after locating a controller via a controller-service, it needs to supply this controller with the law $\mathcal{L}$ it wants to employ, by specifying the text of $\mathcal{L}$ or its URL. The controller then checks if

---

[3] A public distribution version is being finalized as of the time of writing.

law $\mathcal{L}$ is well-formed, and if so, it starts to serve for this client. Only through this hand-shake between a controller and an agent – a procedure called *adoption* of law $\mathcal{L}$ – the agent can start to participate in $\mathcal{L}$-community $\mathcal{C}_\mathcal{L}$. All these kinds of communication between an agent and its controller, including ones mentioned below, are facilitated by a Moses API, while a graphical user interface is provided for human users.

Note that it is quite possible for a single agent, x, to adopt the same law $\mathcal{L}$ more than once, whether connecting to a single controller or multiple controllers. In such a case, however, each adoption results in a distinct membership of x in $\mathcal{C}_\mathcal{L}$, and x participates in this community, representing in effect multiple members. That is, each such membership of x is associated with its own control-state, with respect to which, the locality of the law is strictly preserved. In an application where tighter membership control is necessary, one can choose to deploy a secretary of the community, as explained in [16].

Once x has adopted law $\mathcal{L}$, it may need to distinguish itself as playing a certain role, etc., which would provide it with some distinct privileges under law $\mathcal{L}$. This can be done by presenting certain digital certificates to the controller, as explained in [1]. A simple illustration of such certification is provided by our example law $\mathcal{AP}$ in Sect. 4, under which one may claim some of the roles, stipulated in policy AP.

4   Implementation of the Alarm Policy

We now demonstrate our mechanism to regulate decoupled communication by introducing law $\mathcal{AP}$ that implements, under LGI, policy AP discussed in Sect. 2. We start with some general remarks on the deployment of a law.

In stipulating the actual text of the law, LGI currently supports two languages: (a) a Prolog-like language, introduced in [11], and (b) a restricted version of Java, described in [17]. The former of these languages is employed below. We envision that such stipulation is done by a group of pertinent stake-holders, with the help of computational specialists. In particular, as in law $\mathcal{AP}$, a trustworthy CA may be required, which certifies the status of various role players via issuing and revoking certificates. Note, in general, the use of certificates does not compromise the scalability of our mechanism, because: (a) a CA can be a distributed agency; and (b) the CA does not need to be on-line at all, in order to have a certificate issued by it verified. For more detail on certification, particularly on the treatment of revocation, the reader is referred to [2].

Once stipulated, law $\mathcal{L}$ should be made available to agents that may participate in community $\mathcal{C}_\mathcal{L}$. As explained in Sect. 3.1, the trustworthiness of communal interaction is immune to how the actual text of $\mathcal{L}$ is distributed; e.g., one may send it in an e-mail to his peers, to be used for its adoption by them. If a trustworthy HTTP server is available, one can use it to store the text, and to have it retrieved by the controller during the adoption. For convenience, we also provide an HTTP-based law-server as part of the Moses middleware.

So far, we have assumed that the P/S mediator to be deployed is implemented as a single process. However, this is only for the sake of simplicity of our presentation. In fact, our regulatory mechanism applies to a P/S mediator consisting of multiple, distributed processes, working in concert, just as well[4]. Particularly, no change in law $\mathcal{AP}$ below would be required to regulate the use of such a P/S mediator of a distributed architecture. This is because our regulation is applied *only* to the communication between the mediator and its users, not between the distributed mediator processes that make up the entire P/S service. Note that, in such a case, however, each mediator process has to adopt law $\mathcal{AP}$, and to present a certificate, attesting its mediator role – as a single-process mediator would, which will be explained shortly.

4.1   Law $\mathcal{AP}$ to Regulate Alarms

Law $\mathcal{AP}$, displayed in Figs. 3 and 4, consists of two parts: the preamble and the rule section. The preamble gives this law its name, ap, and contains the following clauses: (a) the cAuthority clause that identifies the public key of the CA, used for the authentication of the controllers that are to mediate $\mathcal{AP}$-messages, as described in Sect. 3.1; (b) an authority clause that identifies admin, represented by its public key, as a CA for certifying various roles played in this community; and finally, (c) the initialCS clause defining the initial control-state of all agents in this community – it is empty in this case.

The rest of the law consists of a set of rules, most of which are followed by a comment (in italic); thus, together with our discussion, the rules should be understandable to the reader. Each rule has a *head*, to the left of symbol :-, and a *body*, to its right. Recall that, as explained in Sect. 3.1, the same law is interpreted individually by the controller associated with each agent in the community. A regulated event triggers, at the controller of the home agent, one rule that has a matching head at a time, if any, in the order in which the rules are written. The rule evaluation proceeds to find a rule that all the goals in its body are attained, given the control-state of this agent; in the absence of such a rule, the regulated event in question is ignored.

In addition to the standard types of Prolog goals, the body of a rule may contain two distinguished types of goals as follows: First, a *sensor-goal*, of the form t@CS, where t is any Prolog term, attempts to unify t with each term in the control-state of the home agent. Second, a *do-goal*, which always succeeds, has the form do(p), where p is one of the primitive operations, mentioned in Sect. 3.1. It appends the term, p, to the ruling of the law. Thus, successful evaluation of a rule body with do-goals leads to a non-empty ruling, and the execution of the primitive operations therein. In what follows, we may speak of this effect as if the said rule itself were to execute the pertinent operations. (By default, an empty ruling implies that the event in question has no consequences – such an event is effectively ignored.) We now discuss how the rules of law $\mathcal{AP}$ implement policy AP.

---

[4] Note that our argument in Sect. 2.2 for communal regulation, as opposed to mediator-based regulation, also applies regardless of the mediator architecture.

$\mathcal{P}$*reamble:*
```
    law(ap).
    cAuthority(publicKeyOfCAuth).
    authority(admin, publicKeyOfAdmin).
    initialCS([]).
```

$\mathcal{R}$1. `certified([issuer(admin),subject(Self),attributes([role(R)])])`
    `:- (R=mediator; R=facilityManager; R=expert(K)), do(+R).`
    Given an appropriate certificate from admin, *a term is inserted to represent the corresponding role.*

$\mathcal{R}$2. `sent(C, subscribe(alarm(AL)), M) :- member(kind(K),AL),`
            `(expert(K)@CS -> AL1=AL`
            `; delete(AL,status(layman),AL2),`
              `append(AL2,[status(expert)],AL1)),`
            `(K=metaAlarm -> expert(K)@CS ; true),`
            `do(forward(C,subscribe(alarm(AL1)),M)).`
    Regulating subscription to alarms: laymen can subscribe to alarms published by experts, and only experts can subscribe to metaAlarm.

$\mathcal{R}$3. `sent(I, publish(alarm(kind(K),text(X))), M) :- clock(T)@CS,`
            `(expert(K)@CS -> S=expert`
            `; S=layman, not(blocked(K)@CS),`
              `not(blocked(kind(K),text(X))@CS)),`
            `A=alarm(kind(K),time(T),informer(I),status(S),text(X)),`
            `do(forward(I, publish(A), M)),`
            `(S=layman -> do(+blocked(kind(K),text(X))),`
                `do(imposeObligation(releaseBlock(kind(K),text(X)),5,min)) ;`
            `true).`
    Regulating publishing of alarms.

$\mathcal{R}$4. `arrived(C, Msg, M)`
        `:- (Msg=subscribe(A); Msg=publish(A)), mediator@CS, do(deliver).`
    A mediator can receive subscriptions and publications.

$\mathcal{R}$5. `sent(M, notify(A), Cs) :- mediator@CS, do(multicast(M, Msg, Cs)).`
    A mediator can notify clients.

$\mathcal{R}$6. `arrived(M, notify(A), U)`
        `:- A=alarm(kind(K),time(T),informer(I),status(S),text(X)),`
            `(S=layman -> expert(K)@CS; true),`
            `(inspector(K)@CS, S=layman ->`
             `imposeObligation(handlingExpire(A,med(M)),10,min) ; true),`
            `do(deliver).`
    An alarm propagated by a mediator is delivered, but a layman does not get an alarm published by another layman.

$\mathcal{R}$7. `obligationDue(releaseBlock(kind(K),text(X)))`
        `:- do(-blocked(kind(K),text(X))).`
    The blocked *term to control the frequency of publishing is removed when the specified amount of time passes.*

Fig. 3. Law $\mathcal{AP}$

Establishing roles: Point 1 of *AP* is implemented by rule $\mathcal{R}1$ as follows: The `certified` event that triggers this rule is generated when the home agent presents its controller a valid certificate, i.e., duly signed by an authority declared in an `authority` clause, in this case admin[5]. As seen in the head of the rule, the `certified` event has as its argument the following representation of the submitted certificate: `[issuer(admin),subject(Self),attributes(role(R))]`. Term `issuer(admin)` tells about the issuer of the certificate, while the `subject` term is used to signify the subject of the certification. `Self` is an LGI built-in variable that is bound to the identifier (id)[6] of the home agent; thus in this case the home agent must have presented a certificate whose subject is the agent itself (i.e., a self-certificate). The `attributes` term describes what is certified about the subject; given R in its argument `role(R)` bound to one of the three roles, (a) a P/S mediator, (b) a facility manager, or (c) an expert on K-alarms[7], it attests that the agent is allowed to assume the role in question. Thus, the rule inserts the binding of R into the control state, treated as the token of the certification in the rest of the law.

Regulating subscription: Rule $\mathcal{R}2$ is triggered when an agent, whose id is bound to C, sends its controller a subscription message of the form `subscribe(alarm(AL))`, addressed to the intended mediator, whose id is bound to M. AL in the message is bound to a list of attribute criteria of this subscription, e.g., `[kind(fire)]`. Except two special cases, explained immediately below, this message is forwarded to M, with no change.

   Here are the special cases: First, the subscription to alarm kind K by a layman, i.e., a home agent without term `expert(K)` in its control-state, is (possibly) transformed; that is, `status(expert)` is placed into the attribute criteria, while all occurrences of `status(layman)`, if any, being deleted. When such a transformed subscription is forwarded to the mediator, it constrains the subscribed alarms to be issued only by experts, denying the chance of laymen subscribing to laymen's alarms. This effectively implements Point 3. Second, a layman's attempt to subscribe to alarms of kind `metaAlarm` is also denied, by requiring the home agent to be a `metaAlarm`-expert, which partially fulfills Point 5c.

   When a message to subscribe to alarms arrives at the controller of the addressed mediator, the corresponding `arrived` event is generated, and handled by rule $\mathcal{R}4$. (Hereafter, we may simply say such a message is, upon its arrival at the agent, handled by the relevant rule.) Note `Msg` is another LGI built-in variable, which carries the entire regulated message. The rule delivers the message to the mediator, after ensuring its legitimacy.

Regulating publication: Rule $\mathcal{R}3$ regulates the publishing of an alarm. Given kind K of the alarm and its description X in the message sent by the home agent, this

---

[5] If the certificate is found invalid, an `exception` event is generated, which is ignored under this law, for the sake of simplicity.

[6] An agent id is of the form: `local-name@domain-name` [1].

[7] Goals `P;Q` and `(P->Q;R)` should read P **or** Q, and **if** P **then** Q **else** R, respectively.

rule adds the following properties before forwarding it to the mediator: (1) id I of the informer; (2) status S, either `expert` or `layman` depending on the informer being a K-expert; and (3) the current time. This ensures the authenticity of the alarm in general, and the informer's status in particular, on which the enforcement of Points 3 and 5b directly relies. The published alarm will be delivered to the mediator by rule $\mathcal{R}4$.

Once the mediator computes the set of clients that have a matching subscription to the given published alarm, the mediator attempts to notify them, which triggers rule $\mathcal{R}5$. Primitive operation `multicast` forwards the given message to a set of recipients, specified in its third argument. Note that $\mathcal{R}4$ and $\mathcal{R}5$, combined, implement Point 2.

When the event-notice propagated by the mediator arrives at each selected subscriber, it is handled by rule $\mathcal{R}6$. This rule ensures that (even under a "faulty" mediator) a layman does not get a K-alarm published by another layman (Point 3), by requiring the recipient to be a K-expert, in that case.

Frequency restriction on laymen: A term, `blocked(kind(K),text(X))`, is inserted into the layman's control state by rule $\mathcal{R}3$ when it publishes a corresponding K-alarm. $\mathcal{R}3$ also imposes an LGI obligation `releaseBlock`, specifying it to come due in 5 minutes, which is handled by $\mathcal{R}7$, to remove the `blocked` term above. Thus, $\mathcal{R}3$, by requiring such a `blocked` term be absent, prevents a layman from publishing the same alarm for the duration of time specified in Point 4.

Rules $\mathcal{R}8$ and $\mathcal{R}9$ allow a facility manager to block a layman from publishing altogether (the remainder of Point 4). Rule $\mathcal{R}9$ ensures that it is not an expert that is blocked, and inserts a term, `blocked(K)`, whose absence is required by rule $\mathcal{R}3$ for a layman's publication to be forwarded to the mediator.

Handling of K-alarms: Rules $\mathcal{R}10$ and $\mathcal{R}11$ allow for a facility manger to assign a K-expert to the duty of a K-inspector (Point 5). In addition, rule $\mathcal{R}11$ implements Point 5a by forwarding subscription to all K-alarms on behalf of this appointed K-inspector.

Rules $\mathcal{R}12$ and $\mathcal{R}13$ allow each K-inspector to send a copy of the alarm to the facility manager, as a proof of noticing it (Point 5b). Note the `fm(FM)` term – inserted by $\mathcal{R}11$ when the appointment message arrived – carries the id of the facility manager.

Point 5c (or its remainder) is implemented as follows. Upon a K-inspector receiving a layman's alarm, rule $\mathcal{R}6$ imposes an obligation, `handlingExpire(A, med(M))` – set to come due in 10 minutes – where A and M are the representation of the alarm, and the mediator that has propagated the alarm, respectively. If this K-inspector acknowledges the alarm in time, resulting in triggering $\mathcal{R}12$ as seen above, the imposed obligation is repealed. Otherwise, on the obligation coming due, $\mathcal{R}14$ sends a `metaAlarm`, carrying the unacknowledged alarm and the id of this K-inspector in the attributes, `text` and `informer`, respectively, to the mediator for publication.

R8. sent(FM, blockLay(K), L) :- facilityManager@CS, do(forward).
R9. arrived(FM, blockLay(K), L)
        :- not(expert(K)@CS), do(+blocked(K)), do(deliver).
A facility manager can block a layman from publishing.
R10. sent(FM, inspectorOnDuty(kind(K),med(M)), X)
        :- facilityManager@CS, do(forward).
A facility manager can send message to put an inspector on duty.

R11. arrived(FM, inspectorOnDuty(kind(K),med(M)), X)
        :- expert(K)@CS, do(+inspector(K)), do(+fm(FM)),
           do(forward(X, subscribe(alarm([kind(K)])), M)).
A K-expert can be appointed as a K-inspector, who is obliged to subscribe to
all K-alarms.

R12. sent(I, ack(A), FM) :- fm(FM)@CS, Obl=handlingExpire(A,med(M)),
           obligation(Obl)@CS, do(repealObligation(Obl)), do(deliver).
R13. arrived(I, ack(A), FM) :- facilityManager@CS,do(deliver).
An inspector can acknowledge a layman's alarm to the facility manager.

R14. obligationDue(handlingExpire(A,med(M))) :- clock(T)@CS,
           do(forward(Self, publish(alarm(kind(metaAlarm),time(T),
              informer(Self),status(layman),text(unack(A)))), M)).
If an alarm received from a laymen is not acknowledged by the inspector, a
metaAlarm is published.

Fig. 4. Law $\mathcal{AP}$ (continued)

5   On the Performance of the Proposed Mechanism

Concentrating only on the access-control aspect of the proposed mechanism, we compare its performance to that of what can be implemented by the P/S mediators themselves. Our measurement of the most recent implementation of the LGI controller shows that each regulated event is processed in about 0.6 ms, on a Sun Fire 280R, UltraSPARC-III server (900 MHz), under the Solaris 2.8 operating system and Java 1.3. (Note that this version still does not incorporate the improvement measures suggested previously in [13].) The general picture that emerges below is as follows: Our mechanism tends to decrease the load on the mediator (in some cases dramatically), reducing the probability of congestion, and to increase the mediator's throughput, but it involves modest increase in latency, when the mediator is not congested.

Note that in this section the analyses and the experiment are based on a single-process mediator. Under a multiple-process, distributed mediator, assuming that the number of clients per mediator node and the frequency of access requests are the same as those of the single-process mediator, the general picture mentioned above should remain qualitatively the same. One notable difference would be that, as the cost of the event-notice routing, which our mechanism

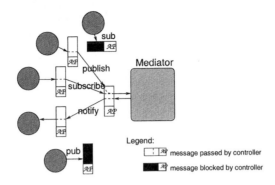

Fig. 5. The effect of the periphery processing

would not affect, becomes the dominating factor of the latency, the overhead on the latency caused by our mechanism should decrease accordingly.

5.1 Load on the Mediator

Our proposed mechanism tends to reduce the load on the mediator, that is, the number of messages received by it, for two reasons.

First, certain messages would be blocked at the periphery by the controllers associated with users (Fig. 5). For example, due to rule $\mathcal{R}3$, implementing policy point 4, if a layman tries to publish the same alarm too frequently, it will be blocked. This is particularly effective in blocking buggy or careless users from bombarding the mediator with a large number of messages, as demonstrated in Sect. 5.2. On the other hand, a mediator-based implementation is vulnerable to such unruly users, who can cause the denial of service to the entire community.

The second factor that can affect the load on the mediator has to do with the maintenance of the status of users, which is relevant to the policy at hand. For example, our AP policy is sensitive to the appointment of an agent as an inspector. Under the proposed communal mechanism, such appointment is carried out by exchanging messages between the users themselves, not involving the mediator. On the other hand, in the mediator-based approach, any change of status relevant to the policy at hand needs to be communicated to the mediator, and thus increases the load on it. This increase might be relatively significant because it is caused by routine interaction between users, which might be much more frequent than alarms that reflect exceptional circumstances. Note that even if certificates are used to establish access rights "off-line," the mediator itself, rather than the periphery, still has to grant (or deny) each access, and it must be made aware of the loss of such rights (e.g., due to the revocation of certificates).

5.2 Congestion Caused by Unruly Informers

We have conducted an experiment that measures the effect of an unruly informer on the performance of P/S services, under (a) the mediator-based access-control,

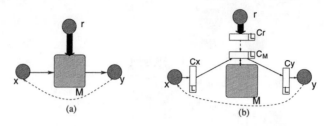

Fig. 6. Coping with an unruly informer

and (b) the proposed decentralized mechanism. The two configurations used in this experiment are depicted in Fig. 6. They both operate under a policy that limits the frequency of publication allowed to any one agent to ten per second. (Of course, this frequency is set well below the threshold to cause congestion to the particular mediator we used.)

In both configurations, essentially the same mediator M is used. In either configuration, one thread of M each handles the in-coming requests from another process, and deposits them in a single queue of M. The processing of user requests, including sending each event-notice to the target subscriber(s), is implemented as another thread (henceforth called the processing thread) that serves one request in the above queue at a time. In configuration (b), the above policy is implemented in LGI similarly to the frequency control on laymen in law $\mathcal{AP}$, while in configuration (a), M's processing thread does some bookkeeping for the time of the most recent publication of each user, based on which each publication request is accepted or rejected. We decided on this implementation for (a), based on the assumption about a realistic access-control module that: (1) it would have to operate on the content of each message (not just on the frequency of all requests alone); and (2) it would not be implemented to have a single processing thread per user, due to rather large resource consumption, as well as difficulty in allowing concurrent operation on the subscription base.

Also, in both configurations, informer x publishes event-notices to M – slowly enough not to cause any congestion – which are conveyed to subscriber y. When y receives each notification, it sends an acknowledgement (directly) to x. Some time after these agents start the communication, 28 s to be exact, a "roguish" agent r begins to publish as fast as it can (in effect, about 1500 publications per second). This publishing lasts 60 s. As an indicator for the latency between x and y, we measure the round-trip time (RTT) of each publication that starts when x publishes it, and ends when x receives y's acknowledgement.

Shown in Fig. 7 is the result of this experiment. In the run for case (a), before r begins its publishing, the RTT remains stable at a few milliseconds. For the duration of r's publishing, the RTT increases linearly, as expected, up to about 15 s, by its end, nearly all of which is spent for the publication to wait in M's queue. After r's publishing ends, it takes quite some time, more than 15 s, for the RTT to return to the normal, while M processes all publications accumulated in its queue.

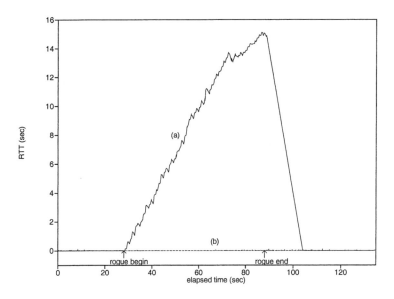

Fig. 7. Congestion caused by r

In contrast, the graph for case (b) is fairly flat throughout, because r's publications are mostly captured by the controller that handles r, and does not transmit more than ten publications per second. Although in the graph it is indistinguishable, the RTT is slightly higher than the normal range of case (a), because of the larger latency under LGI, particularly within a LAN, where this experiment has been conducted (see Sect. 5.3).

5.3   Throughput of the Mediation and End-to-End Latency

Under our mechanism, access-control related computation is carried out at the periphery, i.e., by the controllers associated with users, as depicted in Fig. 5. Since the mediator themselves have less to do per publication, their throughput increases proportionately (with respect to the real-time if the controller runs on a separate host, and to the CPU-time otherwise).

Next, we compare the latency in propagating an authorized notice from informer x to subscriber y through mediator M, *under no mediator congestion*, in two cases: (a) the mediator providing access-control, and (b) each user and the mediator regulated by LGI. These two cases are depicted in Fig. 8, where $T_{\alpha,\beta}$ stands for the time of communication between two processes α and β, while ϵ is used as the time for finding the matching subscriptions, that of the access-control, and that of event-evaluation by the LGI controller. Letting T_a and T_b be the latency in cases (a) and (b), respectively, we consider the *relative overhead* $(T_b - T_a)/T_a$, by following the general discussion in [13].

Based on realistic figures for the communication time, and the time to compute matching subscriptions suggested in the literature, e.g., [3], the relative

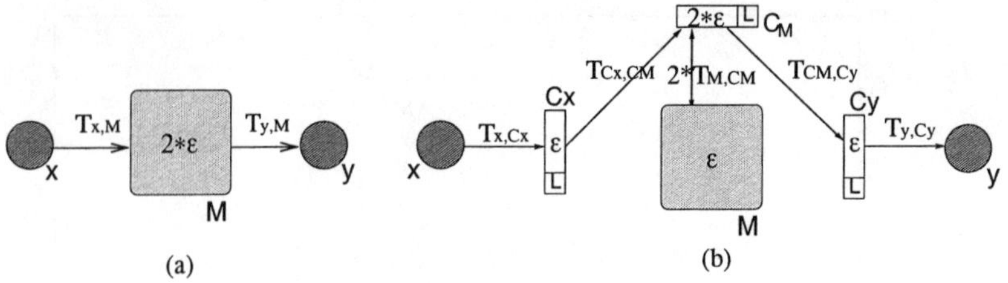

Fig. 8. Two cases for latency analysis

overhead in a WAN setting and that in a LAN setting are: a few percent and several tens of percent, respectively. The former is negligible, and the latter, we view, is acceptable, given in particular the separate controllers running, at least for the mediator, and for its users, to maintain the scalability. This estimate has also been confirmed by measurements obtained in the experiment of Sect. 5.2.

6   Conclusion

Decoupled communication, which requires no direct association between the producers of information and its consumers, is often essential for the integration of distributed and heterogeneous applications. But the indefinite, and potentially global, reach of decoupled communication – the very reason for its power – has a dark side, which may complicate the system using it, making it less predictable, more brittle, and less safe. We have demonstrated these difficulties by taking the P/S paradigm as the representative of decoupled communication, and by using the treatment of alarms in a large hospital as an example application of the paradigm.

We have argued that appropriate regulation of decoupled communication does not lend itself to effective implementation by the P/S mediators themselves, but requires decentralized regulation defined and enforced directly over the agents attempting to communicate with each other. We have shown how such decentralized regulation can be carried out, efficiently and scalably, using the Law-Governed Interaction (LGI) mechanism.

References

1. X. Ao, N. Minsky, T. Nguyen, and V. Ungureanu. Law-governed communities over the internet. In *Proc. of Fourth International Conference on Coordination Models and Languages; Limassol, Cyprus; LNCS 1906*, pages 133–147, September 2000. (available from http://www.cs.rutgers.edu/~minsky/pubs.html).
2. X. Ao, N. Minsky, and V. Ungureanu. Formal treatment of certificate revocation under communal access control. In *Proc. of the 2001 IEEE Symposium on Security and Privacy, May 2001, Oakland California*, May 2001. (available from http://www.cs.rutgers.edu/~minsky/pubs.html).

3. A. Campailla, S. Chaki, E. Clarke, S. Jha, and H. Veith. Efficient filtering in publish-subscirbe systems using binary decision diagrams. In *Proc. of The 23rd Intn'l Conf. on Soft. Eng. (ICSE)*, pages 443–452, May 2001.

4. N. Carriero and D. Gelernter. Linda in context. *Communications of the ACM*, 32(4):444–458, April 1989.

5. P.Th. Eugster, P. Felber, R. Guerraoui, and A.-M. Kermarrec. The many faces of publish/subscribe. Technical report, EPFL, January 2001. DSC ID: 2000104.

6. D. Garlan and D. Notkin. Formalizing dsign spaces: Implicit invocation mechanisms. In *Proc. of VDM'91: 4th Intn'l Sympo. of VDM Europe on Foraml Software Development Methods; LNCS 551*, pages 31–44, Noordwijkerhout, The Netherlands, October 1991. Springer-Verlag.

7. M. Hapner et al. *Java Message Service*. Sun Microsystems Inc., August 2001. Version 1.0.2b, website: `http://java.sun.com/products/jms/docs.html`.

8. IBM Corp. *Gryphon – The system.* website:
   `http://www.research.ibm.com/gryphon/Gryphon/gryphon.html`.

9. G. Karjoth. The authorization service of tivoli policy director. In *Proc. of the 17th Annual Computer Security Applications Conf. (ACSAC 2001)*, December 2001.

10. Z. Miklós. Towards an access control mechanism for wide-are publish/subscribe systems. In *Proc. of Intn'l Workshop on Distributed Event-Based Systems (DEBS'02)*, July 2002.

11. N.H. Minsky. The imposition of protocols over open distributed systems. *IEEE Transactions on Software Engineering*, February 1991.

12. N.H. Minsky, Y.M. Minsky, and V. Ungureanu. Safe tuplespace-based coordination in multiagent systems. *Journal of Applied Artificial Intelligence (AAI)*, 15(1):11–33, January 2001. (available from
    `http://www.cs.rutgers.edu/~minsky/pubs.html`).

13. N.H. Minsky and V. Ungureanu. Law-governed interaction: a coordination and control mechanism for heterogeneous distributed systems. *TOSEM, ACM Transactions on Software Engineering and Methodology*, 9(3):273–305, July 2000. (available from `http://www.cs.rutgers.edu/~minsky/pubs.html`).

14. D.S. Rosenblum and A.L. Wolf. A design framework for internet-scale event observation and notification. In *Proc. of the Sixth European Soft. Eng. Conf.; Zurich, Switzerland; LNCS 1301*, pages 344–360. Springer-Verlag, September 1997.

15. B. Schneier. *Applied Cryptography*. John Wiley and Sons, 1996.

16. C. Serban, X. Ao, and N.H. Minsky. Establishing enterprise communities. In *Proc. of the 5th IEEE Intn'l Enterprise Distributed Object Computing Conf. (EDOC 2001), Seattle, Washington*, September 2001. (available from `http://www.cs.rutgers.edu/~minsky/pubs.html`).

17. C. Serban and N.H. Minsky. Using java as a language for writing lgi-laws. Technical report, Rutgers University, July 2002.

18. C. Wang, A. Carzaniga, D. Evans, and A.L. Wolf. Security issues and requirements for Internet-scale publish-subscribe systems. In *Proc. of the 35th Annual Hawaii Intn'l Conf. on System Sciences*, Hawaii, January 2002.

Performance Comparison of Middleware Architectures for Generating Dynamic Web Content

Emmanuel Cecchet[1], Anupam Chanda[2], Sameh Elnikety[3],
Julie Marguerite[1], and Willy Zwaenepoel[3]

[1] INRIA, Projet Sardes, 655, Avenue de l'Europe, 38330 Montbonnot St Martin, France
{Emmanuel.Cecchet,Julie.Marguerite}@inrialpes.fr
[2] Rice University, 6100 Main Street, MS-132, Houston, TX, 77005, USA
anupamc@cs.rice.edu
[3] Ecole Polytechnique Fédérale de Lausanne, 1015 Lausanne, Switzerland
{sameh.elnikety,willy.zwaenepoel}@epfl.ch

Abstract. On-line services are making increasing use of dynamically generated Web content. Serving dynamic content is more complex than serving static content. Besides a Web server, it typically involves a server-side application and a database to generate and store the dynamic content. A number of standard mechanisms have evolved to generate dynamic content. We evaluate three specific mechanisms in common use: PHP, Java servlets, and Enterprise Java Beans (EJB). These mechanisms represent three different architectures for generating dynamic content. PHP scripts are tied to the Web server and require writing explicit database queries. Java servlets execute in a different process from the Web server, allowing them to be located on a separate machine for better load balancing. The database queries are written explicitly, as in PHP, but in certain circumstances the Java synchronization primitives can be used to perform locking, reducing database lock contention and the amount of communication between servlets and the database. Enterprise Java Beans (EJB) provide several services and facilities. In particular, many of the database queries can be generated automatically.

We measure the performance of these three architectures using two application benchmarks: an online bookstore and an auction site. These benchmarks represent common applications for dynamic content and stress different parts of a dynamic content Web server. The auction site stresses the server front-end, while the online bookstore stresses the server back-end. For all measurements, we use widely available open-source software (the Apache Web server, Tomcat servlet engine, JOnAS EJB server, and MySQL relational database). While Java servlets are less efficient than PHP, their ability to execute on a different machine from the Web server and their ability to perform synchronization leads to better performance when the front-end is the bottleneck or when there is database lock contention. EJB facilities and services come at the cost of lower performance than both PHP and Java servlets.

1   Introduction

Web content is increasingly generated dynamically, a departure from the early days of the Web when virtually all content consisted of static HTML and image files. Dynamic content is used in many online services that need access to current information

M. Endler and D. Schmidt (Eds.): Middleware 2003, LNCS 2672, pp. 242–261, 2003.

such as e-commerce and electronic banking. Also, it is used to customize the look-and-feel of Web pages according to the preferences of each user.

Dynamic Web content is generated by a combination of a Web server, a dynamic content generator, and a back-end database (see figure 1). The Web server serves all static content and forwards requests for dynamic content to the dynamic content generator. The dynamic content generator executes the code that captures the business logic of the Web site and issues queries to the database, which stores the dynamic state of the site.

In more detail, when a Web server receives an HTTP request for dynamic content, it forwards the request to the dynamic content generator. The dynamic content generator executes the corresponding code, which may need to access the database to generate the response. The dynamic content generator formats and assembles the results into an HTML page. Finally, the Web server returns this page as an HTTP response to the client.

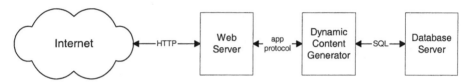

Fig. 1. Typical configuration of a dynamic content Web site.

The implementation of the application logic may take various forms, including scripting languages such as PHP [14] that execute as a module in a Web server such as Apache [4], Microsoft Active Server pages [11] that are integrated with Microsoft's IIS server [12], Java servlets [8] that execute in a separate Java virtual machine, and full application servers such as an Enterprise Java Beans (EJB) server [22]. This study focuses on three software systems for generating dynamic Web content: PHP, Java servlets, and EJB.

PHP is a scripting language in which SQL queries can be embedded. Similarly, Java servlets allow SQL queries to be embedded in the Java code. In both PHP and Java servlets, the application programmer writes the SQL queries. With EJB a number of beans are defined. Session beans implement the business logic of the application, and entity beans implement the persistence services. Roughly speaking, each entity bean corresponds to a database table, an entity bean instance corresponds to a row in the table, and an entity bean member to a column. To access the persistent state, bean methods are called, which in turn issue SQL queries to the database. In contrast to PHP and Java servlets, the SQL queries issued by the beans are generated automatically[1]. Most commonly, the bean methods are called from Java servlets, which in this case only implement the presentation logic of the site.

If only the dynamic content generator accesses the database, both Java servlets and EJB can use Java synchronization mechanisms to offload some of the synchronization and locking typically performed by the database. This can lead to improved performance in the presence of database lock contention.

---

[1] With container-managed persistence. The alternative, bean-managed persistence, in which the application programmer writes the queries explicitly, is not considered in this paper.

PHP executes as a module in the Web server, sharing the same process address space. Both servlets and EJB execute in a separate Java virtual machine, requiring interprocess communication between the Web server and the dynamic content generator. This separation, however, allows an extra degree of freedom in configuring the system, in that the servlets and the EJB can be deployed on a separate machine from the Web server.

Although the computational demands of Java servlets are higher than those of the corresponding PHP scripts, we demonstrate that this extra degree of freedom can be used to improve the performance of Java servlets compared to PHP. In particular, we show that for applications that put significant load on the server front-end, better performance can be achieved by locating Java servlets on a separate machine. The introduction of EJB adds significant overhead that cannot be alleviated by putting the EJB and the associated servlets on separate machines.

To evaluate the performance of these architectures, we use two benchmarks: an online bookstore modeled after the TPC-W specification [20] and an auction site modeled after eBay.com [7]. We perform our experiments on commodity hardware. Each machine contains a 1.33GHz AMD Athlon, 768MB main memory and 60GB disk. The machines are connected to each other and to a set of machines running client emulation software by a switched 100Mbps Ethernet. For the online bookstore, the database server is the bottleneck, and the auction site saturates the server front-end. In all the experiments, the memory, disk and the network are never the performance bottleneck except for one configuration.

The remainder of the paper is organized as follows. Section 2 provides necessary background on PHP, Java servlets, and EJB. Section 3 describes the two benchmarks that we use to evaluate these systems. Section 4 describes our experimental environment and our measurement methodology. Sections 5 and 6 discuss the results of our experiments with the online bookstore and the auction site benchmarks, respectively. Section 7 discusses related work, and Section 8 presents our conclusions.

2   Background

2.1   PHP (Hypertext Preprocessor)

PHP [14] is a scripting language that can be seen as an extension of the HTML language: PHP code can be directly embedded into an HTML page. PHP support generally takes the form of a server module that is integrated into the HTTP Web server. PHP is executed within the Web server process and does not incur any interprocess communication overhead. When the HTTP Web server identifies a PHP tag, it invokes the PHP interpreter module that executes the script. Requests to the database are explicit and are performed using an ad hoc interface.

2.2   Java HTTP Servlets

An HTTP servlet [8] is a Java class that can be dynamically loaded by a servlet engine and runs in a Java Virtual Machine (JVM). After the initial load, the servlet engine invokes the servlet using local calls, but since the JVM is a separate process from the Web server, interprocess communication takes place for each request. Servlets access the database explicitly, using the standard JDBC interface, which is supported by all major databases.

Servlets can use all the features of Java. In particular, they can use Java built-in synchronization mechanisms to perform locking operations[2]. If only the servlet engine accesses the database, locking in the servlet engine can replace some locking in the database, which may reduce database lock contention and communication between the servlet engine and the database.

2.3   Enterprise Java Beans

The purpose of an Enterprise Java Beans (EJB) server is to abstract the application business logic from the underlying middleware. An EJB server provides a number of services such as database access (JDBC), transactions (JTA), messaging (JMS), naming (JNDI) and management support (JMX). The EJB server manages one or more EJB containers. The container is responsible for providing component pooling and lifecycle management, client session management, database connection pooling, persistence, transaction management, authentication, and access control.

We use two types of EJB in our implementations: entity beans that map data stored in the database (usually one entity bean instance per database table row), and session beans that are used either to perform temporary operations (stateless session beans) or represent temporary objects (stateful session beans). As with Java servlets, Java's synchronization mechanisms can be used to offload locking from the database to the application server.

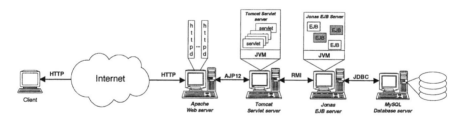

Fig. 2. Using an Enterprise Java Bean server to generate dynamic Web content.

Figure 2 shows an example of an architecture including an EJB server. Java servlets are usually used with EJB to call the bean methods. First, a client sends a request to the HTTP server. The HTTP server invokes the servlet engine using a well-defined protocol (AJP12). The servlet communicates with the EJB server (using RMI) to retrieve the information needed in order to generate the HTML reply. The EJB server in turn calls the database to maintain the state of the beans. These calls are generated automatically.

---

[2] It is possible to do locking using PHP versions 3 and 4 on Unix-like operating systems that support System V Semaphores. We do not consider this possibility in the paper because this feature is not available on all platforms.

2.4   Summary

PHP scripts are easy to write and reasonably efficient, but the database interfaces are ad hoc. PHP code maintenance is awkward because new code needs to be written for each new database to which the scripts need access. PHP scripts execute in the same process (address space) as the Web server, thereby minimizing communication overhead between the Web server and the scripts.

Java servlets access the database using JDBC. This makes them easily portable between databases. Contrary to the PHP interpreter, the servlet engine runs in a JVM as a separate process from the Web server. Therefore, servlets can be placed on a machine different from the one running the Web server. This flexibility can be used to improve load balancing. Also, servlets can use all the Java language features, especially its synchronization mechanisms. Servlets, however, incur the cost of interprocess communications with the Web server.

The EJB architecture offers a level of indirection as it abstracts the application logic from any specific platform or infrastructure. In particular, database accesses are generated automatically as part of the bean methods.

3   Benchmarks

We describe the two benchmarks, which we use to compare PHP, Java servlets, and EJB. We choose these two benchmarks because the first one stresses the database, while the second one stresses the Web server.

3.1   Online Bookstore Benchmark

The online bookstore benchmark implements the TPC-W specification [20], a transactional Web benchmark for evaluating e-commerce systems. Our online bookstore implementation implements all the functionality specified in TPC-W that has an impact on performance, including transactional consistency and support for secure transactions. It does not implement some functionality specified in TPC-W that has an impact only on price and not on performance, such as the requirement to provide enough storage for 180 days of operation.

The database stores all persistent data except for the images, which are stored in the file system of the Web server. The database manages eight tables: *customers*, *address*, *orders*, *order_line*, *credit_info*, *items*, *authors*, and *countries*. The *order_line*, *orders* and *credit_info* tables store the details of the orders that have been placed. In particular, *order_line* stores the book ordered and the quantity and discount. *Orders* stores the customer identifier, the date of the order, information about the amount paid, the shipping address and the status. *Credit_info* stores credit card information such as its type, number and expiry date. The *items* and *authors* tables contain information about the books and their authors. Customer information, including real name and user name, contact information (email, address) and password, are maintained in the *customers* and *address* tables.

We implemented the 14 different interactions specified in the TPC-W benchmark specification. Of the 14 interactions, six are read-only and eight have update queries that change the state of the database. The read-only interactions include access to the home page, new products and best-sellers listings, requests for product detail, and two search interactions. Read-write interactions include user registration, updates to the shopping cart, two purchase interactions, two involving order inquiry and display, and two administrative updates. We use the same Markov model for the distribution of interactions as specified in TPC-W. Interactions may also involve requests for embedded images corresponding to an item in the inventory as well as navigational buttons and logos. All interactions access the database server to generate dynamic content, except for one interaction that involves only static content.

TPC-W specifies three different workload mixes, differing in the ratio of read-only to read-write interactions. The browsing mix contains 95% read-only interactions, the shopping mix 80%, and the ordering mix 50%. The shopping mix is considered the most representative mix for this benchmark. The database scaling parameters are 10,000 items and 288,000 customers. This corresponds to a database size of 350MB, which fits entirely in the main memory of database server. The images stored in the Web server file system use 183MB of disk space.

3.2   Auction Site Benchmark

Our auction site benchmark implements the core functionality of an auction site: selling, browsing and bidding. It does not implement complementary services like instant messaging or newsgroups. We distinguish between three kinds of user sessions: visitor, buyer, and seller. For a visitor session, users need not register but are only allowed to browse. Buyer and seller sessions require registration. In addition to the functionality provided during visitor sessions, during a buyer session users can bid on items and consult a summary of their current bids, their rating and the comments left by other users. Seller sessions require a fee before a user is allowed to put up an item for sale. An auction starts immediately and lasts typically for no more than a week. The seller can specify a reserve (minimum) price for an item.

The database contains nine tables: *users*, *items*, *old_items*, *bids*, *buy_now*, *comments*, *categories*, *regions* and *ids*. The *users* table records contain the user's name, nickname, password, region, rating and balance. Besides the category and the seller's nickname, the *items* and *old_items* tables contain the name that briefly describes the item and a more extensive description, normally an HTML file. Every bid is stored in the *bids* table, which includes the seller, the bid, and a max_bid value used by the proxy bidder (a tool that bids automatically on behalf of a user). Items that are directly bought without any auction are stored in the *buy_now* table. The *comments* table records comments from one user about another. As an optimization, the number of bids and the amount of the current maximum bid are stored with each item to prevent many expensive lookups on the *bids* table. This redundant information is necessary to keep an acceptable response time for browsing requests. As users browse and bid only on items that are currently for sale, we split the *items* table in separate *items* and *old_items* tables. The vast majority of requests access the new items table, thus considerably reducing the database working set.

Our auction site defines 26 interactions that can be accessed from the client's Web browser. Among the most important ones are browsing items by category or region, bidding, buying or selling items, leaving comments on other users and consulting one's own user page (known as myEbay on eBay [7]). Browsing items also includes consulting the bid history and the seller's information. We define two workload mixes: a browsing mix made up of read-only interactions and a bidding mix that includes 15% read-write interactions. The bidding mix is the most representative of an auction site workload.

We size our system according to some observations found on the eBay Web site. We always have about 33,000 items for sale, distributed among eBay's 40 categories and 62 regions. We keep a history of 500,000 auctions in the *old_items* table. There is an average of 10 bids per item, or 330,000 entries in the *bids* table. The *buy_now* table is small, because less than 10% of the items are sold without any auction. The *users* table has 1 million entries. We assume that users give feedback (comments) for 95% of the transactions. The comments table contain about 500,000 comments. The total size of the database, including indices, is 1.4GB.

4   Hardware and Software Environment

4.1   Client Emulation Implementation

We implement a client-browser emulator. A client session is a sequence of interactions for the same client. For each client session, the client emulator opens a persistent HTTP connection to the Web server and closes it at the end of the session. Each emulated client waits for a certain think time before initiating the next interaction. The next interaction is determined by a state transition matrix that specifies the probability to go from one interaction to another.

The think time and session time for both benchmarks are generated from a negative exponential distribution with a mean of 7 seconds and 15 minutes, respectively. These numbers conform to clauses 5.3.1.1 and 6.2.1.2 of the TPC-W v1.65 specification [20]. We vary the load on the site by varying the number of clients. We have verified that in none of the experiments the clients are the bottleneck.

4.2   Application Logic Implementation

In PHP and Java servlets, the application programmer is responsible for writing the SQL queries. To make the comparison fair, we use exactly the same queries to the database in both environments. The only exception is when locking in Java servlets is used. In this case, we remove some "LOCK TABLES" and "UNLOCK TABLES" SQL statements.

With EJB, we separate the presentation logic that remains in the Java servlets from the business logic that is implemented by EJB. The Java servlets are used only as the presentation tier as defined in Adatia et al. [1], to generate the HTML reply from the information retrieved from the bean. We use the session façade pattern [2] represented by figure 3 to implement the business logic. The main business logic resides in stateless session façade beans that access entity beans with container-managed persistence. The entity beans access the database. This design uses the relevant features of the EJB container, and at the same time provides the best performance compared to other designs with entity beans [6].

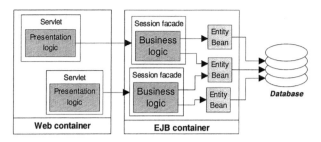

Fig. 3. Session façade design pattern.

4.3   Software Environment

We use Apache v.1.3.22 as the Web server, configured with the PHP v.4.0.6 module, mod_ssl version 2.8.5 and openSSL 0.9.5a. We increase the maximum number of Apache processes to 512. With that value, the number of Apache processes is never a limit on performance.

The servlet engine is Jakarta Tomcat v3.2.4 [19], running on Sun JDK 1.3.1. The EJB server is JOnAS v2.5 [9], an Open Source Java implementation of the EJB speci-fication. We use this EJB server because, to the best of our knowledge, it is the fastest open source implementation [6]. JOnAS is also integrated in production application servers such as the Lutris Enhydra Application Server [10].

We use MySQL v.3.23.43-max [13] as our database server with the MyISAM ta-bles. The MM-MySQL v2.04 type 4 JDBC driver is used for both the servlet and EJB servers.

All machines run the 2.4.12 Linux kernel.

4.4   Hardware Platform

We use four server machines. Each machine has an AMD Athlon 1.33GHz CPU with 768MB SDRAM, and a Maxtor 60GB 5,400rpm disk drive. A number of 800MHz AMD Athlon machines run the client emulation software. We use enough client emu-lation machines to make sure that the clients do not become a bottleneck in any ex-periment. All machines are connected through a switched 100Mbps Ethernet LAN.

4.5   Measurement Methodology

Each experiment is composed of 3 phases. A ramp-up phase initializes the system until it reaches a steady-state throughput level. We then switch to the measurement phase during which we perform all our measurements. Finally, a ramp-down phase sustains the same request rate as the measurement phase to allow for differences in client machines clocks and to allow for all pending requests to terminate. For all ex-periments with a particular application we use the same length of time for each phase, but the duration of each phase is different for the two applications. The online book-store uses 1, 20 and 1 minutes for the ramp-up, measurement, and ramp-down phases, respectively. The auction site uses 5, 30 and 5 minutes. These lengths of time are chosen based on observation of the length of time necessary to reach a steady state and to obtain reproducible results.

To measure the load on each machine, we use the *sysstat* utility [18] that every second collects CPU, memory, network and disk usage from the Linux kernel. The resulting data files are analyzed post-mortem to minimize system perturbation during the experiments.

4.6   Configurations

We experiment with four different configurations, shown in Figure 4.

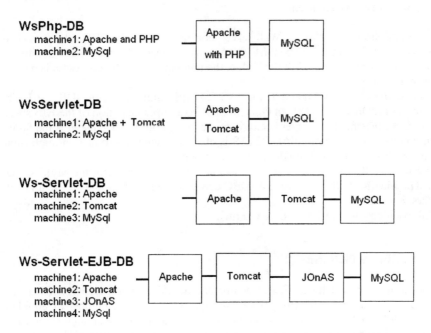

WsPhp-DB
machine1: Apache and PHP
machine2: MySql

WsServlet-DB
machine1: Apache + Tomcat
machine2: MySql

Ws-Servlet-DB
machine1: Apache
machine2: Tomcat
machine3: MySql

Ws-Servlet-EJB-DB
machine1: Apache
machine2: Tomcat
machine3: JOnAS
machine4: MySql

Fig. 4. The four software and hardware configurations evaluated.

We always run the database on a separate machine. PHP is implemented as a server module, so it needs to run on the same machine as the Web server. We refer to the PHP configuration as WsPhp-DB. Servlets can be located on the Web server machine or on a separate machine. We refer to these two configurations as WsServlet-DB and Ws-Servlet-DB, respectively. The configurations WsPhp-DB, WsServlet-DB and Ws-Servlet-DB contain exactly the same database queries. The configurations WsServlet-DB(sync) and Ws-Servlet-DB(sync) perform locking in the servlet engine. They contain the same database queries as WsServlet-DB and Ws-Servlet-DB, except that many of queries that explicitly acquire and release database locks (e.g., "LOCK TABLES" and "UNLOCK TABLES" SQL statements) are removed. For the EJB configuration (Ws-Servlet-EJB-DB), we use four machines, one each for the Web server, the servlet engine, the EJB application server and the database server.

5   Experimental Results for the Online Bookstore

This benchmark contains complex database queries, which stress the database server. For all configurations, the bottleneck is the database server. The bottleneck results either from CPU saturation or from database lock contention. As shown in the next subsections, for this benchmark the database interface (i.e., the set of queries issued to the database) is the key factor that affects the performance. Configurations that have the same database interface have approximately the same throughput.

5.1   Shopping Mix

Figure 5 reports the online bookstore throughput in interactions per minute as a function of the number of clients for the shopping mix, which is the most representative workload for this benchmark.

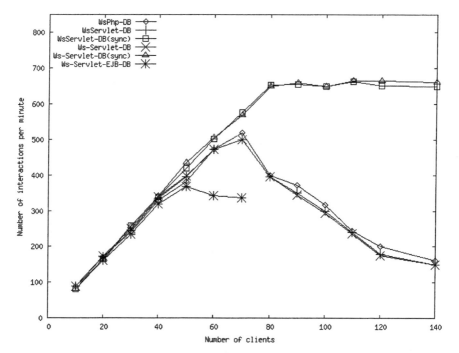

Fig. 5. Online bookstore throughput in interactions per minute as a function of number of clients for the shopping mix.

The PHP configuration WsPhp-DB gives a peak throughput of 520 interactions per minute. As the load increases beyond the peak point, the performance drops because of database lock contention.

The Java servlet configurations WsServlet-DB and Ws-Servlet-DB give approximately the same throughput as the PHP configuration, because these three configurations have the same database interface and contain exactly the same queries. Moving

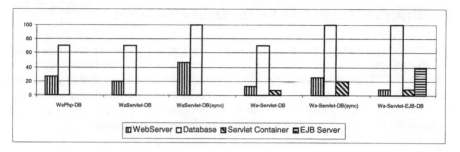

Fig. 6. Online bookstore percentage CPU utilization at the peak throughput for the shopping mix.

servlets to another machine as in Ws-Servlet-DB does not produce any performance gain because the servlets issue the same set of queries and database lock contention remains the bottleneck.

The servlets configurations WsServlet-DB(sync) and Ws-Servlet-DB(sync), which perform some of the locking using the Java synchronization mechanisms, give better performance because of the reduction in database lock contention. The peak throughputs are 663 and 665 interactions per minute, respectively. The bottleneck resource at the peak is the CPU of the database server, which is 100% utilized throughout the peak plateau.

The EJB configuration Ws-Servlet-EJB-DB performs the worst, because it requires too many short queries to maintain the state of beans.

The above results can be further explained by examining Figure 6, which shows the CPU utilization for all configurations and for each machine. For the configurations WsPhp-DB, WsServlet-DB and Ws-Servlet-DB, the CPU utilization of the database is around 70%. It does not reach 100% due to database lock contention. For the configurations WsServlet-DB(sync) and Ws-Servlet-DB(sync), performing some locking operations in the servlets engine alleviates database lock contention and the CPU utilization of the database server reaches 100%. For the EJB configuration Ws-Servlet-EJB-DB, the CPU of the database machine reaches 100%, because the application server issues many short queries to maintain the state of the entity beans.

The other resources (e.g., memory, disk bandwidth, network, process limit) are not the bottleneck for any of the configurations. Memory usage on the database remains constant at 410MB. On the Web server memory usage increases over time as the static images are read into the Linux buffer cache. The memory footprint of the Web server user processes remains as low as 70MB. The traffic between the Web server, the servlet engine, and the database server is very low. Network traffic is the heaviest between the Web server and the clients, but it remains less than 3.5Mb/s. Most of this traffic stems from the static images. Steady-state disk I/O is less than 20 transfers per second for all machines.

5.2   Browsing Mix

Figure 7 shows the throughput using the browsing mix of the online bookstore benchmark. The curves are lower than those in Figure 5, because this workload contains more read queries, which are generally more complex than the update queries.

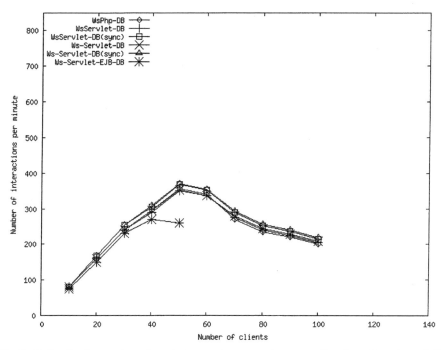

Fig. 7. Online bookstore throughput in interactions per minute as a function of number of clients for the browsing mix.

Fig. 8. Online bookstore percentage CPU utilization at the peak throughput for the browsing mix.

The bottleneck for this mix is invariably the CPU of the database server. There is no lock contention in the database because of the dominance of the read queries. Hence, performing the locking operations in the servlet engine does not yield any noticeable performance gain. For this reason, all configurations, except WS-Servlet-EJB-DB, have the same performance. The performance of Ws-Servlet-EJB-DB is low for the same reason as in the shopping mix.

Figure 8 shows the CPU utilization at the peak throughput for all machines in the different configurations. The figure confirms that the CPU of the database server is the bottleneck for all configurations.

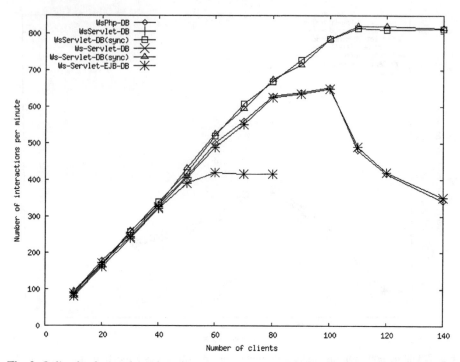

Fig. 9. Online bookstore throughput in interactions per minute as a function of number of clients for the ordering mix.

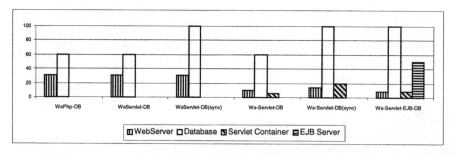

Fig. 10. Online bookstore percentage CPU utilization at the peak throughput for the ordering mix.

5.3   Ordering Mix

The ordering mix contains shorter update queries than the shopping mix and as a result gives higher throughput. Figure 9 depicts the throughput for different configurations, and Figure 10 shows the CPU utilization at the peak point for each configuration.

The configurations WsPhp-DB, WsServlet-DB and Ws-Servlet-DB have approximately the same throughput curves, because the bottleneck is database locking. Figure

10 shows that for these configurations the database server CPU utilization remains around 60%.

Performing the locking operations on the servlet engine, as in WsServlet-DB(sync) and Ws-Servlet-DB(sync), gives much better performance. It reduces the database lock contention and allows the CPU of the database server to reach 100% utilization.

As expected, the performance of the EJB configurations Ws-Servlet-EJB-DB is considerably lower than other configurations.

5.4   Summary

With the database being the bottleneck for the online bookstore, there is little difference between PHP and Java servlets when they use exactly the same queries. Therefore, offloading the servlets to a new machine does not increase throughput. Using Java synchronization mechanisms, it is possible for servlets to perform some locking operations, which reduces lock contention in the database and gives better performance for workloads with a moderate-to-high fraction of writes. The throughput of EJB is lower than with PHP or with Java servlets.

6   Experimental Results for the Auction Site

This benchmark contains mostly short database queries. For example, many update queries correspond to inserting a new bid, buying an item, or leaving a comment. Similarly, the read queries return a list of items that meet specific criteria, show the details of an item, show the history and the comments of a user, or retrieve the status of the user's active bids. This benchmark stresses the dynamic content generator, which communicates with the database and assembles the response. Our measurements show that the bottleneck is the CPU of the dynamic content generator for all configurations except in one case. This benchmark contrasts different implementations of dynamic content generation.

6.1   Bidding Mix

Figure 11 reports the throughput in interactions per minute as a function of number of clients for the bidding mix of this benchmark.

First, we compare WsPhp-DB, WsServlet-DB and WS-Servlet-DB. The PHP configuration WsPhp-DB peaks at 9,780 clients per minute with 1,100 clients. Servlets on the Web server, WsServlet-DB, achieves a lower peak of 7,380 interactions per minute with 700 clients. The best configuration among these three configurations is the one in which the servlets run on a dedicated machine, Ws-Servlet-DB, with 10,440 interactions per minute at 1,200 clients.

These results can be explained by looking at figure 12, which reports the CPU utilization of different machines at the peak throughput for each configuration. When the dynamic content generator runs on the Web server, as in WsPhp-DB and WsServlet-DB, the Web server CPU is the bottleneck with 100% CPU utilization. PHP is more efficient than Java servlets and gives around 33% more peak throughput. We attribute this difference in part to the overhead of communicating between the Web server and the servlet engine, which execute in separate processes. Profiling measurements indicate that, on average, the cost of sending one character of dynamic con-

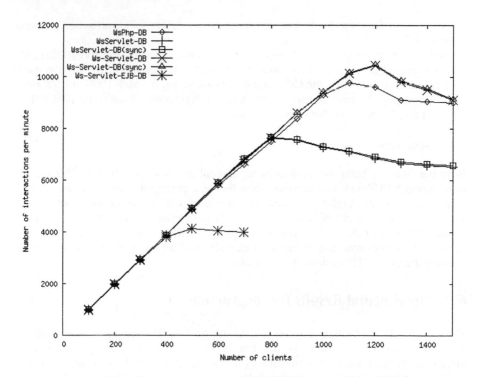

Fig. 11. Auction site throughput in interactions per minute as a function of number of clients for the bidding mix.

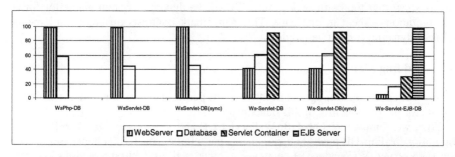

Fig. 12. Auction site percentage CPU utilization at the peak throughput for the bidding mix.

tent between the servlet engine and the Web server is 191 microseconds. In contrast, PHP does not incur such costs. Also, servlets use a type 4 JDBC driver that is written in Java and interpreted. PHP uses a native code database driver, which is presumably faster than the type 4 JDBC driver. Finally, when a dedicated machine is used for the servlets as in Ws-Servlet-DB, the best performance is achieved. The benefit of an extra CPU outweighs the extra communication costs resulting from putting the servlet engine on a separate machine.

Second, consider the configurations WsServlet-DB(sync) and Ws-Servlet-DB(sync). Because the queries in this benchmark are short, the database machine

CPU is at most 62% utilized for all configurations. Also, there is no lock contention in the database. Thus, performing locking in the Java servlets does not increase the throughput. This explains why in figure 11 the throughput curve for WsServlet-DB(sync) coincides with the curve for WsServlet-DB, and Ws-Servlet-DB(sync) coincides with Ws-Servlet-DB.

Finally, the EJB configuration Ws-Servlet-EJB-DB initially exhibits a linear increase in throughput with the number of clients, but stagnates around 500 clients to reach its peak at 4136 interactions per minute. Figure 12 clearly shows that the CPU on the EJB server is the bottleneck resource with average 99% utilization. CPU utilization on all other machines is very modest: 32% on the servlet engine, 17% on the database server, and 6% on the Web server.

None of the other resources (memory, disk, and network) forms a bottleneck for any configuration. For instance, we observe a maximum memory usage of 110MB, 95MB, and 390MB on the Web server, the servlet engine and the database server, respectively. Although the database is much larger than the physical memory of the database machine, most accesses are to records relating to new auctions, which is a small subset. Disk usage is initially high in order to load these records into memory, but then drops off to an average of 0.4 MB/s. The communication between the servlet engine and the database is modest at an average of 1.8Mb/s.

For the EJB configuration Ws-Servlets-EJB-DB, the EJB server uses about 190MB of memory. Although network bandwidth is not a bottleneck, a very large number of small packets are exchanged between the EJB server and the database server (an average of 2,000 packets per second for a total bandwidth of 0.5Mb/s). This large number of small messages results from accesses to fields in the beans that require a single value to be read or updated in the database.

6.2   Browsing Mix

The browsing mix only contains read-only queries. The majority of these queries are short. This results in making the dynamic content generator or the Web server the bottleneck resource rather than the database server.

Figure 13 reports the throughput in interactions per minute as a function of number of clients for the browsing mix workload. The curves follow similar trends as those for the bidding mix. In particular, the PHP configuration WsPhp-DB gives around 25% better peak throughput than the corresponding servlet configuration WsServlet-DB. Moving servlets to a dedicated machine gives the best performance.

Performing locking in the Java servlets does not yield any increase in the throughput. Therefore, the configuration WsServlet-DB(sync) has identical throughput to WsServlet-DB, and Ws-Servlet-DB has identical throughput to Ws-Servlet-DB. The EJB configuration Ws-Servlet-EJB-DB shows the lowest throughput.

Similar to the shopping mix, the disk and memory are never a bottleneck. Also, the network bandwidth is the bottleneck only in the case discussed above.

Figure 14 depicts the CPU utilization of different machines at the peak points for each configuration. The bottleneck resource is the CPU of the server running the dynamic content generator, except for the configurations Ws-Servlet-DB and Ws-Servlet-DB(sync). For these two configurations, the Java servlets run on a dedicated machine. They achieve the highest throughput of 12,000 interactions per minute at 12,000 clients. The CPU of the Web server approaches 100% because of the network

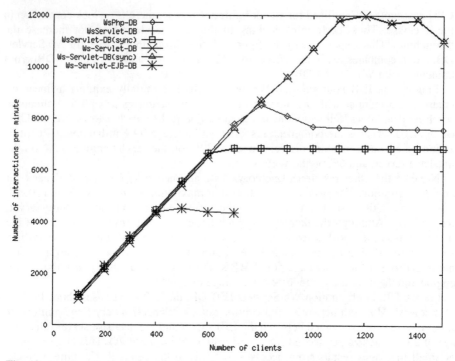

Fig. 13. Auction site throughput in interactions per minute as a function of number of clients for the browsing mix.

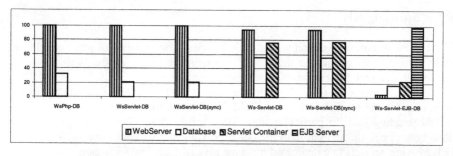

Fig. 14. Auction site percentage CPU utilization at the peak throughput for the browsing mix.

traffic on the Web server. In this configuration the network traffic on the Web server reaches 94Mb/s (80Mb/s to clients and 14Mb/s from the servlet engine).

6.3   Summary

PHP consumes less CPU time than servlets. We attribute this primarily to the fact that it executes in the same process and address space as the Web server. Although an advantage in terms of execution overhead, it restricts PHP to being co-located with the Web server on the same machine. If the Web server is the bottleneck, then better overall performance is achieved by moving the servlet engine to a dedicated machine. Performing locking in the servlet engine does not improve the throughput if there is no database lock contention. EJB offers the most flexible architecture, but even using four machines to run the Web server, the servlet engine, the EJB server and the database, the EJB performance is below that of PHP and Java servlets.

7   Related Work

Cain et al. [5] present a detailed architectural evaluation of TPC-W implemented using Java servlets. They investigate the impact of Java servlets on the memory system, the branch predictor, and the effectiveness of coarse-grain multithreading. Our study is aimed at studying the overall system and at studying differences between system architectures.

Wu et al. compare PHP, Java servlets and CGI as approaches for Web-to-database applications [21]. Their benchmark test is restricted to data retrieval (read) operations, while we use more realistic benchmarks. They only use a configuration where the Java servlet engine runs on the Web server, and even with this configuration servlets outperform the two scripting languages. However, they use PHP3 while we use PHP v4.0.6 that includes a lot of improvements. Our Java servlets environment has a larger overhead than PHP, but the flexibility of servlets allows configurations where the load is balanced among several servers.

The functionalities of Java servlets, PHP and CGI/Perl are compared in Sun's white paper [15]. They analyze the server-side mechanisms provided by each architecture. They conclude that Perl or PHP can help meet short-term goals but present the long-term benefits of using Java servlets for Web-based development, such as platform- and server-independent methods, and portable and reusable logic components. We propose a complementary comparison, focusing on performance, and also including EJB.

The ECperf specification [16] was a first attempt at standardizing the evaluation of EJB servers. Since then, it has been replaced by SPECjAppServer2002 (Java Application Server). SPECjAppServer2002 is a client/server benchmark for measuring the performance of Java Enterprise Application Servers using a subset of the J2EE APIs in a complete end-to-end Web application [17]. The results from SPECAppServer2002 report moderate throughputs (in BOPS or Business OPerations per Second) in view of the hardware platform used to achieve it. This confirms the large software overhead of the currently available implementations of EJB.

In our own earlier work [3], we analyze implementations of three benchmarks (an online bookstore, an auction site, and a bulletin board site) using PHP with the goal of discovering the bottlenecks in each benchmark. In this paper, we extend this work to a comparison of PHP with Java servlets and EJB on two of the benchmarks. We do not use the third benchmark, the bulletin board, in this study because the Web server CPU is the bottleneck for the bulletin board. Therefore, we expect the results for the bulletin board to be similar to the auction site results.

In other earlier work [6] we study the scalability of EJB applications using the auction site benchmark with different enterprise bean types and design patterns. In this paper, we use the session façade design pattern with stateless session beans and entity beans using local interfaces. This design offers the best tradeoff between using EJB services and obtaining high performance.

8   Conclusions

We compare three middleware architectures for generating dynamic content: PHP, Java servlets, and Enterprise Java Beans (EJB). PHP is tied to the Web server. The database interfaces in PHP are ad hoc and have to be written for each database. Java servlets run independently from the Web server. They provide independence from the particular database used by performing all database operations through JDBC. EJB goes one step further and uses a component approach that is platform-independent. EJB splits the business logic and the presentation logic in separate tiers.

In terms of programmability, the number of lines of code in our implementation with Java servlets is higher for the auction site than in the PHP implementation, and about the same for the online bookstore. The presence of the Java tools and the safety properties of the language help in debugging, but the safety properties also necessitate many re-cast's, reflecting well-known trade-offs between typed and untyped (scripting) languages. EJB is easy to use, in that it does not require SQL queries to be written, but our implementation requires more lines of (Java) code than servlets because of the many interfaces that need to be implemented to structure the application logic into enterprise beans. Tools are available, however, that automate the generation of large portions of the EJB code.

In terms of performance, PHP scripts are more efficient than Java servlets. PHP scripts are, however, tied to the Web server and provide limited functionality and runtime support. Java servlets run in a different process from the Web server. This flexibility can be exploited to off-load the servlets to another machine to give better performance when the Web server is the bottleneck. Servlets can use all the Java language features and runtime support. In particular, if servlets are the only application that accesses the database, they can offload some locking operations from the database. This improves performance if there is database lock contention. Enterprise Java Beans offer the most flexible architecture. The EJB server offers many services to the enterprise beans, which capture the application logic. Using EJB represents a trade-off: Expressing the application logic in terms of enterprise beans offers important software engineering qualities such as modularity, portability, and maintainability, but the performance of EJB is lower than both Java servlets and PHP.

References

1. Rahim Adatia et al. – Professional EJB – *Wrox Press, ISBN 1-861005-08-3*, 2001.
2. Deepak Alur, John Crupi and Dan Malks – Core J2EE Patterns – *Sun Microsystems Press, ISBN 0-13-064884-1*, 2001.
3. Cristiana Amza, Emmanuel Cecchet, Anupam Chanda, Alan Cox, Sameh Elnikety, Romer Gil, Julie Marguerite, Karthick Rajamani and Willy Zwaenepoel – Specification and Implementation of Dynamic Web Site Benchmarks – *IEEE 5th Annual Workshop on Workload Characterization (WWC-5)*, Austin, TX, USA, November 2002.
4. The Apache Software Foundation – http://www.apache.org/.

5. Harold W. Cain, Ravi Rajwar, Morris Marden and Mikko H. Lipasti – An Architectural Evaluation of Java TPC-W – *Proceedings of the Seventh International Symposium on High-Performance Computer Architecture*, 2001.
6. Emmanuel Cecchet, Julie Marguerite and Willy Zwaenepoel – Performance and scalability of EJB applications – *Proceedings of OOPSLA'02*, 2002.
7. eBay – http://www.ebay.com/.
8. Jason Hunter and William Crawford – Java Servlet Programming 2nd edition – *O'Reilly, ISBN 0-596-00040-5*, 2001.
9. JOnAS Open Source EJB Server – http://www.objectweb.org.
10. Lutris Enhydra Application Server – http:/www.lutris.com.
11. Microsoft Active Server Pages – http://www.asp.net.
12. Microsoft Internet Information Server – http://www.microsoft.com/iis.
13. MySQL Reference Manual v3.23.36 – http://www.mysql.com/documentation/.
14. PHP Hypertext Preprocessor – http://www.php.net/.
15. Sun Microsystems - Comparing Methods For Server-Side Dynamic Content White Paper – *http://java.sun.com*, 2000.
16. Sun Microsystems – ECperf specification - http://java.sun.com/j2ee/ecperf/, 2001.
17. SPECjAppServer2002 Design Document - http://www.specbench.org/jAppServer2002/docs, 2002.
18. Sysstat package – http://freshmeat.net/projects/sysstat/.
19. Jakarta Tomcat Servlet Engine – http://jakarta.apache.org/tomcat/.
20. Transaction Processing Performance Council– http://www.tpc.org/.
21. Amanda Wu, Haibo Wang and Dawn Wilkins – Performance Comparison of Alternative Solutions For Web-To-Database Applications – *Proceedings of the Southern Conference on Computing*, 2000.
22. Sun Microsystems – Enterprise Java Beans Specifications – http://java.sun.com/j2ee/.

Prefetching Based on Web Usage Mining

Daby M. Sow, David P. Olshefski, Mandis Beigi, and Guruduth Banavar

IBM T. J. Watson Research Center
Hawthorne NY, 10532, USA
{sowdaby,olshef,mandis,banavar}@us.ibm.com

Abstract. This paper introduces a new technique for prefetching web content by learning the access patterns of individual users. The prediction scheme for prefetching is based on a learning algorithm, called Fuzzy-LZ, which mines the history of user access and identifies patterns of recurring accesses. This algorithm is evaluated analytically via a metric called *learnability* and validated experimentally by correlating learnability with prediction accuracy. A web prefetching system that incorporates Fuzzy-LZ is described and evaluated. Our experiments demonstrate that Fuzzy-LZ prefetching provides a gain of 41.5 % in cache hit rate over pure caching. This gain is highest for those users who are neither highly predictable nor highly random, which turns out to be the vast majority of users in our workload. The overhead of our prefetching technique for a typical user is 2.4 prefetched pages per user request.

1 Introduction

Large user perceived latency is a major problem in today's World Wide Web. Many factors contribute to this problem, including transmission latency, DNS name server lookups, TCP connection establishment, and start of session delays at the HTTP servers [3]. Conventional web caching techniques attempt to address part of this problem by temporarily storing recently accessed web content close to the user, on the client device or on a proxy server. These techniques work well when content is reused several times, potentially by several users. However, caching may not reduce latency when there is poor locality of reference and access to dynamic and personalized content.

A complementary approach to reducing latency is to effectively predict user access behavior and use this knowledge to prefetch content close to the user. Several research efforts [7, 2, 6] have studied aspects of prediction and prefetching. These efforts have focused on using the structure and relationship of content to predict user access behavior, and are described in detail in Section 2.

In this paper, we present a novel approach to prefetching that predicts future accesses by learning the usage patterns of individual users. The prediction algorithm mines access logs collected at or near the user. This allows us to focus on the access behavior of individual users rather than on the structure of content at any one Web server. The patterns generated by this technique capture a user's access behavior across multiple Web content servers. These patterns are

M. Endler and D. Schmidt (Eds.): Middleware 2003, LNCS 2672, pp. 262–281, 2003.

used to predict future accesses and to prefetch content to a caching proxy close to the user. The major advantages of this approach are: (1) since we identify patterns about individual users, we can provide differentiated services on a per-user basis, and (2) this is an intermediary-based approach that does not require modifications to the web server and is transparent to content providers.

Our prediction algorithm uses a new learning technique, called Fuzzy-LZ. This technique is an extension of the Lempel-Ziv compression algorithm [31]. Through analytical and experimental evaluation, we show that the predictive capability of this learning technique is proportional to the amount of randomness (which we term *learnability*) in the user's access behavior. We also evaluate the benefit of this learning technique when it is embedded within a web content prefetching test bed.

The following are the key contributions of this paper:

- *Fuzzy-LZ learning technique:* We propose a new learning technique for predicting individual user access patterns taking into account the fact that users access similar but not necessarily identical Web URLs[1]. We evaluate the effectiveness of this technique both analytically and experimentally, and show that the prediction accuracy of this technique is proportional to the randomness of a user's access behavior.

- *Learnability metric:* From complexity measures, we derive a metric called *learnability* which measures the randomness of the access behavior of an individual. This metric enables us to analytically estimate the accuracy with which a user's access behavior can be predicted. We studied a large population of users and found that the access behavior of most users was highly learnable (more than 80% of the users have a learnability measure between 0.65 and 0.85, on a scale of 0 to 1).

- *Prefetching system architecture and evaluation.* We evaluate the learning technique within an experimental web content prefetching system test bed. This test bed models a production enterprise proxy server by replaying the HTTP traffic over a specific time interval. For this workload, we obtained a gain of up to 41.5 % in cache hits over pure caching. The overhead of our prefetching technique for a typical user is only 2.4 pages per user request.

The rest of this paper is organized as follows. Section 2 provides a detailed account of related work in this area. Section 3 describes our Fuzzy-LZ technique for predicting user access behavior, by providing the background necessary to understand the LZ parsing algorithm. Section 3.2 then evaluates the Fuzzy-LZ algorithm, by first defining the learnability metric and then by correlating the Fuzzy-LZ prediction accuracy with learnability. Section 4 describes our evaluation of a content prefetching system testbed that incorporates the Fuzzy-LZ technique and describes the experimental results. Section 5 points to some open issues and concludes.

---

[1] For example, all the news stories related to the Kenyan election on Dec 29th could have similar but not identical URLs on a news web site. This group of similar URLs is treated as a single unit. See Section 3 for details.

2   Related Work

Research related to this work falls into three categories: sequential prediction, web usage mining and prefetching. In this section, we survey the state of the art in each of these fields.

2.1   Sequential Prediction

Our work is built on the theoretical foundations of mature research fields of sequential prediction, information and rate distortion theories. Sequential prediction has developed techniques that predict the next event from a time ordered sequence of events. The work of Lempel and Ziv [12, 31] on complexity and compression of finite sequences produced the LZ algorithm that can be considered a corner stone of this field. Feder et. al. [8] have shown that Lempel and Ziv's work can be used to design efficient and optimal finite state sequential predictors. Inspired by these results, Kumar et. al. [5] used the LZ algorithm to predict the location of a user in a home. Vitter and Krishnan [23] have investigated the use of the LZ algorithm for prefetching from a theoretical perspective. Lossy extensions of the LZ algorithm have been made in [16] for data compression purposes, with interesting links to rate distortion theory [4]. To the best of our knowledge, no one has applied such Lossy compression techniques to machine learning problems in general. Lossless compression algorithms have been successfully applied to a variety of machine learning problems. The links between learning and compression are not accidental. In fact, William of Ockham was the first one to state in the 14th century that the simplest explanations for arbitrary phenomena are always the most reliable. This principle, called the Occam razor principle has been widely applied in machine learning where simplicity is synonymous to conciseness [21].

2.2   Web Usage Mining

Srivastava et. al. [24] define Web Usage Mining as the application of data mining techniques to discover usage patterns from Web data, in order to understand and better serve the needs of Web-based applications. These applications include personalization, site modification, business intelligence, usage characterization, and site improvement applications. Several machine learning techniques have been successfully adapted for general applications. Most of these techniques have been applied to web server logs as opposed to proxy logs (see Section2.3 for the benefits and drawbacks). A notable exception is the work of Kerkhofs et. al. [15] that mines proxy log data. The authors attempt to find association rules [17] between the host parts of URLs to learn user browsing behaviors however they do not apply their technique to prefetching issues.

2.3   Prefetching

Prefetching has garnered a great deal of recent attention as a possible solution for reducing latency and bandwidth consumption on the web. In this section we survey the main theoretical and practical results in this area.

Jiang and Kleinrock [9] have studied the effect that prefetching has on network traffic from a queuing theoretical perspective. The main contribution of their work is the definition of a threshold on the likelihood that a document will be requested by a client. They show that prefetching documents with a likelihood below this threshold degrades the delivery performance of the network.

The Web Collector [27] and PeakJet2000 [18] (a commercial product) are systems that perform prefetching into a local cache based on the hypertext links of the previously downloaded pages. The drawback of this approach is the additional bandwidth load that their system imposes on the network. They improve their cache hit rate from 38.5% to 64.4% by prefetching 10 requests for every request made by the client [27]. Unfortunately, the traffic on the network triples. Our approach addresses this problem by reducing the number of prefetched pages based on information learned from access logs. We only prefetch an average of 2.4 extra pages for each request made by the typical web user and much less for highly predictable users and users with random patterns.

Duchamps [7] and Bestavros [1] separately propose keeping statistics on the "relatedness" of web pages and their embedded links, and use these statistics to make decisions on prefetching. This approach manages to ensure that 62.5% of prefetched pages are eventually used [7] but it completely ignores patterns across different hosts. For instance, this approach is unable to learn that requests to www.cnn.com and www.abc.com are correlated for a given user. Our approach complements Duchamps work and does not limit itself to predict only the accesses available via hyperlinks from the current page.

Davison [6] has proposed a technique that predicts a user's next web request by analyzing the content of the pages recently requested by the user. By prefetching the top 5 URLs predicted by this system, he shows a hit rate improvement over caching of up to 40% for an infinite cache. However, this approach adds a significant computational load on proxies supporting this scheme. Our approach is not as computationaly intensive and prefetches less objects per client request to get similar hit rate improvements.

Yang et. al. [29] have developed a prefetching technique that constructs association rules from web logs by building an n-gram model to predict future requests. They have reported improvements of 6% in fractional latency[2] with the addition of their prefetching module. Palpanas et. al. [20] also proposed a prefetching algorithm based on partial match prediction. Their simulations show that this technique is able to predict up to 23% of user's next web request but it has not been deployed on a real prefetching system.

Both Palpanas et. al. and Yang et. al. perform their mining on Web server logs, whereas we mine proxy server logs. The advantages of mining a proxy server log are: (1) Access patterns across multiple servers can be mined, and (2) to be deployed, the prefetching solution does not require any modifications to the origin servers. However, proxy server logs are more difficult to mine simply because there is much more variability in the requests made by a given user. Despite this, our approach yields a higher prediction accuracy on proxy logs.

---

[2] In [29] the authors define the fractional latency as the ratio of between the observed latency with a caching system and the observed latency without a caching system.

The work of Cohen et. al. [2] presents a different approach to prefetching. They propose a technique that aggregates pages at the web server into groups that they call volumes. In their approach, when a request is processed at the Web server, the Web server serves the request and pushes the entire volume containing the request. Clearly, in order to be widely deployed this approach requires a special protocol between Web servers and proxies for the distribution of volumes. Our approach operates exclusively at the client proxy and is easier to deploy.

Cohen and Kaplan [3] have shown that DNS query time, TCP connection establishment delays and start of session delays at HTTP servers are major causes of large latency. They propose methods for resolving DNS queries and opening up HTTP connections to content servers in anticipation of use. While their work does not predict the next URLs that a user will access, it complements our approach.

3   Predicting User Access Patterns

At the heart of all prefetching middleware lies a mechanism that infers the content that should be fetched in anticipation of its use. Such inferences can either be *informative* or *speculative*. In the former case, inferences are explicitly given to the middleware by an expert. In the latter case, inferences are derived by the middleware from historical data. In this section we focus on the problem of inferencing patterns from historical web usage data, for individual users, in order to learn their web browsing behavior and guide the prefetching middleware in the selection of content to prefetch. We call this problem *the web usage prediction problem.*

We cast this problem as a sequential prediction problem where we attempt to design predictors able to forecast the next URL that a user might access from the set of past URLs that this user has already accessed. Accordingly, inputs to these predictors are time ordered sequences of URLs that have previously been requested by the user. In our experiments, these inputs are obtained from an enterprise proxy server that stores access logs in the NCSA Common Log File Format [14]. We sought to develop an inferencing technique with the following properties:

1. The learning technique ought to be incremental and suitable for online learning, allowing the system to respond in real time to changes in user behavior.
2. The learning technique must be universal. By universal, we mean that it should be able to unconditionally track *any* user behavior. In practice, it should be able to track patterns of users without any knowledge of characteristics of individual users. With this property, we can deploy the same algorithm to a large set of users without having to statistically estimate the behavior of each individual user.
3. The learning technique must be well understood. This property allows us to extensively study the performance of the technique, investigate its optimality and understand its limitations.

4. The learning technique must be able to ignore small differences between similar URLs. This property is crucial for the mining of arbitrary URLs and differentiates this problem from many sequential prediction problems. Indeed, a large portion of URLs on the web are dynamic. The structure of many web sites like www.cnn.com evolves constantly. While a user might always access international news from this site on a daily basis, this user may not access the same URL more than once, simply because news stories are dynamic. Nevertheless, it is clear that the fact that this user periodically accesses the international section of this news site defines a pattern that should be identified by our predictors.

The desired output of the learning technique is a set of patterns of the form:

$$Condition \rightarrow Action$$

The condition is a trigger that defines the state in which a user must be for the pattern to be activated. In this work, the condition is an ordered sequence of URLs representing the last sites visited by the user. The action part of the pattern is a set of URLs. It represents the output of the prediction when the corresponding pattern is activated. In the rest of this section, we propose a novel technique to derive such patterns from user web logs for the web usage prediction problem.

3.1   The Fuzzy LZ Learning Technique

Sequential prediction problems have been addressed extensively in the literature and in particular in [8] from an information theoretical angle. One of the key results of this work is a proof of the efficiency of the well known Lempel-Ziv [12] parsing scheme for universal sequential prediction. It is shown in [8] that this parsing scheme can be used to design finite state predictors that are asymptotically optimal. Inspired by these strong results, we adapt and extend the LZ parsing scheme to solve the web usage prediction problem.

To formalize the problem, we follow [8]. We define U as an infinite sequence representing the sequence of URLs requested by a user. Elements of this sequence belong to Ω, the set of all URL visited. These elements are indexed with discrete time values: $U = \cdots, u_{-2}, u_{-1}, u_0, u_1, u_2, \cdots$. Observations of U are subsequences of U denoted U_i^j where i is the index of the first URL and j the index of the last. Fix the current time at n and imagine an observer that has sequentially received an arbitrary sequence of t URLs $U_{n-t+1}^n = u_{n-t+1}, \cdots, u_{n-1}, u_n$, and wishing to predict the next URL u_{n+1}. Our goal is to design a family of predictors $\{P^t\}, -\infty < t < +\infty$ performing such predictions with a minimal amount of prediction errors. $\{P^t\}$ is a family of functions $P^t : \Omega^t \rightarrow \Omega$, where Ω^t is the t-fold Cartesian product of Ω. The performance of each predictor is measured by its *accuracy*, which is its ability to correctly predict u_{n+1} from the past. Let $A^k_{\{P^t\}}$ be the accuracy of the entire family $\{P^t\}$ over the next k observations of URLs from the current time n. $A^k_{\{P^t\}}$ is equal to the fraction of correct predictions obtained during the testing phase of the learning process.

$$A^k_{\{P^t\}} = \frac{\sum_{i=0}^{k} 1(u_{n+i+1} = P^{t+i}(U^{n+i}_{n-t+1}))}{k}$$

where $1(\cdot)$ is the identity function[3]. Our goal can be translated into a quest for a family of predictors $\{P^t\}$ that maximizes $A^k_{\{P^t\}}$.

Original Incremental Lempel-Ziv Parsing. The Lempel-Ziv (LZ) parsing algorithm was introduced in 1976 in [12]. Soon after, the authors used it to design a universal compression technique [31] that became the standard algorithm for electronic file compression. The success of this algorithm is primarily due to its efficiency, its speed and its incremental nature. To describe how the algorithm works, consider the following example where we attempt to parse the following input sequence of URLs:

$$U^9_0 = a, b, c, a, c, b, b, a, c, b$$

where a, b, and c represent distinct URLs. The LZ algorithm parses this sequence into strings that have not appeared so far. For example, the input sequence U^9_0 is parsed as :

$$\tilde{U}^5_0 = a, b, c, ac, bb, acb,$$

Note that the main difference between U^9_0 and $\tilde{U}^5_0$ is the position of the comas. While elements of U^9_0 are URLs, elements of $\tilde{U}^5_0$ are now sequences of URLs. The key point to remember is that after every coma in $\tilde{U}^5_0$ the algorithm identifies the shortest string that has not been identified before in the parsing.

The LZ parsing has two important properties that allows us to use it for sequential learning problems:

1. As pointed out in [8], this parsing can be modeled as a process of growing a tree, where each new string is represented by a path in the tree. Such trees summarize the subset of all recurrent patterns that were identified by the LZ sequential parsing. Referring back to our desired output, any node in the tree represents the action part of a pattern and the list of ancestors of this node represents the condition part of the pattern. This ancestor list defines the state in which the user is believed to be before accessing the URL represented in the actual node. An example of tree obtained with this algorithm is shown in Figure 1.

2. This parsing can be used to design a family of optimal predictors. The derived trees do not track all the patterns present in the input sequences. Instead, they focus only on the ones with high probabilities. The patterns that are dropped have negligible probability of occurrence. For a formalization of the performance of this technique, please refer to [12, 31, 4, 8].

The LZ parsing has the first three of the four criteria required for our learning solution as described in Section 3. The algorithm is incremental and suitable for online learning problems. It is well understood and has been studied extensively

---

[3] $1(X) = 1$ if X is true. Otherwise, $1(X) = 0$.

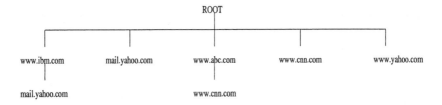

Fig. 1. Output of the original Lempel Ziv parsing algorithm

in the literature [4]. The technique is also universal. But it does not address the fourth criterion, namely the tolerance to small differences between URLs. In the next section, we extend this technique to address this fourth criterion.

Fuzzy-LZ: Fuzzy Extension of the LZ Parsing. While most sequential prediction schemes can be formulated from an information theoretical angle, the problem of mining web usage has a key characteristic that differentiates it from a typical sequential prediction problem. The URL sequence to predict typically evolves with time. As mentioned earlier, the structure of many web sites evolves constantly.

To address this problem, we have extended the LZ parsing scheme by allowing it to make approximate predictions. The main idea is to ignore the small variations in the structure of the URLs composing the input sequence. In essence, we group similar URLs into *clusters*. Instead of predicting individual URLs, we predict clusters of URLs. As a result, our predictors P_t output sets of URLs instead of individual URLs and the prediction accuracy $A^k_{\{P^t\}}$ becomes:

$$A^k_{\{P^t\}} = \frac{\sum_{i=0}^{k} 1(u_{n+i+1} \in P^{t+i}(U^{n+i}_{n-t+1}))}{k}$$

To find such predictors, we first define a semantic distance metric on the space of all possible URLs. Like any other distance metric, this metric quantifies the similarities between elements of its space. This metric is essentially computed by matching the different parts of URLs. Similarities between server names s_1 and s_2 are measured from the index of the last mismatch in their string representation, starting from the end of the strings. We start from the end of the strings because server names become more and more specific as we move from the end of the string to its beginning. Let $\hat{i}_{s_1,s_2}$ denote the index of the last mismatch between s_1 and s_2. Then the distance between s_1 and s_2 that we denote $d_{server}(s_1, s_2)$ is given by:

$$d_{server}(s_1, s_2) = \frac{max\{l(s_1), l(s_2)\} - \hat{i}_{s_1,s_2}}{max\{l(s_1), l(s_2)\}},$$

$l(\cdot)$ being the length function that returns the length of its string argument. To illustrate this, let $s_1 = $ www.yahoo.com and $s_2 = $ mail.yahoo.com. The index of the first mismatch starting from the end of the strings is 11 where the letters l and w do not match. Since $l(s_2) > l(s_1)$, $d_{server}(s_1, s_2) = \frac{l(s_2)-11}{l(s_2)} = \frac{3}{14}$.

Similarities between the path part of URLs are computed in a similar fashion. Let p_1 and p_2 be two valid path names. Let $\hat{j}_{p_1,p_2}$ denote the index of their first mismatch this time. Then the distance between p_1 and p_2 that we denote $d_{path}(p_1, p_2)$ is given by:

$$d_{path}(p_1, p_2) = \frac{max\{l(p_1), l(p_2)\} - \hat{j}_{p_1,p_2}}{max\{l(p_1), l(p_2)\}},$$

To illustrate this, let:
$p_1 = $ /doc/papers/03infocom.tex and $p_2 = $ /doc/papers/2003middleware.tex. The index of the first mismatch is 12, where the characters 0 and 2 do not match. Since $l(p_2) > l(p_1)$, $d_{path}(p_1, p_2) = \frac{l(p_2)-12}{l(p_2)} = \frac{29-12}{29} = \frac{17}{29}$.

Definition 1. *Let u_i, u_j be a pair of URLs. Let $s_{u_i}, p_{u_i}, q_{u_i}$ denote[4] respectively the server name part, the path part and the query part of the URL u_i. We define the semantic distance between u_a and u_b as a real number $d_{URL}(u_a, u_b)$ equal to:*

$$d_{URL}(u_a, u_b) = w_s d_{server}(s_{u_a}, s_{u_b}) + w_p d_{path}(p_{u_a}, p_{u_b}) + w_q d_{path}(q_{u_a}, q_{u_b})$$

where w_s and w_p and w_q are real coefficients.

$d_{URL}(\cdot, \cdot)$ is a distance metric[5]. It always returns a positive real number. This number measures how similar the arguments of $d_{URL}(\cdot, \cdot)$ are. The different weights w_s, w_p and w_q can be used to weigh the importance of the similarities between different parts of the URL. For the web usage prediction problem, we set w_s to 10, w_p to 1 and w_q to zero.

Using $d_{URL}(\cdot, \cdot)$, we have extended the LZ parsing scheme by adding fuzziness in the derivation of the trees. To do this, we define a URL sphere of radius $D, S(u_i, D)$, as the set of all URLs that are within D of u_i according to $d_{URL}(\cdot, \cdot)$. Instead of following the LZ parsing scheme that finds the shortest substring that has not been identified yet, *the key aspect of our proposed parsing is to find the shortest substring of spheres of radius D, that has not been identified yet, D being a parameter of the algorithm.* These spheres are dynamically generated as new URLs from the input sequence of URLs are read.

---

[4] There are more fields present in general URLs. To keep the discussion short, we focus only on the server name, the path and the query string but this definition can easily be extended to all parts of any well formed URL.

[5] To prove this statement, we would have to show that for any URLs $u_a, u_b,$ and u_c, $d_{URL}(u_a, u_b) \geq 0$, $d_{URL}(u_a, u_b) = 0$ iff $u_a = u_b$, $d_{URL}(u_a, u_b) = d_{URL}(u_b, u_a)$ and finally that $d_{URL}(u_a, u_c) \leq d_{URL}(u_a, u_b) + d_{URL}(u_b, u_c)$. The proofs of each of these assertions are trivial, except for the last one, the triangular inequality. An easy way to prove it is to leverage the fact that the length of a match between two URLs is always larger than the length of the match between any of their prefix.

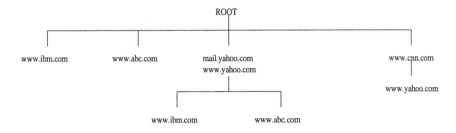

Input Sequence: www.ibm.com, mail.yahoo.com, www.abc.com, www.cnn.com, www.yahoo.com,
www.ibm.com, mail.yahoo.com, www.abc.com, www.cnn.com, www.yahoo.com

Fig. 2. Output of the Fuzzy-LZ Lempel Ziv parsing algorithm

An example of a tree obtained from this procedure is shown in Figure 2. D was set to 4/14 for this example. In contrast with Figure 1, the nodes of the tree shown in Figure 2 are clusters of URLs. In general, as the length of the input sequence increases, the number of nodes generated with the Fuzzy-LZ parsing technique is well below the number of nodes generated by the LZ technique. Hence, Fuzzy-LZ generates less patterns with higher accuracy but the price to pay for this accuracy improvement is the distortion introduced by the clusters.

3.2   Evaluation of Fuzzy-LZ

We have implemented Fuzzy-LZ and performed an extensive number of experiments to evaluate its effectiveness. A key index of the performance of a learning scheme is its *prediction accuracy* $A^k_{\{P^t\}}$. It is equal to the total number of correct URL predictions divided by the total number of requests made by the user. While the prediction accuracy might give an absolute view of the ability of the algorithm to make inferences, it does not take into account the characteristics of input sequences from which patterns are extracted. Indeed, regardless of the efficiency of our predictors, the accuracy of the end results of the predictions made is always bounded by the amount of patterns contained in the input sequence. In what follows, we quantify this amount with the concept of *learnability*. We define learnability and investigate its correlation with the prediction accuracy.

Analytical Evaluation: Learnability. The learnability of a sequence U_1^n is a real number assessing how difficult it is to predict U_1^n. This number is obtained by comparing the number of patterns identified in U_1^n to the number of patterns that would be present in a random sequence with length equal to the length of U_1^n. For example the periodic sequence $a, b, c, a, b, c, a, b, c, \cdots$ has a high value of learnability while most sequences obtained by a random generator would have very low values of learnability. This notion is similar to the notion of complexity of a sequence [13, 8, 12].

Definition 2. *Let $c^{U_1^n}$ denote the number of strings generated by the Fuzzy-LZ parsing of sequence U_1^n of n URLs. Then the learnability of U_1^n that we denote $L(U_1^n)$ is defined as:*

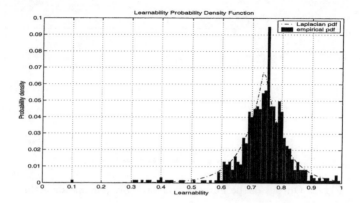

Fig. 3. Learnability probability density function. The mean and variance are respectively 0.7397 and 0.0084. The Laplacian density is obtained from these values

$$L(U_1^n) = 1 - \frac{c^{U_1^n} \log_2 c^{U_1^n} + c^{U_1^n}}{\log_2 \eta_{U_1^n}}, \tag{1}$$

$\eta_{U_1^n}$ denoting the number of different URLs appearing at least once in U_1^n.

Intuitively, $L(U_1^n)$ measures the amount of randomness in U_1^n. To see this, note that $c^{U_1^n} \log_2 c^{U_1^n} + c^{U_1^n}$ is equal[6] to the number of bits required to represent the sphere that contains U_1^n while $\log_2 \eta_{U_1^n}$ is the number of bits required to represent a random sequence of n URLs picked from the set of all URLs that appeared at least once in U_1^n. The ratio $\frac{c^{U_1^n} \log_2 c^{U_1^n} + c^{U_1^n}}{\log_2 \eta_{U_1^n}}$ is a compression ratio. Since this ratio is low for compressible sequences and high for random sequences, $L(\cdot)$ is high for compressible sequences and low for random sequences. Following the Occam Razor principle, we assume that sequences with low learnability are difficult to predict (see Section 2.1).

We have measured the learnablity for a large amount of log data containing the actions of 623 users. The resulting probability density function is shown in Figure 3. The shape of the density is Laplacian with mean 0.7397 and variance 0.0084. Figure 3 shows the distribution of learnability measured on the training set for all these users.

Experimental Results: Prediction Accuracy. From the probability density in Figure 3, we have identified 10 users spanning a range of learnability from 0.45 to 0.85. Our training set is composed of the actions of these users in a time period that starts on August 12 2002 at 12:00 AM and ends on August 15 2002 at 01:59 PM. Our testing set contains the actions that the same users made in a time period that starts on August 15 at 2:00 PM and ends August 16 at 11:59 PM. Using the testing set, we have evaluated the accuracy of the predictions for

---

[6] Please see [4] for a formal derivation of this result in a lossless setting.

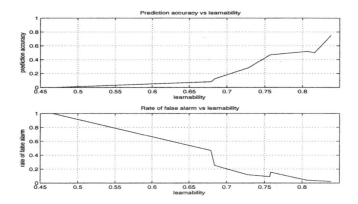

Fig. 4. Learning Effectiveness as a function of learnability

each of these 10 users by counting the number of correct predictions divided by the total number of requests made.

$$\text{prediction accuracy} = p_a = \frac{\text{total number of correct predictions}}{\text{total number of requests}}$$

We also measured the number of times that the predictor made an erroneous prediction. The rate at which such errors are made is called the rate of false alarms:

$$\text{rate of false alarms} = p_{f_a} = 1 - \frac{\text{number of correct prefetch}}{\text{total number of prefetch}}$$

Figure 4 shows the relationship between the prediction accuracy and the learnability. It also shows the relationship between the percentage of false alarms and the learnability. We notice that as the learnability increases, users become more predictable and the prediction accuracy increases while the percentage of false alarms decreases.

4   System Deployment on Experimental Test Bed

To demonstrate the effectiveness of Fuzzy-LZ, we have implemented the approach and deployed it on a system modeled after a real production enterprise proxy. The results presented here focus on the improvement in response time that Fuzzy-LZ is capable of providing for individual users. We compare these results with the results we obtained by using existing, start-of-the-art prefetching algorithms whose cache management is based on optimizing *aggregate* measures obtained for the set of all clients. We begin by describing our approach to designing an experimental test bed that models a production Internet proxy and then present the results obtained from our experiments.

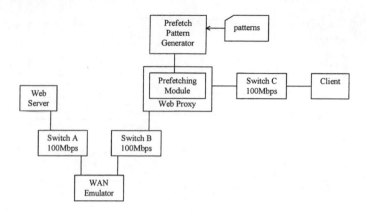

Fig. 5. Experimental test bed

4.1   Experimental Design

The testing environment consisted of four heterogeneous machines: a web server, a WAN emulator, a web proxy and one client machine (Figure 5). The proxy machine was an IBM Intellistation M Pro consisting of a 1.7 GHz CPU with 512 MB RAM. The server machine was an IBM NetVista consisting of a 1.8 GHz CPU with 512 RAM. The WAN emulator was an IBM Intellistation M Pro consisting of a 400 MHz CPU with 128 MB RAM and an IBM thinkpad 770ED consisting of a 266 MHz CPU with 96 MB RAM was used as the client machine. Both client and server machines ran RedHat 7.3, while the proxy ran Windows 2000 and the WAN emulator ran FreeBSD 4.6. Each computer had an 100/10 Mbps ethernet adapter and the three switches in Figure 5 were 100 Mbps fast ethernet switches from NetGear; switch A and B were model FS105 and switch C was a model FS108.

The WAN emulator software used was DummyNet [22], a flexible and commonly used FreeBSD tool. The WAN emulator simulated network environments with different network latencies. For our tests, we set the average round trip time to 200 ms. The latest stable version of the Apache HTTP server, V1.3.20, was executing on the server machine and was configured to run 255 daemons. The proxy machine was also running a version of Apache for Windows 2000, V1.3.26.

Although our test facilities hardware does not necessarily match that of our Internet proxy, we were able to develop traffic patterns in our testing environment that matched those observed by the production proxy server. Specifically, we created a file system on our backend web server that was a shadow of the file set requested at the production proxy server. We also created a traffic generator that created client loads based on the loads observed in the web log files at the production proxy server. The process for achieving this is outlined as a series of tasks in Figure 6.

Step 1: We downloaded the set of web logs from the production proxy server that were collected during the week of August 12 to 16, 2002. This set of five files contained a total of 4,109,814 web log entries in NCSA CLF format.

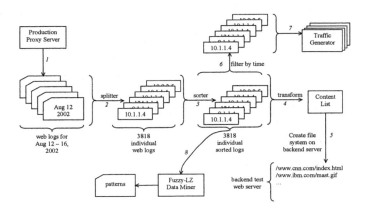

Fig. 6. Web log transformation

Step 2: Using a simple java program, we parsed and split the five log files into 3818 individual log files. Each individual log file contained all the URL requests originating from a specific client IP address[7]. As shown in Figure 6, the individual log files were named after the associated client IP address.

Step 3: Each individual log file was then sorted in ascending order by the log entry timestamp.

Step 4: By parsing all the individual log files we were able to create a file containing a list of unique file names that correspond to each unique URL. Since URL's contain characters that cannot appear in a file name or path, this step requires some transformation on the URL (ie. '%', '#', etc). We sought to develop a file system whose paths and filenames were as close as possible to the paths and filenames given in the requested URLs. In most cases, this meant we simply replaced invalid characters with a valid character. Some URLs were longer than the maximum allowed length of a path and filename on the file system; in these cases, we simply truncated the path and name.

Step 5: We replicated the file system specified in *Content List* on the testbed backend web server. Each file in the content list was reproduced in both size and file path on the web server. The content of each file was simply randomly generated bytes. By using soft links, we were able to save space by sharing files of equal size. In the end, our backend server emulated 32,169 internet web sites, contained 76,033 shared random data files, and 1,885,812 soft links representing the set of unique URL's found in the original proxy log files.

Step 6: Having built a shadow file system on the backend test web server, we ran the set of sorted individual web log files through a filter to obtain all the

---

[7] We identify user's with client IP addresses. We are aware of the limitations of this approach due when IP addresses are dynamically allocated using DHCP. This issue can be resolved using DHCP server logs that tracks not only the assigned IP addresses but also the the media access control address used by the network adapter hardware of the client.

requests for a specific time interval (ie. 12 noon to 1pm on Thursday, August 15th, 2002). This created a set of individual web log files that represented the behavior of each client during the specified time period.

Step 7: Finally, the traffic generator running on the client machine, would fork a process for each of the individual web log files. Each process would read its associated web log file and emulate the behavior of that client by creating the traffic pattern specified in the file. The traffic generator we used was a slightly modified version of the traffic generator described in [19], which is an improved version of the Webstone 2.5 web traffic generator [28]. In addition to the modifications described in [19], we modified the traffic generator to create traffic patterns from individual web log files.

Step 8: As described in Section 3, the Fuzzy-LZ Data Miner reads the individual sorted logs and generates access patterns.

Prefetching System Flow:
Our prefetching system is asynchronous. The prefetching occurs in two phases. The first phase does not use the prefetching module. It corresponds to the standard proxy request loop. All client HTTP requests are intercepted by the Web Proxy. In this first phase, this proxy attempts to serve these requests from its cache. If a requested document is not in the cache, the request is sent to the Web Server. Once the requested content is obtained either from the cache or from the Web Server, it is sent back to the client. The proxy also keeps track of a list of client IP addresses for which prefetching should be performed. After serving the request to the client, the proxy starts the second phase. In this phase, the proxy verifies if the IP address of this client is in the list of clients for which prefetching should be done, in which case it notifies the Prefetch Pattern Generator by sending to it the client IP address and the URL requested. At this time, the proxy ends the processing of this request. The Prefetch Pattern Generator verifies its list of access patterns for this user and sends the corresponding prefetching requests to the Proxy Server. These requests are normal HTTP requests with a special identifier placed in the "From" field of the HTTP request header. When the Web Proxy receives such requests, it identifies them as prefetching requests and passes them to a prefetching module that tries to get the requested content from the Web Server and stores it in the cache.

4.2   Measurements and Results

In this section, we describe the results of our experiments to show that our prefetching system yields an improved cache hit rate, lowers latency, and does not incur significant bandwidth overheads. These results are shown via three plots. The first plot shows the cache hit gain for 10 users spanning the entire spectrum of learnability values. The second plot shows the latency measurements for a "typical" user. A typical user is one whose learnability measure falls on the mode of the distribution, i.e. around 0.75 as seen in Figure 3. The third plot shows the prefetching overhead in terms of the number of requests per second

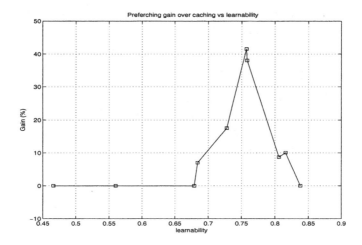

Fig. 7. Cache hit rate gain as a function of learnability

for the typical user. We define the cache hit rate gain as 1 minus the ratio of the prefetching hit rate to the pure caching hit rate. In the first plot, Figure 7, the cache hit rate gain is plotted as a function of the learnability measure. When users are very predictable, i.e., high learnability measures of ≥ 0.84, the cache hit rate gain is negligible. In other words, the cache hit rate of prefetching matches that of caching. This is expected, since predictable users tend to access the same URLs over and over and caching is designed for these scenarios. On the other hand, when users are very random, i.e., low learnability measures of ≤ 0.65, the cache hit rate gain is also negligible. In this case, the lack of identifiable patterns prevents the prefetching system from learning useful access patterns. However, in the middle, i.e., learnability measures between 0.65 and 0.85 where we have more than 80% of the users (see Figure 3), the cache hit rate gain is significant. We believe that within this interval the learnability measure is high enough that the prefetching algorithm can identify sufficient patterns such that it can achieve a non-trivial gain. At the same time, the learnability measure is not so high that the gain is offset by the ability of simple caching systems to benefit from highly predictable user access behaviors.

In the remaining two plots, we track the activity of our typical user (as described above). We performed two experiments: a baseline experiment with only pure caching, and a prefetching experiment with prefetching turned ON. As shown in Table 1, over the course of a one hour interval, prefetching increased the number of cache hits for our user from 86 hits to 122 hits. The latency is measured on the client machine.

In the second plot, Figure 8, the delay (in milliseconds) is plotted against the elapsed time. This plot shows the details of the latency for each request in this time period. The "+" markers indicate each request that resulted in a cache miss during the prefetching experiment. For these requests, the page had to be retrieved from the original server. The "×" markers indicate each request that

Table 1. Experiment summary for a typical user with prefetching ON

Learnability	0.757
Test duration	2PM to 3PM, Aug 15 2002
Total Number of requests	196
Number of cache hits (baseline)	86
Number of cache hits (prefetching)	122
Average delay of cached content ($\times$)	32.02 ms
Average delay of prefetched content (o)	38.11 ms
Average delay of content from the Web server (+)	1747.7 ms

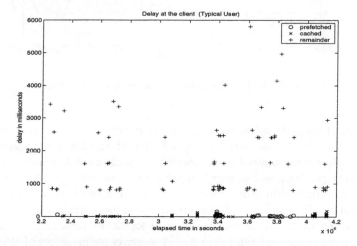

Fig. 8. Latency for each request made by the typical user

resulted in a cache hit during the baseline experiment. The "o" markers indicate all the requests that were not served from the cache in the baseline experiment but were served from the cache in the prefetching experiment. As expected, the latency for those requests served from the cache is less than the latency for those requests requiring an access to the Web Server. Note that the standard deviation for the delay of the "+" markers (server series) is 1127.8 milliseconds while the standard deviation of the delay of the "o" markers (prefetch series) is only 32.7 milliseconds. The standard deviation of the delay of the "$\times$" markers (cached series) is 31.3 milliseconds.

In the third plot, Figure 9, the number of requests per second is plotted against the elapsed time for the prefetch, cached and server series. This plot shows the load that is placed on the proxy server. No more than 4 additional prefetching requests per second are served from the cache for our typical user. The additional load on the network is also low. We measured that 467 extra requests were made by the prefetching module in anticipation of 196 requests made by the user. In other words, for each user requests, there was in average 2.38 prefetching requests issued by the Prefetching Module.

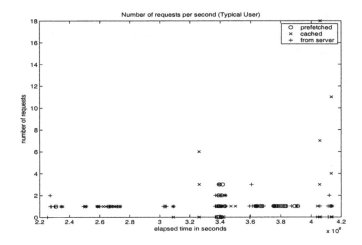

Fig. 9. Number of Requests per second for a typical user

5   Concluding Remarks

This paper has introduced Fuzzy-LZ, a new technique that learns the access patterns of individual users by mining their past access histories. We have shown that this technique predicts user access patterns in proportion to the amount of randomness within a user's access behavior. We have derived from complexity measures a metric called *learnability* that measures the amount of randomness within a user's access behavior. We have measured the learnability of a large-scale system (with 623 users) and found that most users have good learnability (at least 80% of the users have a learnability measure between 0.65 and 0.85 on a scale of 0 to 1). We have implemented and deployed the Fuzzy-LZ learning technique as the predictor within a web content prefetching system. We have seen that the learnability of a user correlates with the overall cache hit rate obtained within the system.

Our conclusion of the gain of Fuzzy-LZ based prefetching over conventional caching can be described in three cases. First, when the access behavior of users is very predictable, the cache hit rate of prefetching matches that of caching. This is not surprising, since predictable users tend to access the same content over and over and caching is designed for this case. Second, when the access behavior of users is very random, the cache hit rate of prefetching also matches that of caching. In this case, the lack of identifiable patterns prevents the prefetching system from learning useful access patterns. Third, when the access behavior of users is neither very predictable nor random, the cache hit rate of prefetching exceeds that of caching by up to 41.5 % with an overhead of only 2.4 prefetched pages per user request for a typical user. Fortunately, the large majority of users in our workload fall within this category.

There are several avenues for future work. First, we plan to perform further evaluations with additional workloads as well as various cache sizes. Second, we believe that we can easily apply the Fuzzy-LZ technique to dynamic content. For example, we can extract general descriptions of the learned clusters and use these descriptions to pre-subscribe users to dynamic content. Finally, we plan to explore the applicability of this technique in pervasive computing environments. Within these environments, user mobility will mean that content cached in one location may not be accessed from the same location, and the increasing heterogeneity of access devices means that content formatted for one device may not be suitable for access by other devices.

References

1. A. Bestavros, Using Speculation to Reduce Server Load and Service Time on the WWW, Proceedings of the 4th ACM International Conference on Information and Knowledge Management, Baltimore, MD, 1995
2. E. Cohen,B. Krishnamurthy and J. Rexford, Efficient Algorithms for Predicting Requests to Web Servers, INFOCOM (1):284–293, 1999
3. E. Cohen and H. Kaplan, Prefetching the Means for Document Transfer: A New Approach for Reducing Web Latency, INFOCOM (2):854–863, 2000
4. T. Cover and J. Thomas, Elements of Information Theory, J. Wiley & Son, 1991
5. S. Das and D. Cook and A. Bhattacharya and E. Heierman III and T.-Y. Lin, The Role of Prediction Algorithms in the MavHome Smart Home Architecture, to appear in IEEE Personal Communications Special Issue on Smart Homes
6. B. Davison, Predicting Web Actions from HTML Content, Proceedings of the The Thirteenth ACM Conference on Hypertext and Hypermedia (HT'02) 2002
7. D. Duchamps, Prefetching Hyperlinks, Proceedings of USITS'99: The 2nd USENIX Symposium on Internet Technologies and Systems, October 1999
8. M. Feider, N. Merhav and M. Gutman, Universal Prediction of Individual Sequences, IEEE Transactions on Information Theory (38):1258-1270, 1992
9. Z. Jiang and L. Kleinrock, An adaptive network prefetch scheme, IEEE Journal on Selected Areas in Communications, 16(3):358–368, April 1998
10. B. Krishnamurthy and J. Rexford, Web Protocols and Practice, Addison Wesley, 2001
11. T. M. Kroeger, D. D. E. Long and J. C. Mogul, Exploring the Bounds of Web Latency Reduction from Caching and Prefetching, USENIX Symposium on Internet Technologies and Systems (1997),
12. A. Lempel and J. Ziv, On the Complexity of Finite Sequences, IEEE Transactions on Information Theory (22):75–81, 1976
13. M. Li and P. Vitanyi, An Introduction to Kolmogorov Complexity and its Apllications, second edition, Springer Verlag (1997)
14. Logging Control In W3C httpd, "http://www.w3.org/Daemon/User/Config/Logging.html"
15. J. Kerkhofs and K. Vanhoof and D. Pannemans, Web Usage Mining on Proxy Servers: A Case Study, Workshop on Data Mining For Marketing Applications, September 2001
16. T. Luczak and W. Szpankowski, A Suboptimal Lossy Data Compression Based on Approximate Pattern Matching, IEEE Trans. Inf. Theory, (43):1439–1451, 1997
17. T.M. Mitchell, Machine Learning, Mc Graw-Hill (1997)
18. PeakJet2000 Software, "http://www.peak.com/peakjet2long.html"

19. D. Olshefski, J. Neih and D. Agrawal, Inferring Client Response Time at the Web Server, SIGMETRICS Proceedings 160–171, Marina Del Rey, CA, June 2002

20. T. Palpanas and A. Mendelzon, Web Prefetching Using Partial Match Prediction, Proceedings of the 4th International Web Caching Workshop, 1998

21. J. Rissanen, World Scientific, Stochastic Complexity in Statistical Inquiry, 1989

22. L. Rizzo, Dummynet: a simple approach to the evaluation of network protocols, ACM SIGCOMM Computer Communication Review, 27(1):31–41, January 1997

23. J. S. Vitter and P. Krishnan, Optimal prefetching via data compression, Journal of the ACM 43(5) 771–793, 1996

24. J. Srivastava, R. Cooley, M. Deshpande and P. Tan, Web Usage Mining: Discovery and Applications of Usage Patterns from Web Data, SIGKDD Explorations 1(2):12–23, 2000,

25. J. Van Leeuwen, (ed.): Computer Science Today. Recent Trends and Developments. Lecture Notes in Computer Science, Vol. 1000. Springer-Verlag, Berlin Heidelberg New York (1995)

26. P. Vitanyi and M. Li, Minimum Description Length Induction, Bayesianism, and Kolmogorov Complexity, IEEE Trans. on Info. Theory (46):446–464, 2000

27. The Web Collector, "http://www.inkey.com/save30/"

28. WebStone, "http://www.mindcraft.com/"

29. Q. Yang, H.H. Zhang and I.T.Y. Li, Mining web logs for prediction models in WWW caching and prefetching, in Knowledge Discovery and Data Mining, 473–478, 2001

30. O. Zaiane, M. Xin and J. Han, Discovering Web Access Patterns and Trends by Applying OLAP and Data Mining Technology on Web Logs, IEEE Advances in Digital Libraries Conference, 1998

31. J. Ziv and A. Lempel, A Universal Algorithm for Sequential Data Compression, IEEE Transactions on Information Theory, (23):337–343, 1977

Distributed Versioning:
Consistent Replication for Scaling Back-End Databases of Dynamic Content Web Sites

Cristiana Amza[1], Alan L. Cox[1], and Willy Zwaenepoel[2]

[1] Department of Computer Science, Rice University, Houston, TX, USA
{amza,alc}@cs.rice.edu
[2] School of Computer and Communication Sciences, EPFL, Lausanne, Switzerland
willy.zwaenepoel@epfl.ch

Abstract. Dynamic content Web sites consist of a front-end Web server, an application server and a back-end database. In this paper we introduce distributed versioning, a new method for scaling the back-end database through replication. Distributed versioning provides both the consistency guarantees of eager replication and the scaling properties of lazy replication. It does so by combining a novel concurrency control method based on explicit versions with conflict-aware query scheduling that reduces the number of lock conflicts.

We evaluate distributed versioning using three dynamic content applications: the TPC-W e-commerce benchmark with its three workload mixes, an auction site benchmark, and a bulletin board benchmark. We demonstrate that distributed versioning scales better than previous methods that provide consistency. Furthermore, we demonstrate that the benefits of relaxing consistency are limited, except for the conflict-heavy TPC-W ordering mix.

1 Introduction

Web sites serving dynamic content usually consist of a Web server, an application server and a back-end database (see Figure 1). A client request for dynamic content causes the Web server to invoke a method in the application server. The application issues a number of queries to the database and formats the results as an HTML page. The Web server then returns this page in an HTTP response to the client.

Fig. 1. Common architecture for dynamic content Web sites

Replication [4, 13, 14, 24] of the database back-end allows improved data availability and performance scaling. Providing consistency at the same time as performance scaling has, however, proven to be a difficult challenge. Eager replication schemes, which provide strong consistency (1-copy serializability [7]), severely limit performance, mainly

M. Endler and D. Schmidt (Eds.): Middleware 2003, LNCS 2672, pp. 282–304, 2003.

due to conflicts [11]. Lazy replication with delayed propagation of modifications provides better performance, but writes can arrive out-of-order at different sites and reads can access inconsistent data.

Recent work has argued that several distinct consistency models should be supplied, since dynamic content applications have different consistency requirements. Neptune proposes three levels of consistency [20]. An extension of this idea proposes a continuum of consistency models with tunable parameters [25]. The programmer then chooses the appropriate consistency model and the appropriate parameters for the application or adjusts the application to fit one of the available models. Adjusting the application may require non-trivial programmer effort.

In this paper we introduce distributed versioning, a technique that maintains strong consistency (1-copy serializability [7]) but at the same time allows good scaling behavior. Distributed versioning improves on our earlier work on conflict-aware schedulers [3] in two ways:

1. A limitation of the previous scheme is the use of conservative two-phase locking which, while avoiding deadlocks, severely limits concurrency. We introduce a novel deadlock-free concurrency control algorithm based on explicit versions, which allows increased concurrency. Distributed versioning integrates this concurrency control algorithm with a conflict-aware scheduler to improve performance over the methods introduced earlier [3].
2. We investigate the overhead of using 1-copy serializability compared to looser consistency models provided by lazy replication. We study this overhead using a variety of applications with different consistency requirements.

In our evaluation we use the three workload mixes (browsing, shopping and ordering) of the TPC-W benchmark [23], an auction site benchmark [1], and a bulletin board benchmark [1]. We have implemented these Web sites using three popular open source software packages: the Apache Web server [5], the PHP Web-scripting/application development language [16], and the MySQL database server [15]. Our results are as follows:

1. Distributed versioning increases throughput compared to a traditional (eager) protocol with serializability by factors of 2.2, 4.8, 4.3, 5.4, and 1.1 for the browsing, shopping, ordering mixes of TPC-W, the auction site and the bulletin board, respectively, in the largest configuration studied.
2. For the browsing and shopping workloads of TPC-W and for the bulletin board, distributed versioning achieves performance within 5% of the best lazy protocol with loose consistency. The auction site's performance is within 25%. The difference is larger in the TPC-W ordering mix, because of the large number of conflicts, but the best lazy protocol does not respect the application's semantics.
3. There is no penalty for enforcing serializability for applications with loose consistency (e.g., the bulletin board).

The outline of rest of the paper is as follows. Section 2 describes the programming model, the consistency model and the cluster design used for distributed versioning. Section 3 introduces distributed versioning. Section 4 describes our prototype implementation. Sections 5 describes the consistency models and the implementation of the different lazy protocols with loose consistency models explored in the paper. Section 6 presents our benchmarks. Section 7 presents our experimental platform and our evaluation methodology. We investigate how distributed versioning affects scaling, and compare it against the other lazy protocols in Section 8. Section 9 discusses related work. Section 10 concludes the paper.

2   Environment

This section describes the environment in which distributed versioning is meant to work. In particular, we describe the programming model, the desired consistency, and the cluster architecture.

2.1   Programming Model

A single (client) Web interaction may include one or more transactions, and a single transaction may include one or more read or write queries. The application writer specifies where in the application code transactions begin and end. In the absence of transaction delimiters, each single query is considered a transaction and is automatically committed (so called "auto-commit" mode).

At the beginning of each transaction consisting of more than one query, the programmer inserts a *pre-declaration* of the tables accessed in the transaction and their modes of access (read or write). The tables accessed by single-operation transactions do not need to be pre-declared. Additionally, the programmer inserts a *last-use* annotation after the last use of a particular table in a transaction. These annotations are currently done by hand, but could be automated.

2.2   Consistency Model

The consistency model we use for distributed versioning is 1-copy-serializability [7]. With 1-copy-serializability, conflicting operations of different transactions execute in the same order on all replicas (i.e., the execution of all transactions is equivalent to a serial execution in a total order).

2.3   Cluster Architecture

We consider a cluster architecture for a dynamic content site, in which a scheduler distributes incoming requests on a cluster of database replicas and delivers the responses to the application server (see Figure 2). The scheduler may itself be replicated for performance or for availability. The application server interacts directly only with the schedulers. If there is more than one scheduler in a particular configuration, the application server is assigned a particular scheduler at the beginning of a transaction by round-robin. For each query of this transaction, the application server only interacts with this single scheduler. These interactions are synchronous: for each query, the application server blocks until it receives a response from the scheduler. To the application servers,

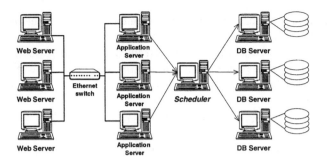

Fig. 2. Cluster design for a dynamic content Web site

a scheduler looks like a database engine. At the other end, each database engine inter-acts with the scheduler as if it were a regular application server. As a result, we can use any off-the-shelf Web server (e.g., Apache) and application server (e.g., PHP), and any off-the-shelf database (e.g., MySQL) without modification. When more than one front-end node is present, an L4 switch is also included. The use of an L4 switch makes the distributed nature of the server transparent to the clients.

3   Distributed Versioning

Distributed versioning achieves 1-copy serializability, absence of deadlock and a high degree of concurrency using a lazy read-one, write-all replication scheme augmented with version numbers, as described next.

3.1   Lazy Read-One, Write-All Replication

When the scheduler receives a write or a commit query from the application server, it sends it to all replicas and returns the response as soon as it receives a response from any of the replicas. Reads are sent only to a single replica, and the response is sent back to the application server as soon as it is received from that replica.

3.2   Assigning and Using Version Numbers

A separate version number is maintained for each table in the database. A transaction is assigned a version number for each table that it accesses (except for single-read trans-actions, see below). As discussed in Section 2.1, each multi-query transaction declares what tables it reads or writes before it starts execution. The tables accessed by single-query transactions are implicitly declared by the query itself. Based on this information, the scheduler assigns table versions to be accessed by the queries in that transaction. This assignment is done *atomically*, i.e., the scheduler assigns all version numbers for one transaction, before it assigns any version numbers for the next transaction. Version number assignment is done in such a way that, if there is a conflict between the current transaction and an earlier one, the version numbers given to the current transaction for the tables involved in the conflicts are higher than the version numbers received by the earlier conflicting transaction.

All operations on a particular table are executed at all replicas in version number order. In particular, an operation waits until its version is available. New versions become available as a result of a previous transaction committing or as a result of last-use declarations (see Section 3.5).

Transactions consisting of a single read query are treated differently. No version numbers are assigned. Instead, the query is simply forwarded to one of the replicas, where it executes after all conflicting transactions complete. This optimization results in a very substantial performance improvement without violating 1-copy serializability.

3.3   1-Copy Serializability and Absence of Deadlock

If transactions have conflicting operations involving one or more tables, then the version numbers for the conflicting tables assigned to the earlier transaction are strictly lower than those assigned to the same tables for the later transaction. Since all conflicting operations execute in version number order at all replicas, all conflicting operations of all transactions execute in the same total order at all replicas. Hence, 1-copy serializability is established.

A similar argument shows that distributed versioning avoids deadlock. For all tables that cause conflicts between transactions, the version numbers assigned to one transaction must be either all smaller or all larger than those assigned to another transaction. Since transactions only wait for the completion of operations with a lower version number than their own, there can never be a circular wait, and therefore deadlock is avoided.

3.4   Limiting the Number of Conflicts

The scheduler sends write queries to all replicas and relies on their asynchronous execution in order of version numbers. At a given time, a write on a data item may have been sent to all replicas, but it may have completed only at a subset of them. A conflict-aware scheduler [3] maintains the completion status of outstanding write operations, and the current version for each table at all database replicas. Using this information, the scheduler sends a read that immediately follows a particular write in version number order to a replica where it knows the write has already finished (i.e., the corresponding required version has been produced). This avoids waiting due to read-write conflicts.

3.5   Reducing Conflict Duration

In the absence of last-use declarations in a transactions, the versions of various tables produced by the current transaction become available only at commit time. The presence of a last-use declaration allows the version to be produced immediately after the time that declaration appears in the application code. This *early release* of a version reduces the time that later transactions have to wait for that version to become available. Early releases do not compromise 1-copy-serializability. All versions are atomically pre-assigned at the beginning of each transaction, and a version release occurs only after the last use of a particular table. Hence, the total ordering of conflicting transactions at all replicas is the same as the one in the system without early releases.

```
begin
    write a
    write b
    write c
end
```

Fig. 3. Sequence of updates in a transaction

```
        1   2   3   4   5   6                          1   2   3   4
T0:     a0,b0,c0                          T0:         a0,b0,c0
T1:                 a1,b1,c1              T1:             a1,b1,c1
```

Fig. 4. Serial execution in conservative 2PL (left) versus increased concurrency in distributed versioning (right)

3.6 Rationale

In our earlier work [3] we use conservative two-phase locking as the concurrency control method for conflict-aware scheduling. We now demonstrate why distributed versioning leads to more concurrency than conservative 2PL.

In both conservative 2PL, and distributed versioning the declaration of which tables are going to be accessed by a transaction is done at the beginning of the transaction. The behavior of the two schemes in terms of waiting for conflicts to be resolved is, however, totally different. In particular, conflict waiting times are potentially much lower for distributed versioning, for two reasons. First, in conservative 2PL, a particular transaction waits at the beginning until all its locks become available. In contrast, in distributed versioning, there is no waiting at the beginning of a transaction. Only version numbers are assigned. Waiting occurs when an operation tries to access a table for which conflicting operations with an earlier version number have not yet completed. The key difference is that at a given operation, distributed versioning only waits for the proper versions of the tables in that particular operation to become available. Second, with conservative 2PL, all locks are held until commit. In contrast, with distributed versioning, a new version of a table is produced as soon as a transaction completes its last access to that table. In summary, the increased concurrency of distributed versioning comes from more selective (per-table) waiting for conflicts to be resolved and from earlier availability of new versions of tables (early version releases).

We illustrate the increase in concurrency with an example. Assume that transactions T_0, and T_1 both execute the code shown in Figure 3, writing three different tables. Assume also that transaction T_0 is serialized before transaction T_1. In conservative 2PL, transaction T_1 waits for the locks on all three tables to be freed by T_0 before it starts executing (see Figure 4). In contrast, with distributed versioning the operations on the different tables are pipelined. This example also clearly demonstrates that, in general, both features of distributed versioning (selective per-table waiting and early availability of versions) are essential. Any single feature in isolation would produce the same behavior as conservative 2PL and thus less concurrency.

One may wonder if similar benefits are not available with alternative 2PL schemes. This is not the case. Selective waiting for locks can be achieved by implicit 2PL, in which locks are acquired immediately before each operation. Implicit 2PL achieves selective waiting, but at the expense of potential deadlocks. Given that the probability of deadlock increases approximately quadratically with the number of replicas [11], any concurrency control algorithm that allows deadlock is undesirable for large clusters. Even if a deadlock-avoidance scheme could be used in conjunction with selective waiting for locks, early releases of locks are limited by the two-phase nature of 2PL, necessary for achieving serializability.

4   Implementation

4.1   Overview

The implementation consists of three types of processes: scheduler processes (one per scheduler machine), a sequencer process (one for the entire cluster), and database proxy processes (one for each database replica).

The sequencer assigns unique version numbers to the tables accessed by each transaction. The database proxy regulates access to its database server by only letting a query proceed if the database has the right versions for the tables named in the query. The schedulers receive the various operations from the application server (begin transaction, read and write queries, and commit or abort transaction), forward them as appropriate to the sequencer and/or one or all of the database proxies, and relay the responses back to the application server. In the following, we describe the actions taken by the scheduler and database proxy when each type of operation is received for processing, and when its response is received from the database.

4.2   Transaction Start

The application server informs the scheduler of all tables that are going to be accessed, and whether a particular table is read or written. The scheduler forwards this message to the sequencer (see Figure 5-a). The sequencer assigns version numbers to each of the tables for this transaction, and returns the result to the scheduler. The scheduler stores this information for the length of the transaction. It then responds to the application server so that it can continue with the transaction. The version numbers are not passed to the application server.

For each table, the sequencer remembers two values: the sequence number next-for-read, to be assigned if the next request is for a read, and the sequence number next-for-write, to be assigned if the next request is for a write. When the sequencer receives a request from the scheduler for a set of version numbers for tables accessed in a particular transaction, the sequencer returns for each table the next-for-read or the next-for-write sequence number, depending on whether that particular table is to be read or written in that transaction. After a sequence number is assigned for a write, next-for-write is incremented and next-for-read is set to the new value of next-for-write. After a sequence number is assigned for a read, only next-for-write is incremented.

The intuition behind this version number assignment is that the version number assigned to a transaction for a particular table increases by one every time the new transaction contains a conflicting operation with the previous transaction to access that table.

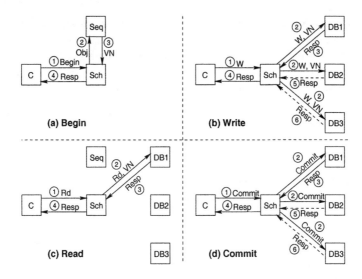

Fig. 5. Protocol steps for each type of query and query response

```
operation            w  w  r  w  r  r  r  w
next_for_read        0  1  2  2  4  4  4  4  7
next_for_write       0  1  2  3  4  5  6  7  7
version assigned        0  1  2  3  4  4  4  7
```

Fig. 6. Sequencer assigned version numbers for a series of operations

For example, Figure 6 shows a series of read and write operations on a particular table, each belonging to a different transaction, in the order of arrival of the transaction's version number request at the sequencer. The figure also shows the version numbers assigned by the sequencer for that table to each transaction and the values of next-for-read and next-for-write. As long as the successive accesses are reads, their transactions are assigned the same version number. Whenever there is a read-write, write-read, or write-write conflict, a higher version number is assigned.

The assignment of version numbers for a particular transaction is *atomic*. In other words, all version numbers for a given transaction are assigned before any version number for a subsequent transaction is assigned. As a result, the version numbers for all tables accessed by a particular transaction are either less than or equal to the version numbers for the same tables for any subsequent transaction. They are only equal if the transactions do not conflict.

4.3   Read and Write

As the application server executes the transaction, it sends read and write queries to the scheduler. In the following, we explain how the scheduler and database proxies enforce the total order for read and write operations necessary for 1-copy-serializability.

Enforcing 1-Copy-Serializability. Both for read and write queries, the scheduler tags each table with the version number that was assigned to that table for this transaction. It then sends write queries to all replicas, while read queries are sent only to one replica (see Figure 5-b and c).

The following rules govern the execution of a query:

– A write query is executed only when the version numbers for each table at the database match the version numbers in the query.
– A read query is executed only when the version numbers for each table at the database are greater than or equal to the version numbers in the query.

If a write query needs to wait for its assigned versions at a particular replica, it is blocked by the database proxy at that replica. If a read query needs to wait, it is blocked at the scheduler until one of the replicas becomes ready to execute the query.

In more detail, the scheduler keeps track of the current version numbers of all tables at all database replicas. The scheduler blocks read queries until at least one database has, for all tables in the query, version numbers that are greater than or equal to the version numbers assigned to the transaction for these tables. If there are several such replicas, the least loaded replica is chosen.

If there is only a single scheduler, then it automatically becomes aware of version number changes at the database replicas as a result of responses to commits or early version releases. If multiple schedulers are present, extra communication is needed to inform the schedulers of version number changes resulting from transactions handled by other schedulers.

Single-Read Transactions. Since a single-read transaction executes only at one replica, there is no need to assign cluster-wide version numbers to such a transaction. Instead, the scheduler forwards the transaction to the chosen replica, without assigning version numbers. At the chosen database replica, the read query executes after the update transaction with the highest version numbers for the corresponding tables in the proxy's queues releases these table versions.

Because the order of execution for a single-read transaction is ultimately decided by the database proxy, the scheduler does not block such queries. In case of conflict, the read query waits at the database proxy. The scheduler attempts to reduce this wait by selecting a replica that has an up-to-date version of each table needed by the query. In this case, up-to-date version means that the table has a version number greater than or equal to the highest version number assigned to any previous transaction on that table. Such a replica may not necessarily exist.

4.4   Completion of Reads and Writes

On the completion of a read or a write at the database (see Figure 5-b and c), the database proxy receives the response and forwards it back to the scheduler.

The scheduler returns the response to the application server if this is the first response it received for a write query or it is the response to a read query. The scheduler keeps track of the state of outstanding writes and updates its internal data structures when one of the database engines sends back a reply.

4.5   Early Version Releases

The scheduler uses the last-use annotation to send an explicit version_release message that increments the specified table's version at each database.

4.6   Commit/Abort

The scheduler tags the commit/abort with the tables accessed in the transaction, their version numbers and a corresponding version_release flag, and forwards the commit/abort to all replicas (see Figure 5-d). The transaction's commit carries a version_release flag only for the tables where early version releases have not already been performed. Single-update transactions carry an implicit commit (and version_release).

Upon completion at a database, the corresponding database proxy increments the version number of all tables for which a version_release flag was included in the message from the scheduler. It returns the answer to the scheduler, which updates its state to reflect the reply. If this is the first reply, the scheduler forwards the response to the application server.

4.7   1-Copy-Serializability

The algorithm achieves 1-copy-serializability by forcing transactions that have conflicting operations on a particular table to execute in the total order of the version numbers assigned to them.

A transaction containing a write on a table conflicts with all previous transactions that access the same table. Therefore, it needs to execute after all such transactions with lower version numbers for that table. This is achieved by the combination of the assignment of version numbers and the rule that governs execution of write queries at a database replica, as seen by the following argument:

1. `next-for-write` counts all the earlier transactions that access the same table. This value is assigned as the version number for the table for this transaction.
2. The database proxy increments its version number every time a transaction that accesses that table completes.
3. Since the transaction is allowed to execute only when its version number for the table equals the version number for that table at the database proxy, it follows that all previous transactions that have accessed that table have completed.

A transaction containing a read on a table conflicts with all previous transactions containing a write on the same table. It follows that it needs to execute after the transaction containing a write on that table with the highest version number lower than its own. This is again achieved by the combination of the assignment of version numbers and the rule that governs execution of read queries at a database replica, as seen by the following argument:

1. `next-for-read` remembers the highest version number produced by a transaction with a write on this table. This value is assigned to the transaction as the version number for this table.

```
operation          w  w  r  w  r  r  r  w
version assigned   0  1  2  3  4  4  4  7
version produced   1  2  3  4  5  6  7  8
```

Fig. 7. Sequencer-assigned version numbers for a series of transactions and the version number produced at the database proxy after each transaction commits

2. The current transaction is not allowed to execute at a database proxy before the version number for that table at that database proxy reaches (at least) the transaction's version number for this table.
3. The algorithm also allows a read query to execute at a database proxy if the database proxy's version number for the table is higher than that of the transaction. The only way this can happen is as a result of a sequence of transactions with reads on the table, and these can execute in parallel without violating the total order on conflicting operations.

In figure 7, using our earlier example, we now add the version numbers produced by each transaction's commit to those assigned by the sequencer. All three reads assigned version number 4 by the sequencer can also read versions 5 and 6 (i.e., versions produced by other concurrent readers). A write is required to wait until all previous readers are done and the version at the database has been incremented to match its own (e.g., the write assigned version number 7).

4.8 Load Balancing

We use the *Shortest Execution Length First (SELF)* load balancing algorithm [2]. We measure off-line the execution time of each query on an idle machine. At run-time, the scheduler estimates the load on a replica as the sum of the (a priori measured) execution times of all queries outstanding on that back-end. The scheduler updates the load estimate for each replica with feedback provided by the database proxy in each reply. SELF tries to take into account the widely varying execution times for different query types. We have shown elsewhere [2] that SELF outperforms round-robin and shortest-queue-first algorithms for dynamic content applications.

4.9 Fault Tolerance and Data Availability

The scheduler and the Web server return the result of an update request to the user as soon as a commit response from any database replica has been received. The schedulers then become responsible for coordinating the completion of the updates on the other database back-ends, in the case of a scheduler, sequencer, or a back-end database failure. To meet this goal, the *completion status*, and all the write queries of any update transaction together with the transaction's version numbers, are maintained in a fault-tolerant and highly-available manner at the schedulers. High data availability is achieved by replicating the state among the schedulers. Additional fault tolerance is provided by also logging this information to stable storage. The details of our availability and fault-tolerance protocol are similar to the ones described in our previous paper [3], in which we also demonstrate that these aspects of our solution do not incur significant overhead in terms of computation, memory, or disk accesses.

5   Loose Consistency Models

In the performance evaluation section of this paper, we compare distributed versioning to a number of replication methods that provide looser consistency than 1-copy serializability. These methods and their implementation are introduced next.

5.1   Definition

We describe the three consistency levels specified in Neptune [20], and the types of dynamic content Web sites for which they are suitable. We further extend these consistency models with an additional model designed to incorporate features from the continuous consistency model spectrum [25].

Level 0. Write-Anywhere Replication. This is the basic lazy consistency scheme that offers no ordering or consistency guarantees. Writes that arrive out-of-order are not reconciled later. This scheme is only applicable to simple services with append-only, commutative or total-updates such as an e-mail service.

Level 1. Ordered Writes. Writes are totally ordered at all replicas, but reads can access inconsistent data without any staleness bounds. This scheme is applicable to services which allow partial updates, and where reads can access stale or inconsistent data such as discussion groups.

Level 2. Ordered Writes and Staleness Control for Reads. Writes are totally ordered at all replicas, and reads satisfy the following two criteria:

- Each read is serviced by a replica which is at most x seconds stale, where x is a given staleness bound.
- Each read of a particular client perceives all previous writes performed by the same client in the correct order.

This consistency model is suitable for sites that need stronger consistency requirements such as auction sites. For example, a client needs to perceive his previous bids in their correct order and should be guaranteed to see a sufficiently recent maximum bid.

Special. Per Interaction or per Object Consistency. This model is application-specific. For each interaction or for each object a consistency model is defined. This approach can be applied to Web sites which have in general strong consistency needs, but where relaxations can be made on a case by case basis, for specific interactions or objects.

5.2   Implementation of Loose Consistency Methods

For Levels 0, 1 and 2, we remove any transaction delimiters and other annotations from the application code. The scheduler and database proxy are modified as follows.

For Level 0, we remove any checks pertaining to in-order delivery of writes at the database proxy. The database proxy still implements conflict resolution, but all writes are handled in the order of their arrival, which may be different at different replicas. No version numbers are used. The scheduler load balances reads among all database replicas.

To implement Level 1, the scheduler obtains version numbers for each write, and the database proxies deliver the writes in version number order, as in distributed versioning. No version numbers are assigned to reads. The scheduler load balances reads among all database replicas.

In addition to the functionality implemented for Level 0 and 1, for Level 2 the scheduler augments its data structures with a wall-clock timestamp for each database replica and for each table. The appropriate timestamp is set every time a database replica acknowledges execution of a write on a table. The scheduler load balances reads only among the database machines that satisfy the staleness bound for all tables accessed in the query, and, in addition, have finished all writes pertaining to the same client connection. A 30-second staleness bound is used for all applications. As in the original scheme described in Neptune, the staleness bound is loose in the sense that network time between the scheduler and the database proxy is not taken into account.

The implementation of Special consistency models is application-specific, and its implementation is deferred to Section 6 where we discuss application benchmarks.

6   Benchmarks

We provide the basic characteristics of the benchmarks used in this study. More detail can be found in an earlier paper [1].

6.1   TPC-W

The TPC-W benchmark from the Transaction Processing Council (TPC) [23] is a transactional Web benchmark designed to evaluate e-commerce systems. Several interactions are used to simulate the activity of a bookstore.

The database contains eight tables; the most frequently used are order_line, orders and credit_info, which give information about the orders placed, and item and author, which contain information about the books.

We implement the 14 different interactions specified in the TPC-W benchmark specification. Of the 14 interactions, 6 are read-only, while 8 cause the database to be updated. The read-only interactions include access to the home page, listing of new products and best-sellers, requests for product detail, order display, and two interactions involving searches. Update transactions include user registration, updates of the shopping cart, two order-placement transactions, two involving order display, and two for administrative tasks.

The database size is determined by the number of items in the inventory and the size of the customer population. We use 100K items and 2.8 million customers, which results in a database of about 4 GB. The inventory images, totaling 1.8 GB, are resident on the Web server.

TPC-W uses three different workload mixes, differing in the ratio of read-only to read-write interactions. The browsing mix contains 95% read-only interactions, the shopping mix 80%, and the ordering mix 50%.

For TPC-W we implement a Special consistency model. This model follows the specification of TPC-W, which allows for some departures from (1-copy) serializability. In more detail, the specification requires that all update interactions respect serializability. Read-only interactions on the retail inventory (i.e., best-sellers, new products, searches and product detail interactions) are allowed to return data that is at most 30 seconds old. Read-only interactions related to a particular customer (i.e., home and order display interactions) are required to return up-to-date data. Even if allowed to read stale data, all queries need to respect the atomicity of the update transactions that they conflict with. We add a number of ad-hoc rules to the scheduler to implement this Special consistency model.

6.2   Auction Site Benchmark

Our auction site benchmark, modeled after eBay [10], implements the core functionality of an auction site: selling, browsing and bidding.

The database contains seven tables: users, items, bids, buy_now, comments, categories and regions. The users and items tables contain information about the users, and items on sale, respectively. Every bid is stored in the bids table, which includes the seller, the bid, and a max_bid value. Items that are directly bought without any auction are stored in a separate buy_now table. To speed up displaying the bid history when browsing an item, some information about the bids such as the maximum bid and the current number of bids is kept with the relevant item in the items table.

Our auction site defines 26 interactions where the main ones are: browsing items by category or region, bidding, buying or selling items, leaving comments on other users and consulting one's own user page (known as myEbay on eBay). Browsing items includes consulting the bid history and the seller's information.

We size our system according to some observations found on the eBay Web site. We have about 33,000 items for sale, distributed among 40 categories and 62 regions, and an average of 10 bids per item. There is an average of 10 bids per item, or 330,000 entries in the bids table. The total size of the database is 1.4GB.

We use a workload mix that includes 15% read-write interactions. This mix is the most representative of an auction site workload according to an earlier study of eBay workloads mentioned in [20].

Although it has been argued that an auction site can be supported by a Level 2 consistency model, as described in Section 5, program modifications are necessary to ensure correct outcome of the auction site with Level 2 consistency. The problem is that the code in several places relies on atomic sequences, which are no longer available in the absence of transactions. For instance, suppose we do not use a transaction for placing a bid. In the transaction for placing a bid, the maximum bid is first read from the item table and then updated if the input bid is acceptable (higher). If reading and updating the maximum bid for an item are not done in a critical section, then if two clients submit bids concurrently, they can both read the same maximum bid value for that item. Assuming that both bids are higher, both will be accepted, and the maximum bid stored in the items table for that item could be wrong (e.g., the lower one of the new bids). Thus, additional code is necessary to verify the correctness of the maximum bid.

6.3   Bulletin Board

Our bulletin board benchmark is modeled after an online news forum like Slashdot [21]. In particular, as in Slashcode, we support discussion threads. A discussion thread is a logical tree, containing a story at its root, and a number of comments for that story, which may be nested.

The main tables in the database are the users, stories, comments, and submissions tables. Stories and comments are maintained in separate new and old tables. In the new stories table we keep the most recent stories with a cut-off of one month. We keep old stories for a period of three years. The new and old comments tables correspond to the new and old stories respectively. The majority of the browsing requests are expected to access the new stories and comments tables, which are much smaller and therefore much more efficiently accessible. Each story submission is initially placed in the submissions table, unless submitted by a moderator.

We have defined ten Web interactions. The main ones are: generate the stories of the day, browse new stories, older stories, or stories by category, show a particular story with different options on filtering comments, search for keywords in story titles, comments and user names, submit a story, add a comment, and review submitted stories and rate comments. None of the interactions contain transactions. For instance, stories are first inserted into the submission table, later moderated, then inserted in their respective tables but not as a part of a multi-query atomic transaction, although each individual update is durable.

We generate the story and comment bodies with words from a given dictionary and lengths between 1KB and 8KB. Short stories and comments are much more common, so we use a Zipf-like distribution for story length [8]. The database contains 3 years of stories and comments with an average of 15 to 25 stories per day and between 20 and 50 comments per story. We emulate 500 K total users, out of which 10% have moderator access privilege. The database size using these parameters is 560 MB.

We use a workload mix which contains 15% story and comment submissions and moderation interactions. This mix corresponds to the maximum posting activity of an active newsgroup, as observed by browsing the Internet for typical breakdowns of URL requests in bulletin board sites [1].

Among the loose consistency models discussed in Section 5, the normal semantics of bulletin boards can be supported by the Level 1 consistency model.

6.4   Client Emulation

We implement a client-browser emulator. A client session is a sequence of interactions for the same client. For each client session, the client emulator opens a persistent HTTP connection to the Web server and closes it at the end of the session. Each emulated client waits for a certain think time before initiating the next interaction. The next interaction is determined by a state transition matrix that specifies the probability to go from one interaction to another. The session time and think time are generated from a random distribution with a specified mean.

7   Experimental Environment and Methodology

We study the performance of distributed versioning and compare them to loose consistency models, using measurement for a small number of database replicas and using simulation for larger degrees of replication. We first describe the hardware and software used for the prototype implementation. Next, we describe the simulation methodology.

7.1   Hardware

We use the same hardware for all machines running the emulated-client, schedulers and Web servers, and database engines (or corresponding simulators). Each one of them has an AMD Athlon 800Mhz processor running FreeBSD 4.1.1, 256MB SDRAM, and a 30GB ATA-66 disk drive. They are all connected through 100MBps Ethernet LAN.

7.2   Software

We use three popular open source software packages: the Apache Web server [5], the PHP Web-scripting/application development language [16], and the MySQL database server [15]. Since PHP is implemented as an Apache module, the Web server and application server co-exist on the same machine(s).

We use Apache v.1.3.22 [5] for our Web server, configured with the PHP v.4.0.1 module [16] providing server-side scripting for generating dynamic content. We use MySQL v.4.0.1 [15] with InnoDB transactional extensions as our database server.

7.3   Simulation Methodology

To study the scaling of our distributed versioning techniques on a large number of replicas, we use two configurable cluster simulators: one for the Web/application server front-ends and the other for the database back-ends. We use these front-end and back-end simulators to drive actual execution of the schedulers and the database proxies.

Each simulator models a powerful server of the given type (Web/application server or database) equivalent to running a much larger number of real servers. The Web/application server simulator takes each HTTP request generated by the client emulator and sends the corresponding queries with dummy arguments to one of the schedulers.

The database simulator maintains a separate queue for each simulated database replica. Whenever the simulator receives a query destined for a particular replica, a record is placed on that replica's queue. The record contains the predicted termination time for that query. The termination time is predicted by adding a cost estimate for the query to the current simulation time. The same method of cost estimation is used as described earlier for load balancing (see Section 4.8). These estimates are relatively accurate, because for the applications we consider, the cost of a query is primarily determined by the type of the query, and largely independent of its arguments. The database simulator polls the queues and sends responses when the simulated time reaches the termination time for each query. The database simulator does not model disk accesses, because profiling of real runs indicates that disk accesses are overlapped with computation. This overlap is partly due to the locality in the application, resulting in few disk accesses for reads, and partly due to the lazy commit style for writes.

8   Results

First, we present a performance comparison of distributed versioning with a conservative 2PL algorithm. Next, we compare the performance of distributed versioning with various loose consistency models.

All results are obtained using a cluster with two schedulers (for data availability). For each experiment, we drive the server with increasing numbers of clients (and a sufficient number of Web/application servers) until performance peaks. We report the throughput at that peak.

The simulators were calibrated using data from measurements on the prototype implementation. The simulated throughput numbers are within 12% of the experimental numbers for all workloads.

8.1   Comparison of Distributed Versioning and Conservative 2PL

Figures 8 through 10 compare distributed versioning to conservative 2PL for the TPC-W shopping mix, the TPC-W ordering mix, and the auction site, respectively. We omit the results for the TPC-W browsing and bulletin board workloads because there is no performance difference between distributed versioning and conservative 2PL. The explanation is that these workloads have low conflict rates. These and all further graphs have in the x axis the number of database engines, and in the y axis the throughput in (client) Web interactions per second. The graphs also show two protocols that only use a subset of the features of distributed versioning. *Dversion - EarlyRel* uses version numbers to selectively wait for the right version of tables, but it does not produce a new version of the tables until commit. Vice versa, *DVersion - LateAcq* waits for the correct versions of all tables at the beginning of the transaction, but produces new versions immediately after the transaction's last use of a particular table. The results clearly confirm the discussion in Section 3.6. With increased conflict rates, distributed versioning produces superior throughput compared to conservative 2PL. Both features of distributed versioning, selective waiting for table versions and early production of new versions, are essential. Without either one of them, improvement over conservative 2PL is minimal.

8.2   Comparison of Distributed Versioning and Loose Consistency Methods

In this section, we investigate the overhead of consistency maintenance for maintaining serializability in distributed versioning. For this purpose, we compare our protocol with

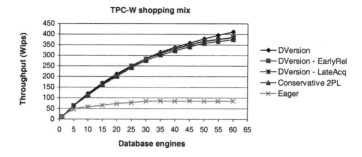

Fig. 8. Comparison of distributed versioning and conservative 2PL for the TPC-W shopping mix

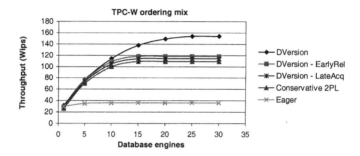

Fig. 9. Comparison of distributed versioning and conservative 2PL for the TPC-W ordering mix

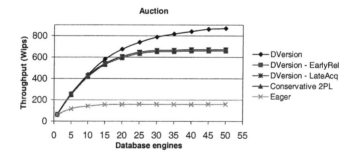

Fig. 10. Comparison of distributed versioning and conservative 2PL for the auction site

all other protocols for all levels of consistency including specialized, and looser than required for each of the three applications. This allows us to detect the overhead of various parts of our solution. For example, we can detect the overhead of in-order delivery for writes or the success of our conflict avoidance and reduction techniques by comparison to the upper bound obtained by assuming that these overheads (for ordering writes or resolving read-write conflicts) do not exist.

Figures 11 through 15 show a comparison of the throughput between distributed versioning protocol (DVersion) and various lazy replication methods. As a baseline, we also include the Eager protocol. These figures allow us to draw the following

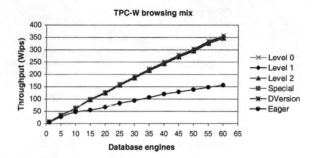

Fig. 11. Comparison of all consistency levels for the TPC-W browsing mix. Special is the specialized consistency level

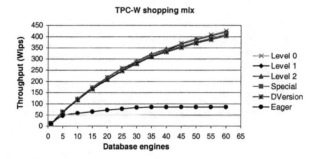

Fig. 12. Comparison of all consistency levels for the TPC-W shopping mix. Special is the specialized consistency level

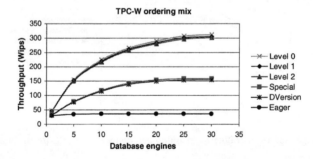

Fig. 13. Comparison of all consistency levels for TPC-W, the ordering mix. Special is the specialized consistency level

conclusions. First, for all applications, the differences between Levels 0, 1, and 2 are negligible. Second, for the workloads with low conflict rates (i.e., TPC-W browsing and bulletin board), there is no difference between any of the protocols. Third, as the conflict rate increases, there is a growing difference between Levels 0, 1, and 2, on one hand, and DVersion on the other. For the largest simulated configuration, these differences are 5%, 25% and 50%, for the TPC-W shopping mix, the auction site, and the TPC-W ordering

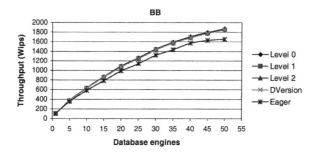

Fig. 14. Comparison of all consistency levels for the bulletin board. Level 1 is the specialized consistency level

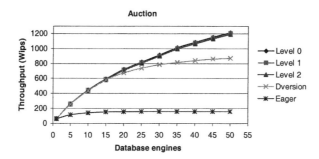

Fig. 15. Comparison of all consistency levels for the auction site. Level 2 is the specialized consistency level

mix, respectively. Fourth, the differences between the Special consistency model and DVersion are small for all workloads of TPC-W. Finally, for the bulletin board, which has no transactional requirements, the overhead of enforcing 1-copy-serializability is minimal.

In a cluster, messages usually arrive in the order that they are sent, and the delay in message delivery is low. Furthermore, interactions between the client and the database are such that at least one database replica must have completed the previous request before the next one is issued. A conflict-aware scheduler directs this next request precisely to that replica. These observations explain the small differences in performance between Levels 0, 1 and 2 for all applications, and between DVersion and Special for TPC-W. Loose consistency models show a benefit, instead, when transactional atomicity is removed, and hence the cost of waiting for read-write conflicts is alleviated. As the number of such conflicts increases, the benefit of loose consistency models grows. Among our applications, this is the case for the TPC-W shopping mix, the auction site, and the TPC-W ordering mix. These results should be viewed with the caveat that, as explained in Section 6, these looser consistency models do not, by themselves, provide the right semantics for these applications. Additional programming effort is required to achieve the right semantics, possibly entailing additional execution time overhead.

9   Related Work

Concurrency control protocols based on multiple versions have been discussed [7] and implemented in real systems [17] to increase concurrency while maintaining serializability in stand-alone database systems. More recently, multiversion ordering [6, 12, 18, 19] has been used and optimized for distributed database systems as well. Most of these systems use transaction aborts to resolve serialization inconsistencies. Some systems targeted at advanced database applications such as computer-aided design and collaborative software development environments [6] use pre-declared write-sets to determine if a schedule conflicting at the object level can be serialized, thus avoiding transaction aborts.

Such systems maintain a history of old versions at each distributed location and need a special scheme for reducing version space consumption and version access time [9], or limiting the number of versions stored [12]. Furthermore, if replication is used at all in these distributed systems, the goal is to increase the availability of a particular version [18]. In contrast, in our versioning concurrency control algorithm we do not maintain old copies of items, all modifications are made in place. The goal of our extra-database algorithm is to allow us to choose the correct version among the different versions of a table which occur naturally due to asynchronous replication. On the other hand, multiversion systems have the advantage that the execution of read-only transactions can be made more efficient by completely decoupling their execution from update transactions [12, 18].

Optimistic replication of data [22] has been used in disconnected mobile devices allowing such devices to perform local updates. In this case multiple versions of the same item can arise with the need of serializing potentially conflicting updates by disconnected clients on all replicas.

Recent work [20, 25] avoids paying the price of serializability for applications that don't need it by providing specialized loose consistency models. Neptune [20] adopts a primary-copy approach to providing consistency in a partitioned service cluster. However, their scalability study is limited to Web applications with loose consistency where scaling is easier to achieve. They do not address e-commerce workloads or other Web applications with relatively strong consistency requirements.

10   Conclusions

The conventional wisdom has been that in replicated databases one could have either 1-copy serializability or scalability, but not both. As a result, looser consistency models have been developed that allow better scalability. In this paper we have demonstrated that for clusters of databases that serve as the back-end of dynamic content Web sites, 1-copy serializability and scalability can go hand-in-hand. This allows for uniform handling of applications and for the use of familiar programming abstractions, such as the use of transactions.

In order to achieve these results, we use a novel technique, called distributed versioning. This technique combines a new concurrency control algorithm based on explicit versions and conflict-aware scheduling to achieve scalability. We have demonstrated that distributed versioning provides much better performance than earlier techniques for providing 1-copy serializability, including eager protocols, and our own earlier work based on conservative two-phase locking. Furthermore, we have compared distributed versioning to various replication methods which only provide loose consistency guarantees. We find that for all our applications, except those with very high conflict rates, the performance of distributed versioning equals or approaches that of looser consistency models.

References

1. C. Amza, E. Cecchet, A. Chanda, A. Cox, S. Elnikety, R. Gil, J. Marguerite, K. Rajamani, and W. Zwaenepoel. Specification and implementation of dynamic web site benchmarks. In *5th IEEE Workshop on Workload Characterization*, November 2002.
2. C. Amza, A. Cox, and W. Zwaenepoel. Scaling and availability for dynamic content web sites. Technical Report TR02-395, Rice University, 2002.
3. Cristiana Amza, Alan Cox, and Willy Zwaenepoel. Conflict-Aware Scheduling for Dynamic Content Applications. In *Proceedings of the Fifth USENIX Symposium on Internet Technologies and Systems*, March 2003.
4. Todd Anderson, Yuri Breitbart, Henry F. Korth, and Avishai Wool. Replication, consistency, and practicality: are these mutually exclusive? In *Proceedings of the 1998 ACM SIGMOD International Conference on Management of Data: June*, pages 484–495, 1998.
5. The Apache Software Foundation. http://www.apache.org/.
6. N. S. Barghouti and G. E. Kaiser. Concurrency Control in Advanced Database Applications. In *ACM Computing Surveys*, volume 23, pages 269–317, Sept 1991.
7. P.A. Bernstein, V. Hadzilacos, and N. Goodman. *Concurrency Control and Recovery in Database Systems*. Addison-Wesley, Reading, Massachusetts, 1987.
8. L. Breslau, P. Cao, L. Fan, G. Phillips, and S. Shenker. Web caching and zipf-like distributions: Evidence and implications. In *Proceedings of the IEEE Infocom Conference*, 1999.
9. Shu-Yao Chien, Vassilis J. Tsotras, and Carlo Zaniolo. Efficient management of multiversion documents by object referencing. In *The VLDB Journal*, pages 291–300, 2001.
10. On-line auctions at eBay. http://ebay.com.
11. Jim Gray, Pat Helland, Patrick O'Neil, and Dennis Shasha. The dangers of replication and a solution. In *Proceedings of the 1996 ACM SIGMOD International Conference on Management of Data, Montreal, Quebec, Canada, June 4–6, 1996*, pages 173–182, 1996.
12. H. V. Jagadish, Inderpal Singh Mumick, and Michael Rabinovich. Asynchronous Version Advancement in a Distributed Three-Version Database. In *Proceedings of the 14th International Conference on Data Engineering*, 1998.
13. P. Keleher. Decentralized replicated-object protocols. In *Proc. of the 18th Annual ACM Symp. on Principles of Distributed Computing (PODC'99)*, May 1999.
14. Bettina Kemme and Gustavo Alonso. Don't be lazy, be consistent: Postgres-R, a new way to implement Database Replication. In *Proceedings of the 26th International Conference on Very Large Databases*, September 2000.
15. MySQL. http://www.mysql.com.
16. PHP Hypertext Preprocessor. http://www.php.net.
17. Postgres. http://www.postgresql.org/docs.
18. O. T. Satyanarayanan and Divyakant Agrawal. Efficient execution of read-only transactions in replicated multiversion databases. In *TKDE*, volume 5, pages 859–871, 1993.
19. D. Shasha, F. Llirbat, E. Simon, and P. Valduriez. Transaction Chopping: Algorithms and Performance Studies. In *ACM Transactions on Data Base Systems*, volume 20, pages 325–363, Sept 1995.

20. Kai Shen, Tao Yang, Lingkun Chu, JoAnne L. Holliday, Doug Kuschner, and Huican Zhu. Neptune: Scalable Replica Management and Programming Support for Cluster-based Network Services. In *Proceedings of the Third USENIX Symposium on Internet Technologies and Systems*, pages 207–216, March 2001.
21. Slashdot: News for Nerds. Stuff that Matters. http://slashdot.org.
22. D. B. Terry, M. M. Theimer, K. Petersen, A. J. Demers, M. J. Spreitzer, and C. H. Hauser. Managing update conflicts in Bayou, a weakly connected replicated storage system. In *Proceedings 15th Symposium on Operating Systems Principles*, pages 172–183, December 1995.
23. Transaction Processing Council. http://www.tpc.org/.
24. M. Wiesmann, F. Pedone, A. Schiper, B. Kemme, and G. Alonso. Database replication techniques: a three parameter classification. In *Proceedings of the 19th IEEE Symposium on Reliable Distributed Systems (SRDS2000)*, October 2000.
25. Haifeng Yu and Amin Vahdat. Design and evaluation of a continuous consistency model for replicated services. In *Proceedings of the Fourth Symposium on Operating Systems Design and Implementation (OSDI)*, October 2000.

Abstraction of Transaction Demarcation
in Component-Oriented Platforms*

Romain Rouvoy and Philippe Merle

INRIA Jacquard Project
Laboratoire d'Informatique Fondamentale de Lille
UPRESA 8022 CNRS – U.F.R. I.E.E.A. – Bâtiment M3
Université des Sciences et Technologies de Lille
59655 Villeneuve d'Ascq Cedex, France
{rouvoy,merle}@lifl.fr

Abstract. Component-oriented middleware becomes the privileged substrate for distributed computing in heterogeneous and open environments. Technically they promote the notion of container as structure to host application components. They transparently take charge of a large set of technical or non-functional services like security or transactions. The transaction service is integrated using a set of transaction demarcation (TD) policies. Nevertheless, they are strongly linked to a specific transactional monitor and they are not often isolated. The main contribution of this paper is to propose a component-based framework to deal with TD policies. Thus, this framework allows one to instantiate several configurations of TD policies with different platforms like EJB, CCM, OSGi, WebServices and several transactional monitors like JTS, OTS, WS-T, BTP, etc. It proposes an extensible abstraction of TD policies. This framework shows that no performance degradation is introduced by the refactoring process.

1 Introduction

Component-oriented middleware such as Enterprise Java Beans (EJB) from Sun Microsystems [1] or the CORBA Component Model (CCM) from the Object Management Group (OMG) [2] becomes the privileged substrate for distributed computing in heterogeneous and open environments. The major reason for this success is that they rationalize the whole process associated to design, development, packaging, assembly, deployment and execution of distributed software. Technically they promote the notion of container as structure to host application components. The containers transparently take charge of a large set of technical or non-functional services like synchronous and asynchronous communication, concurrency, life cycle, activation, persistency, security, transaction, etc. From the transaction point of view, the container has to manage the code related to the transaction management in order to allow the developers to be concentrated on the business code. The delegation of the transaction management is configured via deployment descriptors and the container interprets these descriptors in order to inject the code related to the manipulation of the transaction manager (TM). The different strategies used are identified under the term of transaction demarcation (TD) policies.

* This work is partially funded by RNTL IMPACT and IST COACH projects.

M. Endler and D. Schmidt (Eds.): Middleware 2003, LNCS 2672, pp. 305–323, 2003.
© IFIP International Federation for Information Processing 2003

Nevertheless, every middleware implementation mentioned before and other implementations like .NET from Microsoft [3] or OSGi from Open Services Gateway Initiative (OSGi) [4] are developing their own code for integrating transactions into containers. Moreover, this integration is not often isolated in the container code. It becomes also difficult to introduce new TD policies. And most of the time, containers are strongly linked to the programming interfaces (API) of a specific transactional monitor. For example, EJB containers work with the Java Transaction Service (JTS) [5] while CCM uses the Object Transaction Service (OTS) [6]. But many other transactional monitor specifications exist such as Web Services Transaction Services (WS-T) [7], Business Transaction Protocol (BTP) [8] or more specific ones like the Java Open Transaction Manager (JOTM) [9].

The main contribution of this paper is to propose a component-based framework to deal with TD policies. This framework is independent both of the transaction manager it uses and of the component-oriented platform which uses it. Thus, this framework allows one to instantiate several configurations of TD policies with different platforms like EJB, CCM, OSGi, WebServices and several transactional monitors like JTS, OTS, WS-T, BTP, etc. This framework proposes an extensible abstraction of TD policies through the application of the *Command* Design Pattern [10]. The six standard policies defined in EJB and CCM are supported, but new ones could be designed and included into the framework also. This framework is implemented in the Java language, and has been experimented with the JOnAS J2EE application server [11] using a JTS manager. This framework shows that no performance degradation is introduced by the refactoring process. This framework has also been successfully integrated into JOnAS and OpenCCM [12] platforms using an OTS manager.

This paper presents the scope of transaction demarcation in Section 2. Section 3 establishes the technical challenges. Next, in Section 4 it introduces the Open Transaction Demarcation Framework (OTDF) and its concepts. Then an example of Java implementation of the OTDF is used for illustrating the capabilities of the framework in Section 5. This implementation allows the experimentation of the framework in various situations validating some of its properties and they are presented in Section 6. From there it establishes the lessons of this work in Section 7 and we conclude on perspectives in Section 8.

2   What Transaction Demarcation Is

Transaction demarcation is a way for guaranteeing the transactional context of an invocation. Basically, the transaction policies evaluate if a method should be invoked under an active transaction or not.

2.1   The Policies

Standards like EJB and CCM define a set of six policies in order to cover most of the situations that could happen. These policies are described in Table 1. The description of each policy is:

Supports
   The *Supports* policy is used when a component's operation is able to take transactions into consideration. If a transaction is activated by the client, it may be used by

Table 1. TD policies defined by CCM and EJB

Demarcation Policy	Client Transaction	Container Transaction
Supports	-	-
	Transaction 1	Transaction 1
Never	-	-
	Transaction 1	RAISES(**NEVER**)
Mandatory	-	RAISES(**MANDATORY**)
	Transaction 1	Transaction 1
Required	-	Transaction 2
	Transaction 1	Transaction 1
Not Supported	-	-
	Transaction 1	-
Requires New	-	Transaction 2
	Transaction 1	Transaction 2

the component's operation. On the other hand, if no transaction is activated, the component's operation will be able to execute the same processing without transactional behavior.

Never

The *Never* policy imposes that the selected operation should not be invoked under a transactional context. If the condition is not verified, an exception –specifying that the *NEVER* clause is not respected– is raised. Otherwise, the component's operation is invoked.

Mandatory

The *Mandatory* policy imposes that an operation should be invoked under a transactional context. If the condition is checked then the operation is invoked else the *MANDATORY* exception is raised by the policy.

Required

The *Required* policy is used if an operation requires transactional features. If a transaction has already been activated, the policy propagates this transaction to the operation, else the policy begins a new transaction which would be committed after the invocation.

Not Supported

The *Not Supported* policy checks if a component's operation needs features which could be conflicting with an activated transaction. If a transaction is active, the policy will suspend it for the execution of the method and resume it after.

Requires New

Finally, the *Requires New* policy presents the need for a local transaction for the method. If a transaction is already active, the policy suspends it before beginning a new one. This new transaction is committed just after the execution of the method and the suspended transaction is resumed.

2.2   The Domains

Looking at the TD policies, another organization of these policies could be defined, providing a more structured representation. The goal is to observe each policy for de-

Demarcation

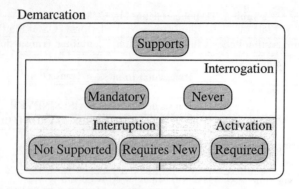

Fig. 1. An Organization of the TD Policies

termining affinities between them. Thanks to this observation, we define the concept of domain. A domain represents the realizable actions of a policy. For example, the *Never* and *Mandatory* policies are only consulting the state of the transaction manager. The *Required* and *Requires New* policies uses the transaction manager in order to activate and validate transactions. Finally, the *Not Supported* and *Requires New* policies need to suspend and resume transactions during their execution. So a repartition of the policies can be obtained and is illustrated in Figure 1.

One can notice that the *Supports* policy is not included inside a domain. The reason is that the *Supports* policy does not interact with any transactional monitor, by consequence no domain could be associated to this policy, while the *Requires New* policy is shared by the activation domain and the interruption domain. The *Requires New* policy requires interruption features for suspending and resuming a possible client transaction and it requires activation features for beginning and validating a container transaction. Each part of this organization defines a domain of interaction with the transaction manager. The domain is both a restriction of the interaction with the transaction manager and a simplification of this interaction specialized in transaction demarcation.

3   Challenges for Transaction Demarcation

This section discusses the main challenges of the integration of transaction demarcation in component-oriented platforms. Figure 2 presents the different challenges encountered when dealing with transaction demarcation. The first challenge is the factorization and the abstraction of the TD policies for addressing more component platforms. The second challenge is the specialization of the TD policies for a given transaction manager. Other technical challenges are more architectural ones and are concerned with organization and extensibility of the TD policies. The following sections detail each of these concerns.

3.1   Transaction Demarcation Abstraction

Most of the platforms define TD policies. The problem is that these policies are implemented inside the scope of a given platform. From a transversal point of view, this code is redundant and needs to be factored between platforms.

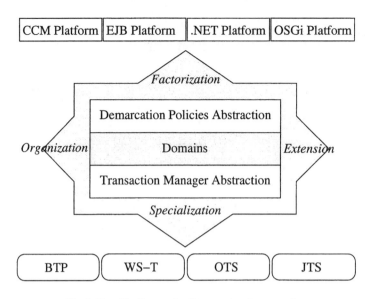

Fig. 2. The Challenges for Transaction Demarcation

But who should address this factorization? It could not be realized by the platform because of the transversality. It could not be realized by the transactional monitor because each policy is designed for interacting with a specific transaction manager which could be different from one platform to another.

So the abstraction of TD policies needs to be addressed by a third party which has to be platform independent as illustrated in Figure 2. This external entity would provide a set of TD policies compliant to the policies defined in the specification of each platform.

3.2 Transaction Monitor Abstraction

Each platform works with a given transactional monitor but is not able to work with other non-compliant transactional monitor. For example, platforms which are able to interact with both JTS and OTS transactional monitors are not prevalent. EJB platforms are working with JTS while CCM ones are working with OTS. But none are able to address more than one type of transactional monitor.

In order to use transaction policies over multiple transaction managers, an abstraction of the transaction manager must be defined and specialized in component transactions as depicted on Figure 2.

3.3 Organization of TD Policies

TD policies could be linked to one or more domains. The domain ensures the connection between type of policies and transaction managers. But domains also introduce a classification of TD policies as mentioned in Section 2.2. This classification needs to be open as the addition of new TD policies could imply the definition of new domains [13].

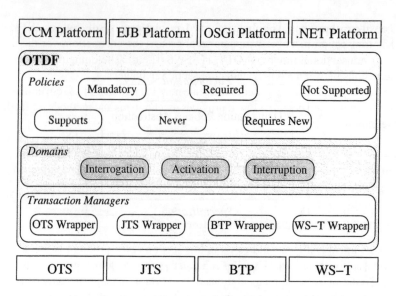

Fig. 3. The OTDF Framework Representation

The domain represents an abstraction of the demarcation as we define an abstraction of the transaction manager. This second level of abstraction allows the specialization and the simplification of the functionalities of the transaction manager for the context of transaction demarcation. Then, policies become easier to design because the technical part is managed by the domain.

3.4 Integration of New TD Policies

TD policies introduced by the CCM and EJB specifications are not covering all domains defined by transactional monitors. Indeed domains like sub-transactions or resources management are not introduced by existing specifications. An open structure must be provided in order to allow the integration of new policies [14]. It means mechanisms for adding new policies and associated domains must be provided.

4 Open Transaction Demarcation Framework

Considering the previous technical challenges, we define the *Open Transaction Demarcation Framework* (OTDF). This framework provides a library of configurable TD policies. It addresses the problem of transaction demarcation over any transactional monitor and is usable from any component-oriented platform.

4.1 Overview

Figure 3 is a structured view of OTDF architecture. OTDF is divided into three parts which are the policies, the domains and the transaction manager wrappers. The policies level considers the types of policies defined in platform specifications (EJB, CCM, etc). The transaction manager wrappers level groups the abstractions for the different models of transactional monitors (OTS, JTS, WS-T, etc). The domains level considers the interactions between a policy and a transaction manager.

The framework is open in order to integrate new TD policies and to cover unexplored domains of transaction demarcation. It provides mechanisms and methods for facilitating this integration.

From a technical point of view, the framework provides an object-oriented and a component-oriented vision of the TD policies. In the meantime the framework is independent of any programming languages as it is designed using the Unified Modeling Language (UML) [15].

4.2   Abstraction of Transactional Monitor

The first technical challenge addressed in this section is the problem of the abstraction of the transactional monitor. Usually, containers strongly adhere to one transactional monitor. Sometimes, the implementations of transaction managers referenced could be changed if they implement the same interfaces. But this variability remains restricted to transaction manager implementations of a same specification (JTS, OTS or WS-T).

In order to provide a better abstraction, the *Wrapper* Design Pattern [10] is used. According to the method, the abstract transaction manager is mapped to a specific implementation of a manager.

The UML diagram of Figure 4 illustrates the application of this design pattern to the transaction manager abstraction.

Our objective is to define a set of transaction manager interfaces with different levels of complexity. Each transaction manager could not implement every potential functionalities addressable by transaction demarcation. For example, JTS monitors are not able to manage nested transactions. So the differences between the transaction manager abstractions need to be identified. By extension, the transaction manager abstraction interfaces would be able to take into account the future evolution of the transaction manager models [16].

The approach for modeling levels of complexity is to define a set of *feature* interfaces. A feature represents a particular property of a transaction manager model. A feature is independent of any other feature. Figure 4 introduces features like configuration, control and interrogation. Because of the fine granularity of features, the interface of a transaction manager could be defined by composing features.

The specialization of the interfaces specifies with a finest granularity the connection between the transaction manager abstraction and a domain. Sometimes, the domain requires more than one feature. But this set of features need to be associated to only one transaction manager. So we define the notion of *scope* for answering this problem. A scope is a composition of features which could be required by a domain. *Scope* interfaces are defined by an extension of the features.

In addition, the combination of features allows also the reproduction of specific models like the Client/Server model of the Java Transaction API as depicted on Figure 4.

When integrating a transaction model, only the elements introducing new functionalities need to be defined using the *Feature* paradigm. If a new domain is introduced with

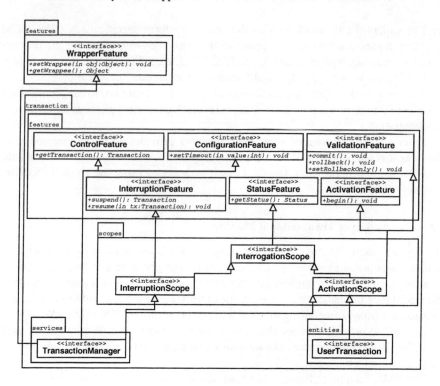

Fig. 4. The Class Diagram of Transaction Manager Abstraction

these features, the associated *Scope* need also to be defined. Other features and scopes are inherited from the framework and the transaction manager abstraction is defined by composing all the features and scopes required for the transaction model.

4.3   Abstraction of Transaction Demarcation

Another technical challenge is the abstraction of the TD policies. In a traditional way, containers implement TD policies using no particular methodology. Most of the time, they check the type of policies they have to activate and the associated treatments are integrated inside the container.

So there are two objectives to reach. Firstly, the extraction of the TD policies from the container. Secondly, we need to burst the block of TD policies into a set of independent TD policies. The first objective is just an extraction of the code managing the transaction demarcation. The other one could be obtained using the *Command* Design Pattern [10].

The root interface *RequestCallController* introduced in Figure 5 is independent of the type of policy implemented. So any TD policy has simply to implement the root interface in order to be compliant with the framework.

The interface *RequestCallContext* offers a generic structure for transmitting parameters to the policies. The lifespan of this interface follows the invocation of a component's method.

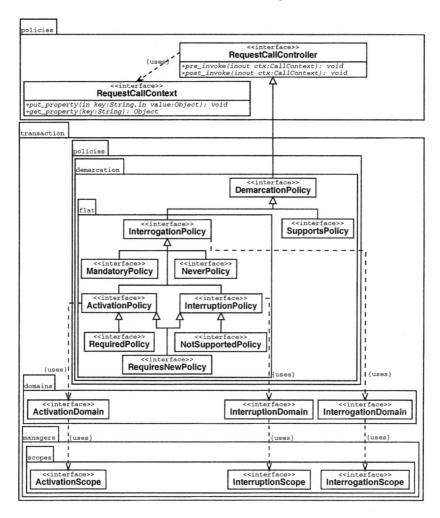

Fig. 5. The Class Diagram of Transaction Demarcation Abstraction

So the information about the associated method and its invocation are not localized with the policy but with the *RequestCallContext*. The consequences of this choice are that this information is defined just before the invocation of the component. And if policies do not contain information about the associated method, they could be shared between the containers.

We define different types of policies which are linked to a specific domain. These types of policies have the same name as the corresponding domains. So the child policies would inherit from the properties defined in the parent interface. The considered properties are the connections to the associated domain.

Thanks to this abstraction, some added values are obtained:

- *identification*: Each TD treatment is associated to a TD policy,
- *adaptability*: By selecting the TD policies to integrate inside the platform,
- *isolation*: By addressing only the TD policy needed, and
- *factorization*: The technical code is delegated to the domain.

4.4   Integration of New TD Policies

The structure of the framework defining independence between platforms and transactional monitors provides a lot of flexibility. A TD policy is composed of a policy and a transaction manager. Thanks to the different abstractions we define (transaction manager and policies), two solutions are possible. They are based on the definition of new transaction manager abstraction and new type of policies. Another solution uses the composition property for defining new policies using existing ones.

Integration of a New Type of Transaction Manager: A solution for defining new TD policies is to integrate –using the abstraction– a new transaction manager abstractions like the BTP abstraction into the framework. As a consequence, all the policies of the framework are associated to the new transaction manager abstraction. A set of new TD policies for the BTP transaction model are obtained using the legacy policies and domains which would be connected to the BTP transaction manager abstraction.

Definition of a New Policy: Another solution consists in defining a new type of policies. An example of this type of policy could be the *Requires New Sub* policy [17]. This type of policy activates a nested transaction inside the scope of an active transaction. The definition of this new policy is based on the abstraction of TD policies. So the new policy has to be associated with the transaction manager which supports nested transactions. The result is a set of new TD policies for a new type of policy using the legacy transaction managers.

Combining Existing TD Policies: Using the *Requires New Sub* policy mentioned before, one could observe that the semantics are incomplete. Indeed the behavior of this policy has not been defined if invoked under no transactional context. How could a new nested transaction be started if no top-level transaction is active? A solution is to say that before beginning the nested transaction, a top-level transaction has to be begun. Another solution is to force the client to invoke the method under a transactional context like it is defined in the *Mandatory* policy. Similar options could be considered also for the case of an invocation realized under a transactional context.

Rather than implementing a policy for each solution which would not be in favor of our process of flexibility, we choose to introduce the notion of TD policy composition. Indeed the composition of the *Required* policy and the *Requires New Sub* policy answer the question mentioned before. The composition of the *Mandatory* policy and the *Requires New Sub* policy provides another solution. Another example is the composition of the *Not Supported* and the *Required* policies. This association simulates the *Requires New* policy.

This combination is realized using a coordinator which organizes the calls to the delegated policies. Next, if delegated policies are themselves a combination of policies, an organization representing a tree of policies could be extracted. So a hierarchy of policies could be defined inside the container. The interesting point is that a hierarchy defines a set of branches and some of them could be preferred to others during the execution.

An evolution of this hierarchy could define "Clever coordinators" in order to switch between the delegated branches or policies depending on a specific clause. The structure of the tree becomes dynamic and the policies executed are different according to the context of the invocation. The framework executes only the policies which are compliant to the execution context.

We are not defining a new organization which could be conflicting with the notion of domain. This hierarchy is only an organization of the policies execution.

5   Java Open Transaction Demarcation Framework

We choose to implement our framework with the Java language [18] essentially for experimental reasons. Many component-oriented platforms are implemented in Java (JOnAS[11], JBoss[19], OpenEJB[20], EJCCM[21], OpenCCM[12], JEFFREE[22]) and as well for transactional monitors (OpenORB TS[23], Tyrex[24], JOnAS TS[11], JOTM[9]).

The multiplicity of implementations allows the experimentation of our framework with various platforms and transactional monitors for the validation of our proposal.

In order to provide several implementations, the framework provides a separated view of interfaces (API) and implementations.

5.1   Transaction Monitor Wrapper

The abstraction of the transaction manager introduces a semantics which is particularly adapted for transaction demarcation. Figure 6 illustrates how a transaction manager could be wrapped and how the semantics introduced by the interfaces is implicitly translated.

From Figure 6, the *UserTransaction* interface inherits from the group of features dealing with activation properties. It also has to implement a configuration feature materialized by the *set_transaction_timeout* method. These features are implemented through the *UserTransaction* interface which defines the features to implement in the scope of a JTS *UserTransaction* interface. So the Java abstraction of the transaction manager needs to be mapped with the transactional monitor used. In this example the wrapped functionalities of the transaction manager are the JTS ones.

The originality of this abstraction comes from the definition of the features which will allow one to extend the abstractions if new transaction models and concepts are defined.

5.2   Transaction Domain

The second level of abstraction is the domain. It models a subset of the functionalities of the transaction manager.

```
public class JTSUserTransactionImpl
   implements UserTransaction {
      protected javax.transaction.UserTransaction tm_ ;

      public void set_transaction_timeout(int seconds) {
          try { tm_.setTransactionTimeout(seconds); } catch(Exception ex) { ... }
      }
      public Status get_status() {
          try { return JTSStatus.jts_to_status(tm_.getStatus());
          } catch (javax.transaction.SystemException ex) { ... }
      }
      public void begin() {
          try { tm_.begin(); } catch (Exception ex)  { ... }
      }
      public void commit() {
          switch(get_status()) {
              case Status.STATUS_ACTIVE :
                  try { tm_.commit(); } catch(Exception ex) { ... }
                  break ;
              case Status.STATUS_MARKED_ROLLBACK :
                  rollback();
                  break ;
          }
      }
      public void rollback() {
          try { tm_.rollback(); } catch(Exception ex) { ... }
      }
      public void set_rollback_only() {
          try { tm_.setRollbackOnly(); } catch(Exception ex) { ... }
      }
}
```

Fig. 6. The JTS Transaction Manager Wrapper

```
public class InterruptionDomainImpl
   extends InterrogationDomainImpl
   implements InterruptionDomain {
      protected InterruptionScope is_ ;

      public void suspend(RequestCallContext ctx) {
          try { ctx.put_property("transaction_suspended", is_.suspend());
          } catch(SystemException ex) { ... }
      }
      public void resume(RequestCallContext ctx) {
          Transaction _tx = (Transaction) ctx.get_property("transaction_suspended");
          if (_tx != null)
             try { is_.resume(_tx); } catch(Exception ex) { ... }
      }
}
```

Fig. 7. An Example of Demarcation Domain: The Interruption Domain

Figure 7 illustrates how to define a domain for abstracting a part of transaction demarcation. But the domain provides a simplification of the TD business code. So the domain has a *RequestCallContext* for storing properties related to the transaction manager. Concretely, the *RequestCallContext* is used for storing the instance of the transaction which is suspended during the invocation of the method. In the case of the

```
public class NotSupportedPolicyImpl
   extends AbstractInterruptionPolicy
   implements NotSupportedPolicy {
     public void preinvoke(RequestCallContext ctx) {
          if (id.get_status(ctx) == Status.STATUS_ACTIVE)
              id.suspend(ctx) ;
     }
     public void postinvoke(RequestCallContext ctx) {
          id.resume(ctx) ;
     }
}
```

Fig. 8. An Example of TD Policy: The Not Supported Policy

InterruptionDomain, the domain requires a set of transaction features which are defined in the *InterruptionScope* interface of the transaction manager.

So from the policy, the developer does not need to manage the propagation of the transaction between the *pre_invoke* and the *post_invoke* methods.

Different possibilities of evolution are possible from the definition of domain. We could define new domains based on the scopes defined by a transaction manager abstraction, this domain would contain the use rules of the selected scope applied to transaction demarcation. But we could also modify the behavior of an existing domain by introducing for example interactivity such as "commit/rollback choice" for the container transactions. The behavior of the TD policy is changed without modifying the content of the policy itself.

5.3 Transaction Policy

Until now, the structure of the framework has been defined and introduced without dealing with the type of policies. Figure 8 presents the implementation of the *Not Supported* policy.

Figure 8 promotes that defining a TD policy is easier than before while being both platform and transactional monitor independent. Moreover, the behavior of a policy becomes easier to understand. One has just to read the code of the policy to understand what it is able to do and could notice that only three lines are necessary to define the policy.

5.4 Platform Usage

This section is an illustration of the integration of JOTDF in a platform which requires TD policies. Most of the time, platforms are not designed for working with JOTDF so an adaptation class for converting the formalisms need to be defined for adapting the framework to the platform.

Figure 9 depicts the mechanism of interception which could be used for integrating TD policies in a component platform. The component is defined by the *Account* interface and the *AccountImpl* implementation class. The component platform generates the *AccountInterceptor* class which would delegate the incoming calls realized by the *Account* interface to its implementation. The interceptor calls also the TD policy through the *DemarcationPolicy* interface just before and after the delegation.

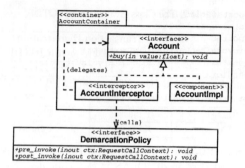

Fig. 9. Interception on a Container hosting Account Components

6   Experimentations

All the design patterns introduced in this paper provide lots of architectural properties. But what about performance? Does this framework introduce a huge overhead to the execution time? Is it really possible to use an EJB platform over an OTS transactional monitor? This section will answer to these questions giving valued results of JOTDF based on various experimentations realized with and without JOTDF.

6.1   Context and Scenario

For evaluating the framework, the computer used is based on an Intel Pentium4 2 GHz with 1024 MB of RAM (DELL Optiflex GX 240). The operating system installed is a Linux Debian based on version 2.4.19-686 of the Kernel. The experimentation is realized on a single computer in order to avoid the interferences generated by the network.

From the software point of view, the Java Development Kit used is the JDK 1.4.1_01 provided by Sun Microsystems. The platform used for the experimentation is an EJB platform working with a JTS transactional monitor. The platform and the transactional monitor are provided by version 2.5.3 of the JOnAS Application Server.

The version of JOTDF used during the experimentation is a basic implementation where we choose to merge the domains and the transaction manager abstraction into one class. This choice illustrates that more or less flexibility could be applied to the framework. A single object is used, which groups the three main domains and the transaction manager abstraction. So each policy would be bound to this object and then will delegate the technical code to the transaction manager.

As an application scenario, a simple example provided with the JOnAS platform is used. This example is a bank account simulation. It uses a container with transaction demarcation features. The bank account is the business component which is tested. A bench component is added and located with the business component on the same component server.

When the bench component is invoked, it activates the business component. Next it produces 10 000 invocations on the bank account component under a transaction, and then it generates 10 000 invocations on the same business component but apart from any transaction.

Table 2. The Class Evaluation of JOTDF

	Transaction Demarcation	
	without JOTDF	with JOTDF
Classes	X TD x Y TM	X TD + Z D + Y TM
Example (6 policies, 3 TM)	6 TD x 3 TM = 18 classes	6 TD + 3 D + 3 TM = 12 classes
New TD	Y classes	1 class
New TM	X classes	1 class

Initially, the standard version of JOnAS is experimented. Next the experiment is started again using a version of JOnAS coupled to the version of JOTDF described in the previous section.

The execution time of the 10 000 calls in each of the four situations is measured. As the business code is negligible, one can consider that the time of crossing of the container and the TD policy is measured. Moreover the difference of time is taken into account more than the absolute values of the measures.

6.2 The Memory Evaluation

Before applying the scenario, a static evaluation of the framework could be realized. It consists with measuring the number of classes and the size of source code used for the management of transaction demarcation. The study is presented in Table 2.

Observing Table 2, much information could be extracted. The "Transaction Demarcation without JOTDF" term considers a basic implementation of transaction demarcation which could be the definition of a TD policy for each type of transaction manager (Y attribute) and each type of policy (X attribute), while the "Transaction Demarcation with JOTDF" term considers the detailed implementation presented in the paper.

Regarding the size of the framework, a basic implementation would provide much more classes than JOTDF. Concerning the extensions of transaction demarcation, the integration of a new TD policy like the *Requires New* policy depends on the number of transaction managers in the basic implementation. In JOTDF, the integration of such a policy results in the definition of only one class. In the same way, the integration of a new transaction manager like the *BTP* transaction manager would introduce as much of the classes as policies in the basic implementation whereas only one class is required in JOTDF. So in JOTDF, the class evolution is linear whereas it would be exponential in a classic implementation.

JOTDF introduces predictability of memory. Indeed JOTDF could share the TD policies between the components of a same component server. So independently of component count, JOTDF uses one instance of the framework. Actually the size of transaction manager depends much more of the number of containers using transaction demarcation features deployed on the server.

6.3 The CPU Evaluation

After the static evaluation, the dynamic evaluation of the framework could be realized. This section presents the results of the scenario execution. The results are presented in Table 3.

Table 3. The Time Evaluation of JOTDF

Policies	JOnAS	JOnAS & JOTDF	Evolution
Supports	17,697 sec	17,569 sec	-0,72 %
Not Supported	18,324 sec	18,302 sec	-0,12 %
Required	31,013 sec	30,963 sec	-0.16 %
Requires New	42,869 sec	42,832 sec	-0,09 %
Never	91,869 sec	90,940 sec	-1,01 %
Mandatory	97,419 sec	97,027 sec	-0,40 %
		Average	-0,42 %

The results presented in Table 3 are explicit, the use of JOTDF does not introduce a higher cost than a handwritten version of TD policies. JOTDF improves the performances of transaction demarcation of the JOnAS platform.

JOTDF also adds better predictability properties. Indeed the invocation does not depend on all TD policies anymore. According to the *Command* Design Pattern, only the cost of TD policy configured influences the cost of invocations. The more policies are used by the platform the better performances can be obtained regarding classical platforms. So the more policy implementation is following our framework the better is the platform performance.

6.4   Example of Heterogeneity in Middleware: EJB over OTS

Another experiment which has been undertaken is an illustration of the new properties obtained thanks to JOTDF. Indeed we try to use an OTS transactional monitor with an EJB platform. These entities are connected through JOTDF.

Thanks to that properties, platforms are no more forced to work with a specific transactional monitor. Going further, heterogenous platforms could execute over a common transaction manager and even in the same transaction.

7   Lessons

This section will discuss several properties about the OTDF framework and its Java implementation JOTDF. Next the advantages and limits of this approach are described. The OTDF framework shows that we obtain:

- **Independence to language:** OTDF is independent of the programming language. It uses no language specific technologies and the architecture could be implemented in any object-oriented programming language.
- **Independence to platforms:** OTDF could be integrated by any platform requiring transaction demarcation. The container calls OTDF where transaction demarcation needs to be applied.
- **Independence to transactional monitors:** OTDF could interact with any transactional monitor once its abstraction has been integrated to OTDF. Special abstractions are linked to a type of transactional monitors like JTS, OTS, WS-T or BTP. So different implementations of a same type uses the same abstraction.

- **Transaction demarcation abstraction:** OTDF defines an abstraction of transaction demarcation which is sufficiently generic in order to be used by most of the existing platforms. Transaction demarcation introduced by OTDF is based on an encapsulation of the method invocation using pre-invocation and post-invocation pattern.
- **Modularity:** The architecture of OTDF is well defined. It uses several types of modules (policies, domains, transaction managers) which could give several entities.
- **Extensibility:** The structure of OTDF has been designed for extensibility. The new transaction manager could be considered and the same for the new TD policies even if they need to define specific domains. OTDF would support new models of transactional monitors thanks to the notion of features presented in the transaction manager abstraction. Considering this architecture, it is easy to introduce new policies with the associated domains, scopes, features and transaction manager abstraction if needed.
- **Dynamic reconfigurability:** OTDF models the connection between the components of the framework. It becomes easy to modify these bindings at runtime.
- **Adaptability:** TD policies are independent entities. The platform could choose and configure the policies required by the specification and use a subset of the policies proposed by OTDF.
- **Component and Aspect:** OTDF is component-oriented, its architecture is modeled using component model. Moreover components could be propagated through several models to the programming level.
  Aspects [25] are a way to treat the separation of concerns. So policies could be integrated in an aspect for adding transaction demarcation properties to an application which has not envisaged such a property during its development.
- **Validation and safety:** The TD policies of OTDF are validated and reliable. The development of new middleware could lean on OTDF for transaction demarcation scope with the confidence of using reliable TD policies. The process of validation is facilitated by the decomposition of a TD policy in three elementary entities which are easier to test and are shared by the TD policies.

The JOTDF implementation proves that one can obtain:

- **No CPU performance degradation:** The benchmark realized shows that even if the performance is not a hard constraint when OTDF has been defined, one can obtain nevertheless interesting results. This is an illustration that architecture and performance are compatible.
- **CPU predictability:** The *Command* Design Pattern provides better predictability and better scalability in terms of CPU computation.
- **Memory predictability:** Sharing policies and factorizing the demarcation management minimize the memory cost of transaction demarcation.

8   Conclusion and Perspectives

This paper has presented a framework for addressing the problem of managing transaction demarcation over heterogenous transactional monitors.

It introduced several technical concerns which could be noticed when the problem of transaction demarcation is studied. The OTDF framework is an answer to these concerns and provides a long-term solution. OTDF provides an architecture based on the abstraction of technical code for keeping only the business code of the demarcation. The separation of concerns used by OTDF provides added values to the framework. Next, OTDF results in a Java implementation called JOTDF. This implementation is then used in several experiments which provide concluding results.

From there, the work begun by OTDF opens three main perspectives. Considering the context of transaction demarcation, OTDF answers many of the actual concerns raised by the current platforms. But OTDF needs to be experimented on other platforms like JBoss, OSGi or EJCCM. OTDF should experiment new policies like the *MandatoryNewSub* [26] in order to validate its extensibility properties. OTDF gives a brief reply to problems of defining a framework for addressing the transactional deployment. The definition of deployment policies could be a track. Finally JOTDF would become a plugin of the JOTM project which targets to provide a framework for addressing all features related to transactions in distributed systems.

Considering a more generic context, OTDF gives a template for the definition of policies for log, security, naming or trading services. Some of them are currently supported by platforms specification like security policies. Other policies are not introduced by specifications but JOTDF could be a template for integrating new policies inside containers.

The other perspective is the integration of the policies with the platform. Different mechanisms could be considered like interception, Aspect-Oriented Programming (AOP) [25] or Meta-Object Protocol (MOP) [27] mechanisms. Another aspect of the integration is to widen the application of policies. Policies could extended to other contexts other than method invocation. Indeed policies could be used for the bind/unbind, create/destroy and activate/passivate events of a component.

References

1. DeMichiel, L., Yalçinalp, L., Krishnan, S.: Enterprise Java Beans Specification Version 2.0 - Public Draft. Sun Microsystems. (2000)
2. OMG: CORBA Components Specification Version 3.0. Object Management Group. (2002) OMG TC Document formal/2002-06-65.
3. Thai, T., Lam, H.: .Net Framework Essentials. O'Reilly (2001)
4. OSGi: OSGi Service Gateway Specification Release 1.0. Open Service Gateway Initiative. (2000)
5. Cheung, S.: Java Transaction Service Specification Version 1.0, Sun Microsystems (1999)
6. OMG: Object Transaction Service Specification Version 1.2. In: CORBAservices : Common Object Services Specification, Object Management Group (2001) OMG TC Document formal/2001-05-02.
7. Cabrera, F., Copeland, G., Cox, B., Freund, T., Klein, J., Storey, T., Thatte, S.: Web Services Transaction Specification Version 1.0, IBM (2002)
8. OASIS: Business Transaction Protocol Specification Version 1.0, Organization for the Advancement of Structured Information Systems (2002)
9. ObjectWeb: Java Open Transaction Manager (2002) *http://www.objectweb.org/jotm*.

10. Gamma, E., Helm, R., Johnson, R., Vlissides, J., Booch, G.: Design Patterns: Elements of Reusable Object-Oriented Software. Addison-Westley Professional Computing, USA (1995)
11. ObjectWeb: Java Open Application Server (2002) *http://www.objectweb.org/jonas.*
12. ObjectWeb: Open CORBA Component Model (2002) *http://www.objectweb.org/openccm.*
13. Barga, R., Pu, C.: Reflection on a legacy transaction processing monitor. In: Proceedings Reflection '96, San Francisco, CA, USA (1996)
14. Procházka, M.: Advanced Transactions in Component-Based Software Architectures. PhD thesis, Charles University, Faculty of Mathematics and Physics, Department of Software Engineering, Malostranské námestí 25, 118 00 Prague 1, Czech Republic (2002)
15. OMG: Unified Modeling Language Version 1.4. Object Management Group. (2001) OMG TC Document formal/2001-09-67.
16. Barga, R., Pu, C.: A Practical and Modular Method to Implement Extended Transaction Models. In: International Conference on Very Large Data Bases, Zurich, Switzerland (1995) 206–217
17. Procházka, M.: Advanced transactions in Enterprise Java Beans. Lecture Notes in Computer Science (2001) 215
18. Gosling, J., Joy, B., Steele, G.: The Java Language Specification. (1996)
19. JBoss Group LLC: JBoss (2002) *http://www.jboss.org.*
20. ExoLab: Open Enterprise Java Bean (2002) *http://openejb.exolab.org.*
21. Computational Physics, I.: Enterprise Java CORBA Component Model (2002) *http://www.cpi.com/ejccm.*
22. ObjectWeb: JEFFREE (2003) *http://www.objectweb.org/jeffree.*
23. SourceForge: OpenORB Transaction Service (2002) *http://openorb.sourceforge.net.*
24. ExoLab: Tyrex (2002) *http://tyrex.exolab.org.*
25. Kiczales, G., Lamping, J., Menhdhekar, A., Maeda, C., Lopes, C., Loingtier, J.M., Irwin, J.: Aspect-oriented programming. In Akşit, M., Matsuoka, S., eds.: Proceedings European Conference on Object-Oriented Programming. Volume 1241. Springer-Verlag, Berlin, Heidelberg, and New York (1997) 220–242
26. Procházka, M., Plasil, F.: Container-interposed transactions. In: Proceedings of the Component-Based Software Engineering special session of the SNPD 2001 Conference, Nagoya, Japan (2001)
27. Robben, B., Vanhaute, B., Joosen, W., Verbaeten, P.: Non-functional policies. Lecture Notes in Computer Science (1999) 74

Optimising Java RMI Programs
by Communication Restructuring

Kwok Cheung Yeung and Paul H. J. Kelly

Department of Computing
Imperial College, London, UK

Abstract. We present an automated run-time optimisation framework that can improve the performance of distributed applications written using Java RMI whilst preserving its semantics.

Java classes are modified at load-time in order to intercept RMI calls as they occur. RMI calls are not executed immediately, but are delayed for as long as possible. When a dependence forces execution of the delayed calls, the aggregated calls are sent over to the remote server to be executed in one step. This reduces network overhead and the quantity of data sent, since data can be shared between calls. The sequence of calls may be cached on the server side along with any known constants in order to speed up future calls. A remote server may also make RMI calls to another remote server on behalf of the client if necessary.

Our results show that the techniques can speed up distributed programs significantly, especially when operating across slower networks. We also discuss some of the challenges involved in maintaining program semantics, and show how the approach can be used for more ambitious optimisations in the future.

1 Introduction

Frameworks for distributed programming such as the Common Object Resource Broker Architecture (CORBA) [9] and Java Remote Method Invocation (RMI) [12] aim to provide a location-transparent object-oriented programming model, but do not completely succeed since the cost of a remote call may be several orders of magnitude greater than a local call due to marshalling overheads and relatively slow network connections. This means that developers must explicitly code with performance in mind, leading to reduced productivity and increased program complexity.

The usual approach to optimising distributed programs in general has been to optimise the connection between the communicating hosts, fine-tuning the remote call mechanism and the underlying communication protocol to cut the overhead for each call to a minimum. Although this leads to a general speed-up, it does not help the performance of programs that are slow due to their structure (e.g. using many fine-grained methods instead of a few coarse-grained methods). Our approach towards solving this problem has been to consider all communicating nodes as part of one large program, rather than many disjoint ones.

We delay the execution of remote calls on the client for as long as possible until a dependency on the delayed calls blocks further progress. At this point, the delayed calls are executed in one step, after which the blocked operation may proceed. By delaying

M. Endler and D. Schmidt (Eds.): Middleware 2003, LNCS 2672, pp. 324–343, 2003.

the execution of remote calls, we build up a knowledge of the context in which calls were made on the client. This enables us to find opportunities for optimisations between calls that would have been lost had the calls been executed immediately.

1.1 Contributions

- We present an optimisation tool which can improve performance of Java/RMI applications by combining static analysis of application bytecode with run-time optimisation of sequences of remote operations. This tool operates on unmodified Java RMI applications, and runs on a standard JVM.
- By aggregating sequences of remote calls to the same server, the total number of message exchanges is reduced. By avoiding redundant parameter and result transfers, total amount of data transferred can also be reduced. When calls to different servers are aggregated together, results can be forwarded directly from one server to another, bypassing the client in some cases.
- We show how run-time overheads can be reduced by caching execution plans at the servers.
- We demonstrate the use of the tool using a number of examples.

The framework presented here provides the basis for a programme of research aimed at extending aggressive optimisation techniques across distributed systems, and deploying the results in large-scale industrial systems. We conclude with a discussion of the potential for the work, and the challenges that remain.

1.2 Structure

We begin in Section 2 with a discussion of related work. We then cover the runtime optimisation framework used to implement our optimisations at a high-level in Section 3. We proceed to cover the optimisations performed in Section 4, and the challenges involved in maintaining the semantics of the original application in Section 5. We then present some performance results in Section 6 and finish off with some suggestions for future work in Section 7 and conclude in Section 8.

2   Related Work

Most work on optimising RMI has concentrated on reducing the run-time overhead of each remote call by reducing the amount of work done per-call or by using more lightweight network protocols. Examples include the UKA serialisation work [14], KaRMI [13], and R-UDP [10]. Similar work has been done on CORBA by Gokhale and Schmidt [7].

Asynchronous RPC [11, 15] aims to overlap client computation with communication and remote execution, replacing results with 'promises', which block the client only when actually used.

A more ambitious approach is the concept of caching the state of a remote-object locally [10]. This works well provided that most operations on cached objects are reads. However, a write operation incurs high penalties for all users of the cached object, since the client has to wait for invalidation of all copies of the object to finish before proceeding.

The first request for invalidated data will also incur an extra delay as the server fetches it from the client that performed the last update.

A later implementation of remote-object caching [5] implements the notion of *reduced objects* where only a subset of the remote-object state is cached on the server. The subset that is cached depends on the properties of the invoked methods — e.g. if a called method only accesses immutable variables, then those variables can be cached on the client without needing to deal with consistency issues.

Neither of these approaches to RMI optimisation conflict with our aggregation optimisations, and although we have not done so ourselves, these optimisations could theoretically be combined. It may be argued that our optimisations are made redundant under certain circumstances (e.g. if the aggregated calls are cached locally).

The concept of aggregating numerous small operations into a single larger operation is very old, and appears in numerous other contexts, especially in the hardware domain. In the context of RPC mechanisms, concepts such as stored procedures in database systems or commands in IBM's San Francisco [3] project are also capable of aggregating calls, but these are explicit mechanisms. Implicit call aggregation is much rarer and harder to implement. One example would be the concept of batched futures [2] in the Thor database system.

3   The Veneer Framework

The RMI optimisations are based on top of Veneer, which is a generalised framework that we have developed for the purpose of easing the development of run-time optimisation techniques. This framework is written in standard Java, using the BCEL [4] library for bytecode generation and the Soot [16] library for program analysis. Veneer is not tied to any particular JVM implementation, which is essential since it is likely be used in a heterogeneous environment. We refer to Veneer as a 'virtual JVM', since it behaves like a highly configurable Java virtual machine, without actually being one.

The framework presents a simplified model of the Java run-time environment, working with what appears to be a simple interpreter, called an *executor*. A basic executor is shown in Figure 1, which executes a method with no modifications whatsoever.

When a method that we are interested in is called, control passes to our executor instead of the original method. The executor is initialised with an *execution plan*, which is essentially a control-flow graph of the method, with executable code-blocks forming the nodes. The executor sits in a loop which executes the current block, then sets the current block to the next block in line to be executed.

The power of this framework lies in the fact that the plan is a first-order object that we can change while the executor is still running, effectively modifying the code that will be executed. The executor has full control over the process of method execution between blocks, such that we can perform operations such as jumping to arbitrary code-blocks, modifying local variables or timing operations if necessary.

We minimise the interpretive overhead by delegating as much work as possible to the underlying JVM, and by making the code-blocks as coarse as possible. There is also an option to permit blocks to run continuously without returning to the executor, though certain block types will always force a return.

The mapping of byte-code to code-blocks in the plan and the methods affected by our framework are determined by a plug-in policy class. The policy class also contains

```
public class BasicExecutor extends Executor{
  public int execute() throws Exception {
    while (block != null
            && !lockWasReleased()) {
      int next = -1;

      try {
        next = block.execute(this);
        block = plan.getBlock(next);
      } catch (ExecuteException e) {
        // Pass control to exception handler
        block = plan.getExceptionHandler(e);

        // Propagate exception if no handler
        if (block == null)
          throw e.getException();

        locals[1] = e.getException();
      }
    }

    return next;
  }
}
```

Fig. 1. Structure of a basic executor

numerous call-back methods that are invoked on certain events, such as the initial loading
of a class.

4   Optimisations

In this section we detail the RMI optimisations that have been implemented. The examples used to illustrate the optimisations are deliberately simplified for clarity.

4.1   Call Aggregation

Delaying calls to form call aggregates is the core technique upon which this project is
based. It is an important optimisation in its own right, and furthermore can also open up
further optimisation opportunities. For example, consider the following code fragment:

```
void m(RemoteObject r, int a) {
    int x = r.f(a);
    int y = r.g(x);
    int z = r.h(y);

    System.out.println(z);
}
```

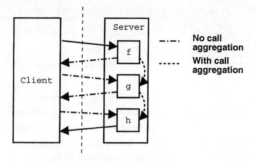

Fig. 2. Example of call aggregation

This program fragment incurs three remote method calls, with six data transfers. However, for this example, we can do better:

- Since all three calls are to the same remote object, they can be aggregated into a single large call, such that the number of times that call overhead is incurred is reduced to one (see Figure 2).
- x is returned as the result of the call to **f** from the remote server, but is subsequently passed back to it during the next call. The same occurs with the variable y. If the values of x and y were retained by the remote object between remote method calls, then the number of communications could be reduced from six to four.
- The variables x and y are unused by the client except as arguments to remote calls on the remote object from which they originated. x and y may therefore be considered as dead variables from the client's point of view, and there is no need for their value to be passed back to the client at all, thereby further reducing the total number of remote transactions down to just two messages with payloads of size *int*.

Client-Side Implementation. We have created a Veneer policy that only affects methods that are statically determined to contain potentially remote method calls. Calls are deemed to be potentially remote if they are invoked via an interface, and have `java.rmi.RemoteException` or one of its super-classes on the throw list. A runtime check is later used to ensure that the potential remote call is actually remote. Note that it is not sufficient just to check that the receiver of the call implements `java.rmi.Remote` since the object could be invoked directly instead of via RMI, and some remote calls may be missed if we are supplied with a non-remote interface that is actually a remote object that implements a remote child of our interface.

The client runs under the control of the Veneer framework using this policy. If the executor encounters a confirmed remote call during the course of execution, then it places the call within a queue and proceeds to the next instruction. Sequences of adjacent calls to the same remote object are grouped together into *remote plans*. Remote plans also contain metadata regarding the calls, such as variable liveness and data dependencies. Calls to other remote objects will not force execution unless the target of the call is defined by a previous delayed call, leading to a control dependency. However, even this condition is relaxed by server forwarding, detailed in Section 4.2.

When a non-remote block is encountered with delayed calls remaining in the queue, a decision has to be made whether or not to force execution of the calls. In general, it is safe to execute the current block without forcing if there are no dependencies between the current instruction and the delayed operations. If dependencies exist or if it is impossible to tell, then we must force execution.

We detect data dependencies by noting attempts to access data returned by RMI calls. Since the results of RMI calls are constructed by deserialising the data returned by the server, there can be no other references to the returned data except for the local that the result of the remote call was placed in. We therefore regard local code that accesses locals that should contain the results of RMI calls as being dependent on the delayed calls.

This scheme is rather conservative, such that even simple assignments from one local variable to another can force the execution of the delayed plans. We hope to improve this in the future using improved static analysis. Also, it cannot detect indirect data dependencies — for example, if the RMI call modifies a remote database which the client proceeds to access using another API, then that access will go unnoticed.

When executing local code in the presence of delayed remote calls, we must ensure that the variables used by the delayed calls are not overwritten or modified by the local code. This is done by making a copy of all locals supplied to the delayed calls that may be touched by the local code.

On forcing execution, the queue of delayed remote plans is traversed, with plans being sent one-by-one, along with the set of data used by the plan, to the corresponding *remote proxy* on the server-side via standard RMI invocation to be executed. The proxy call may either return successfully or throw an exception.

If the call returns successfully, then the variables defined by the plan that are still live are copied back into the locals set of the executing method. If an exception was thrown, then the executor goes through the normal process of finding a handler for the exception within the method, and propagating it up the call chain if one is not found.

The same Veneer policy also runs a remote proxy server on startup, which first registers itself in a naming service via JNDI. The proxy keeps track of all remote objects present on the JVM by inserting a small callback into the constructors of all remote classes at load time[1].

Clients obtain handles to proxies using the standard naming services via JNDI. When a client first encounters a new remote stub, it broadcasts it to all known proxies. The proxy that handles the remote object denoted by the stub will identify itself. Remote plans containing calls on that stub will subsequently be sent to the identified proxy. The stub-to-proxy mapping is cached on the client for speed.

Remote plans sent to the proxy are executed by an executor, which simply executes the calls one-by-one. The calls are made directly on the remote object rather than via another RMI invocation. However, care must be taken due to the semantic differences between local and RMI calls (see Section 5.1).

When finished, the proxy only sends the variables that are live in the client program at the point where execution was forced. The live set is calculated using the metadata supplied with the remote-calls.

---

[1] This may lead to a potential security hole since this may occur before the remote object has been exported for remote access.

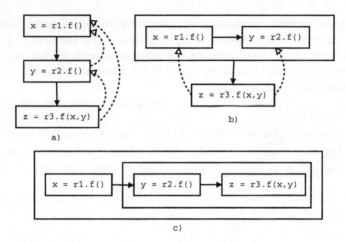

Fig. 3. Implementation of call forwarding: a) Arcs are placed between the calls to r1–r3 and r2–r3 (due to data dependence) and r1–r2 (due to co-location), b) Current cluster is the call to r1 — we append the call to r2 due to the r1–r2 arc, c) Current cluster is the call to r2 — we prepend the call to r3 due to the r2–r3 arc

4.2   Server Forwarding

Server forwarding takes advantage of the fact that servers typically reside on fast connections, whilst the client-server connection can often be orders of magnitude slower. Consider this sequence of calls:

```
x = r1.f();
y = r2.f();
z = r3.f(x,y);
```

The first two methods invoked on *r1* and *r2* are returning objects that are subsequently used as arguments to a method on another remote object *r3*. In this situation, the client is acting as a router for messages between *r1*, *r2* and *r3*. It would be better for *r1* and *r2* to communicate with *r3* directly, such that no constraints are set as to which path is taken between the two servers. Also, if *x* or *y* are dead, then they need not be returned to the client.

Forwarding is also necessary for efficient aggregation of factory patterns. e.g.

```
a = r.newObject();
b = a.f();
```

Without forwarding in place, we would need to force after the call to newObject because a is used as the receiver for the next remote call — without knowing the value of a, we would not where to send the remote plan, or what object to invoke f on.

Implementation. Server forwarding is implemented on top of call aggregation in a preprocessing step just before execution on the remote proxies, by grouping remote plans on differing remote objects together. When a remote proxy encounters a plan that is handled by another remote proxy, it will forward the plan onto that proxy automatically.

At present, the remote plans are composed of straight-line sequences of remote calls to the same object bundled together. We will refer to these units as *call clusters*. We use the following heuristics to decide when to group clusters with differing destinations:

- Plans that are delivered to the same remote proxy should be grouped together
- Plans that are data dependent on one another should be grouped together

We aim to achieve these goals whilst preserving the relative ordering of the calls. First, we build up a graph from the list of call clusters, with an arc between nodes that have a data-dependence or share a remote proxy. We then process the delayed-plan list in order, cluster-by-cluster.

We start by checking if there is an arc from the current cluster to its immediate successor. If there is, then we append it to the current plan. If there is not, then we check for an arc between the parent of the current cluster and the successor, appending to the parent plan if there is. We repeat the process until the check either succeeds, or there are no more parents left to check. At that point, the process is repeated with the successor cluster as the current plan. This process repeats until we have processed all the clusters.

When a remote plan B is appended to a remote plan A, a check is first made as to whether plan A is a call cluster. If it is, then a new plan is created and plans A and B inserted into it, in that order, as children, taking the place of the original plan A. If not, then B is inserted as the youngest sibling of A (i.e. B will be executed after anything already in A will be). The overall effect is that the plans form a multi-rooted tree structure, with call clusters appearing at the leaves. Plans that contain other plans are always sent to the handler of the oldest (i.e. first to be executed) sub-plan.

The algorithm currently gives equal priority to arcs due to co-location and those due to data-dependencies. It is possible to prioritise one type of arc by processing all instances of that type first when traversing through the plan hierarchy, followed by the other type.

We illustrate the process in Figure 3 using the previous example, assuming that *r1* and *r2* are targeted at the same proxy server.

4.3   Plan Caching

These optimisations incur a substantial overhead due to factors such as:

- Overhead of the Veneer runtime
- Maintenance of dependence information for delayed calls
- Pre-processing for server-forwarding
- Transmission of remote plans and metadata

We can reduce some overhead by caching plans on both server and client sides. Instead of building up remote plans by delaying calls as we encounter them, we replace the remote calls with the remote plans built up by delaying those calls previously. When the executor encounters these, it can simply place it directly onto the remote plan queue with minimal overhead.

```
for (int i = 0; i < 1000; i++) {
    r.f();
    r.g();
    if (i % 2 == 0)
        x = r.h();
    else
        x = r.i();
    System.out.println(x);
}
```

Fig. 4. Example of a loop that results in a different remote plan on every iteration

We can only do this for adjacent clusters of remote calls rather than the merged remote plans because the pattern of remote calls might not occur next time. For example, consider Figure 4. During the first iteration, $r.f$, $r.g$ and $r.h$ will be aggregated, but it would not be valid to replace $r.f$ with the aggregated call because the next iteration would result in $r.f$, $r.g$ and $r.i$ being aggregated. However, it is safe to replace $r.f$ and $r.g$ with the aggregate since these always occur together.

We can also take advantage of the fact that the server has seen the plan before to implement a form of data compression. The server can keep a cached copy of the plans that it receives, returning an identifier associated with the cached plan to the client. The client from that point can simply use the identifier to refer to the plan, rather than sending the entire plan every time.

Client-Side Implementation. On the client side, we maintain a list of newly constructed call clusters. After the plans are executed, the clusters are incorporated into the method plan, such that for each cluster, all paths leading to the first call in the cluster are re-routed to the cluster, and the successor of the cluster set to the successor of the last call in the cluster. The embedded remote clusters are delayed similarly to remote calls when encountered, though without the processing required to construct the plan.

After a plan is executed, a list of cache IDs is returned by the server proxy. Cache IDs associated with call clusters are assigned directly to the embedded remote clusters. The cache IDs belonging to compound plans (plans consisting of clusters and other compound plans) are stored in a global cache, which associates a *cache pattern* with a cache ID. The cache pattern is generated by traversing the children plans of the current plan pre-order, adding the cache ID of the plans encountered as we progress.

The cache IDs for all plans are stored as a hash-map from remote server to the cache ID for that server. In all plans, we retain a handle to the last remote server used and the cache ID associated with that server. If the plan is invoked again on the same server, we can re-use the cache ID and avoid a hash-map lookup.

When the plans have been grouped and are about to be sent to the server, we attempt to send cache IDs in preference to the entire plan whenever possible using the following algorithm, starting at the root of the tree:

- If the plan is an embedded cluster, we use the associated cache ID from the embedded cluster directly.
  - If the cache ID is found, then that is used in place of the plan
  - If there is no cache ID, then we must send the entire plan

− If the plan is compound, we:
1. Compute the cache pattern of the plan
2. Lookup the cache ID in the global cache
- If a cache ID is found, then it is used in place of the plan
- If no cache ID is found, then we:
  1. Repeat the algorithm for each child of the plan
  2. If there is a cache ID for the child, then use that in place of the child plan

Server-Side Implementation. On the server side, the remote proxy maintains a cache of encountered plans, indexed by an integer identifier. If a remote plan containing uncached entities is executed, we cache the uncached items and return an array of cache IDs for the overall plan. Since the remote plan forms a tree structure known by both the server and client during the call, cache IDs are returned to the client as a flat array of integers by performing a pre-order traversal of the remote plan, returning the cache IDs as the nodes are encountered. The client uses this information to allocate the correct IDs to the correct clusters.

5   Maintaining Semantics

The optimisations may have changed some of the application semantics due to the difference between executing calls remotely and locally. In this section, we identify and suggest solutions to some of the problems that arise.

5.1   Differences between Local and Remote Calls

A local call and a remote call differ in the way that they pass objects as parameters. Local calls receive their parameters by reference, whereas remote calls receive them by copy. Consider the following code fragment, where r is a remote object:

```
a = r.f(x);
b = r.g(x);
```

Since the arguments to the call are marshalled, using local reference semantics, this would be equivalent to:

```
x'  = x.clone();
a = r.f(x');
x'' = x.clone();
b = r.g(x'');
```

Note that whatever f does to x' is not propagated to x or x'', and similarly the effects of g on x'' are not propagated to x. However, by aggregating calls, the original code is transformed to the equivalent of:

```
x'  = x.clone();
a = r.f(x');
b = r.g(x');
```

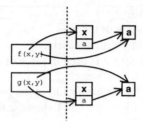

Fig. 5. Effect of sharing under object marshalling — this sharing structure cannot be maintained by copying the parameters one at a time

Now, although the effects of f and g on x' still do not affect x, the effect of f on x' will affect the functioning of g. It is therefore only safe to aggregate the two calls without copying the parameter if we can be sure that f does not change the value of its parameter.

An additional complication is the fact that marshalling preserves sharing between objects. For example, consider the following code:

```
x.a = y;
r.f(x, y);
r.g(x, y);
```

If we denote the arguments received by f as x' and y', and those received by g as x'' and y'', then under conventional RMI, the following properties should hold:

$$x' \neq x'' \tag{1}$$
$$y' \neq y'' \tag{2}$$
$$x'.a \neq x''.a \tag{3}$$
$$x'.a = y' \tag{4}$$
$$x''.a = y'' \tag{5}$$

This rules out copying the arguments separately, since the sharing relationship denoted by equations 4 and 5 would be broken.

Copying Using Serialisation. An easy way to properly copy parameters to a method call is for the server to construct an array containing the variables needed for the next call, serialise it, immediately deserialise the byte-stream into a new array, and supply the new array to the call.

Although this technique also incurs an extra cycle of serialisation and deserialisation, it is still somewhat more efficient than the simpler technique of using RMI calls locally on the server side since it avoids the overhead incurred by going through the stub and skeleton.

Avoiding Argument Copying. An argument to a remote method call need not be copied if any of the following are true:

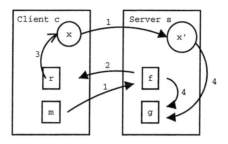

Fig. 6. The callback problem

- The argument is immutable
- All objects reachable via the argument are dead after the call
- The method is guaranteed not to modify the argument

We have currently implemented some simple checks for a subset of the first two conditions. We specifically check for common object types that are known to be immutable, such as instances of `java.lang.String`.

We also introduce the notion of 'flat-types', which are types that do not contain any references. These include common types such as arrays of primitive types such as `int`. If only flat-types are used for the current and subsequent calls, then if an argument is dead and is not aliased by any other argument (which can be done simply by checking if any of the other arguments are equal to it), then we can safely avoid copying the argument.

5.2   Call-Backs

When using Java RMI, it is perfectly possible for a client to act as a remote server, and vice-versa. This creates the possibility for a call-back mechanism, where a call by the client to the server will result in the server calling the client. This can create consistency problems when delaying calls.

Consider a scenario where the server s has managed to obtain a stub to a client c that also acts as a server (see Figure 6). When c calls $s.f(x)$, s makes use of the stub to call the method $c.r$, which has the effect of modifying the object referenced locally on c by x. Since RMI calls are synchronous, if $g(x)$ is subsequently called, the value of x should have been changed.

This causes a problem when aggregating calls, since the value of x that is sent to the server and subsequently operated on by g will be that of the unchanged object. However, since the client c generally does not know how the server s is implemented, it cannot tell in advance if s will modify x via f or not. If we ignore the problem, then g will end up using the old value of x.

A Possible Loophole. It could be argued that we could simply ignore the problem due to the Java memory model in the absence of explicit synchronisation. In the Java language specification [8], the example in 7 is given:

```
class Simple {
    int a = 1, b = 2;

    void to() { a = 3; b = 4; }
    void fro() {
        System.out.println("a=" + a +
                           ", b=" + b);
    }
}
```

Fig. 7. Example to illustrate behaviour of threads accessing shared memory in the absence of synchronisation (from Java language specification)

If to and fro are called from different threads, then a may equal 1 or 3 and b may equal 2 or 4 independently. This is true even if fro executes after to has finished, since there is no obligation for to to write its changes back into main memory immediately without the use of synchronisation.

Since a callback must execute in a different thread from the original caller (since the caller is blocked by the unfinished RMI call), the effects of the callback might not be immediately noticeable by the caller, in theory. In practice this does not happen due to the implementation of RMI flushing the updates to main memory, but the RMI specification [12] itself does not mandate this — in fact, it does not mention synchronisation issues at all.

Proposed Solution. If we wish to ensure that the effects of callbacks are visible, then we can modify the existing protocol to do so. There are two main approaches to solving the problem — by update and by invalidation.

In the update protocol, we need the client to detect when a callback has occurred. This can be done by associating a unique session ID that is associated with the remote plan. This session ID is carried along with the plan to the remote proxy, and to any subsequent remote calls that the proxy may make. Now, if the server calls the client remotely, the client will be able to detect that it is a callback since the session ID will be known to the client. If this happens, then the client sends an updated copy of the variables associated with the session ID to the server before returning from the remote call. The server should use the fresh copy of the variables after the current call is finished.

If an invalidation protocol is used, then the server must inspect the methods being called. If a remote method may result in a callback, then the method is executed anyway, and an exception is thrown back to the client containing information regarding how far execution has progressed. The exception notifies the client of a potential callback situation, such that the client may resend the portion of the remote plan after the method that resulted in a callback, along with an up-to-date copy of the used variables.

6   Experimental Evaluations

We have tested our optimisations with two examples. The first example is a simple, synthetic benchmark to illustrate the potential of the optimisations. The second is an example of a naively written program found in the wild that may benefit from our optimisations.

The tests were performed using the Linux version of the Sun JDK version 1.4.1_01, across a Fast Ethernet network (ping time is 0.1 ms, measured bandwidth is 10.03 MB/s) and over the Internet via a slow ADSL connection (ping time is 98 ms, measured bandwidth is 10.7 kB/s). The client machine in all tests was an Athlon XP 1800+ based PC. The server for the Ethernet test was a 650MHz Intel Pentium-III PC, whilst the server for the ADSL test was a dual-processor 700MHz Pentium-III PC.

For each test, 3 trials of 1000 iterations were performed, and the mean taken as the result.

6.1   Vector Arithmetic

We have evaluated our framework using a simple synthetic benchmark in which the server object provides a single method takes two equal-sized arrays of type double, adds them together, and returns the resulting array. In order to test aggregation, the client application executes a sequence of remote calls of the form:

```
tmp1 = r.add(v0, v1);
tmp2 = r.add(tmp1, v2);
result = r.add(tmp2, v3);
```

This benchmark enables us to easily observe the effect of our optimisation framework as we vary the size of the data, the number of calls aggregated and various parameters of the framework.

We have tested a baseline configuration with no aggregation occurring, and configurations containing from 2–5 aggregated calls. For each configuration, we vary the vector size from 1 to 1024 doubles, doubling the vector size at every step. We test on both the Ethernet and ADSL connections.

We show the results before and after applying the framework on the benchmark program. We have also provided results for a 'hand-optimised' version of the tests (where we provide manually aggregated methods on the server and make the client call these methods) for comparison purposes.

Results. As can be seen in the results in Figures 8(a)–9(e), the optimisations generally result in an overall speedup whenever any aggregation occurs. The exceptions occur when an Ethernet connection is used, with two aggregated calls and argument size of less than 400 bytes. This is due to overhead.

In the baseline case with no aggregation occurring, a slowdown will occur due to the same overhead being occurred but without any compensating speedup from call aggregation. This is easily observable in the Ethernet test, but is not evident in the ADSL test due to the overhead being orders of magnitude smaller compared to the communication times.

If we compare the hand-optimised versus the automatically optimised results for the tests on the Ethernet network, there is a discrepancy of about 0.5 ms per call, which is mainly due to interpretive overhead from the Veneer virtual JVM and the

Table 1. Table of results for the aggregation optimisation applied to the MUD example

Time taken to execute look (ms)	Without optimisation	With optimisation	Speedup
Ethernet	5.4	5.8	0.93
ADSL	759.6	164.9	4.61

call-delaying/plan-building mechanism. However, this overhead remains constant, and is therefore all but invisible when operating across the Internet via ADSL, since it has much greater latencies and is subject to variations that could easily eclipse the 0.5 ms overhead.

6.2 The MUD Example

The MUD (Multi-User Domain) example [6] is a more realistic example that contains call aggregation possibilities. The main candidate for optimisation occurs in the look method of the MudClient class (shown in Figure 10), which retrieves a description of the room and its contents.

This benchmark has 7 aggregated calls with a modest payload — around 100 bytes of textual information in total. We have written a test harness that calls this routine repeatedly, recording the average time per call. Caching and server-side argument duplication have been enabled.

Results. As can be seen in Table 1, the MUD example shows a slight slowdown when operating with an Ethernet network, but a large speedup with operating over the Internet.

The speedup is lower than what we might expect from the vectors benchmark with a similar number of aggregated calls. This is partly because there is very little variable sharing occurring between calls — the sole instance is that between getServer and getMudName, where the result of getServer is used as a receiver for the getMudName method, and is then discarded without ever reaching the client. This is in contrast to the vectors example, where each call uses the result of its predecessor.

We show a breakdown of the time taken to execute the look method in Table 2. As can be seen, the majority of the time in both cases is spent in client-server communication. However, on the Ethernet network, the additional overheads on the client and server side are responsible for about a third of the overall time, while the proportion of time due to overheads is insignificant by comparison when using ADSL (since the overhead remains constant while the communication times have increased). If we could minimise the overheads, then we could achieve as much as a 50% speedup when operating on an Ethernet network.

7 Future Work

Some ideas we have for enhancing the RMI optimisation further are:

- By aggregating calls, we effectively build up knowledge regarding a small portion of the client. This knowledge may enable one to perform some inter-procedural

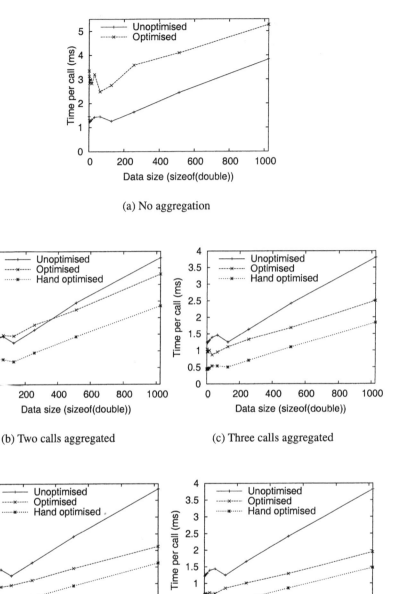

(a) No aggregation

(b) Two calls aggregated

(c) Three calls aggregated

(d) Four calls aggregated

(e) Five calls aggregated

Fig. 8. Results for the vector arithmetic example running on a Fast Ethernet network with varying levels of call aggregation

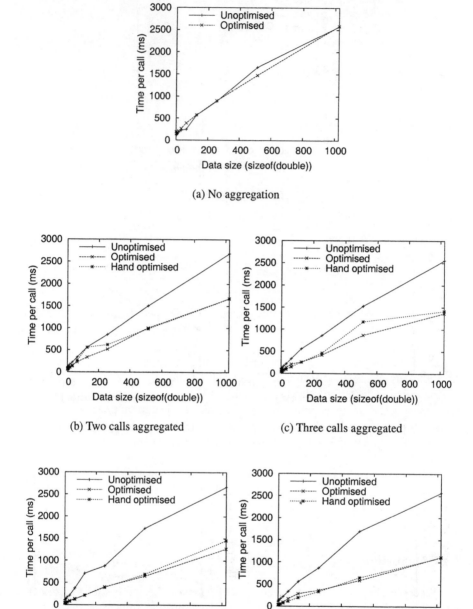

(a) No aggregation

(b) Two calls aggregated

(c) Three calls aggregated

(d) Four calls aggregated

(e) Five calls aggregated

Fig. 9. Results for the vector arithmetic example running over the Internet via a slow ADSL connection with varying levels of call aggregation

```
String mudname = p.getServer().getMudName();
String placename = p.getPlaceName();
String description = p.getDescription();
Vector things = p.getThings();
Vector names = p.getNames();
Vector exits = p.getExits();
```

Fig. 10. Code for the `look` method of the MUD example

Table 2. Table showing a percentage breakdown of the time spent executing 1000 iterations of the `look` method in the MUD example

Factor	Ethernet (%)	ADSL (%)
Remote methods	0.62	0.06
Uncached RMI communication	0.78	0.35
Cached RMI communication	60.51	97.92
Client-side overhead	20.60	0.91
Server-side overhead	15.21	0.61
Argument copying overhead	2.29	0.15

optimisations that are valid for that sequence of calls only by inlining the calls on the server side. The caching facility could serve to cache the optimised code along with the plan.

- As mentioned in Section 4.1, the mechanism to detect data-dependencies triggers too easily. We intend to strengthen this with the aid of escape analysis [17], such that copying the return value of RMI calls into other data structures does not trigger a force unless that structure is visible from outside the current thread of execution.
- At present, loops are effectively unrolled as a remote plan is built up. It may be possible to export the entire loop structure to the server in order to decrease the size of the remote plan.
- Instead of considering simple 'flat-types' to decide when to avoid copying arguments, we can extend the ideas to fully-fledged balloon-types [1] to allow an arbitrary level of type-nesting, provided there are no external references.

8 Conclusion

This paper presents an attempt to extend the scope of run-time optimisation to distributed systems. Conventional optimising compilers, and optimising virtual machines, focus on each node in a system individually. This work explores optimisations which span the nodes of a distributed system. This raises many issues — including security, the potential for failure, and run-time binding of clients to servers.

We have presented a prototype tool which optimises Java RMI applications. The tool is based on a powerful framework, essentially a 'virtual' JVM, which allows the run-time system to re-order blocks of application code subject to data dependence meta-data generated by static analysis. We use this to implement two optimisations of RMI applications: call aggregation, and call forwarding. These, in turn, lead to further optimisations, such as eliminating data transfer across the network for data passed between aggregated calls.

We present performance results for simple examples which demonstrate the performance potential for these optimisations. We also show preliminary results for a more substantial application, which demonstrate that optimisation opportunities do arise in real systems.

Our prototype implementation is based on a very powerful experimental framework, and this incurs some run-time overheads which we hope to reduce in time. There is enormous scope for more powerful analysis and more ambitious optimisations.

Acknowledgements

This project was funded by a studentship and grant from the Engineering and Physical Sciences Research Council (GR/R 15566).

References

1. Paulo Sérgio Almeida. Balloon types: Controlling sharing of state in data types. In *Proceedings of ECOOP '97*, volume 1241 of *Lecture Notes in Computer Science*, pages 32–59. Springer, June 1997.
2. Phillip Bogle and Barbara Liskov. Reducing cross domain call overhead using batched futures. In *Conference on Object-Oriented Programming Systems, Languages, and Applications*, pages 341–354, Portland OR (USA), 1994.
3. R. Christ, S. L. Halter, K. Lynne, S. Meizer, S. J. Munroe, and M. Pasch. SanFrancisco performance: A case study in performance of large-scale Java applications. *IBM Systems Journal*, 39(1), 2000.
4. Markus Dahm. Byte code engineering library manual. Available from http://jakarta.apache.org/bcel/manual.html.
5. John Eberhard and Anand Tripathi. Efficient object caching for distributed Java RMI applications. In *Middleware 2001, Proceedings*, volume 2218 of *Lecture Notes in Computer Science*, pages 15–35. Springer, November 2001.
6. David Flanagan. *Java Examples in a Nutshell*. O'Reilly UK, 2000.
7. Aniruddha Gokhale and Douglas C. Schmidt. Principles for optimizing CORBA internet inter-ORB protocol performance. In *31th Hawaii International Conference on System Sciences*, January 1998.
8. J. Gosling, B. Joy, G. Steele, and G. Bracha. *The Java Language Specification — Second Edition*. Addison-Wesley, 2000.
9. Object Management Group. The Common Object Request Broker: Architecture and specification v2.4.2, February 2001.
10. Vijaykumar Krishnaswamy, Dan Walther, Sumeer Bhola, Ethendranath Bommaiah, George Riley, Brad Topol, and Mustaque Ahamad. Efficient implementations of Java remote method invocation (RMI). In *Proc. of the 4th USENIX Conference on ObjectOriented Technologies and Systems (COOTS'98), 1998.*, pages 19–36, 1998.
11. Barbara Liskov and Liuba Shrira. Promises: Linguistic support for efficient asynchronous procedure calls in distributed systems. In *Proceedings of the SIGPLAN'88 conference on Programming Language Design and Implementation*, pages 260–267, 1988.

12. Sun Microsystems. RMI specification, available at http://java.sun.com/products/jdk/rmi/.
13. Christian Nester, Michael Phillippsen, and Bernhard Haumacher. A more efficient RMI for Java. In *ACM 1999 Java Grande Conference*, pages 152–159, June 1999.
14. Michael Philippsen, Bernhard Haumacher, and Christian Nester. More efficient serialization and RMI for Java. *Concurrency: Practice and Experience*, 12(7):495–518, 2000.
15. R. Raje, J. William, and M. Boyles. An Asynchronous Remote Method Invocation (ARMI) mechanism for Java. *Concurrency: Practice and Experience*, November 1997.
16. Raja Vallee-Rai, Phong Co, Etienne Gagnon, Laurie Hendren, Patrick Lam, and Vijay Sundaresan. Soot - a Java bytecode optimization framework. In *Proceedings of CASCON '99*, pages 125–135, 1999.
17. John Whaley and Martin Rinard. Compositional pointer and escape analysis for Java programs. In *Proceedings of the 14th Annual Conference on Object-Oriented Programming Systems, Languages and Applications*, volume 34 of *ACM SIGPLAN Notices*, pages 187–206, November 1999.

The JBoss Extensible Server

Marc Fleury[1] and Francisco Reverbel[2]

[1] The JBoss Group, LLC
Suite 211, 3500 Piedmont Road, NE, Atlanta, GA 30305, USA
marc@jboss.org
[2] Department of Computer Science, University of São Paulo
Rua do Matão 1010, São Paulo, SP 05508-900, Brazil
reverbel@ime.usp.br

Abstract. JBoss is an extensible, reflective, and dynamically reconfigurable Java application server. It includes a set of components that implement the J2EE specification, but its scope goes well beyond J2EE. JBoss is open-ended middleware, in the sense that users can extend middleware services by dynamically deploying new components into a running server. We believe that no other application server currently offers such a degree of extensibility. This paper focuses on two major architectural parts of JBoss: its middleware component model, based on the JMX model, and its meta-level architecture for generalized EJBs. The former requires a novel class loading model, which JBoss implements. The latter includes a powerful and flexible remote method invocation model, based on dynamic proxies, and relies on systematic usage of interceptors as aspect-oriented programming artifacts.

1 Introduction

Application servers are middleware platforms for development and deployment of component-based software. The application server offers an environment in which users can deploy *application components* — software components, developed either by the users themselves or by third-party providers, that correspond to server-side parts of distributed applications. Most application servers implement one of the industry standards currently adopted for server-side application components: Java 2 Enterprise Edition (J2EE), .NET, and the CORBA Component Model. Each of these standards defines a component model suitable for a class of application components[1].

There is no reason, however, to employ component-based techniques on user applications only. Researchers have presented compelling arguments for also exploiting these techniques *within* the middleware platform [4, 17]. We claim that application servers themselves can (and should) be built in a component-based way, out of dynamically deployable components that provide middleware services to application components. On such a server, extensible and dynamically

---

[1] J2EE actually encompasses two application component models: Servlets/JSP, for web components used by HTTP clients, and Enterprise JavaBeans (EJB), for business components used either by RMI clients or by local clients.

M. Endler and D. Schmidt (Eds.): Middleware 2003, LNCS 2672, pp. 344–373, 2003.
© IFIP International Federation for Information Processing 2003

reconfigurable, two general kinds of components can be deployed: middleware components and application components. In this approach, most of the "application server functionality" is actually realized by a set of middleware components deployed on a minimal server. Due to the requirement differences between middleware components and application components, multiple component models are likely to coexist in a component-based application server: a model for middleware components, plus one or more models for application components.

This paper discusses the design and implementation of JBoss, the extensible, reflective, and dynamically reconfigurable Java application server that pioneered the approach we have just outlined. The JBoss project is at the confluence of research areas such as component-based software development [28], reflective middleware [17], and aspect-oriented programming [8], all of them currently targeted by intense activity. It produced an open-source server whose download statistics [23] since January 2002 have been above 100,000 per month, and have exceeded 200,000 downloads in peak months. The JBoss server includes a set of middleware components that implement the J2EE specification [26], but its scope goes well beyond J2EE. JBoss is open-ended middleware, in the sense that users can extend middleware services by dynamically deploying new components into a running server. To the best of our knowledge, no other application server offers this degree of extensibility.

1.1 The Foundation

An emerging standard, the Java Management Extensions (JMX) [27] specification, provides the foundation for JBoss middleware components. JMX defines an architecture for dynamic management of resources (applications, systems, or network devices) distributed across a network.

In JMX, as in other management architectures, resources must be instrumented to become manageable. One instruments a resource by associating one or more management components with the resource. *Dynamic* management [20] means that one must be able to dynamically load, unload, and evolve these components, without stopping the applications, systems, or devices they instrument. These key requirements for a dynamic management architecture have similar counterparts in the more general field of adaptive middleware.

JMX was chosen as the basis of the JBoss component model for the following reasons: (i) it provides a lightweight environment in which components — as well as their class definitions — can be dynamically loaded and updated, (ii) it supports component introspection and component adaptation, (iii) it decouples components from their clients, allowing components to adapt, and their interfaces to evolve, while their clients are active, (iv) it can be used as a realization of the microkernel architectural pattern [2], to provide a minimal kernel that serves as a software bus for extensions, possibly developed by independent parties, and (v) its usage makes JBoss manageable through JMX-compliant applications.

1.2 The Building

On top of JMX, JBoss introduces its own model for middleware components, centered on the concept of *service component*. The JBoss service component model extends and refines the JMX model to address some issues beyond the scope of JMX: service lifecycle, dependencies between services, deployment and redeployment of services, dynamic configuration and reconfiguration of services, and component packaging.

Nearly all the "application server functionality" of JBoss is modularly provided by service components plugged into a JMX-based "server spine". Service components implement every key feature of J2EE: naming service, transaction management, security service, servlet/JSP support, EJB support, asynchronous messaging, database connection pooling, and IIOP support. They also implement important features not specified by J2EE, like clustering and fail-over.

Rather than attempting to present each of these subsystems, this paper focuses on the EJB subsystem, which we consider a particularly interesting use case for service components. JBoss supports a generalization of the EJB model by using service components as meta components. Its meta-level architecture for generalized EJBs is built upon four kinds of elements: invokers, containers, dynamic proxies, and interceptors. *Invokers* are service components that provide a general remote method invocation service over a variety of protocols. *Containers* are service components that enhance application component classes with predefined and packaged sets of aspect requirements. They provide server-side join points for aspects [16, 8] that crosscut the central concerns of multiple EJB components. *Dynamic proxies*, used as client stubs, provide similar join points at the client side. *Interceptors* implement crosscutting aspects at both sides. Containers, proxies, and interceptors are neither created nor manipulated by initiatives of the server spine, but by actions of an *EJB deployer*, which is a service component itself. In other words, EJB support is pluggable.

1.3 Organization of This Paper

The next section reviews the elements of the JMX architecture that are essential to the understanding of the JBoss service component model. Section 3 presents service components; Sect. 4 describes the meta-level architecture through which JBoss supports generalized EJB components; Sect. 5 summarizes the history of the JBoss project; Sect. 6 discusses ongoing and future work; Sect. 7 examines related work; and Sect. 8 presents our concluding remarks.

2 JMX Foundation

The JMX architecture is shown in Fig. 1. It consists of three levels: the instrumentation level, the agent level, and the distributed services level.

- The *instrumentation level* defines how to instrument resources so that they can be monitored and manipulated by (possibly remote) management applications. The instrumentation of a given resource is provided by one or more *managed beans* (*MBeans*), Java objects that conform to certain conventions and expose a *management interface* to their clients.

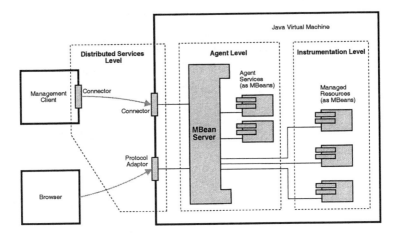

Fig. 1. The JMX architecture

- The *agent level* defines an agent that manages the set of instrumented resources within a Java virtual machine, in behalf of (possibly remote) management applications. The *JMX agent* consists of an in-process server, the *MBean server*, plus a standardized set of agent services: dynamic class loading, monitoring, timer service, and relation service. Agent services are implemented as MBeans; this makes them manageable through the MBean server, like user resources.
- The *distributed services level* specifies how management applications interact with remote JMX agents and how agent-to-agent communication takes place. It consists of *connectors* and *protocol adaptors*, implemented as MBeans. This level is not fully defined at the present phase of the JMX specification process. For information on connectors and protocol adaptors, see [19].

Together, the instrumentation and agent levels define an *in-process* component model. The MBean server provides a registry for JMX components (MBeans) and mediates any accesses to their management interfaces. At registration time, each MBean is assigned an *object name* that must be unique in the context of the MBean server. In-process clients use object names (rather than Java references) to refer to MBeans. To invoke a management operation[2] on an MBean, a local client (typically another MBean) uses the object name of the target MBean. It passes the object name as the first argument in a call to the MBean server's **invoke** method, whose declaration[3] is

```
Object invoke(ObjectName targetName,
              String operationName,
              Object[] params,
              String[] signature);
```

---

[2] *Management operations* are operations that belong to the MBean's management interface.

[3] For clarity, we have omitted any **throws** clauses from the method declarations presented in this paper.

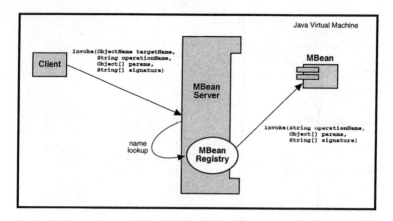

Fig. 2. Method invocation on a dynamic MBean

The MBean server looks up the object name in its registry and forwards the invocation to the target MBean. Figure 2 illustrates this process for a target MBean with a method quite similar to the MBean server's `invoke` method. As we will see shortly, this is the case of a dynamic MBean.

The MBean server introduces a level of indirection that decouples MBeans from their clients. In-process clients of an MBean do not need direct Java references to it. Moreover, clients need no information on the MBean's Java class, nor do they need information (not even at runtime) on the Java interfaces the MBean implements. All they need is the MBean's object name, plus knowledge (possibly obtained at runtime) of its management interface. (We have not yet discussed what would be the management interface of an MBean, but the preceding assertions imply that it does not necessarily correspond to a Java interface.) This very simple arrangement favors adaptation: the absence of references to an MBean scattered across its clients facilitates the replacement of that MBean; the absence of client knowledge about its class and its Java interfaces enables dynamic changes both to the implementation and to the management interface of the MBean.

The *management interface* of an MBean consists of four parts: (i) management attributes, whose values are accessible to clients through the MBean server; (ii) management operations, which clients can invoke through the MBean server; (iii) notifications emitted by the MBean and delivered to registered listeners; (iv) constructors, defined by the MBean's Java class.

2.1 Dynamic MBeans and Standard MBeans

JMX supports two kinds of MBeans,[4] which differ on how they expose to the MBean server their management attributes and their management operations.

---

[4] The JMX specification uses the expression "types of MBeans". We prefer "kinds of MBeans", to avoid confusion with Java types.

```
interface DynamicMBean {
    Object getAttribute(String attrName);
    AttributeList getAttributes(String[] attrNames);
    void setAttribute(Attribute attr);
    AttributeList setAttributes(AttributeList attrs);
    Object invoke(String opName, Object[] params, String[] signature);
    MBeanInfo getMBeanInfo();
}
```

Fig. 3. The DynamicMBean interface

One kind of MBean (the so-called *dynamic* kind) implements a predefined Java interface, regardless of its management interface, and relies on metadata to specify its management interface. The other kind (the so-called *standard* kind) implements a Java interface defined after — and determined by — the MBean's management interface. The kind of an MBean is an implementation detail hidden from clients, which access both kinds of MBeans exactly in the same way.

Dynamic MBeans. By implementing the interface shown in Fig. 3, a *dynamic MBean* provides generic methods for attribute access and operation invocation.

The method getMBeanInfo() returns a self-description of the MBean. The metadata class MBeanInfo supports *MBean introspection*, i.e., from an MBeanInfo instance one can obtain complete information about the management interface of the MBean described by that instance: attribute names and types, operation names and signatures, notification types, Java class name, and Java constructor signatures. The management attributes and operations supported by a dynamic MBean do not necessarily correspond to Java fields and methods, nor do they need to be associated with methods of some particular Java interface implemented by that MBean. They are specified solely by the dynamic MBean's self-description.

Standard MBeans. A *standard MBean* exposes its management attributes and operations by implementing a Java interface named after the MBean's Java class, with the suffix MBean. This interface follows JavaBean-like rules to represent those attributes and operations: it must have a get method for each readable attribute, a set method for each writable attribute, and an additional method for each operation.

As an example, a standard MBean of class Foo must implement a Java interface named FooMBean, whose definition is determined by the MBean's management interface. Suppose the management interface has one attribute and one operation: an integer-valued read/write attribute, whose name is "Count", and an operation named "doSomething", which receives a long parameter and returns a double value. Then FooMBean must be the following Java interface:

```
interface MBeanServer {
    ObjectInstance registerMBean(Object object, ObjectName name);
    void unregisterMBean(ObjectName name);
    ...
    Object getAttribute(ObjectName name, String attrName);
    AttributeList getAttributes(ObjectName name, String[] attrNames);
    void setAttribute(ObjectName name, Attribute attr);
    AttributeList setAttributes(ObjectName name, AttributeList attrs);
    Object invoke(ObjectName name, String opName,
                  Object[] params, String[] signature);
    MBeanInfo getMBeanInfo(ObjectName name);
}
```

Fig. 4. The MBeanServer interface

```
interface FooMBean {
    int getCount();
    void setCount(int value);
    double doSomething(long param);
}
```

Why Two Kinds of MBeans? Standard MBeans are easier to implement, because they relieve their writers from the task of building metadata instances to describe management interfaces. On the other hand, dynamic MBeans are more flexible, as the definitions of their management interfaces can be postponed until runtime. Both kinds of MBeans support some form of evolution of management interfaces. In the case of a standard MBean, however, evolution requires object replacement: one must bind to the MBean's object name an instance of another Java class. Dynamic MBeans support evolution *without* object replacement.

2.2   The MBean Server

The MBeanServer interface appears in Fig. 4. The first two methods shown are a manifestation of the MBean server's role as a registry for MBeans. The remaining ones form a group that parallels the interface DynamicMBean; each of them receives as its first parameter an ObjectName that specifies the target MBean. For brevity, we have omitted several methods, including the ones for MBean creation and those related with JMX notifications.

Clients access MBeans through the MBean server, using its DynamicMBean-like methods. The server's getMBeanInfo method returns metadata that describes the management interface of the target MBean, regardless of kind. Its return value is either a dynamic MBean's self-description or an MBeanInfo instance constructed by the server, most likely at MBean registration time. In the latter case, the MBeanInfo instance contains information obtained through

Java introspection on the *ClassName*MBean interface implemented by a standard MBean whose class is *ClassName*.

The methods for attribute access and operation invocation act differently depending on the kind of the target MBean. If the target is a dynamic MBean, the MBean server simply forwards the invocation to the target MBean through the corresponding method of the DynamicMBean interface. If the target is a standard MBean, the MBean server converts the invocation into a suitable call to the target's *ClassName*MBean interface. As an example, the invocation

```
mbeanServer.getAttribute(targetName, "Count");
```

would be converted into the invocation

```
targetMBean.getCount();
```

Different MBean server implementations may employ different approaches to do such conversions. The simplest approach uses the Java reflection API; in this case the getCount() invocation above would be performed as a reflective call to the *ClassName*MBean interface. The MBean server included in JBoss takes another approach: it avoids the extra cost of reflective calls by applying byte code generation techniques [5]. At MBean registration time, the MBean server performs Java introspection on the *ClassName*MBean interface implemented by a standard MBean and generates the class of a suitable object adapter [11]. The generated adapter implements the DynamicMBean interface and issues non-reflective calls to methods of the *ClassName*MBean interface.

2.3 Reflection in JMX

JMX can be regarded as a reflective architecture. The method getMBeanInfo supports MBean introspection. Object replacement is a simple yet effective form of adaptation at the MBean level: clients refer to MBeans by object names, so the perceived behavior of any MBean can be changed by object replacement. Other forms of adaptation are possible for dynamic MBeans. The agent level includes a dynamic class loading service that facilitates object replacement; this service allows MBeans to be instantiated using new Java classes loaded from remote servers.

3 Service Components

JMX does not include mechanisms for managing dependencies between MBeans, nor does it define a concept of service lifecycle for MBeans. Packaging and deployment of components are also out of the scope of the JMX specification. JBoss addresses all these issues with the notions of service MBean and deployable MBean. *Service MBeans* (also called *service components*) are MBeans whose management interfaces include service lifecycle operations. *Deployable MBeans* (also called *deployable services*), a JBoss-specific extension to JMX, are service

MBeans packaged according to EJB-like conventions, in deployment units called *service archives* (SARs). A service archive contains class files for one or more deployable services, plus a *service descriptor*, which conveys information needed at deployment time.

3.1   Service Lifecycle

A service component may be in the *stopped state* or in the *active state*. At each state transition, one of the following lifecycle operations is invoked on the service MBean:

- `create` — invoked once on each service MBean, after the receiver was created and registered with the MBean server. This operation tells the receiver to complete its initialization and places it in the stopped state.
- `start` — takes a service MBean from the stopped state to the active state. A `start` invocation tells the receiver to do whatever it needs to become fully operational.
- `stop` — takes a service MBean from the active state to the stopped state. A `stop` invocation tells the receiver to undo any actions it took within the `start` operation.
- `destroy` — tells the receiver to clean up its resources. This operation is invoked once on each service MBean, when the receiver is in the stopped state and is about to be unregistered from the MBean server.

The lifecycle operations supported by a service component should be exposed in its management interface. A service MBean is not required to support all four lifecycle operations. For instance, a component with no resources that require clean up does not need a `destroy` operation in its management interface. The set of lifecycle operations in a component's management interface indicates which service lifecycle events are relevant to the component.

3.2   Service Descriptors

Deployable MBeans are service MBeans packaged together with deployment information. Every service archive includes a *service descriptor*, an XML file that contains an `mbean` element for each service component in that deployment unit. An `mbean` element specifies the following information: (*i*) Java class and object name of a deployable MBean, (*ii*) initial values for (some) management attributes of the MBean, and (*iii*) dependencies from the MBean to other deployable MBeans.

Figure 5 shows a service descriptor for a deployment unit with five deployable services. The XML attributes `code` and `name` are mandatory within `mbean` elements; they specify the MBean's class and its object name[5]. The nested `attribute` elements are optional; each such element defines the initial value

---

[5] Strings such as `"jboss:service=WebService"` and `"jboss:service=XidFactory"` contain textual representations of JMX `ObjectNames`.

```
<server>

  <!-- Web server for class loading -->
  <mbean code="org.jboss.web.WebService"
         name="jboss:service=WebService">
    <attribute name="Port">8083</attribute>
    <attribute name="DownloadServerClasses">true</attribute>
  </mbean>

  <!-- XID factory -->
  <mbean code="org.jboss.tm.XidFactory"
         name="jboss:service=XidFactory">
    <attribute name="Pad">true</attribute>
  </mbean>

  <!-- Transaction manager -->
  <mbean code="org.jboss.tm.TransactionManagerService"
         name="jboss:service=TransactionManager">
    <attribute name="TransactionTimeout">300</attribute>
    <depends optional-attribute-name="XidFactory">
            jboss:service=XidFactory</depends>
  </mbean>

  <!-- EJB deployer -->
  <mbean code="org.jboss.ejb.EJBDeployer"
         name="jboss.ejb:service=EJBDeployer">
    <attribute name="VerifyDeployments">true</attribute>
    <attribute name="ValidateDTDs">false</attribute>
    <attribute name="VerifierVerbose">true</attribute>
    <depends>jboss:service=TransactionManager</depends>
    <depends>jboss:service=WebService</depends>
  </mbean>

  <!-- RMI/JRMP invoker -->
  <mbean code="org.jboss.invocation.jrmp.server.JRMPInvoker"
         name="jboss:service=invoker,type=jrmp">
    <attribute name="RMIObjectPort">4444</attribute>
    <depends>jboss:service=TransactionManager</depends>
  </mbean>

</server>
```

Fig. 5. Example of service descriptor file

for a writable attribute in the management interface of the MBean. The nested
depends elements, also optional, specify dependencies from the enclosing MBean
to the MBeans whose object names appear within those elements. The service

descriptor in Fig. 5 specifies dependencies from the transaction manager to the XID factory, from the EJB deployer to the web server, from the EJB deployer to the transaction manager, and from the RMI/JRMP invoker to the transaction manager.

The optional XML attribute `optional-attribute-name`, which appears in one of the `depends` elements in Fig. 5, specifies the name of a writable attribute in the management interface of the enclosing MBean. This writable attribute will be set to the object name enclosed by the `depends` element. In other words, the element

```
<depends optional-attribute-name="SomeAttrName">SomeObjName</depends>
```

is equivalent to the elements

```
<depends>SomeObjName</depends>
<attribute name="SomeAttrName">SomeObjName</attribute>
```

3.3   Dependency Management

JBoss employs a variant of the component configurator pattern [22] to control the lifecycle of deployable services. Deployments of SAR files with service MBeans are handled by a `SARDeployer`, which also acts as a component configurator. A `ServiceController` plays the role of component repository, keeps track of the dependencies between deployable MBeans, and ensures that components with unsatisfied dependencies are disallowed to enter (or to remain in) the active state. The `SARDeployer` and the `ServiceController` collaborate to invoke lifecycle operations on deployable MBeans. They enforce the following protocol:

- When the `create` operation is invoked on a deployable MBean, all deployable MBeans on which the receiver depends have also had their `create` operations invoked. Moreover, the receiver's management attributes have already had their values set to the ones specified in the service descriptor. At this point the target MBean can check if required resources exist. It cannot yet use other deployable MBeans, which are not guaranteed to be operational until they have received `start` invocations.
- When the `start` operation is invoked on a deployable MBean, all deployable MBeans on which the receiver depends have also had their `start` operations invoked.
- When the `stop` operation is invoked on a deployable MBean, all deployable MBeans that depend on the receiver have also had their `stop` operations invoked.
- When the `destroy` operation is invoked on a deployable MBean, all deployable MBeans that depend on the receiver have also had their `destroy` operations invoked.

Deployment/undeployment events drive the lifecycle of deployable services. In response to these events, the `ServiceController` invokes (through the MBean server) service lifecycle operations on deployable MBeans. It issues `create` invocations to ensure that all services on which a given service depends on are created before the service is created, it issues `destroy` invocations to ensure that all services that depend on a given service are destroyed before the service is destroyed, etc.

A word on the intended usage of lifecycle operations on deployable MBeans: `start` and `stop` are expected to be lighter than `create` and `destroy`. One should think of `create` as the (re)configuration hook invoked when a component is (re)deployed, of `destroy` as the clean up hook called when a component is undeployed, and of `stop/start` as suspend/resume operations that are also performed at the very beginning of every undeployment (`stop`) or at the very end of every deployment (`start`).

3.4 Deployment and Undeployment

Deployable MBeans are not the only kind of deployable component that JBoss supports. Besides SARs with deployable MBeans, other types of deployment units are supported as well: plain JAR files with Java classes to be loaded into the server, resource archives (RARs) with resource adapter components, EJB-JARs with EJB components, web application archives (WARs) with servlet/JSP components, and enterprise application archives (EARs) with multi-tier applications.

A `MainDeployer` handles all deployable units by delegating the actual deployment tasks to sub-deployers specific to the various kinds of components: `SARDeployer`, `JARDeployer`, `EJBDeployer`, etc. The set of sub-deployers (and hence the set of deployment units supported) is open-ended. Sub-deployers are service MBeans that register themselves with the `MainDeployer`, which is also a service MBean. The two most fundamental sub-deployers are the `JARDeployer` and the `SARDeployer`. The `MainDeployer`, the `JARDeployer` and the `SARDeployer` are not deployable components: they are created and activated directly by the JBoss boot method. All other sub-deployers are deployable MBeans. This means, for instance, that EJB support (the ability of deploying EJB components into the application server) and servlet/JSP support (the ability of deploying web components) are dynamically deployable features themselves.

The `MainDeployer`'s management interface corresponds to the Java interface partly shown in Fig. 6. The first three operations deal with sub-deployers: registration, unregistration, and listing. The following four operations deal with deployable units of any kind: deployment and undeployment of a unit specified by an URL, check for the presence of a given unit deployed into the server, and listing of all units deployed into the server. Any of the `MainDeployer`'s operations can be invoked from management clients such as the JBoss management console, which is accessible through a web browser, or from remote management applications that access the MBean server through connectors. Moreover, the URL parameter expected by some operations may refer to a deployable unit located at some remote host. If a remote URL is passed to `deploy` operation, a remote

```
interface MainDeployerMBean extends ServiceMBean {
    void addDeployer(SubDeployer deployer);
    void removeDeployer(SubDeployer deployer);
    Collection listDeployers();
    void deploy(URL url);
    void undeploy(URL url);
    boolean isDeployed(URL url);
    Collection listDeployed();
    ...
}
```

Fig. 6. Management interface of the `MainDeployer`

unit will be downloaded to the application server host and then dynamically deployed into JBoss.

Hot Deployment. Deployable components can be conveniently deployed into JBoss simply by dropping deployment units into a well-known directory. This feature is called *hot deployment*. A `DeploymentScanner` monitors the files in that directory and handles every deployment unit found. Not surprisingly, the `DeploymentScanner` is a deployable MBean itself. A thread started by this MBean repeatedly scans the deployment directory and invokes the `MainDeployer` whenever it detects a change. The addition of a new file causes a `deploy` invocation, the removal of an existing file causes an `undeploy` invocation, and a change to an existing file change causes a redeploy (`undeploy` followed by `deploy`) operation.

Class Visibility. We say that a class is *visible* within a server either if the class is already loaded in the server's virtual machine or if it is loadable through the class loading scheme used by the server. For instance, a class in the system classpath might not be loaded, but it is certainly visible.

Unlike servers in which class visibility is statically provided by the system class loader, used to load classes once and for all, JBoss allows visible classes to vary over time. Hot deployment establishes a causal connection from the presence of deployment units in the deployment directory to the visibility, within the server, of the classes contained in those deployment units[6]. If the contents of the deployment directory change, then the set of classes that are visible within the server will also change. Modifications to the deployment directory can cause a given (fully qualified) class name to be associated with different class types at different points in time.

Recall that a Java class type is uniquely determined by the combination of a class loader and a fully qualified class name [18]. In response to changes in the

---

[6] The deployment directory is not the only factor that determines class visibility, which is affected by direct calls to the `MainDeployer` as well.

deployment directory, JBoss instantiates class loaders to dynamically define new class types, which may correspond to "new versions" of previously defined class types.

3.5 Class Loading Issues

A number of Java application servers support some form of dynamic deployment for *application* components. They use variants of a class loading approach that could be called *loader-per-deployment* [21, 14]. A separate class loader, constructed at deployment time and bound to a deployment unit, is assigned to each deployment[7]. This class loader, usually a `java.net.URLClassLoader`, loads class files from the deployment unit it is bound to.

The loader-per-deployment scheme creates a separate namespace for each set of classes loaded from some deployment unit. Components loaded from different deployment units may contain classes with the same name, but these classes will be treated as different types by the Java virtual machine [18]. This approach avoids class clashes between deployment units, but hinders interactions between separately deployed parts. Even though separate namespaces might be convenient for application components, we argue that they are ill-suited for the dynamically deployable parts of an extensible system such as JBoss.

Problems with Hierarchical Loader-per-Deployment Approaches. In order to interact within a Java virtual machine, components need to share non-system classes. The class loader parent delegation model[8] implies that any set of interacting components must be loaded by a set of class loaders with a common ancestor, which loads the collection of classes shared among all those components. Components that share non-system classes require a hierarchical deployment process, in which shared class files are somehow deployed before the components that will share them. Such a process would correspond to a "deployment tree" rooted at the set of shared class files. This approach, however, fosters replication of class files across deployment trees associated with independent (non-interacting) sets of components. Most importantly, experience with earlier versions of JBoss has shown us that hierarchical loader-per-deployment schemes are cumbersome in dynamic environments, specially in the presence of interactions between middleware components developed by different teams.

If a set of components needs to share some non-system class C, then there are dependencies from the component that provides class C to all other components in the set. Component dependencies form a directed acyclic graph, which

---

[7] This description applies to "simple" deployment units (EJB-JARs or WARs). In the case of a "composite" deployment unit (EAR) with multiple EJB and web modules, more than one class loader will be actually created. See [14] for details.

[8] In this model [12], every class loader has a parent class loader. Whenever a class loader is asked to load a class, it first delegates the request to its parent. If the parent fails to load the class, then the class loader attempts to perform the task itself.

in general cannot be reduced to a deployment tree. Moreover, dependencies may change over time, as components are updated. So even if a given set of components currently has a rooted tree as its dependency graph, nothing ensures that future updates to the components will not break the hierarchic structure of that graph. A non-hierarchical approach to class loading is needed to accommodate the general nature of component dependencies.

The J2EE Solution. In spite of their shortcomings, loader-per-deployment schemes are used for application components, by application servers that forbid changes to the individual parts of an application. A component-based application (a complete set of interacting parts) must be deployed as a whole into such a system, so that its components can be loaded by the same class loader or by a suitable class loader hierarchy. Packing together parts that work together is still considered an acceptable rule for application scenarios; it is actually the standard J2EE practice.

3.6   Unified Class Loaders

JBoss employs a new class loader architecture that facilitates sharing of classes across deployment units. A collection of *unified class loaders* acts as a single class loader, which places into a single namespace all classes it loads. Rather than creating its own namespace, each unified class loader adds `Class` objects to a flat namespace shared among all unified class loaders. This is a significant departure from the hierarchical class loading model introduced in JDK 1.2[9].

Instances of `UnifiedClassLoader`, a subclass of `java.net.URLClassLoader`, are registered with a `UnifiedLoaderRepository` MBean. This collection of class loaders behaves like a special kind of `java.net.URLClassLoader` that allows its array of URLs to be updated at any time[10]. To add an URL, create a new `UnifiedClassLoader` for the URL, and register the class loader with the repository. To remove an URL, remove the corresponding `UnifiedClassLoader` from the repository. To load classes, use any of the `UnifiedClassLoaders` in the repository. They are all equivalent and share a single namespace.

Conceptual Description. The class loading strategy is conceptually very simple. The unified loader repository maintains loaded classes in a cache implemented by two hash maps: one that maps class names into `Class` objects, and another that maps class loaders into sets of class names. When a unified class loader is asked to load a class, it first looks at the repository it is registered with and checks if the class is already in the repository's cache. If the class is not

---

[9] JBoss adds `Class` objects to a flat namespace by default, but is also supports "scoped class loading", which creates new namespaces, to allow for concurrent versioning of EAR deployment units. By explicitly specifying scoped class loading, users can have different versions of the same components running simultaneously into a server.

[10] A `java.net.URLClassLoader` has a constant array of URLs, specified by a constructor parameter, and loads classes from these URLs.

cached, the unified class loader attempts to load a class file from its URL. In case it does not find the class file, it iterates through the class loaders registered with the repository until one of them loads the class file. The repository updates its cache whenever a class file is loaded by some unified class loader. On the removal of a class loader from the repository, all classes loaded by the class loader should be removed from the repository's cache. The map from class loaders to sets of class names serves this purpose.

Locking Issues. The actual implementation of unified class loaders, however, is complicated by locking issues. In an attempt to ensure that concurrent threads never load the same class more than once, Java virtual machines typically lock a class loader while the loader is loading a class[11]. Only one thread at a time is allowed to load a class using a given class loader. Under such locking policy, deadlock would occur if the conceptual class loading strategy just described were literally translated into a naive implementation. Suppose that a thread t_1 uses some unified class loader l_1 to load a class c_1 and, at the same time, a thread t_2 uses some unified class loader l_2 to load a class c_2. Assume that neither c_1 nor c_2 is in the repository's cache. Moreover, suppose that the class file for c_1 is in l_2's URL and the class file for c_2 is in l_1's URL. A naive implementation of unified class loaders would deadlock in this scenario.

Deadlock Avoidance. The JBoss implementation avoids deadlocks by using a task scheduler that allocates class loading tasks to a pool of cooperating threads whose elements are temporary owners of unified class loaders. A thread is in the pool as long as it holds some unified class loader's monitor lock. By repeatedly calling the task scheduler to get its next task, each such thread sequentially processes all class loading tasks that must be handled by its unified class loader, including the ones initiated by other threads[12].

---

[11] Depending on the class loaders involved, locking class loaders might actually be a futile attempt to prevent concurrent threads from loading a class more than once. In the case of unified class loaders, locks on class loaders are superfluous and not effective, for the repository is what needs to be locked to ensure that no class gets loaded twice. There should be a way to tell the Java virtual machine not to lock these class loaders. This would be possible if the class loading method directly called by Sun's virtual machines — the method `loadClassInternal` — were not defined as private and synchronized in class `java.lang.ClassLoader`. The method `loadClassInternal` should be protected, rather than private, so that specialized subclasses of `ClassLoader` (such as `UnifiedClassLoader`) could redefine it with no synchronization. With respect to this issue, a member of the JBoss team has filed with Sun a bug report [15] against the Java runtime environment.

[12] If there were a way to tell the Java virtual machine not to lock unified class loaders, then there would be no need for such a deadlock avoidance scheme. Explicit task scheduling appears here merely as an elaborate trick through which JBoss circumvents the Java bug mentioned in the preceding footnote.

3.7   Dynamic Proxy Usage

Since JDK 1.3, the Java reflection API supports a limited form of program adaptation: the late definition of certain object adapter classes called *dynamic proxy* classes. A program can dynamically define a proxy class that implements given interfaces by delegating all method invocations to a generic *invocation handler*, through a type-independent interface. A dynamic proxy instance can be regarded as an object adapter [11] that converts the type-independent interface of its invocation handler into a list of interfaces specified at runtime.

Close interplay takes place between application components, whose interfaces are not known until runtime, and the middleware components that make up the JBoss server. Most of the time such collaboration happens transparently with respect to application components, which perceive themselves as interacting with each other and only occasionally take explicit actions to request middleware services. Enabling transparent collaboration between application components and middleware components, within a platform written in a strongly-typed language like Java, poses a problem: the platform must somehow bridge the gap between the interfaces that are application-specific and those exposed by middleware components. Many application servers bridge this gap with classes statically generated through compilation-based approaches, at the expense of flexibility and developer friendliness. Nevertheless, this is not an option for a system intended to support dynamic deployment of application components whose interfaces are not known in advance. Dynamic proxies are crucially important for JBoss because they can bridge that gap at runtime.

The Dynamic Stub Idiom. Recall how Java RMI handles parameter and return value passing: serializable types are normally passed by value, remote types are normally passed by reference. A *serializable type* is either a primitive type or an instance of a class that implements `java.io.Serializable` or `java.io.Externalizable`. Serialized types are normally passed to other virtual machines in serialized form. A *remote type* is an instance of a class that implements `java.rmi.Remote`. When an RMI parameter or return value is a remote type, a stub for the remote object is normally passed instead of the object.

Note the occurrences of the adverb "normally" in the preceding paragraph. What happens in the case of a remote object that is also serializable? If the object has not been exported (made available to remote clients) through the RMI system , then it will be passed by value. Passing remote objects by value, in serialized form, allows the creation of *custom stubs*. Rather than using stubs generated by RMI tools, a programmer can create his own stub objects, which interact over a *custom protocol* with the remote objects that they represent. Custom stubs should be remote (but not exported) and serializable, so they are passed by value to other virtual machines.

Besides interacting with the remote objects they represent, custom stubs must also implement the application-specific interfaces of these objects. Rather than writing (or creating a tool that generates) a custom stub class for every application interface, one can use dynamic proxies as custom stubs. This is the *dynamic stub idiom*. A dynamic proxy implements the interfaces expected by the application. The invocation handler is the "customized" part of the stub: it uses a custom protocol to interact with the remote object represented by the stub. Dynamic stubs are typically created at the server side and passed by value to other virtual machines. This is possible because dynamic proxy instances are serializable, provided that their invocation handlers are serializable. Section 4.2 describes the key role of dynamic stubs in JBoss.

Conversion of Management Interfaces into Java Interfaces. This is a more prosaic (and very common) usage of dynamic proxies in JBoss. In this use case, a dynamic proxy instance, associated with a given MBean, implements a Java interface whose methods correspond to (possibly a subset of) the MBean's management interface. The proxy has an invocation handler that knows the MBean's object name and forwards method invocations to the MBean, through the MBean server.

4   Meta-level Architecture for Generalized EJBs

The conceptual definition of the EJB architecture [25] relies strongly on the abstract notion of an *EJB container*. In JBoss, a set of meta-level components works together to implement this conceptual abstraction. A *generalized EJB container* is a set of pluggable aspects that can be selected and changed by users. Extended EJB functionality is supported by a meta-level architecture whose central features are:

- usage of MBeans as meta-level components that support and manage base-level EJB[13] components;
- a uniform model for reifying base-level method invocations;
- a remote method invocation model based on dynamic proxies;
- usage of a variant of the interceptor pattern [22] as an aspect-oriented programming [16, 8] technique.

In what follows, we will adopt an EJB standpoint and consider that the base level consists of EJB components. Accordingly, we will refer to EJB interfaces as base-level interfaces. From this perspective, MBeans belong to the meta level, and their management interfaces are meta-level interfaces. Figure 7 shows the meta-level architecture whose elements will be discussed in the following subsections.

4.1   Reified Method Invocations

Interactions between base-level components follow a variant of the message reification model [9]. Inter-component method invocations performed at the base

---

[13] For brevity, we refer to our base-level components simply as EJBs, but it will shortly become clear that they are actually generalized EJBs.

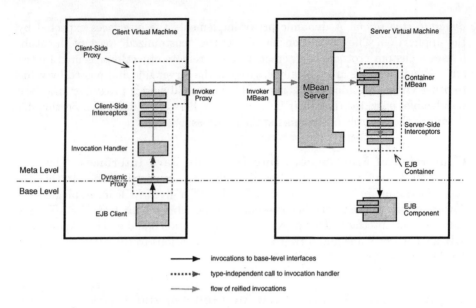

Fig. 7. Meta-level architecture for EJB

level are reified by special `Invocation` objects. Dynamic proxies receive all EJB invocations executed by EJB clients (which may be EJBs themselves) and shift those invocations up to the meta level, by transparently converting them into `Invocation` objects[14].

The gray arrows in Fig. 7 show the flow of reified invocations. The invocation handler creates a reified invocation whenever a method call is issued on the client-side proxy. After traversing a chain of *client-side interceptors*, each reified invocation is sent by an *invoker proxy* to an *invoker MBean* at the server-side, where it is routed through the *container MBean* associated with the target EJB.

Figure 8 lists the fields of a reified invocation. The `objectName` field identifies a container MBean. The `method` and `args` fields specify a method call to be performed on the base-level component associated with that container. The `invocationContext` conveys information that is common to all invocations performed through the same (base-level) object reference. It always includes information on whether the invocation target in an `EJBHome` or an `EJBObject`, and may also specify the id of a particular `EJBObject` instance[15]. Arbitrary invocation-specific information, typically related with non-functional aspects (e.g., security and transactions), is carried within the payload fields.

Note that the class `Invocation` is not serializable, as it has a non-serializable `java.lang.reflect.Method` field. `MarshalledInvocation`, an externalizable

---

[14] The `Invocation` objects are actually created by the invocation handlers of these dynamic proxies.

[15] There is an one-to-one relationship between deployed EJB components and container MBeans, but an EJB component usually has many `EJBObject` instances.

```
class Invocation {
    Object objectName;
    java.lang.reflect.Method method;
    Object[] args;
    InvocationContext invocationContext;
    java.util.Map payload;
    java.util.Map as_is_payload;    // marshalled "as is"
    java.util.Map transient_payload; // not sent to other VMs
    ... //  methods not shown
}
```

Fig. 8. Class that reifies method invocations

subclass of `Invocation`, serves the purpose of allowing reified invocations to be sent across virtual machine boundaries.

No interface along the reified invocation path (see Fig. 7) depends on base-level types: each element in that path provides a Java method or a management operation that takes an `Invocation` parameter. `Invocations` are eventually passed as parameters to an `invoke` operation exposed by all container MBeans:

```
mbeanServer.invoke(
    invocation.getObjectName(),              // target container
    "invoke",                                // operation name
    new Object[] { invocation },             // parameters
    new String[] {                           // parameter types
        "org.jboss.invocation.Invocation"
    }
);
```

Calls to a container's `invoke` operation go through the MBean server's `invoke` method, because the `invoke` operation belongs to the container's management interface.

4.2   Remote Invocation Architecture

A powerful and flexible architecture supports remote method invocations to EJB components deployed in JBoss. The invoker architecture is based on the following points:

- Even though EJB clients expect typed and application-specific interfaces, EJB containers expose a type-independent management operation (`invoke`), which acts as a meta-level gateway to their EJB components. An *invoker* makes this operation accessible to remote clients through some request/response protocol, such as JRMP, IIOP, HTTP or SOAP.

```
interface Invoker extends javax.rmi.Remote {
    String getServerHostName();
    Object invoke(Invocation invocation);
}
```

Fig. 9. Generic invocation interface

- Client-side stubs (or client-side proxies) are dynamic proxy instances that convert calls to the typed interfaces seen by clients into `invoke` calls on remote invokers.
- Each client-side proxy has a serializable invocation handler that performs remote calls on a given invoker, over the protocol supported by the invoker.
- Client-side proxies and their invocation handlers are instantiated by the server and dynamically sent out to clients as serialized objects.

The pattern just outlined is independent of the request/response protocol supported by the invoker. Client-side knowledge of this protocol is confined within the invocation handlers that clients dynamically retrieve from the server along with serialized proxies.

Invokers. An invoker is a service MBean that acts as a protocol-specific gateway, at the meta level, to multiple EJB containers in the JBoss server. All invokers currently available in JBoss are deployable services implemented as standard MBeans. Every invoker exposes an `invoke` method to remote clients. This method takes an `Invocation` parameter and forwards the reified invocation to the container MBean specified by the invocation's `objectName` field.

Figure 9 shows the remote invocation interface exposed by the JRMP invoker, which makes its `invoke` method available to RMI/JRMP clients. Other invokers implement either this interface or very similar ones.

Client-Side Proxies. In order to access an EJB component deployed into a JBoss server, a client must have a reference to a client-side proxy that represents the component. Local calls to application-specific methods are translated by the client-side proxy into `invoke` calls on a remote invoker object. To perform this translation, the proxy — or, more precisely, its invocation handler — must *know* the remote invoker. The exact meaning of "knowing the remote invoker" depends on the protocol over which the proxy interacts with the remote invoker. In the case of a client-side proxy associated with a JRMP invoker, that phrase means "holding an RMI/JRMP reference to the JRMP invoker". For client-side proxies associated with other invokers, the same phrase takes other meanings, such as "knowing the HTTP invoker's URL", or "having a CORBA IOR that references the IIOP invoker".

Invoker Proxies. Everything that is protocol-specific within a client-side proxy is encapsulated within an *invoker proxy*. Regardless of the protocol it supports, each invocation handler holds a local reference to an invoker proxy that implements the `Invoker` interface shown in Fig. 9 [16]. The invoker proxy interacts with a remote invoker, sending `Invocations` and receiving results over a given protocol. Invoker proxies provide a good level of homogeneity to all client-side proxies.

The invoker proxy for a given protocol is created at the server side and bound to a name in a well-known JNDI context. Since invoker proxies are externalizable, they can be sent out to clients along with serialized client-side proxies. Both the creation and the JNDI registration of a given protocol's invoker proxy (e.g., a `JRMPInvokerProxy`) are performed within the `create` operation of the invoker MBean for that protocol (e.g., within the `create` operation of the `JRMPInvoker` service component.)

Local Invocations. In-process calls between components deployed in the same server are optimally handled by a *local invoker* that avoids the cost of marshaling `Invocations`. Local invocations go through client-side proxies and are reified like remote invocations, but in the local case a client-side proxy contains the local invoker itself, not an invoker proxy. Unlike the other invokers, which afford call-by-value semantics, the local invoker provides call-by-reference semantics.

The IIOP Case. For interoperability with CORBA clients written in other languages, IIOP is treated as a special case in JBoss. Even though we have implemented and tested an experimental IIOP invoker that strictly follows the "JBoss invoker pattern", this is *not* the IIOP invoker included in JBoss distributions.

Non-Java clients expect application-specific interfaces to be exposed via IIOP, because they use IDL-generated stubs. In other words, they send out IIOP requests whose operation fields contain application-specific verbs. The invoker pattern, however, leads to an IIOP invoker that implements an IDL interface similar to the Java interface in Fig. 9. Such an invoker could not possibly interoperate with CORBA clients written in other languages, as it would expect IIOP requests with the verb `invoke` in their operation fields. Rather than implementing the invoker pattern, the IIOP invoker included in JBoss follows the standard CORBA/IIOP approach, and hence it does not suffer from language interoperability problems.

Invoker Advantages. JBoss invokers present significant advantages over remote invocation architectures such as CORBA and Java RMI:

---

[16] For the moment, assume that there are no client-side interceptors interposed between the invocation handler and the invoker proxy (see Fig. 7). Interceptors will be discussed in Sect. 4.4.

- *Dynamic generation and retrieval of client-side proxies.* No application-specific stub classes have to be pre-installed in client machines.
- *Extensibility.* Multiple protocols can be simultaneously supported by various invokers and their invoker proxies. Support for new protocols can be added to a running server by dynamically deploying new invoker MBeans.
- *Multiple protocols per EJB.* An EJB component may receive remote invocations over different protocols, i.e., there may be a many-to-many relationship between container MBeans and invoker MBeans.
- *Multiple protocols per client.* Clients receive serialized proxies from other processes and use these proxies to issue remote method calls. Depending on the serialized proxies it receives, a client may employ multiple protocols to interact with various server-side components, without ever being aware of this fact.
- *Separation of concerns.* Invokers draw a very clear separation between middleware concerns inherent to distributed environments (e.g., protocol and fail-over strategy) and other kinds of concerns, either at the middleware level or at the application level.

Together, separation of concerns *and* dynamic retrieval of client-side proxies have far-reaching consequences. Configurable support to failover in clustered JBoss environments is one such consequence. It does not require any special arrangements at the client side, as failover is performed by client-side proxies dynamically retrieved from a JBoss server.

Comparison with CORBA. JBoss invokers afford separation of concerns at a much higher degree than a standard CORBA/IIOP approach. By putting application-specific verbs in a header field of IIOP requests, CORBA effectively forces remote interactions to take place at the base level, rather than at the meta level. We consider this a serious limitation of CORBA/IIOP.

4.3   Containers

When an EJB is deployed into JBoss, a container MBean is created to manage the EJB. Each reified EJB invocation is routed through a container, which provides its EJB with services such as instance pooling, instance caching, persistence, security, and transactions. The container MBean itself does not perform any of these services, it merely aggregates *container plug-ins* that do the real work. A container framework assigns specific responsibilities (bean instance pooling, bean instance caching, and management of bean persistence) to well-defined types of container plug-ins. Besides defining the interfaces that these plug-in types must implement, the framework also accepts a plug-in type — server-side interceptors — whose responsibilities are not specified in advance.

Note that Fig. 7 represents server-side interceptors *within* the EJB container. In JBoss, the abstract notion of an EJB container is realized by a container MBean, together with its set of container plug-ins. Instance pooling, instance caching, and persistence management plug-ins do not appear in that figure (we do not be discuss them in this paper), but they are logically encompassed by the EJB container as well.

JBoss containers are service components implemented as dynamic MBeans. They are created by the `EJBDeployer`, which reads container configurations from XML files.

Container Configurations. A container configuration specifies all information the `EJBDeployer` needs to create a container MBean, its plug-ins, and its interceptors. The configuration defines a Java class for every plug-in and every server-side interceptor, as well as values for configuration parameters. It also defines one or more kinds of client-side proxies that the container will export to EJB clients. For each kind of client-side proxy, it specifies the Java class of every client-side interceptor that will be included in client-side proxies, as well as the invoker MBean (that is, the protocol) that these proxies will use. See [24] for details.

Different kinds of EJBs require containers with different configurations. JBoss has a global configuration file that includes default container configurations for the standard kinds of EJBs (stateless session beans, stateful session beans, entity beans, and message-driven beans). The global configuration file also contains alternative configurations for these kinds of EJBs. A local configuration file, optionally included with a given EJB, may refer to an alternative configuration by its name, in order to specify some non-standard feature such as clustering. Moreover, local configuration files are not constrained to use pre-defined container configurations. A local configuration file may fully define a new container configuration, possibly specifying plug-in and interceptor classes included within the EJB deployment unit.

Generalized EJBs. Local container configurations effectively generalize the EJB model, allowing users to define EJB-like components suited to their needs. For instance, an user that does not need transactions or security can easily create a customized container configuration without transaction or security interceptors, which would otherwise perform superfluous tasks. Local configurations can also be employed to create containers that provide enhanced services. Customized containers can offer assertion capabilities [29] that verify whether component-based applications maintain certain critical properties or not. They can also provide OGSA[17] services in a grid computing environment. These are real examples of enhanced containers, created by JBoss users working on high-confidence systems at MITRE Corporation and by researchers working on the Globus Project, respectively.

4.4   Interceptors as Pluggable Aspects

Pluggable aspects, specified in configuration files written in XML, affect every EJB invocation performed at the base level. Each such aspect corresponds to

---

[17] OGSA is the Open Grid Services Architecture [10] defined by the Global Grid Forum.

```
public abstract class Interceptor
        implements java.io.Externalizable {
    protected Interceptor nextInterceptor;
    public Interceptor setNext(final Interceptor interceptor) { ... }
    public Interceptor getNext() { ... }
    public void writeExternal(final ObjectOutput out) { ... }
    public void readExternal(final ObjectInput in) { ... }
    public abstract Object invoke(Invocation inv);
}
```

Fig. 10. Base class of client-side interceptors

an interceptor that acts directly upon reified invocations. Figure 7 shows two interceptor chains interposed across the reified invocation path: one at the client side, between the invocation handler and its invoker proxy, another at the server side, between a container MBean and its EJB component.

In aspect-oriented terminology, client-side proxies and containers provide *join points* in the invocation path, and interceptors implement *around advice* that runs at those join points. Each interceptor explicitly calls the next element in its chain, so it has complete control over whether the next element will be called or not.

Client-Side Interceptors. These interceptors inherit from the Interceptor class shown in Fig. 10. The field nextInterceptor and the methods setNext and getNext support singly-linked chains of interceptors. Class Interceptor is externalizable and provides default implementations of the externalization methods writeExternal and readExternal. Externalization is crucial for client-side interceptors, as it allows interceptor chains to be built at the server side and dynamically retrieved by clients, along with dynamic proxies. The remaining method, invoke, must be provided by concrete subclasses of Interceptor.

Client-side interceptors typically deal with aspects that involve some form of context propagation from the client to the server (e.g., transactions and security) or handle certain invocations whose processing can be completed at the client side (e.g., getHandle/getHomeHandle calls on EJBObject/EJBHome proxies).

Server-Side Interceptors. Unlike client-side interceptors, server-side interceptors do not need to be externalizable. Rather than inheriting from the externalizable class in Fig. 10, they implement a Java interface that resembles that class, but does not extend java.io.Externalizable or java.io.Serializable.

Server-side interceptor chains are typically longer than client-side ones. Besides dealing with transactions and security at the server side, they handle aspects such as logging, gathering of statistical data, entity instance creation, entity instance locking, detection of reentrant calls, and management of relationships between entities.

5   Project History

There have been four major versions of JBoss. The earliest[18] one (Feb. 1999) was still called EJBoss, a name soon abandoned for trademark reasons. EJBoss was an EJB server that introduced a novel feature — hot deployment — but still used a traditional and compilation-based approach to generate client stubs. JBoss 1.0 (Feb. 2000) was an innovative EJB server that employed a new technology — dynamic proxies — to avoid statically generated client stubs. In version 2.0 (Nov. 2000), JBoss was redesigned and rewritten as a complete J2EE implementation, modularly built around a JMX microkernel. JBoss 2.0 was already an extensible and reflective server that supported server-side interceptors and service MBeans, but not dynamic deployment of service MBeans. Even though invokers were already pluggable in version 2.0, they were container plug-ins, not service MBeans, and there was exactly one invoker (protocol) per EJB container. Version 3.0 (May 2002) featured dynamic deployment of service MBeans, dependency management, unified class loaders, client-side interceptors, and invokers as dynamically deployable MBeans. Multiple invokers per container started to be supported in JBoss 3.2 (first beta release available in Sep. 2002), the version described in this paper.

6   Ongoing and Future Work

Ongoing work includes EJB 2.1 compliance, performance optimizations, and, most importantly, an aspect-oriented programming framework that will allow class, method, field, and constructor pointcuts to be dynamically attached to any Java object. In the near future, this framework should provide the basis for an extended version of the JMX infrastructure within JBoss, as well as for a new implementation of the meta-level architecture described in Sect. 4. Moreover, we expect that close integration with an aspect-oriented programming framework will help JBoss on the move from a generalized EJB model to yet more flexible models for application components.

Another area for future work is on extensions to the metaobject protocol supported by generalized EJB containers. Sensible changes to meta-level elements of the generalized EJB architecture should be allowed in a yet more dynamic way. Management clients, such as the JBoss console, currently can update meta-level attributes and invoke meta-level operations (e.g., a management operation that flushes the instance cache of an entity container). In order to update the container configuration used by some application component, however, they must redeploy the component. (More precisely: they must deploy a new version of the component package, with changes in its local configuration file.) By interacting with the JBoss console, one should be able to add a server-side interceptor or a

---

[18] Except when explicitly stated otherwise, this paragraph informs "final release" dates. Each final release was preceded by a series of alpha and beta releases that started to appear many months earlier.

new protocol (invoker) to a component deployed into a running server, without redeploying the component.

7 Related Work

Support to JMX started to appear in commercial J2EE servers. These systems employ JMX merely as a means to instrument selected parts of the application server and make them manageable through JMX-compliant clients. As far as we know, none of the commercial systems uses JMX as a reflective microkernel architecture at the very basis of the whole server.

A recent paper [3] discusses the performance of EJB applications. It presents a comparative evaluation of the performance of certain applications deployed both on JBoss and on a less flexible server, which relies on compilation to generate stubs and is not built around a reflective microkernel.

FlexiNet [13] is a Java middleware system that exploits reflective techniques in order to support flexible remote method invocation paths (*protocol stacks*, in FlexiNet terminology). Such an invocation path consists of a dynamically generated (and very thin) client-side stub, followed by a client-side chain of metaobjects, which interacts with a server-side chain of metaobjects that ends on the target object. Invocation targets are identified by *names* created by *generators* and resolved by matching *resolvers*. When a name is created, its generator also creates the server-side half of an invocation path. The resolution of the name entails the construction of the client-side half of that path. FlexiNet includes generator-resolver pairs (called *binders*) for various protocols.

Unlike JBoss, FlexiNet does not follow Java RMI conventions to decide whether a method parameter will be passed by value or by reference. Rather than examining the type of the *actual* parameter, it looks at the declared type of the *formal* parameter. The parameter will be passed by reference if its declared type is an interface, and will be passed by value otherwise[19]. Similarly, when passing by value an object with fields that refer to other objects, FlexiNet looks at the declared types of these fields. As standard Java serialization does not provide this semantics, FlexiNet implements its own serialization mechanism. It also implements its own factory of dynamic stubs[20], which differ from the dynamic proxies employed by JBoss in that they cannot implement multiple interfaces. In comparison with FlexiNet, the JBoss remote invocation architecture is considerably simpler, due to its usage of standard Java features (dynamic proxies and object serialization). The serialized form of a dynamic proxy, along with its invocation handler, is the JBoss counterpart of a FlexiNet name. JBoss employs standard Java deserialization as a universal (protocol-independent) "resolver" that converts "names" into client-side stubs.

---

[19] This convention is incompatible with the widely accepted advice that one should favor the use of interfaces (rather than classes) as parameter types. [1]

[20] The development of FlexiNet preceded the inclusion of support to dynamic proxies in the Java reflection API.

Yasmin [6, 7] is a component-based architecture designed with emphasis on distributed applications for network management. The Yasmin model is not Java-based, but it supports hot-deployable components (*"droplets"*) that resemble our deployable MBeans. A major difference, however, is that Yasmin does not address dependence management issues.

OpenCOM [4] is a lightweight component model upon which an adaptive ORB has been implemented. As an in-process model built atop a subset of Microsoft's COM, OpenCOM appears more suitable for very fine-grained components than the JBoss service component model. It supports dependence management, reconfiguration, and method call interception. Nevertheless, OpenCOM does not address deployment issues, nor does it support dynamic loading of component classes from remote locations.

Other component models have been proposed for systems software. Some of these models, which bear less similarity with the JBoss/JMX model than Yasmin and OpenCOM, are discussed in [4].

8   Concluding Remarks

JBoss demonstrates that application servers can be built out of dynamically deployed components that provide middleware services to application components. At the architectural level, its novel contributions include the pioneering usage of JMX as a reflective microkernel architecture, a JMX-based component model with support to dynamic deployment and dependence management, and a meta-level architecture for generalized EJBs. At the implementation level, JBoss innovations include a class loading model that facilitates sharing of classes across deployment units, as well as an "invoker pattern" that relies on serialization of dynamic proxies created at the server side in order to support a general remote method invocation service over multiple protocols.

Researchers have recently advocated "working toward standards for reflective middleware" [17]. The JBoss experience suggests that reflective models based on JMX should be seriously considered as candidates to standardization not only within the network and systems management field, but in the more general Java middleware arena.

Acknowledgements

The JBoss open-source server was designed and implemented by an international team led by Marc Fleury. At the time of this writing, the team has 72 members geographically dispersed across five continents. An up-to-date listing of team members is available at http://sf.net/projects/jboss. Past and present contributors are listed in http://www.jboss.org/team.jsp. Special credit is due to Rickard Öberg, the main designer of JBoss 2.0. His sound decisions are still a major driving force for the project.

The authors wrote this paper as rapporteurs for a group of kernel JBoss contributors that includes Scott Stark, Bill Burke, David Jencks, Sacha Labourey,

Juha Lindfors, Dain Sundstrom, Adrian Brock, Jason Dillon, Christoph Jung, Hiram Chirino, and the authors themselves.

References

1. J. Bloch. *Effective Java.* The Java Series. Addison-Wesley, 2001.
2. F. Buschmann, R. Meunier, H. Rohnert, P. Sommerlad, and M. Stal. *Pattern-Oriented Software Architecture: A System of Patterns.* Wiley, 1996.
3. E. Checchet, J. Marguerite, and W. Zwanepoel. Performance and scalability of EJB applications. In *Conference on Object-Oriented Programming, Systems, Languages, and Applications (OOPSLA'02)*, 2002.
4. M. Clarke, G. S. Blair, G. Coulson, and N. Parlavantzas. An efficient component model for the construction of adaptive middleware. In *Middleware 2001 — IFIP/ACM International Conference on Distributed Systems Platforms*, volume 2218 of *LNCS*, pages 160–178. Springer-Verlag, 2001.
5. M. Dahm. Byte code engineering with the BCEL API. Technical Report B–17–98, Freie Universität Berlin — Institut für Informatik, 1998.
6. L. Deri. *A Component-Based Architecture for Open, Independently Extensible Distributed Systems.* PhD thesis, University of Berne, Switzerland, 1997.
7. L. Deri. Yasmin: A component-based architecture for software applications. In *8th International Workshop on Software Technology and Engineering Practice (STEP'97)*, pages 4–12, London, July 1997. IEEE Computer Society. Also published as IBM Research Report RZ 2899.
8. T. Elrad, M. Aksit, G. Kiczales, K. Lieberherr, and H. Ossher. Discussing aspects of AOP. *Communications of the ACM*, 44(10):33–38, October 2001.
9. J. Ferber. Computational reflection in class-based object-oriented languages. In *Proceedings of the 4th Conference on Object-Oriented Programming, Systems, Languages, and Applications (OOPSLA'89)*, pages 317–326, 1989.
10. I. Foster, C. Kesselman, J. M. Nick, and S. Tuecke. Grid services for distributed system integration. *Computer*, 35(6):37–46, June 2002.
11. E. Gamma, R. Helm, R. Johnson, and J. Vlissides. *Design Patterns — Elements of Reusable Object-Oriented Software.* Addison-Wesley, 1995.
12. S. D. Halloway. *Component Development for the Java Platform.* Addison-Wesley, 2002.
13. R. Hayton and ANSA Team. FlexiNet Architecture. ANSA Architecture Report, Citrix Systems Ltd., Cambridge, UK, February 1999. Available in the ANSA web site (http://www.ansa.co.uk).
14. T. Jewell. EJB 2 and J2EE packaging, part II, July 2001. Available in O'Reilly's OnJava web site (http://www.onjava.com).
15. C. G. Jung. java.lang.ClassLoader.loadClassInternal(String) is too restrictive. Bug report submitted to java.sun.com (bug id 4670071), April 2002.
16. G. Kiczales, J. Lamping, A. Mendhekar, C. Maeda, C. V. Lopes, J.-M. Loingtier, and J. Irwin. Aspect-oriented programming. In *ECOOP'97 — Object-Oriented Programming, 11th European Conference*, volume 1241 of *LNCS*, pages 220–242. Springer-Verlag, 1997.
17. F. Kon, F. Costa, G. Blair, and R. H. Campbell. The case for reflective middleware. *Communications of the ACM*, 45(6):33–38, June 2002.
18. S. Liang and G. Bracha. Dynamic class loading in the Java virtual machine. In *Conference on Object-Oriented Programming, Systems, Languages, and Applications (OOPSLA'98)*, pages 36–44, 1998.

19. J. Lindfors, M. Fleury, and The JBoss Group. *JMX: Managing J2EE with Java Management Extensions.* SAMS, 2002.
20. J. P. Martin-Flatin, S. Znaty, and J. P. Hubaux. A survey of distributed enterprise network and systems management paradigms. *Journal of Network and Systems Management*, 7(1):9–26, 1999.
21. B. Peterson. Understanding J2EE application server class loading architectures, May 2002. Available in TheServerSide.com (`http://www.theserverside.com`).
22. D. Schmidt, M. Stal, H. Rohnert, and F. Buschmann. *Pattern-Oriented Software Architecture: Patterns for Concurrent and Networked Objects.* Wiley, 2000.
23. SourceForge.net. Monthly download statistics for JBoss, December 2002.
    `http://sf.net/project/stats/index.php?report=months&group_id=22866`.
24. S. Stark and The JBoss Group. *JBoss Administration and Development, Edition 2.* JBoss Group, 2002.
25. Sun Microsystems. *Enterprise JavaBeans Specification, Version 2.0*, 2001.
    `http://java.sun.com/ejb/`.
26. Sun Microsystems. *Java 2 Platform Enterprise Edition Spec., v1.3*, 2001.
    `http://java.sun.com/j2ee/`.
27. Sun Microsystems. *Java Management Extensions — Instrumentation and Agent Specification, v1.1*, 2002. `http://java.sun.com/jmx/`.
28. C. Szyperski. *Component Software: Beyond Object-Oriented Programming.* Addison-Wesley, 1998.
29. G. J. Vecellio, W. M. Thomas, and R. M. Sanders. Containers for predictable behavior of component-based software. In *Proceedings of the 5th ICSE Workshop on Component-Based Software Engineering: Benchmarks for Predictable Assembly*, Orlando, Florida, USA, 2002. Carnegie-Mellon Software Engineering Institute.

Flexible and Adaptive QoS Control
for Distributed Real-Time and Embedded Middleware*

Richard E. Schantz[1], Joseph P. Loyall[1], Craig Rodrigues[1], Douglas C. Schmidt[2],
Yamuna Krishnamurthy[3], and Irfan Pyarali[3]

[1] BBN Technologies
Cambridge, MA
{schantz,jloyall,crodrigu}@bbn.com
[2] Vanderbilt University
Nashville, TN
schmidt@isis-server.isis.vanderbilt.edu
[3] OOMWorks, LLC
Metuchen, NJ
{yamuna,irfan}@oomworks.com

Abstract. Computing systems are increasingly distributed, real-time, and embedded (DRE) and must operate under highly unpredictable and changeable
conditions. To provide predictable mission-critical quality of service (QoS)
end-to-end, QoS-enabled middleware services and mechanisms have begun to
emerge. However, the current generation of commercial-off-the-shelf middleware lacks adequate support for applications with stringent QoS requirements in
changing, dynamic environments. This paper provides two contributions to the
study of adaptive middleware to control DRE applications. It first describes
how priority- and reservation-based OS and network QoS management mechanisms can be coupled with standards-based, off-the-shelf distributed object
computing (DOC) middleware to better support dynamic DRE applications with
stringent end-to-end real-time requirements. It then presents the results of experimentation and validation activities we conducted to evaluate these combined OS, network, and middleware capabilities. Our work integrates currently
missing low-level resource control capabilities for end-to-end flows with existing capabilities in adaptive DRE middleware and sets the stage for further advances in fine-grained precision management of aggregate flows using dynamic
adaptation techniques.

1 Introduction and Background

Emerging Trends. Next-generation distributed real-time and embedded (DRE) systems must collaborate with multiple remote sensors, provide on-demand browsing and
actuation capabilities for human operators, and respond flexibly to unanticipated situ-
ational factors that arise at run-time [5]. The distributed computing infrastructure for
these systems must be sufficiently flexible to support varying workloads at different
times during an application lifecycle, yet maintain highly predictable and dependable

* This work was supported by the Defense Advanced Research Projects Agency (DARPA) and
Air Force Research Laboratory under contracts F30602-98-C-0187 and F33615-00-C-1694.

M. Endler and D. Schmidt (Eds.): Middleware 2003, LNCS 2672, pp. 374–393, 2003.
© IFIP International Federation for Information Processing 2003

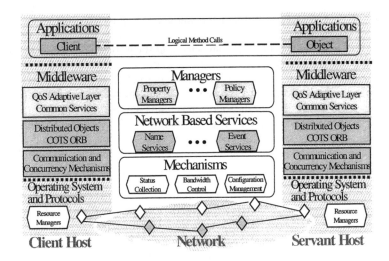

Fig. 1. Layers of Middleware

behavior. Controlling the real-time behavior of such distributed computing systems is one important dimension of the delivered *quality of service* (QoS).

The recent focus on user control over QoS aspects stems from technology advances in historically challenging research areas, such as allocation policies, synchronization of streams in distributed multimedia applications, and assured communication in the face of high demand. The focus on QoS aspects has led to the development of a number of proposed and implemented improvements to commonly available distributed computing infrastructures. When coupled with software that can recognize and react to environmental changes, these improvements form the basis for constructing appropriate adaptive behavior for next-generation DRE systems.

An Overview of COTS Middleware. Requirements for faster development cycles, decreased cost, and reusable solutions motivate the use of *middleware* [25]. Figure 1 illustrates the key middleware layers related to the focus of this paper:

- *Distribution middleware* – This layer encapsulates concurrency, communication, and distribution mechanisms to provide a higher level programming model that automates common programming tasks, such as parameter (de)marshaling, request demultiplexing, and error handling. At the heart of this infrastructure middleware resides some form of Object Request Broker (ORB), such as CORBA [21], Java RMI [32], or Microsoft's COM+ [3].

- *QoS adaptive middleware* – This emerging layer of middleware bridges the gap between an application's QoS needs across its multiple parts and the middleware services and infrastructure that provides QoS. It provides the abstractions necessary to adapt to changing conditions and requirements for applications that can operate in a wide variety of environments and changing conditions. An example of QoS adaptive middleware is the Quality Objects (QuO) framework [34].

Towards an Adaptive COTS Middleware Solution. As network and endsystem performance continues to increase, so too does the demand for more control and manageability of their resources through the middleware interface. In particular, next-generation DRE systems present end-to-end real-time QoS requirements over shared resources and with workloads that can vary significantly at run-time. In turn, this increases the demands on end-to-end system resource management and control, which makes it hard to simultaneously (1) coordinate the management of multiple end-to-end resources and (2) mediate the (possibly conflicting) resource needs across multiple applications, with individual resource mechanisms or managers. In addition, the mission-critical processing aspects of next-generation DRE systems require that they (1) respond adequately to both anticipated and unanticipated operational changes in their run-time environment and (2) ensure that critical capabilities acquire the necessary resources.

Meeting these increasing demands of next-generation DRE systems motivates the need for adaptive middleware-centric QoS management abstractions and techniques. Supporting this adaptive middleware QoS management architecture efficiently, predictably, and scalably requires new dynamic and adaptive resource management techniques that can (1) integrate control and measurement of resources end-to-end, (2) mediate the resource requirements of multiple applications and (3) dynamically adjust resource allocation in response to changing requirements and conditions.

Our prior work has explored many dimensions of QoS-enabled adaptive middleware design and performance, including QoS frameworks, QoS specification and measurement, inserting adaptive behavior into applications, QoS aspects for dependability and survivability, scalable event processing, request demultiplexing, connection management and explicit binding architectures, asynchronous and synchronous concurrent request processing, and IDL stub/skeleton optimizations. This paper focuses on a previously unexamined dimension of QoS-enabled adaptive middleware: *the integration of priority- and reservation-based OS and network QoS management mechanisms with standards-based COTS DOC middleware*. This integration is essential since it enables a new generation of flexible DRE applications that (1) have more precise control over their end-to-end resource management strategies, (2) can be more easily reconfigured and adapted to dynamically changing network and computing environments, and (3) help mature the emerging standards-based COTS infrastructure.

Paper Organization. The remainder of this paper is organized as follows: Section 2 outlines related work on adaptive DRE middleware, including the technologies created during our earlier work on standards-based COTS adaptive DRE middleware that form the basis for the work described in this paper; Section 3 describes the emerging priority and reservation-based resource management mechanisms needed to support dynamic end-to-end QoS management using middleware; Section 4 provides an example DRE application in which we have integrated these resource management services with our earlier adaptive DRE middleware; Section 5 describes empirical results obtained by systematically measuring the behavior of our adaptive DRE middleware in representative application scenarios; and Section 6 presents concluding remarks.

2   Related Work

Distributed object computing (DOC) is the most advanced, mature, flexible paradigm available today for the development of next-generation DRE systems [10]. DOC software architectures are composed of objects that can be distributed or collocated throughout a wide-range of networks and interconnects, thereby shielding applications from many distributed computing complexities. Since conventional DOC middleware historically failed to support more stringent end-to-end application requirements, an increasing body of research has focused on techniques that specify, measure, control, and adapt QoS. This section reviews optimizations and enhancements we and others have made to conventional DOC middleware programming models and implementations so they can support DRE QoS properties and simultaneously allow flexible control and adaptation of key application QoS aspects.

2.1   Our Earlier DRE Middleware Efforts

Our earlier DRE middleware work has focused on TAO and QuO, which leverage Real-time CORBA [20, 21] to provide efficient, scalable, and predictable DRE middleware structures and services, and adaptive QoS management policies, respectively. These technologies serve as the underlying context for adding the specific resource management mechanisms described in Section 3 to manage and control end-to-end DRE performance.

Overview of TAO. TAO [26] is a high-performance distribution middleware targeted for DRE applications with deterministic QoS requirements, as well as best-effort requirements. TAO supports the standard OMG CORBA [21] and Real-time CORBA [20] specifications, whose implementation in TAO ensures efficient, predictable, and scalable QoS behavior for high-performance DRE applications. The following are some of the optimizations in TAO:

- *Optimized IDL Stubs and Skeletons* – TAO's IDL compiler generates stubs / skeletons that can selectively use highly optimized compiled and/or interpretive marshaling/demarshaling [8], thereby allowing application developers to trade off time and space, which is crucial for high-performance DRE applications.
- *Real-time ORB* – TAO's real-time Object Adapter uses perfect hashing and active demultiplexing [22] optimizations to dispatch servant operations in constant time, regardless of the number of active connections, servants, and operations defined in IDL interfaces and TAO's real-time ORB Core [27] uses a multi-threaded, preemptive, priority-based connection and concurrency architecture [8] to provide an efficient and predictable CORBA protocol engine.
- *Run-time Scheduler* – TAO's run-time scheduler maps application QoS requirements (such as bounding end-to-end latency and meeting periodic scheduling deadlines) to ORB endsystem/network resources (such as CPU, memory, network connections, and storage devices) using either static and/or dynamic [7] real-time scheduling strategies.

Overview of QuO. The Quality Objects (QuO) framework [1, 16, 30] is a QoS adaptive layer of middleware that runs on existing DOC middleware (such as Realtime CORBA and Java RMI) and supports distributed applications that can specify (1) their QoS requirements, (2) the system elements that must be monitored and controlled to measure and provide QoS, and (3) the behavior for adapting to QoS variations that occur at run-time. To achieve these goals, QuO provides middleware-centric abstractions and policies for developing DOC applications. Key components provided by QuO to support the above operations include:

- **Contracts** – The operating regions and service requirements of the application are encoded in *contracts*, which describe the possible states the system might be in, as well as which actions to perform when the state changes.
- **Delegates** – Delegates are *proxies* that can be inserted into the path of object inter-actions transparently, but with woven in QoS aware and adaptive code. When a method call or return is made, the delegate checks the system state, as recorded by a set of contracts, and selects a behavior based upon it.
- **System Condition Objects** – System condition objects are *wrapper facades* that provide consistent interfaces to infrastructure mechanisms, services, and managers. System condition objects are used to measure and control the states of resources, mechanisms, and managers that are relevant to contracts.

Our recent work [31] integrating the TAO Real-time CORBA ORB with QuO enables a managed end-to-end path through middleware services. The work reported in Sections 3 though 5 of this paper extends end-to-end middleware control of QoS through the OS and network layers, as well.

2.2 Other Adaptive DRE Middleware Efforts

Meta-programming techniques can be applied to specify middleware QoS behaviors and configure the supporting mechanisms for these QoS behaviors. In particular, the container architecture in component-based middleware, such as Enterprise Javabeans (EJB) and the CORBA Component Model (CCM), provides the vehicle for applying meta-programming techniques that provide QoS assurance control in component middleware. Conan et al [4] use containers together with aspect-oriented software development (AOSD) [14] techniques to plug in different non-functional behaviors. This project is similar to QuO delegates in that mechanisms are provided to inject aspects into applications statically at the middleware level. QuO goes further, how-ever, since it also supports dynamic QoS provisioning via its Qosket mechanisms [24].

de Miguel [17] extends other work on QoS-enabled containers by enhancing an EJB container to support a **QoSContext** interface that allows the exchange of QoS-related information with component instances. To take advantage of the QoS-container, a component must implement **QoSBean** and **QoSNegotiation** inter-faces. A key difference between de Miguel's approach and ours is the QuO delegates and contracts enable the QoS negotiation protocols to be performed transparently to the component implementations.

In their dynamicTAO project, Kon and Campbell [15] apply adaptive middleware techniques to extend TAO so it can be reconfigured at runtime by dynamically linking selected modules, according to the features required by the applications. As with our prior efforts on TAO and QuO, Kon and Campbell provide mechanisms to realize QoS provision in the middleware level. The work described in this paper goes further, however, by integrating QoS provisioning mechanisms at the middleware, OS, and network levels.

The Distributed Multimedia Research Group at Lancaster University has devel-oped a prototype of advanced reflective middleware called Adapt [2]. This middle-ware model concentrates on dynamic composition of objects through open-binding [6], which (1) allows object implementations to be configured dynamically, (2) determines various aspects of object implementations, such as adding or removing methods from an object, and (3) explicitly establishes transport connections between objects that can be used for streaming multimedia data. The Adapt project model also facilitates QoS properties management and monitoring. Compared to the Adapt project, our efforts concentrate on applying QoS provisioning techniques to implement and improve the implementation of an existing middleware standard (CORBA), whereas the Adapt project defines and implements the meta-space of a new middleware framework at a higher level.

3 Managing End-to-End Real-Time QoS via Middleware-Mediated Resource Management Mechanisms

End-to-end QoS requires management and control of the processing resources on nodes in a DRE system and the network resources that connect them. A number of mechanisms for managing these individual resources are emerging, such as mechanisms for (1) prioritizing competing network traffic using standard Internet technologies and (2) reserving prespecified amounts of processor time on COTS host computers. These mechanisms are *necessary* conditions for establishing end-to-end QoS, but they are not *sufficient* by themselves. To achieve end-to-end QoS, therefore, individual resources must be managed in a coordinated manner. Management of an individual resource (e.g., CPU or network connection) will not enable predictable performance if the other complementary resources along an end-to-end path are constrained, unmanaged, or even managed in an uncoordinated manner.

This section describes four emerging mechanisms for managing resources in a DRE system: two each for managing OS and network resources. One pair of mechanisms is predominantly based on a priority paradigm and the other pair is predominantly based on a reservation paradigm. We also discuss how we have enhanced the TAO and QuO middleware to combine and coordinate these mechanisms toward achieving complete end-to-end QoS management capabilities. Section 4 describes the application context for this work and Section 5 then reports our latest experimentation and validation work in using the resource management mechanisms described below separately and in combination.

3.1 Priority-Based OS Resource Management

CORBA (as well as other existing standards-based COTS middleware) has historically lacked features to provide fine granularity allocation, scheduling, and control of key host OS resources necessary to ensure and coordinate predictable platform processing behavior. The Real-time CORBA (RT-CORBA) 1.0 specification [20] defines standard features that support end-to-end predictability for operations in fixed-priority CORBA applications. RT-CORBA (and the TAO implementation) now includes standard interfaces and QoS policies that allow applications to configure the following types of resources:
- *Processor resources* via priority mechanisms, standardized ways of handling thread pools and intra-process mutexes, and a global scheduling service;
- *Communication resources* via protocol properties and explicit bindings; and
- *Memory resources* by bounding buffering requests and the size of thread pools.

Applications typically configure these real-time QoS policies along with other policies when they invoke standard ORB operations. For instance, when an object reference is created using a QoS-enabled RT-CORBA object adapter, the object adapter ensures that any server-side policies that affect client-side requests are embedded within a tagged component in the object reference. This enables clients who invoke operations on such object references to honor the policies required by the target object.

Strict control over the scheduling and execution of processor resources is essential for correct execution of fixed-priority DRE applications. RT-CORBA enables client and server applications to (1) determine the priority at which CORBA invocations will be processed and (2) allow servers to pre-define pools of threads to service incoming invocations in a standard, ORB independent manner.

The fine-grained control of various aspects of ORB implementations is important for predictable behavior. However, establishing a global task priority mechanism that can be mapped to existing lower-level OS priorities and propagated across platforms can be viewed as the key element of RT-CORBA for enabling coordinated end-to-end behavior in a standard and interoperable COTS manner.

3.2   Priority-Based Network Resource Management

Due to its pervasiveness (and the associated cost/availability ramifications), Internet technology is coming to predominate the communication infrastructure for many types of systems. A historic limitation of the Internet technology for DRE applications has been its exclusive reliance on a "best effort" style of resource management. The Internet Engineering Task Force (IETF) realized that Internet Protocol (IP) on its own did not satisfy the requirements for these types of applications, and set up a working group to develop new mechanisms to augment basic IP/TCP. As a result, network resource management capabilities based on Internet technologies are slowly emerging that are more in line with the requirements of DRE computing environments.

In IP networks, data packets contain just enough information for intermediate routers to forward a packet to its destination. Without emerging network traffic management extensions, all IP packets are treated the same and forwarded with "best effort" QoS. If a router between source and destination receives network traffic at a rate faster than it can process, it will drop packets arbitrarily, which is a condition known as *network congestion*. When TCP packets are dropped, the data is lost, and the source host must retransmit the data to the destination host, thereby incurring latencies that are unacceptable to many DRE applications.

The Differentiated Services (DiffServ) architecture [12] provides different types or levels of service for IP network traffic. Individual traffic flows can be made more resistant to dropping (and hence get preferential delivery) by setting the value of each IP packet's DiffServ field with an appropriate value. An IP header has an eight bit DiffServ field that encodes router-level QoS into (1) six bits of DiffServ Codepoint (DSCP), which enables 64 service categories of Per-Hop_Behavior (PHB) and (2) two bits of Explicit Congestion Notification (ECN). A DSCP is added to data packet headers to specify the expected type of service. DiffServ-enabled routers and other network elements use the DSCP to differentiate the network traffic.

We have implemented two enhancements to the RT-CORBA support in TAO that leverage DiffServ capabilities. First, we provided an efficient and flexible way of

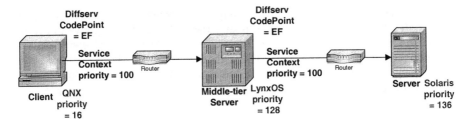

Fig. 2. Example Priority Propagation in RT-CORBA + DiffServ

setting the DSCP by extending the ORB protocol properties on the GIOP request and response packets so that priority can be propagated to requests as they transit the network and OS resources. Based on various factors (such as resource availability, application conditions, and operational requirements), the QuO middleware can change these priorities dynamically by marking application streams with appropriate DSCPs to ensure appropriate priority handling against lower priority competing traffic. Second, we provide a mechanism to map RT-CORBA priorities to DiffServ network priorities. The TAO ORB provides a priority-mapping manager that supports installation of a custom mapping to override the default mapping. Figure 2 depicts how these individual mechanisms are integrated into an end-to-end priority configuration.

3.3   Reservation-Based OS Resource Management

The management of CPU resources in most operating systems has traditionally been handled by assigning priorities to tasks in the system (usually threads or processes) and applying scheduling algorithms to assign each task a share of CPU time. An alternative approach is to reserve sufficient resources *a priori* for the estimated need. While this approach may seem a more natural fit with meeting real-time demands, it is usually more complicated to implement this type of resource management strategy effectively because of issues associated with metering and meeting allocation guarantees while also supporting a priority mechanism for practicality.

The TimeSys Corporation has applied a reservation approach to resource management by implementing a CPU reservation feature in the Linux kernel. The TimeSys Linux kernel is based on resource kernel (RK) [28] work done by the Real-time and Multimedia Systems Laboratory at CMU. An application (or more precisely, a middleware proxy for the application) running on top of the TimeSys resource kernel can specify its QoS requirements for timeliness, and the underlying resource kernel will manage the OS resources so that these requirements can be met.

For CPU resources, TimeSys Linux allows an application to specify its timeliness requirements by specifying parameters for *compute time* and *period*. If the resource kernel can allocate resources that meet these requirements, it grants the application a *reserve*, which guarantees that for every period, the application will have the requested amount of CPU compute time, and will not be pre-empted. Reserving appropriate slices of resources on each of the participating platforms is an alternative to priority based end-to-end management of host processing.

Although TimeSys Linux provides COTS mechanisms for reserving OS CPU resources, the QuO and TAO middleware are responsible for determining who gets the reserved capacity, how much, and for how long. These policy decisions are performed via the higher-level middleware since it retains the end-to-end perspective to set the lower-level OS resources appropriately. We are working with the University of Utah to develop a CORBA-based CPU reservation manager that will (1) be the local agent for setting up reservations on a host and (2) translate various representations of reservation specification into the particular style supported by the TimeSys Linux [23].

3.4   Reservation-Based Network Resource Management

Setting DSCPs as discussed in Section 3.2 makes traffic flows less likely to be dropped due to network congestion in routers. There is no way in this model, however, to *guarantee* a level of service to a traffic flow unless it is the single highest priority traffic at each intermediate step. Just as for the OS-level resource reservations discussed in Section 3.3, it is also desirable to request resources from the network to help guarantee properties, such as latency or bandwidth of network traffic, across some competing flows by reserving appropriate capacity in advance.

To address these issues, the Internet Engineering Task Force (IETF) established a working group to develop a new reserved capacity mechanism to augment IP. The result was the Resource Reservation Protocol (RSVP) specified in RFC 2205 [33], also commonly referred to as IntServ (for Integrated Services). Whereas the DiffServ mechanisms outlined in Section 3.2 merely classify and prioritize packets for different service levels, IntServ reservations allocate and coordinate router behavior along a communication path flow to ensure the reserved end-to-end bandwidth.

RSVP specifies a *signaling* protocol, whereby an application can request a level of service, such as bandwidth, for a certain network flow between a source and destination host. Each router between the source and destination host receives this signaling information, and allocates enough resources to meet the required QoS. The resource reservation is stored in each router so that it can be updated or deleted dynamically.

We have integrated the IntServ mechanisms described above into the QuO and TAO middleware outlined in Section 2.1, where we use them to coordinate end-to-end reservation allocation strategies. The QuO contracts contain the information about the specification of the required reservations. From our prior work on developing intermediate level common distribution services, we utilize the CORBA A/V Streaming Service [19] to set up the (video stream) paths between the communicating CORBA objects. Integrated with that is the ability to attach an RSVP reservation to the underlying network connection as it is setup by the A/V Streaming Service.

4   Applying Managed QoS in DRE Applications

We are applying and evaluating the multi-layered managed QoS approach and mechanisms described in Section 2.1 and Section 3 to complex challenge problems in the avionics and remote sensor processing domains. Certain experimentation platforms involve high speed mobile airborne vehicles, whereas others reside on relatively fixed or slower moving ground platforms. The relevant QoS management includes trading off sensor quality and timeliness, and coordinating resource usage

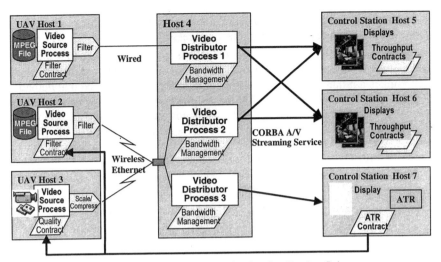

Fig. 3. Architecture of the Evaluation Application Suite

among competing applications, to satisfy changing mission requirements under dynamic, and potentially hostile, environmental conditions.

Figure 3 illustrates the architecture for the application suite that is motivating the specific directions for our work currently being developed and undergoing evaluation. It represents collections of three-stage pipelines that apply QuO, TAO, and TAO's implementation of the CORBA Audio/Video Streaming Service [18] alongside other relevant technologies under investigation to the following three stages:

1. *Sensor sources*, (hosts 1-3) including processes with live camera feeds and those that replay from a file, which send video images to
2. *Distributor processes*, (host 4) which are responsible for distributing the video to
3. *Multiple receivers*, (hosts 5-7) including human-oriented video displays and CPU-intensive image processing software.

This application presents a wide variety of characteristics representative of many or most DRE applications involving constrained resources, varying conditions, and configurations, and varying data and processing characteristics, including:

- *Varying data formats*, including MPEG and PPM, with different data sizes and compression characteristics.
- *Varying network transports*, including wireless, LAN, and WAN, with variable and constrained bandwidth over both noisy and private channels.
- *Varying image processing algorithms*, including image display and image recognition processes (the ATR – automated target recognition – process in Figure 3), with different CPU usage patterns.
- *Varying granularities* of real-time deadlines, ranging from microseconds to milliseconds and seconds.

In particular, managing real-time end-to-end QoS in this context requires supporting and coordinating the following measures of operational effectiveness:

Minimal Frame Rate. Full motion video is typically 30 frames per second (fps), but smooth video is generally perceptible at above approximately 20 fps. Lower frame rates are visibly less smooth, but are viewable as long as other qualities, such as data fidelity and jitter, are controlled. Our DRE application can use frame rates as low as 2 fps for human viewing and lower for image processing.

Minimal Latency. Some uses of sensor information, such as remote piloting, require that the end viewer see an accurate and timely view of what the sensor is collecting, which implies a minimal latency requirement. Studies have indicated that humans can perceive a delay of more than 100-200 ms, so this provides a lower bound for timeliness requirement in cases where the video is meant for human viewing and precision action. In cases where the image is being processed automatically, the important threshold is for the latency to be low enough that there is no more current image. In the case of MPEG-1 where I-frames (full content frames) are two fps, that means a minimum latency of 500 ms.

Minimal Jitter. Controlling the smoothness of the video can have greater impact on the quality of human perception than the frame rate. Controlling the jitter requires control all along the end-to-end path, since it can be affected by changes in the rate at which video is sent, latency of video delivery, and the rate at which frames are displayed. Some typical strategies for reducing jitter, such as buffering, are not as useful in real-time video because of the need for the video to be timely.

Image Quality. The image must be of high enough quality, comprising the image size, pixel depth, etc., for the purpose it is being used. In the case of human viewing, this means the video must be large enough and clear enough to discern the detail that humans need. For automated processing, it means the image must contain whatever important features the processing is intended to detect.

Coordination of Multiple Activities. The middleware, in conjunction with system and application directives, must control and coordinate the QoS so that the necessary allocations and tradeoffs are made to ensure that the highest priority streams and the most important characteristics (e.g., frame rate, latency, and jitter) are favored, even while other, less important characteristics may be minimized or neglected.

Achieving end-to-end QoS requires managing the resources, including CPU and network bandwidth, along the entire path from source to sink. It requires making tradeoffs that consider user requirements, e.g., whether timeliness, fidelity, etc. is the dominant characteristic. In our application architecture, we encode QoS measurement, control, and adaptation directives and policies in QuO contracts that are distributed throughout the application and are responsible for managing the resource and application/data adaptation necessary to achieve an appropriate end-to-end QoS matched to the circumstances relevant at that time.

By incorporating the OS and network mechanisms described in Section 3 that provide lower level resource control capabilities, we can integrate QuO contracts, services such as CORBA Audio/Video Streaming Service, and the underlying TAO Real-time CORBA middleware to establish task and network priorities and reservations end-to-end. These new integrated capabilities complement previous work [13] in which the data/processing characteristics (such as changing the frame rate or image size) were modified as well to satisfy operational requirements.

5   Empirical Results

Section 3 described mechanisms and services useful for managing CPU and network resources. Using the QuO and TAO middleware outlined in Section 2.1 to integrate

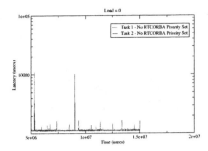 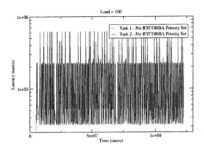

Fig. 4. No DSCP set on either task and no thread priorities; (a) no extra CPU or network load and (b) with extra CPU load and network traffic.

and control these CPU and network resources, we are developing two complementary approaches to end-to-end QoS management:

- *Priority-based* – Using TAO's standard support for CORBA priorities to map to OS priorities and to network priorities based on Real-time CORBA and DiffServ.
- *Reservation*-based – Reserving CPU cycles and network bandwidth based on the TimeSys Linux resource kernel and the IntServ mechanism.

This section describes the results of systematic experiments we have conducted in the context of the application described in Section 4 to evaluate the integration of priority- and reservation-based techniques using standards-based DRE middleware to manage predictable QoS end-to-end.

5.1   Priority-Based End-to-End Adaptive QoS

As discussed in Sections 3.1, RT-CORBA supports the preservation of priorities across threads of activities in DRE applications by (1) mapping the importance of various application activities to corresponding operating system thread priorities and (2) propagating these priorities across the multiple hosts that the activity spans. RT-CORBA is less explicit about the communication transport and network, however. As described in Section 3.2, our approach is to use the RT-CORBA priority not only for mapping to thread priorities and application scheduling requirements, but also to map to DiffServ network priorities for end-to-end predictability and performance.

Empirical Results for Prioritization. We conducted a set of experiments to evaluate the improvement in predictability and performance when using RT-CORBA priorities to map to thread priorities and network DSCPs. The experiments consisted of two video senders transmitting video to two receiver servants under the following conditions:

- *Control runs*, using senders with no priorities and no network management, with and without contending CPU load and network traffic.
- *Experimental runs* with extra CPU load and network traffic, using thread priorities; DiffServ priorities; and thread priorities and DiffServ priorities combined.

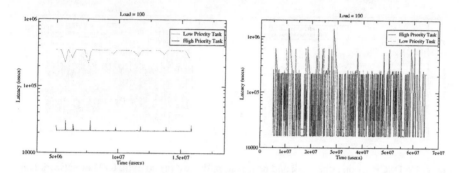

Fig. 5. Tasks with different priorities; no DSCP set on either task; and with introduced CPU load; (a) no traffic congestion and (b) with traffic congestion.

This experiment tests the hypothesis that combined management of thread and network resources results in improved performance and predictability compared with no resource management and management of either one individual resource alone.

The testbed consisted of 4 PCs with 1 GHz AMD Athlon processors and 512 MB RAM, running Redhat Linux 7.1, with a 100 M bits-per-second (bps) Ethernet network. The sender machine hosted two identical tasks playing the role of video senders, generating GIOP messages at the rate of approximately 1.2 Mbps, the approximate bandwidth of MPEG video at 30 frames-per-second (fps). The receiver machine hosted two servants activated in two separate Portable Object Adapters (POAs), which dispatch operations to servants. A third machine played the role of a DiffServ-enabled router, while a fourth machine generated cross traffic in excess of 90 Mbps. We introduced continuous additional CPU load by making 100 consecutive calls to a function checking for large prime numbers.

Figure 4 illustrates the control runs, with both sender tasks having no RTCORBA (thread) priority and no network management of the video stream traffic. Figure 4a indicates the results with no extra load introduced, either in the CPU or in the network. As long as resources are plentiful, the latency of the video traffic for both streams was approximately 1.5 ms, with occasional spikes to approximately 10 ms. When extra network and CPU load was introduced, as illustrated in Figure 4b, performance and predictability degraded significantly. Latency fluctuates widely between a few milliseconds to nearly a second for both streams.

Figure 5 illustrates the results of the first set of experimental runs, evaluating the ability of thread priority alone. As mentioned above, the hypothesis is that while the thread priority mechanism defined by the RT-CORBA specification alone might improve performance and predictability, it is only a partial solution and cannot, by itself, lead to end-to-end QoS. To test this hypothesis, we set one sender task as high priority and the other low priority and increased the CPU load. Figure 5a illustrates that the higher priority task (sender 1) exhibits significantly lower latency than the lower priority task (sender 2).

When network traffic is introduced, however, thread priorities are not sufficient to maintain QoS. The system becomes unpredictable even with RTCORBA priorities set, as Figure 5b illustrates. In fact, there is a possibility of a priority inversion when the high priority task finishes after the low priority task. As expected, the RT-CORBA

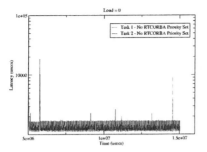 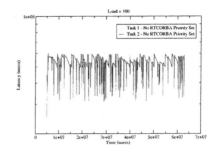

Fig. 6. Tasks with no thread priorities but with DSCP set on either task; and with introduced network traffic; (a) no CPU load and (b) with CPU load.

mapping to thread priority has no capability to maintain QoS when the network is the bottleneck. Figure 6 illustrates the efficacy of Diffserv alone. In the presence of introduced network traffic, Diffserv is sufficient to maintain predictable performance (Figure 6a). However, when extra CPU load is also introduced, the system experiences unacceptable jitter (Figure 6b). In contrast, Figure 7 illustrates the results of the experiment in which we use RT-CORBA priorities for mapping to both thread priorities and DSCPs. In this experiment, both senders get thread priorities and their DSCP set, giving them preferential treatment over the competing CPU load and network traffic, with sender 1 having the higher priority thread and higher network priority. Both senders become much more predictable, while sender 1's stream exhibits lower latency than sender 2's. Priority-based thread control combined with priority-based DiffServ network management is thus able to provide better end-to-end performance and predictability in the face of CPU and network contention than either can do individually.

5.2   Reservation-Based End-to-End Adaptive QoS

The previous sections described priority-based mechanisms for ensuring end-to-end QoS performance of applications. Priority mechanisms do not always work as well, however, in systems with unpredictable and dynamic load scenarios as they do in more static systems, where the load is periodic and the system is not affected to a significant degree by the external environment [29]. Priorities serve best to reflect relative timing requirements of tasks. Likewise, reservations serve best to reflect the absolute timing requirements of each task, when and if they are known.

Below, we describe experiments conducted with reservation-based resource management mechanisms in the context of the video streaming application and the CORBA Audio/Video Streaming Service outlined in Section 4. These results illustrate how the reservation resource mechanisms described in Sections 3.3 and 3.4 can be used in conjunction with adaptive DRE middleware to provide end-to-end QoS as an alternative to, or in concert with, priority-based techniques. The experiments evaluate network and CPU mechanisms separately and in conjunction with application adaptation, providing another step toward our ongoing research objective of a comprehensive end-to-end capability for QoS adaptive middleware.

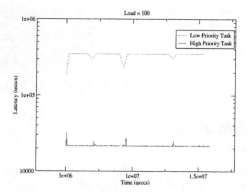

Fig. 7. Task 1 with High Thread Priority and DSCP set and with traffic and CPU load

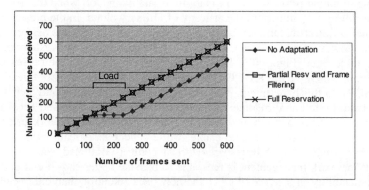

Fig. 8. Predictability of Image Delivery using Network Reservation

Empirical Results for Network Reservations. We conducted a set of experiments on the video delivery application to evaluate the effectiveness of network reservation to increase the predictability and performance of data delivery. Our experiments included two types of RSVP reservations: full reservations (1.2 Mbps, enough to support 30 fps) and partial reservations (670 Kbps). Since partial reservations are not sufficient to support full rate video (i.e., 30 fps), we experimented with using QuO-based frame filtering also, i.e., reducing the video frame rate to a rate that the network (and network reservation) can support. In these experiments, we conducted experiments in every one of the following possible combinations:

1. No frame filtering and no reservation
2. No frame filtering and partial reservation
3. No frame filtering and full reservation
4. Frame filtering and no reservation
5. Frame filtering and partial reservation
6. Frame filtering and full reservation (This combination is included for completeness only. With a full reservation, no frame filtering is necessary.)

Table 1. Summary of Network Reservation Experimental Results

	Under Load		
	% Frames Delivered	Average Latency	Standard Deviation
No Adaptation	0.83%	324 ms	NMF
Partial Reservation	43.9%	742 ms	190.6
Full Reservation	100%	190 ms	42.3
No Reservation; Frame Filtering	95.04%	276 ms	146.6
Partial Reservation; Frame Filtering	99.18%	187 ms	143.6
Full Reservation; Frame Filtering	100%	171 ms	63.5

The sender/distributor and receiver boxes were 750 MHz Pentium III laptops with 512MB RAM, with 10 Mbps Ethernet between them. The video sender sent MPEG-1 video (approximately 1.2 Mbps for 30 fps) for 300 seconds. After 60 seconds elapsed, an extra 43.8 Mbps network load was generated for 60 seconds, then discontinued. The frame filtering cases dynamically reacted to network load by filtering frames down to 10 fps or 2 fps, whichever the network would support.

Figure 8 summarizes the predictability of video delivery in experiments 1, 5, and 6. With no adaptation, almost all of the frames sent while the system was under load were lost. With a partial reservation and frame filtering, the middleware dropped less important intermediate frames, but successfully delivered all full content frames (i.e., I-frames). With a full reservation, all frames were delivered successfully.

Table 1 describes the predictability (number of frames delivered), performance (latency), and jitter (standard deviation) under load of all the experimental cases. It illustrates that network reservation greatly increases the predictability and performance, and reduces the jitter when the system is heavily loaded.

Empirical Results for CPU Reservations. As with the priority-based experiments, end-to-end QoS reservations need to consider image processing as well as image delivery. To measure the ability to control the predictability of the CPU processing requirements of the application, we constructed an experiment where image frame data was transmitted from a client program to a CORBA middleware-based image processing server, simulating the automatic target recognition (ATR) function shown in Figure 3 of our application architecture. In the image-processing server, we ran three different computationally intensive edge detection algorithms (Prewitt, Sobel, and Hirsch algorithms [11]) from the Tools for Image Processing library [9].

We ran the experiments by sending many images to the image-processing server in the following different runs:

- Two *control* runs, which processed images with (1) no competing CPU load and (2) competing CPU load (and no CPU management) and
- An *experimental* case, where images were processed with competing CPU load and with CPU reservations added.

Table 2. Summary of CPU Reservation Experimental Results

Algorithm	No Load		Competing CPU Load		CPU Load & CPU Reservation	
	Av. Proc. Time (ms)	Std. Dev.	Av. Proc. Time (ms)	Std. Dev.	Av. Proc. Time (ms)	Std. Dev.
Kirsch	44.3	0.08	56.5	11.8	44.5	0.87
Prewitt	44.6	0.09	51.5	9.2	44.7	0.16
Sobel	45.3	0.12	59.8	12.9	45.7	0.84

We ran these experiments on a Pentium-III 850 MHz machine with 480 megabytes of RAM, running Red Hat Linux 7.1 with version 2.4.7-timesys-3.0.145 of the Timesys real-time Linux kernel. We used four images in PPM format, 400x250 pixels, 300,060 bytes, and in RGB color. The sender continuously sent the images to the receiver via a CORBA interface. The receiver processed the image by invoking the Kirsch, Prewitt, and Sobel edge detection algorithms in sequence. We executed the algorithms without load, with competing CPU load, and with competing CPU load and a CPU reservation, and recorded the time that each algorithm took to process the image. The results are summarized in Table 2.

These results show that under load, the execution time of the edge detection algorithms increased significantly – Kirsch by +41%, Prewitt by +13%, and Sobel by +30%. The execution times of the edge detectors varied more than when there was no load, as illustrated by the higher standard deviations. This result may be explained by the fact that the load added was variable and not sustained.

Adding a CPU reservation reduced the execution time under load to values that are comparable to those exhibited with no load. The variability in the execution times was also much less than in the experiment with load but with no CPU reservation. CPU reservations therefore did its job as expected to reduce the latency and increase the predictability of executing tasks when there is competing CPU load.

Our short-term future plans involve combining CPU and network reservation mechanisms in a middleware controlled end-to-end QoS management capability for our video streaming application.

6   Concluding Remarks

This paper describes recent advances we have made towards developing adaptive DRE systems with end-to-end QoS management by integrating and testing a variety of emerging operating system and network resource management mechanisms with our earlier work on standards-based COTS DRE middleware and adaptive QoS management frameworks. As our work becomes more completely integrated as common middleware – and is complemented with appropriate resource management binding and scheduling services and policies – it is enabling a new generation of flexible DRE applications that (1) have more precise control over their end-to-end resource management strategies and (2) can be easily reconfigured and adapted to dynamically changing network and computing environments.

Most cost effective, near term solutions to end-to-end system QoS management need to rely on underlying COTS components, such as operating systems, networks, and CPUs. To provide an effective end-to-end solution, however, mechanisms for managing resources at these architectural levels must be integrated with middleware. Until recently, capabilities for managing these resources outside of the narrow host or intra-network perspective were either missing, primitive, or non-standard. The attention being focused on QoS issues for distributed systems has prompted activities that have led to a variety of new mechanisms for low level resource control. Accordingly, our current R&D activity is focused on two topics:

1. How to integrate these emerging individual mechanisms effectively to form a consistent end-to-end control model and
2. How to integrate these low-level mechanisms with higher levels of middleware that can provide end-to-end and system-wide policies and strategies needed to complete our vision.

While this paper indicates that we are making significant progress, we have not yet achieved our final integration milestones. The results in Section 5 illustrate how we have made fundamental progress in separately supporting the two dominant paradigms: priority-and reservation-based approaches. We have demonstrated the effectiveness of implementations of these mechanisms (sometimes integrated, sometimes in isolation) to do what they were intended to do. We have made progress on integrating these low-level controls with higher-level middleware abstractions and policy mechanisms intended to unify the individual elements of the system. All of that work is continuing. After we have integrated, tested, and validated all of the individual mechanisms end-to-end, as well as with the upper levels of middleware for individual flows, we will then focus on the aggregate management policies and adaptive behavior that these levels of middleware are intended to enable. When all of these attributes are in place, we can then provide a more detailed decomposition of the roles and interfaces required to provide a complete service.

Ultimately, we contend that priority- and reservation-based approaches will both have their place in complex DRE application systems. It will therefore be important not only to provide both a consistent end-to-end priority and reservation capability stand-alone, but to characterize, understand, and manage the patterns of their individual use and the interplay and interactions between them.

One promising research direction is to combine priority-based mechanisms in conjunction with reservation mechanisms, using the priority paradigm to drive who gets reservations and to what degree. Since OS reservation allocation mechanisms are newer and have been applied less often than priority mechanisms, they also lag priority-based mechanisms in coordinating and standardizing the reservation mechanisms across distributed systems. Our future work aims at redressing this imbalance.

QuO and TAO software are available in open-source format at http://www.dist-systems.bbn.com/tech/QuO and http://deuce.doc.wustl.edu/Download.html.

References

1. BBN Technologies, "Quality Objects (QuO)", http://www.dist-systems.bbn.com/papers.
2. G. Blair, G. Coulson, P. Robin, M. Papathomas, "An Architecture for Next Generation Middleware," Proceedings of the IFIP International Conference on Distributed Systems Platforms and Open Distributed Processing, London, England, 1998.
3. D. Box, Essential COM, Addison-Wesley, Reading, MA, 1997.
4. D. Conan, E. Putrycz, N. Farcet, M. DeMiguel, "Integration of Non-Functional Properties in Containers," Proc. of the 6th International Workshop on Component-Oriented Programming, Budapest, Hungary, 2001.
5. B. Doerr, T. Venturella, R. Jha, C. Gill, and D. Schmidt, "Adaptive Scheduling for Real-time, Embedded Information Systems", Proceedings of the 18th IEEE/AIAA Digital Avionics Systems Conference (DASC), St. Louis, Missouri, Oct 1999.
6. T. Fitzpatrick, G. Blair, G. Coulson, N. Davies, P. Robin, "Supporting Adaptive Multimedia Applications through Open Bindings," International Conference on Configurable Distributed Systems, Maryland, 1998.
7. C. Gill, D. Levine, and D. Schmidt, "The Design and Performance of a Real-Time CORBA Scheduling Service", Real-Time Systems, The International Journal of Time-Critical Computing Systems, special issue on Real-Time Middleware, vol. 20, num. 2, 2001.
8. A. Gokhale and D. Schmidt, "Optimizing a CORBA IIOP Protocol Engine for Minimal Footprint Multimedia Systems", Journal on Selected Areas in Communications special issue on Service Enabling Platforms for Networked Multimedia Systems, vol. 17, num. 9, Sep 1999.
9. S. Grigorescu, C. Grigorescu, and A. Jalba. Tools for Image Processing, Version 0.0.1. http://www.cs.rug.nl/~cosmin/tip/, 2002.
10. M. Henning and S. Vinoski, "Advanced CORBA Programming With C++", Addison-Wesley, 1999.
11. S. Hlavac and R. Boyle Image Processing, Understanding, and Machine Vision, 2nd edition. PWS Publishing Company, Pacific Grove, CA, 2nd edition, 1999.
12. IETF, An Architecture for Differentiated Services, http://www.ietf.org/rfc/rfc2475.txt
13. Karr DA, Rodrigues C, Loyall JP, Schantz RE, Krishnamurthy Y, Pyarali I, Schmidt DC. Application of the QuO Quality-of-Service Framework to a Distributed Video Application. Proceedings of the International Symposium on Distributed Objects and Applications, September 18-20, 2001, Rome, Italy.
14. G. Kiczales, "Aspect-Oriented Programming", Proceedings of the 11th European Conference on Object-Oriented Programming, Jun 1997.
15. F. Kon, F. Costa, G. Blair, and R. Campbell, "The Case for Reflective Middleware," CACM, June 2002.
16. J. Loyall, R Schantz, J.. Zinky,and D. Bakken, "Specifying and Measuring Quality of Service in Distributed Object Systems", Proceedings of the 1st IEEE International Symposium on Object-oriented Real-time distributed Computing (ISORC), April 1998.
17. M deMiguel, "QoS-Aware Component Frameworks," The 10th Int'l Workshop on QoS, Florida, 2002.
18. S. Mungee, N. Surendran, Y. Krishnamurthy, and D. Schmidt, "The Design and Performance of a CORBA Audio/Video Streaming Service," Design and Management of Multimedia Information Systems: Opportunities and Challenges, Idea Publishing Group, 2000.
19. Object Management Group, "Control and Management of Audio/Video Streams, OMG RFP Submission (Revised), OMG Technical Document 98-10-05", Oct 1998, Framingham. MA.
20. Object Management Group, "Realtime CORBA Joint Revised Submission", OMG Document orbos/99-02-12, March 1999.

21. Object Management Group, Real –Time CORBA 2.0: Dynamic Scheduling Specification, OMG Final Adopted Specification, *September 2001*, http://cgi.omg.org/docs/ptc/01-08-34.pdf.

22. I. Pyarali, C. O'Ryan, D. Schmidt, N. Wang, V. Kachroo, and A. Gokhale, "Applying Optimization Patterns to the Design of Real-time ORBs", Proceedings of the 5th Conference on Object-Oriented Technologies and Systems, San Diego, CA, May 1999.

23. J. Regehr and J. Lepreau. "The Case For Using Middleware To Manage Diverse Soft Real-time Schedulers," In *Proc. of the International Workshop on Multimedia Middleware*, Ottawa, Canada, October 2001.

24. R. Schantz, J. Loyall, M. Atighetchi, P. Pal. "Packaging Quality of Service Control Behaviors for Reuse," *Proceedings of the 5th IEEE International Symposium on Object-oriented Real-time distributed Computing (ISORC 2002)*, April 29 - May 1, 2002, Washington, DC.

25. R. Schantz and D. Schmidt, "Middleware for Distributed Systems: Evolving the Common Structure for Network-centric Applications," Encyclopedia of Software Engineering, Wiley and Sons, 2002.

26. D. Schmidt, D.Levine, and S. Mungee, "The Design and Performance of Real-Time Object Request Brokers," Computer Communications, April 1998.

27. D. Schmidt, S. Mungee, S. Flores-Gaitan, and A. Gokhale, "Software Architectures for Reducing Priority Inversion and Non-determinism in Real-time Object Request Brokers", Journal of Real-time Systems, special issue on Real-time Computing in the Age of the Web and the Internet, Kluwer, 2001.

28. TimeSys Corporation. *TimeSys Linux R/T User's Manual*, 2.0 edition, 2001.

29. Timesys Corporation. Predictable Performance for Dynamic Load and Overload, Version 1.0. http://www.timesys.com/files/whitepapers/Predictable_Performance_1_0.pdf, 2002.

30. R. Vanegas, J. Zinky, J. Loyall, D. Karr, R. Schantz, and D. Bakken, "QuO's Runtime Support for Quality of Service in Distributed Objects", Proceedings of Middleware 98, the IFIP International Conference on Distributed Systems Platform and Open Distributed Processing, Sept 1998.

31. N. Wang, D. Schmidt, A. Gokhale, C. Gill, B. Natarajan, C. Rodrigues, J. Loyall, R. Schantz. "Total Quality of Service Provisioning in Middleware and Applications," Microprocessors and Microsystems spec. issue on "Middleware Solutions for QoS-enabled Multimedia Provisioning over the Internet", 2003.

32. A. Wollrath, R. Riggs, and J. Waldo, "A Distributed Object Model for the Java System", USENIX Computing Systems, MIT Press, vol. 9, num. 4, Nov/Dec 1996.

33. L. Zhang, S. Deering, D. Estrin, S. Shenker, and D. Zappala, "RSVP: A New Resource ReSerVation Protocol," *IEEE Network*, September 1993

34. J. Zinky, D. Bakken, and R. Schantz, "Architectural Support for Quality of Service for CORBA Objects", Theory and Practice of Object Systems, vol. 3, num. 1, 1997.

Large-Scale Service Overlay Networking
with Distance-Based Clustering

Jingwen Jin and Klara Nahrstedt*

Department of Computer Science
University of Illinois at Urbana-Champaign, USA
{jjin1,klara}@cs.uiuc.edu

Abstract. The problem of service routing (or dynamic service composition) has recently emerged as a consequence of the distributed composable services model residing in middleware layer(s). However, existing solutions are mostly suitable for small- or medium-scale service overlay networks, as service routing is performed over flat overlay topologies such as a mesh. Due to their increasing routing information maintenance costs, these flat (single-level) topology solutions cannot cope with large-scale service overlay networking. For better scalability, in this paper, we provide a hierarchical service routing framework, which comprises three parts. In the first part, we organize the overlay network nodes into clusters based on their Internet distances. We then construct a hierarchically fully connected (HFC) topology based on the clustering result. In such a topology, nodes within a cluster are considered fully connected, and the clusters themselves are also fully connected by their border nodes. In the second part, a hierarchical state information distribution protocol will be provided so that each node in the system maintains full state of the nodes in its own cluster and aggregate state of other clusters in the system. In the third part, we present how service paths can be computed hierarchically in a divide-and-conquer fashion. Through simulation tests, we demonstrate that while achieving much better scalability, our framework provides also as good and efficient service paths as single-level mesh solutions.

Keywords: service routing, dynamic service composition, clustering, topology aggregation, hierarchical routing

1 Introduction

The concept of overlay networking has recently been brought up for supporting various kinds of middleware and application services. However, most of the existing work, such as [1–6], targets at small- or medium-scale overlay networks, as the constructed overlay topologies are mostly meshes of single level. These

---

* This work was supported by the DARPA grant, F30602-97-2-0121, NSF grants CCR-9988199 and EIA 99-72884 EQ, and NASA grant NAG2-1406. Jingwen Jin is also supported by CAPES/Brazil.

M. Endler and D. Schmidt (Eds.): Middleware 2003, LNCS 2672, pp. 394–413, 2003.
© IFIP International Federation for Information Processing 2003

single-level, flat network organizations do not scale, because of their increasing routing information maintenance cost. To achieve scalability, in this paper, we introduce a middleware framework for hierarchical service routing that reduces routing information maintenance cost by means of topology abstraction and state information aggregation. In correspondence to these mechanisms, service routing will also be done hierarchically. Assuming that each node in the system maintains partial global state (full state of the nodes in its own cluster and aggregate state of other clusters in the system), hierarchical routing shares advantages of source routing and distributed routing [7].

Although hierarchical (data) routing at the network layer has been extensively studied in the literature [8–10], hierarchical service routing in distributed, overlay service networks (middleware and application layer) presents several additional challenges that need special efforts. (1) While at the network layer, clusters are defined manually by humans based on certain properties of the network (e.g., location, administrative domain, or connectivity), an overlay service network has a virtual, fully-connected topology[1]. Hence the first problem is *how to identify virtual clusters and how to define connectivity between nodes and clusters*. (2) In a clustered service overlay network, the second problem is *how service routing information should be aggregated and distributed*. (3) Compared to data routing, service routing exhibits two new constraints: service functionality and service dependency, that make traditional data routing solutions inapplicable [11]. While solutions such as [11, 12, 5] exist for service routing over flat, single-level topologies, *how can a single-level topology solution be extended to solve the hierarchical service routing problem?*

We address these challenges as follows. For the first problem, as delay (proximity) will be used as a performance metric when seeking service paths, we will use proximity as a metric for clustering services. Since services are located in proxies, the distance between a pair of services can be represented by the distance between the proxies in which the services are located. Thus the problem of clustering services by their proximity amounts to the problem of clustering proxies by their proximity. To achieve this goal, a combination of mechanisms (for distance map obtainment and clustering) will be adopted in this paper, so that the clustered overlay proxy network is congruent with the underlying physical network. Once the clusters (of proxies) have been detected, we will create the topology in such a way that nodes within a single cluster are fully connected, and the clusters themselves are also fully connected by their border nodes. Therefore, any pair of intra-cluster nodes can communicate to each other directly, and any pair of inter-cluster nodes can communicate to each other via their border nodes. We name such a topology an HFC (Hierarchically Fully-Connected) topology. Figure 1 depicts an example of a bi-level HFC topology. This topology design choice stems from the following observation. Service routing exhibits some different features (e.g., service functionality and service dependency) than data routing that make the use of partial mesh topologies, which is suitable for

---

[1] An overlay service network creates a virtual, fully-connected topology with nodes, called proxies, carrying value-added middleware or application services.

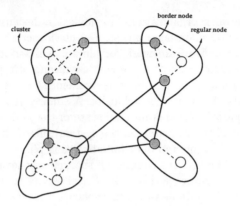

Fig. 1. An example of HFC topology: nodes within each cluster are fully connected, and clusters are fully connected by their border nodes (in shadow).

data routing, not as suitable. This is so because, in data routing, nodes simply participate as relays, and pass data as is to their neighboring nodes; however, in service routing, as the data traverses, nodes may be required to process it differently using different services. Since how services are to be composed (the service dependency issue) is mostly resolved at the runtime, two runtime-defined neighboring services may appear to be several nodes apart in a statically configured partial mesh. In other words, meshes configured statically do not reflect well service dependency needs that are resolved at execution time. In fact, highest efficiency in service paths can be only achieved if the overlay network is considered fully connected (assuming the underlying physical network does not partition). We thereby try to make the hierarchical topology as fully connected as possible. While large networks cannot afford full topologies, after having done proximity-based clustering, small groups of nearby nodes will afford to be fully connected. In a bi-level HFC hierarchy, two nodes (thus also the services installed on them) are at most two nodes away. By limiting the number of hops between any pair of services will potentially increase service path efficiencies.

For the second problem, because service routing involves functionality as the basic requirement, and certain performance metrics for optimization purposes, we will need to maintain two pieces of information: service functionality (or capability) of the nodes and performance status of single or aggregated nodes/links, by using a hierarchical state information distribution protocol. Topology aggregation with QoS parameters has been studied in [9, 13]. We need to further solve the service capability information (SCI) aggregation problem. Assuming that each service can be uniquely named, and a single proxy's SCI is represented as a set of service names, we can aggregate SCI of a group of proxies as the union of their individual SCI sets. State information will be further discussed in Section 4. In this paper, we will only consider delay as our service path performance metric, QoS parameters such as bandwidth, machine capacity, and machine volatility [11], will not be considered at this point.

For the third problem, we will adopt the solution developed in our previous work [11] for intra-cluster service routing, and use a modified version for inter-cluster service routing. The resulting solution will perform hierarchical service routing in a top-down, divide-and-conquer fashion, in a sense that a single node with partial global state of the system first resolves the inter-cluster service routing problem, and then let certain proxies inside those clusters along the path to find intra-cluster service routes.

The rest of the paper is structured as follows. In Section 2, we describe the assumptions made throughout this paper. Section 3 presents the details about HFC-topology construction. Section 4 provides a hierarchical state information distribution protocol so that when stabilized, each node in the overlay network topology has a partial global state of the system. In Section 5, we show how hierarchical service path finding can be performed. Section 6 is devoted to performance study/comparison of the presented solutions in several aspects, against other topology organization methods. Section 7 concludes the paper with some future directions.

2   Assumptions

2.1   Service Model

This research is based on the composable services model [14–17], assuming services can be composed together to perform more complex tasks. Such a model allows dynamic customization of services, and is useful, for example, in multimedia application delivery or in Web applications where customizations are specially desirable to overcome various kinds of Internet heterogeneities or to cater to end-users' special needs. As two application instances that may make use of the composable services model:

- An MPEG video stream may undergo a series of transformations for customization: (1) be watermarked for copyright protection; (2) be converted from MPEG to H.261 to reduce bandwidth requirement; (3) be incorporated with a background music, under user's request; (4) be compressed, again, for less bandwidth requirement.
- A Web document may (under user's request): (1) be translated to another language; (2) be merged with another document residing on a certain machine; (3) be formatted.

Service composition has to follow certain dependency relations due to either operational constraints[2] or input/output constraints[3]. We use the notation $s_i \rightarrow s_j$ to denote that service s_i is to be followed by service s_j. A service request is

---

[2] For copyright protection, watermarking may need to be applied before any other service operations.

[3] For example, if two transcoding services, *MPEG2JPEG* and *JPEG2H261* are to be composed, then the former should be applied before the latter due to the data-type constraints of input/output.

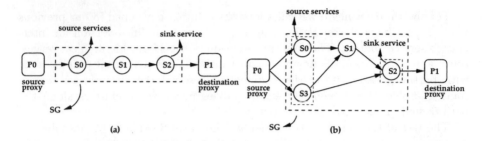

Fig. 2. Two example service requests (source proxy + SG + destination proxy). (a) service request with linear SG: $s_0 \to s_1 \to s_2$; (b) service request with non-linear SG which contains three possible configurations: $s_0 \to s_1 \to s_2$, $s_3 \to s_1 \to s_2$, and $s_3 \to s_2$.

to find a service path, between a pair of source and destination nodes, such that it satisfies a linear or non-linear service dependency graph (service graph or SG for short), as depicted in Figure 2. While a linear service graph contains only one single service configuration, a non-linear service graph may contain multiple feasible service configurations, because a path that leads from any source service to any sink service is said to satisfy the request (a feasible configuration).

2.2   Overlay Networks

In order to carry out the customizations, services need to be available at certain locations between the multimedia server and client. Since it is not scalable performing all customizations at the end points (server and client), proxies have been introduced to facilitate the deployment of applications[18]. We thus assume in this paper that composable services are installed on these media proxies. We do *not* assume active services or any type of dynamic downloading of services; i.e., in this work, services are statically installed on proxies. The reason that active services are not assumed here is that we believe in the current Internet, they are still hard to be widely deployed, as most system administrators may not allow dynamic installations of software in their systems due to security concerns. The no-active-services assumption generally implies that proxy nodes become different in terms of functional capabilities.

Given a distributed, composable service overlay network, applications demand support from middleware so as to automate processes of locating and composing services. The service path finding problem is, given a service request (source proxy + SG + destination proxy), to find an efficient mapping between services and proxies, so that the end-to-end path is efficient in terms of delay or other QoS metrics [11]. In this paper, we will only consider delay as a performance metric when performing service path finding. A concrete service path may have the form: $sp = \langle -/p_0, s_1/p_1, \ldots, s_n/p_n, -/p_{n+1} \rangle$, where p_0 and p_{n+1} are source and destination proxies, respectively, and s_i/p_j means that service s_i is mapped onto proxy p_j (note that $-/p_i$ means no service is mapped onto p_i, i.e., p_i acts as a message relay.).

3   HFC Topology Construction

As long as the underlying physical network does not partition, a set of overlay nodes can be considered fully connected. However, under such an overlay topology consideration, routing information distribution cost becomes unfeasibly high for a large overlay network, because each proxy would have $n - 1$ neighbors. A more scalable way is to consider the overlay network as a mesh [1, 4–6]. However, static mesh configurations do not take the service dependency issue, which is mostly resolved at execution time, into consideration. The general consequence of this is two neighboring services will likely appear to be several nodes apart, so that in order to reach one service from another, several intermediary proxy nodes will need to participate in the service path as message relays. Therefore, mesh topologies would incur longer service paths than the fully connected topology. Besides, although in terms of state information maintenance scalability, mesh is better than the fully connected topology, without topology abstraction and state information aggregation, the improvement is still not sufficient for larger-scale overlay networks.

A common approach to achieving scalability is to organize large networks into clusters/groups, so that topology abstraction becomes possible to reduce the size of global state [19, 9, 8]. Our HFC topology has the following basic properties:

1. **distance-based clustering:** Nodes are clustered by their proximity in the Internet.
2. **connectivity:** All intra-cluster nodes are fully connected among themselves, and all clusters are fully connected by their border nodes. Later on, we will call links crossing two clusters *external links*, and all other links within single clusters *internal links*.
3. **border node selections:** The border nodes between two clusters are selected to be the two closest nodes belonging to the two clusters.
4. **visibility:** Each cluster is visible by its border nodes from outside.

An HFC topology makes service routing in a large-scale overlay network feasible and efficient because of the following reasons. First, clustering allows topology abstraction so as to reduce the state information maintenance overhead. Second, clustering based on the proxies' proximity makes small groups of closely located proxies afford to be fully connected to best cater to runtime-defined service dependency needs. Third, the border node selection rule maximizes routing efficiency between clusters due to geometric properties. Also due to geometric properties, for clusters of reasonable sizes, it's very unlikely that a single node will be selected to be border nodes to all other clusters in the system, which improves load balancing on border nodes. Lastly, when dealing with hierarchical topologies, the most common way of topology aggregation is to represent a group of nodes as a single logical node [19]. Such a representation is simplest, but also introduces too much imprecision [20]. In our framework, we will make all border nodes of a cluster (several nodes instead of a single one) represent a group. Such a visibility feature will help find efficient service paths with better precisions. This issue will become clearer in Section 5.

The construction of an HFC topology follows three major steps: distance map obtainment, clustering, and selection of border nodes.

3.1   Distance Map Obtainment

As end-to-end latency is an important application-level measurable metric that gives a good reflection of the underlying physical network [21, 22], we will use this metric to represent Internet distances. Suppose n is the number of nodes in the overlay network, if we are to get a complete distance map for the clustering purpose, then $O(n^2)$ end-to-end measurements are needed, and $O(n^2)$ entries will be in the map, which is an expensive operation. However, in [22], the researchers made two interesting observations, that will allow us to reduce the complexity of the work significantly. Through real-world Internet distance measurements, the authors in [22] observed that: (1) Internet hosts can be mapped into a k dimensional coordinate space such that the geometric distance between every pair of nodes more or less reflects the network distance (round-trip propagation and transmission delay) between the nodes; (2) without directly measuring the distance between a pair of nodes x and y, this distance information can be calculated (predicted) if we know the distances between x and a set of common landmark nodes L, and the distances between y and L. Therefore, to obtain the complete distance map of n overlay proxies, we do the following:

1. Set up a small group of m landmarks - L, and let each of them measure the distances between itself and all other landmarks. To minimize the effect of Internet noises, we take the minimum value of several measurements.
2. Map the obtained distance map of L into a k-dimensional geometric space S with minimum error. This is a function minimization problem solvable by mathematical methods such as [23].
3. Each proxy obtains the coordinates of L, and measures the distances between itself and L in order to be able to derive its own coordinates relative to L's positions, again through some function minimization method [23]. To minimize Internet noises, the minimum of several measurements should be taken.

Using such an approach, a complete distance map of n proxies can be obtained by using $O(m^2 + nm)$ measurements and will only have $O(kn)$ of entries ($n \gg m$ and $n \gg k$), compared to $O(n^2)$ measurements and $O(n^2)$ entries in a genuine approach. Note that the goal of setting up the landmarks is to provide to regular proxies some reference points in the geometric space - S; the landmarks will not participate in any other activities.

3.2   Clustering by Graph Theory

We assume a particular proxy - P - is elected to perform the clustering operations once all of the proxies have reported their own coordinates to it. Clustering is a big and old research area spanning several fields. Many clustering methods exist

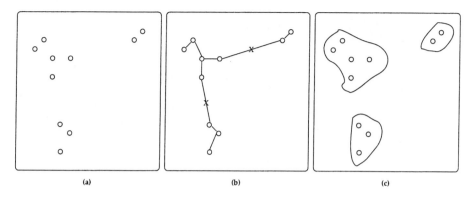

Fig. 3. (a) A set of n nodes in space S; (2) an MST connecting the nodes (inconsistent edges are marked with X; (3) clusters detected by removing the inconsistent edges in (b).

in the literature for different objectives, and most of them are guided by certain laws or principles [24]. Among them, we cite the famous Gestalt principle of grouping by *proximity*. Based on this principle, Zahn [25] demonstrated how the minimum spanning tree (MST) can be used to detect clusters. We adopt this method to detect proxy clusters as follows.

1. Construct the MST for the set of n nodes in S.
2. Identify inconsistent edges in the MST.
3. Remove the inconsistent edges to form connected components and call them clusters.

The crucial step in the algorithm is the definition of inconsistency. We consider an edge to be inconsistent when its length is significantly larger than the average of nearby edge lengths [25]. Let a denote the length of the link being examined - l, and let T_l and T_r denote the left and right sub-trees connected by l, whose average length of links is denoted by b. We say that l is inconsistent if $a/b > k$, where k is a selected number, e.g., 2, 3, ...

In this work, we concentrate on clustering an overlay network of size n using one computation. However, in the real world, we should allow proxies to join and leave dynamically. While we can let future proxies join clusters of their nearest neighbors, multiple joins and leaves may deteriorate the quality of clustering. Hence some kind of re-structuring mechanism needs to be devised. We leave this as our future work.

3.3   Selection of Border Proxies

We also let P carry out the border proxies selection operation. As stated, in the HFC topology, clusters are fully connected by their border proxies. Thus, between every pair of clusters, a pair of border proxies is selected. For maximum routing efficiency, the two border proxies between a pair of clusters are

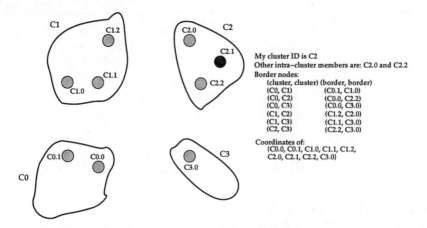

Fig. 4. Information learned by $C_{2.1}$ from P.

selected to be the pair of nearest proxies belonging to the two clusters. Let $X = \{x_1, x_2, \ldots, x_m\}$ and $Y = \{y_1, y_2, \ldots, y_n\}$ denote two clusters, and let $[x_b, y_b]$ denote their border proxies, where $x_b \in X$ and $y_b \in Y$, then for all other pairs of proxies $[x_i, y_j]$ (such that $x_i \neq x_b$, $y_j \neq y_b$, $x_i \in X$, and $y_j \in Y$), $distance(x_i, y_j) \geq distance(x_b, y_b)$.

Once the proxy P is done with clustering and border node selection, it will distribute the relevant topology information to each proxy in the system. In particular, each proxy in the system will learn the following from P: (1) its own cluster's ID and membership information, i.e., who are other members belonging to this cluster; (2) the cluster IDs in the system and their border proxies; (3) coordinates of all members within the cluster and coordinates of all border proxies in the system. Figure 4 depicts the information learned by $C_{2.1}$ from P.

4   Service Routing Information Distribution

As stated in Section 1, service routing needs two pieces of information: distance and service functionality/capability. Since each proxy has already the relevant coordinates information that allows itself to derive distances between any intra-cluster nodes and between any pair of clusters (represented by the corresponding border nodes), only the service capability information needs to be further distributed. Each proxy will maintain two Service Capability Tables, one for all proxies in its own cluster - SCT_P, and the other for all clusters in the system - SCT_C. The following protocol will be adopted for distribution and maintenance of the nodes' service capability information.

1. **Local State:** Every proxy p_i in the system periodically distributes its local service capability information through a *local state* message[4] to all of the

---

[4] In a *local state* message, p_i lists the names of services installed on p_i.

proxies within its own cluster. A proxy p_j that receives a *local state* message will update its SCT_P.

2. **Aggregate State:** Each border proxy p_b periodically aggregates the service capability information of its own cluster and distributes it through an *aggregate state* message[5] to the neighboring border nodes in other clusters. A border node p'_b that receives such a packet updates its own SCT_C, and is responsible for forwarding it to other proxies of its own cluster. Any proxy that receives a forwarded *aggregate state* packet simply updates its own SCT_C.

5   Hierarchical Service Path Finding

In [11], we provided a generic, global-view-based approach to finding optimal service paths in flat topologies. Due to the service functionality and service dependency restrictions in service routing, no existing solutions for data routing (e.g., Dijkstra's Algorithm) can be directly applied to solve the service routing problem. In [11], we showed how to map the service topology and service request information into a directed acyclic graph (which we call service DAG), to make a classical shortest-paths algorithm applicable for computation of optimal service paths. The main objective of the mapping phase was to get rid of the complexities caused by the two restrictions stated above, so that any path that leads from the source node of the service DAG to the sink node of the service DAG would be a viable service path, and applying a shortest-path algorithm will return us a shortest service path in terms of a given metric.

Since in the HFC framework, the topology and state information has been abstracted at certain point, we will not be able to find a concrete service path in one single step. Instead, we will have to perform service path finding hierarchically, first at the cluster level and then at the proxy level. With only an abstract state of other clusters in the system, no single proxy is able to find a concrete service path solely on its own, unless all requested services can be satisfied in the local cluster. The general idea of hierarchical service routing is to first let some proxy (e.g., the destination proxy specified in the request) look for a cluster-level service path, so that to which cluster each service is mapped to is defined. Later, the proxy can let certain nodes of those particular clusters decide which specific in-cluster proxies will be the concrete providers of those services and combine their decisions to obtain the final service path. Figure 5 depicts a picture of hierarchical service routing at high level. We will call such a service path finding mechanism *divide-and-conquer*. Different than in [11], which finds optimal solutions in terms of a given performance metric, now we can no longer guarantee that the resulting service paths are optimal. That is, although we sought to optimize distance independently at two levels of service routing, the overall service path may not be optimal due to topology abstractions.

---

[5] In an *aggregate state* message, p_b lists the names of all services available in its entire cluster. Assume $S_1, S_2, \ldots, S_m$ are the sets of services available at proxies $p_1, p_2, \ldots, p_m$ in a certain cluster C_i. Then the aggregate service set S of this cluster is the union of all S_i's; i.e., $S = S_1 \cup S_2 \cup \ldots \cup S_m$.

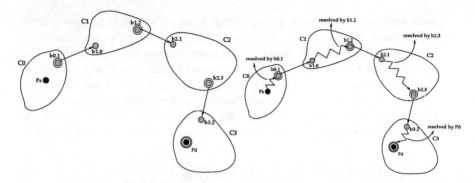

Fig. 5. Hierarchical routing at high level: (a) A single node - p_d - first computes an inter-cluster service path connecting certain border nodes; (b) certain nodes within each cluster individually compute intra-cluster service paths and return their answers to p_d to form the final service path.

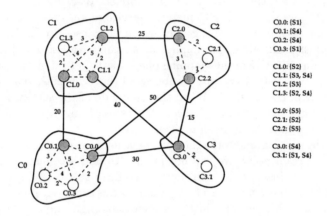

Fig. 6. The service topology (network topology + services) of the example.

In parallel to describing the general procedures of hierarchical service routing below, we provide a small example for better illustration. The topology, as well as the detailed service capability information, are shown in Figure 6. There are four clusters, C_0, C_1, C_2, and C_3, whose elements (proxies) are labeled as $C_{0.0}$, $C_{1.2}$, ..., according to how they are clustered, to ease our reading. Services available at each proxy are listed at the right side of the figure.

5.1   Inter-cluster Service Path Finding

Without loss of generality, we assume a service request, which comprises a source proxy, a service graph, and a destination proxy, and issued by a client, is sent to the destination proxy, and the output of this destination proxy will feed into the client's input.

1. **map:** Based on the aggregate state information maintained at p_d, find instances of the requested services in all clusters in the system by looking up p_d's SCT_C, and construct a service DAG as described in [11].

   Example: Based on the aggregate global state perceived by C2.1 (Figure 7(a)), map the service request (Figure 7(b)) into a service DAG(Figure 7(c)) by finding instances of each service in SCT_C. The two end nodes of such a service DAG are, respectively, the IDs of the clusters in which the source and destination proxies fall; p_d knows its own cluster's ID, and can query the source proxy for the source proxy's cluster ID. Note that the distance labeled on each link between a pair of clusters - C_i and C_j, is the distance between the border proxies of two clusters. The distance is zero if $C_i = C_j$. Although for simplicity the example only considers linear service graph, the solution can be easily extended to also consider non-linear service graphs, as shown in [11].

2. **apply shortest-paths algorithm:** On top of the service DAG, a shortest-path algorithm such as Dijkstra's algorithm, or DAG-shortest-paths algorithm can be applied to compute a shortest path. We will call the resulting path a CSP (Cluster-Level Service Path). Such a CSP is a service path comprised by possibly several external clusters, whose fine-resolution states are not known at p_d.

   Example: Although simply applying a classical shortest-paths algorithm (e.g., DAG-shortest-paths algorithm) on top of the service DAG would result in a cluster-level shortest service path, whose total distance is the sum of the lengths of external border links making up the path, we modify the DAG-shortest-paths algorithm in such a way that selection of a shortest path also takes into account internal distances as much as possible. If, in the service topology of Figure 7, there are two cluster-level service paths (*path 1:* $C_0 \rightarrow C_1 \rightarrow C_2$ and *path 2:* $C_0 \rightarrow C_3 \rightarrow C_2$) that both satisfy the given request, just judging from the external links, the proxy $C_{2.1}$ would see no difference between the two, because both paths have their total external link lengths of 45. However, if $C_{2.1}$ considers the internal distances between the border nodes as well, the latter might be a preferred path because: (1) in *path 1*, the service path will leave C_0 from $C_{0.1}$, enter C_1 from $C_{1.0}$, leave C_1 from $C_{1.2}$, enter C_2 from $C_{2.0}$, and finally reach the destination - $C_{2.1}$, the total distance will be no less than $20 + 5 + 25 + 2 = 52$; (2) in *path 2*, the service path will leave C_0 from $C_{0.0}$, enter C_3 from $C_{3.0}$, leave C_3 from $C_{3.0}$, enter C_2 from $C_{2.2}$, and finally reach the destination - $C_{2.1}$, the total distance will be no less than $30 + 15 + 1 = 46$. At this point, we have no way to know how long the intra-cluster service paths will be, but since the lower-bound distance of path 1 is higher than that of path 2, there's no reason for us not to prefer the latter to the former. In order to take the internal distances into account, we need to add a back-tracking procedure before performing the regular *relax* procedures in a classical shortest-paths algorithm. Details of such back-tracking verification are omitted from this paper. Readers can find similar mechanism used in [11]. The shortest service path is shown in bold lines in Figure 7(c).

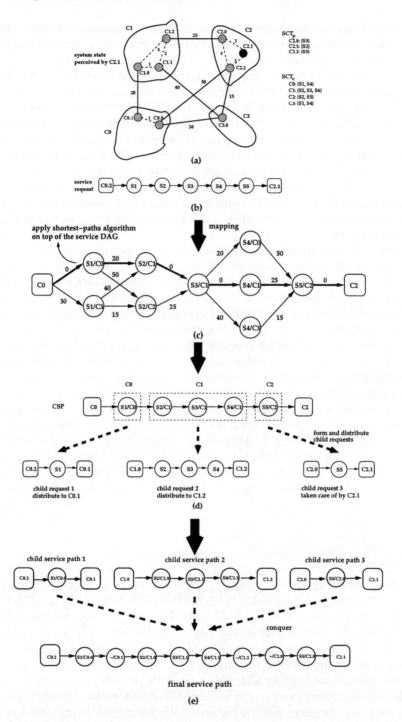

Fig. 7. Inter-cluster service routing (steps performed by the destination proxy $C_{2.1}$ of the service request).

3. **distribute child service requests (divide):** Dissect the original service request into smaller portions, and distribute these child requests to the corresponding clusters.
   Example: Once getting a shortest cluster-level service path, the destination proxy $C_{2.1}$ is responsible for dissecting the original request into pieces. Starting from the source node in the CSP, a new child request is formed for a consecutive set of nodes if these consecutive nodes are all mapped into the same cluster. For each child request, the selection of source proxy and destination proxy is done as follows. Let $\langle C_0, C_1, \ldots, C_n \rangle$ denote the sequence of clusters making up the CSP, and let the notation $b_{i,j}$ denote the border node inside cluster C_i connecting to cluster C_j, then in general, the source proxy of a child request i is $b_{i,i-1}$, and the destination node is $b_{i,i+1}$. If it is the first child request ($i = 0$), the source proxy is that indicated in the original service request; and if it is the last child request ($i = n$), the destination node is that indicated in the original service request. Figure 7(d) shows the dissected child service requests. The first two child requests are to be sent to $C_{0.1}$ and $C_{1.2}$, respectively, and the third one will be taken care of by $C_{2.1}$ itself.
4. **compose child service paths (conquer):** Wait for results of those child service requests to arrive, and compose all child service paths into a single one. This is the final service path.
   Example: The destination proxy $C_{2.1}$ waits for all child service paths[6] to arrive, and combine them as shown in Figure 7(e).

5.2   Intra-cluster Service Path Finding

Since at the cluster level, proxy p_d only knows in which cluster each requested service should be located, it will rely on some in-cluster proxies to further decide which proxy, specifically, will be the concrete provider of each service. A proxy p_x, upon receiving a child service request that consists only of services satisfiable by p_x's cluster, will compute an optimal intra-cluster service path by using the solution described in [11]. The basic procedure consists of two steps: mapping and applying shortest-paths algorithm on top of the obtained service DAG. Different from the mapping step done for inter-cluster service routing above, where each service is mapped into a cluster by looking up SCT_C, now each service will be mapped onto concrete proxies by looking up p_x's SCT_P. After completing the computation of a shortest child service path, p_x sends the result (child service path) back to p_d for it to be composed with others.
   Example: Computations of intra-cluster service paths are shown in Figure 8.

6   Performance Studies

In this section, we conduct simulation tests to study the performances of our hierarchical framework. The simulations are done by using the well-known simulator $ns2$, and our Internet topologies are generated following the *transit-stub*

---

[6] Computations of child service paths are shown in Section 5.2.

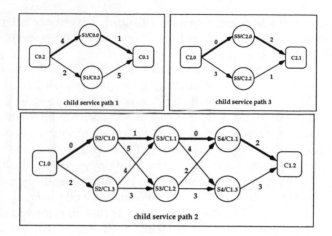

Fig. 8. Computations of child service paths. Shortest paths are indicated with bold lines.

model [26]. We will measure performances of the HFC framework in two aspects: state information maintenance overhead and service path efficiency.

6.1 State Information Maintenance Overhead

The biggest advantage of hierarchical routing is that state information maintenance overhead is reduced through topology abstraction. We will study the performance of the HFC topology by comparing it to that of single-level topologies. Since state in service routing includes two pieces of information: distance and service capability, we will quantify their overheads separately. Overhead is quantified in number of *node-states*; if a single node p keeps n node-states for particular state (either distance or service capability), it means that p maintains that many entries in its corresponding state table where each entry can be either for a single node or for a cluster, depending on situations.

Coordinates-Related Overhead: In this work, since we used coordinates-based distance map in the HFC framework, we will also assume this for single-level topology service routing. In a single-level topology, each proxy is required to keep coordinates of all proxies in the system. Therefore, assuming n is the size of the overlay network, the per proxy coordinates-related overhead is n node-states. However, in an HFC topology, each proxy is only required to keep the coordinates of its local cluster nodes and the coordinates of all border nodes in the system. We set up overlay topologies of different sizes: 250, 500, 750, and 1000 proxies, on top of physical topologies generated by using the TS model [26]. Each overlay topology is tested on top of 10 different physical topologies. Figure 9(a) shows the results averaged over 10 tests.

Service-Capability-Related Overhead: In a single-level topology, each proxy again, needs to maintain service capability information for all proxies (n nodes)

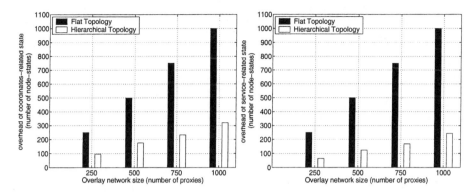

Fig. 9. (a) Number of coordinates-related node-states kept at a single proxy; (b) number of service-related node-states maintained at a single proxy.

in the system. However, in the HFC framework, the number of such nodes perceived at a single proxy is the sum of the number of nodes in each proxy's own cluster plus the number of clusters in the system. Figure 9(b) shows results of the simulation tests with the same setups as above.

While in flat topologies, both overheads would increase linearly with constant one, the increases are much slower in the hierarchical case (with dramatically smaller constants), meaning the HFC framework scales much better than flat topologies. Although theoretically in the worst case, hierarchical organizations may not produce advantages, for example, when most of the nodes fall into one cluster, such undesirable phenomena did not happen in our simulation tests, and we think that extremely unbalanced network node distribution would not happen in practice either. We intend to analyze the node distribution issue further in our future study. Also note that in all of the simulations of this paper, coordinate spaces of two dimensions are used. It would be also interesting, in the future, to quantify the precisions of the distance maps obtained by using coordinate spaces of different dimensions, and see their impact on clustering.

6.2 Service Path Efficiency

The goal of service routing is to find *efficient* service paths. Since in this paper, we only consider distance as the routing metric, we say that for a single service request, a shorter path is more efficient that a longer one. We will compare path efficiencies achieved by our hierarchical service routing framework (HFC with topology abstraction) against those of regular mesh-based solutions. At the same time, we will also quantify the performance losses solely caused by topology aggregation. Hence we will compare path efficiencies achieved by our HFC framework against those achieved by HFC without topology abstraction. To be fair, performances will be compared in the same simulation environments. We wrote programs to generate random simulated environments for overlay topolo-

Table 1. Simulation test environments.

physical topology	landmarks	proxies	clients	services/proxy	service req. length
300	10	250	40	4-10	4-10
600	10	500	90	4-10	4-10
900	10	750	140	4-10	4-10
1200	10	1000	120	4-10	4-10

gies with 250, 500, 750, and 1000 proxies. Table 1 shows the settings. We conduct two sets of tests for different purposes.

We first compare path efficiencies of hierarchical service routing against those of regular meshes. A regular mesh is constructed with the following rules: each proxy creates links to its 1-4 nearest neighbors, and 1-2 randomly chosen, farther located neighbors (to make the topology connected). In a single-level (mesh) topology solution, each node maintains global state of the system. Thus, a single node is able to find an optimal service path by applying the methods described in [11]. The first two bars in each 3-bar set of Figure 10 show the average service path lengths obtained for the two tests. Each point in the figure corresponds to the average result of up to 5 runs (on top of 5 different physical topologies), with 1000 client requests per each run. We see that despite the distance information imprecision introduced in the HFC framework, the performance of the HFC framework is still comparable to (actually slightly better than) single-level mesh solutions. This is the case because in the HFC topology, the number of hops between two overlay nodes (or neighboring services) is constrained to no more than two. As predicted, this feature potentially increases service path efficiencies.

The biggest disadvantage of hierarchical routing is that path efficiencies may get compromised due to routing information imprecision. Thus, it is interesting to examine the performance degradation caused solely by topology aggregation in hierarchical service routing (i.e., performance compromise of doing hierarchical service routing). For this purpose, we compare performances achieved by HFC topologies in two cases. In case one, we perform the topology aggregation as described throughout this paper. In the second case, we do *not* perform any topology abstraction or state information aggregation on top of the HFC topology. Therefore, each proxy will have full state of the whole system. The last two bars in each 3-bar set of Figure 10 give us a comparison between the two; the differences between the two show the performance deterioration caused by the distance imprecision in hierarchical service routing.

7   Conclusions

In this paper, we have presented a hierarchical service routing framework that solves the three challenges described in Section 1, and studied its performances through simulations. Despite the distance imprecision introduced in hierarchical service routing, our framework achieved path efficiencies as good as regular single-level mesh solutions, while also achieving scalability.

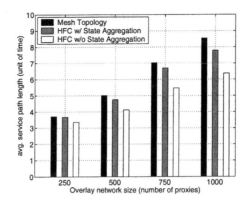

Fig. 10. A comparison of service path lengths.

Service routing is still a new area. To the best of our knowledge, this is the only work so far dealing with hierarchical *service* routing. We expect this research area to be further explored in the future. Some of the improvements that we can think of for our HFC framework can be dynamic membership and QoS. The framework so far does the clustering operations all at once. However, in the real world, we should allow proxies to join and leave dynamically. While we can let future proxies join clusters of their nearest neighbors, multiple joins and leaves may deteriorate the quality of clustering. Thus some kind of re-structuring mechanism needs to be devised. Also, many applications are QoS demanding. How to embed QoS (e.g., network bandwidth, machine load, machine volatility) into hierarchical service topologies, and properly aggregate those pieces of information into meaningful service routing state, are important issues.

Acknowledgments

This material is based upon work supported by DARPA (under Award No. F30602-97-2-0121), NSF (under Awards No. CCR-9988199 and EIA 99-72884 EQ), NASA (under Award No. NAG2-1406), and CAPES/Brazil. Any opinions, findings, and conclusions or recommendations expressed in this publication are those of the authors and do not necessarily reflect the views of the awarding agencies.

The authors would also like to thank the anonymous reviewers for their helpful comments.

References

1. Y. Chu, S. G. Rao and H. Zhang. A Case For End System Multicast. In *Proc. of ACM SIGMETRICS*, pages 1–12, Santa Clara, CA, Jun 2000.
2. J. Liebeherr, and M. Nahas. Application-Layer Multicast with Delaunay Triangulations. In *Proc. of Sixth Global Internet Symposium (IEEE Globecom 2001)*, San Antonio, Texas, Nov 2001.

3. Jingwen Jin and Klara Nahrstedt. mc-SPF: An Application-Level Multicast Service Path Finding Protocol for Multimedia Applications. In *Proc. of IEEE International Conference on Multimedia and Expo (ICME2002)*, Lausanne, Switzerland, Aug 2002.

4. D. Xu, K. Nahrstedt,. Finding Service Paths in a Media Service Proxy Network. In *Proc. of SPIE/ACM Multimedia Computing and Networking Conference (MMCN'02)*, San Jose, CA, Jan 2002.

5. Xiaohui Gu, Klara Nahrstedt, Rong N. Chang, Christopher Ward. QoS-Assured Service Composition in Managed Service Overlay Networks. In *Proc. of The IEEE 23rd International Conference on Distributed Computing Systems (ICDCS 2003)*, Providence, Rhode Island, May 2003.

6. Jingwen Jin and Klara Nahrstedt. On Construction of Service Multicast Trees. In *Proc. of IEEE International Conference on Communications (ICC2003)*, Anchorage, Alaska, May 2003.

7. S. Chen, K. Nahrstedt. An Overview of Quality-of-Service Routing for the Next Generation High-Speed Networks: Problems and Solutions. *IEEE Network Magazine*, 12(6):64–79, 1998.

8. King-Shan Lui, Klara Nahrstedt, Shigang Chen. Hierarchical QoS Routing in Delay-Bandwidth Sensitive Networks. In *Proc. of IEEE Conference on Local Computer Networks (LCN 2000)*, Tampa, FL, Nov 2000.

9. Turgay Korkmaz and Marwan Krunz. Source-Oriented Topology Aggregation with Multiple QoS Parameters in Hierarchical Networks. *ACM Transactions on Modeling and Computer Simulation*, 10(4):295–325, Nov 2000.

10. F. Hao and E. W. Zegura. On Scalable QoS Routing: Performance Evaluation of Topology Aggregation. In *Proc. of IEEE INFOCOM*, Tel Aviv, Israel, Mar 2000.

11. Jingwen Jin, Klara Nahrstedt. QoS Service Routing for Supporting Multimedia Applications. Technical Report UIUCDCS-R-2002-2303/UILU-ENG-2002-1746, Department of Computer Science, University of Illinois at Urbana-Champaign, USA, Nov 2002.

12. Sumi Choi, Jonathan Turner, and Tilman Wolf. Configuring Sessions in Programmable Networks. In *Proc. of IEEE INFOCOM*, Anchorage, Alaska, Apr 2001.

13. King-Shan Lui, Klara Nahrstedt. Topology Aggregation and Routing in Bandwidth-Delay Sensitive Networks. In *Proc. of IEEE Globecom 2000*, San Franscisco, CA, Nov-Dec 2000.

14. F. Kon, R. Campbell, M. D. Mickunas, K. Nahrstedt, and F. J. Ballesteros. 2K: A Distributed Operating System for Dynamic Heterogeneous Environments. In *Proc. of the 9th IEEE International Symposium on High Performance Distributed Computing*, Pittsburgh, Aug 2000.

15. S. D. Gribble, M. Welsh, R. von Behren, E. A. Brewer, D. Culler, N. Borisov, S. Czerwinski, R. Gummadi, J. Hill, A. Joseph, R.H. Katz, Z.M. Mao, S. Ross, and B. Zhao. The Ninja Architecture for Robust Internet-Scale Systems and Services. *Special Issue of Computer Networks on Pervasive Computing*, 2001.

16. Xiaodong Fu, Weisong Shi, Anatoly Akkerman, and Vijay Karamcheti. CANS: Composable, Adaptive Network Services Infrastructure. In *Proc. of Third USENIX Symposium on Internet Technologies and Systems*, San Francisco, CA, Mar 2001.

17. A. Ivan, J. Harman, M. Allen, and V. Karamcheti. Partitionable Services: A Framework for Seamlessly Adapting Distributed Applications to Heterogeneous Environments. In *Proc. of IEEE International Conference on High Performance Distributed Computing (HPDC)*, Edinburgh, Scotland, Jul 2002.

18. A. Fox, S. Gribble, Y. Chawathe, and E. Brewer. Adapting to Network and Client Variation Using Infrastructural Proxies: Lessons and Perspectives. *IEEE Personal Communications*, Aug 1998.

19. The ATM Forum. *Private Network-Network Interface Specification Version 1.0 (PNNI 1.0)*, Mar 1996.

20. B. Awerbuch, Y. Du, B. Khan, and Y. Shavitt. Routing Through Teranode Networks with Topology Aggregation. In *Proc. of IEEE ISCC*, Athens, Greece, Jun 1998.

21. Sylvia Ratnasamy, Mark Handley, Richard Karp, Scott Shenker. Topologically-Aware Overlay Construction and Server Selection. In *Proc. of IEEE INFOCOM*, New York, NY, Jun 2002.

22. T. S. Eugene Ng, Hui Zhang. Predicting Internet Network Distance with Coordinates-Based Approaches. In *Proc. of IEEE INFOCOM*, New York, NY, Jun 2002.

23. J. A. Nelder and R. Mead. A Simplex Method for Function Minimization. *Computer Journal*, 7, 1965.

24. Erich Rome. Simulating Perceptual Clustering by Gestalt Principles. In *Proc. of 25th Workshop of the Austrian Association for Pattern Recognition*, Berchtesgaden, Germany, Jun 2001.

25. C.T. Zahn. Graph-Theoretical Methos for Detecting And Describing Gestalt Clusters. *IEEE Transactions on Computers*, C 20, 1971.

26. E. Zegura, K. Calvert, S. Bhattacharjee. How to Model an Internetwork. In *Proc. of IEEE INCOFOM*, Apr 1996.

A Step Towards a New Generation of Group Communication Systems*

Sergio Mena, André Schiper, and Paweł Wojciechowski

Ecole Polytechnique Fédérale de Lausanne (EPFL)
School of Computer and Communication Sciences
1015 Lausanne, Switzerland
{first.last}@epfl.ch

Abstract. In this paper, we propose a new architecture for group communication middleware. Current group communication systems share some common features, despite the big differences that exist among them. We first point out these common features by describing the most representative group communication architectures implemented over the last 15 years. Then we show the features of our new architecture, which provide several advantages over the existing architectures: (1) it is less complex, (2) it defines a set of group communication abstractions that is more consistent than the abstractions usually provided, and (3) it can be made more responsive in case of failures.

1 Introduction

1.1 Context

Group communication has been widely argued to be an important enabling technology for building fault-tolerant applications in distributed systems [6]. Traditionally, applications can be made tolerant to crashes by replicating critical processes. In such a context, the group communication system (or middleware) manages the interaction between the process replicas across the network. The implementation of group communication middleware in a system with process crashes and unpredictable communication delay is a difficult task. Therefore, it is important to have a clean design of the group communication's architecture, with a well-understood set of programming abstractions provided by each component of the system.

In the dynamic group communication model, processes are organised into groups. The membership of a group can change over time, as processes *join* or *leave* the group, or as crashed processes are *removed* from the group. The current set of processes that are members of a group is called the *group view*.

* Research funded by the EPFL grant "Semantics-Guided Design and Implementation of Group Communication Middleware", by the Swiss National Science Foundation under grant number 21-67715.02, and partially by OFES under contract number 02.0328, as part of the IST MIDAS project (2001-37610).

M. Endler and D. Schmidt (Eds.): Middleware 2003, LNCS 2672, pp. 414–432, 2003.

Processes are added to and deleted from the group view via *view changes*, handled by a *membership* service. Communication to the members of a group is done by various *broadcast* primitives. The basic "reliable" broadcast primitive in the context of a view is called *view synchronous broadcast*, or simply *view synchrony*[1] [13]. The semantics of view synchronous broadcast can be enhanced by requiring messages to be delivered in the same order by all processes in the view. This primitive is called *atomic broadcast*[2] [13]. Moreover, different research groups distinguish between the *primary partition* membership and *partitionable* membership [13]. The discussion of these two models is outside the scope of this paper. In our work, we focus on the primary partition model, in which processes observe the same sequence of views. Primary partition membership is adequate for managing replicated servers, even in the case of link failures and/or network partitions.

The difficulty of implementing a group communication middleware can be formally explained by theoretical impossibility results, such as the impossibility of solving consensus in an asynchronous system when processes can crash [17]. These impossibility results can be overcome by strengthening a little bit the system model [10]. Even though many experimental group communication systems have been implemented during the last decade, so far the use of group communication middleware has not yet become a common practice when building fault-tolerant applications. We think that one of the reasons is the complexity of specifications of group communication services, which makes it difficult to understand the services provided by these systems. Another reason is the complexity of the systems itself.

1.2   Traditional Group Communication Architecture

In [13], Chockler *et al.* describe a comprehensive set of specifications of group communication services, which correspond to the most popular implementations. These specifications can serve as a unifying framework for the classification, analysis and comparison of the group communication systems that have been implemented over the last fifteen years.

The first observation we made is that all the implemented group communication systems we are aware of, adopt the same basic architecture, in which the group membership and view synchrony services are the basic components in the system. The guarantees provided by these two basic components are then used to implement other group communication services, e.g., atomic broadcast. We call this architecture the "traditional architecture".

---

[1] Basically, view synchrony ensures that between two consecutive views v and v', processes that are members of v and v' deliver the same set of messages broadcast to the group. View synchrony is sometimes called *virtual synchrony*. *View synchronous broadcast* is actually the best denomination, but we keep the term *view synchrony* to be consistent with the group communication literature.

[2] Atomic broadcast is also called *total order broadcast*.

1.3   Contribution: A New Architecture

In this paper we propose a new architecture with two key features that distinguish it from traditional architectures.

The first key feature is atomic broadcast (instead of group membership and view synchrony) as the basic component. The atomic broadcast component is then used to build other group communication services on top, e.g., group membership. Such an architecture has better separation of concerns. For example, the group membership service usually has to deliver new group views with guarantees that resemble those provided by the atomic broadcast. Therefore it seems logical for the atomic broadcast service to be more primitive than the group membership service. This architecture is formally supported by the new specification of group communication given in [32].

The second key feature of our new architecture is the absence of the view-synchrony service. This traditional service, which has a rather complex specification [13], is replaced by a new service called *generic broadcast* [29, 28]. Generic broadcast has a simpler specification than view-synchronous broadcast, but at the same time provides a more general service.

In our opinion, the reason for adopting the traditional architecture in the implementation of group communication systems seems more historical than justified by some strong arguments against other architectures. At the time when the first group communication systems (such as Isis) were built, it was not clear how to implement fault-tolerant atomic broadcast protocols without reconfiguration to exclude crashed processes. In later years, when the first papers appeared that suggested a different implementation of atomic broadcast (for example [9]), the traditional architecture had been already well established and the new implementations of group communication systems usually closely followed this initial approach.

In this paper, we compare different variants of the traditional architecture and argue that our new architecture is not only more elegant than the traditional architecture, but also has several advantages, which make it an interesting choice for designing and implementing new generations of group communication systems. The rest of the paper is organized as follows. Section 2 presents examples of the traditional group communication architecture. Section 3 describes our new architecture. Section 4 discusses the advantages of the new architecture compared to the traditional architecture. Finally, Section 5 concludes the paper.

2   Existing Group Communication Architectures

In this section we present the architecture of existing group communication systems. Since it is not possible (and also not really worth) to present the architecture of all group communication systems that have been implemented, we have selected here the most representative architectures. At the end of the section we abstract from the specific architectures and draw some general conclusions.

We have divided this section into two parts: *monolithic* and *modular* systems. As the name suggests, monolithic systems do not allow the system to be easily customized to the user needs; modular systems allow the user, using off-the-shelf components, to build the protocol stack that fits his/her needs.

Among all existing monolithic systems, we have chosen to present Isis [7, 6], Phoenix [25], RMP [34, 27], and Totem [2]. Among modular systems the most representative one is Ensemble [21]. There are many other group communication systems but their architecture overlap with the ones presented here. Transis [14], Relacs [3], and Newtop [16] architectures overlap with Totem and Ensemble. JavaGroups [4] is strongly inspired by Ensemble (it can even be configured to use an Ensemble stack). The group communication protocol suite implemented in the Appia framework [26] is also strongly inspired by Ensemble. The membership service presented in [23] uses a token based approach as in Totem or RMP.

2.1 Monolithic Systems

Isis. Isis was the first system to propose group communication [7, 8]. It is a monolithic *primary partition* system, i.e., when a network partition occurs, the computation can only proceed in one partition of the network, called the *primary partition*. The Isis architecture is depicted in Figure 1. The main layers are the following[3]:

- The *group membership* layer, which is responsible for maintaining the membership of groups. This layer handles *joins* (request to join the group) and *leaves* (request to leave the group). The layer also excludes processes that are suspected to have crashed. The group membership layer ensures that processes deliver the successive views in the *same total order*.
- Group membership does not provide any semantics for communication. For that reason, the group membership layer needs to be extended with a layer providing a semantics for the messages broadcast to the current group members. This semantics is called *view synchrony* (see Section 1).
- The upper layer provides *atomic broadcast*: it ensures that messages are delivered in the same order by all processes. Atomic broadcast is implemented using the view synchrony layer [8].

Phoenix. The Phoenix architecture [25] is a variation of the Isis architecture (Fig 2). The basic layer solves the *consensus* problem [10][4]. Membership (primary partition) and view synchrony are provided by the same layer: both the membership problem and view synchrony are solved using the underlying consensus layer. Similarly to the Isis architecture, atomic broadcast is provided on top of the view synchrony/membership layer.

The main limitation of Isis is to provide the membership service at the level of *processors*. In case of partition, this leads the service to kill all processes on

---

[3] The architecture corresponds to the protocol described in [8]. Since we do not discuss *causal order* in the paper, the Isis causal order protocol does not appear here.

[4] In the consensus problem, each process p_i starts with an initial value v_i, and all correct processes must agree on a common value v that is one of the initial values v_i.

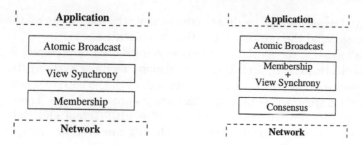

Fig. 1. Isis architecture   **Fig. 2.** Phoenix architecture

processors that are not in the primary partition. This drawback is prevented in Phoenix, which provides the membership service at the level of *processes*. This allows the computation to proceed in all partitions. Consider for example link failures leading to the following situation: the primary partition of some replicated service S is in some network component Π_1, and the primary partition of some other replicated service S' is in some other network component Π_2. A client process in Π_1 can read/update the service S and read S', while a client in Π_2 can read/update S' and read S.

RMP. RMP [34, 27] is another monolithic group communication system, whose architecture differs from the Isis and Phoenix architectures (see Figure 3). The RMP protocol has been influenced by Chang-Maxemchuk's atomic broadcast algorithm [11]. In RMP, the membership layer is split into two parts: *fault-free* membership and *fault-tolerant* membership.

The fault-free membership handles joins and leaves in the absence of failures, using the underlying atomic broadcast layer: joins/leaves are implemented using atomic broadcast. This totally orders joins/leaves with respect to any other application message that is issued using atomic broadcast, i.e., it ensures the *view synchrony* property in the absence of failures. However, the atomic broadcast protocol blocks in case of a process crash. The role of the fault-tolerant membership layer is to avoid blocking by excluding processes that are suspected to have crashed. The fault-tolerant membership protocol, based on a two-phase commit protocol [5] among the surviving processes, is completely different from the fault-free protocol. This fault-tolerant protocol has also the responsibility to ensure the view synchrony property, i.e., it orders view changes with respect to application messages that are atomically broadcast.

Totem. Unlike the architectures presented so far, Totem [2] – while being a monolithic architecture – is a representative of the systems based on the *partitionable membership* model.

Similarly to RMP, Totem uses an atomic broadcast algorithm based on a rotating token. Total order is provided by the middle layer of the architecture depicted in Figure 4 (the layer handles also flow control). The lower layer membership protocol, apart from detecting failures and defining views, recovers token and messages that had not been received by some members when failures occur.

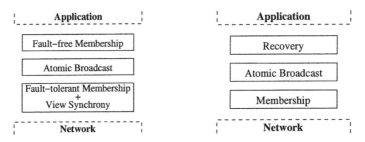

Fig. 3. RMP architecture   **Fig. 4.** Totem architecture

The top *recovery* layer completes the membership layer, by ensuring the (extended) view synchrony property[5]. When the membership layer is invoked, e.g., to exclude a process, it does not enforce the (extended) view synchrony property. This is ensured by the recovery layer.

2.2   Modular Protocol Stacks

Unlike monolithic systems, modular systems allow users to customize the protocol stack to their specific needs. Horus [31] (the successor of Isis) and the re-implementation of Horus in the OCaml language called Ensemble [21] are the best representatives of modular group communication stacks. The idea is to use a set of off-the-shelf components and to compose them using the Horus/Ensemble framework to obtain a protocol stack with the functionalities customized to the user requirements. Similarly to Horus, Ensemble is based on the partitionable membership model. A sample Ensemble protocol stack is depicted in Figure 5. A few explanations are needed:

- A component, e.g., *stable*, can be placed at many places in the stack. The choice of the place has an impact on efficiency. For example, the role of the *stable* component is to detect messages stability[6]. When stability is detected by the *stable* component, an event is delivered to the layer below, and travels down from layer to layer until it reaches the bottom of the stack. At this point the event is bounced back, and travels up through the stack from component to component, until it reaches the top of the stack. The notification of stability occurs during the *upwards* travel of the event.
- The application is not the uppermost layer in the stack. The reason is that it would take more time to convey events from the network level to the application. The most efficient layering leads placing components active in *normal* scenarios *below* the application, and components that handle *abnormal* scenarios *above*.

---

[5] Extended view synchrony [13] extends the view synchrony property, defined in the context of the primary partition model, to the partitionable membership model.

[6] A message is stable at a process when the process knows that the message has been delivered at all destinations.

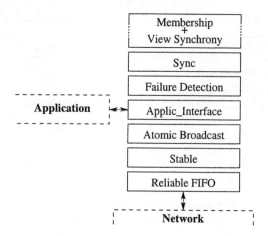

Fig. 5. Ensemble sample protocol stack

Apart from these generalities, here are comments about the Ensemble stack example depicted in Figure 5:

– The *atomic broadcast* component only orders messages in the absence of failures, or more precisely, when the system is stable (since Ensemble provides a partitionable membership service). Without additional membership layers, the different atomic broadcast protocols used would block in case of failures (e.g., upon crash, or disconnection).
– *Sync:* The layer implements a protocol for blocking a group during view changes, i.e., for preventing the broadcast of new messages during view changes.
– *Membership:* Actually, this is not a single layer, but a protocol suite, which includes various components, e.g., *merge*, *inter*, *intra*, etc. It is important to note that even though the membership component appears above the atomic broadcast component, it does not rely on it at all; a correct stack can have the membership components without the atomic broadcast component.

2.3   Discussion

The first observation from the above overview is that an architecture is necessarily influenced by the underlying algorithms. In other words, the architectures that have been presented differ because they rely on different algorithms (for membership, for view synchrony, for atomic broadcast, etc.). However, even though these architectures differ, they share some common features.

Group Membership and Failure Detection Are Strongly Coupled. *Failure detection* is a lower level mechanism than *group membership*. Failure detection gives notification of (possible) process failures (or disconnection) without worrying about inconsistencies (e.g., process p might suspect process r, whereas

q might never suspect r). On the other hand, group membership gives *consistent* failure notification[7].

However, none of the architectures that we have presented exploits this difference: group membership and failure detection are strongly coupled. In most of the architectures, the failure detection component does not even appear explicitly: it is completely hidden within the group membership component. Even in the architectures where the failure detection component is not hidden in the group membership, it directly interacts with the group membership, and only with it. In other words, other components learn about suspicions from the group membership component, not from the failure detection component. The group membership component acts as a failure detection component for the rest of the system.

Atomic Broadcast Algorithms Rely on Group Membership. A corollary of the previous observation is that, in all the above architectures, atomic broadcast algorithms rely on the group membership component; all these algorithms require the help of group membership to avoid blocking in the case of the failure of some critical process.

Basically these atomic broadcast algorithms operate in two modes: (1) a failure-free mode, and (2) a failure mode. A failure notification received from the group membership leads the protocol to switch from the failure-free mode to the failure mode. Here are two examples:

- In Isis and Phoenix, atomic broadcast is implemented using a fixed *sequencer* process. In the normal mode, the sequencer process attaches sequence numbers to messages that are atomically broadcast. However, the protocol blocks if the sequencer crashes. The notification of the failure of the sequencer is needed to prevent blocking, and to switch to the failure mode. In the failure mode the algorithm ensures that if one process has received a sequence number for some message m, then all correct processes receive the same sequence number for m. Once this is ensured, a new sequencer is chosen, and the algorithm returns to the normal mode.
- In RMP and Totem, processes form a logical ring and atomic broadcast is implemented using a rotating *token*. In the normal mode, the token is passed over the ring of processes. A process holding the token can attach a sequence number to the messages it wants to broadcast. If one process crashes, the ring is broken, and the token may be lost. The failure mode is needed to recover from this situation.

This dependency of atomic broadcast on group membership is visible in the above stacks, where the membership component is *below* the atomic broadcast component. This is only partially true for RMP (see Figure 3), in which the dependency of atomic broadcast on group membership holds only in case of

---

[7] The notion of *consistency* differs in the primary and in the partitionable membership service.

failures (failure-free membership is implemented using atomic broadcast). This dependency of atomic broadcast on group membership also holds in Ensemble, even though the atomic broadcast component is below the membership component in the stack in Figure 5: in Ensemble, as already explained, the layering of components does not reflect functional dependencies.

The Consensus Abstraction Is Barely Used. When the consensus problem was defined in the early eighties [18], it was largely considered as a theoretical problem, with little practical relevance. Since then, the practical importance of consensus for solving problems such as atomic broadcast, (primary partition) group membership or view synchrony has been recognized. Nevertheless, except for Phoenix, no consensus component appears in the implementations.

Notice that this comment about consensus applies only to the primary partition systems, since the role of consensus in the context of partitionable group membership and extended view synchrony [13] (the counterpart of view synchrony in the context of partitionable membership) is not clear.

3   The New Architecture

We present now our new architecture. We proceed in three steps, starting with an overview at the same level of details as the architectures presented in Section 2 (allowing comparison). Then in Section 3.2, we present the augmented version of the architecture with a new key component: *generic broadcast*. Finally in Section 3.3, we describe the full version of the architecture with additional details.

3.1   Overview of the New Architecture

Figure 6 shows an overview of our new architecture. At this level of details, we can already see three important features[8]:

- Atomic broadcast does not rely on group membership, but *group membership relies on atomic broadcast.*
- There is no *view synchrony* component.
- Group membership and failure detection are decoupled.

Group Membership Relies on Atomic Broadcast and Not the Opposite. All the systems that have been described in Section 2 rely on atomic broadcast algorithms that require a perfect failure detector, i.e., a failure detector that makes no mistakes. This failure detector is denoted by $\mathcal{P}$ in [10]. The group membership service, when placed below atomic broadcast, emulates the perfect failure detector $\mathcal{P}$ by forcing incorrectly suspected processes to crash.

---

[8] Note that Figure 6 does not mean that the application can only interact with the Group Membership component (the component just below the application).

Instead, we propose to use an atomic broadcast algorithm requiring a $\Diamond\mathcal{S}$ failure detector (much weaker than $\mathcal{P}$), which allows to make mistakes by suspecting correct processes: $\Diamond\mathcal{S}$ allows even an unbounded number of wrong suspicions. Such an atomic broadcast algorithm is given in [10]: it is based on a sequence of instances of consensus (see the *consensus* component in Figure 6 below the total order broadcast component). This algorithm is able to work without blocking even if up to $f < n/2$ crashes occur. As a result, this algorithm does not have to rely on a group membership service.

Since the group membership component does not need to appear *below* the atomic broadcast component, it can be placed *above*: this means that group membership can be implemented using atomic broadcast, which is quite natural, since views need to be totally ordered. This generalizes the solution of RMP (Sect. 2.1). However, because of the limitations of the atomic broadcast algorithm used by RMP (it assumes a perfect failure detector, emulated by the membership service), RMP could use the solution only in the absence of failures: RMP's atomic broadcast relies on membership in case of failures.

It might appear to the reader that inverting the group membership component and the atomic broadcast component in the stack is just moving the complexity from one component to the other (the more complex component being the lowest in the stack). This is not true. It should be noted that any solution that implements (primary partition) group membership *below* atomic broadcast, actually has two algorithms to solve the same ordering problem: one specific solution to order membership changes, and one general (in the context of atomic broadcast) to order application messages. This only observation suggests that such architectures are not optimal.

There Is No View Synchrony Component. There is no view synchrony component in Figure 6. This component is replaced by a more powerful component, called *generic broadcast*, which is discussed below.

Group Membership and Failure Detection Are Decoupled. The strong coupling between failure detection and group membership in the architectures described in Section 2 was motivated by the atomic broadcast algorithms (requirement of a perfect failure detector emulated by the membership service). These architectures could not exploit the distinction between failure suspicion and membership exclusion (only process exclusions could be exploited by the atomic broadcast algorithm).

Decoupling group membership from failure detection has the following advantage: failure detections do not necessarily lead to process exclusion. This also means that decisions to exclude processes are no more taken by the group membership component. We come back to this issue below.

3.2   Augmented Version of the New Architecture

We introduce now the key component of our new architecture, namely *generic broadcast* (see Figure 7).

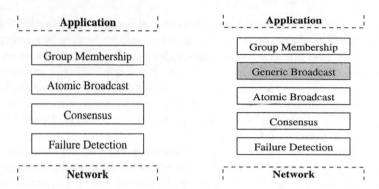

Fig. 6. New architecture: overview   **Fig. 7.** New architecture with the Generic Broadcast component

Generic Broadcast Component. Generic broadcast is a powerful group communication primitive proposed recently [29, 30]. It is generic in the sense that the ordering of messages is defined by a conflict relation on the messages. If two *conflicting* messages m and m' are broadcast, then generic broadcast delivers them in the same order on all destination processes. However, if m and m' do *not* conflict, then generic broadcast does not order them (which is less expensive). So, if all messages conflict, then generic broadcast is equivalent to atomic broadcast. If no message conflicts, then generic broadcast reduces to reliable broadcast. As we explain below, generic broadcast favourably replaces view synchrony.

In terms of the implementation of our architecture, we assume here a thrifty implementation of generic broadcast that uses atomic broadcast [1]. In such a solution, atomic broadcast is not necessarily called in every run. Atomic broadcast is used only when conflicting messages are broadcast (see [1] for an extended discussion of the notion of *thrifty* implementation of generic broadcast).

Active and Passive Replication. Since a group communication middleware is supposed to provide abstractions for the replication of critical components, it is natural to confront the abstractions provided so far with the needs of replication techniques. Our preliminary architecture (Fig. 6) provides atomic broadcast, which allows us to implement active replication [33], also called state machine approach (in active replication, the client requests are sent to all servers using atomic broadcast, and every server processes the request).

Atomic broadcast is not needed in passive replication. Instead, view synchrony provides the right abstraction, see for example [20]. However, our new stack does not provide such an abstraction. We illustrate in the next section how generic broadcast can be used in place of view synchrony. More generally, as shown in [32], view synchrony does not need to be considered as a basic abstraction. View synchrony follows rather from adequate specifications of dynamic group communication [32].

Generic Broadcast Instead of View Synchrony for Passive Replication.
In passive replication, the client sends its request to only one server, the *primary*.
Only the primary processes the client request; before sending the response back
to the client, the primary updates the state of the backups. This is done by an
update message, sent from the primary to the backups. The standard solution
consists in relying here on *view synchrony*.

With generic broadcast[9], the solution consists in considering two types of
messages (Fig. 8): (1) *update* messages, and (2) *primary change* messages. The
update messages are used by the primary to update the state of the backups.
The *primary change* messages are used by the backups to change the new primary, when the current primary is suspected to have crashed. A *primary change*
message does not lead to the exclusion of the old primary, which remains in the
view. If the primary has actually crashed, a new view will be installed to exclude
it after a very long timeout (see *Monitoring Component*, Section 3.3).

The conflict relation between *update* and *primary change* messages is as
follows:

	update	primary change
update	*no conflict*	*conflict*
primary change	*conflict*	*conflict*

This conflict relation ensures that (1) *primary change* messages are totally ordered, (2) *update* messages are totally ordered with respect to *primary change*,
and (3) *update* messages are not ordered with respect to other *update* messages.
For illustration, consider a replicated server with three replicas s_1, s_2, s_3 (which
define the group s) and the following scenario (Figure 8):

- The server s_1 is initially the primary.
- At time t, s_1 receives a client request, processes it, and generic-broadcasts
  the *update* message to the group s.
- Approximately at the the same time t, server s_2 suspects s_1 to have crashed,
  and generic-broadcasts the *"primary-change(s_1)"* message to the group s.
  Upon delivery of this message, all servers (including s_2) modify their view
  from $[s_1; s_2; s_3]$ to $[s_2; s_3; s_1]$, which leads the servers to consider s_2 to be the
  new primary[10].

Since these two messages conflict, we have only two possible outcomes:

1. All members of s deliver the *update* message before the *primary-change*
   message.

---

[9] In this example we have to assume FIFO generic broadcast, i.e., the FIFO point-to-
point property in addition to the ordering properties of generic broadcast. The same
FIFO property is required in the context of the solution based on view synchrony.

[10] Views are here *lists* of processes, rather than *sets* of processes. The primary is the
process at the head of the list. Note that the delivery of the *primary-change(s_1)*
message does not lead to the exclusion of s_1.

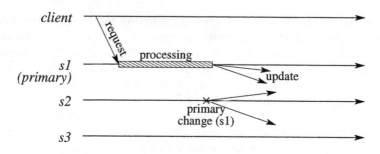

Fig. 8. Generic broadcast for passive replication

2. All members of s deliver the *primary-change* message before the *update* message.

In case 1, the primary change occurs logically *after* the handling of request req by s_1. In case 2, the primary change occurs logically *before* the handling of the request. This means that the processing of the request by s_1 must be ignored. The client will timeout, learn that s_2 is the new primary, and reissue its request to s_2.

3.3 Full Version of the New Architecture

The full version of our architecture, which includes all components and all interfaces between components, is given in Figure 9. The additional components are:

− the *reliable channel* component,
− the *monitoring* component.

Note that in Figure 9, the operations on the generic broadcast component are called *abcast* (invocation of atomic broadcast) and *rbcast* (invocation of reliable broadcast)[11]. The conflict relation is the following:

	rbcast	abcast
rbcast	*no conflict*	*conflict*
abcast	*conflict*	*conflict*

In other words, in the context of the passive replication example, *rbcast* should be used for the *"udpate"* message, and *abcast* for the *"new primary"* message. Of course, generic broadcast can be initialized with a different conflict relation table.

We explain now briefly the role of the *reliable channel* and *monitoring* components.

---

[11] See [32] for a precise specification.

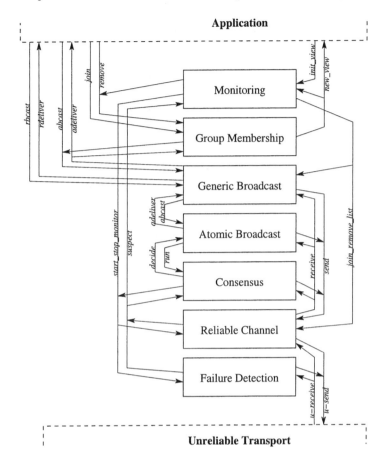

Fig. 9. New architecture: full version

Reliable Channel Component. The *reliable channel* component ensures the following property: if a correct process p sends message m to some correct process q, then q eventually receives m. This abstraction can be easily implemented on top of TCP [15].

Monitoring Component. In our architecture, the decision to exclude a suspected process from the membership is not made by the group membership component[12]. The decision is made by the monitoring component, which then calls the *remove* operation of the *membership* component.

The separation of concerns between the *failure detection* component and the *monitoring* component allows for very flexible policies. On the one hand, the *consensus* component of process p could ask the *failure detection* component

---

[12] The operations on the membership component are *join* – to add a process to the group, and *remove* – to remove a process from the group (including itself).

to use a *small* timeout value (e.g., in the order of seconds) to suspect some other process q. Typically, this suspicion would *not* lead to the exclusion of q. On the other hand, the *monitoring* component of p might ask the *failure detection* component to use a large timeout value (e.g., in the order of minutes) to suspect q. Here a suspicion would lead the *monitoring* component to call the *membership* component to *remove* q. However, to make such a decision, the monitoring component may also interact with the *monitoring* component of other processes, and for example decide on the removal of q only after having learned that a threshold of other processes also suspect q.

Still another exclusion policy can be expressed, which is relevant when process p sends message m to process q. The *reliable channel* component at p buffers m, until $ack(m)$ is received from q (which acknowledges reception of m by q). If q crashes, m might stay in p's buffer forever. In this case, the only way to discard m is to exclude q from the membership (if q is excluded from the membership, there is no more obligation for q to deliver m, i.e., m can be safely discarded). This is called *output-triggered* suspicion in [12]. The *monitoring* component can exclude processes based on output-triggered suspicions (which should be based on long timeout values).

4   Assessment of the New Architecture

We stress now on the advantages of the new architecture compared to the traditional architectures presented in Section 2.

4.1   Less Complex Stack

With traditional architectures, the ordering problem is solved in two places: (1) within the group membership component for views, and (2) within the atomic broadcast component for messages[13]. From a conceptual point of view this is not optimal, and introduces an unnecessary complexity. This redundancy has disappeared in the new architecture, where the ordering problem is solved only once (in the atomic broadcast component).

Actually, in the traditional architectures the ordering problem is even solved in a third place, namely in the view synchrony component, which orders messages with respect to view changes. In our new architecture, this additional ordering problem is also solved in the same place, namely in the atomic broadcast component. Indeed, when the generic broadcast component detects a message conflict (e.g., between a reliable broadcast and atomic broadcast view change message), then it calls the atomic broadcast component. The details can be found in the thrifty generic broadcast algorithm [1].

Altogether, from the point of view of the ordering problem, the new architecture is less complex than traditional architectures. Smaller complexity usually leads to easier maintenance.

---

[13] In RMP, ordering is performed in two different places only in case of failures.

4.2   More Powerful Stack (Provides More Functionalities)

The new suite of components provides functionalities which are not present in traditional stacks. The prominent example is generic broadcast, which extends the ordering provided by view synchrony. Consider for example a replicated service managing client bank accounts, with deposit and withdrawal operations (withdrawal does not allow to withdraw more than available). Both classes of operations update the state of the server, but deposit operations are commutative, i.e., they do not need to be ordered with respect to themselves. This ordering typically can be solved using generic broadcast. Traditional stacks do not provide any specific solution: atomic broadcast would have to be used both for deposit and withdrawal operations. This would induce a non-necessary overhead.

On a more minor issue, the fact that failure suspicions can be generated in two distinct places is not without benefit. Depending on the context, the monitoring component can take the decision to exclude a process from the membership either (1) based on notification from the failure detector component, or (2) based on notifications from the reliable channel components, or (3) it could wait for notifications from both components.

4.3   Higher Responsiveness

Group communication allows the implementation of fault-tolerant replicated services. Performance of group communication is usually measured in failure-free executions. However, performance of group communication in case of failures often is equally important.

Consider for example the latency of atomic broadcast, i.e., the time elapsed between the atomic broadcast of m and the first delivery of m. In case of failures, the timeout used to detect failures represents an important part of this latency. So, reducing the latency in case of failures requires failure detection timeouts to be as small as possible. However, reducing failure detection timeouts increases the probability of false suspicions. Decoupling failure suspicions from process exclusions plays here an important role.

In traditional architectures, wrong failure suspicions have a high cost: the cost of excluding the wrongly suspected processes, followed by the cost of the join operation (with the costly state transfer operation) in order to include again the process in the membership. This has forced traditional systems to adopt large failure detection timeout values. In our stack, where failure suspicions are decoupled from exclusions (i.e., false suspicions lead to a small overhead), timeouts can be chosen to be smaller. This leads to a gain in efficiency in case of failures, e.g., to higher responsiveness.

4.4   Minor Efficiency Issue

Traditional systems have another responsiveness problem, namely in the context of view changes. This problem is not related to failures, since view changes may be triggered by *join* requests, and *remove* requests that are not exclusions. The traditional solution in the context of membership changes ensures that messages broadcast before the membership change are delivered before the membership change takes place. This property is called *sending view delivery* (see [13]). However, in order to ensure this property without discarding messages, processes must stop sending messages while the membership change protocol is running (see for example the *Sync* layer of Ensemble, Section 2.2). To prevent this undesirable *blocking* problem, which reduces responsiveness, alternate and more complex solutions to handle membership changes have been proposed [19, 24]. These solutions implement a weaker property called *same view delivery* [13]. The implementation based on generic broadcast does not lead to blocking: the solution "naturally" implements the *same view delivery* property without additional complexity [32].

5   Conclusion

Existing group communication systems (GCS) can be classified according to two dimensions: (1) the *membership model* dimension, and (2) the *structuring* dimension. The *membership model* dimension allows the classification of GCS as either (i) *primary partition* GCS, or (ii) *partionable membership* GCS. The *structuring* dimension allows the classification of GCS as either (i) *monolithic* or (ii) *modular*. Isis, falls into the category *primary partition/monolithic*, while Ensemble falls into the category *partitionable/modular*.

This paper has introduced a third dimension: the *protocol* dimension. With respect to this third dimension, existing GCS can be characterized as *GM-VS*[14]: (1) membership is the basic component in the stack, and (2) view synchrony is the basic communication abstraction. The paper has presented an alternate solution that could be called *AB-GB*[15] based: (1) atomic broadcast is the basic component, (2) no view synchrony as such is provided, and (3) the GCS provides generic broadcast (instead of view synchrony) as a more powerful abstraction.

We have started the implementation of this new architecture, using two different protocol composition frameworks: Appia [26] and Cactus [35, 22]. The two implementations share the same protocol code at each module, and differ only in the way interactions (events) are routed across modules in each of the frameworks.

References

1. M. K. Aguilera, C. Delporte-Gallet, H. Fauconnier, and S. Toueg. Thrifty generic broadcast. In *Proceedings of the 14th International Symposium on Distributed Computing (DISC'2000)*, October 2000.
2. Y. Amir, L.E. Moser, P.M. Melliar-Smith, D.A. Agarwal, and P.Ciarfella. The Totem Single-Ring Ordering and Membership Protocol. *ACM Trans. on Computer Systems*, 13(4):311–342, November 1995.

---

[14] *Group Membership - View Synchrony.*
[15] *Atomic Broadcast - Generic Broadcast.*

3. O. Babaoglu, R. Davoli, L. Giachini, and M. Baker. Relacs: A communication infrastructure for constructing reliable applications in large-scale distributed systems. In *Proceedings of the 28th Hawaii Interntional Conference on System Sciences*, volume II, pages 612–621, Jan 1995.
4. Bela Ban. *JavaGroups 2.0 User's Guide*, Nov 2002.
5. P.A. Bernstein, V. Hadzilacos, and N. Goodman. *Concurrency Control and Recovery in Distributed Database Systems*. Addison-Wesley, 1987.
6. K. Birman. The Process Group Approach to Reliable Distributed Computing. *Comm. ACM*, 36(12):37–53, December 1993.
7. K. Birman and T. Joseph. Reliable Communication in the Presence of Failures. *ACM Trans. on Computer Systems*, 5(1):47–76, February 1987.
8. K. Birman, A. Schiper, and P. Stephenson. Lightweight Causal and Atomic Group Multicast. *ACM Trans. on Computer Systems*, 9(3):272–314, August 1991.
9. T. D. Chandra and S. Toueg. Unreliable Failure Detectors for Asynchronous Systems. In *proc. 10th annual ACM Symposium on Principles of Distributed Computing*, pages 325–340, 1991.
10. T.D. Chandra and S. Toueg. Unreliable failure detectors for reliable distributed systems. *Journal of ACM*, 43(2):225–267, 1996.
11. J. M. Chang and N. Maxemchuck. Reliable Broadcast Protocols. *ACM Trans. on Computer Systems*, 2(3):251–273, August 1984.
12. B. Charron-Bost, X. Défago, and A. Schiper. Broadcasting messages in fault-tolerant distributed systems: the benefit of handling input-triggered and output-triggered suspicions differently. In *Proceedings of the 20th IEEE Symposium on Reliable Distributed Systems (SRDS)*, pages 244–249, Osaka, Japan, October 2002.
13. Gregory Chockler, Idit Keidar, and Roman Vitenberg. Group communication specifications: A comprehensive study. *ACM Computing Surveys*, 33(4):1–43, December 2001.
14. Danny Dolev and Dalia Malki. The Transis approach to high availability cluster communication. *Communications of the ACM*, 39(4):64–70, 1996.
15. Richard Ekwall, Péter Urbán, and André Schiper. Robust TCP connections for fault tolerant computing. In *Proc. 9th International Conference on Parallel and Distributed Systems (ICPADS)*, pages 501–508, Chung-li, Taiwan, December 2002.
16. Paul D. Ezhilchelvan, Raimundo A. Macedo, and Santosh K. Shrivastava. Newtop: A fault-tolerant group communication protocol. In *International Conference on Distributed Computing Systems*, pages 296–306, 1995.
17. M. Fischer, N. Lynch, and M. Paterson. Impossibility of Distributed Consensus with One Faulty Process. *Journal of ACM*, 32:374–382, April 1985.
18. M.J. Fischer. The consensus problem in unreliable distributed systems (A brief survey. In *Proc. Int. Conf. on Foundations of Computations Theory*, pages 127–140, 1983.
19. R. Friedman and R. van Renesse. Strong and Weak Virual Synchrony in Horus. In *15th IEEE Symp. on Reliable Distributed Systems (SRDS-15)*, pages 140–149, Niagara-on-the-Lake, Ontario, Canada, September 1996.
20. R. Guerraoui and A. Schiper. Software-Based Replication for Fault Tolerance. *IEEE Computer*, 30(4):68–74, April 1997.
21. Mark Hayden. The Ensemble system. Technical Report TR98-1662, Department of Computer Science, Cornell University, January 8, 1998.
22. Jun He, Matti A. Hiltunen, Mohan Rajagopalan, and Richard D. Schlichting. Providing transparent qos customization for CORBA objects, 1997.
23. Matti A. Hiltunen and Richard D. Schlichting. A configurable membership service. *IEEE Transactions on Computers*, 47(5):573–586, 1998.

24. J. Sussman I. Keidar and K. Marzullo. Optimistic virtual synchrony. In *19th IEEE Symp. on Reliable Distributed Systems (SRDS-19)*, pages 42–51, Nurnberg, Germany, October 2000.
25. C. Malloth. *Conception and Implementation of a Toolkit for Building Fault-Tolerant Distributed Applications in Large Scale Networks*. PhD thesis, Federal Institute of Technology, Lausanne (EPFL), 1996.
26. Hugo Miranda, Alexandre Pinto, and Luís Rodrigues. Appia, a flexible protocol kernel supporting multiple coordinated channels. In *Proceedings of The 21st International Conference on Distributed Computing Systems (ICDCS-21)*, pages 707–710, Phoenix, Arizona, USA, April16–19 2001. IEEE Computer Society.
27. Todd Montgomery. Design, implementation, and verification of the reliable multicast protocol. Master's thesis, West Virginia University, Dec 1994.
28. F. Pedone and A. Schiper. Handling Message Semantics with Generic Broadcast Protocols. *Distributed Computing*. Submitted for publication.
29. F. Pedone and A. Schiper. Generic Broadcast. In *13th. Intl. Symposium on Distributed Computing (DISC'99)*. Springer Verlag, LNCS 1693, September 1999. Extended version to appear in ACM Distributed Computing, 2002.
30. F. Pedone and A. Schiper. Handling Message Semanticas with Generic Broadcast Protocols. *Distributed Computing*, 15(2):97–107, april 2002.
31. Robbert Van Renesse, Kenneth P. Birman, Bradford B. Glade, Katie Guo, Mark Hayden, Takako Hickey, Dalia Malki, Alex Vaysburd, and Werner Vogels. Horus: A flexible group communications system. Technical Report TR95-1500, Department of Computer Science, Cornell University, Apr 1996.
32. André Schiper. Dynamic Group Communication. Technical Report, EPFL, March 2003.
33. F.B. Schneider. Replication Management using the State-Machine Approach. In Sape Mullender, editor, *Distributed Systems*, pages 169–197. ACM Press, 1993.
34. Brian Whetten, Todd Montgomery, and Simon M. Kaplan. A high performance totally ordered multicast protocol. In *Dagstuhl Seminar on Distributed Systems*, pages 33–57, 1994.
35. Gary T. Wong, Matti A. Hiltunen, and Richard D. Schlichting. A configurable and extensible transport protocol. In *INFOCOM'01*, April 2001.

A Middleware-Based Application Framework for Active Space Applications

Manuel Román and Roy H. Campbell

Department of Computer Science
University of Illinois at Urbana-Champaign, Urbana, IL 61801
{mroman1,rhc}@cs.uiuc.edu

Abstract. Ubiquitous computing challenges the conventional notion of a user logged into a personal computing device, whether it is a desktop, a laptop, or a digital assistant. When the physical environment of a user contains hundreds of networked computer devices each of which may be used to support one or more user applications, the notion of personal computing becomes inadequate. Further, when a group of users share such a physical environment, new forms of sharing, cooperation and collaboration are possible and mobile users may constantly change the computers with which they interact; we refer to these digitally augmented physical spaces as Active Spaces. We present in this paper an application framework that provides mechanisms to construct, run or adapt existing applications to ubiquitous computing environments. The framework binds applications to users, uses multiple devices simultaneously, and exploits resource management within the users' environment that reacts to context and mobility. Our research contributes to application mobility, partitioning and adaptation within device rich environments, and uses context-awareness to focus the resources of ubiquitous computing environments on the needs of users.

1 Introduction

Future ubiquitous computing will surround users with a comfortable and convenient information environment that merges physical and computational infrastructures into an integrated habitat. Context-awareness should accommodate the habitat to the user preferences and tasks, group activities, and the nature of the physical space. We term this dynamic and computational rich habitat an Active Space. Within the space, users will interact with flexible applications that may move with the user, may define the function of the habitat, or collaborate with remote applications. The research described in this paper builds on experiments with applications conducted in a prototype active meeting room (Figure 1). We have currently developed fourteen applications that we use regularly in our seminars, meetings, and presentations.

The Active Space consists of the Gaia middleware OS[1] managing a distributed system composed of four 61" wall-mounted plasma displays, a video wall, 5.1 audio system (Dolby Digital), touch screens, IR beacons, badge detectors, and wireless and wired networks connecting 15 Pentium-4 PCs running Windows 2000 and Windows CE based Compaq iPaq PDAs. Gaia supplies services including event delivery, entity presence detection (devices, users, and services), context notification, a space repository to store information about entities present in the space, and a context-aware file system.

M. Endler and D. Schmidt (Eds.): Middleware 2003, LNCS 2672, pp. 433–454, 2003.

Fig. 1. Prototype Active Meeting Room Hosting a Slide Show Application

The application experiments examine how to construct applications that use multiple devices simultaneously, take advantage of resources contained in the user habitat, exploit context information (e.g., location and social activity), benefit from automatic data transformation and can alter their composition dynamically (e.g., attaching and detaching components) to adapt to changes in the Active Space, and move with the users to different Active Spaces.

The problem we focus in this paper consists on providing an application framework that leverages the functionality provided by the Gaia middleware OS to assist developers in the construction of Active Space application. The application framework addresses three issues: (1) defining an application model that can accommodate the requirements of Active Spaces including dynamically changing the cardinality, location, and quality of input, output, and processing devices used by an application; (2) providing a mapping mechanism that allows defining applications' requirements generically and automatically mapping them to the resources present in a particular Active Space; and (3) implementing a flexible policy driven application management interface that allows customizing applications to the dynamic behavior of Active Spaces.

The paper continues with a description of the issues we consider are key for Active Space applications (Section 2), a description of the application framework including information about the application model (Section 3), the mapping process (section 4), and the application management functionality (Section 5). Section 6 explains how the application framework addresses the issues listed in Section 2, Section 7 presents an example of an application we have built using the framework, and Section 8 discusses performance evaluation. We present related work in Section 9, and conclude in Section 10.

2   Active Space Applications' Key Issues

Based on our experiments, we define an Active Space application as a collection of dynamically assembled components that fulfill the requirements of a user or a group of users. Dynamism is probably the most important aspect of an Active Space application, and requires a flexible component based application architecture capable of changing its own composition at run-time. We have identified a number of issues that are common to most Active Space applications. These issues are the cornerstones of our application framework, which effectively simplifies the development of Active Space applications. We list these issues next.

2.1   Resource-Awareness

Ubiquitous computing scenarios contain hundreds of resources, including devices (e.g., sensors, displays, and CPUs), services (e.g., file management, printing, and temperature controller), and applications (e.g., slideshow presenter, music player, and calendar). In order to exploit these resources, Active Spaces must provide functionality to discover existing resources, functionality to store information about resources including their capabilities, their availability, and their cardinality, and functionality to query for specific resources.

2.2   Multi-device

In an environment where users are surrounded by hundreds of devices, the notion of interacting with a single device becomes inappropriate. Users may utilize different devices at different times, or may use multiple devices simultaneously to accomplish a well defined goal, as long as certain security and availability policies apply. This "post-pc" scenario requires a new model for application construction that allows partitioning applications into different devices as required by users and their associated context (e.g., time of the day, location, current task, and number of people). Application partitioning allows distributing functional aspects of an application (e.g., application logic, output, and input) across different devices. Remote terminal systems (such as X-Windows) allow redirecting the application output and input to different devices. However, they do not provide support to redirect the application output to one device and the input to another device. And for the same application, it is not possible to redirect multiple outputs to different devices. The type of application partitioning we seek is conceptually similar to the one proposed by Myers et al. [2], and provides fine grained control to choose a target device for each individual application functional aspect, as well as support for altering the application partitioning at run-time.

The application partitioning must be: (1) dynamic, so it may vary at run-time according to changes in the Active Space (e.g., new devices introduced in the space, or new people entering the space), and (2) reliable, in such a way that guarantees application integrity even when the application is distributed across different devices.

2.3   User-Centrism

Resource-awareness and the multi-device approach convey a third essential property: user-centrism. To accommodate application partitioning into multiple devices that vary over time, we bind applications to users and map the applications to the resources present in the users' current environment.

Abowd et. al.[3] use the term "everyday computing" to denote the type of applications associated with users that do not have a clearly defined beginning and end. Users may start these applications and use them for several days, months, or even years. Applications may be periodically suspended and resumed but not terminated. These applications are bound to users, and take benefit of the resources present in the users' environment.

User-Centrism requires applications to (1) move with the users, (2) adapt according to changes in the available resources (it may imply data format transformation, or internal application composition, or both), (3) provide mechanisms to allow users to configure the application according to their personal preferences, and (4) allow more than one user to participate in the same application.

2.4   Run-Time Adaptation

Active spaces are highly dynamic environments, where changes are the norm. Devices may be added to and removed from the space at any time, existing software entities may crash or new ones may be added dynamically, and users may enter and leave the space to start and stop participating in existing tasks. All these properties require applications capable of reacting to such changes at run-time. We consider two types of adaptation, functional and structural.

Application functional adaptation (i.e. changing the behavior of the application algorithm) is an important feature that has already been applied to traditional applications by means of reflection [4-8].

Adaptation of the interactive components' composition (altering the number and location of the components the user utilizes to interact with the application) does not apply to traditional interactive applications running on desktops due to, at least, three main reasons:

1. Usage pattern for interactive desktop applications is different from the one observed in Active Space applications. Desktop users sit in front of the computer and use the local peripherals to interact with the application. If users move to a different computer, they restart the application or start a remote session (e.g. X-Windows, and Windows Terminal Services); it is not possible to split the application among several devices dynamically. On the other hand, Active Space applications' users are not bound to a single device; they can move freely around the space and use any available device; therefore, they expect the application to move and duplicate functionality to different devices dynamically.
2. From an abstraction or granularity point of view, the desktop computer defines the execution environment, and therefore, there is no concept or need for splitting the application across different machines. However, in an Active Space, the Active Space itself (not the individual devices it contains) defines the execution environment (different abstraction granularities). Therefore, devices contained in the Ac-

tive Space become execution nodes of a larger computing abstraction. From this perspective, applications require functionality to alter their composition dynamically to adapt to changes in the Active Space, and alter the application composition to use the most appropriate execution nodes according to user preferences and context parameters.

3. Most interactive desktop applications are disconnected from external context attributes, and therefore, there is no need to adapt the application composition. The strong connection with context attributes in Active Spaces requires the application to adapt to new scenarios dynamically.

As an example of structural adaptation, consider a user reading a confidential document in an active office display. When the context of the Active Space indicates that another user is entering, the application moves the document to the user's personal PDA to protect confidentiality. This requires attaching a new application component (the one on the PDA) and removing an existing one (the one in the display).

2.5   Mobility

Application partitioning and user-centrism require applications to be mobile. There are at least two different types of mobility: intra-space mobility and inter-space mobility. Intra-space mobility is related to the migration of application components inside an Active Space and is the result of application partitioning among different devices. Inter-space mobility concerns moving applications across different spaces, and is a consequence of user-centrism (users are mobile by definition).

2.6   Context-Sensitivity

One of the main differences between an Active Space and a traditional distributed system is the utilization of the physical and digital context associated to the space as a default computational parameter. Context is one of the most important properties in ubiquitous computing [9] and therefore applications must be able to access and alter existing context information. Context may trigger both functional and structural adaptation. As an example of functional adaptation, a news broadcasting application may select different types of news depending on who is in the room, the time of the day, or the mood of the users. And as an example of structural adaptation, a music application may use a user's laptop to play the music if there are other people present in the room; or may use the audio system of the room, the displays (to present the list of songs), and the room's speech recognition system to control the application when the user is alone.

2.7   Active Space Independence

Active spaces are characterized by containing a collection of heterogeneous devices. Furthermore, different Active Spaces have different number of resources. These two properties - heterogeneity and device cardinality – complicate the development of Active Space portable applications. Applications cannot make any assumption about the number and type of devices they will find in different Active Spaces. Traditional operating systems successfully address the issue of heterogeneity by providing software abstractions to represent the real hardware devices. However resource cardinality is not normally a concern in traditional operating systems, which can assume certain hardware configurations. For example, most personal computer operating systems can safely assume the existence of peripherals such as one monitor, one keyboard, one mouse, one audio device, one video card, and some storage device. Unfortunately, this does not apply to Active Spaces. While an active meeting room can have several devices such as displays, keyboards, and mice, an active car may not have any display, keyboard, or mouse. However, it may offer additional resources (e.g., speakers, and microphone) that make it possible to use the application prior to dynamic adaptation of the application.

Active space applications must be able to run in heterogeneous Active Spaces without requiring developers to customize the applications for each environment. Users must be able to use the same applications in their active home, active car, and active office.

3   Application Model

We have implemented an application framework that simplifies the development of applications for Active Spaces. The application framework models applications as a collection of distributed components, reuses the application partitioning proposed by the Model-View-Controller pattern[10], and covers all the aspects presented in Section 2. The application framework is implemented on top of a Middleware Operating System (Gaia OS), defines an application model, implements functionality for application mapping, and implements a number of application management protocols. In this section, we present the application model and describe the application mapping, and the management protocols in the following sections.

The application model consists of five components: Model, Presentation (generalization of View), Controller, Adapter, and Coordinator. The Model, Presentation, Controller, and Adapter are the application base-level building blocks and are strictly related to the application domain functionality. The Coordinator manages the composition of the four base-level components and implements the application meta-level. It stores information about the composition of the application components and exports functionality to access and alter the component composition (e.g., attaching and detaching presentations and controllers, and listing current presentations). Figure 2 illustrates the application model.

3.1   Model

The Model component implements the logic of the application, stores and synchronizes the application's state, and provides an interface to access the application functionality. The Model maintains a list of listeners and it is responsible for notifying them about changes in the application's state to keep them synchronized. There is no restriction on the implementation of the Model, which can be built as a single component or as a collection of distributed components. A Model can be as simple as an

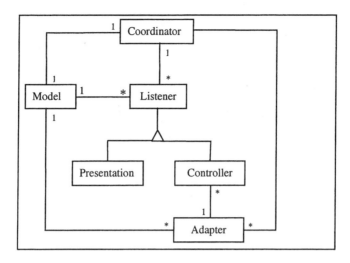

Fig. 2. Application Model UML Diagram

integer with associated methods to increase, decrease and retrieve its value and representing a counter, or as complicated as a specific data structure with some related methods representing information about a document concurrently manipulated by a group of users

3.2   Presentation

The Presentation transforms the application's state into a perceivable representation, such as a graphical or audible representation, a temperature or lighting variation, or in general, any external representation that affects the user environment and can be perceived by any of the human senses. The Presentation generalizes the scope of the View component of the MVC, which was originally defined as a graphical representation rendered on a display. An important difference with MVC views is that presentations are output entities and do not handle user inputs. This behavior is required to model non-graphical presentations such as a music player, which cannot coordinate input events. Presentations are implemented as listeners that can be attached to and detached from the Model dynamically. When a Presentation is attached to a Model, the application framework invokes the *attach* method on the Presentation and assigns the Model's reference to the Presentation. Presentations use this method (attach) as a constructor to obtain and present the application data when they are first attached to the Model. When a Presentation is detached from a Model, the middleware infrastructure invokes the *detach* method on the Presentation so the Presentation stops presenting the application's data and releases used resources. All presentations must implement the *notify* method, which is invoked by the Model whenever there is a change in the application's state. The implementation of the notify method is Presentation dependent; however, the common behavior consists on retrieving the new application state from the Model (using the Model's interface) and updating the Presentation's data, which affects the output perceived by the users.

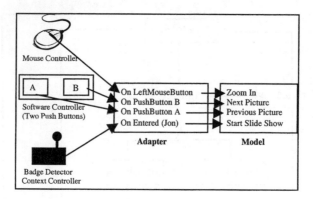

Fig. 3. Adapter Example.

3.3   Controller

A Controller is a component (i.e., hardware and software) capable of altering the application's state through the Model's interface. Examples of hardware controllers are mice, keyboards, and active badges. Examples of software controllers are GUIs (e.g., MVC and PAC[11] based) containing widgets that can be associated with user defined events, and context controllers, which are entities that process different context properties and synthesize specific context events that change the application's state. Encapsulating context in controllers has all the benefits described by Salber et. al. [12], and simplifies the development of applications that can easily react to changes in the context.

Controllers are implemented as Model listeners and therefore receive notifications from the Model (notify method) so they can be synchronized with the application state. Controllers that do not require being synchronized with the Model (e.g. array of push buttons and mouse) simply ignore the notifications. Similarly to presentations, controllers implement *attach*, *detach*, and *notify* which are invoked when the Controller is attached to, detached from, and notified by the Model.

3.4   Adapter

This component coordinates the interaction between controllers and the application Model. It maps method calls generated by controllers into requests to the application Model dynamically, therefore decoupling controllers from specific models.

Figure 3 illustrates an example of an Adapter translating the events received from three controllers into method requests for the Model. The Adapter's mappings can be set dynamically using the *setMapping* method.

According to the application model, it is possible to associate more than one Adapter with the same application. Depending on configurable properties (e.g., type of Controller, user utilizing the Controller, or context properties such as location) different adapters can be activated at different times, therefore changing the effect of controllers on the application.

3.5   Coordinator

Active space applications are a collection of distributed components composed of a Model and a number of presentations, controllers, and adapters. The dynamic nature of these applications challenges traditional interactive applications in terms of number and location of application components. In most of the cases, traditional interactive applications run in a single device and therefore those issues are not a concern. For an Active Space application, the number and location of presentations and controllers depends on the number of users, the nature of the space, and the activity taking place in the Active Space. After an Active Space application is started, it is common to add and remove presentations and controllers, or move these components to different devices contained in the space.

The Coordinator encapsulates information about the application components' composition (i.e., application meta-level) and provides an interface to register and unregister presentations, controllers, and adapters. The Coordinator provides also functionality to retrieve run-time information about the composition of the application components, and allows for fine-grained control over the composition rules. This functionality does not exist in traditional MVC, where changing the application composition is not normally required. For example, a user entering an active office containing several plasma displays may want to move the calendar application Presentation from his or her PDA to the active office. As a result, the application reconfigures itself to use all plasma displays to present different views of the calendar simultaneously (e.g., monthly, daily, and weekly view), and uses a touch screen, a keyboard, and speech recognition simultaneously to accept data and commands from the user.

The Coordinator monitors the status of the application components and reacts to failures according to user defined policies. For example, if a component of the application stops running, the Coordinator detects it and automatically unregisters the component from the application. This is the default policy, and can be overridden by users.

4   Application Mapping

The proposed application mapping mechanism provides functionality to build applications that can be used in heterogeneous Active Spaces.

Applications based on the application framework are independent of a particular Active Space by using generic application descriptions that list the application components and their requirements. These descriptions are used to create a specific application description that uses resources present in the Active Space, which match the application requirements listed in the generic description. The application framework defines two types of application descriptions: the application generic description (AGD), and the application customized description (ACD).

The AGD (Figure 4, left) is an Active Space-independent application description that lists the components of an application and their requirements. The AGD uses name-value pairs to describe the component's requirements and it is used as a template from which concrete application configurations (i.e., ACDs) are generated. The description contains a list of application components consisting of one Model, one Coordinator, zero or more presentations, and zero or more controllers. Every compo-

| Model {
ClassName JukeboxModel
Cardinality 1 1
Requirements
    device=ExecutionNode
    and OS=Windows2000
}
Presentation {
ClassName MusicPlayer
Cardinality 1 *
Requirements
  device=ExecutionNode
  and type=AudioOutput
  and OS=Windows2000
}
Controller {
ClassName ListViewer
Cardinality 1 *
Requirements
  device=ExecutionNode
  and Type=TouchScreen
  and OS=Windows2000
  or OS=WindowsCE
Mappings
  selectedEntryChanged =
  playSong
}
Coordinator {
ClassName Coordinator
Cardinality 1 1
Requirements
device=ExecutionNode
  and OS=Windows2000
} | Application =
{
Model =
{{
 ClassName="JukeboxModel",
 Hosts={{ "amr1.as.edu"}},
}}
Presentation =
{{
  ClassName ="MusicPlayer",
  Hosts={{"amr2.as.edu"}}
}},
Controller =
{{
  Classname ="ListViewer",
  Hosts={{"plasma1.as.edu"},
    {"pda1.as.edu"},
    },
  AdapterMappings = {
    {"selectedEntryChanged"
    ,"playSong"},
    }
}},
Coordinator =
{{
  ClassName ="Coordinator",
  Hosts={{"amr3.as.edu"}},
}},
} |

Fig. 4. Music Jukebox AGD (left). Music Jukebox ACD customized for an active meeting room (right).

nent entry includes a component name, an optional field with the parameters required, a field with the component cardinality (minimum and maximum number of instances of the component allowed), and a list of requirements for the component, which include information such as for example, required operating system, and hardware platform. The mapping mechanism uses the requirements to query the Active Space Middleware Operating System (Gaia in our case, also referred to as meta-OS) to obtain a list of matching entities. Finally, the Controller can include an optional number of mappings for the Adapter (if no mappings are defined, the Adapter simply forwards the requests).

The ACD is an application description that customizes an AGD to the resources of a specific Active Space. The ACD consists of information about what specific components to use, how many instances to create, and where to instantiate the components. The Controller component includes the mappings specified in the AGD.

Figure 4 (left) presents the AGD defined for an application called Music Player, which provides functionality to organize and play a collection of music files using resources present in the ubiquitous computing environment. The Model, for example, is implemented by a component named JukeboxModel, has a cardinality of one (a Music Jukebox application has exactly one Model), and requires an ExecutionNode device running Windows 2000. Gaia uses the term Execution Node to abstract any device capable of hosting the execution of Gaia components (e.g., Model, Presentation, Controller, Adapter, and Coordinator). Figure 4 (right) illustrates an ACD customized for a prototype active meting room.

The mapping mechanism receives an AGD and a target Active Space, and generates and ACD customized for such space, according to a mapping policy. The diversity of resources present in an Active Space allow for multiple application configurations. This behavior contrasts with applications running in desktop computers where applications have a fixed number of resources. For example, the music player application presented in Figure 4 could be customized to the active meeting room with one to as many song selectors as compatible execution nodes present in the space, and as many music player presentations as devices with audio output capabilities present in the space. If we also count the personal devices introduced by the users, the possible configurations are even larger.

The mapping mechanism offers two modes of operation: manual and automatic. In the manual mode of operation, users interact with a GUI that parses an application AGD and allows them to drive the mapping process by choosing the devices where the different application components will be instantiated. The automatic mode uses a service called ACDGenerator, which does not require user intervention and uses policies to drive the ACD generation process.

Based on our experience using a prototype Active Space, ACDs are not generated each time an application is started. Instead, ACDs are generated once (when no ACD is available for a specific application and a specific Active Space) and reused later on, as long as the configuration of the Active Space does not change. For example, we often use a Presentation Manager application to present slide-shows. We have a number of default ACDs for this application that allows us to instantiate the application using the displays on the left side of the room, right side of the room, and all available displays (each one using an appropriate touch-screen to instantiate the Controller, located in the appropriate side of the room). When a user selects an application, he or she is presented with a list of default configurations. However, the user is also allowed to create his or her own ACD (which can be saved and reused later).

5   Application Management

This section describes the application management functionality provided by the application framework, including instantiation, adaptation, suspension and resumption, mobility, reliability, and termination. Because of the dynamic nature of Active Spaces, there is no single algorithm for the different management tasks that fits all possible Active Space scenarios. We use policies (e.g., scripts, and services) that leverage the interfaces exported by the application framework services to perform each of the management tasks. Policies allow users and developers to customize each of the application management tasks according to their preferences, the nature of the Active Space, or the specific type of application. The use of policies allows also creating libraries with groups of policies customized to specific Active Spaces and tasks (e.g. active home, active office, and classroom assistant).

5.1   Application Instantiation

Active space applications are a collection of distributed components that interoperate using inter-process communication mechanisms such as RPC. A component is the smallest distributable execution unit in the system; it can have several formats, including an executable, a dynamic library, and a java class. Unlike traditional applications, Active Space application components do not necessarily share the same address space, or even the same machine. Therefore, they require an instantiation mechanism capable of starting application components in any device present in the Active Space and responsible for assembling the components together.

The application ACD contains information about the components required for the application, their names, initial parameters, and their target execution nodes. The application framework leverages the functionality provided by Gaia OS to instantiate the application components and to assemble them together. There are two default instantiation policies: *strict* and *best-effort*. Due to the distributed nature of Active Space applications, the instantiation mechanism must take into account the possibility of components crashing during the instantiation, and therefore must define what actions to take in case of failures. The *strict* policy guarantees that the application will be instantiated only if all components of the application are successfully created and connected. The *best-effort* policy guarantees that the application will be started if the Model, Coordinator, and at least one Presentation and Controller are successfully created and connected. This policy is useful in situations where the application has duplicated presentations and controllers, and therefore, if some of the presentations or controllers crash it does not affect the usability of the application.

5.2   Application Termination

Terminating an application requires removing all application components from all machines. The application Coordinator's interface provides a method that automatically contacts all application components and terminates them. The Coordinator uses the meta-level information that it stores to locate the appropriate components.

Although the default Coordinator implementation terminates all components, an alternative implementation could disconnect the interactive components from the application (presentations and controllers) and terminate the Model and the Coordinator. This approach keeps the interactive components running (although disconnected from any application) so they can be re-used by another compatible application.

5.3   Application Suspension and Resumption

The Model and the Coordinator are the only two components that maintain state. The Model stores state related to the functional aspect of the application (application base-level) while the Coordinator stores information about the application composition (application meta-level). Presentations and controllers are both stateless, and obtain the state from the Model.

The Coordinator provides two methods to save the state of the application. The *saveState* method provides support to save the state of the application related to the application base-level. That is, the state relevant to the application functionality (e.g.

current song being played, and volume). The default Coordinator implementation forwards the request to the Model of the application, which is responsible for saving the state in some appropriate format. The method receives a Gaia Context File System path[13], where it can save the data. This data can be accessed remotely from different Active Spaces. Saving the application state persistently is application dependent. The second method related to state saving is called *generateCurrentACD*, and it provides functionality to generate an ACD that matches the current application layout, including the number of components, their location, and their names. The returned ACD can be used to re-instantiate the application, creating the same number of components, and in the same locations. The ACD is only useful if the application is resumed in the same space where it was suspended, and the space still has the resources the application used (mobile devices might not be present anymore). Otherwise, the ACD can be used to learn about the number of components the application had before it was suspended, and negotiate with the new space to find appropriate new resources. This is the task of a specific instantiation policy. The application framework provides a default policy to suspend and resume an application in the same Active Space.

5.4   Application Reliability

When an application is composed of a collection of distributed components running on multiple machines simultaneously, reliability becomes a key factor. The application must be able to monitor the status of the different components, detect faulty components, and react accordingly. Furthermore, due to the diversity of applications, reliability must be configurable at different granularities such as per-application instance basis or per-application type basis.

Current implementation of the application framework encapsulates the reliability policies in the Coordinator. The default policy detects when an application component stops functioning and automatically detaches it from the application using the Coordinator's interface. However, this policy can be replaced with more sophisticated strategies such as for example, automatically restarting and reassembling the crashing component.

5.5   Application Mobility

The application framework provides support for both inter and intra-space mobility. Intra-space mobility is implemented as a library that interacts with the Middleware Operating System to create and terminate components, and with the Coordinator to attach and detach new and terminated components. For example, moving a Presentation requires creating a new instance of the Presentation, attaching it to the application via the Coordinator, and terminating the original instance. The only difference with duplicating is that the latter does not terminate the original instance.

Inter-space mobility is implemented by a service (Mobility Service) that reuses the application management suspension and resumption methods. The service interacts with the Middleware Operating System to detect people leaving and entering the space. When a user leaves, the service obtains a list of associated applications and suspends them. Then, when the user enters an Active Space, the service resumes the suspended applications. More details about mobility can be found at [14].

6   Addressing the Active Space Application Development Key Issues

This section details how the application framework presented in this paper addresses the issues listed in Section 2. Resource-Awareness (first issue) is addressed by the Gaia Middleware Operating System; the application development middleware services simply leverage the existing functionality (Gaia OS Space Repository) to find resources present in the current environment and relevant to the application. Multi-Device utilization (second issue) is supported by the application model defined by the middleware. The functional decomposition of applications into a Model, a number of presentations, controllers, adapters, and a Coordinator to manage all previous components, simplifies the mapping of different application aspects to different (heterogeneous) devices. Furthermore, implementing each functional unit as a distributed component allows instantiating them in different devices. User-Centrism (third issue) is supported by the intra- and inter-Active Space application mobility functionality provided by the Application Management. Users can move and duplicate components across the Active Space and can move to different Active Spaces and have their applications following them. Run-Time Adaptation (fourth issue) allows controlling the composition of the application dynamically. This functionality is implemented by the application Coordinator (functionality to attach and detach components dynamically) and it is supported by the distributed nature of the Application Model. Application mobility (fifth issue) is directly supported by the Application Management Functionality via the inter- and intra-Active Space mobility protocols. Context-Sensitivity (sixth issue) is supported by the Application Model by means of context Controller. These are controllers that receive context information and trigger changes in the application accordingly. The Controller is the mechanism to introduce context in the application, but it does not provide functionality to synthesize context information from sensors. Instead, it relies on existing services, such as the Gaia OS Context Service. Finally, Active Space Independence is supported by the Application Mapping mechanism, which supports the generation of Active Space customized ACDs .These ACDs allow portability of applications across heterogeneous Active Spaces.

The application framework provided by Gaia meta-OS covers the challenges related to Active Spaces and simplify the development of portable applications. Application developers focus on the functionality related to the application (e.g., playing music or collaboratively editing a document) and leverage the functionality provided by the application framework to supports tasks that are common to most Active Space applications (e.g., mobility, multi-device utilization, and context-awareness).

7   Music Player Example

We present in this section the Music Player Application, an application based on our application framework that provides functionality for playing music files taking benefit of the resources contained in the Active Space where the application is instantiated. The application base-level provides functionality for managing a collection of music files distributed among different devices located in different Active Spaces, allows selecting, controlling, and playing a specific song in the user's current location, and

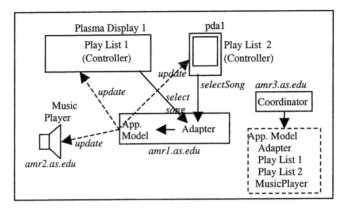

Fig. 5. Music Application Composition.

exports information about the play list contents, as well as the currently selected song. The application provides also functionality to register, unregister, duplicate, and move presentations and controllers dynamically, adapts to context changes, and uses mobility policies to follow the user to different Active Spaces.

7.1   Implementation Details

In this example we focus on our active meeting room (Figure 1), managed by Gaia OS. Figure 4 illustrates the AGD for the music application, which consists of a Model, a Presentation (player), a Controller, and a Coordinator. The Coordinator automatically instantiates a default Adapter that maps the events from the Controller (e.g. entry selected) into method requests to the Model (e.g. play). The MusicPlayer Presentation interacts with a commercial-off-the-shelf application to play the audio. The response time of the application is within an acceptable range from an interactive point of view. For example, selecting a song requires less than a second to execute and manipulating the meta-level (duplicating, moving, attaching and detaching presentations and input sensors) takes from 3-6 seconds depending on the request.

7.2   Instantiating and Using the Application

We describe in this section the Music Application's instantiation process. The user enters the active meeting room, registers his or her PDA, and selects a strict instantiation policy to create the application according to the ACD illustrated on the right side of Figure 4. The diagram depicted in Figure 5 illustrates the resulting application partitioning.

When the user selects a song using the PDA's Controller, this sends an event (selectedEntryChanged) to the Adapter with the name of the song. The Adapter sends a request to the Model (playSong), which sends an update to the music player Presentation, and to the two controllers (List Viewers). The player gets the music data from the Model and starts playing, and the list viewers get the name of the currently selected song and highlight the name in their list.

8   Performance Evaluation

The main goal of the application framework is to provide support for the construction of a new type of applications we refer to as Active Space applications. In order to evaluate the framework, we have focused on whether or not the functionality provided is sufficient, rather than performance. Both Gaia OS and the application framework are built on top of Orbacus, which is an efficient and fast CORBA implementation, and CORBA UIC[15], a customized and efficient minimalist CORBA ORB. Therefore, the response time of the system is well within an acceptable interactive response time and comparable to interactive desktop applications.

In order to evaluate the application framework, we have built fourteen applications that have allowed us to validate the framework. The fourteen applications show that the application framework is generic enough to cover a large range of interactive Active Space applications.

We present in this section a performance evaluation for a slideshow application we use regularly in our Active Space (Presentation Manager). The application consists of a Model that keeps information about the state of the slideshow (e.g., slideshow name, slideshow file's path, and current slide), a Presentation that uses Microsoft Power Point to render the slides (via the COM interface), and a VCR Controller with functionality to start and stop the slideshow and navigate the slides. The application allows presenting synchronized slides in multiple displays simultaneously, and can also have multiple VCR controllers attached simultaneously. Furthermore, it provides functionality for intra- and inter-space mobility (default application framework functionality). We present next, a performance evaluation for application instantiation, moving a Presentation (slide viewer) from one display to another (intra-space mobility), navigating slides, and terminating the application. All the tests were performed in our prototype Active Space, which has a 1Gb Ethernet network, 802.11b, 15 Pentium IV at 1.2 GHz with 256MB of RAM, and 4 61" Plasma displays. All the times presented are the average result of ten experiments.

Figure 6 illustrates the average time required to instantiate the Presentation Manager application, which consists of a Model, a Coordinator, a number of presentations (one, two, three, and four, each in a different display), and one or zero controllers. Each configuration corresponds to a different ACD. The time was calculated from the time we start the application until the first slide is displayed by all presentations. The average time increases linearly as the number of presentations increases. The time required to start Microsoft PowerPoint in one machine by double-clicking the icon and starting the slideshow is 0.85 seconds (no Gaia OS or application framework). Starting the Presentation Manager with one Presentation and one VCR Controller takes 2.18 seconds, while the same application without the VCR Controller requires 1.13s. These times include creating the Model, the Coordinator, a Presentation, and one or zero controllers, and assembling them together using the Coordinator interface. All components except the VCR Controller are implemented as DLLs and creating them requires loading them in a pre-created process (Component Container). The VCR Controller, on the other hand, is an executable. Creating a new executable takes longer than loading a DLL (at least in Windows), which explains the 1.05 additional seconds required to instantiate the application with the Controller. Based on the previous results, the impact of the application framework is negligible. According to Figure 6, there is a penalty of approximately 1s for each additional Presentation. This number is the time required to create the PowerPoint COM object plus the time required by this object to render the first slide (the Presentation creates the COM object and sends requests to display slides). It is possible to improve the instantiation time. Our current instantiation policy instantiates all presentations sequentially, and therefore, it waits until a Presentation is properly created before creating a new one. It is possible to implement an optimistic instantiation policy that uses asynchronous method invocations (it does not wait for a response) and simply checks at the end whether or not all components were created successfully (interacting with the Gaia OS Space Repository). In this case, the time would be significantly smaller, regardless the number of presentations because all presentations would be instantiated in parallel.

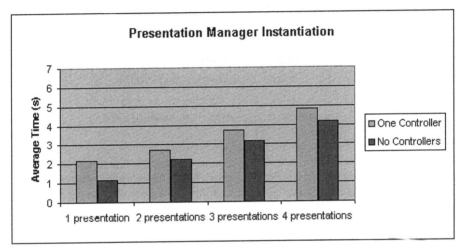

Fig. 6. Average time to instantiate the Presentation Manager application.

Next experiment calculated the time required to move a Presentation (slide) from one display to another. This time included creating a Presentation in the execution node associated to the target display, attaching it to the Coordinator, unregistering and terminating the original Presentation, and finally the time required by the new Presentation to display the current slide (the new Presentation gets the current state by interacting with the Model). The average time based on ten experiments was 2 seconds.

Based on our experience with all the applications, the interactive application response time is similar to a desktop application. For example, in the case of the Presentation Manager, the time it takes to move to the next or previous slide since we press a button in a VCR Controller (running on a wireless connected PDA or on a wired connected touch screen) is the same as in a standard Power Point application running on a PC (e.g., pressing the space bar), which is on average below a second. This time includes sending an RPC request over the network from the VCR Controller to the Adapter, the Adapter mapping the request to the appropriate method request for the Model, sending an RPC to the Model, the Model updating the current slide number and sending a notification (asynchronous RPC) to the presentations (the notification includes the slide number), and the presentations parsing the notification and rendering the appropriate slide via the PowerPoint COM object. Presentations cache the slideshow file locally at the beginning of the slideshow so they only ask for the file once (they obtain the file from the Gaia Context File System). The time is bounded by the Power Point rendering engine, not by the mechanisms implemented by the application framework

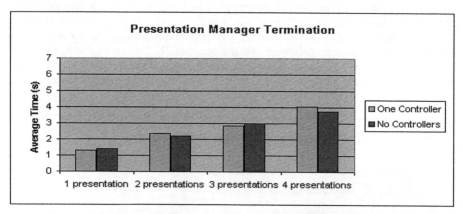

Fig. 7. Average time to terminate the Presentation Manager.

Our next performance evaluation calculates the time required for terminating the application. The Coordinator exports a method that implements this functionality. The method interacts with the Model, Presentation(s), Controller(s), and Adapter(s), notifies them that they are being unregistered from the application (the components can then implement cleaning-up procedures including resource release), and uses the Gaia Component Management Core functionality to terminate all components, including itself. In the Presentation Manager application, the only components that implement clean-up functionality are the Presentations. When they receive the notification, they stop rendering the slide and terminate the execution of the PowerPoint COM object. For our experiment, we calculated the execution time of the Coordinator's *terminateApplication* method. We used the same configurations as in the instantiation experiments, that is, one, two, three, and four presentations, once with a VCR Controller, and the second time without the VCR Controller. Figure 7 illustrates the termination times. In this case, the average time for terminating an application with or without a VCRController is roughly the same (the time required by Windows to terminate the VCR Controller executable is negligible).

Finally, suspending and resuming an application is similar to terminating and instantiating an application respectively, with additional required time to save the state (suspend) and restore the state (resumption). We have performed some experiments suspending and resuming Presentation Manager in the same Active Space (we reuse the same ACD). The time to save the state stored by the model and the coordinator is on average 30ms (using Gaia's distributed file system), while the time to restore the state took, on average, 50ms. Therefore, the time required to suspend and resume an application is bounded by the termination and instantiation times.

Based on the performance evaluation and on our experience with the rest of Gaia applications, the Application Framework does not introduce any overhead on the overall application response time, compared to most traditional desktop applications.

9   Related Work

The Pebbles [2] project is investigating partitioning user interfaces among a collection of devices. Pebbles is mostly concerned with issues related to GUIs, and the proposed infrastructure does not provide functionality for dynamically altering the partitioning layout. Our application framework focuses on the application composition, management, adaptability and configurability, and provides reflective functionality that allows altering the application structure at run-time.

BEACH [16] is a component-based software infrastructure that provides support for constructing collaborative applications for active meeting rooms. BEACH applications are similar to the applications we propose in that they contemplate one user exploiting multiple devices at the same time, dynamic reconfigurations, integration of the physical space, interoperation among all resources contained in the space, and they rely on a software infrastructure to access resources contained in the space. However, the main differences between BEACH and our approach are that BEACH concentrates on collaborative applications while we consider both collaborative and single user applications, BEACH is customized for meeting room-like environments while our framework can be used in different scenarios.

Graspable Interfaces [17] presents an evolutionary model for GUIs where physical objects are used to interact with applications. This approach distinguishes time-multiplexed input devices from space-multiplexed input devices. Our framework combines both concepts and defines the time-space-multiplexed model.

The PIMA [18] and I-Crafter [19] projects propose a model for building platform independent applications. Developers define an abstract application that is automatically customized at run-time to particular devices. PIMA and I-Crafter generate applications for a single device, while we consider applications partitioned across devices. However, we can leverage the functionality provided by both approaches to dynamically generate application presentations customized to specific devices.

The Presentation-Abstraction-Controller[20] (PAC) is a framework that specifies interactive application components and their interrelation rules. The Presentation defines the concrete syntax of the application (i.e., input and output behavior of application), the Abstraction corresponds to the semantics of the application (i.e., functions that the application is able to perform), and the Control maintains the consistency between abstractions and presentations. PAC combines the input and output mechanisms in the Presentation component, while MVC requires two components, namely View and Controller. In PAC, Presentations do not need to know the details about the Abstraction. This functionality is encapsulated in the Control, which keeps Presentations and Abstractions synchronized. The advantage is that in PAC, all control functionality is encapsulated in the Control component, while in MVC, the functionality is distributed across View-Controller pairs. The Abstraction-Link-View[21] (ALV) is also a framework to build interactive applications that are used by multiple users simultaneously. Its goal is to maximize the separation between the user interface and the application logic. The main rationale behind ALV is to foster human-to-human communication and share common data during the interaction to facilitate the interaction. ALV is based on constraints, which allows registering a function with a specific variable. Shall the variable change, the function is automatically invoked. Constraints allow for fine grained control over the synchronization rules, which contrasts with MVC, where the View is responsible for determining what changed in the Model. The

Abstraction implements the semantics of the application, the View presents the information managed by the Abstraction to the user and coordinates user input, and the Link stores all constraints and implements the functionality for synchronizing Views and the Abstraction. Every application has at least one View per user. The Link allows the View and the Abstraction to ignore each other, which simplifies application development and encourages component reuse. The Active Space application framework described in this paper, although reusing the original concepts from MVC, uses techniques present in PAC and ALV.

Projects such as Stanford's iROS [22] and CMU's Aura [23] provide a middleware infrastructure to manage ubiquitous computing environments. However, none of them provides an explicit middleware infrastructure customized to support application development.

10 Conclusions and Future Work

This paper presents our application framework for designing and building user-centric, resource-aware, context-sensitive, multi-device, mobile applications. These applications are bound to users instead of devices, can take benefit of resources present in the users' environment, can react to changes in the environment, and can be partitioned among different devices.

The application framework defines an application model that provides a component (Coordinator) to access and modify the composition of the application dynamically, implements a mechanism to define applications abstractly and manually or automatically map them to arbitrary environments, uses flexible policies to separate the basic application construction and modification functionality from particular strategies.

We have successfully implemented the functionality described for Gaia OS and the application framework, and have fourteen applications that prove that the framework simplifies the design and implementation process. Furthermore, the flexibility and dynamism of such applications has simplified the interaction with Active Spaces such as our prototype active meeting room. The framework allows integrating existing components including Microsoft COM objects (e.g., Power Point) as presentations, controllers, and models, and extends the functionality of these components by allowing users to move the component across different devices, and even extend them for collaborative environments. Integrating existing components is done by having a Presentation, Controller, or Model wrapping the existing components and delegating the application framework-related requests to the wrapped component.

Although we have not fully reached the proposed customizable habitat vision yet, we believe that the application framework presented in this paper is a valid solution to program existing device rich environments.

Acknowledgements

This research is supported by the National Science Foundation grant NSF 98-70736, NSF 9970139, and NSF infrastructure grant NSF EIA 99-72884

References

1. Roman M, Hess CK, Cerqueira R, Ranganat A, Campbell RH, Nahrstedt K: Gaia: A Middleware Infrastructure to Enable Active Spaces. IEEE Pervasive 1:74-82, 2002
2. Myers BA: Using Hand-Held Devices and PCs Together, Communications of the ACM, vol 44, 2001, pp 34-41
3. Abowd GD, Mynatt ED: Charting Past, Present, and Future Research in Ubiquitous Computing. ACM Transactions on Computer-Human Interaction 7:29-58, 2000
4. Costa FM, Blair GS, Coulson G: Experiments with an architecture for reflective middleware. IOS Press 7:313-325, 2000
5. Kon F, Singhai A, Campbell RH, Carvalho D, Moore R, Ballesteros FJ: 2K: A Reflective, Component-Based Operating System for Rapidly Changing Environments. Paper presented at the ECOOP'98 Workshop on Reflective Object-Oriented Programming and Systems, Brussels, Belgium, July 1998 1998
6. Kiczales G, Rivires Jd, Bobrow DG: The Art of the Metaobject Protocol. MIT Press, 1991
7. Kiczales G: Beyond the Black Box: Open Implementation. IEEE Software 13:137-142, 1996
8. Blair G, Coulson G, Robin P, Papathomas M: An Architecture For Next Generation Middleware. Paper presented at the IFIP International Conference on Distributed Systems, Platforms, and Open Distributed Processing, Lake District, England, September 1998
9. Dey AK: Providing Architectural Support for Building Context-Aware Applications, PhD Thesis in Computer Science. Atlanta, Georgia Institute of Technology, 2000, pp 188
10. Krasner GE, Pope ST: A Description of the Model-View-Controller User Interface Paradigm in the Smalltalk-80 System. Journal of Object Oriented Programming 1:26-49, 1988
11. Coutaz J: PAC: An object-oriented model for dialog design. Paper presented at the INTERACT'87: The IFIP Conference on Human Computer Interaction, Stuttgart, Germany, 1987
12. Salber D, Dey AK, Abowd GD: The Context Toolkit: Aiding the Development of Context-Enabled Applications. Paper presented at the CHI'99, Pittsburgh, May 1999
13. Hess C, Campbell RH: A Context-Aware Data Management System for Ubiquitous Computing Applications. Paper presented at the International Conference in Distributed Computing Systems (ICDCS 2003), Providence, Rhode Island, May 19-22, 2003 2003
14. Roman M, Ho H, Campbell RH: Application Mobility in Active Spaces. Paper presented at the 1st International Conference on Mobile and Ubiquitous Multimedia, Oulu, Finland, 2002
15. Roman M, Kon F, Campbell RH: Reflective Middleware: From Your Desktop to Your Hand. IEEE Distributed Systems Online. Special Issue on Reflective Middleware, 2001
16. Tandler P: Software Infrastructure for Ubiquitous Computing Environments: Supporting Synchronous Collaboration with Heterogeneous Devices. Paper presented at the Ubicomp 2001: Ubiquitous Computing, Atlanta, Georgia, September 30 - October 2 2001
17. Fitzmaurice GW: Graspable User Interfaces, PhD Thesis in Computer Science. Toronto, University of Toronto, 1996
18. Banavar G, Beck J, Gluzberg E, Munson J, Sussman JB, Zukowski D: An Application Model for Pervasive Computing. Paper presented at the 6th ACM MOBICOM, Boston, MA, 2000
19. Ponekanti SR, Lee B, Fox A, Hanrahan P, Winograd T: ICrafter: A Service Framework for Ubiquitous Computing Environments. Paper presented at the Ubicomp 2001: Ubiquitous Computing, Atlanta, Georgia, September 30 - October 2 2001
20. Coutaz J: PAC, an Object Oriented Model for Dialog Design. Paper presented at the Human Computer Interaction. INTERACT 1987 1987

21. Hill RD: The Abstraction-Link-View Paradigm: Using Constraints to Connect User Interface to Applications. Paper presented at the CHI May 3-7 1992
22. Johanson B, Fox A, Winograd T: Experiences with Ubiquitous Computing Rooms. IEEE Pervasive Computing Magazine 1:67-74, 2002
23. Sousa JP, Garlan D: Aura: an Architectural Framework for User Mobility in Ubiquitous Computing Environments. Paper presented at the IEEE/IFIP Conference on Software Architecture, Montreal, August 25-31 2002

A Proactive Middleware Platform
for Mobile Computing*

Andrei Popovici, Andreas Frei, and Gustavo Alonso

Department of Computer Science
Swiss Federal Institute of Technology (ETHZ)
ETH Zentrum, CH-8092 Zürich, Switzerland
{popovici,frei,alonso}@inf.ethz.ch

Abstract. An obvious prerequisite for mobile computing devices is the
ability to adapt to different computing environments. Otherwise the devices are forced to carry with them everything they may eventually need
during their operational life time. This is neither desirable nor feasible,
thereby hinting at the need for dynamic adaptation. The idea would be to
let the environment be proactive and adapt the application rather than
forcing the application to adapt itself to every possible environment. In
this paper we present a platform for doing exactly this. Applications
running on our modified JVM can be extended at run time with new
functionality. Through this platform, mobile devices can acquire on-the-
fly any functionality extension they may need to work properly in a given
environment. The functionality extensions are local in time and space:
they are active only on a specific site and just for the time they are
needed. The platform can be used in both centralized settings (with a
base station providing the extensions) or in self configuring mode (extensions are provided by peers). In this paper we describe the platform,
how to use it and report on one of the several prototypes that have been
constructed.

1 Introduction

Device proliferation challenges existing software architectures and creates new
types of yet unsolved problems. For instance, a large number of mobile nodes, potentially heterogeneous in nature, is hard to configure and administrate
[SGGB99]. Similarly, devices that are continually moving from one location to
another need to be able to adapt themselves to the new locations. Otherwise,
the devices need to be overprovisioned in terms of functionality so that they can
operate in as wide a range of settings as possible. Such an approach bloats the
applications, making them more complex and resource hungry. Moreover, there
will always be situations that were not foreseen in the design or settings that

---

* The work presented in this paper was supported (in part) by the National Com-
petence Center in Research on Mobile Information and Communication Systems
(NCCR-MICS), a center supported by the Swiss National Science Foundation under
grant number 5005-67322.

M. Endler and D. Schmidt (Eds.): Middleware 2003, LNCS 2672, pp. 455–473, 2003.

have changed since application deployment. In those cases, the application will simply no longer function.

In almost all forms of mobile computing, whether it is *nomadic* (a mobile device that changes location and needs to work with different fixed infrastructures) or *ad-hoc* (mobile devices that want to spontaneously interact with each other), the key to deal with such problems is adaptability. The basic idea is that for a mobile device to work properly at a given location, it must adapt itself to that location in both time and space. Spatial adaptation implies adopting the policy and requirements of the *current location*. Time adaptation implies adopting the *current policies and requirements* of the actual location. Both can change at any time and in completely unexpected ways.

To avoid limiting the adaptation capabilities of mobile devices, we suggest not to rely entirely on the abilities of the application. Instead, we argue that there is a need for proactive environments capable of adjusting and extending the functionality of mobile devices. Note that this allows to naturally address both spatial and time adaptation. When a mobile device enters a new computing environment, the environment provides the necessary extensions so that the device can operate in that location at that moment. Of course, the device should be able to discard the extensions once it leaves that particular location. The environment can be anything: a base station, a community of devices interacting spontaneously, or just another device.

As an example of such proactive adaptation, consider a mobile robot used in different production halls. Every time the robot enters a particular hall, it is the hall (e.g., a base station supervising the hall) that adapts the robot to the task at hand. For instance, in one hall it might be necessary to keep track and log every single movement performed by the robot. In another hall, it might be necessary to make sure the robot does not perform certain actions. In yet another hall, every movement of the robot must be sent to another robot that mirrors exactly the movements of the first robot. As soon as the robot fulfills its task and leaves a give production hall, the behavior extensions and additional functionality explicitly added by that hall are discarded.

An advantage of this proactive adaptation is that the program controlling the robot does not need to be aware of any of the extensions appended at run-time. Thus, the program can be kept small and focused on controlling the robots, leaving any adaptation to extensions acquired on the fly. Another advantage is that proactive adaptation allows to extend the functionality of the robot in multiple ways, ways that may not have been foreseen at the time the robot was constructed. Finally, it is possible to change the policies and requirements of a production at any time. Newly arrived robots will simply acquire new extensions that reflect the new policies. Robots already in the hall will be adapted by removing the old extensions and replacing them with the new ones. Moreover, bugs, fixes, or evolution of the software running in the robot can be done through extensions so that the robot is kept functional until there is an opportunity to replace the code in the robot.

Similar scenarios for adaptability exists in a multitude of mobile computing applications. An example are PDAs entering a building being adapted with an encryption layer, a persistence module, and a filter that prevents using certain resources. Another example are accounting modules being added to mobile devices (e.g., lap-tops) to bill them for the use of services in a given location. In all these examples, the key aspect is that applications do not need to establish beforehand what they can and cannot do. Adaptation takes place through a proactive environment capable of delivering the necessary extensions to the mobile devices, devices that must carry a platform to dynamically acquire, apply, and discard extensions as needed.

In this paper we describe a complete system that can be used to implement such scenarios. The system comprises two layers. The first layer resides in each mobile device and provides the support for adaptation, i.e., it provides the ability to apply *run-time extensions* to applications. For this first layer we use the PROSE dynamic AOP system [PGA02,PAG03]. The second layer is in charge of distributing and managing the extensions. This second layer typically resides in a base station but can also be embedded in mobile devices for exchanging extensions in a peer-to-peer manner. This layer is implemented using MIDAS (MIddleware for ADaptive Services), a Jini [AWO+99] based system that can deliver extensions to mobile devices using a wireless network. Together, the two layers can be used to extend the functionality of either single devices or entire communities of mobile devices.

The rest of the paper is structured as follows. Section 2 motivates the proposed architecture by looking at the infrastructure and requirements. Section 3 presents the core functionality of the system to enable adaptive nodes, and illustrates the concepts of MIDAS. We then show in Section 4 how to use MIDAS for adapting robots in an industrial setting. Section 5 concludes the paper.

2   Motivation

In this section we state the requirements for proactive adaptation and discuss an infrastructure that could address these requirements. We also comment on related work.

2.1   Requirements

As pointed out in the introduction, adaptation is a key approach to deal with the variety of computing environments and changing settings that a mobile application will encounter during its operational life time. Such adaptation can be achieved in many different ways. However, feasible solutions must take into account a number of important requirements.

A first requirement is for the extension mechanism to be generic rather than application specific. In the same way mobile devices cannot foresee all possible situations they will encounter, it is also not possible to predict which applications will require adaptation. Furthermore, since proactive adaptation requires a certain infrastructure, it is also not reasonable to provide such infrastructure on an application basis. Whatever the infrastructure is, it must work with a wide range of applications.

A second requirement is for the extension mechanism and supporting infrastructure to be entirely symmetric. In other words, if a mobile device is capable of receiving extensions, it should also be able to provide extensions to other nodes. Such ability does not need to be used in all cases but should not be excluded by design. For reasons of space, we concentrate in this paper mostly on solutions involving a base station although the ideas presented and the system being described can be used without modification in a peer-to-peer setting.

Finally, and for obvious practical reasons, the mechanism used for adaptation through functionality extensions must be secure to avoid that it is misused and tampered with. Secure adaptation involves two aspects: making sure that the extension comes from a trusted party and making sure that the extension does not access system resources if it is not supposed to do so.

2.2   An Infrastructure for Proactive Adaptation

Interactions between clients and service providers have been traditionally supported by middleware. Traditional middleware mainly helps to provide a uniform view of a system, in spite of the possible heterogeneous nature of the underlying components. The middleware also provides functionality that facilitates the development of applications over such heterogeneous components. For instance, the Corba Component Model [CCM97]) adapts services with transparent middleware functionality for implicit context, authentication and authorization, etc.

In conventional settings, such service adaptation is based on a fixed server architecture. What we propose is to make any mobile computing environment act as a middleware server capable of adapting at run time any application entering that environment. Since doing so for any possible mobile computing environment would be next to impossible, we have concentrated our first efforts in Java based applications. Hence, the idea is to provide a nomadic infrastructure [BCKP95] where applications running on a JVM can be provided with extensions (also written in Java) that modify their behavior. The problem turns then into how to adapt Java programs at run time and how to manage and distribute Java extensions under the constraints imposed by the requirements listed above. In what follows we describe step by step how these two problems can be solved.

2.3   Related Work

The type of adaptation we advocate is somewhat different from the conventional notions of adaptation and context awareness [SAW94]. What we propose is to dynamically extend or modify the functionality of an application. This is different from adaptation based in sensing the environment and choosing between different pre-programmed options. It is also different from adaptation based in obtaining data about the environment (either by the application itself or the environment provides the data) and changing behavior according to an established program.

In what we propose, adaptation means adding functionality that was not there before. This is difficult to achieve with current technologies. The reason is that there is no generic way to augment at run-time the functionality of an application unless this was foreseen at development time.

The explicit participation of the environment in the adaptation of underlying applications has been explored in the Odyssey system [NSN+97]. This form of adaptation is known as application-aware adaptation. Application-aware adaptation has been used, for instance, to hide the effects of mobility using replication and cache consistency techniques. Conceptually, this work is related to our approach since it also advocates an active implication of the infrastructure in the adaptation of applications.

The same need to shift a part of the adaptation logic away from the application has lead to approaches that propose new software architectures to support adaptive systems [ECDF01,KF01]. Thus, ICrafter [PLF+01] advocates the move of intelligence from the end-points to the resource-rich infrastructure. ICrafter uses pattern matching techniques to overcome the need for standardized interfaces, and relies on user interface generators to create functionality for new services. The user interface generators in the ICrafter design roughly correspond to the application-aware infrastructure we want to associate to each location. However, it is application specific and some of the ideas might be difficult to generalize. In our case, we use aspect-orientation techniques [KLM+97,OL01,BH02] to ensure an application and adaptation neutral platform.

Finally, it is worth mentioning the ongoing work in dynamic and adaptive middleware. An example is an adaptive service layer in CORBA [ZBS97] that provides horizontal support for the simultaneous adaptation of several applications. A step further is represented by reflective middleware [APW01, CBCP1, BC01], which opens the definition of the infrastructure and allows to dynamically reprogram the service layers. Implementations of reflective middleware can be found at the CORBAng [EGK+99] project which uses meta-models to structure a meta-space. Some approaches [YK01] even propose dynamic hardware-reconfiguration to support adaptability. The Cactus project [HSH+99,CHS01] is another good example of how adaptive software systems can be used in distributed environments. While these approaches represent considerable progress, we believe our approach complements them by addressing a more generic form of adaptation.

3   System Architecture

In a first step, we describe how to extend the functionality of an application at run-time. In a second step, we describe the management layer for extensions.

3.1   Step 1: Generic Support for Run-Time Extensions with PROSE

There are many similarities between the problems addressed by conventional middleware architectures for fixed computing and the type of adaptations we envision for mobile settings. For example, when the problem of passing implicit context information along a remote call translates into *adding* functionality at a *large number* of points in the execution of an application, such as all incoming and outgoing method calls.

In such cases, it is not sufficient to instantiate new components into an existing service. One must actively modify existing components. With this in mind, we turned to *Aspect Oriented Programming* (AOP) [KLM+97] as the most suitable approach to address this problem.

AOP allows adding extensions to an existing application. AOP is originally intended for extensions that cannot be easily expressed using traditional object-oriented techniques like inheritance. The description of such extensions is based on the concept of *aspects*, the part of a software system that affects the behavior of a component. An aspect is defined by a *crosscut* and a *crosscut action*. A simple aspect example may be:

before methods-with-signature *'void *.send*(byte[] x,..)'*
do encrypt(x)

This aspect specifies that in all methods whose name starts with "send", and which receive a byte array as a parameter, the byte array must be first encrypted. The crosscut of this aspect is the collection of method entries in a given application that matches the specified signature patterns. In AspectJ [XC02,LK98], e.g., crosscuts contain patterns for matching the invocations of method(s) of a set of classes, access and modification of objects fields, and exception handling. The crosscut action (here, the encryption of the byte array) is the code to be inserted at (before or after) the points defined by the crosscut. The act of inserting the new code, thereby changing the behavior of the application, is performed by a so called *weaver* tool. Weavers are typically based on a preprocessor or a specialized compiler as AOP was originally designed as a compile time technique.

Such platforms for aspect-oriented programming [XC02] are not appropriate for expressing run-time adaptations, because they bind aspects (extensions) and application classes at compile-time. The alternative is to modify the application code at run-time. For this purpose, we have developed PROSE[1] (PROgrammable extenSions of sErvices), a system in which aspects are first-class Java entities, and all related constructs are expressed using the base language, Java [PGA02,PAG03]. PROSE allows programmers to:

- adapt the functionality of a *running* application by dynamically injecting an extension
- make adaptation secure by providing the appropriate protection from malicious extensions that may use the proactive adaptation as a trapdoor.

Addressing Run-Time Adaptation in PROSE. To add functionality at run-time, PROSE leverages the fact that most modern JVMs [Sun02,SOT+00]

---

[1] PROSE is available for download from our web site http://prose.ethz.ch

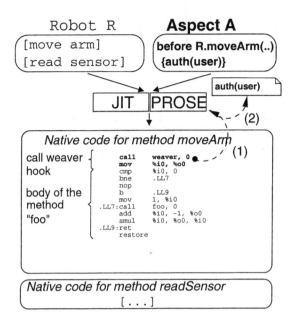

Fig. 1. The run-time adaptation process in PROSE

uses a just-in-time (JIT) compiler. A JIT compiler continuously translates at run-time code being interpreted by the JVM into native code. The native code is equivalent to the Java byte-code, but can be executed more efficiently. PROSE adds extension functionality by instructing the JIT-compiler to insert additional actions (advice code) when transforming the bytecode into native code.

Consider as an example the problem of extending the behavior of a robot R. For simplicity, assume that the movements of the robot are controlled by only two methods, *moveArm* and *readSensor*. An aspect A defines the policy for the robot actions in a given production hall. A will be woven through the robot application whenever R enters the production hall. For simplicity, we consider that A adds the middleware functionality for authorization. With this, each execution of *R.moveArm* is dynamically extended such that it is preceded by a call to *auth(user)*. By this transparent authorization, the production hall has the ability to prevent the robot from executing actions on behalf of clients that are not authorized. Figure 1 shows how PROSE modifies the translation of Java bytecode into native code. R's functionality is translated into native code, and PROSE adds *minimal hooks* (or *stubs*) before the actual code of the methods. Stubs must be woven at *all* potential join-points in R's code (such as field changes, method boundaries, exception throws and handlers, etc.). In our case two native instructions are added before the native code corresponding to *moveArm*. Every time *moveArm* is called, PROSE is notified (step 1). When this happens, PROSE checks whether any additional action must be executed, and eventually executes all actions corresponding to that join-point (step 2).

This layer of indirection – the stub code – leads to an increase of the resulting code size (since code is added at locations where no advice is needed). However, given the small size of the minimal hooks, the impact on performance is small [PAG03].

Addressing Secure Execution in PROSE. Functionality extensions received from foreign hosts, could contain malicious code. To prevent this, PROSE was designed in such a way that the extension code is entirely isolated from the original code of the application. This allows practically any Java application to use the standard Java security model [SM] to run in a sandbox the extensions received from remote hosts . Through this, PROSE defines an *aspect sandbox* in which interceptions, although spread through various components, are treated as if they belong to the same component.

With PROSE on every mobile node we gain the capabilities of AOP together with the ability to perform the weaving at run-time without disrupting the application. With this, we achieve the necessary generality as well as the support for dynamic adaptation we are aiming at.

3.2   Step 2: Extension Management with MIDAS

When every mobile node runs on a PROSE-enabled JVM, it can be extended at run-time – provided that an extension is woven into the system at the right time and place. Adding and removing extensions, and guaranteeing that the right extensions are inserted into the appropriate nodes is an important task that guarantees the locality of adaptations. This task – the *extension management* – is provided in our architecture by MIDAS. MIDAS builds on top of PROSE and provides the following services:

extension distribution: discover new nodes joining a local environment, distribute extensions to them and then activate these extensions using PROSE,

locality of adaptations: keep extensions alive for the time a mobile device reaches that location, revoke extensions for those nodes that leave the location, and allow the replacement of obsolete extensions with new ones in case the local policy evolves or it is changed, and

security: enhance the sandbox security model provided by PROSE with a trust model in which extensions are accepted by mobile nodes only if they come from a trusted party.

Addressing Extension Distribution. To achieve this goal, MIDAS separates nodes into two roles. *Extension base* nodes contain a list of extensions. They discover new nodes joining the network and send extensions to the newcomers. *Extension receivers* can get extensions from extension bases. We assume that each extension receiver has PROSE activated on its JVM. When it obtains an extension from an extension base, it immediately inserts the extension using the PROSE API. Extension receivers also discard extensions when they leave a network or lose contact with the extension base.

By appropriately assigning extension base and extension receiver roles, one can achieve various forms of adaptations. At one extreme, each node can contain an extension base. When it joins a new community, it distributes its extensions and receives others from the existing nodes. This type of organization is appropriate for creating an information system infrastructure in an entirely ad-hoc manner. At the other extreme, each physical location may have a base station as extension base. All other nodes (e.g., the mobile nodes) are extension receivers. This organization is appropriate for adaptations that correspond to infrastructure and organizational requirements. Between the two extremes, many other configurations are possible.

Addressing Revocation of Extensions. The proactive platform must be designed for device mobility. This implies that extensions must transiently adapt a service (for as long as the service is working in a given space). To model this behavior, the extensions are *leased* to each node (i.e., to the adaptation service of a node). It is the responsibility of each extension base to keep alive the functionality it has distributed among nodes. When a node leaves a given space, the leases on the extensions acquired in that space fail to be renewed and they will be discarded. Each extension is notified before leaving a proactive space so that it can execute a shut-down procedure ensuring that all current operations are completed and a consistent state is achieved. The revocation service is achieved as follows:

1. each MIDAS extension base keeps track of its extension activity (what nodes where adapted, at what point in time) and optionally implements a simple roaming algorithm to deal with nodes migrating between areas.
2. each MIDAS extension receiver keeps track of what extensions have been obtained from what base. If a MIDAS base fails to keep a given extension alive, the extension is immediately withdrawn from the system. By autonomously withdrawing extensions, extension receivers address the space and time dimension of adaptations.

Addressing Security. The layer of security provided by PROSE (in which extensions are run in a sandbox) is enhanced by MIDAS with an additional layer of verification. In MIDAS each extension instance has to be signed. This ensures that the received extension has been instantiated and configured by a trusted entity. The verification of the originator of an extension is done before insertion of the extension in PROSE. Each extension receiver node (and thus each mobile device) may define its preferences and trusted entities.

3.3   Example of MIDAS

The best way to describe how MIDAS works is through an example. Consider a service m_R exported by a robot (R). Figure 2.a illustrates this situation. What

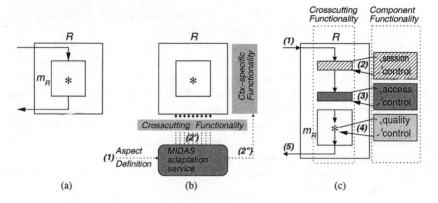

Fig. 2. (a) Remote method call of m_R on a node (b) Node containing the adaptation service and (c) Remote method call of m_R after the node is adapted.

we would like to do is to adapt the functionality m_R of robot R as the robot enters a production hall. This adaptation occurs through the adaptation service that the robot carries with it (Figure 2.b).

The first step in the adaptation process is to detect the adaptation service of the node. For service detection and brokerage, one can use existing platforms for spontaneous networking. In our case, we have chosen Jini [AWO+99]. The adaptation service advertises itself as a Jini service, thereby announcing its presence to the environment (assume for simplicity that the environment is a base station). The environment recognizes the adaptation service and, therefore, knows that the node can be adapted. Let's assume the production hall has a set of predefined adaptations. Furthermore, assume that these adaptations implement an access control policy and a quality assurance mechanism that logs persistently all changes to the state of a robot (represented as $*$ in Figure 2) in a database associated to the production hall.

The two adaptations are sent to the adaptation service of the new node as aspects specifying how and where the application has to be changed (step 1 in Figure 2.b). The activation of the aspects comprises two steps. The first is to include in m_R the code necessary to trap the execution at the appropriate points (step 2' in Figure 2.b). The second is to instantiate the extensions that will carry out the adaptation (step 2" in Figure 2.b). Once the adaptation service has activated the incoming aspects, node R reaches the state shown in Figure 2.c.

At this stage, the node is adapted and its functionality has been modified (Figure 2.c). When m_R is invoked (step 1, Figure 2.c) and before the method m_R is executed, a first interception occurs (step 2, Figure 2.c). This first interception is used to call a module that extracts session information like the callers identity. After the execution of this first extension is completed, another interception occurs (step 3, Figure 2.c) that will invoke the access control extension. The access control extension uses the session information to determine whether the call should be completed or not depending on the policy defined as part of the extension. If the call can be completed, the execution of m_R begins. Assume that as part of this execution, the robot changes its internal state (*). These changes are intercepted and propagated by the quality control extension (step 4, Figure 2.c) to a database at the base station. Once the changes are safely stored, execution of m_R resumes and, upon completion, the results are returned to the caller (step 5, Figure 2.c).

The important issue to understand in this procedure is that R needs to carry neither the interception points nor the extensions. All R needs is a PROSE enabled JVM and have the adaptation service. The rest is provided by the context and dynamically added to the application.

For simplicity we have omitted many details of the execution of the adaptations. In addition to the ones described, there are other adaptations that are transparently added to R. These adaptations take care of marshaling and unmarshaling arguments, adding and removing MIDAS specific information to each call, etc. Of the extensions used as examples, the session management extension is an implicit extension needed to implement other extensions (like the access control). When an extension that requires session information is added to a node, the session management extension is automatically also added to that node. The access control extension is an example of an adaptation that does not require to know the source code. It is enough to know the published interface of m_R. There are also many useful extensions which don't know anything of the application, not even the interface. For instance, it is very easy to design an extension that will encrypt every outgoing call from an application and decrypt every incoming call. Another example is a variant of the logging extensions that records every call to an application.

4   Application Development for Proactive Environments

We have already used MIDAS to implement several prototypes and various forms of extensions (e.g., [PA02,PAG03]). These prototypes have been used for testing and benchmarking. They provided us with feedback on the overall functionality, and we could determine how easy was for a programmer to start working with an extensions.

4.1   Basic Design

Once the adaptive middleware infrastructure is in place, developers can start to design concrete environments that impose their own policy and services to all applications within their boundaries. This involves identifying the necessary adaptations, identifying where they will take place, and building all the interfaces required by the environment. In the case of the robots, we employ the RCX controller available in Lego's Robotics Invention System [Leg] as the platform for developing the robots. For communication purposes we use Jini, although any other protocol for spontaneous interaction (e.g., [LCX+01]) could be considered.

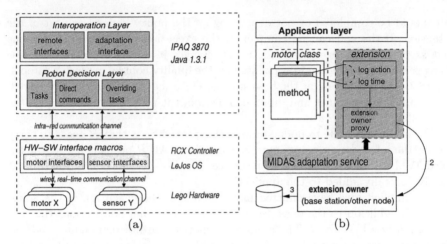

Fig. 3. (a) Software architecture in each robot and (b) the extension application for hardware monitoring.

Figure 3.a shows the basic architecture of the software attached to each robot. The upper layer defines the functionality for inter-operation with other nodes. Depicted from left to right, this layer defines (i) the services the node makes available to other nodes, like event processing, interface publishing, or lease management (provided by Jini in this case) and (ii) the adaptation service of MIDAS.

The second layer defines the application logic of the robot. This layer defines small programs (tasks) that define an objective for the robot (e.g., searching for a particular object). A task is a basic program that decides what the robot is going to do. A task is broken into activity requests (hardware macros) that are sent to the lower layers, modeling the hardware. A good example of a hardware macro would be, e.g., "turn left 30 degrees". A task is also notified whenever an event of interest is detected by the sensors. When this happens, the hardware completely freezes its activity and notifies the robot application layer of the occurred event (e.g., a touch sensor identified an obstacle). A task may decide to continue the interrupted command, or abort it and continue with a new sequence task.

Although the task model allows robot autonomy, there are situations in which a robot must be controlled by a human. Imagine, for example, that a robot reaches a dead end and is not capable of autonomously leaving that space. The *direct mode* layer is basically an interface that allows direct connection to the robot hardware. The *overriding layer* is a way to override an existing task without using the direct mode.

Both the inter-operation layer and the robot application layer are implemented as Java programs running on a H3870 iPAQ PDA.

The third layer contains software models and macros for operating all operative parts of the robot, e.g., motors and sensors. This layer offers a homogeneous

Fig. 4. A plotter prototype integrated in the proactive platform.

view of the underlying hardware, and it is implemented using the LeJOS [Jos02] operating system running on LEGO's RCX device controller. LeJOS is a tiny Java VM operating system, with a footprint of less than 20 kBytes. The hardware entities have been encapsulated in a Device class with Sensor and Motor as sub-classes. For each particular device (e.g., light sensor, motion sensor) further sub-classes are added to the system.

4.2 Application

Of the several prototypes developed using this architecture, we will describe here the plotter of Figure 4. This robot acts as the head of a printer as it moves a marking pen across three dimensions. The same robot can be used to control any other device in a similar manner (a saw, a scalpel, a drill, an electric contact, etc). Movement across each dimension is controlled by a motor. The overall movement is determined by a drawing program that exports a drawing interface as a Jini service. The program and the robot do not contain any code beyond that related to drawing.

4.3 Adaptation Example

An first example of adaptation is a hardware monitoring and logging extension. The idea is to record every movement of the robot and to store these movements persistently. Figure 3.b shows the situation after the robot has received an extension that monitors hardware activities. For each one of the motors, any calls to their proxy objects will be intercepted by the added extension (the gray box). For each method invocation of the motor proxy, the extension logs the time when the command was issued, its duration, as well as the identity of the robot (1). This data is first locally stored and then asynchronously sent to a base station (2). At the base station, the data is stored in a database (3).

```
1  class HwMonitoring extends Aspect {
2      // the remote owner
3      RemoteOwner ownerProxy;
4
5      // the interception specification
6      public void ANYMETHOD(Motor thisMotor, REST params)
7          {
8              ownerProxy.post(thisMotor.getId(),System.currentTimeMillis(),...)
9          }
10 }
```

Fig. 5. An extension for remote monitoring.

The extension for hardware monitoring and logging is very concise. A simplified version of it is depicted in Figure 5. It is a 100% Java class compiled and instantiated on the base station. Line 6 specifies that entries and exits of *any* methods belonging to a Motor class must be intercepted. The REST parameter indicates that the signature of the method (specific arguments) are not important. Once intercepted, PROSE will call ANYMETHOD (lines 6-9). This method does the actual logging by calling the ownerProxy object.

It is important to notice that neither the robot nor the program controlling the robot is aware of the extension. The extension can be added or removed as needed. If the robot is moved to a different location, that location can add a new extension that indicates where the data must be sent for persistent storage. Or, within the same location, the extension can be exchanged for a new one that indicates that the data must be sent to a program that shows the movements in a graphic display. Similar extensions could be used, for instance, to disable certain movements of the robot, or certain combination of movements, to replay sequences of movements, etc. A clear advantage of this form of adaptability is that devices only need to carry their basic functionality. Anything else are location specific adaptations inserted or extracted as needed.

4.4 Applications of the Adaptation Example

The simple monitoring and logging extension described can be used in many forms. We have developed several such applications by making the base station itself available as a Jini service. One can, thus, connect to the base station and query the database that stores all movements performed by robots being monitored by the base station. Figure 6 is a screen-shot of a client application connected to the base station. On the left side, it displays a list of all the motor actions ever executed by the robot named robot:1:1. Out of the action list, a selection was transferred to the right panel. The right panel allows manipulations of these movement sequences. Some examples of useful manipulations are:

Remote Replication. If the robot is being controlled by a human, it is possible to use the extension to monitor all the moves and feed them to an identical robot

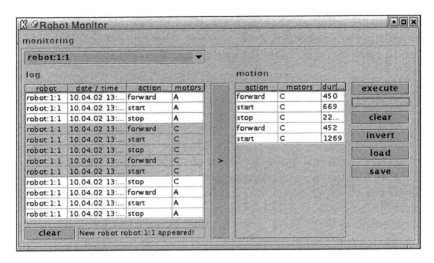

Fig. 6. A screen-shot of a simple hardware monitoring tool.

in a remote location (or to a collection of identical robots in other locations). That way one can either duplicate the work or follow up what is being done. It is also possible that the replication of the work takes place at a scale different from what is being done by the original robot. The only thing needed is to amplify or reduce the extracted sequence of movements to adjust it to the new scale.

Simulation. In difficult or important situations, one may want to record all movements performed. That way, if an accident or failure occurs, one can replay a part of the sequence of movements to see if the failure can be reproduced or better understood. This feature is particularly interesting if the failure is due to the interaction between different robots: the system can be instructed to replay the sequence of movements of all robots at the right relative time, thereby reproducing the interaction between them.

Control. It is possible that when the robot is used in certain locations, one might want to limit what the robot can do. For instance, one may forbid movements beyond certain coordinates so that certain parts of the paper remain untouched. If a drill is used, one may prevent lateral displacement of the drill when it is brought down. For this, the monitoring extension only needs to incorporate the coordinates or sequence of movements that are not allowed and simply check before allowing the movement to take place.

Again, the relevant point in all these potential applications is that none of them require to have any code in the robot. Depending when and how the robot is used, adaptations are added and removed as needed. Moreover, new adaptations can be easily designed as the use of the robots changes or evolves over time. This greatly simplifies the design of the software for the robot itself but also makes the maintenance of the adaptations much more manageable (compared with the case where they are embedded in every robot). This feature makes the approach highly attractive in many industrial settings.

4.5   Discussion

Our experience with the platform for proactive adaptation has been extremely encouraging. One of our initial goals was that the programming of extensions should be easy to use by application programmers. We have had this expectation confirmed during the past year, as students involved in projects and courses had to use MIDAS for exercises and development projects. Indeed, if a student was proficient in Java, a few days sufficed for the student to be able to program extensions.

This user experience lead to new applications we did not consider in the beginning. One example is a security extension that intercepts readings of all sensors of the robots. The security aspect intercepts all service calls and decides, *before* the execution of the application logic, whether the remote caller has the right to execute the intercepted method. If the access is denied, the execution is ended with an exception. Another example are applications where the "age" of the device corresponds to the trust associated to that device. A proactive context can add an extension that records the "birth date" of a device. The very same extension may intercept all service invocations of all possible devices and decide how to proceed depending on the device's age. We are at this stage considering other alternatives also suited for ubiquitous computing environments [KZ01].

One important issue is the cost of having a platform for run-time adaptation activated in each node. When no extensions are added, an overhead of about 7% (measured using a SPECjvm benchmark [SPE]) could be observed. When adding a do-nothing extension that traps method entries, all methods not affected by interceptions are not slowed down. For those methods where interceptions are performed, an overhead of roughly 900ns can be expected. For comparison, a void non-intercepted interface call costs 700ns on a Pentium 2, 500 MHz CPU. We measured the overhead of extensions implementing security, transactions and orthogonal persistence. In all cases the cost of the interceptions was much less then the cost of executing the additional functionality, indicating that the platform overhead is negligible. The results of these measurements are described in [PAG02].

Future Work. MIDAS heavily relies on the Jini infrastructure. As Jini is required on all participating nodes, a resource-scarce device would need a full Java runtime environment. To reduce this resource consumption, some parts of MIDAS are being re-implemented to obtain a smaller footprint. Further we are looking at tuple spaces [Gel85,LCX+01] to get a more flexible and expressive platform for distributing extensions.

5   Conclusion

In this paper we have presented a generic platform for proactive middleware. The platform supports the adaptation at run time of applications by extending their functionality with new code that enhances, modifies or controls the functionality already present in the application. We have described the architecture in detail and shown with an example how it can be effectively used in different industrial settings. We are aware that the type of proactiveness we propose is not suitable to all form of mobile computing. Nevertheless, our experience in developing several prototypes using the proposed platform show that the technology works quite well in nomadic settings, where high-end mobile nodes like PDAs, laptops or robots interact using wireless networks. Such devices cover already a wide range of mobile computing applications. The prototypes built also demonstrate that our approach can help to significantly reduce some of the cost associated to the maintenance of widely distributed systems and simplify the process of developing software capable of working in mobile computing scenarios.

References

[APW01]   D. Arregui, F. Pacull, and J. Willamowski.   Rule-Based Transactional Object Migration over a Reflective Middleware.   In *Middleware 2001: IFIP/ACM Intl. Conf. on Distributed Systems Platforms*, volume 2218 of *LNCS*, pages 179–196, 2001.

[AWO+99] K. Arnold, A. Wollrath, B. O'Sullivan, R. Scheifler, and J. Waldo.   *The Jini Specification*. Addison-Wesley, Reading, MA, USA, 1999.

[BC01]   G. S. Blair and G. Coulson. The Design and Implementation of Open ORB version 2. *IEEE Distributed Systems Online Journal*, 2(6), 2001.

[BCKP95] R. Bagrodia, W. Chu, L. Kleinrock, and G. Popek. Vision, Issues, and Architecture for Nomadic Computing. *IEEE Personal Communications*, 2(6):14–27, 1995.

[BH02]   J. Baker and W. Hsieh. Runtime Aspect Weaving Through Metaprogramming. In *1st Intl. Conf. on Aspect-Oriented Software Development, Enschede, The Netherlands*, pages 86–95, April 2002.

[CBCP01] M. Clarke, G. S. Blair, G. Coulson, and N. Parlavantzas.   An Efficient Component Model for the Construction of Adaptive Middleware. In *Middleware 2001: IFIP/ACM Intl. Conf. on Distributed Systems Platforms*, volume 2218 of *LNCS*, pages 160–178, 2001.

[CCM97]   CORBA Component Model RFP. Available at http://www.omg.org/docs/orbos/97-05-22.pdf, 1997.

[CHS01]   W.-K. Chen, M. Hiltunen, and R. Schlichting. Constructing adaptive software in distributed systems. In *Proc. of the 21st Intl. Conf. on Distributed Computing Systems (ICDCS-01)*, pages 635–643, Los Alamitos, CA, April 16–19 2001. IEEE Computer Society.

[ECDF01] C. Efstratiou, K. Cheverst, N. Davies, and A. Friday. An Architecture for the Effective Support of Adaptive Context-Aware Applications. *LNCS*, 1987, 2001.

[EGK+99]   F. Eliassen, V. Goebel, T. Kristensen, T. Plagemann, A. Andersen,
           H. Rafaelsen, W. Yu, G. Blair, F. Costa, G. Coulson, and K. Saikoski.
           Next generation middleware: Requirements, architecture, and prototypes.
           In *The Seventh IEEE Workshop on Future Trends of Distributed Comput-
           ing Systems*, pages 60–, Tunisia, South Africa, December 1999.

[Gel85]   D. Gelernter. Generative communication in Linda. *ACM Transactions on
           Programming Languages and Systems (TOPLAS)*, 7(1):80–112, 1985.

[HSH+99]   M. A. Hiltunen, R. D. Schlichting, X. Han, M. M. Cardozo, and
           R. Das. Real-time dependable channels: customizing qoS attributes for
           distributed systems. *IEEE Transactions on Parallel and Distributed Sys-
           tems*, 10(6):600–612, June 1999.

[Jos02]   Jose Solorzano. leJOS, Java for the RCX. www.lejos.org, 2002.

[KF01]   E. Kiciman and A. Fox. Separation of Concerns in Networked Service Com-
           position. Position Paper Workshop on Advanced Separation of Concerns
           in Software Engineering at ICSE 2001, Toronto, Canada, May 2001.

[KLM+97]   G. Kiczales, J. Lamping, A. Menhdhekar, C. Maeda, C. Lopes, J.M. Lo-
           ingtier, and J. Irwin. Aspect-Oriented Programming. In Mehmet Akşit and
           Satoshi Matsuoka, editors, *In Proc. of ECOOP'97 Jyväskylä, Finland*, vol-
           ume 1241 of *LNCS*, pages 220–242. Springer-Verlag, New York, NY, June
           1997.

[KZ01]   Tim Kindberg and Kan Zhang. Context authentication using constrained
           channels. Technical Report HPL-2001-84, HP Labs, 2001.

[LCX+01]   T. J. Lehman, A. Cozzi, Y. Xiong, J. Gottschalk, V . Vasudevan, S. Landis,
           P. Davis, Bruce K., and P. Bowman. Hitting the distributed computing
           sweet spot with TSpaces. *Computer Networks (Amsterdam, Netherlands:
           1999)*, 35(4):457–472, March 2001.

[Leg]   Lego. Lego mindstorms robotics invention system. At
           http://mindstorms.lego.com, 2002. Lego Mindstorms.

[LK98]   C. V. Lopes and G. Kiczales. Recent Developments in AspectJ. In Serge
           Demeyer and Jan Bosch, editors, *Object-Oriented Technology: ECOOP'98
           Workshop Reader*, volume 1543 of *LNCS*, pages 398–401. Springer, 1998.

[NSN+97]   B. D. Noble, M. Satyanarayanan, D. Narayanan, J. E. Tilton, J. Flinn,
           and K. R. Walker. Agile Application-Aware Adaptation for Mobility. In
           Sixteenth ACM Symposium on Operating Systems Principles, pages 276–
           287, Saint Malo, France, 1997.

[OL01]   D. Orleans and K. Lieberherr. DJ: Dynamic Adaptive Programming in
           Java. In *Reflection 2001: Meta-level Architectures and Separation of Cross-
           cutting Concerns*, Kyoto, Japan, September 2001. Springer Verlag.

[PA02]   A. Popovici and G. Alonso. Ad-Hoc Transactions for Mobile Sevices. In
           *Proc. of the 3rd VLDB Intl. Workshop on Transactions and Electronic
           Services (TES '02)*, Hong Kong, China, August 2002.

[PAG02]   A. Popovici, G. Alonso, and T. Gross. Design and evaluation of spon-
           taneous container services. Technical report no. 368, Computer Science
           Department, Swiss Federal Institute of Technology, 2002.

[PAG03]   A. Popovici, G. Alonso, and T. Gross. Just in time aspects: Efficient dy-
           namic weaving for java. In *2nd Intl. Conf. on Aspect-Oriented Software
           Development, Boston, USA*, 2003.

[PGA02]   A. Popovici, T. Gross, and G. Alonso. Dynamic Weaving for Aspect Ori-
           ented Programming. In *1st Intl. Conf. on Aspect-Oriented Software Devel-
           opment, Enschede, The Netherlands*, April 2002.

[PLF+01]   S. R. Ponnekanti, B. Lee, A. Fox, P. Hanrahan, and T. Winograd. ICrafter: A Service Framework for Ubiquitous Computing Environments. *LNCS*, 2201, 2001.

[SAW94]   B. Schilit, N. Adams, and R. Want. Context-Aware Computing Applications. In *IEEE Workshop on Mobile Computing Systems and Applications*, Santa Cruz, CA, US, 1994.

[SGGB99]   E.G. Sirer, R. Grimm, A.J. Gregory, and B.N. Bershad. Design and Implementation of a Distributed Virtual Machine for Networked Computers. In *Symposium on Operating Systems Principles*, pages 202–216, 1999.

[SM]   Sun Microsystems. The Java Security Model. http://java.sun.com/.

[SOT+00]   T. Suganuma, T. Ogasawara, M. Takeuchi, T. Yasue, M. Kawahito, K. Ishizaki, H. Komatsu, and T. Nakatani. Overview of the IBM Java Just-in-Time Compiler. *IBM Systems Journal*, 39(1):175–193, 2000.

[SPE]   Spec - The Standard Performance Evaluation Corporation. SPECjvm. Web access http://www.spec.org/osg/jvm98/.

[Sun02]   Sun Microsystems. *Java 2 Platform, Standard Edition, v 1.4.0: API Specification*, 2002. java.sun.com/j2se/1.4/docs/api/.

[XC02]   Xerox Corporation. The AspectJ Programming Guide. Online Documentation, 2002. http://www.aspectj.org/.

[YK01]   S. S. Yau and F. Karim. Reconfigurable Context-Sensitive Middleware for ADS Applications in Mobile Ad-Hoc Network Environments. In *5th International Symposium on Autonomous Decentralized Systems (ISADS)*, pages 319–326, March 2001.

[ZBS97]   John A. Zinky, David E. Bakken, and Richard E. Schantz. Architectural Support for Quality of Service for CORBA Objects. *Theory and Practice of Object Systems*, 3(1), 1997.

A Flexible Middleware System
for Wireless Sensor Networks*

Flávia Coimbra Delicato, Paulo F. Pires, Luci Pirmez,
and Luiz Fernando Rust da Costa Carmo

Núcleo de Computação Eletrônica – NCE & Computer Science Department – DCC
Federal University of Rio de Janeiro
P.O Box 2324, Rio de Janeiro, RJ, 20001-970, Brazil
{fdelicato,paulopires,luci,rust}@nce.ufrj.br

Abstract. The current wireless sensor networks (WSN) are assumed to be designed for specific applications, having data communication protocols strongly coupled to applications. The future WSNs are envisioned as comprising of heterogeneous devices assisting to a large range of applications. To achieve this goal, a flexible middleware layer is needed, separating application specific features from the data communication protocol, while allowing applications to influence the WSN behavior for energy efficiency. We propose a service-based middleware system for WSNs. In our proposal, sensor nodes are service providers and applications are clients of such services. Our main goal is to enable an interoperability layer among applications and sensor networks, among different sensors in a WSN and eventually among different WSN spread all over the world.

1 Introduction

Recent advances in micro-electro-mechanical systems (MEMS) technology, wireless communications, and digital electronics have enabled the development of low-cost, low-power, multifunctional sensor nodes that are small in size and communicate over short distances. These tiny sensor nodes, which consist of sensing, data processing, and communicating components, leverage the idea of sensor networks based on collaborative effort of a large number of nodes [3].

A wireless sensor network (WSN) is composed of a large number of such sensor nodes, which are densely deployed either inside the monitored phenomenon or very close to it and are interconnected by a wireless network. Sensor networks can play the role of a highly parallel, accurate and reliable data acquisition system.

Typically, sensors are devices with limited energy and processing capabilities, deployed in an ad-hoc fashion and communicating through low bandwidth wireless links. Sensor nodes have to operate unattended, since it is unlikely to service a large number of nodes in remote, possibly inaccessible locations. Therefore, energy saving is a crucial requirement in such an environment.

Examples of sensor networks include military networks for intruder detection, networks for environment monitoring, parking lot networks, surveillance networks and so on.

---

* This work is partially supported by the Brazilian funding agency CAPES

M. Endler and D. Schmidt (Eds.): Middleware 2003, LNCS 2672, pp. 474–492, 2003.
© IFIP International Federation for Information Processing 2003

Sensor tasks usually have high-level descriptions, such as "report the detection of any 10 tons four-legged animal in region X". However, individual sensor nodes typically provide very simple and low level functionalities. Therefore, to meet a complex sensing task, sensor nodes must coordinate among themselves and the individually collected data must be aggregated to provide more accurate and significant results. The coordination among sensor nodes must take into account their heterogeneity and their individual features such as location, sensor type and residual energy.

Sensor data are transmitted from multiple acquisition sources toward one or more processing points, which may be connected to external networks. Since sensors monitor a common phenomenon, it is likely to appear significant redundancy among data generated from different sensors. Such a redundancy can be exploited to save transmission energy, through filtering and data aggregation procedures in-network. Also to save energy, the short-range hop-by-hop communication is preferred over the direct long-range communication to the final destination. Therefore, to achieve energy efficiency, applications should be able to dynamically change the network behavior, for example, influencing the way sensor data are routing throughout the network.

Current works [6,12,13,14] consider sensor networks as being designed for specific applications, with data communication protocols strongly coupled to the application. In fact, the network requirements and organization, as well as the way data should be routed, change according to the application. In spite of the application specific behavior of the current sensor networks, many authors [17] envision the future sensor networks as being composed of heterogeneous sensor devices and assisting to a large range of applications for different groups of users. To achieve this goal, a middleware service is needed to provide a layer of abstraction that separates application specific requirements from underlying data dissemination protocols.

A middleware for WSN should support the implementation and basic operation of a sensor network, such as described in [23]. This is a non-trivial task, since WSNs have some unique features, such as the resource constraint of nodes (energy, storage and processing) and the high dynamic and fault prone characteristics of the WSN environment. Furthermore, sensor nodes in the same network can be heterogeneous regarding their processing and storage capabilities. To deal with the intrinsic characteristics of sensor networks, some software design principles for WSN have been proposed in [18] and have been used by most of the WSN specific protocols. These principles are the adoption of localized algorithms, data-centric communication and the utilization of application-specific knowledge. A WSN middleware must take into account such design principles.

We propose a distributed middleware system for sensor networks sitting above the data dissemination protocol. Our approach is motivated by the fact that despite of the advantages of the middleware technology, current works on WSN do not consider such a technology in the design of WSNs. The proposed system addresses the specific requirements of WSN and it is based on the concept of services. Services are defined as the data provided by the sensor nodes and the applications (for instance, a filtering program) to be executed on such data. Clients access the sensor network submitting queries to those services.

Services are published and accessed through an XML-based language (Extensible Markup Language [27]) named WSDL language (Web Services Description Language) [25]. WSDL is used for describing services available on the Web, named *Web services*, in a standardized way. One important point is that a Web Service, despite of its name, needs not necessarily exist on the World Wide Web. A Web Service can live anywhere on the network (Inter- or intranet).

By adopting the Web Services paradigm, we propose an interoperability layer for sensor networks systems that is generic and flexible, providing the basic functionalities required for any WSN. Such a middleware layer is composed of the SOAP protocol [29] and interfaces provided by WSDL documents. Using specific data dissemination protocols for sensor networks, such as direct diffusion [12] and LEACH [10], among others, and the service-based middleware layer, we intend to offer a flexible and powerful way of manipulating, extracting and exchanging data from sensor networks. Applications access the sensor network and modify the underlying data dissemination behavior through a common and application independent interface provided by the middleware layer.

The middleware interface provides a mechanism through which application specific code (such as programs to data filtering and data fusion) can be injected and triggered inside the network, allowing energy efficiency in data dissemination, thus increasing the WSN performance and time life. The middleware also enables the generation and communication of high level tasks, as well as the coordination of such tasks among nodes, even if the nodes have heterogeneous features. In order to suit to the WSN resource constraint and fault prone, the proposed middleware is designed to be robust and fault tolerant, demanding little processing and storage requirements, and keeping the messages exchanged as short as possible.

Our approach enables the construction of generic sensor networks capable of meeting the requirements of a large range of independently designed applications. Furthermore, the use of standard protocols in the middleware layer provides the necessary mechanisms to enable the interoperability among different networks.

The present work describes the main features and the components of the proposed middleware service. The paper is organized as follows. Section 2 covers the background concepts. Section 3 presents the components of the proposed middleware system. Next, Section 4 details the system operation and Section 5 presents the related work. Section 6 discusses system features according to the specific requirements of sensor networks. Finally, Section 7 outlines the conclusions and future works.

2   Background

This section presents some background concepts needed for the comprehension of the remaining of the paper. The concepts outlined encompass WSN, middleware systems (generic and specific for WSN) and Web services technology.

2.1   Wireless Sensor Networks (WSN)

Most of the wireless sensor networks work as a reliable data capture network. Data are collected in the distributed sensors and relayed to a small number of exit points, called sinks, for further processing.

The dissemination of information in a WSN is done by nodes performing measurements and relaying data through neighboring nodes to reach some sink in the network. Data sent by different nodes can be aggregated in order to reduce redundancy and minimize the traffic and thus the energy consumption. To enable data aggregation in network in an efficient way, application-specific code, such as data caching and collaborative signal processing should occurs as close as possible to where data is collected. Such a processing depends on attribute-identified data to trigger application-specific code and hop-by-hop processing of data [9].

WSN can be classified in proactive and reactive networks, according to the class of the target application. In proactive WSNs, nodes periodically (in a pre-defined interval) sense the environment and transmit data of interest. In reactive WSNs, nodes react immediately to sudden and drastic changes in the value of a sensed attribute. The later is well suited for time critical applications.

Once the type of network is defined, protocols that efficiently route data from nodes to users have to be designed. Several WSN specific protocols have been proposed in the last few years [6,9,10,12]. Some protocols are sender-initiated [14] while others are receiver-initiated [12]. Some protocols are based on a flat network topology [12, 14] while others are based on a hierarchical topology [6,10]. In the latter case, protocols adopt a cluster-based approach and make use of some algorithm for cluster formation [24] requiring the coordination among nodes in a cluster.

For large-scale networks, grouping nodes in clusters can be beneficial for a number of reasons [24]. From a routing perspective, clustering allows network protocols to operate in a hierarchical fashion, breaking transmissions into different levels. Such an approach is highly fault-tolerant, providing better isolation and recovery of network problems. Clustering can also be beneficial for data collection algorithms. Some applications do not require the data collection from all nodes during all time. Cluster members can collaborate about recent data measurements and determine how much information should be transmitted to the user application. By averaging data values collected within the cluster, the algorithm can trade data resolution for transmission power [24]. Finally, clustering can help dealing with non ideal distribution of sensor networks. In areas where there are a redundant number of sensors, a clustering algorithm can be used to select which nodes better represent data samples for the region and which ones can be put in a power-save mode, thus saving energy and increasing the lifetime of the network as a whole.

Most of WSN protocols rely on localized algorithms and data-centric communication, besides to exploit application-specific knowledge in the data dissemination. Localized algorithms are a special kind of distributed algorithms that achieve a global goal by communicating with nodes in a restricted neighborhood. Such algorithms scale well with increasing network size and are robust to network partitions and node failures [18]. Data-centric communication introduces a new style of addressing in which nodes are addressed by the attributes of data they generate (sensor type) and by their geographical location, instead of by their network topological location. Finally, the use of application knowledge in nodes can significantly improve the resource and energy efficiency, for example by application-specific data caching and aggregation in intermediate nodes [18].

Regardless the specific protocol adopted, all protocols depend on some mechanism for representation of user application queries and of generated sensor data, and for execution of application-specific processing triggered by pre-defined data attributes. Data-centric protocols represent queries and data through high level descriptions (meta-data) and disseminate such descriptions in the network instead of the collected raw data. When a cluster-based approach is adopted, a further mechanism for representation of coordination messages exchanged among nodes is needed.

2.2   Middleware Technology

Middleware technologies free application designers of explicitly dealing with problems related to distribution, such as heterogeneity, scalability, resource sharing, and the like. Middleware provides application designers with a higher level of abstraction, hiding the complexity introduced by distribution.

The term middleware is widely used to denote a layer comprised of groups of generic services sitting below user applications. Typical middleware services include directory services, service discovery, transaction management, and provide different types of transparencies, such as location transparency and fault transparency. CORBA [16], J2EE and J2ME [22], and COM [15] are examples of traditional middleware technologies. The use of middleware systems speeds up the development and deployment of new applications, leaving to the developers only the task of designing business specific components.

Traditional middleware technologies have been developed assuming the requirements of fixed distributed systems. Such systems are composed of fixed devices, with high processing and storage capabilities, usually permanently connected to the network through continuous and high bandwidth connections. These distributed systems operate in a relatively static execution context. For static context we mean the bandwidth is high and continuous and the location of the devices and services hardly ever changes.

WSN are a category of ad-hoc networks having all the features of such networks and some further constraints. Devices in WSN have low processing and storage capabilities, can be mobile or not, can be destroyed or suffer battery depletion and are subject to environmental dynamics. Furthermore, they are typically connected through wireless links with low capability and error prone. The adopted communication paradigm is typically asynchronous and event-driven.

The essential requirements for WSN middleware include providing mechanisms that assure the efficient use of communication resources available and that allow the dynamic configuration of user applications. Besides, it must be robust, fault tolerant, lightweight and with short storage requirements, given the WSN low capabilities.

One additional requirement concerns the execution context information. Middleware collects information on the execution context, such as actual location of a device, value of network bandwidth, latency, available remote services, etc. Most of middleware developed for traditional distributed systems adopts the principle of transparency. By transparency, we mean that such a context information is used privately by middleware and not shown to the applications. For example, middleware may discover a congestion in a portion of the distributed system and therefore redirect requests to access data to a replica residing on another part of the distributed system, without informing the application about this decision [5]. In the other hand, in WSN, applications must be aware of context information, in order to accomplish some strategy for efficient use of the scarce network resource. Such a feature is named principle of awareness. By awareness we mean that information about the execution context (or part of it) is passed up to the running applications, that are now in charge of taking strategic decisions [5].

The next section gives a more detailed view of WSN middleware characteristics.

2.3   WSN Middleware Requirements

The main purpose of middleware for sensor networks is to support the development, maintenance, deployment and execution of sensing-based applications. This includes mechanisms for formulating complex high-level sensing tasks, communicating those tasks to the WSN, coordination of sensor nodes to split the tasks and distribute them to the individual sensor nodes, data fusion for merging sensor readings of individual sensor nodes into a high-level result, and reporting the result back to the task issuer. Moreover, appropriate abstractions and mechanisms for dealing with the heterogeneity of sensor nodes should be provided [5]. All mechanisms provided by a middleware system should respect the special characteristics of WSN, mainly the energy efficiency, robustness, and scalability. The communication style to be adopted should typically be asynchronous, event-driven and data-centric.

Another unique feature of WSN middleware is the application knowledge in sensor nodes. Traditional middleware is designed to accommodate a wide variety of applications without necessarily needing application knowledge. Middleware for WSN, however, has to provide mechanisms for injecting application knowledge into the WSN [18].

A further characteristic addresses the concepts of time and location of sensed events. Since WSNs monitor real world data, time and spatial information are relevant, being key elements for fusing individual sensor readings. Therefore, support for time and location management should be tightly integrated into a middleware for WSN [5].

Finally, it is important to note that the scope of middleware for WSN is not restricted to the sensor network alone, but also covers external networks connected to the WSN (such as Internet) as well as the applications interested in querying sensor data through such external network.

Despite of the advantages of the middleware technology, current works on WSN are not considering such a technology in the network design. WSNs have been built with a high degree of dependency between the applications and the underlying communication protocol. Such a dependency generates rigid systems, with sensor networks being specifically designed to particular applications.

In fact, WSN applications should be able to access the network and modify the underlying data dissemination behavior in order to achieve energy efficient. The adoption of a middleware service provides a flexible, application independent layer that allows the interaction among different applications and the WSN, separating the data communication functionalities from the application specific processing.

In this work, we propose a middleware layer for sensor networks that aims to meet their specific requirements. Our proposal is based on the concept of service, and on the Web services technology. The next section gives an overview on the Web services technology.

2.4   The Web Services Technology

Web services can be define as modular programs, generally independent and self-describing, that can be discovered and invoked across the Internet or an enterprise intranet. Like component-based middleware systems, Web services expose an interface that can be reused without worrying about how the service is implemented.

Unlike current component-based middleware [15, 16, 22], Web services are not accessed via protocols dependent on a specific object-model. Instead, Web services are accessed via ubiquitous Web protocols and data formats, such as Hypertext Transfer Protocol (HTTP [7]) and XML [27], which are vendor independent.

The *Web Services Description Language* (WSDL) [25] is an XML language for describing the interface of a Web service enabling a program to understand how it can interact with a Web service. Each Web service publishes its interface as a WSDL document (an XML document) that completely specifies the service's interface so that clients and client tools can automatically bind to the Web service.

A WSDL document defines services as collections of network endpoints or ports [25]. Besides, messages and port types are defined. *Messages* are abstract descriptions of the data being exchanged, and *port types* are abstract collections of operations. In WSDL, there is a separation between the *abstract* definition of messages and their *concrete* network implementation. This allows the reuse of abstract definitions of *messages* and *port types*. The concrete protocol and data format specification for a particular port type defines a reusable *binding*. A *port* is specified by associating a network address with a reusable binding. A *service* is defined as a collection of ports.

The SOAP protocol extends XML so that computer programs can easily pass parameters to server applications and then receive and understand the returned semi-structured XML data document.

Since the Web services technology uses XML as the encoding system, data is easily exchanged between computing systems with incompatible architectures and incompatible data formats. WSDL completely describes the Web service interface, while SOAP completely describes parameters, data types and exceptions included in a message being exchanged between Web services.

The Web services technology is based on a flexible architecture named SOA (service-oriented architecture [8]). In a service-oriented architecture three roles are defined: a service requestor, a service provider and a service registry.

A service provider is responsible for creating a service description, publishing that service description to one or more service registries, and receiving Web services invocation messages from one or more service requestors.

A service requestor is responsible for finding a service description published to one or more service registries and for using service descriptions to invoke Web services hosted by service providers. Any consumer of a Web service is a service requestor.

The service registry is responsible for advertising Web service descriptions published to it by service providers and for allowing service requestors to search the collection of service descriptions contained within the service registry. The service registry role is to be a match-maker between service requestor and service provider.

Besides the roles just described, three operations are defined as part of SOA architecture: publish, find and bind. These operations define the contracts between the SOA roles.

The publish operation is an act of service registration or service advertisement. When a service provider publishes its Web service description to a service registry, it is advertising the details of that Web service description to a community of service requestors.

The find operation is the logical dual of the publish operation. It is the contract between a service requestor and a service registry. With the find operation, the service requestor states a search criterion, such as type of service. The service registry matches the find criteria against its collection of published Web services descriptions.

The bind operation embodies the client-server relationship between the service requestor and the provider [8]. It can be sophisticated and dynamic, such as on-the-fly generation of a client-side proxy based on the service description used to invoke the Web service, or it can be a static model [8].

Besides to comply to the SOA pattern, the Web service technology can be factored into three protocols stacks [8]: the wire stack (or exchange format), the description stack and the publish and discovery stack.

The wire stack represents the technologies that determine how a message is sent/received from the service requestor to the service provider. The stack is composed of three levels. The first level is a network protocol, which can be an Internet wire protocol, such as HTTP [7], or sophisticated enterprise-level protocols. The second level is the data encoding mechanism that is based on XML. The third level refers to XML messaging layers. For XML messaging, Web services use SOAP [29], which acts as a wrapper to XML messages, guaranteeing a solid, standard-based foundation for Web services communication.

The description stack provides aspects of a service that are important to the service requestor. In Web services, XML is the basis of service description. The XML Schema specification (XSD) [28] defines the canonical type system. Besides this level, the next levels of the stack are the descriptions of the service interface, the service concrete mapping and the service endpoint. An endpoint defines the network address where the service itself can be invoked. All of those levels use WSDL [25], which is an XML-based language for describing the interface of Web services. WSDL is a very flexible model for services descriptions but it is also rather verbose. A typical sensor device has very limited capacities. So, a more compact mechanism for data representation is needed. One example of such a mechanism is the WAP Binary XML Content Format (WBXML [26]). This format defines a compact binary representation for XML, intended to reduce the size of XML documents for transmission and to simplify parsing them.

The publish and discovery stack corresponds to the directory service for Web services. Service providers need a publication mechanism so that they can provide information about the Web services they offer and service requestors need well-defined find APIs for using such Web services.

3   Proposed Middleware Service

Our work proposes a distributed middleware system for sensor networks sitting above the data dissemination protocol and basing on the Web services technology. Such a middleware aims to provide a generic and flexible interoperability layer allowing different user applications to access and extract data from sensor networks.

The main goal of our middleware is to provide an interoperability layer:

- among user applications and the WSN, allowing the execution of data queries and of application specific processing in-network;
- among different sensors in the same WSN, allowing data communication and sensors coordination according to an underlying protocol;
- eventually, among different sensor networks.

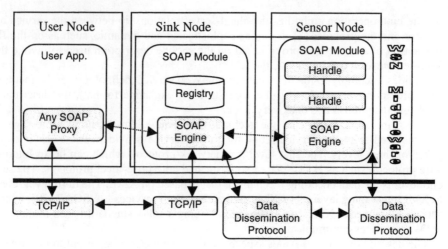

Fig. 1. System Architecture.

The proposed system is based on the Web services technology. Web services are built according to a pattern called service-oriented architecture (SOA) and they can be described by a trio of interoperability stacks [8] (see Section 2.4).

Section 3.1 describes the sensor network physical components considered in the proposed system. Section 3.2 describes the roles played by the middleware components in agreement with the SOA pattern, while Section 3.3 describes such components according to the Web services interoperability stacks.

3.1   Sensor Network Physical Components

In our system, we consider a sensor network as comprising of two main physical components: sensor nodes and sink nodes. Our distributed middleware runs in both sensor and sink nodes above the data dissemination and the location services. Furthermore, a proxy provides the communication interoperability between user applications and the sensor network (Fig. 1). It is important to note that this proxy is not coupled to our middleware design, neither it is required to be built with any specific technology. It is actually a generic proxy responsible for generating SOAP messages to be exchanged between the user application and the WSN.

A **sensor node** can contain one or more specialized sensing devices. Furthermore, it can have routing and data aggregation capabilities. Thus, the routing function is distributed among all nodes. We assume that all the sensor nodes have enough processing and storage capacities to store and execute aggregation programs.

Sink nodes provide an interface through which external systems can obtain the information collected by the sensor network. Such interfaces can be accessed locally or remotely (i.e., through the Internet). Sink nodes can also aggregate data, but they do not have sensor devices. We assume that they are more powerful regarding to processing and communication capabilities than sensor nodes.

3.2 System Components According to the Service-Oriented Architecture Pattern

The proposed system is based on the concept of service-oriented architecture (SOA) [8] (see Section 2.4). A user application querying data from a sensor network plays the role of a **service requestor**. Sink nodes act primarily as **service providers** to the external environment. They provide the service descriptions of the whole sensor network, and they offer access to such services. At the same time, sink node act as **requestors** to the sensor nodes, requesting their specialized services, in order to meet the user application needs. Sensor nodes are **service providers**, providing data and programs (for application-specific processing). Sensor nodes send their services description to sink nodes, thus executing the basic publish operation. Sink nodes also act as **registries**, keeping a repository with services descriptions of each sensor type existing in the sensor network.

In our system, the functionality of the **publish** operation is accomplished through the Publish_content operation, and the functionalities of **find** and **bind** operations are both accomplished through the Subscribe_interest operation.

Our system groups the functionalities described by the operations find and bind in one single operation. Sink nodes provide the services description interface and, at the same time, provide access to such services. The user application interacts only with sink nodes, and sink nodes in its turn access sensor nodes services passing the resulting data to the application. In fact, the operation find is only accomplished internally by the sink nodes, which consult their repositories of services descriptions. When an application submits a query to the sensor network, it is actually executing a bind to the services supplied by the sensor nodes. However, the application only interacts with the sink. The operation Subscribe_Interest is translated by the sink to a **find** operation followed by a **bind** to the sensor nodes that can meet the application request.

3.3 Interoperability Stacks

In our system, the **wire stack** is composed of the SOAP protocol and an underlying data dissemination protocol. We do not make assumptions about the underlying protocol. Instead, we provide a generic interface for a class of protocols. The **description stack** has all of its levels based on WSDL documents, in the document-centric approach [8]. The functionalities of the **publish and discovery stack** are accomplished by a software module executing in sink nodes. Sink nodes act as service registry agents. During the network configuration, sensor nodes send messages publishing their services and sink nodes keep a repository with such descriptions. Besides such functionalities, sink nodes act as interceptors for network services requests. External applications access the network via sink nodes. Sinks receive requests and direct such requests to sensor nodes according to the information stored in the sink repository.

In the next sections we detail the wire and description stacks. We do not describe the discovery stack in detail since it is not relevant to this work.

The Wire Stack: The Communication Framework. Users applications interested in submitting queries to the sensor network must access some sink node. The communication between user applications and sink nodes can be accomplished through conventional TCP/IP sockets. Applications must generate a SOAP message describing the user interests. Such a message is generated based on the sensor network service descriptions stored in the sink repository. Services descriptions are written in WSDL language. Since WSDL is an open and ubiquitous standard for services description, there are many tools [11] for automatic generation of SOAP proxies. Proxies build SOAP messages and receive back query results thus, they represent the software interface among applications and sink nodes. The proposed WSN middleware provides a service interface allowing user applications to interact with the sensor network system in an application-to-application communication style, offering more flexibility than a direct user interface. Instead of submitting queries in a proprietary and pre-defined format, specified through the user interface, applications are free to choose the way they want to view and receive data.

All the communication inside the sensor network is accomplished using the underlying data dissemination protocol and formatted as SOAP messages. The sending and receiving of SOAP messages by a SOAP node is mediated by a binding to an underlying protocol. SOAP messages can be transported using a variety of underlying protocols. The SOAP specification includes a binding to HTTP. Additional bindings can be created by specifications that conform to the binding framework. Specific bindings for each data dissemination protocol should be defined as needed.

The SOAP protocol is responsible for defining exchanging rules and messages format in our system. In order to reduce the messages size, thus saving energy in sending/receiving, the XML compact binary representation [26] is adopted for SOAP messages exchanged inside the sensor network

The SOAP module, as well as a module representing the data dissemination protocol must be present in every node in the network.

SOAP Module. The SOAP module in our system is composed of three main components: the SOAP engine, a set of handles and a binding with the underlying protocol. The SOAP engine acts as the main entry point into the SOAP module. It is responsible for coordinate the SOAP message's flow through the various handles and for ensuring that the SOAP semantics are followed. Handles are the basic building blocks inside the SOAP module and they represent the messages processing logic. Three kinds of handles are defined: common handles, transport handle and specific handle. Common handles are responsible for marshalling/unmarshalling of messages, header and attachments processing, serialization, conversions of data type to the types supported by the local software, among any other basic functions. The transport handle `Matching_Data` is specifically built for sending and receiving messages through the underlying protocol. The handle `Matching_Filter` is a sensor's specific handle which is built for representing the activation of application-specific programs inside the network. More details about the use of specific handles are described in Section 4.

Sink nodes contain common handles only. Sensor nodes contain, besides common handles, the transport handle `Matching_Data` and the Web services specific handle `Matching-Filter`.

The Services Description Stack: WSDL Documents. The generic services provided by a sensor network are described through a WSDL document. In that document, port types elements (see Section 2.4) contain two types of service descriptions: descriptions of services provided by sensor nodes and descriptions of services provided by sink nodes. Each service port type contains operations, which can be thought as system APIs. Those operations contain parameters, defined in the document through messages. Bindings of operation definitions to their concrete implementation should be defined according to the underlying protocol. The WSDL language allows a binding to be defined through SOAP or directly to a lower level protocol. A port identification, indicating the place containing the operation implementation, can be done through any unique identifier, as a device address.

The operations defined for the Web services specified in our system address the requirements of a generic sensor network. Despite of the data dissemination protocol adopted, a WSN needs mechanisms to: represent user queries and sensor data; represent and trigger application specific code; and to represent coordination messages in cluster-based approaches. The following operations aims to provide such mechanisms.

Publish_Content: used by the sensor node to create and disseminate a SOAP message containing its service descriptions. Services include types of sensing data and filters existent in the sensor node.

Publish_Data: used by sensor nodes to create SOAP messages communicating generated data.

Subscribe_Interest: used by an application to submit a query to a sink node. The query includes the interest description and the filters to be activated.

Subscribe_Filter: used by an application in a sink node to inject a new filter in the network. A filter contains the attributes to be matched for its execution and the syntax to invoke the filter program.

Join_Cluster: used by sensor nodes to declare their intention to join in a cluster.

Advertising_Leader: used by the elected leader node to announce its identity to the others cluster members.

4   System Operation

Sensor networks have an initial setup stage comprising of four different phases: deployment, activation, local organization and global organization [23]. Deployment is the physical placement of sensors in the target area. In order to reduce energy consumption, sensor nodes reside in a sleep state until the deployment. Therefore, sensors need to undergo an activation phase after they are scattered in the region of interest. The local organization phase includes the neighbors' discovery. During the global organization phase, nodes establish the communication path to some sink in the network. It is essential that all nodes reach a sink through some path so that their data can be delivered to the application. After the organization phase, each node is supposed to know and distinguish the nearby nodes. Any unique identifier can be used as a node identifier, as for example, its MAC address or a device serial number. When adopting a hierarchical, cluster-based protocol, besides the phases just described, the WSN initial organization includes a phase for clusters formation, in which nodes group themselves in clusters with a chosen leader or cluster-head responsible for the management of the communication among cluster members.

```
<SOAP-ENV:Envelope xmlns:m0="http://SensorDescTypes" ...
  <SOAP-ENV:Body>
    <m:PublishContent xmlns:m="http://namespace">
      <parameter ID="MAC_ADDR" NetworkID="NET_ID">
        <m0:TTL unit="Seconds">3600</m0:TTL>
        <m0:Type>Motion</m0:Type>
        <m0:DataDomain>
          <m0:Value>Four Legged Animal</m0:Value>
          <m0:Value>Two Legged Animal</m0:Value>
          <m0:Value>Creeper Animal</m0:Value>
        </m0:DataDomain>
        <m0:GeographicLocation unit="LatLong">
          <m0:x>35.00</m0:x> <m0:y>-23.00</m0:y>
        </m0:GeographicLocation>
        <m0:Energy unit="J">1</m0:Energy>
        <m0:Confidence>
          <m0:Max>1.0</m0:Max> <m0:Min>0.2</m0:Min>
        </m0:Confidence>
        <m0:DataRate unit="mSeconds">
          <m0:Max>10</m0:Max> <m0:Min>1000</m0:Min>
        </m0:DataRate>
      </parameter>
    </m:PublishContent>
  </SOAP-ENV:Body>
</SOAP-ENV:Envelope>
```

Fig. 2. SOAP configuration message.

Our middleware system operates according to four different steps: intial setup, interest advertisement, data advertisement, and (optionally) cluster formation. We discuss each one of those steps in the next sections.

4.1   Step 1 – Initial Set Up

In our system, during the local and global organization phases, nodes exchange SOAP configuration messages (Fig. 2), describing the services (data and filters) supplied by them. Such messages include the node and network identification (the latter used when there are several interconnected sensor networks), a TTL (sensor time-to-live), sensor type(s), geographical location, current amount of energy, maximum and minimum confidence degrees, maximum and minimum acquisition intervals (data rate), filters that exist in the node and specific information of each sensor type. The SOAP configuration message is broadcasted in the network using the functionality of the underlying data dissemination protocol. When a sensor node receives a configuration message, it can decide to transmit it or not. If the message describes a sensor type matching its own features or if a similar message has already been sent before, the node does not need to transmit it again. Sinks keep entries for each different sensor type, therefore their repositories scale with the number of sensor types.

Sink nodes store the content of received configuration messages in a local repository. Such a repository is based on soft-state, since active sensors in a particular instant of time can be inactive in a subsequent instant. It is important that every sink in the network has the complete knowledge on all existent sensor types. Sinks may periodically exchange messages, so that all sinks contain the same information.

Since configuration messages traverse intermediary nodes until reaching a sink, such nodes can also store messages exploiting their content, for example, extracting geographic and energy information when disseminating interests through the network. The information about sensor geographical location can be used when the underlying protocol implements some kind of location-based routing optimization [31]. The data dissemination protocol adopted can be further optimized considering the sensor current energy in the decisions about routing. The optimization procedures based on geography location or current energy are included as application-specific programs in the network, and are executed only when the application asked for it.

4.2   Step 2 – Interest Advertisement

Applications requesting data from a sensor network should subscribe an interest in some sink. An interest contains the sensor type, the data type, the geographical location of interest, the acquisition interval (data rate) and the acquisition duration. For time critical applications, a threshold value can be included, as a limit from which the sensors must inform data, regardless the current data rate.

Applications can request the activation of application-specific programs existent in nodes. Furthermore, new programs can be injected in the network. A program description contains an identifier and a list of data types with their respective values. The identifier is used to trigger the execution of the appropriate program already existent in the sensor node when such a node receives data matching the values specified in the program description. When injecting a new program, it is transported as a SOAP message attachment [29].

SOAP messages advertising interests (Fig. 3) are disseminated in the sensor network using the underlying data dissemination protocol. A handle responsible for matching data to interests, named Matching_Data handle is provided as part of the middleware layer.

4.3   Step 3 – Data Advertisement

A sensor generates data in an initial rate specified in its configuration message. The sensor only sends SOAP data advertisement messages if it had received a previous interest message advertising interests matching its own data type. Sensors change their acquisition interval according to the received SOAP interest messages. When detecting data for which they have received an interest, sensors issue data advertisement messages.

SOAP messages advertising data contain the data type, the instance (or value) of that type that was detected, the sensor current location (sensors can be mobile), the signal intensity, the confidence degree in the accomplished measurement, a timestamp, and the current sensor amount of energy.

The message dissemination involves a matching stage among data and interests, and the possible execution of filters. The matching data to interest stage is accomplished by the handle Matching_Data. The handle Matching_Filter matches

```
<SOAP-ENV:Envelope xmlns:m0="http://SensorDescTypes" ...
  <SOAP-ENV:Body>
    <m:SubscribeInterest xmlns:m="http://namespace">
      <parameter>
        <m0:SensorType>Motion</m0:SensorType>
        <m0:DataType>Four Legged Animal</m0:DataType>
        <m0:DataRate unit="mSeconds">20</m0:DataRate>
        <m0:Duration unit="Seconds">20</m0:Duration>
        <m0:Area>
          <m0:PointA unit="LatLong">
            <m0:x>35.00</m0:x> <m0:y>-23.00</m0:y>
          </m0:PointA>
          <m0:PointB unit="LatLong">
            <m0:x>35.02</m0:x> <m0:y>-23.03</m0:y>
          </m0:PointB>
        </m0:Area>
        <m0:Threshold>0</m0:Threshold>
      </parameter>
    </m:SubscribeInterest>
  </SOAP-ENV:Body>
</SOAP-ENV:Envelope>
```

Fig. 3. SOAP message advertising interests.

data to programs and dispatches programs execution whenever it is necessary. The resulting (possibly aggregated or filtered) data are delivered to the dissemination layer as a new SOAP data advertisement message to be sent along the network.

4.4   Step 4 – Cluster Formation

Cluster-based protocols have additional cluster formation and cluster-leader election phases according to a specific algorithm [24]. After nodes are relatively confident that they are aware of their neighbors (organization phase), the next task is to form relationships with nearby nodes resulting in clusters. Clusters should contain a manageable number of nodes that are close [24]. Usually cluster formation algorithms include a step in which nodes declare their interest in joining in a particular cluster as a leader and a further step of deciding which node will be the leader, advertising the chosen node to the other cluster members. Specific code representing the algorithm must be injected in the network in a interest advertising message. Two messages are needed to accomplish the functionality of a generic cluster algorithm: the Join_cluster message is used by nodes advertising their desire of joining in a cluster and the Advertising_Leader message announces the elected cluster leader. Join_cluster messages contain the node identification, a timestamp and the node current energy amount. The node energy can be considered or not for the cluster algorithm being used. Join_cluster messages can be multicasted or broadcasted in a target area, according to the underlying data dissemination protocol. Advertising_Leader messages contain a timestamp and the elected leader node identifier.

5   Discussion

In this section we discuss the features of the proposed middleware system according to the specific requirements sketched for WSN presented in Sections 2.2 and 2.3.

Efficient Usage of WSN Resources. The content of SOAP messages includes information on node energy and geographical location. Both information are parameters for resource usage optimization algorithms. Application specific code implementing such algorithms is deployed in sensor nodes and triggered by SOAP messages containing some pre-defined data values.

Robustness and Fault Tolerance. The proposed middleware system is fully distributed, with application specific code deployed in every sensor node and with the information on services provided by the WSN being replicated in every sink node. Such a distributed feature naturally increases the system robustness and fault tolerance.

Lightweight and Short Storage and Energy Requirements. SOAP is a lightweight protocol. We have implemented a compact version of the SOAP engine, which requires minimal processing capacities, to run inside the sensor network. To allow access to the WSN through the internet, sink nodes, which are not energy constraint nodes, have installed a standard SOAP engine. The SOAP messages exchanged through the system as well as the WSDL documents stored in repositories are represented with the XML binary compact format, in order to reduce their length. The use of the compact format also reduces the message payload and thus the energy spent in message transmission.

Statement and Communication of High Level Tasks and Coordination among Nodes. Functionalities of node coordination as well as the communication of high level tasks are accomplished through generic SOAP messages defined by the middleware system (see Section 4).

Data Fusion and Data Filtering. Data filtering and aggregation programs can be loaded in sensor nodes during the WSN deployment or they can be injected on-the-fly as SOAP message attachments. Such programs are triggered when pre-defined data arrive in sensor nodes containing the programs code. The trigger data are defined by interest advertising SOAP messages.

Support to Nodes Heterogeneity. Such a support is a central feature of our proposal. Since our middleware system is based on the ubiquitous XML technologies, we naturally address the interconnection among different sensor nodes in a WSN, or even among different WSNs throughout our middleware layer.

Awareness and Application Knowledge. User applications and the middleware layer exchange execution context information, such as nodes energy and location, in order to carry out optimization strategies for the efficient use of WSN resources.

6   Related Work

There are some projects addressing the development of middleware for WSN, such as [1,19,20,21]. The Smart Messages Project [21] is based on agent-like messages containing code and data, which migrate throughout the sensor network. NEST [1] provides microcells as a basic abstraction. They are similar to operating system tasks with support for migration, replication, and grouping. SCADDS [19] is based on a paradigm called Directed Diffusion, which supports robust, data-centric and energy-efficient delivery and in-network aggregation of sensor events. Most of these projects are in an early stage focusing on developing algorithms and components for WSN, which might later serve as a foundation for future middleware systems.

In [4] a distributed sensor network middleware service is presented whose purpose is power conservation. Such a service sits on top of the network routing layer and performs data placement and caching as a strategy to conserve battery power. That work does not address the representation of user queries and sensor data.

The Intentional Naming System is an attribute-based name system operating in a overlay network over the Internet [2]. It provides a method based on late binding to cope with dynamically located devices. Despite of having several features desirable for a middleware for sensor networks, INS was designed for more generic mobile networks, offering a sophisticated hierarchical attribute matching procedure. However, they do not address the specific requirements of WSN, nor provide mechanisms which deal with interoperability issues.

Our proposal has some similarities with [30], a database approach for WSN systems. Such a work exploits the sensor computation capabilities to execute part of the query processing inside the network, using query proxies. In their distributed approach, relevant data is extracted from the sensor network, when and where it is needed. The primary difference from our work is that they adopted a relational data base approach, based on XML an SQL queries optimization. Their system performs aggregations in the network as specified by a centrally computed query plan. We propose a totally distributed service approach, based on the ubiquitous standards WSDL and SOAP.

7   Conclusions and Future Works

In this paper, we have presented a middleware service for sensor networks. We claim that the future wireless sensor networks should provide a ubiquitous, standardized access through a common and application independent interface. The contributions of this work are three-fold. First, we propose an interoperability layer separating the data dissemination functionality from the application-specific processing. Second, we have defined an ubiquitous middleware architecture for WSN based on the Web services technology, where sink nodes are modeled as Web Services that expose services provided by the network using a standard service interface. Third, we propose the use of the WSDL language and SOAP protocol, already recognized as Internet standards, as the mechanisms for describing services and formatting messages used by the underlying communication protocol.

We do not couple our proposal to any particular underlying data dissemination protocol. Instead, we provide a generic interface between the middleware layer and the underlying protocol layer.

The proposed approach offers high expressiveness and flexibility when designing sensor networks, allowing the interoperability of heterogeneous sensor. In our approach, sensor networks can be used as a system for supplying data for different applications and users. Our main goal is to provide the underpinning for building more general purpose networks, instead of strictly task-specific ones, in order to assist a large range of users, possibly spread all over the world, sharing a common interest in a specific application area. Since energy saving is a key element in WSN design, our proposal makes an effort to keep the amount of spent energy in the same level as current WSN systems. It is important to note that energy consumption in data processing in WSNs is assumed to be order of magnitude smaller than in data transmission [12]. Therefore, the additional processing needed for parsing SOAP messages should be insignificant to the system. For this reason, our approach addresses energy saving in data transmission by adopting a compact binary XML format in the messages exchanges inside the WSN.

Currently, we are working on the implementation of the SOAP module as described in this paper. We have already defined the WSDL documents for describing the WSN services and the SOAP messages format and content. We expect that the experimental results prove the system feasibility and beside, the total energy spent in transmission and processing do not overcome the values found in current WSN protocols.

References

1. A Network Virtual Machine for Real-Time Coordination Services. Available in: www.cs.virginia.edu/nest
2. Adjie-Winoto, W., Schwartz, E., Balakrishnan, H., Lilley, J.: The design and implementation of an intentional naming System. 17th ACM Symposium on Operating Systems Principles (SOSP '99). Published as Operating Systems Review, 34(5):186–201, Dec. 1999
3. Akyildiz, I. et al.: Wireless sensor networks: a survey. Computer Networks, 38(4):393–422, March 2002
4. Bhattacharya, S., Abdelzaher, T.: Data Placement for Energy Conservation in Wireless Sensor Networks. Department of Computer Science, University of Virginia. Submitted to ICDCS 2002. Available in: http://www.andrew.cmu.edu/~weizhang/wsn/documents/fin_sagnik_journal.pdf
5. Capra, L., Emmerich, W., Mascolo, C.: Middleware for Mobile Computing (A Survey). UCL Research Note RN/30/01. Available in: http://www.cs.ucl.ac.uk/staff/L.Capra/publications.html. July 2001
6. Choksi, A.: Hierarchical Routing in Sensor Network, CS-672: Seminar on Pervasive and Peer-To-Peer Computing, Storage & Networking. Term-Paper Submission, Rutgers University. Available in: http://www.cs.rutgers.edu/~achoksi/presentation/CS672_paper_ankur.pdf . 2001
7. Fielding, R. et al.: RFC 2616. Hypertext Transfer Protocol -- HTTP/1.1. Available in: ftp://ftp.rfc-editor.org/in-notes/rfc2616.txt. June, 1999
8. Graham, S. et al.: Building Web Services with Java: Making Sense of XML, SOAP, WSDL, and UDDI. Sams Publishing, 2002
9. Heidemann, J. et al.: Building Efficient Wireless Sensor Networks with Low-Level Naming. In Proc. of the ACM Symposium on Operating Systems Principles (146-159). Chateau Lake Louise, Banff, Alberta, Canada. Oct. 2001. Available in: http://www.isi.edu/~johnh/PAPERS/Heidemann01c.html
10. Heinzelman, W., Chandrakasan, A., Balakrishnan, H: Energy-Efficient Communication Protocol for Wireless Microsensor Networks. In Proc. of the 33rd Hawaii International Conference on System Sciences (HICSS '00), Jan. 2000
11. IBM White Paper, Web Services Toolkit. Available in: http://www.alphaworks.ibm.com/tech/ Webservicestoolkit. April 2002

12. Intanagonwiwat, C., Govindan, R., Estrin, D.: Directed diffusion: a scalable and robust communication paradigm for sensor networks. In Proc. of the ACM/IEEE International Conference on Mobile Computing and Networking - MobiCom 2000 (56-67), Boston, MA, USA, Aug 2000
13. Krishnamachari, B., Estrin, D., Wicker, S.: Modeling Data-Centric Routing in Wireless Sensor Networks. Available in: http://www2.parc.com/spl/members/zhao/stanford-cs428/readings/Networking/ Krishnamachari_infocom02.pdf. 2002
14. Kulik, J., Heinzelman, R. B., Balakrishnan, H.: Negotiation-based protocols for disseminating information in wireless sensor networks. ACM Wireless Networks 2000. Available in: http://citeseer.nj.nec.com/ 335631.html, 2000
15. Microsoft Corporation, "The Component Object Model Specification". Available in: http://www.opengroup.org/pubs/catalog/ax01.htm, Oct. 1995
16. OMG (Object Management Group). The Common Object Request Broker: Architecture and Specification. Revision 2.0. July 1995
17. Qi, H., Kuruganti, P. T., Xu, Y.: The Development of Localized Algorithms in Wireless Sensor Networks, Invited Paper - Sensors 2002, 2, (286-293), 2002
18. Römer, K., Kasten, O., Mattern, F.: Middleware Challenges for Wireless Sensor Networks. ACM SIGMOBILE Mobile Computing and Communications Review, Vol. 6, Number 2, 2002
19. Scalable Coordination Architectures for Deeply Distributed Systems. Available in: http://www.isi.edu/div7/scadds
20. Sensorwebs Project. Available in: basics.eecs.berkeley.edu/sensorwebs
21. Smart Messages Project. Available in: http://www.rutgers.edu/sm
22. SUN Microsystems, "Enterprise JavaBeans Specification 2.0. Sun Microsystems". Available in: http://java.sun.com/products/ejb/docs.html, August 2001
23. Ulmer, C., Alkalai, L., Yalamanchili, S.: Wireless Distributed Sensor Networks for In-Situ Exploration of Mars, Work in progress for NASA Technical Report. Available in: http://users.ece.gatech.edu/ ~grimace/research/reports/nasa_wsn_report.pdf
24. Ulmer, C.: Organization Techniques in Wireless In-situ Sensor Networks. Report. Available in: http://users.ece.gatech.edu/~grimace/research/.
25. W3C (World Wide Web Consortium) Note, "Web Services Description Language (WSDL) 1.1". Available in: http://www.w3.org/TR/2001/NOTE-wsdl-20010315
26. W3C (World Wide Web Consortium) Note, "WAP Binary XML Content Format". Available in: http://www.w3.org/TR/wbxml/, June 1999
27. W3C (World Wide Web Consortium) Recommendation, "Extensible Markup Language (XML) 1.0 (Second Edition)". Available in: http://www.w3.org/TR/REC-xml, Oct. 2000
28. W3C (World Wide Web Consortium) Recommendation, "XML Schema Part 0: Primer". Available in: http://www.w3.org/TR/xmlschema-0/, May 2001
29. W3C(World Wide Web Consortium) Note on Simple Object Access Protocol (SOAP) 1.1, Available in: http://www.w3.org/TR/SOAP/, May 2000
30. Yao, Y., Gehrke, J. E.: The Cougar Approach to In-Network Query Processing in Sensor Networks. Sigmod Record, Volume 31, Number 3, September 2002. Available in: http://www.cs.cornell.edu/ johannes/papers/2002/sigmod-record2002.pdf
31. Yu, Y., Govindan, R., Estrin, D.: Geographical and Energy Aware Routing: a recursive data dissemination protocol for wireless sensor networks. Available in: http://citeseer.nj.nec.com/461988.html

A Middleware Service for Mobile Ad Hoc Data Sharing, Enhancing Data Availability

Malika Boulkenafed and Valérie Issarny

INRIA-Rocquencourt
Domaine de Voluceau, Rocquencourt, BP 105
78153 Le Chesnay Cédex, France
{Malika.Boulkenafed,Valerie.Issarny}@inria.fr
http://www-rocq.inria.fr/arles/

Abstract. It is now commonplace for a person to use lightweight wireless computing devices, and to make his/her data available to other people's devices using todays various networking capabilities (infrastructure-based WLAN, ad hoc WLAN, GSM, etc.). Middleware platforms initially developed for stationary distributed systems cannot be directly applied in such a mobile environment. They must adapt their functionalities so as to best cope with possible resource constraints (energy, storage) of mobile terminals as well as with the various types of wireless networks that are now available. In this paper, we present a middleware service that allows collaborative data sharing among ad hoc groups that are dynamically formed according to the connectivity achieved by the ad hoc WLAN. Our service enhances, in particular, data availability within mobile ad hoc collaborative groups, and integrates a new adaptive data replication protocol for mobile terminals, combining both optimistic and conservative schemes. Our service has been designed so as to minimize energy consumption and optimize data availability and storage consumption.

Keywords. Middleware services, data availability, collaborative work, ad hoc networks, mobile computing, wireless networks.

1 Introduction

Given the current advances in the field of mobile computing concerning both lightweight devices and wireless networking capabilities, middleware infrastructures have to adapt their services to better support this mobile wireless environment and the new classes of applications that result from it. Lightweight computing devices (e.g., PDA[1], third generation mobile phones, hand-held computers, etc.) are becoming increasingly available for a large range of users. In addition, low-power and short-range wireless connectivity among these devices (e.g., Bluetooth, IEEE 802.11, MANET[2], HiperLAN, OWS[3], and HomeRF in the

---

[1] Personal Digital Assistants.

[2] Mobile Ad hoc NETwork

[3] Optical Wireless Solution

M. Endler and D. Schmidt (Eds.): Middleware 2003, LNCS 2672, pp. 493–511, 2003.
© IFIP International Federation for Information Processing 2003

context of PAN[4]) are increasingly flexible, especially with the advent of protocols supporting ad hoc communication (e.g., Bluetooth, IEEE 802.11, MANET) and enabling a collection of mobile hosts with wireless network interfaces to form a temporary network without the need for any established infrastructure or centralized administration [11], [13]. Middleware infrastructures initially developed for stationary distributed systems cannot be directly applied in such a mobile environment. Therefore, widely accepted middleware platforms have specified their *wireless* or *mobile* variants (e.g., wireless CORBA). Indeed, mobile devices are resource-scarce (low amount of persistent storage, limited battery power, etc.). It is therefore necessary to adapt all system functionalities and in particular functionalities related to data management (adequate coherency and replication management protocols), which is the focus of our paper. In this context, a number of services and/or protocols have been proposed regarding specific problems raised by mobility, such as disconnected operations (e.g., [9], [12], [15], [17], [20], [23], [25], [26], [27] and discovery of services [3].

Since it became commonplace to find users equipped with lightweight devices and short-range wireless interfaces, new needs for adapted functionalities that account with the various connectivities enabled by today's networking capabilities have emerged. There are scenarios in which no wired or wireless networking infrastructure is available, either because it may be economically impractical or physically impossible to provide the necessary infrastructure. Therefore, ad hoc networks are particularly suitable. Ad hoc networks represent the latest trend in distributed computing; work in this area has mainly dealt with routing protocols [1], [19], [24], [18] without taking into account data management within these networks. However, ad hoc networks are particularly well suited to form small groups of devices that are in the communication range of each other, in order to share and manipulate common data when the fixed networking infrastructure is not available. This requires devising adequate data management that allows the user to work in a collaborative manner and to benefit from the flexibility of ad hoc networks, thus supporting the notion of *mobile collaborative ad hoc groups*.

An example of mobile collaborative ad hoc group is a working meeting regarding some international cooperation (e.g., a European research project), which takes place in a hotel conference room, somewhere in a convenient destination easily reachable by all partners. An other example is a network gaming session, which may happen at any place (e.g., a cafeteria, train, lounge, etc.). Consider the first example. Representatives from each project partner meet periodically to work in a collaborative manner on the project. In order to facilitate travel arrangement, project partners choose a European meeting location that is easily reachable by all of them. Usually, they book a hotel, which unfortunately does not always provide any facility to support this kind of meetings, except may be a projector and an insufficient number of sockets. Attendees bring their project data on their wireless devices, which range from laptops to PDAs. It means that these devices have heterogeneous capacities in terms of persistent storage, and

---

[4] Personal Area Network.

battery. Furthermore, attendees do not bring all project data. Thus, data are already distributed between the attendees' devices according to both the attendees' contribution and the capacity of their devices. Every attendee must be able to easily access any project data brought by others, even if not locally cached on his device. This can be done either using floppy disk, or memory card, but it does not allow any coherency management of such replicated data. Fortunately, attendees' devices are equipped with wireless interface cards. Thus, they would like to be able to share their data using the wireless network even if there is no existing networking infrastructure in the meeting hotel, provided that some security guarantees are given regarding the wireless communication. The solution to this requirement is to use ad hoc networking (e.g. IEEE 802.11b WLAN in ad hoc mode) with adequate data management functionalities, which support secure mobile ad hoc collaborative groups. These functionalities subdivide into two core categories:

1. Secure group management that ensures: (i) transparent group creation using a discovery service to detect trusted partners (their devices) that *belongs* to the group; (ii) adaptation to the group dynamics, so that members can leave or join the group at any time; (iii) secure group communication through an encryption protocol that must account with devices' resources and network connectivity.
2. Data management that ensures: (i) that members access the most recent data version available within the ad hoc group, (ii) data coherency within the group through a conservative coherency protocol to effectively support collaborative work, since members must have the same version of shared data; (iii) adaptive data replication to avoid data loss if the devices storing them suddenly disconnect.

There is the need for a middleware service guaranteeing collaborative data sharing within mobile ad hoc groups and enhancing data availability while meeting the above constraints, by making adequate tradeoffs among data replication, data coherency, and resource consumption on mobile devices. Most of the replication mechanisms that have been proposed for mobile environments do not manage replication with respect to the mobile devices' resources or more generally with respect to the execution context. They all assume that mobile devices have enough cache to contain a user's entire working set of data. This is not a reasonable assumption when the system runs on an environment containing hand held devices with reduced storage capacities. In addition, these systems rely on infrastructure-based networks (e.g., reachability of a base station), and do not offer the possibility of forming ad hoc collaborative groups. These systems, further, maintain coherency of replicas optimistically, which means that they allow updates to be performed independently on any replicas. Although this is convenient for stand-alone mobile devices, it does not match the requirement of accessing a uniform version of the shared data within collaborative ad hoc groups.

This paper presents a middleware service for data sharing within a mobile ad hoc collaborative environment that addresses the aforementioned requirements. It supports secure group management and provides an adequate solution to enhance data availability with respect to mobility constraints (connectivity, device resources) through an adaptive availability scheme that deals with data coherency and replication, in a way that minimizes energy and storage consumption. Our adaptive replication protocol ensures data availability despite the dynamics of the collaborative groups according to the users' specific situation (e.g., profile of the device in use, network connectivity, etc.).

This paper is organized as follows: Sections 2 and 3 are the core of this paper. Section 2 presents functionalities of the middleware service necessary to support secure mobile ad hoc collaborative groups. Section 3 presents our contribution concerning data availability management within ad hoc collaborative groups. Our contribution lies in the integration of both conservative and optimistic coherency management within an adaptive data replication protocol for enhanced availability according to group dynamics and devices' specific situations. Section 4 assesses the proposed service in terms of local storage and communication overhead, response time, and energy consumption. It is shown that using our protocol, generated meta-data overhead is negligible, response time grows linearly with data update size, while group size affects it slightly. Finally, Section 5 concludes, summarizing our contribution and discussing our current and future work.

2   Middleware Service for Data Sharing within Collaborative Mobile Ad Hoc Groups

Ad hoc networks enable users equipped with lightweight computing devices and wireless interfaces to form a temporary network without the need for any established infrastructure. It is quite interesting to exploit such flexibility to allow them to share and manipulate some data in a collaborative manner (e.g., working meeting, network gaming, etc.) provided that some guarantees regarding security are given. Therefore, a mobile middleware platform should include a service that provides a number of functionalities so as to best cope with mobile collaborative ad hoc groups.

The secure group management functionalities (see §2.1) include discovery of peer mobile terminals that are in the communication range of each other. Then, to form a collaborative group, all the peer terminals should authenticate themselves. Authentication requires a trusted third party (e.g., the home server of the European project) to issue a digital certificate, which is stored on any device that previously authenticated with the given third party. Then, peers that can trust each other build a secure ad hoc group in order to share data and collaborate. Groups are restricted to one hop ad hoc networks, because we consider that the collaborating peers are usually located in the local communication range of each other. However, every peer is free to leave the group, as well as, new trusted peers can join it at any time.

Data sharing within the group is then carried out by making sure that each peer within the ad hoc group has complete knowledge of all the data cached/stored within the group. Access to such data from any of the mobile terminals, belonging to the group, leads to copying it locally, if not already cached. Data coherency is maintained by enforcing a conservative coherency protocol that takes into account mobile devices and wireless network constraints, and provides an effective support for collaborative work, since collaborating users must have the same version of the shared data (see §2.2). Finally, in order to enhance data availability and prevent data miss, useful data for collaborative work have to be rationally replicated on peer devices, with respect to the devices' resources (storage space , energy, etc.) as further detailed in Section 3.

2.1   Secure Group Management

Security is of crucial importance in our context, it is therefore mandatory to ensure end-to-end privacy and integrity of the user's data. However, as our platform aims to run on resource constrained terminals, it is necessary to balance strong security enforcement with resource consumption, and in particular energy. For authentication purposes, a trusted third party (e.g., home server) issues Digital Certificates (DC) [21] to users' devices after proper verification of their IDs. The use of DC avoids the need for a trusted, online, third party. A DC includes the user's public key, validity period, the domain name (defined by the home server, e.g., the name of the European project) to which the user belongs, etc. The DC is signed by the trusted third party's private key. Thus, when two nodes wish to authenticate each other upon joining/creating a group, they announce each other with their Digital Certificates. Each of them then verifies the genuineness of the certificate by using the signature on the certificate (every peer must know the third party's public key). Then, the authenticated peers participate in a Group Key Agreement (GKA) protocol to come up with a common secret. A GKA protocol is essentially a contributory protocol designed to provide all the participants with a shared secret key over an open network. This secret is a symmetric key and can be used for securing all further communication. It has to be renewed upon group composition change or at the end of some prefixed security interval. Many such protocols have been proposed in the literature [2], [6], [7], [14].We are currently examining their adaptation for mobile ah hoc environment with respect to devices' resource constraints. In particular, note that the authentication protocol can be integrated with the Group Key Agreement (GKA) protocol thus saving on communication costs.

Group management builds upon a discovery protocol that aims to dynamically detect new peers that are in the communication range of a given group[5], and those that have left it. This task is addressed by service discovery protocols, like SLP (Service Location Protocol), Jini[6], UPnP[7] (Universal Plug and Play), SDP (Bluetooth Service Discovery Protocol) and Salutation[8] [3]. SLP offers a

---

[5] Notice that a singleton peer is consider as a group.

[6] http://www.sun.com/jini

[7] http://www.upnp.org

[8] http://www.salutation.org

decentralized mode that does not require any *Directory Agent* to collect service announcements in a centralized database. Therefore, it is particularly suitable for ad hoc networks. Each mobile terminal then periodically advertises for the domains[9] it belongs to (e.g., the European project) using its Digital Certificate. When it meets other mobile terminals in its communication range (remember that we consider one hop ad hoc networks) that are advertising for the same domain (i.e., peers that it can trust), the group creation takes place after proper devices authentication.

For a given period of time, a peer is chosen to lead the group. The leader then checks the value of the *group variable*, which gives the group composition, with the list of nodes' IDs returned by the discovery service. If these two values differ, the group must integrate the (potential) newcomers, and/or discard the (potential) nodes that have left. In addition, the group leader makes sure that peers belonging to the group have a global view of data cached within the group and other peers situation (available resources for collaboration). The leader election ensures that the same peer will never be a leader for two successive periods, in order to distribute the charge of group management over all the peers involved (see [4] for more details).

2.2   Data Management

Data management ensures that the user accesses the most recent data version available within the ad hoc group, and guarantees data coherency within the group. It enforces, within the ad hoc group, a conservative coherency protocol that accounts with mobility constraints (devices' resources, network connectivity) (see [5] for more details). This stems from our concern for effectively supporting collaborative work within ad hoc groups. Therefore, peers belonging to an ad hoc group must access the same version of shared information.

The coherency protocol is based on two elements: an *exclusive writer protocol* adapted to mobile environments, and a log, named *Coherency Control List* (CCL). The *exclusive writer protocol*, used within ad hoc groups, builds upon a distributed token management protocol: a unique *token*, is associated with each shared data and created upon first access to the data within an ad hoc group. Each peer must request the token ownership to be able to modify the corresponding data. Therefore, only the peer that owns the token is allowed to modify the data. However, local data can be manipulated (read/write) independently within disjoint groups, provided that the data are synchronized when a group is joined. Update propagation for a given shared data occurs only when any member of the group tries to access the data, because if a group member updates its local copy of particular data, propagation of this update is not necessary if none of the other group members wants to read or update the same data (either cached locally or not). Furthermore, updates are propagated only to the peer which is to access the data. This follows from our aim to save energy by reducing communication among peers.

---

[9] As defined by its home server, e.g., the European project.

The Coherency Control List is used for incremental lazy update propagation, and serves two purposes: (i) achieving coherency among replicas within an ad hoc group by the lazy update propagation from the current token owner to the peer which is to access its copy; (ii) handling divergences due to non-synchronized concurrent updates in different ad hoc groups which may ultimately require user intervention since fully automated conflict resolution can not be achieved [8], [23].

3   Adaptive Data Replication for Enhanced Availability

To enhance data availability, an adaptive data replication protocol with respect to mobile devices constraints is used. In the context of collaborative work within mobile ad hoc groups, data may become unreachable if the peers storing them suddenly disconnect. On the other hand, excessive or systematic data replication in order to address unforeseen disconnection leads to unnecessarily overloading the group's peers and in particular to greatly increasing their energy consumption and storage space. Thus, useful data for collaborative work within a group have to be rationally replicated on peer devices, with respect to the devices' resources. Following our assumptions, mobile users are able to form ad hoc groups and to share their data in a collaborative manner. As previously stated, existing mobile distributed systems do not manage replication with respect to devices' resources, nor support transparent collaborative data sharing within ad hoc groups, although some of them support collaborative database applications within infrastructure-based WLAN [8]. We aim to achieve data availability within mobile collaborative ad hoc groups through an adaptive peer-to-peer data replication protocol with respect to devices' specific profiles in order to minimize resource consumption (in particular energy).

Each peer caches the set of data necessary for its local autonomy and/or collaborative work. When a peer meets other trusted peers in its local communication range, they form a collaborative ad hoc group. Then, any peer within the group knows about the other peers' situations. Peers profiles serve to identify whether peers can be involved in increasing data availability according to their specific situation. A profile thus indicates: (i) available local storage space for sharing, (ii) whether the peer is able to store replica files other than those that are accessed on the peer depending on available energy, and (iii) expected time within the group, following user's indications (e.g., a diary). Notice further that by construction of ad hoc group management each peer knows both the data that are stored on the various peers of the group, and the situation of each of these peers. Our replication scheme then distinguishes two replica types for a data: (i) Work Replicas are stored on the peer according to data access, either before joining or when part of the group, and (ii) Preventive Replicas are generated by replicating/updating data among the Work Replicas, in order to maintain an up-to-date copy of the data within the collaborative group depending on the peers' profiles. The choice of which peers should store Preventive Replicas is determined by combining the peers' profile with semantic relationships between already stored data on the considered peer and the generated Preventive Replica (see §3.2).

3.1   Peers Profile

Within a collaborative ad hoc group, data are distributed among peers belonging to the group. The main reason for data miss is peer disconnection. We can distinguish two types of disconnections: (i) voluntary disconnection, e.g., when the user does not want to stay within the group any longer; and (ii) involuntary disconnection, essentially due to a low battery for power-unplugged devices. Therefore, we define the peer's profile, in order to anticipate decreasing availability generated by these disconnections. The peer's profile provides the following information:

- **Available energy:** this can be approximated using the monotonously decreasing linear function[10]:

$$Energy(t) = init - \frac{init}{battery} \times t \tag{1}$$

  where $init$ is the initial battery value at the time the peer joined the group, and $battery$ is the estimated battery life defined as a function of the peer's charge and is periodically recomputed. $Energy(t)$ serves to determine whether the peer is able to replica files other than those that are accessed locally. Indeed, receiving a new replica involves wireless communication and thus energy consumption [10].
- **Expected time within the group:** this can be estimated using,e.g., user's indications or his/her diary. It can be approximated by the following linear function of time:

$$Time(t) = cst - t \tag{2}$$

  where cst is the expected time spent within the group.
- **Available local storage space for sharing:** this is given by the function $Space(t)$, whose value depends on the peer's replication rate and has to be recomputed periodically.

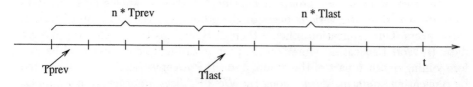

Fig. 1. Group Profile Update Periodicity

---

[10] Notice that we consider power-unplugged devices

The profile of any peer is always locally available. The ad-hoc group profile is then periodically updated by gathering fresh profiles from the peers belonging to the group. This period is dynamically adapted according to the group's evolution, considering that peers' mobility has a greater impact than changes in individual profiles. Indeed, peers' motion leads to modifying the number of replicas within the group. So, by adapting the update of the group profile to the group's dynamics, we control the replication rate while minimizing communication. The period is initially set to a given value T. Using *statistical modal class* the duration of the period T is adapted every n periods as follows. Let t be the current time and $\gamma = \frac{C_{prev}}{C_{last}}$, with C_{last} being the number of changes[11] over the last n periods (i.e. over $[t - (n \times T), t]$) and C_{prev} being the number of changes over $[t - (2 \times n \times T), t - (n \times T)]$ (see Figure 1). Then, if γ is smaller than one, T should be decreased for the next n periods because the group has been changing less frequently over the last n periods than it changed over the n previous periods. The new value of T then becomes equal to:

$$T' \times (1 + \frac{C_{prev} - C_{last}}{n}) \tag{3}$$

with T' being the previous value of T. On the other hand, T should be increased if γ is larger than one. We get the following new value for T:

$$T' \times (1 - \frac{1}{n \times C_{last}} \times \sum_{i=1}^{max_c} (i \times n_{ci})) \tag{4}$$

where max_c denotes the maximum number of changes over a period for the last n periods of duration T' and n_{ci} gives the number of periods during which there were i changes over the last n periods.

Over a given period T', we can associate one of the following attributes with each peer's profile functions $Energy(t)$, $Time(t)$, and $Space(t)$. Considering $Energy(t)$, we have:

– *Optimal*, the function is maximal over T' and superior to the given threshold e_{th}. This thresholds is tuned by the user or the application. Let G be a group of n peers, $Energy_i(t)$ is the function for available energy estimation for $peer_i$'s profile. $Energy_i(t)$ is *optimal* if and only if

$$\forall t \in [0, T'], \forall j = 1, ..., n \wedge j \neq i/peer_j \in G$$
$$Energy_i(t) \geq e_{th} \wedge Energy_i(t) \geq Energy_j(t) \tag{5}$$

– *Acceptable*, the function is *acceptable* over T' if it is not *optimal*, but still greater that the threshold. $Energy_i(t)$ is *acceptable* if and only if

$$\forall t \in [0, T'], Energy_i(t) \geq e_{th} \tag{6}$$

– *Weak*, the function is considered to be *weak* over T' if it goes below the given threshold. $Energy_i(t)$ is *weak* if and only if

$$\exists t \in [0, T'], Energy_i(t) \leq e_{th} \tag{7}$$

---

[11] By changes we mean peers' motion that leads to joining or leaving the group

Table 1. Peer's profile classification

$Energy(t)$	$Time(t)$	$Space(t)$	**Peer's Profile**
Optimal	Optimal	Optimal	Optimal
Optimal	Optimal	Acceptable	Optimal
Optimal	Optimal	Weak	Acceptable
Optimal	Acceptable	∀	Acceptable
Optimal	Weak	∀	Weak
Acceptable	Optimal	∀	Acceptable
Acceptable	Acceptable	∀	Acceptable
Acceptable	Weak	∀	Weak
Weak	∀	∀	Weak

The definition of attributes is applied similarly to functions $Time(t)$, and $Space(t)$, using their respective thresholds t_{th}, and s_{th}.

Then, combining the functions' attributes, we associate the previous attributes to the peer's profile as indicated in Table 1. An *optimal* profile designates a peer able to actively collaborate and share its resources within the ad hoc group. In contrast, a *weak* profile designates a peer with few resources, and hence, unable to share them within the group.

The attributes of $Energy(t)$, $Time(t)$, and $Space(t)$ do not have the same weight for determining the profile attributes. Indeed, $Energy(t)$, and $Time(t)$ indicate, respectively, the available energy and the expected time within the group. Moreover, they represent the evaluation of parameters that can generate a peer's disconnection. Thus, if one of them has a *weak* attribute, the peer's profile is considered *weak*. On the other hand, $Space(t)$ does not have the same influence on a peer's profile. Therefore, even if $Space(t)$'s attribute is *weak*, a peer's profile is still *acceptable* because replacement policies can be used to release some storage space. A peer's profile attributes serve to adapt replication to the peer's available resources.

3.2   Work and Preventive Replicas

When a peer joins a group, its locally cached data are considered as Work Replicas (WR). Furthermore, Work Replicas are generated upon access demands to non locally cached files. Those replicas are stored locally on the requesting peer regardless of its available resources. A replacement policy (LRU) is used in order to release storage space and hence delete old or seldom accessed Work Replicas provided that at least an other Work Replica is cached within the group.

Within an ad hoc group, updates among Work Replicas are lazily propagated. Therefore, coherency checks, based on CCLs, are performed upon actual access to Work Replicas. Their coherency is managed following the *log-based exclusive writer* as described in Section 2.2.

When the profile of a peer p caching the latest version of a Work Replica (p is the last writer on this replica) becomes *weak*, p propagates an update (if not already done) to another Work Replica stored on a peer with an *optimal* profile

Table 2. Replicas Management within an Ad Hoc Group

Within an Ad Hoc Group		Events	Actions
Their are many WRs	only one replica is up-to-date	the peer caching the up-to-date replica becomes *weak*	update a WR, that becomes also a PR
	many WRs are up-to-date	a peer caching a WR becomes *weak*	Do nothing
Their is one WR	-	the peer caching the WR becomes *weak*	create a PR on an appropriate peer

if one exists, or with an *acceptable* profile otherwise. This updated Work Replica also becomes a Preventive Replica (PR). Notice that the lazy update propagation is no longer respected in this case, updates are systematically propagated to the Preventive Replica. If peer p is the only peer caching this Work Replica (determined using the group variable), then a new replica (Preventive Replica) has to be created, as summarized in Table 2. The choice of which peer should store the new Preventive Replica is determined by combining its profile with semantic relationships between data as further described below.

Preventive Replicas serve to maintain an up-to-date copy within the group. This is actually our minimal replication rate. Some peers can already cache Preventive Replicas created within other ad hoc groups. These replicas are considered to be Work Replicas when these peers join a new group and become part of the peers' regular local cache. Furthermore, a Preventive Replica within an ad hoc group becomes a Work Replica when: (i) an access demand is made on it; (ii) a new Work Replica is created within the group on a peer with at least *acceptable* profile (see Table 1). This can happen either when a new peer joins the group, or a peer belonging to the group requires an access to the given replica.

The choice of which peer of an ad hoc group, should store a Preventive Replica is first guided by its profile. Therefore, peers with *weak* profiles are never going to be selected to store a Preventive Replica. Then, peers already caching a corresponding Work Replica are chosen. In this case, the chosen Work Replica is updated regardless of lazy update propagation. Hence, it also becomes a Preventive Replica. If none of the peers with an *optimal* or an *acceptable* profile are caching a corresponding Work Replica, then we rely on semantic relationships between data cached on peers and the Preventive Replica to be created.

Let p_1 be a peer caching the latest version of a Work Replica f_1W. The profile of p_1 becomes *weak* so p_1 has to create a Preventive Replica. Assuming, that none of the peers caching f_1W has a convenient profile, then p_1 has to chose a peer caching the most semantically related set of data to f_1W in order to create its Preventive Replica. The choice of semantically related data is specific to data type. For instance, when considering files, the peer p_1 chooses semantically related set of files to f_1W as follows:

- as a general rule, files cached on p_1 or in the same directory as f_1W are the most closely related. File naming also provides important clues to semantic relationships, e.g., files with the same name but different extensions are closely related.

Table 3. Selecting a Peer for Caching a Preventive Replica

Profile	Is Caching a Work Replica	Is Caching Semantically Related Data	Peer's Selection
Optimal	true	∀	Optimal Selection
Optimal	false	true	Acceptable Selection
Optimal	false	false	Weak Selection
Acceptable	true	∀	Acceptable Selection
Acceptable	false	true	Acceptable Selection
Acceptable	false	false	Weak Selection
Weak	∀	∀	Not Selected

- p_1 computes semantic distances between $f_1 W$ and locally cached files, as described in [16], in order to create clusters of semantically related files. Notice that $f_1 W$ can belong to different clusters. Peers locally caching n files belonging to $f_1 W$'s clusters are considered to be semantically related to $f_1 W$. The parameter n is tuned by the user or the application.
- After the clustering operation, p_1 orders the peers according to their eligibility to store the Preventive Replica. Table 3 gives all the cases involved in a peer's selection for storing a Preventive Replica. *Optimal* selection peers are the best candidates to store the Preventive Replica. Otherwise, a peer among *acceptable* selection peers is chosen. If there are no *optimal* or *acceptable* selection peers within the group, then a *weak* selection peer is chosen. A *weak* selection peer does not cache Work Replicas or semantically related data, but its profile allows it to become involved in increasing data availability. However, if the group contains only not selected peers, data availability cannot be maintained without compromising these peers' resources, which are already *weak*.

4   Assessment

In order to evaluate our collaborative ad hoc group and data availability management protocol in terms of performance and data overhead, we have implemented our middleware service within a file system. The resulting distributed file system for mobile ad hoc data sharing [22], [4] is implemented in Objective Caml 3.04[12]. Performance measurements concern in particular the group management, coherency management, and replication protocol. They have been done on a platform of ten laptops (Compaq Armada M700, M300, and Toshiba Satellite 1800-911) with a 500 MHz Pentium III CPU, 256 KB of cache, 200 MB of RAM and a 10 GB hard disk running under Linux Mandrake release 7.1 (2.2.15-4mdk) operating system. The wireless LAN is IEEE 802.11b in ad hoc mode using the Lucent 11Mb WaveLAN "'SILVER"' PC Card wireless interface.

Figure 2 gives the time taken for creating a group, leaving and joining a group, which are linear with the group size. The main cost of group creation lies in detecting trusted peers and sending the meta-data (group composition,

---
[12] http://caml.inria.fr/index-eng.html

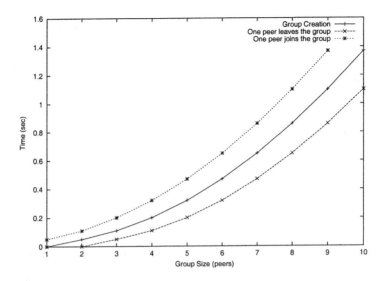

Fig. 2. Group Management Overhead

Table 4. Cost of Getting the Token

Group size (*peers*)	2	3	4	5	6	7	8	9	10
Time (*sec*)	0.00949	0.01281	0.01982	0.02129	0.02645	0.02977	0.03493	0.03825	0.04341
Energy (*mW.sec*)	1.58	2.91	5.4	6.67	9.08	11.87	15	18. 51	22.38

CCLs, profiles, etc.) by the group leader so as to allow peers belonging to the group to have a global view of shared data and other peers' profiles.

Table 4 shows that the cost, in terms of response time and energy consumption, of getting the token (without the updates) to modify a data, is constant within a particular group. Note that the cost of an additional peer in terms of response time is only about 0.005 sec. However, the cost of one additional peer in terms of energy depends on the group size. Indeed, being in ad hoc mode means that even non destination peers consume energy when messages are being sent. That is why, adding one peer to a group of three peers does not have the same energy impact as adding one peer to a group of ten peers. However, the cost in terms of energy consumption still very low. Note that being idle in an ad hoc configuration costs 843 mW.sec.

The cost, in terms of response time, of getting updates is proportional to the update size, as depicted in Figure 3. Using our coherency protocol, getting access to coherent data locally depends on the update size, while group size affects only slightly the performance of our protocol. However, the energy consumption depends on both the group size and the update size. It is given (based on equations from [10]) by:

$$\varepsilon_{msg} = (0.1 + 0.25 * n) * size + 221 + 163 * n \tag{8}$$

where n is the ad hoc group size and *size* the update size.

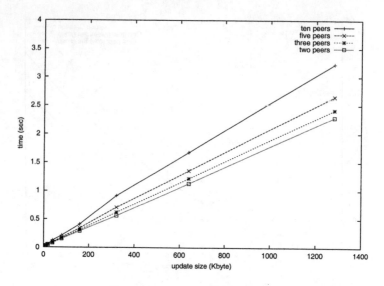

Fig. 3. Cost of Getting Updates

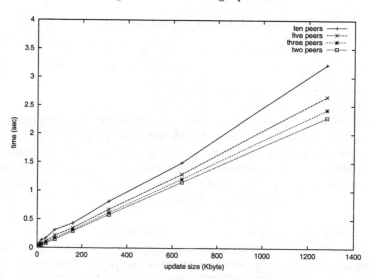

Fig. 4. Lazy Update Propagation

Figure 4 and 5 show the benefits of our coherency management protocol (lazy update propagation) in terms of response time. Indeed, the response time, when lazily propagating updates (in the case of write operations) ranges from 0.0269 sec to 3.219 sec according to the group size and the update size, as depicted by Figure 4. However, when the updates are propagated whenever they occur, which corresponds to an optimistic coherency management (note that peers belonging to group are in the communication range of each other), the re-

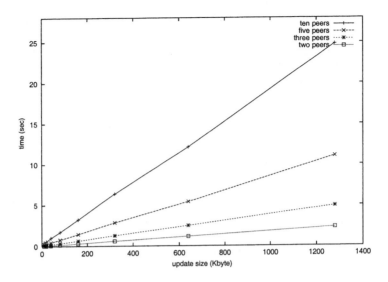

Fig. 5. Optimistic Update Propagation

sponse time (in the case of write operations) ranges from 0.0361 sec to 24.8 sec according to the group size and the update size, as depicted by Figure 5. Let compare these two coherency management protocols for a given scenario. Initially, we have an ad hoc group of four peers, all caching the data. We have made four successive write operations by different peers, and we suppose that update size is 640 Kbytes for each write operation. Following our protocol, the time taken to first write access a coherent data file is equal to 0.019 sec, for the second successive write operation it is equal to 1.20 sec, for the third it is equal to 1.22 sec, and for the last write operation to 1.27 sec (this results from our lazy update propagation). However, if the updates are propagated whenever they occurs, in the same scenario, the time taken to write access a coherent data file is equal to 3.639 sec per write operation. Thus, by lazily propagating updates, we save time and communication for the four write operations, which is equivalent to 7218 mW of energy consumption.

Concerning the data overhead introduced by our availability management protocol, we can distinguish two types of overhead: the local storage overhead, it includes the data necessary for coherency and replication management (group composition, CCLs, profiles, etc.) and that are locally stored; the message overhead, which includes the data sent within messages in addition to the actual updates. The local storage overhead is given by (in Bytes):

$$
\begin{aligned}
Local\_overhead = 3 \times int + 2 \times bool + (5 \times real + 16 \times char) \times p \\
+ \sum_{j=1}^{G}(16 \times char \times p_j + int \times Modif_j) + \sum_{i=1}^{W+R}(16 \times char + size\_ccl_i)
\end{aligned} \tag{9}
$$

$$
size\_ccl_i = int + \sum_{j=1}^{G}(16 \times char \times p_j + int \times Modif_j)) \tag{10}
$$

Where p is the number of peers caching locally the data, $Modif$ is the number of write operations, G is the number of different group configurations where updates occur, W is the number peers waiting for write, R is the number peers waiting for read, and int, $real$, $char$, and $bool$ the sizes of respectively integer, real, character, and boolean variables. The message overhead[13] is given by (in Bytes):

$$Message\_overhead = 2 \times int + file\_name \times char$$
$$+ \sum_{j=1}^{G}(16 \times char \times p_j + int \times Modif_j) + sum_{i=1}^{W+R}(16 \times char + size\_ccl_i)$$
$$(11)$$

Where $file\_name$ is the length of the file name. In these equations we considered that peer's ID is a string of 16 characters.

Using our availability management protocol, the local storage overhead as well as the meta-data sent in addition to the updates are negligible regarding the average size of data files, e.g., the message overhead represents 0.41 percent of the whole message to be sent. Further evaluations using simulation should be done, in order to measure the performances of our protocol within different scenarios and profiles including high peers mobility, this is part of our future work.

5 Conclusion

Mobile ad hoc networks are particularly suitable to form small collaborative groups in order to share and manipulate common data. Until now, work concerning ad hoc networks mainly deals with routing protocols without taking into account data management within these networks. Data management over wireless networks relies essentially on adequate replication management for enhanced availability. Manipulating data within mobile ad hoc collaborative groups requires two core functionalities:

1. Secure group management that ensures: (i) transparent group creation using a discovery service to detect trusted partners (their devices) that *belongs* to the group; (ii) adaptation to the group dynamics, so that members can leave or join the group at any time; (iii) secure group communication through an encryption protocol that must account with devices' resources and network connectivity.
2. Data management that ensures: (i) that members access the most recent data version available within the ad hoc group, (ii) data coherency within the group through a conservative coherency protocol to effectively support collaborative work, since members must have the same version of shared data; (iii) adaptive data replication to avoid data loss if the devices storing them suddenly disconnect.

Existing distributed systems that deal with mobility do not manage replication with respect to wireless devices resources, nor support transparent collaborative data sharing within ad hoc WLAN groups.

---

[13] Notice that profile's parameters are not involved in the message overhead

Therefore, we have designed and presented a middleware service that allows collaborative data sharing among ad hoc groups that are dynamically formed according to the connectivity achieved by the ad hoc WLAN. Our service enhances, in particular, data availability within mobile ad hoc collaborative groups, and integrates a new adaptive data replication protocol for mobile terminals.

We believe that data availability is a crucial requirement in such environment, and it is one of the prominent QoS criteria for collaborative work. Our replication protocol is based on a combined coherency management (using both optimistic and conservative schemes) in order to account for various connectivity as enabled by today's wireless networking capabilities. It is further based on two replica types: Work Replica, and Preventive Replica. The former is generated according to access demands to non locally cached files, and benefits from the lazy update propagation following our *log-based exclusive writer* coherency protocol. The latter serve to maintain an up-to-date copy within the group, and is generated according to the profile of the peer holding the latest version of the corresponding Work Replica. The choice of which peer should store a Preventive Replica is determined by combining the peers' profile with semantic relationships between locally stored files and the generated Preventive Replica.

It is shown that using our middleware service, the meta-data overhead generated is negligible, the response time grows linearly with update size, while group size affects it slightly, and, the lazy update propagation saves time and energy consumption. We are further working on evaluating performances of our protocol, by simulating various scenarios and peers' profiles.

Acknowledgments

The authors would like to acknowledge the work carried out by Raghav Bhaskar and Daniel Augot regarding security management in mobile ad hoc networks and their proposition to adapt group key agreement protocol to such environment. We would like also to acknowledge the contribution of David Mentré, Anis Ben-Arbia, and Animesh Pathak to the design and the implementation of the ad hoc group management protocol and the coherency management protocol. This work has been partially funded by the ITEA VIVIAN Project (ITEA 99040).

References

1. Micah Adler and Christian Scheideler: Efficient communication strategies for ad-hoc wireless networks. In *ACM Symposium on Parallel Algorithms and Architectures*, pages 259–268, 1998.
2. G. Ateniese, M. Steiner, and G. Tsudik: New multiparty authentication services and key agreement protocols. *IEEE Journal of Selected Areas in Communications*, 18(4):pp. 1–13, 2000.
3. C. Bettstetter and C. Renner: A comparison of service discovery protocols and implementation of the service location protocol. In *Proceedings 6th EUNICE Open European Summer School: Innovative Internet Applications*, 2000.

4. Malika Boulkenafed, Anis Ben Arbia, David Mentré, and Valérie Issarny: AD-HocFS: Sharing files in wlans, 2002.
   http://www-rocq.inria.fr/solidor/work/AdHocFS.html.
5. Malika Boulkenafed and Valérie Issarny: Coherency management in ad-hoc group communication. In *Proc. of the joint VIVIAN-ROBOCOP workshop on Software Infrastructures for Component-Based Applications on Consumer Devices*, Lausanne, Switzerland, September 16, 2002.
6. M. Burmester and Y. Desmedt: A secure and efficient conference key distribution system. In LNCS Springer, editor, *Proc. of Eurocrypt'94*, pages pp. 275–286, 1995.
7. W. Diffie, D. Steer, L. Strawczynski, and M. Weiner: A secure audio teleconference system. In LNCS Springer, editor, *Proc. of Crypto'88*, 1988.
8. W. K. Edwards, E. D. Mynatt, K. Petersen, M. J. Spreitzer, D. B. Terry, and M. M. Theimer: Designing and implementing asynchronous applications with bayou. In *Proc. of the Symp. on User Int. Software and Tech.*, Banff Alberta (Canada), Oct. 1997.
9. Todd Ekenstam, Charles Matheny, Peter L. Reiher, and Gerald J. Popek: The bengal database replication system. *Journal of Distributed and Parallel Databases*, 9(3):187–210, 2001. citeseer.nj.nec.com/449358.html.
10. L. Feeney and M. Nilsson: Investigating the energy consumption of a wireless network interface in an ad hoc networking environment. *In proc. of the IEEE Infocom*, 5(8), 2001. www.sics.se/ feeney.
11. J. D. Gibson: *The Mobile Communication Handbook*. CRC Press, 2nd edition, 1999.
12. Richard G. Guy, Peter L. Reiher, David Ratner, Michial Gunter, Wilkie Ma, and Gerald J. Popek: Rumor: Mobile data access through optimistic peer-to-peer replication. In *ER Workshops*, pages 254–265, 1998. citeseer.nj.nec.com/guy98rumor.html.
13. T. Imielinski: *Mobile Computing*. Kluwer Academic Publishers, 1996.
14. M. Just and S. Vaudenay: Authenticated multy-party key agreement. In *Proc. of ASIACRYPT'96*, 1996.
15. John Kubiatowicz, David Bindel, Yan Chen, Patrick Eaton, Dennis Geels, Ramakrishna Gummadi, Sean Rhea, Hakim Weatherspoon, Westly Weimer, Christopher Wells, and Ben Zhao: Oceanstore: An architecture for global-scale persistent storage. In *Proceedings of ACM ASPLOS*. ACM, November 2000. citeseer.nj.nec.com/kubiatowicz00oceanstore.html.
16. Geoffrey H. Kuenning: Seer: Predictive File Hoarding for Disconnected Mobile Operation. PhD thesis, University of California, Los Angeles, May 1997.
17. P. Kumar and M. Satyanarayanan: Supporting application-specific resolution in an optimistically replicated file system. In *Proceedings of the 4th Workshop on Workstation Operating Systems*, 1993.
18. Haiyun Luo, Paul Medvedev, Jerry Cheng, and Songwu Lu: A self-coordinating approach to distributed fair queueing in ad hoc wireless networks. In *INFOCOM*, pages 1370–1379, 2001. citeseer.nj.nec.com/luo01selfcoordinating.html.
19. Sergio Marti, T. J. Giuli, Kevin Lai, and Mary Baker: Mitigating routing misbehavior in mobile ad hoc networks. In *Mobile Computing and Networking*, pages 255–265, 2000. citeseer.nj.nec.com/marti00mitigating.html.
20. Cecilia Mascolo, L. Zanolin, and Wolfgang Emmerich: Xmiddle: an xml based approach for incremental code mobility and update. *Journal of Automated Software Engineering*, 9(2), 2002.

21. Alfred J. Menezes, Paul C. van Oorschot, and Scott A. Vanstone: *Handbook of Applied Cryptography*. CRC Press, 4th edition edition, 1996. http://www.cacr.math.uwaterloo.ca/hac/.

22. Davide Mentre, Malika Boulkenafed, and Valérie Issarny: ADHOCFS: A serverless file system for mobile users. Research Report 4303, INRIA-Rocquencourt, 2001.

23. K. Petersen, M. J. Spreitzer, D. B. Terry, M. M. Theimer, and A. J. Demers: Flexible update propagation for weakly consistent replication. In *Proc. Symp. on Operating Systems Principles (SOSP-16)*, pages 288–301, Saint Malo, Oct. 1997.

24. Amir Qayyum: *"Analysis and evaluation of channel access schemes and routing protocols for wireless networks"*. PhD thesis, University of Paris Sud, Orsay, France, November 2000.

25. P. Reiher, J. Popek, M. Gunter, J. Salomone, and D. Ratner: Peer-to-peer reconciliation based replication for mobile computers. In *European Conference on Object Oriented Programming '96 Second Workshop on Mobility and Replication*, 1996. citeseer.nj.nec.com/5097.html.

26. M. Satyanarayanan, James J. Kistler, Puneet Kumar, Maria E. Okasaki, Ellen H. Siegel, and David C. Steere: Coda: A highly available file system for a distributed workstation environment. *Journal of IEEE Transactions on Computers*, 39(4):447–459, 1990. citeseer.nj.nec.com/satyanarayanan90coda.html.

27. H. Yu and A. Vahdat: Design and evaluation of a continuous consistency model for replicated services. In *Proc. of the 4rd Symposium on Operating Systems Design and Implementation*, 2000. citeseer.nj.nec.com/yu00design.html.

Author Index

Alonso, Gustavo   455
Amza, Cristiana   282

Bacon, Jean   62
Banavar, Guruduth   262
Beigi, Mandis   262
Bhola, Sumeer   202
Boulkenafed, Malika   493
Briot, Jean-Pierre   123

Campbell, Roy H.   143, 433
Cecchet, Emmanuel   242
Chanda, Anupam   242
Chen, Mao   83
Chen, Yuan   182
Cox, Alan L.   282

Delicato, Flávia Coimbra   474

Elnikety, Sameh   242

Fiege, Ludger   103
Fleury, Marc   344
Fox, Geoffrey   41
Frei, Andreas   455

Gärtner, Felix C.   103

Huang, Ling   1

Issarny, Valérie   493

Jin, Jingwen   394
Joseph, Anthony D.   1

Kasten, Oliver   103
Kelly, Paul H.J.   324
Krishnamurthy, Yamuna   374
Kubiatowicz, John   1

LaPaugh, Andrea   83
Loyall, Joseph P.   374

Marguerite, Julie   242
Medvidovic, Nenad   162
Mena, Sergio   414

Merle, Philippe   305
Mikic-Rakic, Marija   162
Minsky, Naftaly H.   222
Murata, Takahiro   222

Nahrstedt, Klara   394

Olshefski, David P.   262

Pallickara, Shrideep   41
Peschanski, Frédéric   123
Pietzuch, Peter R.   62, 202
Pires, Paulo F.   474
Pirmez, Luci   474
Popovici, Andrei   455
Pyarali, Irfan   374

Ranganathan, Anand   143
Reverbel, Francisco   344
Reynolds, Patrick   21
Rodrigues, Craig   374
Román, Manuel   433
Rouvoy, Romain   305
Rust da Costa Carmo, Luiz Fernando   474

Schantz, Richard E.   374
Schiper, André   414
Schmidt, Douglas C.   374
Schwan, Karsten   182
Shand, Brian   62
Singh, Jaswinder Pal   83
Sow, Daby M.   262

Vahdat, Amin   21

Wojciechowski, Paweł   414

Yeung, Kwok Cheung   324
Yonezawa, Akinori   123

Zeidler, Andreas   103
Zhao, Ben Y.   1
Zhou, Dong   182
Zhou, Feng   1
Zhuang, Li   1
Zwaenepoel, Willy   242, 282